RESISTANCE, REBELLION AND REVOLUTION IN HUNGARY AND CENTRAL EUROPE: COMMEMORATING 1956

RESISTANCE, REBELLION AND REVOLUTION IN HUNGARY AND CENTRAL EUROPE: COMMEMORATING 1956

Edited by

LÁSZLÓ PÉTER and MARTYN RADY

Hungarian Cultural Centre London,
UCL 2008

RESISTANCE, REBELLION AND REVOLUTION IN HUNGARY AND
CENTRAL EUROPE: COMMEMORATING 1956

EDITED BY LÁSZLÓ PÉTER and MARTYN RADY

Studies in Russia and Eastern Europe No. 3
(formerly SSEES Occasional Papers)

ISBN: 978-0-903425-79-7

Copies of this publication and others in the School's refereed series can be obtained from the
Publications Office, SSEES, UCL, Gower Street, London WC1E 6BT.

Front cover: Revolutionaries on a truck, Budapest, October 1956.
Published by courtesy of the American Hungarian Federation <http://www.hungary1956.com>.

Typeset and Printed by Q3 Print Project Management Ltd,
Loughborough, Leics.

Contents

Preface

The Hungarian Cultural Centre in London is proud to be associated with this, the third volume on the history of Hungary which the Centre has supported and co-published. Like its predecessors on Lajos Kossuth and on British-Hungarian Relations, the present work demonstrates the sustained interest in Great Britain in the field of Hungarian history. The collection draws together British, Hungarian and North American historians and thus illuminates the continued scholarly exchange between both countries and continents. Hungary's first king, St Stephen, wrote that *unius lingue uniusque moris regnum imbecile et fragile est*. This is the heritage we have been building on for more than a thousand years. We may similarly observe that a country's history is all the more strongly understood when it is discussed and written about by scholars coming from more than just one nation.

The Hungarian Cultural Centre in London was opened in Covent Garden in 1999. From the very start its mission has been to familiarize the British people and the rest of the world with all the treasures that were spread to Europe by the Hungarians, as well as to highlight the values that Hungary owes to foreign cultures, in this way emphasizing Hungary's role as a bridge for inter-cultural communication. The present work comports entirely with this aim, as well as having its focus on one of the most important events in post-war Hungarian and European history – the Revolution of 1956.

Katalin Bogyay

State Secretary for International Affairs
Hungarian Ministry of Education and Culture
Director of the Hungarian Cultural Centre (1999–2007)

October 2007

Acknowledgements

The editors are most grateful to the Hungarian Cultural Centre in London and to the Hungarian Ministry of Cultural Heritage which funded the present volume as well as the conference held on 21–22 September 2006 from which it draws. The editors acknowledge the support of Katalin Bogyay, formerly director of the Hungarian Cultural Centre; the current director of the Hungarian Cultural Centre, Ildikó Takács; George Kolankiewicz and Robin Aizlewood, successive directors of UCL-SSEES; the Hungarian Embassy in London and His Excellency Béla Szombati; the Centre for the Study of Central Europe at UCL-SSEES; the MB Grabowski Fund; and the advice and assistance of Christine Fernandes, Kelly Peaston, Susie Rizvi, Peter Sherwood, Clare Thomas and Trevor Thomas.

The Editors

Introduction

László Péter

Resistance to established political authority, rebellion and revolution are common terms that are all too frequently taken for granted. There is, however, no public or scholarly consensus about which events qualify as rebellion, revolt, uprising or revolution. Nor is there any agreement on the explanations of these events. The lack of consensus on the subject should not be overlooked when considering the history of Central Europe, and of Hungary in particular, because this region has probably experienced more than its fair share of public convulsions. Social upheavals have throughout history taken a wide variety of forms and some reflection on the different uses of the terms used to describe them may help to improve historical understanding and terminological clarity. The uses of the word revolution appear to justify my contention that the term is unsuited to analysis.

In this introduction I will briefly survey the social upheavals of the past and the terms in which they were described in order to substantiate my argument. The notions of resistance, rebellion and revolution presuppose the existence of organized society with some central authority. Convulsions occur when the central authority loses its ability to enforce its laws and order breaks down. We may go back to ancient Egypt, a riparian society with a strong central government. There were no rules concerning the succession to the Pharaoh in Egypt and to the rulers of other riparian societies: dynasties were replaced through political violence frequently accompanied by social and religious change. As the nature of the monarchy in Egypt was theocratic, a revolt – a rebellion against the ruler – was not only wrong in itself but also sacrilege, a disturbance of the divine order.

The first to study changes of government was probably Plato. That a Greek should have been the earliest to be concerned with the subject is unsurprising because in the city states of Greece power was frequently disputed and a variety of forms of government made their appearance. Plato thought that although the state could be run by a single ruler (monarchy) or by a minority (aristocracy) or by the majority (democracy), it was the first and third forms from which all the others derived.[1] Change in government, frequently violent, was more than the displacement of the incumbent ruler. It occurred because governments were founded on unsound ideas of justice misusing the precept of equality, and this engendered civil discord. He made the perceptive observation, valid for violent changes of political regimes in general, that, 'in any form of government

---

I am obliged to Angus Walker who recast some of my unclear arguments.
1   Plato, *The Laws*, Book III, § 693.

revolution always starts from the outbreak of internal dissention in the ruling class.'[2] Apart from his appeal for the establishment of the Ideal State, his practical advice was to attain harmony and stability by a balance between the conflicting forces through a mixed form of government.[3]

Aristotle offered a more comprehensive account of changes in government. He distinguished between constitutions that served the common interest and those that served only the personal interests of the rulers, which were perverted forms of government. He then argued in the *Politics*[4] that the distinction could be applied to a categorization based on number. Rule by the One, the Few or the Many produced three types of constitution that served the common interest: monarchy, aristocracy and polity. The perverted form of each was to be found in tyranny, oligarchy and democracy, making six types of rule in all. The last two, oligarchy and democracy, also had a class basis in that they respectively represented rule by the rich and by the poor. Constitutions were modified or overthrown as a result of discontent or as the outcome of a struggle between factions with conflicting views on justice and equality. The polity, the mixed constitution, offered stability more than the other forms because it produced a balance between the rich and the poor. In general, in Aristotle, what was later called 'revolution' was a form of political rather than social change. Polybius, drawing on the history of republican Rome, elaborated the concept of the mixed constitution but otherwise, notwithstanding the violent history of Rome, for centuries no one attempted to develop Aristotle's theories any further. Changes of government in the ancient world were frequently violent. In Egypt, in the Roman and in the Byzantine empires, succession was not based on rules or established conventions, apart from the acceptance that the overthrow of a ruler was legitimized by its success. Christianity rejected the use of force against an autocratic ruler and required passive obedience from the faithful. Yet political power was frequently transferred by violence. The strengthening of the secular authority of the monarchs in Western Europe and the revival of classical learning in the twelfth century changed Christian attitudes to the use of force. Aquinas, the Angelic Doctor, accepted the Philosopher's advice that the best government was a 'judicious admixture' of forms headed by a king. If he was appointed by a superior, then 'the remedy against tyrannical excess must be sought from him.' Where, however, the ruler was elected by the community, they could reduce his power and even depose him should he abuse his position by becoming a tyrant.[5] These ideas were taken much further in the writings of Marsilius of Padua and William of Ockham. The Conciliarists argued that as the 'body politic' consisted of the head and the members, the whole body of citizens (or its 'weightier part') formed a corporate body which either directly or in a general council of its representatives could make decisions affecting every member of the political body. Otherwise government would be arbitrary and, as St. Augustine had already observed, bad government was but great larceny. The community possessed, it

---

2   Plato, *The Republic*, ch. XXIX.
3   Plato, *The Laws*, Book VI, § 757.
4   Aristotle, *Politics*, Book III, ch.7.
5   St Thomas Aquinas, *On Princely Government*, Book I, ch. 6.

was argued, an inherent power to constitute its government, correct its wrongs and if necessary to depose it. Although the Conciliar movement failed in the fifteenth century, it exerted a seminal influence on the republican aspirations of the liberal and constitutional movements of later times.

In Italy the city states, as in ancient Greece, experienced abrupt and violent changes of government. This prompted the first use of the term 'revolution' to describe such changes. It was derived from the Latin *revolutiones* used in astrology. The underlying notion was that, as in astrology, the planets continually circled and occasionally and recurrently came into conjuncture determining significant events. By analogy, reversals of political power were referred to as *revoluzioni*. For Machiavelli, such a revolution was the aim of anyone seeking to fulfil his political ambitions. There was no theoretical substance to these ideas. They simply represented the acknowledgement that force was everything. Power could only be maintained and allegiance secured by a display of willingness to use violence. A ruler was always vulnerable to conspiracies and to the violence of other ambitious men. Machiavelli accepted that losers in power struggles were likely to be assassinated. Writers in other European countries occasionally also justified the killing of a tyrant in some circumstances. William Barclay, in 1600, a defender of the monarch's absolute authority, dubbed these authors as 'monarchomachs'.

The Reformation brought more sophisticated ideas about resistance to authority. Revolution and revolt that, in Machiavelli, suggested that political change associating a circular movement, were now used to imply a change from the horizontal circling of the planets to the rotation of a vertically positioned Wheel of Fortune where change was a movement from below. In other words, the idea that the political order was threatened by individuals was replaced by the notion that a constitution could be changed by a rising of the people, an insurrection. The Reformation meant that rulers and subjects frequently professed different versions of Christianity. The differences sometimes led to uprisings. The Calvinist author of the well-known *Vindiciae contra tyrannos* (1581) advocated insurrection against a Catholic monarch on the grounds that God appoints kings but the people put the sceptre into their hands. This dictum was an early instance of a more fully-developed contractual theory of political obligation. All its elements can be found in earlier writings but they were now put together in such a way as to constitute a new theoretical account of subordination within a political system where the people are seen for the first time as individual and irreducible elements of the polity, each with their own ability to decide upon its form of government. In its most radical form, the doctrine held that since the people had agreed to set up rulers over themselves for certain purposes they had therefore the right to resist or remove them when they departed from these purposes, i.e. broke their contract. When the contract was broken, the people could even separate themselves from the rest of the kingdom: this theory was used to justify the Dutch revolt against Spain and the American War of Independence. Government had to be based on the express consent of the governed, as Jefferson's classic formulation in the American Declaration of Independence asserted.

1789 radically changed the focus of political analysis.. As John Dunn remarks, 'the combined intellectual and political impact of the French revolution [...] transformed "revolution" into a central term in the interpretation and practice of modern politics.'[6] Explanations of the causes of revolutions became inseparable from the assessment of their political merits. The French Revolution had a powerful effect on public attitudes everywhere. It glorified the word 'Revolution'. Before 1789 the execution of Charles I in England was a part of the 'Great Rebellion' or 'Civil War', which became the 'English Revolution' only after the 'Great French Revolution'. Paradoxically, the orderly replacement of government, in line with Locke's principles, in 1688 acquired the label at the time as the 'Great' and after 1789 as the 'Glorious Revolution'. The French Revolution became the universal paradigm for whatever was modern and progressive. When an American journalist asked Chou En-Lai what he thought were the consequences of the French Revolution, the Chinese leader's thoughtful response was that 'it was too early to say.' The concept of revolution became associated with the principle of democracy and Hannah Arendt argued that a striving for the creation of a political order that guaranteed liberty was implicit in all revolutionary activity in spite of the counter-evidence that revolutions can just as easily lead to the establishment of regimes that are simply alternative systems of oppression, as in Iran.

After 1789, the word revolution had, as its most important although not exclusive connotation, the idea that it presaged the complete re-making of society. As Thomas Paine put it in 1791, 'what we now see in the world, from the Revolutions of America and France, are a renovation of the natural order of things.'[7] There was a belief that revolutions provided the means for realizing what was held to be the perfectibility of mankind. A 'true revolution', according to this usage, was not merely a revolt against tyranny, the struggle to turn the political order upside down. It involved the total rejection of an inefficient *ancien régime* and the creation of a new social order in its entirety. 1789 created the professional revolutionary: the self-conscious activist and dreamer of a society remade.

Revolution as a fundamental discontinuity in social development was to be a recurrent preoccupation in social and political thought in the nineteenth century. Saint-Simonians held that industrial development entailed revolutionary social and, therefore, political change. Marx combined the insights of Adam Smith and Hegel to argue that revolutions universally marked transitions from one, inevitable, stage in economic and social development to another. According to Marx, in each society the forces of production, which make up society's economic underpinning, develop more rapidly than the relations of production constituted by slavery, feudalism and capitalism, the political superstructure of society. When the political system becomes a constraint on the new forces of production, revolution made it possible to reach a higher stage of social development. Revolutions are carried out by the previously economically disadvantaged social classes. The slave owners are replaced by feudal landlords and they in turn by the bourgeoisie. Eventually, Marx predicted, the bourgeoisie would be replaced through a socialist revolution by the proletariat which would lead to the

---

6 John Dunn, 'Revolution' in Terence Ball *et. al.* (eds), *Political Innovation and Conceptual Change*, Cambridge, 1989, p. 337.
7 Thomas Paine, *Rights of Man*, London, 1791, Pt. 1, Conclusion.

establishment of the communist, classless society. This was the conclusion of an inexorable historical process.

Revolutions in Europe did not, however, follow the Marxist pattern. France in 1830, in 1848 and in 1871 repeated the conflicts of 1789 before settling down to a 'bourgeois' democracy. Not only did Marx fail to understand the mechanics of political change but he made the even more fatal mistake of failing to grasp the overwhelming importance of nationalist movements. 1848, the year of revolutions over the whole continent (save Russia), has (based on G.T. Trevelyan's quip) been sometimes unhelpfully described as the great turning point of European history at which, however, history stubbornly refused to turn. It is true that the autocrats, humiliated by urban uprisings in the spring, were all back in the saddle by the end of 1848. Nevertheless, the new ideology of liberal nationalism provided an impetus for the institution of representative governments in many parts of Europe. Nationalist ideology was a potent force for change in two respects. The Austrian, Russian and Ottoman empires were unable to suppress their national movements. Furthermore, the antagonisms between competing national groups proved intractable. Revolutions and wars of independence determined the emergence of modern nations; they were emblematic of national identity and aspirations. Indeed, British colonies that were given their independence often felt that their legitimacy lacked a critical element and were given to exaggerating the strength and violence of any demands for independence that had been voiced before achieving sovereignty.

How did the social and intellectual changes in Western Europe affect the rest of the continent? By the eighteenth century the modern form of the social contract introduced by Hobbes and developed by Locke provided the underpinning for moderate as well as radical and revolutionary politics in Central Europe. The German professors of the natural law school, the impeccably unoriginal Christian Wolff of Halle and the much respected Karl Anton Martini, tutor to the sons of Empress Maria Theresa, relied in their arguments on contract theory in its least provocative form. They held that the power of the monarch originated in the people. Once power was transferred to the monarch, however, the people did not have the right to resist the monarch's enactments. In 1790, under the influence of Rousseau and the events in Paris, the radical implications of the contract theory made their appearance. Péter Ócsai Balogh, a judge and an influential leader of the Hungarian nobility, in an anonymous but widely circulated manuscript, argued that because Emperor Joseph, by contravening the Pragmatic Sanction, had broken the contract with the People the thread of succession had been broken – *filum successionis interruptum* obtained. Political power reverted to the People and they could now elect a king from outside the line of the Habsburgs or negotiate with Leopold II over a new contract to be enacted at his coronation in a revised Inaugural Diploma. Although the nobility finally settled with Leopold for much less, the radical conclusions of the contract theory remained an undercurrent in Hungarian politics. They resurfaced in April 1849 when, under the spell of Lajos Kossuth, the Hungarian parliament deposed the Habsburg dynasty. But contract theory could be a double-edged sword. The response from the 'Austrian' side after the defeat of the revolution was the *Verwirkungstheorie*: the claim that Hungary had forfeited all her historic rights on account of rebellion against the monarch.

In the twentieth century, the political upheavals predicted by Marx were to be found not in the developed economies of capitalism but in countries peripheral to the development of market societies. The revolts against the colonial powers that broke out in many parts of the world were inspired by intellectuals rather than by a spontaneous uprising of the masses. Yet the Bolshevik takeover in Russia in 1917 gave a new twist to the concept of revolution. Lenin argued that revolutions occurred when, in addition to the objective economic conditions analysed by Marx, the subjective conditions, the existence of a party of organized and dedicated revolutionaries also obtained. The so-called 'Great Russian Revolution' was in fact a *coup d'ét☐t* by Lenin's followers, a small minority. There were very few communists in the countries in Eastern Europe when they were occupied by the Soviet army at the end of the Second World War. Yet with the active help of the Soviet occupying power, Moscow-trained Stalinists had within a few years seized power in the region. The communists destroyed the old social order and established command economies and one-party rule. This transformation was justified by the claim that a social revolution had taken place. Because this claim did not match with what most people experienced at the time, rhetorical substitutes had to be found. The class struggles of the past, the rebellions and independence movements against the Russian, the Habsburg and Ottoman empires were lumped together as the 'revolutionary progressive inheritance' which had been sustained and brought to fruition by the 'revolutionary' activities of the communists. In Hungary, the Bocskai revolt (1604), the Rákóczi rebellion (1703–1711) and, above all, the revolutions in 1848 and in 1918 were deployed by the regime as surrogates for the required, but absent, social revolution. After 1956 the party became a good deal less enthusiastic about the 'revolutionary tradition', but it maintained the claim that it had spearheaded a revolution after 1945 and substituted a new social system for the old one. This thesis enabled the authorities to claim that events were in line with Karl Marx's teaching but, being conspicuously circular, it was inadequate to legitimize the new social order. Yet it was important for the regime to insist on its revolutionary credentials.

In Hungary the events of 1848 and 1956 reinforced the use of the word 'revolution' as a value judgement but not as an analytical term. The defenders of the communist regime in 1956 and after were obliged to insist that the political convulsion was a 'counter-revolution'. Like the transformation in 1848, the events of 1956 have been described by Hungarians of all classes as a 'national revolution' and the word has still not lost its seductive power. The fundamental meaning has shifted from the notion of a political disruption to the idea that some political process was thought of as progressive. In 1989, when the communist system in the region collapsed, when the Czechs had a 'velvet revolution' and the Romanians a violent revolution, the Hungarians claimed that they had had a 'negotiated revolution' and had carried out a political transformation that patently did not involve any institutional discontinuity.

It is everywhere recognized that what took place in October 1956 in Hungary was a significant event in twentieth century history. Most active supporters of the events at the time and after called 1956, without hesitation, a revolution. But more detached observers in newspapers and in books on politics have referred to 1956 as a 'revolt' or an 'uprising' as frequently as a revolution. Half a century later, the appellations are as imprecise as ever. On its fiftieth anniversary, *The Times* referred to 1956 as an 'uprising'. His Royal

Highness the Prince of Wales invited guests to commemorate the 'Hungarian Revolution'; yet the Speaker of the House of Commons held a reception that, apparently after consultation with the Foreign Office, was designated as a celebration of the anniversary of the 'Hungarian Uprising'; the Hungarian Ambassador commemorated the 'Revolution and Freedom Fight'. Political scientists are equally divided. Peter Calvert argued that Hungary in 1956 had a 'revolution, for it did succeed, if only momentarily, in achieving control of the state.'[8] Those who eschew the use of the word 'revolution' and characterize 1956 as a 'revolt' or an 'uprising' do so perhaps either because it ultimately failed or because they consider 1956 as a national rising against foreign domination.

The originally violent connotation of 'revolution' has been gradually watered down over time. By the end of the eighteenth century the word could be applied not only to the bloody consequences of 1789 but also, as we have already noted, to the peaceable events of 1688 as the 'Glorious Revolution'. Since 1789 the term revolution has been applied indifferently to any discontinuous change in a political system, violent or otherwise. A meritorious rather than a descriptive term, 'revolution' is often used, in corrupting language and thought, through *contr☐dictio in ☐diecto*, as three examples from Hungarian history demonstrates. The mantra phrase, widely used by Hungarian historians about 1848, is 'lawful revolution'. After 1945 'revolutionary legality' justified the police terror through the 'people's courts' against the opponents of communists. And, as we have already noted, the entirely peaceful political transformation in 1989 has been labelled as a 'negotiated revolution'.

Is it possible to rescue the terminology from the semantic confusion that clearly prevails in its use in describing the events of 1956 in Hungary and elsewhere? Are we able to find a proper place for resistance, rebellion and revolution in a dictionary? Resistance to authority is normally used descriptively: it is directed against particular policies rather than against the political regime as such. It is possible to argue that the uses of words like 'revolt' and 'uprising' are also descriptive and present no problem in finding a place for them in a dictionary. 'Rebellion', on the other hand, has a pejorative connotation. Generally understood as a failed attempt to overthrow either the incumbent of established authority or the whole system of rule, it has, however, a descriptive basis that qualifies for a categorical place in the dictionary. The word revolution has, however, since the French Revolution of 1789 been carrying so much normative baggage that it would be impracticable to look for consensus on its use. As John Dunn points out (1989) 'revolution' has been used to label a large number of political episodes which lack a unitary causal explanation: 'the extreme promiscuity of its modern usage now precludes its being judged to express a single clear concept.'[9] Indeed, political convulsions can be described from a variety of legitimate perspectives. And it follows that any definition of revolution is bound to be informed by a set of judgements about the value of those events and not by reference to any analytical construction that can, or is indeed meant to, meet with common agreement. Any definition of the term is therefore bound to be a self-conscious, deliberate stipulation rather than merely the application of common usages of the word.

---

8   Peter Calvert, *Revolution*, London, 1970, p. 143.
9   Dunn, 'Revolution', p. 345.

Revolutionary Contexts

Rebellion, Civil War and Revolution: Scotland, Ireland and England in the 1640s

Michael Braddick

Leaving aside the distinctions between them, rebellion, riot, civil war and revolution have in common the fact that they are non- or extra-institutional means to political ends. There is a dividend in setting aside these taxonomical difficulties and concentrating instead on the relationship between institutional and non-institutional politics, differing but connected realms of political activity: doing so throws light on the differing forms both of institutional and informal politics. What follows is a very brief overview of patterns in such non-institutional politics – the expression of grievances outside the normal or accepted channels of court politics or representative institutions – in early modern England, with such questions in mind. It will focus in particular on the mid-seventeenth century crisis in the three Stuart Kingdoms. This, I hope, points to a way of understanding the relation of civil war and regicide to long-term political development in England, as well as a point of comparison with the contemporaneous crises in Ireland and Scotland (perhaps even beyond). In doing so, we move beyond the problematic characterization of that conflict as a 'revolution' or 'rebellion' with the attendant difficulties which have preoccupied the previous generation of scholarship on these conflicts, and focus instead on what was the original interest of these arguments: how to place this crisis in the longer term history of English politics.

In the highly specialized scholarship on early modern England, the study of non-institutional politics belongs more to social history and popular politics ('politics out of doors' is an oft-used term of art) than to the political history which has dominated recent scholarship on the English civil war and revolution. A key theme in this social history is the decline of 'peasant rebellion' and the development instead of forms of riot which represent forceful petitioning. From the great Peasant Revolt of 1381 to the mid-, or perhaps late sixteenth century regional risings were possible on the basis of peasant grievances, mobilized and organized over relatively wide territories with the support of middling social groups, and occasionally led by disaffected barons. These regional rebellions therefore represented, among other things, social coalitions. During the sixteenth century the spread of commercial agriculture disrupted the potential for such coalitions, driving a wedge between the economic interests of the middling sort and the poorer sort. The result was the birth of traditions of plebeian riot, no longer activated on the basis of an alliance with the middling sort, but seeking redress for economic and social grievances independently; often, in fact, appealing to the crown over the heads of their richer neighbours. Another element of the declining prospects for social coalitions in support of regional rebellions is the withdrawal of the aristocracy, the transformation of regional magnates into a court aristocracy, seeking patronage and influence, rather than mobilizing their tenants and neighbours as a power base independent of the crown. By the late sixteenth century, English aristocrats conformed closely to the ideals of the renaissance courtier, and the last magnate rebel, the earl of Essex was unable to mobilize support.[1]

The 'decline of peasant rebellions' in England is of course a much more complex question than this, and each instance of rebellion and riot is worthy of (and has often received) detailed treatment. But, even in summary form like this, it is clear that the forms of non-institutional politics which we can observe in sixteenth and seventeenth century England changed as the forms of state authority shifted – accounts of state formation have a kind of corollary in accounts of the shifting forms of non-institutional mobilization. As the middling sort assumed larger roles in local administration, and identified their interests more closely with the gentry and social order, they were less likely to have shared interests with plebeian rioters. As regional magnates were drawn into court politics as renaissance courtiers, their interests were expressed through the institutions of Tudor government, and they were less likely to try to raise their tenants in support of a political position.[2]

Considering revolt, rebellion, riot and revolution as varieties of non-institutional politics we can see how they were all shaped by the changing limits and practicalities of institutional politics. In most cases, too, they were adjuncts to institutional politics rather than a repudiation of them: extra-institutional as much as non-institutional forms of expression. In general, in fact, we might assume that as institutions form, are sustained and decay, they call forth differing forms of such politics. We might think here of the growth of transnational peace and anti-globalization movements in response to the declining capacity of national governments to operate independently in the face of global political problems. There is also, of course, a penumbra of semi-institutional politics – lobbying, patronage and other forms of informal pressure, which can shade into more active forms of mobilization outside the normal channels of government. Riots in sixteenth and seventeenth-century England were often the pursuit of legal suits by other means, for example; and the earl of Essex had been driven to revolt following a long period of unsuccessful manoeuvring to secure more influence at court.[3]

Most recent work on plebeian popular politics has emphasized the sophistication of political and legal ideals. Routine engagement with the institutions of the state, church and law equipped ordinary people with a command of official discourses, which could

---

1   The best overview is Anthony Fletcher and Diarmaid MacCulloch, *Tudor Rebellions*, 5th edition, Harlow, 2004, see here, esp. ch. 10. For the politics of crowds, see John Walter, *Crowds and popular politics in early modern England*, Manchester, 2007.

2   For state formation, see Michael J. Braddick, *State formation in early modern England, c. 1550–1700*, Cambridge, 2000; the classic study of the transformation of the aristocracy is M. E. James, *Society, politics and culture: studies in early modern England*, Cambridge, 1988. For the importance of civic humanism in English political culture, see Marku Peltonen, *Classical humanism and republicanism in English political thought, 1570–1640*, Cambridge, 1995.

3   Walter, *Crowds*; for negotiation, see also Michael J. Braddick and John Walter, *Negotiating power in early modern society: order, hierarchy and subordination in Britain and Ireland*, Cambridge, 2001, esp. intro., chs. 4, 5, 7. For Essex, see James, *Society, politics and culture*, ch. 9.

be deployed to their advantage.[4] Riots then took the form of forceful representations of the implications of official discourses – for example to jog local authorities to intervene in the grain market in order to ensure supplies of affordable food. Force was deployed with discipline – rarely against persons, very rarely with lethal consequences, and always against identifiably 'political' targets. Once again, we can see the forms of non-institutional politics changing in relation with the development of state institutions – in this case in the political languages used to legitimate the position of rioters – and how these forms of non-institutional politics form a continuum with semi-formal lobbying and pressure. This appropriation of official discourse is evident more continuously in the negotiation of power in routine circumstances: the calls of the poor to their social superiors to make good on their claims to have the benefit of their country at heart and to offer material support, for example.

On this view, then, riot in early modern England was an extension of institutional politics, shaped in relation to the formal structures of power, but conducted without a social coalition in support. These forms of political activity existed in symbiosis with institutional politics – both as a kind of twin to the forms of institutionalized politics and as dependent on the discourses of institutional politics for modes of legitimate expression. What issues necessitated mobilization outside the formal channels of government, who was interested in participation, and the forms of language used to express discontents were all products not just of grievances and interests, but of the institutional structures available for their expression.

Civil war in England, 1642–1648

The conflicts of the mid-seventeenth century have not figured in many recent accounts of these issues.[5] Paradigmatic explanations for the war used to make a close connection between high and low politics, but in ways that are now discredited. Marxists argued that pressure for constitutional change reflected the interests of emerging political classes, in opposition to a dominant landed elite in alliance with the crown. Whig historians, who accepted the case that there was pressure for constitutional change did not see it as a reflection of class interest, but did also presume some harmony between constitutional change and the interests of the lower orders. Both views were associated with the view that the war had long-term causes – in the structural conditions of social and economic life, or the inevitability of constitutional crisis. War was seen as a more or less predictable consequence of structural political conflicts, and the revolution of 1649 as a more or less natural outgrowth of the war and the political conflicts that had caused it. Lawrence Stone's classic study of the causes of the English revolution, for example,

---

4 See in addition to the works cited above, Steve Hindle, *The state and social change in early modern England, 1550–1640*, Harlow, 2000; Andy Wood, *Riot, rebellion and popular politics in early modern England*, Basingstoke, 2002.

5 The outstanding exception is recent work by John Walter, especially *Understanding popular violence in the English revolution: the Colchester plunderers*, Cambridge, 1999. Another notable exception is Wood, *Riot, rebellion and popular politics*. For fuller reference to recent work by Walter, Wood, Cressy and others, see Michael Braddick, *God's Fury, England's Fire: a new history of the English civil wars*, Harmondsworth, 2008.

took as its end-point 1642, seven years prior to the regicide – the processes in train at the start of the civil war evidently explained how the rest of the conflict unfolded. [6]

Revisionist work has unpicked these connections: between class and party; between conflicts before the war and the causes of the fighting; between the causes of the war and of the revolution; and has therefore emphasized the contingent causes of both war and revolution arising from it.[7] Revisionists have also been sceptical about the connection between popular and national politics, emphasizing the problems of writing a social history of political allegiance. The problems here are two-fold – evidential and method-ological. In general, it is possible to find an indication of allegiance for only a fraction of the population and at a fixed moment in time. There are methodological difficulties both in interpreting this snapshot of allegiance and inferring its roots, although this can often be augmented with more qualitative contemporary (or at least near-contemporary) comment. While impressive analyses of popular allegiance have been developed in the face of such objections, it is possible for those sceptical about this enterprise to continue to advance them.[8] A further difficulty which is less emphasized, but which seems to me no less significant, is capturing fluidity. Anyone who has left us detailed materials on which to base an account of their civil war allegiance seems to exemplify the truth that there were more than two sides, that allegiance to one of the two armies was therefore shifting, offered with differing degrees of commitment, and changed as the political programmes being championed by the armies evolved. These were armed coalitions which attracted changing and variable commitments from among the same populations.

A further and equally central concern of revisionism was to debunk heroic accounts of the war – particularly the modernization narratives that championed the history of the war and revolution as an episode in the history of progress. This gave rise to an allied emphasis on hesitant, conservative and neutralist politics, and on the horrors and trauma that were the costs paid for the radicalism. One of the factors making for shifting alle-giances was the calculation about whether the political disagreements were really worth a war, or continuing the war, and so on.[9] This sat well with the cutting edge of research in social history, which had tended to emphasize the village study, pursued through an anthropological lens. This kind of analysis tended to see the village as a closed world (despite the evidence of high population turnover), with a distinct set of politics (prima-rily those of social structure – hierarchies of wealth and gender in particular) which

---

6   Lawrence Stone, *The causes of the English revolution, 1529–1642*, revised edition, London, 2001. The
    most penetrating introduction to the debate is Ann Hughes, *The causes of the English civil war*, 2nd edition,
    Basingstoke, 1998. Ronald Hutton, *Debates in Stuart history*, Basingstoke, 2004, is also penetrating and
    offers a revisionist perspective.
7   The leading figures in these respects are Conrad Russell, *The causes of the English revolution*, Oxford,
    1990, and Russell (ed), *The origins of the English civil war*, London, 1973; and John Morrill, *The nature
    of the English revolution*, Harlow, 1993, and *Revolt in the provinces: the English people and the tragedies
    of war, 1630–1648*, second edition, Harlow, 1998.
8   The most sophisticated studies of allegiance are David Underdown, *Revel, riot and rebellion: popular
    politics and culture in England, 160-3-1660*, Oxford, 1985, and Mark Stoyle, *Loyalty and locality:
    popular allegiance in Devon during the English civil war*, Exeter, 1994. For the sceptical revisionist
    response to Underdown, see Morrill, 'The ecology of allegiance in the English Revolution. With a reply
    by David Underdown', *Journal of British Studies*, 26, 1987, 4, pp. 451–79.
9   Morrill, *Revolt in the provinces*; Morrill (ed), *Reactions to the English civil war, 1642–49*, Basingstoke,
    1982; Ronald Hutton, *The royalist war effort: 1642–1646*, 2nd edition, London, 2002.

operated over the *longue-durée*. Anthropological methods and an interest in structure, *Annaliste*-style, produced an emphasis on particular kinds of politics which moved to slow rhythms, and were played out in distinctive local arenas.[10] A consequence of this was to reinforce the separation between analysis of the causes, course and consequences of civil war (increasingly analysed in terms of the short-term and contingent), and of village politics.[11]

I have argued elsewhere that this has been to the disadvantage of an understanding of the civil war and the political creativity to which it gave rise. If we concentrate on mobilization – non-institutional politics as a means to influence the direction of institutional politics – we have a means to reconnect high and low politics, with benefits for an understanding of the course and consequence of the war. My analysis moves forward from there by emphasizing mobilization rather than allegiance as a way of reconnecting high and low politics; and by emphasizing creativity rather than 'radicalism', a term which tends to limit the range of thought which historians analyse. Mobilization brings together sensitivity to precise political context, with the cultural history of representation, and the sociology of politics and political communication. Overall this also provides a context for intellectual history, although I have no claims to expertise in that area.[12]

A key question here is why established institutions of government failed to function in channelling and resolving political conflict between 1640 and 1642 despite the very evident commitment of all partisans to sustaining the life of those institutions. There was a widespread belief that a party was actively trying to dissolve the two crucial institutions of government – church and state. In order to save these institutions it was necessary to mobilize support outside them. This process prompted another party to form, also intent on saving the church and state, but this time by shoring up monarchical authority against populist mobilization. Ironically, of course, this involved no small amount of populist mobilization. Non-institutional politics in England in 1641 and 1642 were driven by the need to mobilize outside the institutions of government in order to protect them, and these mobilizations were driven by differing views of where the major threat to their integrity arose from.[13]

---

10 Keith Wrightson is the key figure here. His dazzling and hugely influential study of *English society, 1580–1680*, London, 1982, has been of seminal importance. For a brilliant overview of this strand of scholarship, see Keith Wrightson, 'The politics of the parish in early modern England', in Paul Griffiths, Adam Fox and Steve Hindle (eds.), *The experience of authority in early modern England*, Basingstoke, 1996, pp. 10–46.

11 Wrightson's *English society* contains only the briefest index entries to the civil war.

12 Michael J Braddick, 'Mobilisation, anxiety and creativity in England during the 1640s' in John Morrow and Jonathan Scott (eds), *Liberty, Authority, Formality* (forthcoming, Manchester, 2007/8). See also Braddick, 'The English revolution and its legacies (the Neale Lecture for 2004)' in Nicholas Tyacke (ed.), *The English Revolution c. 1590–1720* (forthcoming, Manchester, 2007/8).

13 For this analysis, see Braddick, *God's Fury*, chs. 4–7. It is deeply indebted to Anthony Fletcher, *The outbreak of the English civil war*, London, 1981, and to the work of Peter Lake, especially 'Antipopery: the structure of a prejudice', in Richard Cust and Ann Hughes (eds), *Conflict in early Stuart England: studies in religion and politics, 1603–1642*, Harlow, 1989, pp. 72–106; and Lake, 'Anti-Puritanism: the structure of a prejudice', in Kenneth Fincham and Peter Lake (eds), *Religious politics in post-Reformation England: essays in honour of Nicholas Tyacke*, Woodbridge, 2006, pp. 80–97.

Another feature of this crisis bears again on the larger question of the forms of non-institutional politics – how they are shaped by changing means of mobilization. Print has long been recognized to be crucial to the course of the political crisis in England. Christopher Hill had earlier argued that the radicalism of the period represented an eruption into the open of previously suppressed forms of expression. This gave rise to a long-running debate about the nature of early modern censorship – in a moment of zeal Hill had likened it to the suppression of political expression in late communist Romania – and to the significance of changes in the book trade during the 1640s. I have argued elsewhere that the effect of print was often to amplify, generalize and accelerate other forms of mobilization: crowds, petitions and demonstrations. The collapse of censorship and the dramatic shift of output towards short, time-sensitive and ephemeral publications was an adjunct to political mobilization. But print also had a distinctive role in encouraging the development of more exaggerated positions through the iterative effect of printed debate about church and state in the absence of disciplines over that debate.[14]

England saw a conflict over the nature and future of institutions pretty much universally agreed to be crucial to the social and political order – national church, crown and parliament. The difference was not over the identity of those institutions, nor even over the terms which could be used to describe them, but over the threat to them and the means necessary to protect them. Those differences were canvassed outside the institutions of government – in demonstrations, petitioning campaigns and in print. Following the king's withdrawal from parliament in January 1642, the paper battles were carried out into the institutions of local government, where a partisan inflection was given to the deliberations of bodies normally understood to offer the univocal opinion of the 'country': assizes, quarter sessions and their grand juries. Militias and strong-points were seized as defensive measures, armies were raised and ultimately a battle was fought. This gave rise the following year to full-scale warfare, in which the respective causes were refined and publicized in order to obtain the support necessary to fight, but in that process the meaning of key terms became increasingly unstable, so too the rules governing political argument. Plurality was exacerbated by divisions within the coalitions, particularly on the parliamentary side, over war aims, peace terms and the meaning of the conflict. This gave rise to creativity – in the ways that opinions were circulated, the deployment of existing forms of political argument and the development of substantive arguments that were highly innovative.

It has long been noted that England was the last of Charles's kingdoms to rebel, the one to produce the most spontaneous armed royalism and that the rhetorical differences between the two sides were slight.[15] Against this, it has been similarly persistently noted that the civil war signalled the opening of the 'epic years of the English imagination'.[16] A number of explanations have been offered for this apparent paradox: my own centres on mobilization. Activists seeking support outside the institutions of government competed for control of the standard terms of political discourse, producing a problem

---

14 Braddick, 'Mobilisation, anxiety and creativity'.
15 See especially Conrad Russell, *The fall of the British monarchies 1637–1642*, Oxford, 1991.
16 G.A. Pocock, quoted in J.C. Davis, 'Political thought during the English revolution', in Barry Coward (ed), *A companion to Stuart Britain*, Oxford, 2003, pp. 274–96.

of credibility. It became difficult to know what was happening, to agree what it meant and even to agree the terms on which such issues could be decided. Many responses to this situation were anxious, but some were creative – seeking new ways to ground truth claims, to interpret the meaning of events and new rules on which to base these claims.

These conditions gave rise, among other things, to many attempts to re-establish disciplines over knowledge production – both in print and elsewhere. They often shared three key features – to secure sound empirical data, establish agreed rules of interpretation, or create institutions which can guarantee truth claims. This was a golden age for English astrology and Baconianism, which offered clear rules on all three issues, as well as for more obviously political speculation. We might think of John Milton's famous argument in *Areopagitica* for a market in opinion, which would give rise to knowledge, and of Thomas Hobbes's attempts to arrive at political truths through a philosophical political science, for example. An identifiable political process – mobilization – helps to contextualize rapid change in the conditions of knowledge production – creativity as well as innovative discursive and communicative strategies.[17]

The Scottish revolution

Much of the most important recent work on the 1640s has demonstrated that it is impossible to treat the causes and course of this crisis in England independently of the politics of the other Stuart kingdoms. The collapse of institutional politics in England was a product first of responses to a revolution in Scotland and then to a rebellion in Ireland. The fate of three kingdoms was tied together by confessional politics, in particular, which made it impossible to take a position on the internal affairs of one kingdom without reference to events in the other two.[18] However, although it was a shared crisis, in terms of mobilization and creativity England was distinct: a civil war that produced a revolution. Attention to politics in Scotland and Ireland throws the distinctiveness of this English experience of a wider crisis into sharper relief.

The plurality of mobilizations in England contrasts sharply with Scotland. Outraged by a new Prayer Book associated in Scottish minds with dilute English protestantism and the power of bishops, Scottish presbyterians carried through a revolution. They first brought pressure to bear on existing institutions in ways that were to become familiar in England – through crowds, petition, print and then armed demonstration. When Charles's government tried to face down the opposition the conflict escalated, leading to the signing of a national Covenant in 1638. This bound its signatories to stand together in defence of the true religion, and to stand with the king in the defence of the true religion. It was signed very widely indeed, in fact almost universally, and gave a clear historical and legal account of what the true Scottish religion was. Here was the first contrast with what was to happen in England two years later – the possibility of agreeing a text for settlement allowed for a united front in opposition to crown policy. A second contrast was that in Scotland, rather than simply battling for control of existing

---

17 Braddick, 'Mobilisation, anxiety and creativity'; Braddick, 'English revolution and its legacies'.
18 For a succinct narrative from this perspective and further references, see David Scott, *Politics and war in the three Stuart kingdoms, 1637–49*, Basingstoke, 2004.

institutions, the Covenanters created a revolutionary body – the Tables – which had no previous constitutional existence.[19]

Scottish Presbyterians then promoted a double covenant, which seemed to imply that obedience to the monarch was dependent on the monarch's credentials as godly ruler: a form of resistance theory that was, to some extent at least, respectable in Reformation Europe. On the basis of this double covenant and in the light of an agreed version of the past, present and future of the Scottish Kirk, they were able to defend their corner by force of arms, behind a manifesto and through a body established for that purpose – the Tables. This has been characterized as oligarchic centralism – an elite political movement which harnessed rather than unleashed popular feelings. This Covenanting revolution was remarkably successful, securing a climb-down from Charles I on the substance of the issue and a tacit acknowledgement that he should deal with this revolutionary authority – the Tables – whose role was justified by the Covenant.

In Scotland the discipline of the Kirk, particularly the Kirk sessions, offered an institutional basis for a more or less unanimous mobilization around a clearly defined cause.[20] This was co-ordinated at a national level by a revolutionary body – the Tables – and supported in the General Assembly. In England control of existing institutions – parishes, grand juries, parliament – was contested, and there was no revolutionary body promoting a unified opposition to the crown. Scotland produced Samuel Rutherford; civil war followed when it seemed, in a three kingdom context, that the achievement of the consensual religious aims had gone too far in eroding the authority of the monarchy. In Scotland, revolution led to civil war.[21]

Ireland: Baronial revolt to confessional war

It was the success of the Covenanters which led to the summoning of parliament in England in 1640. The failure of that parliament to resolve English political difficulties resulted to a considerable extent from the outbreak of rebellion in Ireland in 1641.

English policy in Ireland during the sixteenth century had not initially been based on expropriation and colonization, but rather on the transformation of local elites into a court aristocracy. This was failing by the mid-sixteenth century, when it became overlain with a confessional divide: the reformation failed among the native Irish and old English settlers, so that their exclusion from power was doubly-determined – an exaggerated view was that they were neither civil nor Christian. In order to secure royal authority it was increasingly thought necessary to plant civil and Christian settlers,

---

19 The principal works are David Stevenson, *The Scottish revolution 1637–44: the triumph of the Covenanters*, Edinburgh, 2003, and Allan I. Macinnes, *Charles I and the making of the Covenanting movement, 1625–1641*, Edinburgh, 1991.

20 For the social and cultural embrace of the Kirk, see Margo Todd, *The culture of Protestantism in early modern Scotland*, New Haven, 2002.

21 For the later history of Covenanting period, see David Stevenson, *Revolution and counter-revolution in Scotland, 1644–1651*, London, 1977. For Rutherford and Covenanting political thought, see John Coffey, *Politics, religion and the British revolutions: the mind of Samuel Rutherford*, Cambridge, 1997; Coffey, 'Samuel Rutherford and the political thought of the Scottish covenanters', in John R. Young (ed.), *Celtic dimensions of the British civil wars: proceedings of the second conference of the Research Centre for Scottish History, University of Strathclyde*, Edinburgh, 1997, pp. 75–95.

whose influence would transform Ireland. By the 1630s this meant that power was in the hands of newcomers, on planted land, of a religion quite different from that of the rest of the population.[22]

In the late 1630s, as Scotland and the English parliament seemed to be falling into the hands of puritans completely hostile to Catholic interests, Catholic elites in Ireland felt the crown to be the safeguard of their future, and calculated that now might be the time to throw their weight behind the crown, against these puritans. They planned a rising in Ulster and a plot in Dublin, confident that they could control disorder in order to make a forceful representation to the king about their aspirations. The rising led to a polarization of English and Scottish politics, as puritans demanded that it be crushed, and completely disowned by the crown; while the crown seemed to hesitate on both points. In the meantime Irish peasant unrest ran out of the control of the leadership, leading to violent dispossession of protestant settlers and the development of a confessional war. English and Scottish armies invaded with this view, and helped to create what they had feared.[23] The dolorous consequences of this live on, of course.

Conclusion

What is often now discussed as a single crisis can also be seen as the intersection of three distinct forms of non-institutional politics in a shared crisis: a revolution defined by Calvinist resistance theory; a baronial revolt which gave way to confessional and ethnic violence; and the effects of multiple and overlapping mobilizations in favour of differing views of the future of existing institutions. Each case is of course intrinsically important and interesting; Ireland for the development of the confessional politics which have been so important for its subsequent history; Scotland for what might be one of the more successful Calvinist revolutions in early modern Europe; and England for its unusual creativity and the open-endedness of the resultant political speculation.

England's freedom, declared by the revolutionary regime in 1649, was certainly highly unusual in a European context. This unusual radicalism arose from ingredients which were common to many conflicts in early modern Europe. Threats to the true religion as locally understood, concerns about the future of representative institutions and problems arising from trying to govern multiple kingdoms were hardly unique to the Stuart kingdom. However, some of the resolutions possible elsewhere were not possible in England – this could not resolve into a separatist movement, or result in partition or confessional separation since these political conflicts did not follow territorial or ethnic divisions and represented a battle within a single church. Neither was deposition a serious possibility, although it was floated at various points, and the reversionary interest was unpromising. Instead, the English were locked into a debate about how to interpret apparently shared values and for control of institutions universally agreed to have an important and legitimate role in religious and political life. England in the 1640s

---

22 Braddick, *State formation*, ch. 9, offers a brief overview and full references. Nicholas Canny, *Making Ireland British 1580–1650*, Oxford, 2001, is authoritative and comprehensive.

23 Nicholas Canny, 'What really happened in Ireland in 1641?', in Jane H. Ohlmeyer (ed), *Ireland from independence to occupation 1641–1660*, Cambridge, 1995, pp. 24–42; Canny, *Making Ireland British*, chs. 8–9; Scott, *Politics and religion*.

saw tremendous intellectual creativity because there was no obvious political exit, and no apparent hope of rhetorical solution. Instead new grounds were sought on which to construct secure knowledge of the social and political world. This arose from rhetorical and a formal institutional conservatism, which effectively locked political conflict in, without allowing the exits afforded to other rebels in early modern Europe. This in turn suggests that we might start to compare England's creativity to other civil wars, rather than other revolutions.

Forms of non-institutional politics in Ireland and Scotland reflect patterns of institutional life in those kingdoms, and forms of political discourse which enjoyed legitimacy there: differing forms of revolt, rebellion, riot and revolution have to be understood against the full range of possibilities for the expression of political interests. I have argued elsewhere that institutional changes during the 1640s were important to long-term processes of state formation in England and the wider territories of the Stuart crown.[24] I would also suggest that we can place this experience in a longer history of non-institutional politics in those territories too. Certainly against the background of the larger narrative of non-institutional politics in sixteenth- and seventeenth-century England, the civil war also assumes considerable significance. The decline of the social coalitions behind regional rebellions in England gave way to riot, but also to the foundation of extra-local ideological coalitions, mobilized in print and other ways.[25] These had a pre-civil war history, but a much more impressive post-civil war future. The experience of partisan political mobilization represents a key point in the development from Peasants' Revolt to the reign of King Mob.

---

24 Braddick, *State formation*.
25 For particular important studies on the theme of partisan politics, see Tim Harris, *London crowds in the reign of Charles II: propaganda and politics from the Restoration until the Exclusion Crisis*, Cambridge, 1987; Harris, *Politics under the later Stuarts: party conflict in a divided society, 1660–1715*, Harlow, 1993; Mark Knights, *Politics and opinion in crisis, 1678–1681*, Cambridge, 1994; Knights, *Representation and misrepresentation in later Stuart Britain: partisanship and political culture*, Oxford, 2004.

'The Bloody Project': Ethics and the Experience of Revolutionary Selfhood in Leveller and Jacobin Practice

Brodie Richards

By studying the practices of the Levellers and the Jacobins this essay examines how the practice of revolution raised the question of who it is good to be and, in doing so, enabled the formation, within ethical practice, of a Leveller and Jacobin subjectivity. The articulations, debates and struggles over the good not only shaped the event of revolution, but also the agent of revolt, in his ethical subjectivity, and presented him with the possibilities of selfhood that his action came to express and manifest. For the men and women who engaged as Levellers and Jacobins, the problem of revolution was not strictly social or political – that of determining the right laws and structures for a new socio-political order – it was ethical. In his practice, the revolutionary was forced to question himself about how to act and how to live *as* a revolutionary. For revolutionaries, the problem thus became of how they should engage themselves in the practice of revolution, of being who they ought to be, and the question of how to be 'good' and 'true'. The questioning the revolutionary agent directed to his own self, and the care he devoted to his self, was not confined to the problem of establishing a relationship with moral obligations that defined rules for acting and living.[1] Rather, what was more primary than obligation was the fact that the event embodied the practice of orientating oneself to and encountering the good within practical agency. The practice of revolt expressed an ascetic practice and discourse that enabled the agent to constitute himself as the moral agent of revolt and to experience a relationship to his own self that was produced by his own ascetic practice of ethical self-transformation.[2] Becoming a revolutionary was bound to the task of determining a relationship with what was good,

---

1   My use of the term 'care of the self' and its relationship with ethics is derived from the work of Michel Foucault, specifically: Foucault, *The Use of Pleasure* (The History of Sexuality, vol 2), trans. Robert Hurley, New York, 1990, and *The Care of the Self* (The History of Sexuality, vol 3), trans. Robert Hurley, New York, 1986.

2   Foucault drew the distinction between a history of moral codes, a history of moral behaviour and a history of ethics. He defined the history of ethics as the historical study of 'the way in which individuals are urged to constitute themselves as subjects of moral conduct'. The history of ethics studies within a given period 'the models proposed for setting up and developing relationships with the self, for self-reflection, self-knowledge, self-examination, for the decipherment of the self by oneself, for the transformations that one seeks to accomplish with oneself as object.' The term 'ascetics' refers to the practices and discourses that shaped the way the subject formed an ethical relationship to his own self. See Foucault, *The Use of Pleasure*, p. 29.

articulating values about what was admirable and what was not, and constituting oneself according to an articulation about what made political life meaningful.[3]

This essay will focus on the Levellers of the English Civil War and the Jacobins of the French Revolution. My aim is to use these two historical examples to highlight the problem of ethics as it presents itself in the practice of revolt and to study how the experience of ethics raised for the agent the problem of his own selfhood. Studying revolutionary ethics also enables us to address one of the main themes of the present collection: the question of what moves the individual to revolt against a system that he perceives as oppressive. In the act of revolting, the ethical discourse on what is good and who is good shaped the agency of the revolutionaries and offered them not only justification for their action, but a compelling vision of the necessity of their action and of their own moral worth as agents engaged in redefining the nature of their community.

Any historical study of revolution confronts the fraught question of what a revolution is. In summary the issue reduces to which of the two dynamics, the political or the social, shapes the nature of revolution. Marxist historiography has conceptualized the nature of revolution as shaped by economic processes and as representing the political expression of socio-economic change and class struggle. The agent of revolution is formed by these economic and social structures and acts according to the interests of class. In response to Marxism, a considerable body of work emphasizes the political nature of revolution, focusing on the centrality of state formation, radical movements, ideological conflict and a political struggle for power. By this measure, revolution is about liberty, democracy and power. Within this debate, the normative historiography of revolution has been led to prioritize the examination of revolt as politics and as a process of social change and class struggle, focusing on the agent as an ideology, a social class, a party and a personality. In doing so, these studies on revolution have prioritized the historical transformations that the politics of revolution has produced within the social and political structures. Nevertheless, the question of the nature of revolution compels us also to consider the question of moral agency and to examine the effect that the practice of revolution had in the formation of ethical subjectivities, the distinctive consciousness and capacity to revolt of the agents who practised revolution.

The practice of revolution constituted the formation of revolutionary selfhood. The creation of these subjectivities, both Leveller and Jacobin, offered the agents of revolt the possibility of experiencing, within their practice, certain forms of political agency. The self-understanding they achieved as agents was shaped by the moral discourse on the good and the ethical practices of self-formation. These discourses and practices constituted the possibility of considering oneself a political agent who embodied an ethical capacity to revolt and the freedom to engage in the foundation of a political community.

Studying the formation of these revolutionary subjectivities draws on a body of twentieth-century philosophical work that has challenged the concept of subjectivity embodied within normative historiography. This philosophical work enables the

---

3   The importance of the ethical distinction between 'right' and 'good' and the centrality of the concept of the good for the experience of selfhood is outlined by Charles Taylor, *Sources of the Self: The Making of Modern Identity*, Cambridge, MA, 1989, pp. 3–107.

historian to consider the question of revolutionary selfhood in a new way. The philosophical insights of the philosophers of language –thinkers as diverse as Heidegger, Wittgenstein, Habermas and Foucault, to name only a few – structure, and enable this essay to study, the question of how revolutionary politics problematized the experience of being revolutionary and produced the possibility for the ethical experience of selfhood.[4] These thinkers share a common theoretical assumption about the constitutive force of language, its embodiment within practice, and the centrality of historical processes and events in situating possibilities for shaping the meaning of selfhood.[5] The locus of the human capacity for self-realization shifts from the self-conscious mind to temporally specific practices, both discursive and non-discursive, which situate the agent within historical processes that enable the production and constitution of historical subjectivities. These historical experiences of agency, marked by multiplicity and temporality, are embodied in acts of speaking and doing, not in the act of a pure consciousness.

From this perspective, the ascetic practice of the Levellers and Jacobins points not to an ideology, mentality, or consciousness that the agent adopted in order to shape his action, but to a practice – to the act of revolt itself. His action is justified, explained, outlined – shaped – by a moral discourse about 'the good'. His everyday practice confronts him with the question of being good insofar as he acts, and the event itself calls upon him to determine how to act by raising the question of what is right and good. The revolutionary event thus prefigures the ethical problem rather than the ethical problem pre-figuring the event: the agent 'finds' his ethics within the revolutionary project itself. This paper does not seek to reconstruct the Jacobin or the Leveller moral self-consciousness *before* he revolted, or examine what the qualities of that thought and self-consciousness can tell us about how he revolted. Instead, I want to study how the practice of this revolt compelled the agent to question himself about who he was as an agent. His act of revolt raised the question of who he was, presenting the problem of the self to those who engaged as revolutionaries. Within the events that shaped the Leveller and the Jacobin, the practice of revolt came to express the possibility for the subject to identify capacities within his own self as a political agent and to experience a freedom that was constituted as an asceticism of ethical self-transformation.

Before turning to the separate case studies that I have proposed, I want to speak about the general field of problematization that the Levellers and Jacobins shared. Both Leveller and Jacobin practice emerged within a political situation where the question of

---

4   The essential works for my study of this philosophical critique of modern subjectivist philosophy and for understanding how to use these theories on language, agency and selfhood for the study of revolt have been: Martin Heidegger, 'The Fundamental Question of Metaphysics', in *Introduction to Metaphysics*, trans. Gregory Fried & Richard Polt, New Haven, 2000, pp. 1–54; Michel Foucault, *The Archaeology of Knowledge and The Discourse on Language*, trans. A.M. Sheridan Smith, New York, 1972, pp. 3–70; Charles Taylor, 'Hegel's Philosophy of Mind', *Human Agency and Language*, Cambridge, 1985, pp. 77–96 Jürgen Habermas, 'An Alternative Way out of the Philosophy of the Subject: Communicative versus Subject-Centred Reason,' *The Philosophical Discourse of Modernity*, Cambridge, 1990, pp. 294–326.

5   The theory of language as constitutive is outlined by Heidegger when he refers to 'the naming force of language and words'. As he explains, 'for words and language are not just shells into which things are packed for spoken and written intercourse. In the word, in language, things first come to be and are.' Heidegger, 'The Fundamental Question of Metaphysics', p. 15.

community was being forcibly raised and problematized. This problematization emerged in a dynamic situation that included widespread debate, the proliferation of the written and spoken word, a violent struggle over the values and structures that were proposed, and the experience of radical change in the nature of government, citizenship and in the structures of communal life. The Levellers and Jacobins developed their political practice in response to this situation claiming the right, duty and capacity to offer solutions. In the midst of this conflict over values and the nature of community, both the Jacobins and the Levellers revolted against the traditions and norms of their political society. Their revolt was tied to the practice of proposing a new project for the creation and preservation of the community – the Levellers proposed in their *Agreement of the People* to radically alter the foundations and norms of English society; for their part, the Jacobins sought to make France a republic, and, in the absence of the king, to re-order the political society around the moral and political structures of a secular republic. Both the Levellers and the Jacobins claimed to speak for the community – they invited groups that had been traditionally silenced to participate visibly and forcibly in the establishment of the new community. Both movements were willing to use violence to secure the new community, and they suggested that the purity of their vision, its sanction by the laws of nature, reason and God, justified the violence that would be used. Both the Levellers and the Jacobins aimed their bow, with an aggressive and organized hand, with a disciplined and ascetic stance and – to paraphrase Camus – the bow bent, the wood complained, and at the moment of supreme tension, the Leveller and the Jacobin, inflexible and free, released an unswerving arrow against tyrants.[6]

In the August of 1648, at the height of the English Revolution, *The Bloody Project* circulated London, responding to the crisis by asking the following question: 'Can there be a more bloody Project then to engage men to kill one another, and yet no just cause declared?'[7] This question propelled Leveller discourse to question for themselves, 'upon what grounds with a good conscience can you engage your selves, or perswade others to engage in killing and slaying of men?'[8] The argument developed by *The Bloody Project* expressed two primary questions addressed by the Levellers' ethical discourse: who was compelled to engage in settling the kingdom? What obligations did their engagement placed upon them as agent? First, what concerned the Levellers, and the problem they raised repeatedly, was that 'the people', as a group, would be used by the various factions – whether king, army or parliament – for their own self-interested ends. As they warned their readers: 'The King, Parliament, great men in the City and Army, have made you but stairs by which they have mounted to Honour, Wealth and Power.'[9] In response to this concern, the Levellers appealed to all citizens of England to consider the nature of their engagement for themselves. This appeal was asserted in the phrase that one finds throughout Leveller tracts, that the agent should 'look about you.'[10] The Levellers agreed that the political situation not only concerned everyone, but compelled all as a duty to engage in settling the commonwealth, and the individual was

---

6   Albert Camus, *The Rebel*, trans. Anthony Bower, New York, 1956, p. 306.
7   William Walwyn, *The Bloody Project* (1648), in Jack R. McMichael and Barbara Taft (eds.), *The Writings of William Walwyn*, Athens, GA, 1989, p. 307.
8   ibid, p.303.
9   ibid, p. 306.
10 *Looke About You: A Word in Season to a Divided Nation* (1647). E408(3).

expected to engage according to his own conscience and judgement. As a result, the Levellers admonished the common man to use his own powers of judgement and decide for himself how to act. It is from the *Poore Wise-mans Admonition* that we see the clearest statement of this concern:

> Although you and your families are they who in all publicke calamities do suffer most, yet seem you altogether insensible of your owne danger untill it be directly upon you, you looke not into public affaires yourselves, but trust wholly upon others; and if they either through weaknesse, wilfulnesse, corruption or treacherie faile in their trust or turne oppressors and tyrants, ye remain liable to be deluded and betrayed by them into tumults, wars, miseries and bondage. But believe it, you have need to look about you, and that verie quickly, to see into affaires your selves, and understand how things go, for you are likely very speedily to be put upon the greatest triall of your wisdom and faithfulness that ever men were put upon.[11]

When he was admonished, attacked and eventually imprisoned for his actions, John Lilburne defended himself by claiming, 'I did look well about me before I did what I did.'[12]

Secondly, Leveller ethical discourse was intimately concerned with the question of duty and obligation. The violence of war compelled the Levellers to assert a strict sense of moral obligation. Leveller practice was based on the insistence that the agent's engagement within the political struggles must follow the dictates of the laws of nature and God: the agent must engage out of necessity and according to the opportunity presented by God.[13] The political crisis within England was interpreted as such an opportunity, when God presented the English with the opportunity to settle the fundamental laws of their community.[14] As the *Manifestation* asserted: 'God hath so blest that which has been done, as thereby to cleer the way, and to afford an opportunity which these 600 years has been desires, but could never be attained, of making this a truly happy and wholly Free Nation.'[15] The agent was being called by God for this task, and it was the agent's duty to respond to this calling with care and circumspection. The agent must look upon the situation and determine what the ends of his engagement were, and what authority sanctioned his engagement. The Levellers consistently challenged the king, the parliament and the grandees of the army regarding these moral issues, insisting

---

11 *The poore Wise-mans Admonition* (1647), in A. L. Morton (ed.), *Freedom in Arms: A Selection of Leveller Writings*, New York, 1975, p. 123. For a similar instruction to soldiers, advising them to 'look well about you' see *Sea-Green & Blue, See Which Speaks True* (1649), British Library [hereafter BL], Thomason Tracts, E 559 (1), 8; *The English Souldiers Standard* (1649), in Morton, *Freedom in Arms*, p. 232.

12 *The Picture of the Councel of State* (1649), in William Haller and Godfrey Davies (eds), *The Leveller Tracts 1647–1653*, New York, 1944, p. 202.

13 The concept of necessity was central within the legal and moral tradition of this time, where one finds the expression 'necessity has no law' often used to defend the act of revolt. For Leveller use of the concept, see Richard Overton, *An Appeale from the degenerate Representative Body* (1647), in Don M. Wolfe (ed.), *Leveller Manifestoes of the Puritan Revolution*, New York, 1944, p. 160. The concept was central to the narratives that the Levellers wrote about their arrest and imprisonment. For example, see Richard Overton, *The Commoners Complaint: Or, A Dreadfulwarning From Newgate, to the Commons of England* (1647), in William Haller (ed.), *Tracts on Liberty in the Puritan Revolution, 1639–1647*, vol 3, New York, 1965, pp. 374–392.

14 The concept of opportunity was particularly emphasized in the sermons of the period. See thus Thomas Goodwin, *Zerubbabel's Encouragement to Finish the Temple* (1642), BL, Thomason Tracts, E 147 (13); Stephen Marshall, *The Right Understanding of the Times* (1647), BL, Thomason Tracts, E 369 (5).

15 John Lilburne, et al, 'A Manifestation' (1649) in Haller and Davies, *Leveller Tracts*, p. 227.

that parliament and the army had deviated from the ends that were present in its actions of the early 1640s, while accusing the army and the parliament of toppling one system of oppression for another.

Nevertheless, when we study Leveller practice and ethical discourse we can note that the call from God was not only about common duty and what was right – it was also a call to the good. Grounded in their practice of looking into affairs for themselves and their concern for the nature of the engagement, the Levellers proposed the *Agreement of the People* as a means to settle the commonwealth.[16] In the practice of promoting the *Agreement of the People,* the Levellers questioned themselves about political activity as an ethical problem. It was the practice of proposing the Agreement that raised the question of who it was good to be and specified the ethical subject of this Agreement. Not only were the 'well-affected' recognized as the only proper agents of the Agreement, the Agreement also specified that the organization, promotion and participation within the Agreement must be confined to 'fit' persons. What distinguished Leveller practice from the practice of Parliament was that the Levellers proposed that an agent could make himself 'fit', whereas parliament remained tied to the discourse that defined being fit with the status of owning property. The Levellers, together with the agitators in the Army, claimed that by engaging with the war and settlement of the commonwealth, they had become 'fit' persons. Leveller discourse appealed to their uprightness, their affections for the cause and their energetic and active service as the grounds for considering themselves 'fit' to participate in the settlement of the nation. This discourse suggested that their affections, actions and character exemplified their 'public-spirit' and the Levellers outlined the ethical practices that the agent must use to shape his own 'public-spirit'. For example, this discourse outlined the centrality of association and friendship for maintaining the proper affections for the cause and the importance of reading and writing for forming oneself as an agent able to serve the community.

In the *Manifestation*, the Levellers presented the most detailed ethical discourse about their action and themselves as agents. As they wrote, it was the aspersions cast upon them that necessitated they 'open their breasts and shew the world our insides.' In response, the Levellers presented a detailed moral characterization of their action, their aims, and themselves as agents, so that 'the world may clearly see what we are, and what we aim at.'[17] Arguing that no man is born for himself, the *Manifestation* insists that the agent is obliged to engage for 'the advancement of communitive happiness'.[18] Being good according to the dictates of an impartial conscience was the grounds for being serviceable and useful to the Commonwealth, and the Levellers presented themselves in their service as models of 'public-spiritedness'. As they concluded: 'we aim not at power in our selves, our Principles and Desires being in no measure of self-concernment.'[19] The Leveller discourse on themselves characterized who the agent must be in his relationship with the good and how he must act as an agent of revolt, bringing forth

---

16 The Levellers produced three versions of an Agreement: *An Agreement of the People* (1647); *Foundations of Freedom: Or an Agreement of the People* (1648); *An Agreement of the Free People of England* (1649). All three can be found in Wolfe, *Leveller Manifestoes.*
17 Lilburne, et al., *A Manifestation*, pp. 279, 284.
18 ibid, p. 227.
19 ibid, p. 282.

the question of ethical subjectivity. Shaped by this discourse, Leveller practice was constituted as an ascetic that defined, justified, and constituted the Leveller claim to embody a mode of ethical being within their political agency. The Levellers offered themselves as a model for the common man, and extended the possibility of being fit to the agent who fought, who petitioned, who wrote pamphlets and who demonstrated in the street. The battle that divided the parliament from the Levellers was more than an ideological battle over how to settle the kingdom; it was a battle of over who was fit to be an agent of settlement and who the agent must be, in his selfhood, to participate in the settlement.

Similarly, within the French Revolution, Jacobin discourse problematized the revolutionary as an ethical agent. His 'self' was the source of intense debate and passion, and through intense ascetic and political work he was expected to be 'revolutionary' toward his own self. It was only through the care he devoted to his own self that he could shape his own conduct according to the principles of republican virtue and form himself according to the good that was defined by the revolution. Speaking of the 'revolutionary man' and of his relationship to the revolution, Saint-Just suggested that since 'his aim is to see the Revolution triumph', he ought to 'watch himself when he speaks of it.' Saint-Just elaborates on the subject of the 'revolutionary man' who he says is 'inflexible, but temperate and sensible. He lives simply, without affecting the luxury of false modesty. He is the irreconcilable enemy of every lie, indulgence, and affectation' and 'the soul of honour'. Saint-Just then instructs his readers that the 'revolutionary man' ought to know 'that if the revolution is to triumph he must be as good now as once he was bad: and his morality is not a clever pose, but something heart-felt and fundamental.'[20] The Jacobins insisted that being revolutionary was defined by the agents' relationship with 'the good' and through this insistence Jacobin discourse intensified the problematization of the relationship between the ethical subject and political action.

This intensification was produced by the political conditions of 1792, when the revolutionary project was redefined as a project for founding a republic. The foundation of the republic was problematized as a moral act and the focal point of Jacobin discourse on moral regeneration was the need to create Republicans. As Maximilien Robespierre remarked, 'it is not only a vain word that constitutes the republic; it is the character of the citizens.'[21] The nature of revolutionary agency and selfhood was constituted through a discourse on the 'true Republican' and through the institutions and practices that were meant to enable the citizen to shape himself as a republican and a revolutionary. As the Lyons Surveillance Committee remarked: 'to be truly Republican, each citizen must experience and bring about in himself a revolution equal to the one that has changed France.'[22] In responding to the problem of moulding 'true Republicans' fit for a republic and a democratic society, the Jacobins developed ethical practices for the 'care of the

---

20 Louis Antoine Saint-Just, 'Sur la Police Générale, sur la justice, le commerce, la législation et les crimes des factions', (26 Germinal an II) in *Oeuvres Complètes*, ed. Michèle Duval (Paris, 1984), p. 809.
21 Maximilien Robespierre, *Lettres a Ses Commettans*, No. 1 (1972), in *Oeuvres Complètes de Robespierre*, vol 5, ed. Gustave Laurent, Paris, 1961, p.17.
22 'Instruction adressée aux autorités constituées des départemens [*sic*] de Rhone et de Loire, par la Commission temporaire' (Lyon, 16 November 1793), in Walter Markov and Albert Soboul (eds.), *Die Sansculotten von Paris*, Berlin, 1957, p. 224.

self' that were a central concern for the goals of regeneration and virtue. The moral discourse on the 'true Republican' was essential to the Jacobin Terror, whereby individuals were forced to direct their attention on themselves, to decipher, recognize, and observe themselves, thereby establishing a certain relationship to themselves as the ethical agents of revolt.

The practices of *civisme* – embodied in service, solidarity and sacrifice – offered the agent the means to exemplify, through his words, actions, and mode of being, the embodiment of a 'revolutionary life' (*vie révolutionnaire*). The citizen was constantly expected to perform 'acts of *civisme*' and he was expected to prove the *civisme* of his own being through his republican virtues. Throughout the republic, the system of terror that governed France imposed the discourse of *civisme* on the citizen. Bearing a certificate of *civisme* constituted the citizen's membership in the moral community of the Republic and it defined his solidarity with other republicans. Within the system that regulated the certificates of *civisme*, revolutionaries were examined by the revolutionary committees and were compelled to scrutinize themselves in self-examination. The practice of self-examination demanded that the revolutionary give narrative accounts of his actions and develop a discourse about his own 'revolutionary life' that presented his self to personal and public scrutiny.[23] These narratives were tied to the moral practices that the revolutionary developed as the means to shape his conduct and mode of being – practices that were developed within the popular societies and within the structures of moral education. Within these moral institutions, the practical experience of *civisme* was defined within three fundamental republican activities: service, solidarity and sacrifice. They were fundamental because they formed three practical conditions through which the question of being republican was enabled for the republican agent. First, the republican must serve the republic and this service was made possible through a wide variety of political practices and institutions of the republic. Secondly, the republican must define himself and act in solidarity with the republic and other republicans. Thirdly, the republican must make sacrifices for the republic. Within the demands of *civisme* – its practices and discourses – the nature of selfhood was presented as a pressing concern for citizenship and the revolutionary was embodied within a process of moral transformation through which he had to make his own self the object of his care

The problem of ethics is exemplified by the case of the Chemin family, a father and son, who lived in the Section Révolutionnaire. Both men, in separate instances, were arrested as suspects, their *civisme* was questioned, and the nature of their 'revolutionary life' was scrutinized. Appealing to the Committee of Public Safety for release, they presented their conduct, character and 'true republicanism' as evidence of their moral worth as revolutionaries. In the discourse of both men, their 'life' as a revolutionary was placed at the centre of a narrative that was meant to define the nature of their *civisme* as it was embodied in their words, actions and mode of being. The discourse and practice of examining Chemin père and Chemin fils reveals the moral discourse of the revolutionary, the institutions through which the discourse was expressed and the practices

---

23 For an example of such narratives, see Magnier, *Ma Vie Patriotique* (13 Fructidor an II); *Certificat de Civisme du C. Saint-Félix* (n.d), BL, F. 1021 (17); Garebeuf, *Précis du Mémoire et Pièces Justificatives du Civisme de Garebeuf* (n.d.) BL, R 674 (26).

that offered the presentation of selfhood as fundamental to revolutionary politics. In this dialogue between institutions, the question of the revolutionary self was presented, and we find the fundamental ethical problems of revolutionary agent defined.

The examination of these two agents was centred on the problem of what constitutes the good republican. When comparing the two tracts that defend the revolutionary life of each agent, we can see how each narrative articulated the three fundamental republican activities that structured the ethical problem of being a true and good republican.[24] First, both were presented as having actively served the republic. For example, the elder Chemin was described as someone who frequented the popular society, was commissioner in the Section and had been a member of the Committee of Surveillance. Secondly, the sacrifice of each agent was highlighted. Their active involvement in the revolutionary *journées* was emphasized for both men; their 'revolutionary existence' included having energetically and without hesitation joined in the street fighting that accompanied the fall of the Bastille, the revolution of 10 August and the revolution of 31 May. Chemin père defended his son suggesting that his energetic support for the Revolution was exemplified by how, in 1789, he 'carried himself with his brothers-in-arms to all the places where the revolution summoned patriots.'[25] Chemin père's sacrifice was presented by the Section with particularly high esteem, for one of his sons had fought and died for the republic in the Vendée. Finally, both men were characterized as exemplars in respect of their familial relations, political associations and practices, and the bonds of republican solidarity that they had demonstrated. They shared in the values of the republic, they propagated them to others, and they offered themselves as a model of emulation for others. Chemin fils was praised as a writer, not only for a journal he had written and printed, but for a series of educational works composed for children and citizens with little education. He was specifically praised for the way he presented 'in a simple and naive manner, the principles of morality, liberty, equality, and true republicanism'.[26] In this discourse on the nature of his action and selfhood, the sources insisted that the revolutionary in question had 'shown himself' (*se montrer*) through his conduct and his words. Being present at the popular society, engaging in the revolutionary *journées*, donating money, and writing republican tracts were how the agent revealed his republican self and shaped himself through a practice of self-transformation. Within their ascetic practice, and the moral discourse on *civisme*, Jacobinism created a specific meaning of revolutionary politics that was shaped by the problem of ethics and republican selfhood.

The act of revolt makes the agent intimately concerned with life and death; with love and honour; and with truth and good. Death stalked the Leveller and the Jacobin, and was a persistent concern. The agent participated in the struggles of his time armed not only with values and programmes, but armed with the presentation of his body, his practice, and his selfhood as embodying the nature of the good. Elsewhere in this volume,

---

24 'Des Citoyens de la Section Révolutionnaire aux Representants du peuple, membres du Comité de Salut public et de Sureté Générale', (Paris, n.d.) in Markov and Soboul, *Die Sansculotten von Paris*, pp. 362–366; C. Chemin,'Aux Citoyens Representans composant le Comité du Sureté Générale', (Paris, 28 floréal, 1794) in Markov and Soboul, *Die Sansculotten von Paris*, pp. 366–368.

25 Chemin, 'Aux Citoyens Representans composant le Comité du Sureté Générale', p. 368.

26 ibid.

Paul Hollander has raised the question of how we can account for the choice to sacrifice oneself and what moves the individual to engage in the perilous act of revolt.[27] For the Levellers and the Jacobins the answer was clear: the rebel acts in the name of love. Against the ethics of self-interest and self-preservation, Leveller and Jacobin moral discourse called upon the agent to encounter the good within the practices the agent performed on behalf of his community. For the Leveller and the Jacobin, to love the community in service, in sacrifice, and in solidarity with his fellow citizens, was to be raised to a higher good, beyond personal interest, while it marked the achievement of a selfhood that was conditioned by his asceticism and his ethics. Leveller and Jacobin both spoke against the 'self' when it was equated with egotism, personal interest and avarice. Nevertheless, when defining whom they were as agents of revolt, they presented a 'self' that was an ascetic achievement. Their moral discourse presented the revolutionary self as a model of beauty and good, while presenting their own agency as the embodiment of a meaningful political engagement.

In claiming to speak for the community about its needs and its fundamental structures, the Levellers and Jacobins grounded their status in their ethics; their revolt embodied the problem of who the agent must be, in his ethical subjectivity, if he was to participate in the foundation of the new community. The experience of politics, citizenship and agency was tied to an ethical articulation and an ethical practice of selftransformation. Nevertheless, the practical expression of this ethics was intimately tied to violence and exclusion. The Leveller and the Jacobin waged war in the name of this selfhood. The Leveller admonished the 'malignant' elites as much as the 'neuters' who failed to respond to the common cause. The *Agreement of the People* that the Levellers sought to implement gave these two figures no place within the founding of a new community. Nevertheless, while the Levellers aimed 'at the conversion of all, and the destruction of none', the Jacobins waged a war on 'suspects' for whom the Republic offered death, exile and imprisonment.[28] The Jacobin discourse on the relationship between political action and the nature of a 'good life' justified the deprivation of life for political agents who did not conform to their articulation of the nature of being good and the content of a beautiful and meaningful political existence. Shaped by an ethical discourse on 'the good' and the ethical problematization of revolutionary selfhood, the advent of Jacobin politics transformed modern revolutionary agency. It has been a disquieting transformation. Forced to use violence in order to secure moral transformation, Jacobin practice could offer some a vision of freedom, beauty and selfhood that nourished an extraordinary energy for securing rights, fighting oppression, and devoting oneself to the cause of the community and its needs; to others, however, it offered death, exclusion, intimidation and deprivation. From the Jacobin, the politics of revolution not only learned the art of terror, but came to consider terror as the tool justifiably wielded by those who embodied the 'truth' and the 'good' within their ethical subjectivity. Being a 'true' revolutionary – ascetic and disciplined – licensed a 'Bloody Project' that the Levellers would not have understood as 'public-spirited'.

---

27 See below, pp. 201–8.
28 Lilburne *et al.*, *A Manifestation*, p. 280.

The Revolutionary Moment and the 'Lost Treasure' of Democracy: 1989 in the Light of Hannah Arendt, Walter Benjamin, and Slavoj Žižek[1]

Tim Beasley-Murray

Normality and Narcissism

When the West gazes at Central and Eastern Europe today, it is easy to forget that less than two decades ago this region was convulsed by revolution. The French revolution inspired in those who observed it from beyond the borders of France feelings of joy and terror in equal measure. It created a radically new world. The October Revolution consisted of ten days that shook the world and left it shaken to its core. What terror, by way of contrast, was inspired by the revolutions of 1989 to which, in the Czechoslovak case, the epithet 'velvet' was so aptly ascribed?[2] With the epithet, 'velvet', the danger of revolutionary fervour is muffled by the swish of an evening gown and domesticated into the plush of the bourgeois interior. And what joy did the revolutions of 1989 inspire that could result not in the sublimity of books nine and ten of Wordsworth's *The Prelude* but in the banality of The Scorpions' soft rock ballad, 'The Wind of Change'?[3] 1989 seems not to have shaken the world to its core and its revolutions seem to have changed very little. By undoing the perceived historical aberration of communist rule, they appear to

---

1   I should like to thank Séan Hanley, Simon Pawley, and Kieran Williams for their helpful comments on drafts of this essay. In particular, I am grateful to Kieran Williams for what I have to say below on 1989 and juridification, and to Simon Pawley for his perspicacious and careful reading of my text.
      This essay is also published in Peter J.S. Duncan (ed.), *Convergence and Divergence: Russia and Eastern Europe into the Twenty-First Century*, UCL-SSEES Studies in Russia and Eastern Europe, London, 2007.

2   It might be argued that it is memory and the stories that are told later, rather than contemporaneous observation, that have imparted the sense of drama and terror to events like the Russian and French Revolutions. In relation to the Russian case, this function of memory and narrativization is treated by Frederick Corney in his *Telling October: Memory and the Making of the Bolshevik Revolution*, Ithaca, NY, 2004. Nevertheless, it is worth considering what it is that makes the revolutions of 1989 so unmemorable and so little amenable to the telling of dramatic stories.

3   In *The Prelude* we read of Wordsworth's youthful reaction to the French Revolution: 'O pleasant exercise of hope and joy! / For great were the auxiliars which then stood / Upon our side, we who were strong in love! / Bliss was it in that dawn to be alive, / But to be young was very Heaven!' Book X, 690–94 (1805 version), in William Wordsworth, *The Prelude: a Parallel Text*, ed. by J. C. Maxwell, Harmondsworth, 1986, p. 440. 'The Wind of Change' by the German band, The Scorpions, was the soundtrack for East Germany and much of Europe in the period between its release in 1990 and German reunification in October 1991. With lyrics by Klaus Meine, it goes as follows: 'I follow the Moskva / Down to Gorky Park / Listening to the wind of change / An August summer night / Soldiers passing by / Listening to the wind of

23

have returned the world to its natural course. This process of renormalization means that Central and Eastern Europe now looks little different from Western Europe. It may perhaps seem a little bit more down-at-heel and little bit more vulgar, but, as the traces of communist abnormality are gradually eroded, the landscape that emerges is one that is familiar to the western gaze.[4] And the western eyes that perceive this post-revolutionary landscape of normality are full of self-love.

The introduction of liberal democratic politics and the implementation of liberal-economic policy have been brewed together to produce a miraculous cream that can be applied to the face of Old Europe's liberal democracy and its ageing institutions. The youthful desire of New Europe to become even more western than the Old appears to be proof that the West was right all along: that its moral values are superior, and that its liberal political and economic order are natural, normal and necessary. Each accession criterion fulfilled, each EU norm adhered to, has represented a satisfaction of the West's narcissism. All this has conspired to make the processes of transition and accession, for the West, a slow-burning, masturbatory love affair.

It does not matter that some westerners, particularly academics who study the region, are ambivalent about the process of Central and Eastern Europe's renormalization. In nostalgic mode, whether by proxy or not, such observers secretly wish to prolong the experience of the exotic that adheres in the traces of communist rule. The West's appetite for communist kitsch is evidence of this.[5] Likewise, many western academics find post-communist aberrations from normality more alluring than the normal (and, of course, as research projects, a better source of funding). This fascination with traces of enduring abnormality is, however, again an act of narcissism. In the frisson of voyeurism, the West finds its own sense of superiority reinforced, again and again. The West mixes moral repugnance with semi-pornographic leering at the political and social problems of Central and Eastern Europe: the selling of babies and sex, human rights abuses by populist governments, xenophobic nationalism, skinhead crimes against

---

change / […] Take me to the magic of the moment / On a glory night / Where the children of tomorrow dream away / in the wind of change / The wind of change / Blows straight into the face of time / Like a stormwind that will ring the freedom bell / For peace of mind / Let your balalaika sing / What my guitar wants to say.' See <http://www.80smusiclyrics.com/artists/scorpions.htm> [accessed 20 April 2007].

4   This is, of course, a western perspective. From more of an eastern perspective, a different question arises: how did life under state-socialism, that seemed so normal, dissolve in an extraordinary moment, and then reconfigure itself as a liberal democratic and capitalist order that so quickly took on the appearance of normality. This is the question that underpins Yurchak's book, tellingly entitled *Everything was forever, until it was no more*. Here, talking about the 'last Soviet generation' of the 1980s, Yurchak refers to the 'profound experience of the Soviet system's permanence and immutability and the complete unexpectedness of its collapse' that stands in paradoxical contrast to the fact that that collapse 'appeared unsurprising when it happened'. Alexei Yurchak, *Everything was forever, until it was no more: the last Soviet Generation*, Princeton, NJ, 2005, p.1. Normality seems to be like a bowl of treacle into which one drops a pebble: with remarkable speed, the viscous practices of everyday life absorb and cover over the extraordinary event. Lefèbvre's work on everyday life provides an insight into this process. See Henri Lefèbvre, *Critique of Everyday Life*, trans. John Moore, London, 2002. For an analysis of the both revolutionary and normalizing role of everyday practices in the events of 1989 and in the absorption of East Germany into West Germany, see Joe Moran, 'November in Berlin: the End of the Everyday', *History Workshop Journal*, 57, 2004, pp. 216–234

5   This is an appetite that Central and Eastern European artists have known cleverly how to exploit. Witness the global success of the Russian Sots Art movement.

Roma, and so forth.[6] Abnormalities must be perceived in order to highlight normality and to display the necessary nature of that normality. Thus, Central and Eastern Europe's failure to achieve western liberal-democratic norms as well as its success in doing so are double sources of western self-congratulation.

There might, however, be a good reason for the western narcissism. It is possible that the revolutions of 1989 contain a pertinent lesson for Europe as a whole. As Slavoj Žižek puts it:

> Why was the West so fascinated by the dissolution of Communism in Eastern Europe? The answer seems obvious: what fascinated the Western gaze was the *reinvention of democracy*. It is as if democracy, which in the West shows more and more signs of decay and crisis and is lost in bureaucratic routine and publicity-style election campaigns, is being discovered in Eastern Europe in all its freshness and novelty. The function of this fascination is thus purely ideological: in Eastern Europe, the West seeks for its own lost origins, its own lost original experience of 'democratic invention'.[7]

If Žižek is right that the events of 1989 in Central and Eastern Europe constituted a reinvention of democracy, if they brought to light again what Žižek terms the 'treasure that causes democratic enthusiasm and that the West has long ago lost the taste of',[8] then it is a constant imperative to return to that moment in order to seek again a treasure that Central and Eastern Europe now seems also to have mislaid.[9] This is narcissism once again, but perhaps, this time, a productive narcissism.

Žižek I: Revolution as a passing point of seriousness

It is easy to forget that the regimes of Central and Eastern Europe were, in theory, revolutionary democratic regimes. 'Really existing' revolutionary democracy may have been a travesty, but, like any travesty, it used the discourse and political concepts of the real thing. For Žižek, the revolutionary moment of 1989 was to be found in that instant when the joke that was 'really existing' revolutionary democracy was suddenly taken seriously. In the Monday demonstration of 1989 in Leipzig the slogan on the lips of the crowd was '*Wir sind das Volk*'. According to Žižek, what is revolutionary about this slogan is that it seeks to make real the promise of true democracy that was inherent in

---

6 Žižek's comments on Central and Eastern European liberal intellectuals also apply to their Western counterparts: 'liberal intellectuals refuse [nationalism], mock it, laugh at it, yet at the same time stare at it with powerless fascination.' Slavoj Žižek, *Tarrying with the Negative*, Durham, NC, 1993, p. 212

7 Žižek, *Tarrying with the Negative*, p. 200.

8 ibid. This is an implicit reference to a chapter title of Arendt's *On Revolution*, 'The Revolutionary Tradition and its Lost Treasure'. Hannah Arendt, *On Revolution*, Harmondsworth, 1990, p. 215. This intertextual allusion is revealing since Žižek rarely refers to Arendt in his work.

9 The approach that I take here is philosophical rather than social-scientific in orientation. Social science approaches have proved remarkably impotent in their treatment of the events of 1989. See *East European Politics and Societies*, 13, 1999, 2, an issue devoted to an assessment of the legacy of 1989. The various contributors fail to produce any coherent answer to the question that frames this round-table special issue, 'Were the events of 1989 revolutions?', exactly because of the normative social-science taxonomies that they use. A (perhaps both more modish and, in some senses, more old-fashioned) emphasis on the revolutionary spirit seems to be of greater use. I must also point out that my arguments here emerge primarily from a reading of events in East Germany and Czechoslovakia, events with which I am most familiar. Nevertheless, (also in a non-social-scientific vein) these arguments on the fate of the revolutionary spirit are intended to apply, in broad terms, to the experience of the region as a whole.

the sick joke of the German Democratic Republic. By working seriously within the discourse of revolutionary democracy to which the regime paid lip-service, the demonstrators acted in a genuinely democratic and revolutionary spirit. The people, the real people, not the false people as constituted by the party and the comedic institutions of the state, laid claim to power.

In Žižek's analysis, this moment of revolutionary democracy, however, is no more than a passing point. One might describe this as a point between the 'normalization' of Communist-party rule (as in Czechoslovakia of the 1970s) and the 'renormalization' that I have already described. He describes this passing point as follows:

> In spite of betrayed enthusiastic expectations, something did take place in between, in the passage itself, and it is in this Event which took place in between, this vanishing mediator, in this moment of democratic enthusiasm, that we should locate the crucial dimension obfuscated by later renormalization.[10]

What caused this moment to vanish? Žižek observes that the crowds of Monday demonstrators stopped chanting '*Wir sind das Volk*' and began chanting '*Wir sind ein Volk*'. The shift from definite to indefinite article, writes Žižek, marked 'the closure of the momentary authentic political opening, the reappropriation of the democratic impetus by the thrust towards reunification of Germany, which meant rejoining Western Germany's liberal-capitalist police/political order'.[11] As '*das Volk*' the people were the subject of their own discourse, free to choose their own, qualitatively new path. As '*ein Volk*' the people became the object of the pre-existing discourse of reunification. As one people, they were propelled along a path that was already mapped out in advance: the magical yellow-brick road of capitalist gold that would lead them back home, not, in this case, to Kansas, but to the equally mythical paradise of the West German *Vaterland*. The moment of a collective revolutionary subject had passed and the crowd had become the collective object that constitutes the masses in liberal democracy.

Žižek II: The fate of the relation between the State and the individual

The experience of politics has changed dramatically with the fall of the Berlin wall. With the change from state-socialist regimes to liberal democracies, a paradoxical change has occurred in the relationship between the state and the individual. It is common to think of the state-socialist regimes of Central and Eastern Europe as undemocratic. According to this commonplace, in these undemocratic societies the organs of the state were not interested in listening to the voice of the people. In reality, nothing was further from the case.

Under state-socialism, the state did not use democratic elections to listen to their people as a whole, but (whether though its organs of secret police or the political officers in the work place) it was passionately committed to hearing the voices of its citizens as individuals.[12] This may have occurred by subterfuge, surveillance and in an atmosphere

---

10 Slavoj Žižek, 'A Leftist Plea for "Eurocentrism"', *Critical Inquiry*, 24, 1998, 4, pp. 988–1009 (p. 1004)
11 Žižek, 'A Leftist Plea', p. 990.
12 A recognition of the perverse interest of the state-socialist regime in the individual contradicts thinkers like Václav Bělohradský (a Czech émigré philosopher whose thought has been influential on Václav Havel) for whom state-socialism represents the apogee of impersonalism and the brutal victory of western rationalist universalism gone wrong. See Václav Bělohradský, *Kríze eschatologie neosobnosti*, London, 1982.

of fear, but, nevertheless, the relationship between the state and its citizens existed on the level of the individual. An artistic representation of this relationship is to be found in Karel Kachyňa's film of 1969, *Ucho* (The Ear), in which a government official returns from a reception with the gradually dawning suspicion that he is likely to be purged. He and his wife, who know that their house is bugged by the secret police as a matter of course, spend a night of fear in constant dialogue, political and intimate, with the organs of the state. This is the travesty of democracy under state socialism where the state listens to the individual's most mundane utterances with the greatest interest. As a more everyday example of this intimate relationship one need only think of the practice, or at least the wide-spread perception of the practice, of the use of undercover informers and the maintenance of individual files on individual citizens.

In the events of 1989 the state-socialist travesty of democracy became genuine drama. A result of the intimate relationship between the state and individual citizens was the conviction, at first amongst dissidents and then amongst the citizens more generally, that their opinions counted for something. The large-scale demonstrations of 1989 expressed the fact that this conviction, previously held for the most part only by intellectuals, had spread to the people as a whole. It was, then, the existence of the travesty of the listening state that enabled the great manifestation of true democracy in the autumn of 1989, a manifestation that both brought democracy into being and abolished it at one stroke.

The liberal democracy that followed this momentary manifestation of true democracy is something entirely different. Whilst liberal democracy allows its individual citizens the opportunity to have their say within the framework of multi-party democracy, the relationship between the individual and the state is, in fact, a relationship on the collective and abstract level of quantity. Between these infrequent opportunities to stand up and be counted but certainly not listened to, it is clear that the state has no interest in the views of its citizens. One need only witness the British state's studious indifference to its citizens' views on subjects such as, on the liberal side of the equation, the war in Iraq, and, on the rightist side of the equation, the rights of homeowners to use violence in defence of their property. Whilst Kachyňa's portrayal of the travesty of the state's concern for the individual is an artistic representation of state-socialism, the artistic representation of the liberal-capitalist state's attitude to the individual is to be found in Kafka.[13]

In the transition from state-socialism, the relationship between state and individual has been transformed from one of concern into one of indifference. That the liberal-democratic state is aware of the oddness of this relationship can be seen in the recourse of major political parties to focus groups. Focus groups represent another form of travesty of the listening state in which, behind a mask of interest in the individual citizen's individual views, the state seeks out what is representative (and hence unindividual) in its citizens. The admittedly grotesque opposite of the focus group was to be found under

---

13 I refer here, in particular, to the indifference of the organs of the law to the individual in Kafka's *The Trial*. Deleuze and Guattari argue for the anti-capitalist and revolutionary nature of Kafka's writings in Gilles Deleuze and Félix Guattari, *Kafka: pour une littérature mineure*, Paris, 1975. A less speculative and more document-based interpretation of Kafka's politics is to be found in Ritchie Robertson, *Kafka, Judaism, Politics, and Literature*, Oxford, 1985. Robertson labels Kafka a 'romantic anti-capitalist', p. 140.

state socialism in the bright focus of the secret police interrogation, a thoroughly individual encounter that could have serious individual consequences.

Nonetheless, if the state-socialist state was interested in hearing what its citizens had to say on an individual level, a corollary to this was its lack of care for them as a collective body. It mattered little to the state-socialist regimes that their people as a collective body were living in relative poverty in comparison to their neighbours in Western Europe, or that their personal freedoms were limited. It mattered only when they began to take decisions as individuals by joining in dissident political activity or applying to emigrate.[14] Similarly, liberal democracies are genuinely interested in their citizens as a collective and make efforts to care for public health, bring down unemployment, and improve education. Their citizens, however, are only important to them in so far as they assume a collective symbolic function. Where the state socialist regime was interested in the specific human being, say, Václav Havel or Adam Michnik, and not in the well-being of the average Czech or Pole, liberal democratic regimes are interested only in the average: not Mrs Smith who happens to live in Worcester but Worcester Woman; not Mr Jones who happens to live in Basildon, but Basildon Man. Whilst the culture of sound-bite politics and the media's obsessive desire for individual illustrations of political matters may seem to highlight the individual, liberal-democratic regimes become concerned with such figures only in so far as they become representatives of a collective group and symbols of something larger than themselves. The result is an absolute reversal of de Tocqueville's view, enthusiastically endorsed by Hayek: 'Democracy attaches all possible value to each man; socialism makes each man a mere agent, a mere number.'[15]

The socialist state was not interested in the collective but in the individual; the liberal-democratic state is not interested in the individual but in the collective. In the transition between these systems, however, there is a moment in which the barrier between the individual and collective is sublated and the state is forced to respond to its citizens in the spirit of democracy. This is moment in which I suggest that democracy comes into being and destroys itself. Such a view provides a further interpretation of Žižek's comment on the shift from the definite article, *das Volk*, to the indefinite article, *ein Volk*. The indefinite article gave a definite direction towards a reunification that was suddenly mapped out in advance, unlike the freedom of the definite article which contained so many indefinite pathways. In chanting '*Wir sind das Volk*', the crowds were laying claim to their definite individuality; in chanting '*Wir sind ein Volk*', the crowd suddenly became an indefinite collective.

It might not worry us that the liberal democracy that emerged triumphant from the aftermath of the revolutionary movements of 1989 seems not to be interested in the individual. After all, some might say that it is better that the state should leave the individual well alone. Nevertheless, it is important to recognize that political and social structures are also invested with a libidinal economy.[16] One might posit that the albeit perverse intimacy between state and individual that existed under state socialism provided

---

14 State-socialist regimes, thus, did not deny the right to travel to their people as a whole but rather to individuals.
15 Alexis de Tocqueville, quoted in Friedrich von Hayek, *The Road to Serfdom*, Chicago, IL, 1944, p. 25.
16 It is such a psychoanalytic approach that underlies Žižek's work.

chimerical satisfaction of libidinal needs. The withdrawal of this perverse intimacy has led (only for a time, and only in the case of some societies and some social sectors) to a significant sense of lack and to a consequent displacement of libidinal energies onto other objects, most notably, the nation as mystical body. For, in so far as an individual identifies with the nation *qua* organic unity as the primary political unit, rather than with the state *qua* instrument of convention, he or she does so on a plane that transcends (or, put more correctly: mythically precedes) the split between state and individual. Žižek makes a similar point:

> The problem of Eastern Europe's nationalist populism is that it perceives Communism's 'threat' from the perspective of *Gemeinschaft*, as a foreign body corroding the organic texture of the national community; this way, nationalist populism actually imputes to Communism the crucial feature of capitalism itself. In its moralistic opposition to the Communist 'depravity,' the nationalist-populist Moral Majority unknowingly *prolongs* the thrust of the previous regime toward State qua organic community. The desire at work in this symptomatic substitution of Communism for capitalism is a desire for capitalism cum *Gemeinschaft*, a desire for capitalism, without the formal-external relations between individuals. Fantasies about the 'theft of enjoyment.' the reemergence of anti-Semitism, etc., are the price to be paid for this impossible desire.[17]

According to this, the mystical union of the individual member of the nation with the nation itself is a reworking of the travestied intimacy between individual and state under state socialism.

This, then, might serve to explain, in part, the not inconsiderable successes of the populist nationalism and the far-right in post-1989 Central and Eastern Europe as a displacement of desire.[18] The author of a newspaper piece on the far-right's success in Saxony hits the nail on the head, without, perhaps, realizing that he has done so:

> An alarmed German media has given differing explanations for the NPD's rise. They include the fact that the communists ran the area until 1989; the unemployment rate of 18%; and disillusionment with Germany's red-green government in Berlin. But the phrase most frequently mentioned in Königstein is 'bürgernah', which, loosely translated, means 'close to the people'. While German politicians have argued endlessly, and often abstrusely, about economic reforms, the NPD has quietly built up its local base. Since the late 90s it has fielded well-known candidates for key elections. And it has assiduously gathered support among its core constituency – the young – with barbecues, discos and canoeing trips.[19]

The truth here is that, by means of the chimerical 'closeness to the people' that is a constituent part of nationalist ideology (and not merely in barbecues, discos and camping trips), the far-right supplies the satisfaction of desires that the abstract indifference of the liberal democratic state is unable to fulfil.

Neither the chimerical unity of the national community in far-right and nationalist ideology nor the travesty of intimacy between state and individual in state socialism encapsulate the genuine spirit of democracy. Nevertheless, the chimera and the travesty that they represent constitute, perhaps, at least formally, a better approximation of

---

17 Žižek, *Tarrying with the Negative*, p. 211.
18 These limited successes are, it must be noted, often overemphasized and overdramatized by the Western media for the sort of reasons that I have described above. Perhaps what is at stake here is more the relative failure of liberalism in Central and Eastern Europe.
19 Luke Harding, 'Nazis out!', *The Guardian*, 11 February 2005, <http://www.guardian.co.uk/germany/article/0,2763,1410544,00.html> [accessed 26 December, 2007].

democracy than liberal-democratic indifference. The lesson that the revolutions of 1989 and what has followed teach us is that the structural failure of the liberal-democratic state to provide a genuinely democratic relationship between itself and the individuals of which it is made up is a serious failure indeed.

In his *Philosophy of Right*, Hegel posits civil society as an intermediate sphere of reconciliation between the overly concrete forms of identification in family life and the overly abstract demands of the state.[20] Similarly, for de Tocqueville, and neo-Tocquevilleans such as Putnam, the voluntary associations of civil society provide smaller-scale activities with which citizens as individuals freely identify themselves and, hence, that school them for participation in the larger-scale activity of democratic politics.[21] In both conceptions, civil society, the product and prerequisite of capitalism, is the means by which the general institutions of the state, on the one hand, and a society that consists of particular individuals, on the other, are reconciled. Since the changes of 1989 in Central and Eastern Europe, civil society has been hailed as the democratic panacea, in recognition, in part, of the inability of the liberal-democratic state to respond to its citizens in a concrete way. And yet, as Mudde and others have argued, rather than Western-sponsored NGOs with their lofty, pluralist aims, it is the often explicitly anti-democratic and anti-liberal organizations of what has been termed 'uncivil' society that best express the democratic spirit:

> In many ways, then, the 'uncivil movements' like the ones studied in this volume, are more authentic representatives of civil society in post-communist Europe. Not only do they indeed fill the space between the household and the (national) state. They also play an important role in the process of democratisation, be it directly or indirectly (by provoking 'civil' movements to respond to their challenge). Moreover, unlike many prominent 'civil' organisations in Eastern Europe, which are elite-driven NGOs detached from society, many 'uncivil' organisations are true social movements, i.e. involved in grass-roots supported contentious politics.[22]

These voices, with their demands for war-veterans' rights, ethnic purity and so forth, are voices that the liberal-democratic order treats with a mixture of fascinated horror and practical indifference. Nevertheless, despite their ostensibly anti-democratic aims, then, these 'uncivil' and (from a Western perspective) abnormal movements of Central and Eastern Europe may best channel the political-libidinal energies that also were to be seen in 1989.

Benjamin: Revolution as interruption

It is strange now for us to think back to 1989 and imagine that the integration of Central and Eastern Europe into the Western liberal-democratic and liberal-economic order

---

20 See G. W. F. Hegel, *Elements of the Philosophy of Right*, trans. by H. B. Nisbet, ed. by Allen W. Wood, Cambridge, 1990.

21 See Robert Putnam, *Making Democracy Work: Civic Traditions in Modern Italy*, Princeton, NJ, 1992.

22 Cas Mudde, 'Civil Society in Post-Communist Europe: Lessons from the Dark Side', in Petr Kopecký and Cas Mudde (eds), *Uncivil Society? Contentious Politics in Post-Communist Europe*, London, 2003, pp. 157–70 (p. 164). The 'uncivil' movements that this volume deals with include the Croatian war veterans' movement, Hungarian skinheads, the protest movement of Ukrainian miners, and Poland's nationalist *Samoobrana* (self-defence) movement.

might have appeared to some to be only one of a set of competing possibilities.[23] There is a tendency to accept the inevitability of the path, the yellow brick road, that (it turns out) history has taken. It is in this context that Walter Benjamin's thoughts on revolution may be of assistance.

For Benjamin, the sense of the present as the only conceivable state of affairs, that is, the sense of the present as determined by progress, is itself catastrophe:

> The concept of progress must be grounded in the idea of catastrophe. That things are 'status quo' *is* the catastrophe. It is not an ever-present possibility but what in each case is given. Thus Strindberg [...]: hell is not something that awaits us, but this life here and now.[24]

Catastrophe is not the threat of earthquakes, volcanoes, or the unruliness of the mob. Catastrophe is the conviction that the present with all its ills (poverty, inequality and violence) is necessary and normal. In opposition to this, Benjamin conceives of revolution as the interruption of the catastrophe that is historical evolution. Benjamin articulates this view in a striking reworking of Marx's famous image: 'Marx says that revolutions are the locomotive of world history. But perhaps it is quite different. Perhaps revolutions are the grasp for the emergency brake by the human race travelling on the train.'[25] It is the sudden recognition of catastrophe all around that forces the proletariat to pull the revolutionary emergency brake that brings history to an end.

The revolutions of 1989 were just such a moment of interruption when citizens pulled the emergency brake in the train of history. But what went wrong? The creaky train of Socialism shuddered to a halt. The travellers clambered down onto the tracks, somewhat stunned at their own actions, gazed round for a minute at the open fields of freedom, and immediately took fright at the vertiginous sight of their own agency.[26]

---

23 It is particularly difficult for many to imagine that democracy and the free market are not naturally and necessarily yoked together, and that reforms in the one sphere might not be reliant on reforms in the other, and *vice versa*. In this context, however, as Boris Johnson comments, China provides a salutary case that baffles those on the right: 'The longer you spend in the new China, watching the oxyacetylene lamps on the building sites at 3 a.m., the clearer it is that Francis Fukuyama was wrong when, in 1989, he pronounced that the fall of Soviet communism meant the end of history. Systematically, methodically, and with the connivance of their entire political establishment and their growing bourgeoisie, the Chinese are making a mockery of the claim that free-market capitalism and democracy must go hand-in-hand.' Boris Johnson, 'They Love Capitalism but not Elections', *The Spectator*, 22 April 2006, <http://www.spectator.co.uk/archive/features/15196/they-love-capitalism-but-not-elections.thtml> [accessed 20 April 2007]. To those on the left, this mockery comes as less of a surprise.
24 Walter Benjamin, *The Arcades Project*, trans. and ed. by Howard Eiland and Kevin McLaughlin, Cambridge, MA, 1998, p. 473
25 Walter Benjamin, 'Parapolimena to "On the Concept of History"', in *Selected Writings IV*, trans. by Edmund Jephcott and others, ed. by Howard Eiland and Michael W. Jennings, Cambridge, MA, 2003, pp. 401–11 (p. 402)
26 It is possible here to think of the story of the Grand Inquisitor in Dostoevsky's *The Brothers Karamazov*. The Grand Inquisitor accuses Christ as follows: 'You want to enter the world, and You go with empty hands, with some vague promise of freedom which they, in their simplicity and innate stupidity, could not even comprehend and which frightens them and overawes them – for nothing has ever been so intolerable to man and to human society as freedom!' Fyodor Dostoevsky, *The Brothers Karamazov*, trans. by Ignat Avsey, Oxford, 1994, p. 316. The implicit question that Dostoevsky raises is of how freedom may be acted upon, despite and in the face of its burdens.

Like agoraphobics on a day-trip to the Hungarian plain, they rushed towards the only vehicle that would take them away from the desolate open space of freedom: a train moving slowly and inexorably on an adjacent track. Gratefully, they pulled themselves aboard the train of Liberal Democracy and free-market economics.[27] But now the revolutionary moment had passed. The agoraphobic citizens had committed themselves to another path of inevitability, mere passive travellers again who had sacrificed their capacity for radical change and action.[28]

Arendt I: Revolution as natality

With the concept of action, I now turn to Arendt. In her phenomenological analysis of human behaviour in *The Human Condition*, Hannah Arendt distinguishes different modes of human endeavour. Work, on the one hand, is the unending and repetitive pattern of behaviour that provides us with our material need. It is an activity that we must undertake to ensure our survival. It is, hence, rooted in mortality, necessity and repetition. Action, by contrast, is the ability to produce the entirely new, to produce that which has never been. It is rooted in natality, freedom, and in the capacity for new beginnings. In a tone that is close to Benjamin, Arendt comments: 'The miracle that saves the world, the realm of human affairs, from its normal, "natural" ruin is ultimately the fact of natality, in which the faculty of action is ontologically rooted.'[29] In her concrete analysis of political history, revolutions embody man's capacity for action and hence embody the spirit of freedom that saves him from ruin.

In *On Revolution* Arendt notes that pre-modern revolutions conceived of themselves as restorations, renovations, and as returning a corrupt state of affairs back to their correct order. Such, for example, is Locke's use of the term, revolution, in the Second Treatise on Government.[30] Nevertheless, Arendt notes that in modern revolutions, by which she means those of the eighteenth century onwards, something new emerges.

---

27 One might argue, in a Benjaminian vein, that this shinier train, also driven by a narrative of progress, is, nevertheless, similarly heading for catastrophe. In the case of free-market economics, the rocks that lie ahead on the line may quite likely be the ecological and environmental catastrophe that the logic of capitalism seems unable to avoid. In this sphere, as elsewhere, it is matter of summoning up the courage to pull the emergency brake.

28 This is not to say, however, (in line with the established, popular image in Western discourse of Central and Eastern European citizens as incapable of making 'mature' and rational decisions) that the choice to board the Liberal-democratic express was not a rational one. Nor do I ignore the irrefutable existence of external factors, operating globally, that influenced these choices. My concern here, however, is with the revolutionary spirit as it is expressed in the agency of its participants.

29 Hannah Arendt, *The Human Condition*, Chicago and London, 1998, p. 247.

30 See John Locke, 'The Second Treatise of Government: An Essay Concerning the True Original, Extent and End of Civil Government', in Locke, *Two Treatises of Government*, ed. by Peter Laslett, Cambridge, 1988, pp. 265–428, especially 414–15 (§§ 223–25).

The modern concept of revolution, inextricably bound up with the notion that the course of history suddenly begins anew, that an entirely new story, a story never known or told before, is about to unfold, was unknown prior to the two great revolutions of the eighteenth century. [...] Crucial then to any understanding of revolutions in the modern age is that the idea of freedom and the experience of a new beginning should coincide.[31]

Arendt argues that these revolutions started with the aim of restoring an old political order. The American Revolution began with the demand of the colonists for a restoration of their rights that they felt had been abused by the British crown. In the midst of their struggle for this restoration, however, a revolutionary pathos of an entirely new beginning asserted itself. This new beginning manifested itself in independence and a new constitution. In this new beginning spoke the voice of freedom.

The story of the revolutions of 1989 represents a curious inversion of the great revolutions of the eighteenth century. Initially, the utopian dreams of the demonstrators (centred on the East German *Neues Forum* and their counterparts in Czechoslovakia, Slovenia and elsewhere) were imbued with a vital sense of natality. As Jiří Suk puts it in his study of the events of 1989 in Czechoslovakia: 'It was a revolution that very few expected and that's why almost nobody had prepared for it. For that reason the general impression that it evoked was all the more profound and spectacular: a revolution whose participants were improvising.'[32] This improvization was imbued with natality. Part of this was the sense that it might be possible to create something radically new that would be neither the old socialism of the East nor the old capitalism of the West. Swiftly, however, this discourse of new beginnings was drowned out by a discourse of restoration and return, couched in various terms: the discourse of *Wiedervereinigung*, a 'return to Europe', a restoration of inter-war capitalist democracy.[33]

Evidence of this can be seen in the way in which constitutional arrangements were come to. For Arendt, constitution-making is fundamental act of freedom. Thus, the

---

31 Arendt, *On Revolution*, pp. 28–29. The real newness of the revolutions of 1989 consisted in the fact that they were dramatic political changes that occurred largely without the violence that this quotation refers to (with the exception of Romania). Arendt is insistent that revolutions 'are not even conceivable outside the domain of violence': Arendt, *On Revolution*, p. 18. 1989 showed another path and that path is arguably its most important legacy. It might be argued, however, that, whilst the revolutions of 1989 were accompanied by little violence, they were nevertheless conducted with a sense, experienced by their participants, of the permanent danger of violence.

32 Jiří Suk, *Labyrintem revoluce. Aktéři, zápletky a křižovatky jedné politické krize (od listopadu 1989 do června 1990)*, Prague, 2003, p. 35. This study documents and analyses, in great detail and at great length, the events of November 1989 to June 1990 with a particular focus on Civic Forum. With extensive quotations that include records of private conversations, it is also an invaluable source of material.

33 Habermas, in an influential article from 1990, describes the events of 1989 variously as 'rectifying' and 'catching-up' revolutions that were meant to enable a return to constitutional democracy after the aberration of communism. He explicitly refers to the fact (and implicitly to Arendt) that the revolutions of 1989 seemed to hark back to the sense of the term, revolution, current before the great revolutions of the eighteenth century. Jürgen Habermas, 'What does Socialism mean Today? The Rectifying Revolution and the Need for New Thinking on the Left', *New Left Review*, o. s. I/183, 1990 (Sept-Oct), pp. 3–21. Williams, also using Arendt, argues that dismissing the revolutionary nature of 1989 because of its restorationist tendencies is misguided: 'If east European revolutionaries claim that they want only to "re-turn" to Europe, and establish "normal" European institutions, they are simply using the same rhetorical devices of many earlier revolutionaries and will end up innovating in ways they never foresaw or intended.' Kieran Williams, 'Introduction', in Elizabeth Skomp and Roman Žyla (eds), *Harmony and Discord: Moving towards a New Europe*, London: School of Slavonic and East European Studies – University College London, 2003, pp. xi-xvi (xiii). Williams's optimism, however, seems not yet to have been vindicated.

American Federalist Papers and the meeting houses in which they were debated as the basis of the American constitution represented a new political space in which the revolutionaries mapped out their new beginning.[34] In agoraphobic Central and Eastern Europe, however, for the most part the space of constitution-making quickly became uninhabited waste ground or given over to political horse-trading at 'round tables' of dubious legitimacy.[35] The negotiated nature of constitutional transition in Central and Eastern Europe meant that constitution-making tended not to represent a radical break.[36] The process of constitution-making was marked by tortured compromise with the past, not a radical break with it. The Latvian constitution, uniquely but illuminatingly, is simply a readoption of the constitution of 1922.[37] The abandonment of natality in the failure to seize the opportunity of constitution-making was a part of the process in which the revolutionary treasure slipped from the people's grasp.[38]

Arendt II: Liberation and freedom; the social and the political

Arendt's *On Revolution* makes a distinction between two possible aims of revolutionary activity: liberation and freedom. For Arendt, liberation defines itself negatively as an attempt of the people to free itself from oppression, whether this be the oppression of tyranny or the oppression of material need. Freedom, by contrast, has a positive content: it is the right of the people to enter the *polis*, the right to admission to participation in

---

34 It must be noted, however, that Arendt is guilty in *On Revolution* of overplaying the radically innovative nature of constitution-making in North America. The American constitution did not emerge out of a void but grew out of a tradition of constitutional thought that extended back to the period of English Civil War and that included documents like the Instrument of Government that established Cromwell's Lord Protectorship in 1653.

35 Elster notes the impact of personal and group interests in the framing of post-1989 Central and Eastern European constitutions that meant that the process of drawing up constitutions was far from the creation of new space of freedom, as envisaged by Arendt. See Jon Elster, 'Forces and Mechanisms in the Constitution-making Process', *Duke Law Journal*, 45, 1995, 2, pp. 364–96.

36 Suk speaks of 'constitutional continuity' as a characteristic of the process of constitution-making in Czechoslovakia. Suk, *Labyrintem revoluce,* p. 29. Referring to the distinction in writing on constitution-making between preservative and transformative constitutions, Wydra suggests a complex relation between conservative and innovative tendencies: 'Whilst east European constitutions have a strongly preservative character, as they resort to national, pre-communist traditions [...] from an experiential perspective, however, what appears as preservative in east European constitutionalism can be seen as fundamentally transformative, as it has been shaped by active attempts to transform communism.' Harald Wydra, *Communism and the Emergence of Democracy*, Cambridge, 2007, p. 214. For a full, empirical account of the protracted and largely conservative process of constitution-making after 1989, see Rett R. Ludwikowski, *Constitution-making in the Region of Former Soviet Dominance*, Durham, NC, 1996, pp. 110–92.

37 Similarly, the Hungarian constitution is an extensively revised version of the communist constitution of 1949.

38 In this context one might comment that, whilst the revolutions of 1989 gave up on natality in the sphere to which it is appropriate, namely politics, the quality of natality was preserved in the sphere of the nation. It follows that the Slovak nationalist slogan, 'starý národ, mladý štát' (an ancient nation, a young state), contains a truth but only in its inversion: with independence in 1993, it was the Slovak nation that was still young, but its form of state was depressingly old. In 1994, under the populist-nationalist government of Vladimír Mečiar, a history book of this title and of extremely dubious historical veracity (including grand and false claims about the 'Slovak' nature of the Great Moravian Empire, and so forth) was provided to all schools to supplement more conventional textbooks. See M. Ferko *et al, Starý národ - mladý štát*, Bratislava, 1994

public affairs. It is an adherence to the goal of freedom, rather than satisfaction with mere liberation, that defines a revolution in an authentic sense:

> Only where change occurs in the sense of a new beginning, where violence is used to constitute an altogether different form of government, to bring about the formation of a new body politic, where the liberation from oppression aims at least at the constitution of freedom can we speak of revolution.[39]

Whilst these goals are related, in so far as liberation precedes and is, moreover, a precondition for the constitution of freedom, they may also work against each other. In Arendt's analysis of the French revolution, the revolutionaries, appalled at the sheer material need of *les malheureux* whom the revolution had ushered onto the stage of history, turned their attention away from the constitutional establishment of a political space of freedom and redirected their energies towards the liberation of the populace from their social burdens. It was through this neglect of what Arendt terms the 'political question' of freedom in favour of the 'social question' of liberation from material necessity that the French Revolution lost the revolutionary treasure that it had so briefly possessed.[40]

In the case of the revolutions of 1989, likewise, a concern for mere liberation soon drowned out the voices that called for the establishment of freedom. Admittedly, the demands of the various dissident groups in the region before 1989 focused on freedom and public participation. The conception of dissent as the creation of a 'parallel *polis*' expressed an ardent desire for admission to the public sphere.[41] As Václav Havel put it in his 'The Power of the Powerless' (1979), 'in societies under the post-totalitarian system, all political life in the traditional sense has been eliminated. People have no opportunity to express themselves politically in public.'[42] The explicit goal of those who constituted what Havel terms the 'hidden sphere' of dissent to emerge into the bright sun of public participation was (*contra* those arguments that suggest that Czech dissidents merely collapsed politics into ethics) a quintessentially political goal, a goal that was concerned with freedom. Similarly, in the Monday marches in Leipzig and in the use of the street and the square as sites of demonstration in cities throughout the region, the growing revolutionary crowds sought to claim the public sphere for themselves.

---

39 Arendt, *On Revolution*, p. 35.
40 As Arendt puts it: '[..] the multitude rushed to the assistance of the French Revolution, inspired it, drove it onward, and eventually sent it to its doom. When they appeared on the scene of politics, necessity appeared with them, and the result was that the power of the old regime became impotent and the new republic was stillborn; freedom had to be surrendered to necessity, to the urgency of the life process itself. [...] Meanwhile, the revolution had changed its direction; it no longer aimed at freedom, the goal of the revolution had become the happiness of the people.' Arendt, *On Revolution*, pp. 60–61. Needless to say, the absolute division that Arendt posits here between politics and economics and her insistence that the former should not embroil itself in the latter are extremely problematic positions, not least for the Marxist tradition.
41 The phrase, 'the parallel *polis*', was first used by Václav Benda as the title of a *samizdat* publication of 1978 and was subsequently picked up by Havel and others.
42 Václav Havel, 'The Power of the Powerless', trans. by Paul Wilson, in Václav Havel *et al*, *The Power of the Powerless*, ed. by John Keane, London, 1985, pp. 21–96 (49). Havel uses the term 'post-totalitarian' here to refer to the post-Stalinist state-socialism of 1970s normalization.

The revolutions of 1989, however, did not terminate in a new agora within a new *polis*, open to all. Whilst public participation was enormously extended through the adoption of multi-party democracy and through other measures in the dismantling of the one-party state, the space of that participation quickly became the relatively private spaces of the polling booth or the (smoky) back-rooms where deals were cut by the new political parties.[43] Liberation was the order of the day. Arendt notes that the corner stone of liberation as a negative phenomenon is liberation from restraints on freedom of movement. Ultimately, it was this sort of liberation (what Blackstone describes as 'the power of locomotion [...] without imprisonment or restraint'[44]) that played the decisive role in the revolutions of 1989: first, in the flow of train-loads of East Germans down through Hungary and over the newly opened border into Western Europe; and, second, and (most iconically) in the crowds who scaled and burst through the Berlin wall.[45] These trajectories ultimately led to the non-political spaces of relatives' sitting rooms, Mercedes-Benz showrooms, and the aisles of West German supermarkets. For, in East Germany and elsewhere, the social question overpowered the political question. The goal of the revolution swiftly became economic not political: the happiness of the people, defined in material terms, and not their freedom; the alleviation of their relative poverty in comparison with Western abundance.[46] Enthusiasm for democracy and freedom of speech was soon transformed into an enthusiasm for *Begrüßungsgeld*, BMWs, and a share of the booty of privatization and restitution.[47] For all the problems with Arendt's rigorous separation of the social and the political, there is no doubt that

---

43 Arendt's *On Revolution* thoroughly condemns modern electoral democracy for its abdication of the public sphere to representatives. Arendt's preferred model would be a federation of small councils of participating citizens. Such a model, in her view, might go some way to resurrect the spirit of the *polis* for modern times. It is worth noting Arendt's enthusiasm for the revolutionary events of Hungary 1956 and, in particular, for the workers' councils that sprang up during the course of those events. For Arendt, in Hungary 1956 'the rise of the councils, not the restoration of parties, was the clear sign of a true upsurge of democracy against dictatorship, of freedom against tyranny': Hannah Arendt, *The Origins of Totalitarianism*, 2nd enlarged edn, Cleveland, OH, 1958. This second edition includes a chapter on Hungary 1956 that was omitted from subsequent editions. Arendt's view of 1956 and other systems of council democracy has received criticism for its inconsistencies and for its tendency to distort facts to fit theories. See John F. Sitton, 'Hannah Arendt's Argument for Council Democracy', *Polity*, 20, 1987, no 1, pp. 80–100. It is also worth noting at this point that one of the most significant political acts of the post-1989 period, the split of Czechoslovakia in the so-called velvet divorce, was committed by the most distant of representatives, without popular consultation, and with a questionable level of popular support.

44 Quoted in Arendt, *On Revolution*, p. 32. Blackstone's definition echoes the minimal definition of freedom in Hobbes: 'LIBERTY or FREEDOME, signifieth (properly) the absence of Opposition; (by Opposition, I mean externall Impediments of motion;)': Thomas Hobbes, *Leviathan*, ed. Richard Tuck, Cambridge, 1991, p. 145.

45 I witnessed these crowds at first-hand, having arrived in Berlin on 12 November 1989. I celebrated my 18th birthday on 19 November, drinking beer on the top of the wall between the Brandenburg Gate and the Reichstag.

46 Whatever the material discrepancies between East and West, the economic situation of Central and Eastern Europe could scarcely be compared with the poverty of the French revolutionary masses which Arendt describes as a 'state of constant want and acute misery whose ignominy consists in its dehumanizing force': Arendt, *On Revolution*, p. 60. There is nothing dehumanizing about having a reasonable health-care system but not having bananas.

47 *Begrüßungsgeld* was the term for the 100 DM 'welcome money' that the West German state gave to each arriving East German citizen. This system was originally designed for only small numbers of claimants. Following the fall of the Berlin wall, chaotic scenes ensued as huge numbers of East Germans queued at West Berlin banks and *Sparkassen*, wishing to claim their allowance of West German currency.

the shift in the goal of 1989 from freedom to free market signalled the passing of the revolutionary moment.[48]

Arendt III: The limits of revolution; juridification

Freedom and liberation, in Arendt's account, are characterized by different temporal structures. Where liberation may be a one-off act (throwing off the yoke of oppression), the creation of freedom is an activity that must be sustained. This mode of action, in practical terms, places extreme demands on the physical endurance of its actors and their continuing commitment to public business (over the private concerns of their households). Put crudely: at some point the flesh is weak and one must leave the *polis* and return to the *oikos* in order to perform the actions of necessity: sleep, eat, wash, have sex. Suk demonstrates graphically how attempts to prevent the normalization of Civic Forum, to keep it something special, fluid, and unjuridified (that is to say: all attempts to preserve the freedom-establishing qualities of action and novelty), ultimately collapsed for two main reasons: first, the demands of such a mode of acting took too great a toll on the participants; and secondly, because such demands resulted in a self-selecting and hence exclusive group of participants who were able to live up to them.[49]

It is this second reason that was most fatal to the conception of revolution as experiment and natality. The problem is best summed up by Havel himself in his words to his inner circle, following a secret meeting on 15 December 1989 with Marián Čalfa, interim Communist prime minister from 10 November 1989 to 18 January 1990:

> I'm in an absurd situation, because I've just taken part in a discussion behind closed doors [*kabinetní jednání*, literally, 'cabinet negotiations'] and in private [*mezi čtyřma očima*, 'between four eyes', i.e. only the two of them were present] with Čalfa. My feeling is, and maybe I'm stupid, but my feeling is that these were the most important discussions there have ever been. [...] But the paradoxical thing about it all is that we are opponents of 'politics behind closed doors' [*kabinetní politika*] and that all of this has to be kept completely secret, not from the StB [the secret police] but from our people and from the public, not least that part of the public that suspects us of politicking behind closed doors. [...] So for the meantime I ask you to keep everything that I am about to say to yourselves, to keep as silent as the grave, and not to tell anyone anything about it.[50]

This is scarcely Havel's 'living in truth'.[51] Moreover, this quotation reveals the fate of the public realm under the pressures of revolutionary activity. The forum of revolution, open to all, has become the '*kabinet*' of politicking in which an inner circle makes deals with the highest representative of the former regime. If one examines the spatial metaphors of this passage, one sees an opposition between open spaces (the public and, implicitly, the forum) and closed spaces (the '*kabinet*' and the grave) in which Havel's supposedly revolutionary movement is forced to locate itself with the latter term.

---

48 This process took place at astonishing speed. Speaking of the Czechoslovak case, Suk notes that 'the first months of 1990 demonstrated that economics had become the form of politics *par excellence*'. Suk, *Labyrintem revoluce*, p. 32

49 Suk, *Labyrintem revoluce*.

50 Václav Havel, conversation with his inner circle, quoted in Suk, *Labyrintem revoluce*, p. 230.

51 This is Havel's notion, drawn largely from Masaryk and Patočka, of the authentic way to exist in inauthentic circumstances, discussed extensively in 'The Power of the Powerless'. It is the cornerstone of his conception of dissent.

Havel's inclusive 'adhocracy' had become an exclusive oligarchy.[52] A realization of this combined with growing demands from outside the inner circle for inclusion in the sphere of decision-making.[53] It was this that led to the development of more fixed institutions, and more transparent, and perhaps dismayingly normal methods of selection and procedure. Nevertheless, in this process of normalization and juridification, something of the revolutionary spirit died.

The fate of radical innovation in democratic practices was part of a more general drive away from free experimentation and towards normative modes of behaviour and towards law. As Williams puts it in his review of Suk's book:

> What happened to [Civic Forum] in the eight months covered by this book reflects what befell the country as a whole, in that the revolutionary spirit quickly yielded to juridification; the great rallying cry of 1989 was not freedom, but rule of law. When one reads [Civic Forum's] first programmatic statement, 'Co chceme' (What we want) of 26 November 1989, one finds topping the list of demands *právo* (law), embodied in a new constitution and an independent judiciary with broad review powers. By December 1989, Suk shows, the locus of action had shifted from [Civic Forum and The Public against Violence, Civic Forum's Slovak equivalent] (and the crowds on the squares) to the legislatures.[54]

There seems to be a contradiction here within the revolutionary movements that evolved out of dissent. On the one hand, we find in dissent a sense of the stultifyingly administered nature of life under state-socialism and corresponding demands for the freeing up of life.[55] On the other hand, we find a sense of the arbitrary and extra-legal character of the state-socialist regime and corresponding demands for the reestablishment of law and for legitimate juridification. The sense that the communist regime and its laws had been, from this perspective, extra-legal meant that this was a revolution that acted not only in the name of freedom but also in the name of limitation.[56] To grasp the nature of this contradiction is to grasp something of the nature of the revolutionary spirit of 1989 and hence to understand its fate.

---

52 'Adhocracy' is a term that Havel used to describe his conception of improvisational and unregulated 'anti-politics'. Suk shows that Havel takes the term from the work of the American futurologist, Alvin Toffler. Suk, *Labyrintem revoluce*, p. 35.

53 Suk includes a letter written to Havel by Ivan Dejmal, a signatory of Charta 77 and, at the time, the chairperson of the ecological section of Civic Forum, that illustrates the resentment felt at the transformation (under the pressure of day-to-day politics) of the organization from an open and inclusive one into something that resembled a closed oligarchy. Referring to 'you [*Ty*, the informal second-person pronoun] and the group of people around you' it complains that 'we have practically no influence on what you [plural] do. The plenary session of Civic Forum, where previously that would have been possible, has been gradually put on the back burner with the explanation that you don't have time for it because you are so busy negotiating with the government.' Ivan Dejmal, letter to Václav Havel, in Suk, *Labyrintem revoluce*, pp. 242–43 (p. 242).

54 Kieran Williams, Review of Jiří Suk, *Labyrintem revoluce. Aktéři, zápletky a křižovatky jedné politické krize (od listopadu 1989 do června 1990)*, in *Central Europe*, 3, 2005, 1, pp. 91–92 (p. 92).

55 These are demands that, in part, reflect and grow out of the 'bohemian' milieu of the cultural and political underground and its emphasis on alternative life-styles. Thus, Peter Uhl describes Czechoslovak society of the 1980s as a 'bureaucratic dictatorship' that cannot tolerate alternative communities: 'here any form of expression that is not under bureaucratic control is necessarily disruptive.' Peter Uhl, 'The Alternative Community as Revolutionary Avant-garde', trans. by Paul Wilson, in Václav Havel *et al*, *The Power of the Powerless*, pp. 188–97 (p. 192)

56 Hence, one of the many epithets commonly applied to the events of 1989 in Czechoslovakia: the 'self-limiting' (*sebeomezující*) revolution.

Conclusion

These perspectives on 1989 may be of limited use. It might sensibly be argued that nothing new could be born out of 1989, that the weary railway passengers of Central and Eastern Europe had no choice but to board the liberal-democratic express (that, after all, was rather better than the socialist stopping-train that they had been on up to that point), and that the normality that has now been achieved is better than the abnormality of secret police surveillance and repression. If this is the case (and it might well be), one could go on to argue that any talk of revolution as interruption, of natality and *Neues Forum* is nonsense and, moreover, nonsense of unpardonable and patronizing naivety.

To suggest that Central and Eastern Europeans should have behaved differently is to assume a moral high ground that it is not ours in the West to take. (As we should be well aware, our own democratic and revolutionary spirit is far from healthy.) Such a suggestion only expresses an unfair and schoolmasterly disappointment at the East's inability to outstrip us in the lessons of democracy and rediscover the revolutionary treasure for us. Žižek describes with eloquence the disappointment that the aftermath of 1989 brought about in Western observers:

> The passage from actually existing socialism to actually existing capitalism in eastern Europe brought about a series of comic reversals, in which sublime democratic enthusiasm was transformed into the ridiculous. The dignified East German crowds gathering around Protestant churches and heroically defying Stasi terror all of a sudden turned into vulgar consumers of bananas and cheap pornography; the civilized Czechs mobilized by the appeal of Václav Havel and other cultural icons all of a sudden turned into cheap swindlers of Western tourists. [57]

As he goes on to argue, this disappointment and sense of 'betrayed enthusiasm' was mutual:

> The East, which began by idolizing the West as the example of affluent democracy, finds itself in a whirlpool of ruthless commercialization and economic colonization. [...] It is clear that the protesting crowds in East Germany, Poland, and Czechoslovakia wanted something else, a utopian object of impossible fullness designated by a multiplicity of names (*solidarity, human rights*, and so forth) *not what they effectively got.*[58]

Despite this, a sense of shared, if varying disappointments may help keep alive a sense of the importance of democracy and the revolutionary spirit that sustains it. If this is the case, the thought of thinkers such as Arendt, Benjamin and Žižek, directed towards 1989, may provide a cool gaze that reveals a vision of a new and not yet existing Europe. This is to be found in the space that was opened up in the transitory revolutionary moment of 1989. It may have been a space that was quickly closed down. Nevertheless, the critical perspective of that space may aid in doing away with narcissism, defamiliarizing normality, and in revealing the revolutionary treasure of democracy that needs to be rediscovered again and again.

---

57 Žižek, 'A Leftist Plea', pp. 1003–04.
58 ibid, p. 1004.

Resistance and Rebellion in Early Modern Hungary

Ius resistendi in Hungary

László Péter

It is a safe assumption to make that some political precepts and ideas have existed throughout recorded history. These ideas probably include the duty of government to maintain order; protect the lives and property of the subjects; sustain justice; secure rights based either on some natural quality or on service; the precept of freedom from unjustified interference; the obligation to keep agreements; and the duty of obedience to established authority. All of these may be considered near perennial features of social life. And so is resistance to authority and even the removal of those in power in some circumstances. For the duty of obedience to established power can never be unlimited. Even in fully autocratic states, resistance to authority, when successful, was habitually justified. By improving on Mommsen's definition, Charles Diehl described Eastern Rome as an 'autocracy tempered by revolution and assassination.'[1] Accordingly, if and when usurpation of power was accomplished, the authority of the successful new ruler was recognized as legitimate because the deposed incumbent was apparently inadequate or unworthy. On the other hand, when the challenger failed, he was labelled as merely a rebel. In sum, resistance to authority, and even tyrannicide, has been justified in society, *post factum* but not *ex ante*. It is apparent, therefore, that the subject did not have the right of resistance to established authority.

Resistance to authority as a right developed, after some antecedents, in medieval Europe where temporal authority was based on custom and was held therefore to be limited. In his classic monograph on divine right and the right of resistance in the early middle ages Fritz Kern argued that the subject 'owed his ruler not so much obedience but fealty' and fealty was conditional: it had to be reciprocal in character.[2] Custom based on fealty produced the beneficiary system of landownership with its hierarchy of donor-donee relationships, based on fidelity, in which each side possessed rights as well as obligations towards the other. Whenever one side failed to meet its customary obligations, the other side invoked resistance on the offending side as a customary right. The donor-donee relationships did not engender the complex social hierarchy east of the Elbe, typical in Western Europe. In kingdoms like Bohemia, Hungary and Poland, there were only two levels and the donation of land was largely confined to the ruler, as donor,

---

1   Charles Diehl, 'The Government and Administration of the Byzantine Empire', in *The Cambridge Medieval History*, vol 4, 1936, p. 729.
2   Fritz Kern, *Kingship and Law in the Middle Ages*, Oxford, 1948, pp. 87–89.

and the noble as donee.[3] Yet even here, the customary right of resistance was as vigorously exercised as in the western parts of the Continent.

In Hungary, the medieval structure remained a firm foundation on which the right of resistance to authority was based for much longer than in the western part of the Continent. Indeed, a convenient way to tease out the specific features of the Hungarian resistance to established political authority is to compare it to the growth of comparable features elsewhere. In western Christendom, the age of Reformation split the Church into rival confessions. This was the chief reason for the rise of what was to prove to be the durable theory of social contract, which evolved in the sixteenth century, although at first only to protect the faith of particular religious minorities. Radical Calvinists and Jesuits no longer justified resistance as a customary right based on mutual fidelity and obligations, but on contract and agreement, as a deliberate act by the people. Accordingly, because the people had agreed to establish government for certain ends, they thereby had the right to resist and even remove the holders of power if they neglected or contravened those ends. In its radical form, social contract theory justified rebellion by the people or rather some notables acting for them. The right of resistance in England, Holland and France was later refined, largely under the influence of Locke, by the assumption that the social contract had created a civil society, to which everybody consented, prior to the setting up of government which was to use power for certain ends as a trustee on behalf of the community. And when the government by persistent misrule broke its trust, it was argued, it dissolved itself and the right to form a government reverted to the people. The people, i.e. civil society, then simply erected a new government without any major social upheaval. Rebellion by the people was, therefore, no longer necessary, as it had been in the religious wars of the sixteenth century, in order to change the government. The contract theory, although ill-defined and uncertain in its application, gave rise in the eighteenth century to constitutional systems based on the idea of government by consent.

Developments in Hungary were almost invariably affected by the changes that took place in Western Europe. The Church was the important contact between the West and Hungary. The country's educated groups were for centuries provided by the clergy, many of whom visited the universities of Bologna, Paris, later Germany, Vienna and Cracow. Yet Hungary retained the medieval forms of resistance in a robust form for much of its history. The precept of resistance, later called *ius resistendi*, was formally enacted by King Andrew II in the Golden Bull of 1222.[4] The background to this *decretum,* a royal charter of liberties, was a political upheaval which the king faced after his return from a crusade to the Holy Land. He was compelled to replace the high officers of the kingdom with a new set of personnel. As Andrew complained to Pope Honorius III 'an immense crowd' had assembled, demanding that the king should desist from what they viewed as harmful practices which amounted to abuses of royal authority, and that he should confirm the liberties that St Stephen, the holy king, had

---

3   The terms 'donor' and 'donee' are not quite appropriate because the donated land was not a fief but an
    allodium, a reward for past services without specific future obligations.
4   ⁴Gyula Kristó, 'Az 1222. évi Aranybulla', in György Székely (ed.), *Magyarország története*, Budapest,
    1984, vol 2, pp. 1320–32; László Kontler, *Millennium in Central Europe,* Budapest, 1999, p. 77; Pál
    Engel, *The Realm of St Stephen*, London, 2001, pp. 93–95; Bryan Cartledge, *The Will to Survive*, London,
    2006, pp. 21–22.

granted to the nobility. The provisions which included many previously unrecorded privileges, listed under 31 headings, began with the promise that the king would every year on the day of Saint Stephen hear the cases of the *servientes regis*,[5] propertied soldiers subject to the king alone, who might freely assemble in Székesfehérvár. The privileges included the exemption from taxes, limits on the military duties of the nobles and their right not to be arrested without first being summoned and sentenced by due judicial process.[6] These privileges applied to the *comites*, later called barons, the high rank of the nobility as well as the rising lower rank, the *servientes regis,* a term that appeared for the first time in 1217.

The last paragraph of the *decretum*, clause 31, stipulated the famous sanction, the penalty attached to the infringement of the enacting clauses: 'Should we, or any of our successors, at any time seek to violate this disposition of ours, both the bishops and other lords and nobles of the *regnum* collectively and singly, present and future can, by this authority, be free in perpetuity to resist and oppose us and our other successors without the imputation of high treason.'[7] In contrast to the liberties which this charter granted to the *servientes regis* (later called the untitled nobility, in contrast to the titled nobles who formed the higher rank), it is generally held today by medievalists that the charter confined the sanction of resistance to the bishops and the higher rank (from which the baronial class developed).[8]

It was a generally popular habit, and historians were no exception, to boast that the Hungarian constitution was as old, if not older, than the English. Scholars habitually compared the Magna Carta and the Golden Bull.[9] As both charters were the products of societies with institutions based on customary systems of privileges and mutual fidelity, it is not surprising that there should be some similarities. The right of resistance (although in very different forms) was enacted in both – just as it was asserted elsewhere in Europe. The vast differences between English and Hungarian social conditions, however, make comparisons quite unrealistic.[10] Nor is there any evidence that the Magna Carta, which had been issued just seven years earlier in 1215, influenced the

---

5 On the emergence of this group, see Martyn Rady, *Nobility, Land and Service in Medieval Hungary*, Basingstoke & New York, 2000, pp. 35–38, The 1287 enactment of the Golden Bull referred to 'nobiles regni Ungarie universi, qui servientes regales dicuntur', János M. Bak *et al.*, *Decreta Regni Mediaevalis Hungariae* (hereafter *DRMH*), 5 vols, 1989–2005, vol 1, p. 40. This *decretum* was analysed by Jenő Szűcs, *Az utolsó Árpádok*, Budapest, 1993, pp. 125–31.

6 'nisi prius citati fuerint et ordine iudiciario convicti', *DRMH*, vol 1, p.32.

7 Clause 31 of Andrew II's Golden Bull of 1222: 'Statuimus etiam quod, si nos vel aliquis successorum nostrorum aliquo umquam tempore huic disposicioni contraire voluerint, liberam habeant harum auctoritate sine nota infidelitatis tam episcopi quam alii iobagiones ac nobiles regni nostri universi et singuli presentes ac posteri resistendi et contradicendi nobis et nostris successoribus in perpetuum facultatem.' *DRMH*, vol 1, p.35. József Gerics in exploring the provenence of the 'universi et singuli' term demonstrated the influence of canon law on the sanction, 'Az Aranybulla ellenállási záradékának értelmezéséhez', in Iván Bertényi (ed.), *Ünnepi tanulmányok Sinkovics István 70. születésnapjára*, Budapest, 1980, pp. 99–108.

8 Alajos Degré, 'Az ellenállási jog története Magyarországon', *Jogtudományi Közlöny*, June 1980, p. 367; József Gerics, *A korai rendiség Európában és Magyarországon*, Budapest 1987, p. 259.

9 The Protestant Pál Ráday, chancellor to Rákóczi, might have been, as Ágnes R. Várkonyi has suggested, the first who in 1706 compared the Golden Bull to the Magna Carta, *Magyarország története 1686–1790*, vol 1, Budapest, 1989, p. 327; László Péter, 'The Holy Crown of Hungary, Visible and Invisible', *Slavonic and East European Review*, 81, no 3, pp. 488 n. 362.

10 Ferenc Eckhart, *Magyar alkotmány- es jogtörténet*, Budapest, 1941, p. 33.

revolt that forced Andrew to enact the Golden Bull. The subsequent history of the two charters, however, reveals some notable similarities. It used to be claimed that each had been the source of continuous constitutional developments, while in fact both went into eclipse shortly after their enactments, and then were rediscovered and later cherished as the fountain-heads of a continuous progress towards representative institutions. Constitutional development has in fact been discontinuous in most countries.

The Golden Bull changed neither the social nor the political conditions of the country. The new holders of high office had already by December 1222 lost their positions to the old set of barons. Government practices went on unchanged to the dismay of the Church. In 1231 under pressure from Pope Gregory IX, Andrew confirmed the liberties of the privileged classes.[11] Yet in this *decretum*, the sanction found in the Golden Bull was replaced by a new sanction: 'the king freely consented' to the authorization that the archbishop of Esztergom might admonish and even excommunicate him or his successors should the liberties granted in the charter be infringed.[12] Béla IV, Andrew's son and successor, hoped to consign the 1222 charter to oblivion.[13] He restored royal authority by claiming the *ius regium* (i.e. *ius coronae*) to repossess royal land which had been lost under his predecessors. Towards the end of his rule in 1267, Béla, under pressure from his son, the future Stephen V, issued a short, ten-paragraph charter confirming the liberties of the whole nobility.[14] But once again, instead of the sanction of the Golden Bull, excommunication by the church figured in the text instead of clause 31.

In the last decades of the thirteenth century, royal power was debilitated by the emergence of strong baronial groups which generated political instability and general insecurity. Partly in order to counterbalance the oligarchs, the nobility organized itself horizontally into local autonomous counties, assembled in their own *generales congregationes* (in 1289 the term *parlamentum publicum* can be found) and a few token nobles were also invited to the royal council.[15] No evidence has been found so far, however, that in this period the sanction of resistance laid down in the 1222 charter was referred to or even remembered. After 1308, the Angevin kings, by replacing the old baronial groups with their own supporters, had considerable success in restoring royal authority. The county assemblies lost much of their earlier competence.[16] Yet it was under this new dynasty that the Golden Bull resurfaced. In 1318 when the bishops were engaged in conflict with Charles Robert, they produced a copy of the 1222 Bull, with its clause 31. Alajos Degré could be right in suggesting that the bishops knew that they could not rely on the 1231 or the 1267 charters since the Holy See as a supporter of the Angevin kings would not apply the sanction of excommunication provided in them.[17] It is also possible that the bishops hit upon a copy of Andrew's charter accidentally. When Charles Robert's son, Louis I, faced discontent among the nobility he felt strong and secure enough to re-enact in 1351, with some

---

11 *DRMH*, vol 1, pp. 36–39.
12 Eckhart, *M. alk. tört.*, pp. 34–35.
13 Rady, *Nobility*, p. 40.
14 Szűcs, *Az utolsó Árpádok*, pp. 131–36.
15 ibid, pp. 293–96.
16 Engel, *The Realm*, pp. 179–81.
17 Degré, 'Az ellenállási jog', p. 368.

important changes to the rules governing the inheritance of land, the 1318 version of the Golden Bull.[18] Although from this time onward, the kings at their coronation confirmed the Golden Bull, including clause 31, it is far from clear whether the sanction of Andrew II's Bull acquired the prominent position in the constitution which later became attributed to it.

After the death of Louis, royal power once more collapsed. In a kingdom where institutions were poorly developed, the ruler's capacity to persuade rested to a large extent on the land which he had available for distribution. This land was given out, however, as allodial property and might only revert to the ruler in the event of the owner's death without heir or treason. The royal fisc thus became attenuated and, along with it, the bonds of *fidelitas*. The transition in the 1380s from the Angevin dynasty to the Luxemburgs further eroded the loyalty felt by noblemen to the ruling house. Sigismund, elected king in 1387, had to start all over again. Weakened by the disastrous Battle of Nicopolis against the Ottomans, at the diet of Temesvár in 1397, Sigismund confirmed the rights of the nobility by re-enacting most clauses of the Golden Bull. Yet clause 31 was not among them.[19] Nor did the 'league' of office-holder barons who imprisoned Sigismund for six months in 1401 or the barons who rebelled against him in 1403, offering the crown to Ladislas of Naples, so far as we know, invoke the sanction of Andrew II's Bull. Sigismund eventually succeeded in overcoming the opposition (as Béla IV and Charles Robert had done before him and Matthias Corvinus was to do subsequently) by replacing, through patient effort, a large part of the baronial class with *homines novi*, his own supporters. After Sigismund's death in 1437, when central authority collapsed for two decades, the parties to the fierce political conflicts did not refer expressly to clause 31 of the Golden Bull. It emerges from János Bak's studies that it was only after the death of King Matthias in 1490, in the Jagiellonian period (1490–1526), that clause 31 became permanently a chief point of reference. Weary of Matthias's innovations, the barons at the diet were determined, as a chronicle noted, to elect a king 'whose plaits they could hold in their hands'.[20] They elevated the pliable Wladislas II to office.

István Werbőczy, leading judge at the court from 1502 and the political leader of the party of the nobility expressed in his work a new self-confidence of the untitled nobility which flexed its muscles for a fight with the barons and the king. Werbőczy listed in a single passage (the so-called *primae nonus*) in his customary, the *Tripartitum*,[21] the nobility's four cardinal privileges: (1) the right to be free of arrest without the due legal process; (2) to be subject only to the lawfully crowned king; (3) exemption from servile obligations and from payment of taxes and to provide military service only in defence of the kingdom.

---

18 *DRMH*, vol 2, p. 9.
19 Franciscus Döry *et al. Decreta regni Hungariae 1301–1457*, Budapest 1976, p.158 and *DRMH*, vol 2, pp. 23 and 176.
20 Janos M. Bak, *Königtum und Stände in Ungarn im 14.-16. Jahrhundert*, Wiesbaden, 1973, p. 62.
21 *Tripartitum opus iuris consuetudinarii inclyti regni Hungariae*, *DRMH*, vol 5, 2005, 473 pp. The first edition of 1517 is published here together with its English translation.

The fourth (not to mention the others) and last one is that if any of our princes and kings should venture to act contrary to the liberties of the nobles, then, as stated and expressed in the general decree of the most illustrious prince, our former Lord King Andrew the Second, called 'of Jerusalem' (which decree every Hungarian king is wont to swear on oath to observe before the Holy Crown is placed on his head), they have the liberty in perpetuity to resist and oppose him without the imputation of high treason.[22]

Werbőczy stretched the scope of clause 31 of Andrew's Bull, hitherto a sanction, and elevated it to the status of a cardinal privilege or *ius* and he referred to the contents of the Golden Bull as *sacra decreta*.[23] Furthermore, he did not predicate the right of resistance on the nobles *universi et singuli* as it had been in the Golden Bull, but on the *communitas* in which, as he emphasized repeatedly, all nobles, including the most powerful ones and the poorest, 'enjoy one and the same liberty' (*una eademque libertatis gaudent*). The *communitas* of the nobility existed as a separate repository of law side by side with the crown.[24] I shall return to this point after a brief summary of the practice of *ius resistendi* until the end of the Habsburg Monarchy.

Following the disaster inflicted on the kingdom by the Ottomans at Mohács in 1526, the nobility elected as king the Archduke Ferdinand, a Habsburg who until János Zápolya's death in 1540, had to tolerate a rival king. The foreign hereditary possessions of the new dynasty and the occupation of central Hungary by the Ottomans enabled the crown to create a new titled nobility of princes, counts and barons and to subordinate the Hungarian royal administration to the imperial offices in Vienna. The diet still retained, however, substantial powers in respect of protecting the nobility's *jussai* (rights). Also, Transylvania, a separate principality under the Sultan's suzerainty, became after 1547 a new counterweight to the Habsburg court. Although its princes regarded their country as a part of the Holy Crown of Hungary, Transylvania sometimes cooperated and at other times rebelled against the Habsburg king.[25] The unsuccessful Fifteen Years' War of the Habsburgs together with the Hungarian and Transylvanian nobility and Moldavia and Wallachia against the Ottoman empire introduced the 'Time of Troubles', open conflicts between the imperial court and the estates of Hungary and of Transylvania.[26]

István Bocskai, a magnate in eastern Hungary, was the leader of the first major rising against the Habsburg monarch in 1604. Supported by the nobility, many towns and soldier-herdsmen, the 'heyducks', the Calvinist leader fought, among other things, for religious liberties. In justifying the rebellion against the monarch he did not however use Calvin's arguments (which he may have known) or indeed the social contract theory in any form. Bocskai and also the assembled estates referred regularly to the rights

---

22 'Quarta (ut reliquas pręteream) & ultima est quod si quispiam regum & principum nostrorum libertatibus nobilium in gernerali decreto excellentissimi principis quondam domini secundi Andreę regis cognomento Hierosolymitani (ad quod observandum quilibet regum Hungariæ priusquam suum sacro caput dyademate coronaretur sacramentum pręstare solet) declaratis & expressis contravenire attemptaret, extune sine nota alicuius infidelitatis liberam illi resistendi & contradicendi habent in perpetuum facultatem', ibid, p.56. Only some kings included in their coronation oaths observance of the Golden Bull.

23 *Tripartitum*, II: 6, para. 6.

24 On the appearance of the *communitas* in Hungary, see Gerics, *A rendiség*, pp. 250–64.

25 See Kontler, *Millennium*, pp. 148–49.

26 The social consequences of the 'Time of Troubles' were summarized by Kálmán Benda in 'Hungary in Turmoil, 1580–1620', *European Studies Review*, 8, 1978, pp. 281–304.

enshrined in the *primae nonus* of the *Tripartitum*.[27] When the estates at the diet at Korpona in 1605 pleaded they should be spared of punishment for their rebellion, the king's representative promised that they would not once they had renewed and kept their allegiance to the king. The estates then declared that they had not acted unlawfully: 'When the king acts against the rights and the laws of the *ország* they can resist him according to the *primae nonus* without incurring the charge of infidelity'[28] This amounted once more to an extended reading of clause 31. While Werbőczy had predicated the right of resistance on the rights enshrined in the Golden Bull, Bocskai extended the rights to cover the *ország jussai* in general, i.e. the rights of Hungary and Transylvania as separate political Lands within the Habsburg Monarchy. This extended interpretation of the *primae nonus* then influenced the princes of Transylvania who justified their armed conflicts with the crown as actions intended to protect the Protestant religion and Hungarian liberty. Imre Thököly, the leader of a major revolt in Upper Hungary against Habsburg rule, announced in 1684, with reference to the provision of resistance, that the law of Andrew II subsumed 'the spirit of Hungarian liberty, the proper limit of rule, the judge and avenger of the subject that is able to wash out completely the stain of rebellion.'[29] Not surprisingly, when a few years later Emperor Leopold I, with the help of an international army, expelled the Ottomans from Hungary his position was strong enough to force major changes through a pliant diet. The diet felt gratitude for the liberation of the country and was afraid that the court would, on the basis of *ius gentium,* apply the *Verwirkungtheorie* to Hungary as a conquered land and replace the country's institutions with some other system. The court at the diet secured in Article II of 1687 the agnatic hereditary succession of the dynasty to the Hungarian crown. Equally important was Article IV according to which, as the statute 'explained', only some wicked rebels had understood by clause 31 of Andrew II's decree that the *status et ordines*, i.e. the diet, could ever rise up against the legitimate king. For this reason the diet consented to the court's request that the clause relating to the right of resistance should be deleted from Andrew's law which was to be observed in all other aspects.[30] In addition, Article I also expressly excluded clause 31 from Joseph's coronation oath. Significantly, the same exclusion was repeated in the coronation oath of Charles III (VI) in 1711, of Maria Theresa in 1741, of Leopold II in 1790, of Francis I in 1792, in the 'Inaugural Diploma' of Ferdinand V in 1836, and even in the coronation oaths of Franz Joseph in 1867 and of Charles IV in 1917.[31]

---

27 Ferenc Eckhart, 'Bocskay és hiveinek közjogi felfogása', in *Károlyi Árpád Emlékkönyv*, Budapest, 1933, pp. 135–38.
28 ibid., p. 137.
29 Quoted by Gyula Szekfű, *Magyar történet*, vol 4, Budapest, 1935 (hereafter *Magyar tört.*) p. 203.
30 As regards article 31, the statute declared that its 'probum sensum, nonnisi quorundam privatorum prava interpretatio, in alienum praevaricatum ne fors, detorquere studuisset: saniorumque suae majestatis sacratissimae fidelium statuum et ordinum nunquam ea mens fuisset; quod juxta illum (per malevolos et seditiosos obversum) contra legitimum regem, et dominum suum. quispiam armis consurgere et sese erigere queat.' For this reason the article 'mediante praesenti articulari constitutione exclusae, et semotae.' *Corpus Juris Hungarici*, 1657–1740, ed. Dezső Márkus, Budapest, 1900 (hereafter *CJH*), p. 336
31 In Law III of 1917 (the Inaugural Diploma), Charles IV promised to keep the customs and laws of the kingdom 'kivéve mindazonáltal dicsőült II. András 1222. évi törvényének azon megszüntetett záradékát, amely igy kezdődik: Quodsi vero Nos, ezen szavakig: in perpetuum facultatem.' *CJH*, 1917, Budapest, 1918, p. 10.

The fact that a statement formally referring to the abolition of the *ius resistendi* by statute remained a permanent feature of the investiture in the royal office until the very end of the Habsburg Monarchy, may already suggest that the issue of resistance retained political significance after 1687. In fact, only the loyalist section of the nobility acquiesced in its abolition and its omission never attained general acceptance by the political class. The *ius resistendi* had to be expressly declared abolished in the royal oath because only the statute, ordained by the king in agreement with the diet, had abolished it – custom had not.[32] In the Hungarian system custom could always rescind statute (*desuetudo*) and in the oath the king vowed to maintain intact the custom of the Land. The greatest protracted armed rebellion against Habsburg authority based on the customary right of resistance, leading in 1707 to the *abrenuntiatio* of the house of Habsburg, lasted from 1703 to 1711. Its charismatic leader, Ferencz Rákóczi, in his proclamation *Recrudescunt inclitae gentis Hugariae vulnera* listed under 21 long headings the grievances of the Hungarian nation. The first one objected to the taking away of the free election of the king 'which custom maintained for centuries unimpaired'. The second heading vehemently protested against the shameful abrogation of Andrew's 'great law' which conferred 'never ceasing power to resist the king when he degrades the laws'.[33] The Senate presided over by Rákóczi in January 1706 demanded the restoration of the *ius resistendi*.[34] So the leaders of the revolt took entirely Thököly's view of clause 31 and held its abrogation to be unlawful.[35] For a few years, the uprising united practically the whole country, not just the nobility, under Rákóczi, and it shook the Monarchy to the core. The rebellion ended in a settlement at Szatmár with an amnesty (although the leader and his entourage opted for exile) and confirmation of the nobility's customary rights. In sum, Werbőczy's elevation of clause 31 to a cardinal *ius* during the Time of Troubles became an effective weapon in the hands of the nobility against the crown. Andrew's *decretum* was remembered only through the *Tripartitum*. Also, the medieval view that attributed a kind of reality to *ius* which preserved its multivocal character was, through Werbőczy, transmitted to modern times, a point to which I shall return at the end of this paper.

In the age of enlightenment, through administrative reforms, the powers of the crown were used more extensively and efficiently. In 1723, succession in the crown was extended to the cognatic line of the dynasty. These changes were counterbalanced by the nobility which secured in 1741 article VIII the provision, with reference to the *primae nonus* of the *Tripartitum*, that fundamental rights, *fundamentalia jura*, could not even be brought before the diet for discussion. This meant that basic customary rights were subject neither to revision nor even interpretation by the diet.[36] In the eighteenth century, the social centre of opposition to Vienna was no longer the mostly loyal aristocracy but the *bene possessionati,* the well-to-do untitled nobility, later called

---

32 On the role of custom see István Szijartó, *A diéta, a magyar rendek és az országgyűlés 1708–1792*, Budapest 2005, pp. 40–43.

33 Béla Kŏpeczi, *A Rákóczi–szabadságharc és Európa*, Budapest 1970, pp. 35–36.

34 Miklós Asztalos, *II Rákóczi Ferenc és kora*, Budapest 1934, p. 200.

35 Szekfû, *Magyar tört.*, vol 4, p. 288.

36 *CJH*, 1740–1835, p. 24, and see the proper interpretation of this habitually misunderstood clause in István Ereky, *Jogtörténelmi és közigazgatási jogi tanulmányok*, Eperjes, 1917, vol 1, p. 184 n 2.

gentry.[37] The source of their rising influence was the vital distinguishing institution of the country: the local county, which they controlled by elected officials and which, in contrast to the other lands and kingdoms of the Monarchy, preserved its autonomy (if not quite independence) in its relations with the royal offices. Furthermore, the deputies of the fifty counties constituted the *sanior pars* of the diet's lower house. As diets were now called irregularly, the county assemblies, in cooperation with each other, became the habitual foci of resistance to the decrees enacted by the central authorities. They practised *vis inertiae* against taxes and recruitment not granted by the diet and against various other measures which in their view diminished their rights. They may have merely put the objectionable decrees *ad acta*, filed in the archives.[38] The assembly could, furthermore, formally declare opposition to its implementation or send a letter to the central authority, the council of lieutenancy, or charge the county's chief elected officer, the *alispán*, with so doing. The response of the central government to obstructive, recalcitrant counties was to dispatch a royal commissar backed by army units to restore authority. After 1780, when Joseph II failed to arrange his coronation and through reforms, introduced by octroi, began to dismantle the Hungarian system of customary privileges, opposition by the counties to the new measures became general from 1787. The nobility in their assemblies and in an enormously large pasquiline literature again demanded restoration of the *ius resistendi*.[39] Joseph's new and unlawful system collapsed in 1789. The county deputies at the diet convoked by Leopold II in 1790, insisted on the reenactment of clause 31 of Andrew's Bull. Leopold was able to resist the demand only through a new settlement in which the rights of the nobility were once more confirmed. In Article X Hungary was described as *regnum liberum et [...] independens*, which possessed its own *constitutio*,[40] and in article XII the monarch was made to promise that royal decrees would be issued outside the diet only in cases where statute law was unaffected. The county was, from this time onwards, cherished as the 'bastion of the constitution'.

In the next round of conflict between the crown and Hungary after the Napoleonic wars, when the counties resisted the financial measures imposed on the country by Francis I, the monarch was forced in 1825 to convoke the diet after a period of thirteen years in which it had not met. This event opened up the age of liberal nationalism in which some of the *bene possessionati* deputies of the counties spearheaded the introduction of social reform and of responsible government. This bid for power prepared the way for the major conflict between the crown and Hungary in 1848. The Hungarian liberal nationalists, followers of Count István Széchenyi, aimed at dismantling the whole system of privileges and certainly did not want to restore the anachronistic *ius resistendi*. Yet even the Liberals did not entirely shed the ingrained attitudes on resist-

---

37 See on this István Szijártó's monographs, *A diéta,* esp. pp. 17–19, 359–68, and *Nemesi társadalom és politika,* Budapest, 2006, pp. 100–41.

38 See the history of a case in county Somogy in 1765–1771, in István Szijártó, *Rendiség és rendi intézmények a 18. századi Magyarországon,* Candidate dissertation, Budapest 1997, pp. 1–2.

39 See Győző Concha, *Az 1790/1-diki országgyűlés,* Budapest, 1907, vol 2, pp. 9, 21, 32, 38.

40 Largely under the influence of Montesquieu, the nobility designated its customary rights as a constitution. See László Péter, 'Montesquieu's Paradox on Freedom and Hungary's Constitutions 1790–1990', *History of Political Thought,* 16, 1995, pp. 79–80.

ance. Ferencz Deák's draft Penal Code of 1843 punished for treachery those (officials) who were involved in the preparation of unlawful royal orders and also those who obeyed them. On the other hand, resistance to 'anti-constitutional measures' did not constitute rebellion. 'Does not this amount to the smuggling the right of resistance into the text of the codex?' – asked János Varga.[41]

The conceptual framework supporting the liberal political programme was provided by contractualism. The theory of social contract had been well known in Hungary since the age of the Enlightenment. Mediated by the German natural law school and particularly by the obsessively state-interventionist Christian Wolff, the social contract theory, in its mildest possible form, became a part of the curriculum in the University of Vienna under Baron Karl Anton Martini, tutor to the leading personalities of the Monarchy. The monarch, according to Martini's teaching, was the source of the law. It was everybody's duty to obey the ruler because the power to make law had been transferred to the monarch in an agreement, a contract, by the people. Subjects, therefore, did not have the right of resistance although their representatives had the right to be consulted, particularly on measures that affected their fundamental natural rights. Martini's textbooks, published in the 1760s, were followed by the leading university jurists in Hungary, all government officials – Lakits, Rosenmann, Schwartner, Cziráky, Virozsil and others – who classified Hungary as a *monarchia limitata* rather than a *monarchia mixta* in which political power was shared between the monarch and the estates. Other jurists, influenced also by the social contract assumption of the natural law school, emphasized the role of agreements between the crown and the political community. They represented the views of the county nobility. Barits, Aranka, Geörch, to mention only a few, held a dualistic view of political power. They presumed that political authority was based on two legitimate sources: the monarch and the political community; Hungary was a constitutional monarchy (in fact a *monarchia mixta*).[42] There were also radical representatives of the Enlightenment who combined the medieval *ius resistendi* with the theory of social contract. In an anonymous work, József Hajnóczy inferred from the social contract the right of resistance and argued that Andrew II's clause expressed the natural right of civil society from which no nation could be deprived by law.[43]

Contractual arguments affected the vocabulary used at the diet. While jurists were concerned with the social contract, the county officials and the deputies at the diet were preoccupied with the political contract between the crown and the nation. It was an easy transition to understand the feudal nexus of a purely customary system, based on mutual trust between king and nobility, as agreements based on statutory enactments which imposed contractual rights and duties on the parties. Hungary's rights or *jussok* (L. *ius/ iures* = H. *jussok*) – so went the argument – were enshrined in statutes which were, in fact, contracts between the crown and the nation. Due to this shift, the statutes became an independent legal source. They existed side by side with custom and were the principal point of reference cited in support of the list of *gravamina* presented to the

---

41 János Varga, *Deák Ferenc és az első magyar polgári büntetőrendszer tervezete* (Zalai Gyűjtemény, 15), Zalaegerszeg, 1980, p. 91.
42 See Péter, 'The Holy Crown', pp 472–74.
43 Kálmán Benda, *A magyar jakobinus mozgalom iratai*, Budapest 1957, vol 1, p 323.

monarch's government in the *diaetalis tractatus*, the negotiations leading, from time to time, to settlements with the crown.[44] The April Laws in 1848 laid the foundations of a Hungarian civil society and established a separate Hungarian government, but as a settlement it turned out to be a complete failure. The Batthyány government claimed rights which the April Laws did not grant. The conflict led to war between Hungary and the Empire and then the Schwarzenberg government imposed by octroi the March Constitution on the whole Monarchy, emasculating the April Laws. In a direct response to this, the Hungarians drew on the radical implications of the contractualist theory in the Declaration of Hungarian Independence drafted by Lajos Kossuth in April 1849. The Declaration of the National Assembly provided a long account of the 'perfidious acts' of the Habsburg dynasty which had ever since 1527 repeatedly broken the bilateral agreements by which they were elevated to the royal office. This historical account provided justification for the 'lawful representatives of the nation' to restore to Hungary its inalienable natural rights. The Assembly declared Hungary to be an independent European state whose territorial integrity was inviolate; 'deposed, debarred and banished' the house of Habsburg in the name of the nation; declared peace towards all its neighbours; left the determination of the form of the state to the following parliament and appointed 'by unanimous acclamation' Lajos Kossuth as governor-president.[45] After the defeat of the Hungarian army in August 1849, the centralist and unconstitutional Bach regime was imposed on the country. That the nobility engaged in 'passive resistance' against the regime was a cliché that emerged largely after the collapse of the Bach regime in 1859. Nevertheless, its usage in Hungary could have been the source of its emergence in the vocabulary of politics in other languages (another, more likely source is, of course, India). But no research has, so far that I know, been carried out on the provenance of this term.

After the collapse of Kossuth's independent course, Ferencz Deák, the 'sage of the nation', became undisputed leader. He and his followers also believed that Hungary and the dynasty had been historically tied together by contracts, especially by the fundamental contract of the 1723 Pragmatic Sanction through 'mutually dependent conditions'. Unlike Kossuth, they did not derive from the idea of contract its radical corollary: that it could be terminated. When the contract was broken by one side, the essence of Deák's argument was that the other side should resist until the contract was restored through *diaetalis tractatus*.[46] This moderate use of contractualist politics led to a lasting constitutional settlement in 1867.

Apart from the first few years after 1867 political support for the Settlement (labelled inaccurately and unfairly as the 'Compromise') was never very strong. Deák's ideas could never compete with Kossuth's vision of Hungary endowed with the 'right' to be a fully independent state. The county remained an important centre of resistance against the new system. Although, through the establishment of representative government, it had lost most of its political power, its autonomy was restored which induced county

---

44 This change was examined in László Péter 'The Irrepressible Authority of the *Tripartitum*', in *DRMH*, vol 5, p. xvii.

45 Istvan Barta (ed.), *Kossuth Lajos összes munkái*, vol 14, Budapest 1953, pp. 894–912, esp. pp. 895, 910–11.

46 Manó Kónyi, *Deák Ferencz beszédei*, Budapest, 1903, vol 3, pp. 35, 40, 47–48.

Heves, later followed by others, to pass resolutions opposing the Settlement even as early as 1867. Heves went on resisting until 1869. The government, following established practice, suppressed the resistance by dispatching a royal commissar. For this it was fiercely attacked by the opposition in the House of Representatives (hereafter the House). Prime Minister Tisza did his best to weaken county autonomy by building up local institutions under ministerial control. His successor in 1891 even tried to introduce an appointment system for all county officials, which many liberals demanded. The bill the government introduced faced such robust obstruction in the House that the whole question of the county's position was postponed indefinitely. County autonomy was still widely regarded by the political class as a constitutional guarantee of Hungary's rights.[47] Half-domesticated, never a pussycat, the county was ordinarily docile but now and again it reverted to type with wild-cat strikes of *vis inertiae*. No longer its own master, the county nevertheless still remained an effective forum of resistance. Its ability to cooperate with others ensured the wide dissemination of its influence. There were other foci of resistance: Forty-eighter clubs, university student associations, and an expansive literature in which jurists provided novel interpretations of the laws in an attempt to establish new national rights (*nemzeti jussok*). There were riots, demonstrations against the government in the capital and, above all, there was vigorous opposition in parliament. All these forces often worked together.

Most of them came together in creating the constitutional crisis of 1905–06. Parliament resolved that the counties should obstruct the implementation of the decrees issued by the 'unconstitutional' Fejérváry government. The counties used the traditional *vis inertiae* rather than lawful procedure in their resistance. The government then, as earlier, sent commissars to restore order, although this move frequently led to further unrest because, as was now claimed, the commissar was an institution alien to the Hungarian constitutional system.[48] County officials duly carried out the 'sealing-wax revolution' (*pecsétviasz forradalom*). Sealing up the committee rooms, the traditional locus of their power, they broke up the chairs of the commissars (the *széktörés* is a medieval form of resistance to authority)[49] while the commissars were pelted with eggs by mobs on their arrival. When István Tisza, backed by the House's majority, changed the standing orders to control obstruction, the minority opposition broke the furniture of the House on 13 December 1904 to demonstrate that parliament had lost its authority.

Parliamentary obstruction was after 1867 the major form of resistance to government authority. Like the *vis inertiae* of the counties this form of resistance also had a long background in history and it survived into the age of representative government. The

---

47 László Péter, 'Die Verfassungsentwicklung in Ungarn', in Helmut Rumpler & Peter Urbanitsch (eds.), *Die Habsburgermonarchie 1848–1918*, vol 7, part 1 ('Verfassung und Parlamentarismus'), 2000, Vienna, pp. 492–96.

48 On street disturbances in Hungary, see Alice Freifeld, *Nationalism and the Crowd in Liberal Hungary, 1848–1914*, London, 2002, ch. 10; on political disorder between 1903–1906 see László Péter, 'The Army Question in Hungarian Politics 1867–1918', *Central Europe*, 2006, no 2, pp.97–101; on the (robust) 'guerrilla war' of the counties under gentry rule against the government in 1905–6, see József Horváth, *Az 1905/6 évi vármegyei ellenállás története,* Budapest, [1907], pp. 10–11, 45–51, 65–67, 228–31, 320, 335; on Budapest's (lukewarm) resistance see Sebestyén Szőcs, *Budapest székesfőváros részvétele az 1905–1906 évi nemzeti ellenallásban*, Budapest, 1977, pp. 92, 95–96.

49 Cf. *A Magyar nyelv történeti – etimológai szótára*, Budapest 1976, vol 3, p. 700.

rowdiness of the *jurati* (secretaries of the deputies) whenever a government supporter addressed the House in the Reform era had antecedents as early as the seventeenth century. The April Laws of 1848 put an end to this form of resistance.[50] When representative government was restored in 1867, the loosely construed rules of the House's standing orders, which allowed unlimited debate over bills, weakened the authority of the chair and made it easy for any determined minority to obstruct the work of the House.[51] The Forty-eighters, followers of Kossuth, filibustered the bill on franchise reform brought in by the Lónyay government in February 1872. The *obstruckció* spread like bushfire in the House because the Forty-eighters argued that the bill overrode national rights. The government eventually caved in, losing a large part of its legislative programme. The possibility of obstruction, even though unexercised for years, remained a threat which inclined the government to avoid contentious legislation. Obstruction was employed in 1886 and with great ferocity in 1889, in both cases over the common army (its existence itself was seen as an affront to Hungarian liberty). In 1899, the Bánffy government was the first to fall as a direct outcome of obstruction. Parliamentary obstruction created a protracted political crisis in 1903 when the army question swept away three governments and drove the country, indeed the whole Monarchy, into the constitutional crisis of 1905.[52]

The remedy against parliamentary obstruction by minorities is, of course, the reform of the standing orders which many parliaments carried out in the nineteenth century. Yet Hungarian politicians, apart from István Tisza's group, were most reluctant to enforce the majority principle. For the country had a constitutional rather than a parliamentary system of government. The wide powers of the king, supported by the resources of the whole Empire, left parliament in an insecure position. Restricting free speech in parliament by the reform of the House's standing orders, it was argued by many moderate politicians, would alter the constitutional balance between the nation and the crown more heavily in favour of the latter. In Hungary, therefore, *obstrukció* was not considered to be an aberration but a necessary feature of parliamentary life. Lajos Mocsáry summed up the system as 'parliamentary tyranny tempered by obstruction.'[53] Tisza, putting through the reform of the Standing Orders in 1912, finally obliterated the systematic obstruction in the House. This made it possible more easily to dispatch business but at the cost of some of the House's political strength.

* * *

It has clearly emerged from this cursory review of Hungarian politics in the periods following Mohács that resistance to authority was essentially about resistance to alien Habsburg rule by native, national forces. This is such a plausible way of looking at the subject that no historian would dissent from it. I would not do either. Yet the subject has a deeper aspect: the conflict between the two sides was not merely political but structural. For each side existed as a distinct repository of rights, a fact which is significant

---

50 *CJH*, 1948, Law IV paras 10–14.
51 On parliamentary obstruction, see Péter, 'Die Verfassungsentwicklung', pp. 469–72.
52 See Péter, 'The Army Question', pp. 97–100.
53 Péter, 'Die Verfassungsentwicklung', p. 471.

because it goes a long way towards explaining the depths and the indestructibility of the conflicts between the crown and Hungary as a *communitas* of the *Land* (*ország*). This structural dualism had already emerged in the Middle Ages, centuries before the Habsburg succession. Far from being a peculiarly Hungarian feature in medieval Europe, in many other countries institutions also had a binary character. Whereas elsewhere in Europe this feature disappeared, in Hungary the medieval system survived much longer, partly perhaps because the crown did not go native.

This is not the place (at the end of this paper) to offer a proper account of the emergence of the *communitas*[54] i.e. *regnum* in its *ország* sense of a political community, which developed side by side to the crown, i.e. *regnum* designating royal authority. In a purely customary system, which Hungary had, reference to 'old custom' already presupposed a notion of 'we', i.e. a community in some vague sense. Simon Kézai's Chronicle written in the thirteenth century, was the first history of the *communitas*. It became the source for Thuróczy's Chronicle of the 1480s which, in turn, provided the basis for Werbőczy's views.[55] By then, the *communitas* had become a corporation: an *ország* (*regnum*) endowed with rights, *jussok* and obligations towards the crown. *Ius* was the legal and moral basis of the community's social norms. In the sixteenth-century translations into Hungarian of Werbőczy's customary, somebody's *jussa, igaza, igazsága* conflated law, truth and justice.[56] The multivocal use of *ius* shaped the Hungarian mental outlook for centuries which, mixing up the real with the desirable, may go a long way to explain why so many of the resisters' aims were unrealistic.

What may be called the 'let's kidnap the emperor' syndrome is a good example of the political naïveté associated with the images of *jus*. The historical background of this recurring adventure-dream was the political crisis of Sigismund's rule. In April 1401 the king was arrested and kept in captivity for six months by leading barons, led by the archbishop and the palatine, until Sigismund met some of their demands.[57] This episode fixed the imagination of malcontents for generations to come. The syndrome first occurred after the Peace of Vasvár (1664) in which General Montecuccoli, having defeated the Turkish army, concluded peace as if his army had been the defeated one. Hungary was rife with discontent and conspiracies. Leading men planned to kidnap Emperor Leopold in Austria and keep him in a castle in Hungary until he remedied the country's grievances. The palatine disagreed but conspiracies went on until 1671 when the court brutally suppressed the movement.[58]

A classic case of the syndrome is also the Gáspár Noszlopy conspiracy. After the collapse of Kossuth's independent Hungary in 1849 the country was teeming with conspiracies against the unconstitutional Bach regime. Kossuth's agents planned to organize a popular uprising to prepare Kossuth's return from abroad. Noszlopy, one of the participants, did not find the plan radical enough. His plan was to capture Emperor

54 On the emergence of the concept of *communitas*, see Jenő Szűcs, *Nemzet és történelem,* Budapest 1974, pp. 444–64; Rady, *Nobility, Land and Service,* ch.10.
55 Péter Váczy, 'A népfelség elvének magyar hirdetője a xiii. században' in *Károlyi Árpád Emlékkönyv,* Budapest, 1933 p 563 n.54.
56 See *DRMH,* vol 5, pp. xiii-xv.
57 Engel, *Realm of St Stephen,* pp. 206–08.
58 Gyula Szekfű, *Magyar tört.,* vol 4, pp. 174–77.

Franz Joseph in Kecskemét, during his visit to Hungary in June 1852, and make him endorse the nation's demands. The kidnapping was to be carried out by a posse, decked out in sparkling hussar uniforms so as to inspire the ordinary people to rise up against the regime. The reliable tailors of Kecskemét were ordered to work in great secrecy at night on the uniforms. Unfortunately, when Franz Joseph passed through Kecskemét, only a fraction of the uniforms were ready, the kidnapping had to be postponed, and soon after the police (which, as in the seventeenth century, knew all about the plan) picked up the participants.[59] Conspiracies do not fit the Hungarian political mentality (successful conspirators are disciplined and sophisticated in the art of deception; that Hungarians can't keep secrets is a commonplace).

The syndrome survived even the collapse of the Habsburg Monarchy. Zoltán Böszörményi, a leader of the sprouting Right Radical movements in the 1930s prepared an uprising in the Great Plain, including once more Kecskemét, as a preliminary to marching on Budapest to establish a military dictatorship. The conspirators bought up staff officers' uniforms to impress the populace. The rising began in May 1936 and was easily put down by the local authorities.[60]

The multivocal character of *ius = igaz*, transmitted by Werbőczy to modern times, was clearly recognized by Ignácz Frank. The respected law professor asked in his textbook: 'What do we understand by the words truth, justice and law?' (*igaz, igazság és törvény*). The gist of his detailed analysis of usages was that *igaz, igazság* meant, first of all, that which corresponded to reality (the Latin *veritas*, the German *Wahrheit*). Secondly, it meant justice (*justitia, Gerechtigkeit*), that 'each receive his due'. Thirdly, *ius* was used to mean *ius quod quis habet; das Recht was man hat*: his liberty, power, property, claim or obligation. But *ius* did not mean law; for that *törvény* was the right word which, as in the sense of *Gesetz*, also embraced custom and other legal sources.[61]

The untested, hypothetical conclusion of this paper is that the mentality based on *ius* which developed in relations between the crown and the political class was transmitted to other social and political conflicts before and even after structurally-dualist politics came to an end in 1918. For instance, uses of the word *igazság* (justice) in the twentieth century remained multivocal. *Igazságot Magyarországnak* was a much used slogan in political campaigns against the Trianon Treaty. The aviation pioneer, György Endresz, put on his airplane 'Justice for Hungary' when he flew from New York to Budapest in 1931. After 1956, a publication bore the title: *Mi az igazság a Nagy Imre ügyben?* (What is the truth about the Imre Nagy case?). Truth and justice are conflated in the common usage of other East European languages. It is well known that *pravda* in Russian could mean either truth or justice or law. Apparently the same applies to Serbo-Croat and Bulgarian.[62] It would be well worth exploring this subject comparatively.[63]

---

59 See Albert Berzeviczy, *Az absolutismus kora Magyarországon, 1849–1865*, Budapest, 1922, vol 1, pp. 299–300.
60 C.A. Macartney, *October Fifteenth*, Edinburgh, 1961, vol 1, p. 159.
61 Ignácz Frank, *A közigazság törvénye Magyarhonban*, Buda, 1845, vol 1, pp. 8–11.
62 I am grateful to Dr Catherine MacRobert (Oxford, LMH) for providing this information.
63 I have benefited from János M. Bak's critical comments on the first draft. Angus Walker has also read the manuscript. I am grateful for his many suggestions.

Bocskai, Rebellion and Resistance in Early Modern Hungary

Martyn Rady

Stephen Bocskai led in 1604 the first significant rebellion against Habsburg rule in Hungary. From inauspicious beginnings, and relying at first upon only a few hundred heyducks[1], Bocskai rapidly accumulated an army that was capable of ejecting the foremost Habsburg generals from the kingdom. Elected in the next year prince of Hungary, and a few months later, prince of Transylvania, Bocskai forced Emperor Rudolf II (King Rudolf I of Hungary) to retreat entirely from his political and confessional objectives. In the Peace of Vienna, concluded in 1606, the Habsburg court conceded religious freedom to Hungary, acknowledged Transylvania's independence, and placed limits on the fiscal and military demands that might be laid upon the kingdom. The peace of 1606 was guaranteed by the Upper and Lower Austrian, Bohemian, Moravian and Silesian estates, thus laying the basis for their future political cooperation. Moreover, in the settlement that he worked out with the heyducks, Stephen Bocskai established an important military counterweight to Habsburg ambitions in the region which served to prolong both Transylvanian independence and Hungary's privileged position within the Habsburg Monarchy for much of the seventeenth century.

And yet, Bocskai was an unlikely rebel, for throughout his career he had shown himself to be a stalwart supporter of the Habsburg cause. Certainly, we may observe that the political circumstances of the sixteenth and early seventeenth centuries were conducive to intrigue and that it was not unusual for Central European courtiers, noblemen and princes to alter their political allegiances. Those whose home was in the Partium, as Bocskai's was, may perhaps, on account of this region's ambivalent situation, have been particularly given to ambiguity. Nevertheless, Bocskai's biography demonstrates a remarkable consistency in respect of his commitment to an alliance between Transylvania and the Habsburgs and to a unified Hungarian kingdom under Habsburg suzerainty. Between the ages of ten and nineteen, Bocskai had served as a page in Maximilian II's court in Prague. There he had learned – and here I follow Kálmán Benda's analysis – that the only force capable of matching the Turks in Central Europe was the Habsburgs' own. Várad (Oradea), the principal city and redoubt in the Partium, and Gyulafehérvár (Alba Iulia), the prince of Transylvania's seat, were in this respect quite unequal to Prague and Vienna.[2] Upon his return to Transylvania in 1576, Bocskai

---

1 The heyducks (*hajdúk*) were originally cattle-drovers of the plain, living as freemen outside seigneurial authority. Forming their own self-governing communities, they also acted as freebooters and mercenaries, and may usefully be compared to the cossacks of the Polish-Lithuanian and Russian steppe.

2 Kálmán Benda, *Bocskai István*, 2nd edition, Budapest, 1993 (first published 1942), pp. 13, 35.

entered the service of the Báthori family where he rapidly established himself as a leading adviser to the principality's ruler. Bocskai's rise to influence owed much to his family's close connections to the Báthoris which were cemented by his sister's marriage to the prince's brother, the voivode Christopher. Following Christopher's death in 1581, Bocskai became guardian to his infant son, Sigismund, who was subsequently elected prince of Transylvania. Sigismund assumed power in his own right in 1588, at the age of sixteen, and Bocskai continued to remain in his nephew's service. Over the next decade he accumulated by donation of the prince several score properties, including some of the most important castles and redoubts in both the Partium and Transylvania.[3] In 1592 he was appointed captain of Várad and *főispán* (lord-lieutenant) of Bihar, positions which gave him command of one of the main gateways into Transylvania. Shortly thereafter, he was appointed supreme commander of the principality's forces. Family connection thus combined with wealth and military office to make Bocskai the most powerful man within the Transylvanian principality.

Over the next eight years, Bocskai worked in collaboration with the prince to bring about a revolution in Transylvanian foreign relations. Hitherto, Transylvania had largely followed a policy laid down by the predominantly protestant estates of political neutrality under Turkish patronage. Sigismund's own inclinations impelled him, however, like Bocskai in the direction of a Habsburg alliance. As a Catholic, Sigismund naturally looked towards the Habsburgs and towards joining together with the Catholic powers against the Turks. His patronage of the Jesuits and regard for his pro-Habsburg confessor, Alfonso Carillo, were a frequent source of recrimination at meetings of the Transylvanian diet. Both the Transylvanian diet and the prince's own council proved, however, resistant both to cooperation with the Habsburgs and to forsaking Turkish patronage. As their leaders indicated, recalling previous rapprochements, 'that [Habsburg] gruel has burnt our mouths once already', and, 'until Christian arms have retaken Buda, you should not go against the Turks for there is no one who will defend Transylvania.'[4] Sigismund not only ignored this advice, but in a remarkable coup conducted in August 1594, he had ten leaders of the estates opposition seized and murdered. Bocskai was not only implicated in the plot but also benefited both from the victims' confiscated land and from the 25 wagons of moveable goods of which their heirs were relieved.[5] Two months later, Transylvania formally joined the papal- and Habsburg-led Holy League and thus entered the 'Fifteen Years War' (1591–1606) against the Turks.[6]

Sigismund was never more, however, than an unwilling ruler and he was happy to negotiate the princely office for a safer home, a good-sized palace and a cardinal's hat, particularly after the Turkish war began to go badly for him. Bocskai was signally active in urging Sigismund's various abdications (he abdicated altogether on four occasions) and, in particular, his ceding office to Rudolf II. For while Sigismund's own interest in

3   Elek Jakab, 'Uj adatok Bocskay István életéhez', *Századok*, 28, 1894, pp. 771–98 (pp. 774–76).
4   Kálmán Benda, *A Bocskai-szabadságharc*, Budapest, 1955, p. 10; Benda, *Bocskai István*, p. 28.
5   Benda, *Bocskai István*, pp. 43–4; Jakab, 'Uj adatok', pp. 773, 780.
6   An excellent introduction to the impact of the Fifteen Years War on Hungary is provided by Daniel P. David, 'The Fifteen Years' War and the Protestant Response to Habsburg Absolutism in Hungary', *East Central Europe/L'Europe du Centre-Est*, 8, nos 1–2, 1981, pp. 38–51.

abdication was largely motivated by what he might obtain in exchange, in Bocskai's view a transfer of power to Rudolf would ensure that the Habsburgs were more likely to lend military support to the principality's defence. In 1597, Sigismund did indeed abdicate in Rudolf's favour and imperial commissioners took over the principality's government. Disappointed, however, with the palace provided him in Silesia, Sigismund soon returned, only to abdicate again the next year and hand over the princely office to his cousin, Cardinal Andrew Báthori. Although never elected by the Transylvanian estates, Emperor Rudolf continued, however, to press his claims to the principality. In 1600 Transylvania was occupied, at least nominally on his behalf, by the Wallachian voivode, Michael the Brave, and Andrew Báthori was slain. Once again, imperial commissioners were appointed to administer the principality. On this occasion, however, an imperial army led by the captain of Kassa, Giorgio Basta, followed in their wake. The depredations of Basta's soldiery, although typical of the mercenary-armies of the time, earned him and his imperial master an abiding reputation in both Hungary and Transylvania for misgovernment. Moreover, in order to cover the costs of war and mercenary-service in Hungary and Transylvania, the Habsburg court resorted to ever more drastic remedies – overturning tax exemptions, exacting forced loans, and confiscating the properties of individual noblemen.[7]

Although Bocskai was instrumental in Sigismund's transfer of office to Rudolf and never recognized Andrew as prince, he was distrusted by the imperial commissioners and was accordingly deprived of the captaincy of Várad and of command of the principality's forces. Moreover, his support for a Habsburg alliance and role in the murder of the estates opposition had rendered him notorious in the eyes of the Transylvanian diet. Accordingly, in 1600 the diet brought charges of treason against him and confiscated his lands.[8] It was only with difficulty that Bocskai was able to keep control of his most important properties in the Partium. With Basta's troops occupying Transylvania, Bocskai now considered it expedient to go to Prague to petition Rudolf for the return of his lands. He spent almost two years there, from 1600 to 1602, in conditions that the leading, pro-Bocskai chronicler describes as 'honourable custody' (*tisztességes fogság*), but which certainly also involved advising the ruler on Transylvanian affairs.[9] Whatever the exact circumstances of his sojourn in Prague, it is nevertheless evident that Bocskai played no active role in Sigismund's two restorations to office in 1601–02 (he abdicated again on both occasions), in Basta's murder of Michael the Brave, or in the vain rebellion of the Transylvanian nobility against Basta's army in 1601. Indeed, his commitment to a Habsburg alliance remained consistent. As he wrote on one occasion to Sigismund, Rudolf's forces commanded all the gateways to Transylvania. The principality was powerless to defend itself against both the Turks and Tatar raiders, and could only be kept safe by collaborating with the Habsburgs.[10]

---

7 For the state of the Hungarian and imperial finances at this time, see the succinct exposition by László Makkai, 'A Habsburgok és a magyar rendiség a Bocskai-felkelés előestéjén', *Történelmi Szemle*, 17, nos 1–2, 1974, pp. 152–82 (pp. 160–3).

8 Benda, *Bocskai István*, p. 93.

9 Szamosközy, vol 4, p. 161; Benda, *Bocskai István*, pp. 98–100.

10 Benda, *Bocskai István*, p. 99.

In late 1602, Bocskai returned to the Partium without having succeeded in recovering his lost Transylvanian properties. It must have been a bleak homecoming, for in his absence his wife had died still without child, while the surrounding countryside bore only too clearly the scars of war. Over the next two years, Bocskai evidently began to reconsider the policy which he had for promoted for over two decades. In place of a Habsburg alliance, he now began to think in terms of a policy aimed against the Habsburgs. Accordingly he opened in March 1604 discussions both with the Porte and with the leaders of the Transylvanian opposition now sheltering on Turkish-held territory. Although there was certainly some mention of Bocskai assuming the office of prince, his own negotiations were cautious and his commitments vague, and he never entered into any formal treaty with either the Turks or the Transylvanian malcontents.[11] Nevertheless, in September 1604, Bocskai's dealings were revealed to Basta's successor as imperial captain of Kassa, Giacomo Belgiojoso, who immediately saw in them evidence of treason. Refusing both the invitation to explain himself to Belgiojoso and the advice of friends that he throw himself on Rudolf's mercy, Bocskai began to muster and to fortify his principal redoubts thereby compelling Belgiojoso to move against him militarily.[12]

For four centuries, historians have considered the autumn of 1604 as the decisive moment in Bocskai's career, when (as we might put it) he crossed the 'moral threshold' from loyalty to rebellion. As the historian Szamosközy put it, Bocskai now 'began to think of himself and of his nation.' (*Kezde gondolkodni maga és nemzete felől*).[13] By this measure (and as Szamosközy himself understood matters), the personal destruction which Bocskai faced was akin to the devastation of the country caused by the passage of warfare, the depredations of imperial mercenaries, and Rudolf's general misrule. Such psychological linkages are, however, always hard to prove. One is bound also to ask just what Bocskai had been thinking about over the last two decades if it was only now that he began to ponder over himself and the nation. Moreover, it is evident from his negotiations with the Turks and exiles that Bocskai's breach with his earlier policies was not sudden but the product of a gestation of no less than six months, and so well before his collision with Belgiojoso. Under these circumstances, we should probably imagine a longer process of rumination whereby Bocskai gradually began to see a convergence of his own interests with those of other groups in Hungarian society. This convergence was intimately connected not only to the general condition of the kingdom and principality brought about by a dozen years of warfare but also to the issue of religious tolerance.

In the opening years of the seventeenth century, Rudolf embraced a new zeal in respect of the Catholic faith which may or may not be related to the rise of a 'Spanish

---

11 Andrea Molnár, *Fürst Stefan Bocskay als Staatsmann und Persönlichkeit im Spiegel seiner Briefe, 1598–1606*, Munich, 1983, p. 38. Molnár indicates the possible role of Ottoman diplomacy in originally 'detaching' Bocskai from the imperial side. See ibid, p. 71.

12 Makkai indicates correctly that it was Bocskai rather than Belgiojoso who prompted hostilities – see László Makkai, 'A Bocskai felkelés' in (eds) Zs. P. Pach and R. Ágnes Várkonyi, *Magyarország története 1526–1686*, vol 1, 1987, pp. 709–73 (p. 713). Even as late as 5 October, a week after Bocskai had started mustering, Belgiojoso was still seeking a negotiated settlement. See László Nagy, 'Okmányok a Bocskai szabadságharc idejéből', *Hadtörténelmi Közlemények*, 3, nos 3–4, 1956, pp. 291–332.

13 Benda, *A Bocskai-szabadságharc*, p. 14; see also Szamosközy, vol 4, p. 237.

party' in the imperial court.[14] In the case of Hungary, however, the opportunity to impose the Counter-Reformation was afforded by a curious semantic windfall. In 1603, the royal cities of Hungary had collectively complained to Rudolf in respect of articles included in the draft decree of the recent diet at Pozsony (Bratislava) which undermined their monopoly of the urban wine trade. Their appeal included reference to the ruler's *patrocinium* over them and to their status as a *peculium coronae*. Rudolf's chancellery accordingly rewrote the fourteenth article of the decree in favour of the cities and sealed the new version.[15] This seemingly minor episode carried wide implications. First, the ruler had demonstrated that he might unilaterally alter a draft decree of the diet even after it had been debated and approved both by himself and by the estates. Secondly, the cities had used in their petition a most ill-advised vocabulary which might be interpreted as acknowledging their status as the king's private property. As a secretary in the imperial chancellery noted, by their own admission the cities of Hungary constituted 'Kammergut'.[16] They were thus the pawns of Hungary's king and so might be treated in the same way as cities in the hereditary Austrian lands.[17]

The consequences were not long in coming. In January 1604, Belgiojoso entered Kassa (Košice) and drove the Lutheran clergy out of the city's main church. Later that year, Lőcse (Levoča) was also repossessed for the Counter-Reformation. Well might the cities and their confessional allies now complain at the diet which met in April that *peculium coronae* did not mean *peculium regis* and that they might still practise whatever religion they chose.[18] The response of the Archduke Matthias, who presided over the diet, was terse. The cities belonged to the crown and thus to the king, and the ruler might determine their religious disposition by virtue of his plenitude of power and of his apostolic authority.[19] Moreover, the heresy laws, as enacted over the course of the last century, should at last be put into effect and, in any case, the churches in which most protestants worshipped had originally been built and paid for by Catholic lords and patrons.[20] The diet broke up with no agreement having been reached in the matter of religion. Following, however, the example of 1603, the chancellery secretary, Himmelreich, now inserted with the Archduke's consent, a final article to the decree of the diet, expressly banning protestant worship and prohibiting the diet from all further discussion of religious matters.[21]

Although a Calvinist by upbringing, Bocskai had served Sigismund Báthori, notwithstanding his promotion of the Jesuits and his restoration of a Catholic bishop to the see

---

14 R.J.W. Evans, *Rudolf II and His World: A Study in Intellectual History, 1576–1612*, Oxford, 1973, pp. 68–9.

15 *Magyar országgyűlési emlékek* (*Monumenta comitalia regni Hungariae* [1526–1606]), (eds) Vilmos Fraknói, Árpád Károlyi, 12 vols, Budapest, 1874–1917, (hereafter *MOE*), 10, pp. 274, 319, 338.

16 *MOE*, 10, pp. 319–20.

17 See thus, Kálmán Benda, *Habsburg-absolutizmus és rendi ellenállás a XVI. – XVII. században*, Budapest, 1975, p. 38; Makkai, 'A Habsburgok és a magyar rendiség', p. 166.

18 *MOE*, 10, p. 511. See also, ibid, p. 597. The debate hinged on the meaning of *corona*: the cities and their allies understood the crown as the *regnum* in its organic sense and as involving membership of the political nation; the ruler saw the crown as an abstraction of the royal person.

19 *MOE*, 10, p. 572.

20 *MOE*, 10, pp. 519–22.

21 Article 22 of the *decretum* of 1604. Although repudiated both in 1606 and in the decree of the 1608 diet, Article 22 continued to be included in the *Corpus Juris Hungarici*.

of Transylvania. Writing in the mid-1590s, the papal nuncio had recorded Bocskai's apparent indifference in matters of religion.[22] Nevertheless, as part of his negotiations in 1604 over acquiring the princely office for himself, Bocskai evidently thought it worthwhile to play the part of an 'enthusiastic Calvinist'.[23] Left with a poor hand, this was the card which he now dealt, raising the standard of religious liberty and confessional freedom. By this route, he was immediately able to enlist heyduck mercenaries, formally in imperial service but left for too long unpaid, and to a large extent motivated by a chiliastic interpretation of Calvinist belief. At first, only a few hundred joined his camp, but their experience in warfare soon told to their advantage and brought others onto Bocskai's side. In a decisive engagement fought on 15 October the heyducks ambushed a portion of Belgiojoso's army on the road between Álmosd and Diószeg. The next day, Debrecen fell. In the mean time, representatives of the five leading Upper Hungarian cities (Kassa, Lőcse, Eperjes [Prešov], Bártfa [Bardejov] and Kis-Szeben [Sabinov]) entered into an alliance to defend protestant worship by force, thus providing both further allies and the money with which to enlist mercenaries. As heyduck captains acting on Bocskai's behalf explained to envoys of the cities, 'We have rebelled and taken arms for the Christian religion, for Our Lord Jesus Christ, and for Hungary, our dear homeland.'[24] By the end of the month, Kassa had opened its gates to Bocskai's heyducks and Belgiojoso's forces were in fast retreat. A brief counter-offensive by Basta petered out with the onset of winter. The imperial troops thus returned westwards, leaving much of Upper Hungary open to Bocskai's forces. When at the beginning of 1605, Rudolf judged it prudent to summon a diet to Pozsony to stem the rebellion, only five counties bothered to send delegates.[25]

Over the course of 1605, Bocskai consolidated his power and broadened the base of his support. His rebellion now drew to its side the nobility, including some of the wealthier landowners in western Hungary. In order to achieve the nobility's cooperation, the heyducks were brought under control, placed under the command of noble officers, and bought off with money voted by the cities and by promises of land. The territorial grants and collective ennoblements which Bocskai made to some 10,000 heyducks formed the basis of what later became the seven 'heyduck towns' and of a permanent military force guarding the Partium and Transylvania.[26] For its part, legitimization of the authority which Bocskai had gathered was not slow in coming. In February 1605, a rump diet met in Marosszerda to elect Bocskai prince of Transylvania. A second diet, which gathered in September, this time with full representation, elected him anew and installed him formally in office. Meanwhile in April 1605, Bocskai was elected prince of Hungary at a meeting of the Hungarian estates at Szerencs in Abaúj county. It is possible that even at this late stage Bocskai contemplated assuming the royal office,

---

22 Benda, *Bocskai István*, p. 51.
23 József Thúry, 'Bocskay István fölkelése', *Századok*, 33, 1899, pp. 21–43, 115–33 (p. 32).
24 Benda, *A Bocskai-szabadságharc*, p. 70; see also, Lajos Kemény, 'Lippay Balázs, Bocskay főkapitánya Kassa városához', *Hadtörténelmi Közlemények*, 1914, pp. 473–4.
25 *MOE*, 11, pp. 105, 118.
26 István Rácz, 'Hajdútelepítések és kiváltságok', in (ed.) György Módy, *A hajdúk a magyar történelemben*, Debrecen, 1969, pp. 47–68 (pp. 48–9). The number of these settlements was supplemented by heyduck villages settled on private estates.

for in early May he compelled the *alispán* (deputy-lieutenant) of Árva county to take an oath of allegiance 'to the crown of noble Hungary and to its elected king'.[27] Conceivably, it was the absence of the Holy Crown, a vital constitutive element of Hungarian kingship, which dissuaded Bocskai from assuming the royal dignity. Certainly, in November, 1605, he received the gift of a crown from the Sultan, but he always regarded this as a personal distinction and not as a mark of office. Finally, in December 1605, the Hungarian diet elected Bocskai palatine and thus to a position which the Habsburg rulers had left vacant for more than forty years.[28]

Bocskai's rebellion was unprecedented in the history of Habsburg Hungary. It therefore required the type of *post factum* justification in society to which successful revolts normally aspire.[29] Although Bocskai's speeches may well have been subsequently embellished, there can be little doubt that Bocskai himself was a formidable orator with a profound mastery of the Hungarian language. Nevertheless, he seldom addressed the causes of his rebellion but rather left its explanation to his supporters and to representatives of the Hungarian diet. The accounts given by these tended, however, to differ according to whether the intended audience was domestic or foreign, and thus whether rendered in Hungarian or Latin. As far as the 'national' audience was concerned, Bocskai's supporters stressed in addition to the ruin of the country for which Rudolf was held responsible, the divine mission to which the new prince of Hungary and Transylvania had been appointed. In their address to the prince, the diet meeting at Szerencs in 1605 thus likened Bocskai to a line of Old Testament rulers: 'Believing this in full conviction, that as God chose, dedicated and elevated David when He took him from the sheep-folds, Moses from his shepherding, and Saul from the dust, so God in concert with us has on this day dedicated, chosen and confirmed Your Highness as prince among us.'[30] In similar fashion, the same meeting of the diet applauded Bocskai as the 'Moses of the Hungarians', who 'by the gracious and goodly will of the Lord God' had been sent to deliver his people from captivity.[31]

We will not find in any of this conventional Calvinist resistance theory, explaining the right or even duty of 'lesser magistrates' to take up arms against oppression. Nevertheless, the references to Moses are instructive. In the *Institutes of the Christian Religion*, Calvin proposes two routes by which tyrants might be overthrown. In the first place, 'Constitutional defenders of the people's freedom' have an obligation to curb the rule of tyrants. Calvin identifies among the number of these defenders, the ephors of Sparta, the tribunes of Rome and – as he adds cautiously – 'perhaps there is something similar to this in the power exercised in each kingdom by the three orders, when they hold their primary diets'.[32] Alternatively, though, God Himself might intervene directly: 'Herein is the goodness, power and providence of God wondrously displayed. At one

---

27 Ferencz Kubinyi, 'Esküminta Bocskay idejéből', *Századok*, 33, 1899, pp. 657–8.
28 *MOE*, 11, p. 402. Bocskai's name is, however, omitted from the *Liber Dignitariorum Saecularium* held in the Hungarian National Archive.
29 See László Péter's contribution here, p. 41.
30 *MOE*, 11, p. 153.
31 Kálmán Benda, 'A kálvini tanok hatása a magyar rendi ellenállás ideológiájára', *Helikon*, 1971, pp. 322–30 (p. 327).
32 *Institutes of the Christian Religion*, Chapter 20 ('Of Civil Government'), Section 31 (trans. Thomas Norton, London, 1599).

time He raises up manifest avengers from among His own servants and gives them His command to punish accursed tyranny and deliver His people from calamity when they are unjustly oppressed [...]. Thus He rescued His people Israel from the tyranny of Pharaoh by Moses [...].'[33] For those attending the diet of Szerencs, which opened with a service in a Reformed church, the analogy was clear. Bocskai was the avenger of his people, appointed by God to liberate Hungary from Habsburg bondage.

There was already by the early seventeenth century a strong literary tradition of 'Hebraic patriotism' which associated the Hungarians and Transylvania with Israel and with the early history, wanderings and tribulations of the Jews.[34] The Moses motif was thus readily taken up by Bocskai's supporters and combined with other biblical allusions. According to one contemporary commentator, Bocskai was instructed by divine counsel to liberate Pannonia. He was thus 'our Moses', a 'Christian Gideon' and, moreover, a likeness of Christ himself: 'From Bihar county and from a little village, you arose to our defence, as Christ came from the manger and from little Nazareth for the world's redemption.'[35] It was, however, the image of Moses which prevailed, so that upon his own death Bocskai was indeed transported metaphorically to Mount Horeb.[36] Indeed, so convinced was Bocskai himself in the aptness of the Moses and other biblical allusions that he even deployed these in correspondence with Rudolf: 'God has been with me in this; account for my position through my acting on God's secret counsel; like Moses from his shepherding, David from the sheep-pen, like the fleeing Jehoshaphat, whom God made prince and king over His people.'[37]

Appeals rooted in the Calvinist imagery of resistance were only rarely, however, directed at foreign audiences for whom the reformed faith often constituted a heresy. Thus, the manifesto of the Szerencs diet which was addressed in Latin 'before God and the whole Christian world' catalogued Rudolf's misdeeds: his high taxes and confiscations, the misdeeds of his troops, his disregard for the Hungarian constitution and attempt to reduce the kingdom *in provinciae formam*, his overspending on a lavish crown, the absolute rather than ordinary power that he practised, and so on. The diet was additionally at pains to stress that it was not opposed to kings in general, but only to those who were tyrants.[38] Apart from a fleeting reference to Rudolf's emulation of Nebuchadnezzar (a theological 'own goal' since Calvin had expressly written on why Nebuchadnezzar should have been obeyed!),[39] biblical references were eschewed in favour of a long list of Rudolf's alleged crimes. Nevertheless, once the rebellion was stripped of its lawfulness in Calvinist rhetoric and reduced to a catalogue of wrongs, its justification became more elusive. Were Rudolf's crimes really sufficient to permit active resistance to his rule? Accordingly, Bocskai and the estates now turned their

33 ibid, Book 20, Section 30.
34 Graeme Murdock, *Calvinism on the Frontier 1600–1660: International Calvinism and the Reformed Church in Hungary and Transylvania*, Oxford, 2000, pp. 261–4.
35 Gyula Bisztray, Tibor Klaniczay, Lajos Nagy, Béla Stoll, *Régi magyar költők tára. XVII század*, vol 1, Budapest, 1959, pp. 256–8.
36 ibid, p. 290.
37 Graeme Murdock, *Beyond Calvin: The Intellectual, Political and Cultural World of Europe's Reformed Churches*, Basingstoke and New York, 2004, p. 74.
38 *MOE*, 11, pp. 168–84.
39 *Institutes of the Christian Religion*, Chapter 20, Section 27.

attention to vindicating their rebellion by reference to the customary rights that were considered as belonging to the political nation and which had been given formal expression in Werbőczy's *Tripartitum*.[40]

The famous resistance clause included in the Golden Bull of 1222 was a historical curiosity that had never been invoked during the Middle Ages. It was, however, mentioned as a right belonging to the noble community in Stephen Werbőczy's code of customary law, the *Tripartitum*, published in 1517. In his account of the four privileges and chief liberties of noblemen, given in Part One, article 9 of the text, Werbőczy thus explained, 'if any of our princes and kings should venture to act contrary to the liberties of the nobles, then, as stated and expressed [in the Golden Bull of Andrew II] [...], they have for ever more the liberty to resist and oppose him without the taint of infidelity.'[41] The inclusion of this clause in the *Tripartitum* was plainly controversial and a subsequent redraft of Hungary's laws commissioned by Ferdinand I omitted it completely.[42] Despite these concerns, the *Tripartitum* was not deployed during the course of the sixteenth century for its public law content. Certainly, it was used extensively in the courts, but almost entirely as a guide to procedural and private law.[43] There are, however, strong hints in the furious debate attending the legal condition of Hungary's cities that some recourse was now had to the *Tripartitum* from the point of view of public law. Thus at the Gálszécs diet of 1604, the Upper Hungarian estates complained to Belgiojoso that the cities constituted *membra regni* and that their status as *peculia* of the crown should be understood accordingly. The terms in which the estates cast their remonstration are close to the text of the *Tripartitum* itself and to its own explanation of the relationship of Hungarian nobles to the crown.[44] We should also note that the expression, *peculium*, which is a civilian term, was (to my knowledge) completely unknown at this time in Hungary except for a single passage of the *Tripartitum* where its author flaunts his classical learning.[45]

Reliance upon the text of the *Tripartitum* is, however, explicit in justifications of the support given to Bocskai's revolt. The Szerencs diet thus referred directly to the content of the *Tripartitum*, 'according to which we may take arms against His Majesty in our defence for our lives and liberty.'[46] Likewise, the appeal made by the same diet to Christendom concluded with the observation that 'the laws of Hungary allow free contradiction and insurrection against such a king who violates the laws of the kingdom.'[47] Again, in negotiations with imperial envoys, the representatives of the estates gathered at Korpona in 1605 expressly footnoted the *Tripartitum*'s text, 'For if

---

40 Molnár, *Fürst Stefan Bocskay*, p. 28
41 *Tripartitum*, I. 9 [4]. We use here the English-language translation given in Werbőczy, *The Customary Law of the Renowned Kingdom of Hungary*, eds and trans. by János M. Bak, Péter Banyó and Martyn Rady, (Decreta Regni Mediaevalis Hungariae, 5), Idyllwild, CA, and Budapest, 2005.
42 Alajos Degré, 'Az ellenállási jog története Magyarországon', *Jogtudományi Közlöny*, 35, no 6, 1980, pp. 366–71 (p. 368).
43 Martyn Rady, 'Stephen Werbőczy and his *Tripartitum*' in *The Customary Law of the Renowned Kingdom of Hungary*, pp. xxvii-xliv (pp. xl-xli)
44 *MOE*, 10, p. 597; *Tripartitum*, I. 4.
45 *Tripartitum*, I. 5.
46 *MOE*, 11, p. 154.
47 ibid, p. 180.

the king goes against the laws and decrees of the kingdom, it is possible to resist him without the taint of infidelity. Part I. Title 9.'[48] The same principle was written into the draft peace-terms agreed with Rudolf in early 1606. It was here laid down that the rebels would return to Rudolf's side and be faithful to him, but 'not without detriment to the permanent laws and liberties of the kingdom', by which may be understood their rights of rebellion and resistance.[49] It may well be, as Eckhart has argued, that the conception put forward by the rebels was an essentially medieval one: that the king was bound by the laws of the kingdom and that if he transgressed these, then he might be overthrown.[50] This is, however, to miss the larger literary context. Bocskai's supporters were in Werbőczy's text able to find legal justification for their insurrection and thereby to revive the principle of lawful resistance as first enunciated in the Golden Bull of 1222. And, indeed, from this point onwards, the right of resistance would enter into the public law of the kingdom, as an essential ingredient for rendering rebellion lawful. As Imre Thököly was to remark in 1684, on the occasion of his own rebellion against the Habsburg Leopold I, the right of resistance constituted 'the spirit of Hungarian freedom, the true regulator of government, the judge and avenger of subjects, which may completely and entirely erase the stain of rebellion.'[51] Although the right of resistance was officially repudiated by the Hungarian diet in 1687, it lingered on sufficiently in the Hungarian customary tradition to make it seem worthwhile to every subsequent Habsburg ruler to affirm in his coronation oath its continued abolition.[52] In seeming confirmation of their misgivings, both Ferenc Rákóczi in the early eighteenth century and the noble counties in their opposition to Joseph II at the century's end relied upon the resistance clause as justification for their respective revolts.[53] In short, it was Bocskai's rebellion which reintroduced to Hungarian politics the Golden Bull's right of resistance as mediated through Werbőczy's *Tripartitum*.

Bocskai's rebellion concluded with the Peace of Vienna of 1606 which recognized Transylvania's independence, and conceded almost entirely the demands of the Hungarian estates, including freedom of religion, the withdrawal of mercenary forces, and a commitment to remedy the most flagrant abuses of Rudolf's rule. As part of the negotiations over the terms of the peace, Bocskai resigned his title of prince of Hungary in exchange for the title of 'prince of the empire'.[54] Bocskai himself died at the end of the year, maintaining in his will the need for an independent Transylvania as a counter-weight to Habsburg ambitions in Hungary.[55] For one, however, who had spent most of his career not in opposing the Habsburgs but instead in seeking an alliance with them, the title that he took to his grave was perhaps not an unfitting epitaph.

---

48 ibid, p. 452.
49 ibid, pp. 699, 860.
50 Ferenc Eckhart, 'Bocskay és hiveinek közjogi felfogása', *Károlyi Árpád Emlékkönyv*, Budapest, 1938, pp 133–141 (pp. 138–9).
51 Degré, 'Az ellenállási jog', p. 369.
52 László Péter, 'The Holy Crown of Hungary, Visible and Invisible', *Slavonic and East European Review*, 81, no 3, 2003, pp. 421–510 (p. 445).
53 See László Péter's contribution here, pp. 49–50; also, Degré, 'Az ellenállási jog', p. 370.
54 *MOE*, 12, pp. 695, 737.
55 Thúry, 'Bocskay István fölkelése', p. 28.

The Rákóczi Revolt as a Successful Rebellion[1]

István M. Szijártó

The professionalization of history, that is the establishment of the institutionalized discourse of history, happened mainly in the nineteenth century, at the same time as national states emerged in Europe. This coincidence has had profound effects on historians' approach towards the past. The dominance of the national question in Hungarian public thought prescribed how, for instance, events that took place in the eighteenth century should be viewed a century later and, indeed, how they have been seen ever since. Every Hungarian pupil of nine years or more knows that there was a war of independence in Hungary led by Prince Ferenc II Rákóczi. They know this, because they know that there is something *called* the 'Rákóczi-*szabadságharc*'. (The exact translation of the term is 'freedom fight' or 'fight for freedom'). But that there was such a fight for freedom is, as with other interpretations of history, actually an invention of historians.

History became an institutionalized discourse in Hungarian society in the second half of the nineteenth century. By its end, in Hungary as elsewhere in Europe, the roots of historicism and positivism had fused together in a methodologically-oriented discipline of history (*Geschichtswissenschaft, történettudomány*). In this process, historicism preserved the ideas that historical events are singular; that reality can only be comprehended as a part of the historical process; and that history conveys meaning in itself – but it had lost Humboldt's or Ranke's belief in God. Positivism, on the other hand, had lost the drive to establish laws in history, keeping only the fetishism of sources and its preference for analyses which remain close to these sources. In the second half of the nineteenth century, however, the older romantic school of writing history also continued to influence the historiographical scene in Hungary.

In 1972, when Jenő Szűcs wrote about Observant Franciscan friars preparing the peasant rebellion of 1514 with their social criticism, and then becoming its spiritual leaders,[2] his analysis evoked in his readers the intellectual debates that had preceded the revolution of 1956. The popularity of Szűcs's thesis about 1514 and the impact of his work is inseparable from this fact. In similar fashion to Jenő Szűcs's study, which acquired a wider significance on account of the time of its publication and of its contemporary resonances, the history of the early eighteenth century carried implications of its own in the context of the later nineteenth century. The experience of the revolution and

---

1   I would like to express my thanks to Mrs. M. Lofmark for helping me with this English text.
2   Jenő Szűcs, 'A ferences obszervancia és az 1514. évi parasztháború. Egy kódex tanúsága', *Levéltári Közlemények*, 43, 1972, pp. 213–263.

war of independence in 1848–49 became the focal point around which Hungarian national consciousness crystallized and through which everyday perceptions were refracted. Recollection of 1848–49 served as the basis for the passive resistance of the Hungarian political class prior to 1867 and, after the Compromise, it served as the emotional basis to the opposition Party of Independence. And just as 1848–49 was deemed a valiant failure, so also was the Rákóczi rebellion, for it too had failed to bring Hungary the independence that it sought.

One of the major figures of the romantic school of history in Hungary was Kálmán Thaly (1839–1909). He started publishing his newspaper articles about the grave of Prince Ferenc II Rákóczi in Istanbul in 1862, at the age of 23. Two years later he was elected a corresponding member of the Hungarian Academy of Sciences. To quote his biographer, Ágnes R. Várkonyi, he was 'a historian with a poet's soul', and so the 'age of Rákóczi was brought to life not by the historian but by the poet; the historian simply gave context to the figures that he had earlier brought to life.' Thaly's first monograph on János Bottyán, a general of Ferenc II Rákóczi, published the next year, achieved immense popularity.[3] The last lines of the book are these: 'We are not able to mark the general's grave in the ruined graveyard; its mound has been levelled with the ground that already carries only his fame, concealing his ashes as a treasure. Could we mark his grave, we might write on his gravestone the following, next to his coat of arms:

> He lived for the country, he defended her cause to the end,
> He died, and after his death liberty has fallen to the ground.
> Happy hero! ... he could still take hope to his grave
> And he could not see the sad end of the sacred fight.
> Happy hero! he at least did not die in exile!
> He used to guard his country; and now the country guards his ashes.[4]

When reading these sentences on Bottyán, did not Thaly's readers think of Sándor Petőfi, the young poet who fell in battle in the last days of the War of Independence in 1849, and who has lain in an unmarked grave ever since?

Kálmán Thaly was a prolific historian of the age of Rákóczi, who published several books and dozens of source publications, including contemporary verse that were partly his own, *à la* Macpherson. He was prone also to 'adjust the sources to the romantic images that were dear to his heart', instead of (as Ágnes R. Várkonyi writes) changing the views he had formed of the 'kuruc' rebels in his youth. His vision of the Rákóczi rebellion was accepted by the general public. From 1878 to 1909, Kálmán Thaly was member of parliament for the opposition Party of Independence, and later its deputy chairman, which immensely increased his scholarly authority.[5] Gyula Szekfű later claimed that Thaly's victory over the rival historians, that is romanticism's victory over positivist historiography, had catastrophic consequences:

---

3   Ágnes R. Várkonyi, *Thaly Kálmán és történetírása*, Budapest, 1961, pp 17, 43, 68, 84, 436.
4   Kálmán Thaly, *Bottyán János. II. Rákóczi Ferencz fejedelem vezérlő tábornoka. Történeti életrajz a kuruc-zvilág hadjárataival*, Pest, 1865, p. 501.
5   Várkonyi, *Thaly Kálmán*, pp. 129, 133, 196, 314.

[...] assisted by his emotions, building on the lack of political and social education for the masses, he accepted the fight and won a victory. Historians with a western historical and a wider literary education, especially those with a more delicate sense of taste, could not compete with Thaly's rude polemical style but had, instead, to listen with mute irritation to the general public's praise of Thaly as Rákóczi's historian.[6]

By 1896, when the thousand-year anniversary of the Hungarian conquest of the Carpathian Basin was celebrated, Prince Ferenc II Rákóczi came to represent the full national independence of Hungary. The repatriation of his remains was granted in 1904 as a political concession that was made by Franz Joseph almost personally to Kálmán Thaly, and Rákóczi's re-burial on 29 October 1906 took place in the single period when Thaly's party was in government (1906–10).[7]

In the context of the fiftieth anniversary of the Hungarian revolution of 1956, there is no need to explain the statement that participants in a war of independence can have a variety of personal interpretations of the struggle in which they engaged, and that several different historical interpretations of any event can be read into the evidence of the past. Although for Ferenc II Rákóczi himself, the period between 1703 and 1711 might be best described as an unsuccessful war of independence, it is still up to the historian to choose whether or not to adopt this interpretation.

Rather than following in the footsteps of the romantic historiography of the later nineteenth century and presenting the Rákóczi revolt as an unsuccessful war of independence, or giving its events a revisionist analysis, as has been done by several historians (especially in respect of the Treaty of Szatmár in 1711 which ended the revolt with a compromise), I would like to suggest a different interpretation. Not being a historian of the age of Rákóczi, I shall try to evaluate it without analysing it. I shall regard this event as a 'black box'. Neglecting its content, I shall look exclusively at its input-output relations, that is: I would like to look at what Hungary was like both before the Rákóczi revolt and after it, and to compare the two conditions. To do so, I shall use one quantitative measure: taxation. The argument which follows may thus be one-sided, but will still, I trust, prove relevant.

The Rákóczi revolt can also be regarded as the last in a succession of seventeenth-century rebellions by the Hungarian estates against the rulers, but it had its peculiarities. First, it was not animated by confession; it was not simply the revolt of the Protestant Hungarian estates against the Catholic Habsburgs. Moreover, the support of the principality of Transylvania was not of decisive importance. We should also stress that the revolt enjoyed significant popular support. Therefore, I shall develop my argument along two lines: investigating the case of noble taxation on one hand, and the changes of the amount of the yearly contribution on the other, in the hope that the latter tells us about the situation of the commoner taxpayers, the so-called *misera plebs contribuens*.

In the period of the Ottoman wars, the landed nobility often took part in paying the main state tax, the so-called contribution (along with fulfilling their other obligations

---

6   Gyula Szekfű, *A száműzött Rákóczi*, Budapest, 1913, p. 372.
7   Katalin Mária Kincses, '"Minden különös ceremonia nélkül". A Rákóczi-kultusz és a fejedelem hamvainak hazahozatala', *Hadtörténelmi Közlemények*, 116, 2003, pp. 46–76 (pp. 49, 51, 67, 71).

like sending troops to serve under the king's banner or taking up arms themselves in the noble levy of fighting men).[8] For a long time, they paid a special (and minor) tax for guarding the crown jewels.[9] In the middle of the sixteenth century and from the end of the eighteenth, the landed nobility paid for gifts made to the king, queen, and sometimes other members of the dynasty.[10] Carrying the burdens of the noble levies of fighting men was also far from insignificant. After 1670, we encounter a major change. Although its trigger was a specific event, the Wesselényi-conspiracy against Leopold I, what followed certainly comported with Central-European trends. During the course of the Thirty Years War, rulers established standing armies, and, supported by them, set out to eliminate the dualism of king and estates in politics.[11] The decisive moment in Hungary was 1670: the diet lost its prerogative to vote for the contribution, which was assessed and collected by the army instead, very often using force. A part of this was to be paid by the privileged. In February 1672, an unprecedented five-forint tax was levied on each nobleman.[12] It was met by a very determined resistance and the measure was withdrawn.[13] Nevertheless, Leopold I ordered on 6 June 1671 that half of the 40-forint tax which was assessed on each *porta*, the usual basis for taxation, should be paid by landlords.[14] In the 1690s, the petty nobility entered the group of the taxpayers along with those peasants that earlier had not paid the contribution.[15] In the years around 1700, a representative body of the Hungarian estates (the so called *concursus*) repartitioned the contribution, without having the right to determine its amount. In 1696, the *concursus* insisted on the nobility's immunity from the contribution, but backed down in 1698. The *concursus* then agreed to a part-payment by the

8   See the following acts of parliament: Art. 28 of Act 1542 (Diet of Besztercebánya); Arts 23 and 25 of Act 1548; Art. 4 of Act 1556; Art. 3 of Act 1595; Art. 3 of Act 1600; Art. 2 of Act 1601; Art. 5 of Act 1638; Art. 25 of Act 1647; Art. 5 of Act 1655 and Art. 8 of Act 1659. See Dezső Márkus (ed.), *Magyar Törvénytár*, vols 2, 3 and 4 for the years 1526–1608, 1608–1657, 1657–1740, Budapest, 1899–1900.

9   See the following acts of parliament: Art. 4 of Act 1635; Art. 33 of Act 1647; Art. 15 of Act 1655; Art. 10 of Act 1659; Art. 50 of Act 1662 and Art. 36 of Act 1681. Art. 6 of Act 1630 and Art. 8 of Act 1638 do not specify if this special tax was to be paid by the privileged. In Art. 96 of Act 1649, however, payment for the guards of the crown jewels was exceptionally asked from the *misera plebs contribuens*.

10 See the following acts of parliament: Art. 5 of Act 1546; Art. 42 of Act 1559; Art. 4 of Act 1791; Arts 3 and 4 of Act 1792. From the middle of the 16th to the middle of the 18th century, however, the coronation gift was levied on the commoner taxpayers, see Art. 2 of Act 1563, Art. 3 of Act 1572 (second *decretum*), Arts 10 and 11 of Act 1613, Art. 33 of Act 1622, Art. 9 of Act 1625, Art. 9 of Act 1638, Art. 150 of Act 1647, Arts 13 and 14 of Act 1655, Art. 3 of Act 1681, Arts 4 and 6 of Act 1715 and Art. 3 of Act 1741 (ibid, and Dezső Márkus (ed.), *Magyar Törvénytár*, vol 5, for the years 1740–1835, Budapest, 1901. That is, I do not agree with József Hajnóczy who claimed that the coronation gift was paid by the landlords up to 1655 and only by the peasants thereafter. ([Hajnóczy József], *De diversis subsidiis publicis dissertatio*, no place, 1792, p. 158.) In the 18th century, acts of parliament no longer indicated who was required to pay for the coronation gift, since it had become evident that peasants had to – until changed at the end of this century.

11 Gerhard Oestreich, 'Ständetum und Staatsbildung in Deutschland', in Oestreich (ed.), *Geist und Gestalt des frühmodernen Staates. Ausgewählte Aufsätze*, Berlin, 1969, pp. 281–289.

12 László Benczédi, 'Rendi szervezkedés és a kuruc mozgalom (1664–1685)', in Ágnes R. Várkonyi (ed.), *Magyarország története 1526–1686*, 2nd edition, Budapest, 1987, vol 2, p. 1192.

13 István Nagy, 'A Magyar Kamara adóigazgatási tevékenysége a XVI.–XVII. században', *Levéltári Közlemények*, 66, 1995, pp. 29–51 (p. 48).

14 ibid; the royal decree of 25 May, 1672 was similar to this. See Kálmán Benda (ed.), *Magyarország történeti kronológiája*, vol 2, Budapest, 1982, p. 493.

15 Ágnes R. Várkonyi, 'A Habsburg-abszolutizmus berendezkedése Magyarországon (1686–1703)', in Győző Ember & Gusztáv Heckenast (eds.), *Magyarország története 1686–1790*, vol 1, Budapest, 1989, pp. 96–97.

privileged,[16] although not so much as they were finally required to pay: 250 000 forints of the four-million-forint total.[17] After 1707, the nobles were also expected to pay taxes to Rákóczi's *kuruc* state.[18]

After 1711, the above-mentioned taxes (the contribution, the tax imposed for the guarding of the crown jewels, and the various gifts) were no longer paid by the nobility even in part. Until the French Wars at the end of the century, noble levies of fighting men were only raised in 1741 and 1744.[19] On the other hand, the petty noble groups that made up the vast majority of the Hungarian nobility still had to pay a *taxa* for most of the century. We cannot therefore speak of the tax immunity of the complete Hungarian nobility, not even in the eighteenth century – and even less so in the early modern period. It is, however, true that the landed nobility of Hungary acquired an almost complete tax immunity after the Rákóczi rebellion, that this immunity of taxation became a specifically Hungarian feature in the Habsburg Monarchy after the reforms of Haugwitz in the late 1740s, and that their exemption was increasingly regarded as an abuse by representatives of the enlightened state.[20]

Examining the commoner-taxpayers' situation, let us look at the yearly amount of the contribution. Figure 1 shows various, partly contradictory figures for the amount of the annual contribution of Hungary between 1680 and 1770.[21] It is clear that the Rákóczi rebellion brought a major change in this respect. The sum fell from something between two and seven million forints to an amount between one and 2.5 million forints a year (Figure 2). If we try to draw conclusions from the data which seem to be most reliable for the troubled years at the turn of the century, and compare them to the average tax of the successive years, we can say that the amount of the contribution decreased from three to four millions to 1.5 – 2 million forints (Figure 3).

All in all, once we cease judging the Rákóczi revolt by the token of independence, then there is no reason to consider it unsuccessful. When we consider the pre-1703 and post-1711 states of affairs in taxation, which is one field only, but a complex and crucial one, it is evident that the balance of the Rákóczi revolt was definitely positive. For the

16 Ágnes R. Várkonyi, 'A Habsburg-abszolutizmus és a magyarországi jobbágyság a XVII.–XVIII. század fordulóján', *Századok*, 99,1965, pp. 679–718 (p. 686).

17 Országgyűlési Könyvtár (Parliamentary Library, MSS), Gyurkovits-gyűjtemény, *Acta concursus regni Hungariae pro elaboranda methodo regulamenti militaris et norma in contribuendo stabilienda, in diem 20 julii anno 1698 convocati, ac mense octobris eodem anno conclusi per Georgium Gyurikovits anno 1840 collecta*, p. 104.

18 Benda (ed.), *Magyarország történeti kronológiája*, vol 2, p. 542.

19 In the years around 1800, these were raised more frequently and the *subsidium* (the extraordinary war subsidy) was paid overwhelmingly by the nobles. However, this period falls outside of the chronological focus of this essay.

20 In the Austrian provinces, noble land was taxed from 1749. In the same year, earlier sporadic taxation was also transformed into regular taxpaying in the Czech provinces as well.

21 Várkonyi, 'A Habsburg-abszolutizmus berendezkedése', pp. 96–97.; József Zachar, *Habsburg-uralom, állandó hadsereg és magyarság 1683–1792*, Budapest, 2004, pp. 72–74; P. G. M. Dickson, *Finance and Government under Maria Theresa 1740–1780*, 2 vols, Oxford, 1987, vol 2, pp. 186–187; Emma Iványi, *Esterházy Pál nádor közigazgatási tevékenysége (1681–1713)*, Budapest, 1991, pp. 145, 201; Dezső Szabó, 'Az állandó hadsereg beczikkelyezésének története III. Károly korában', *Hadtörténelmi Közlemények*, 11, 1910, pp. 35, 44, 50, 352–354, 370, 375, 383, 560–563, 581–582; Magyar Országos Levéltár (Hungarian National Archive), N71 Fasc. 3 QQQQ NB, *Specificatio subsidiorum ab anno 1715 pactatorum, et resolutorum*.

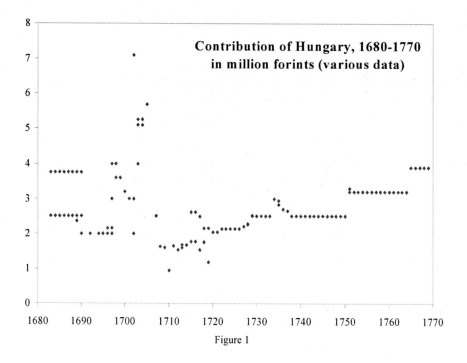

Figure 1

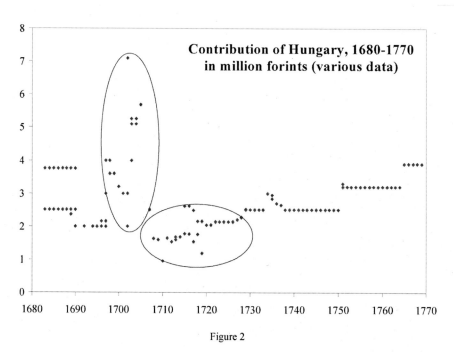

Figure 2

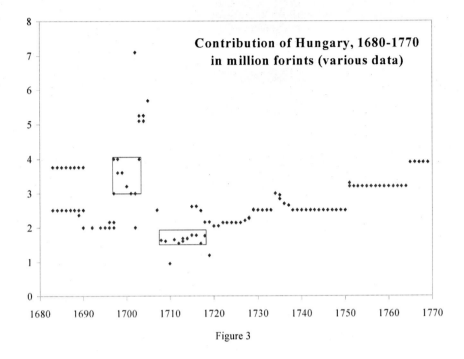

Figure 3

estates, the fight won back their – although not complete – control over taxation, leaving them in a strong position that – despite its gradual erosion – maintained the dualism of king and estates in eighteenth-century Hungarian politics, even though this was an anachronism at the time. Moreover, the landed nobility had won an immunity from the most onerous state tax that they had not enjoyed in the seventeenth century.

The fact that the majority of the political class in Hungary was satisfied with this arrangement is amply demonstrated by the fact that Ferenc II Rákóczi was only followed into exile by a narrow group of supporters, while others like his chancellor Pál Ráday became leaders of the Protestant opposition at the diet in 1712. We can also recall a later event. In 1741, the Hungarians had a realistic chance of toppling the Habsburgs, but unlike the Czechs, they chose to support Maria Theresa. The events of 1741 testify to the statement that the 1711 arrangements were acceptable, even prefer-able to the Hungarian political elite, and as a result of their stance, Hungary was left out of Haugwitz's refoms. This put her on a historical *Sonderweg* in the Habsburg Empire, increasingly diverging from the path of development in the other Habsburg provinces.

We might argue that the Rákóczi revolt was widely supported in Hungary by the peasantry because of the overwhelming burdens they had been forced to carry in the years around 1700. If so, this is another reason why the rebellion was a success. The fact that the prerogative to raise taxes was recaptured by the estates also brought very tangible results for the peasantry: a probable reduction of the annual tax burden of the country by a half. Stronger estates meant lower taxes. If we concentrate on the behaviour of the majority of the participants in the revolt, and not on Rákóczi himself and the narrow group of his most faithful supporters, and if we try to find political and material goals behind the behaviour of these actors, we cannot escape the conclusion that the Rákóczi revolt was more successful than not.

At the beginning of this essay, I tried to place the romantic historiography of the Rákóczi rebellion into a historical context. Let me finish by returning to the same line of argument. Looking at some important interpretations of the post-1711 decades of eighteenth-century Hungarian history, as written in the twentieth century, it is not difficult to establish which are the values in the sign of which they were composed. One of the first Hungarian representatives of social history, Imre Wellmann, wrote the introduction to the eighteenth-century volume of the influential *Cultural History of Hungary* (1941).[22] He writes of the country in an emotional style, especially of its destruction in the early 1700s. He strongly identifies himself with the common people, without completely discarding the old nationalistic tone (e.g. when speaking of the national minorities or presenting the events of 1741). Politically, Wellmann regarded the eighteenth century as a fight between outdated estates and strong absolutism, and he considered it tragic that the latter was represented by a foreign dynasty, working in foreign interests, even though it sought to promote new ideas, the public good and humanity. The estates of Hungary are given their *raison d'être* only by the contemporary need to defend national interests. Evidently, in terms of the eighteenth century, Wellmann would have put himself on the side of a national absolutism.

Approximately a decade earlier, the leading figure of the Hungarian *Geistesgeschichte* school, Gyula Szekfű, published the eighteenth-century part of the classic interwar account, *Hungarian History* (jointly edited with Bálint Hóman).[23] Szekfű's values do not significantly diverge from those of Wellmann. Evidently, Szekfű did not sympathize with the Hungarian estates of the eighteenth century. He points out that it is a mistake to regard them as an off-shoot of West European constitutional development, but sees them rather as a vestige of the Middle Ages. It is still with a measure of national pride, however, that he claims that it was exclusively the Hungarian estates that could force absolutism to a compromise in the Europe of that day. This ambiguity is characteristic of the overall picture that he presents of the problem. Szekfű seems to stand for an absolutism that had enlightened elements, but he leaves the door open for the estates, as representatives of the nation, to take the lead through their own modernization. His judgement on the estates is thus not so harsh as Wellmann's.

In the unfinished Marxist overview of the history of Hungary, the volume on the period 1686 to 1790 was published last: only in 1989. The politics of the period were here discussed by Győző Ember.[24] Ember writes that absolutism won the fight against the estates everywhere in the eighteenth century, but had to conclude a compromise with the estates in Hungary. Nevertheless, as the development of the 'forces of production' resulted in a certain modification in the 'relations of production', and enlightened

---

22 Imre Wellmann, 'Barokk és felvilágosodás felvilágosodás', in Wellmann (ed.), *Barokk és felvilágosodás*, Budapest, 1941 [= Sándor Domanovszky (ed.), *Magyar művelődéstörténet*, vol 4].
23 Bálint Hóman & Gyula Szekfű, *Magyar történet*, vol 6, Budapest, undated.
24 Győző Ember, 'Magyarország a Habsburg-birodalomban', in Ember & Gusztáv Heckenast (eds.), *Magyarország története 1686–1790*, vol 1, Budapest, 1989.

absolutism was introduced, this also resulted in a suppression of the estates in Hungary. The state, as the instrument and vehicle of new social and productive forces, extended its influence to more and more domains of life. Ember's view of the estates is harsher than those of Wellmann or Szekfű, because he makes progress, seen in its Marxist sense, and not the nation the touchstone. By his measure, the fact that absolutism was foreign and the estates Hungarian changes nothing, and the historian may only disapprove of the Habsburgs if it can be shown that they treated Hungary disadvantageously and in a way that could not be justified by reference to the interests of the empire.

Domokos Kosáry's classic monograph on eighteenth-century Hungary was published in 1980.[25] The Enlightenment provides the magnetic pole which orientates his judgement. In Kosáry's view, the role of the positive hero is played out by those noblemen who stepped out of the late Baroque and moved towards the Enlightenment. The estates are accordingly presented in a disadvantageous light. In Kosáry's view, 'old-fashioned feudal nationalism' and 'pre-nationalism' do not give a *laissez-passer* for 'old-fashioned feudal tendencies'.[26]

The earlier romantic historiography identified itself fully with the Hungarian estates fighting the Habsburgs. With the coming of the methodologically-oriented discipline of history, historians sought to reconcile progress with the struggle for nationhood. This 'bridge-building' explains Wellmann and Szekfű's ambivalent judgement on the eighteenth-century Hungarian estates. The former announced a milder, the latter a harsher judgement, but not even Wellmann could set himself completely against the estates, since (as he thought) they represented the national interests in the eighteenth century.

Under Mátyás Rákosi's Stalinist regime, this line was continued by coupling nationalist and communist thought. When the revolution in 1956 showed nationalism as a double-edged weapon for communists, the dominant line was also modified in historiography. Following the so-called 'Erik Molnár debate', we can witness the fast decline in the importance of the national approach. Progress alone remained the benchmark – and the judgements passed on the Hungarian estates became unambigously negative. We can see this both in the chapters written by Győző Ember, as also in Domokos Kosáry's great work.

I think that it is fully legitimate to place social progress and the discernment of national values at the centre of present-day historical narratives. But other points of view may also be acceptable. The change in direction in German historiography is, in this respect, edifying. After the Second World War, traditions had to be re-evaluated. Earlier, the national approach and – as far as the early modern period was concerned – the building of the national state had been favoured. In this narrative, the princes played the part of positive heroes, as they took the first steps on the road that led to the nine-teenth-century unification of Germany. After the Second World War, however, when the end of this road was shown to have been a catastrophe, the early modern German estates were no longer seen as merely swimming against the tide of history when they

---

25 Domokos Kosáry, *Művelődés a XVIII. századi Magyarországon*, Budapest, 1980.
26 ibid, p. 342.

fought the princes, but they were given instead the role of the precursors of constitutionalism.[27]

I would argue that it is now time that democratic values take their place among the central values upon which Hungarian historian base their judgements. In this way, we might also find that the estates of Hungary in the eighteenth century represented in some way the principle of constitutionalism. Although in that age, this could not rest on the political representation of the complete population, the institutions of the Hungarian estates still, at least by eighteenth-century standards, realized a wide political participation.

The Rákóczi revolt brought tax immunity to the landed gentry, lower taxes for the *misera plebs contribuens*, and a political structure that not only conserved a significant autonomy for Hungary within the Empire, but also opened up (by the standards of the age) wide room for political participation. By these measures, it might be justly regarded as not so much an unsuccessful war of independence but rather as a successful rebellion.

---

27 The first important publication suggesting a different evaluation was F. L. Carsten, *Princes and Parliaments in Germany*, Oxford, 1959. See also Helmut Neuhaus, *Das Reich in der frühen Neuzeit*, Munich, 1997, pp. pp.58, 65; Rudolf Endres, *Adel in der frühen Neuzeit*, Munich, 1993, pp. 113–114.

Rebellion or revolution? The Case of the Hungarian 'Jacobins'

Orsolya Szakály

The reputation of the 'Jacobin'[1] conspiracy of 1794 is ambiguous. It has often been celebrated as a radical departure in the democratization of Hungarian politics, as the first, albeit abortive, attempt to abolish privileges and to establish a Hungarian republic based on equal rights and general political representation. By this measure, the 'Jacobin' movement was revolutionary, at least in its intentions. Nevertheless, the whole movement has also been dismissed as the brainchild of an immoral adventurer, Ignác Martinovics, and of a few gullible individuals. The conflicting historical interpretations of the 'Jacobin' movement rely to a great extent on the political persuasion of the historians who are doing the interpreting.[2] Conservative historians[3] acknowledge it as an attempt to gain independence for Hungary, albeit one that was discredited by the 'demonic' figure of its leader. Liberal[4] and Marxist[5] historians, on the other hand, have tended to view the movement as a precursor of the radical social changes of the nineteenth and twentieth centuries, and to celebrate its desire to overhaul the feudal political system.

The full extent and membership of the Hungarian 'Jacobin' conspiracy of 1794 is not known. The lack of sources leaves huge gaps in our understanding of the manifold and sometimes conflicting aims of those who were involved. In this way, as in many others, it was similar to the political unrest that characterized the last year of Joseph II's reign, and in particular the attempt to de-throne the Habsburg dynasty in Hungary in 1789–90. In the present chapter, I will draw parallels between the two events and show that the 'Jacobin' movement was in many ways a continuation of the former. Moreover, I will argue that rather than being revolutionary, in respect of its power-base and membership,

---

1   The conspiracy of 1794 was coined 'Jacobin' by the authorities in order to blacken the reputation of those involved. They did not have any contact with the Jacobin government of France. The leader of the Hungarian movement, Ignác Martinovics, claimed that he could secure French support, but this was one of his many lies. The programme of even the more radical wing of the movement shows more similarity with the French constitution of 1791 than with any later developments in France. Hence, I use the term 'Jacobin' in inverted commas.

2   Kálmán Benda, 'A magyar jakobinus mozgalom történeti irodalmának rövid áttekintése', in Kálmán Benda, *Emberbarát vagy hazafi? Tanulmányok a felvilágosodás korának magyarországi történetéből*, Budapest, 1978, pp. 213–31. For earlier studies, see Domokos Kosáry, *Bevezetés a magyar történelem forrásaiba és irodalmába*, vol 2. 1711–1825, Budapest, 1954, pp. 507–18.

3   For example Vilmos Fraknói, *Martinovics élete*, Budapest, 1921.

4   For instance Mihály Horváth's history of Hungary: Horváth, *Magyarország történelme*, vol 8, 2nd edn, Pest, 1873.

5   The first Marxist analysis of the movement that was reproduced in different forms: István Kató, 'A magyar jakobinus-mozgalom néhány kérdéséről', *Századok*, 84, 1950, 2, pp. 199–234.

the Jacobin movement had the potential to become the last attempt at redressing the structure of power-relations between the Habsburg dynasty and Hungary through the traditional path of rebellion.

Anyone who has consulted the two large volumes of source publication on the Hungarian 'Jacobin' movement[6] would be surprised at my assertion that we lack sources for this episode of Hungarian history. Arguably, the Hungarian 'Jacobins' suffer from overexposure, due to the fascination of Marxist historiography with incidents of class struggle. Some elements of the 'Jacobin' movement, notably its republicanism and anti-feudal tendencies, fitted the Marxist categories neatly. As a result, many of the writings on the 'Jacobins' are hopelessly tendentious. The two volumes of sources themselves are, however, still valuable. Compiled by Kálmán Benda (not a Marxist himself), they include seminal pieces of Hungarian political literature from the first half of the 1790s. These, although for the most part not directly connected with the 'Jacobin' movement, point to the continuity between the conspiracy and the political upheaval at the very end of Joseph II's reign. The volumes also contain the programmes of the Hungarian 'Jacobins', documents concerning their treason trial, and a selection of their seized papers. Nevertheless, we have to bear in mind that the source-base itself is biased. Several months had elapsed between the first few arrests in August 1794 and the larger clamp-down that followed in December. Between those two dates there was plenty of time to dispose of sensitive material.[7] Furthermore, the movement was organized in a cell-like fashion: new members were recruited directly by a current member and were obliged to win over two more persons to the cause. Consequently, most members knew only three others in the movement. Moreover, these people were often their kith and kin and so most of those involved, with the signal exception of Martinovics who was an outsider, had a vested interest in covering for each other.

No such comparable pool of primary sources is available for the political unrest affecting the county nobility in 1789–90.[8] Nonetheless, it is clear that theirs was a traditional rebellion in so far as it constituted a public act of defiance. The political tension between Joseph II and the Hungarian estates never actually manifested itself in armed conflict, but the Hungarian counties refused to raise troops and to provide supplies for the Habsburg army.[9] This, together with the unfavourable international situation in which the Habsburg Empire found itself, particularly the threat of Prussian military intervention, succeeded in forcing the restoration of the 'Old Order' in Hungary when, in early 1790, the dying Joseph II revoked almost all of his reforming decrees concerning Hungary. Nevertheless, it would be wrong to see the events of 1789–90

---

6 *A magyar jakobinusok iratai*, ed. Kálmán Benda, 2 vols, Budapest, 1952–57; vol 1: *A magyar jakobinus mozgalom iratai*, Budapest, 1957, and vol 2: *A magyar jakobinusok elleni felségsértési és hűtlenségi per iratai, 1794–1795*, Budapest, 1952.

7 Éva H. Balázs, 'A bitó, a börtön üzenet volt. Kétszáz éve végezték ki a magyar jakobinusokat', in H. Balázs, *Életek és korok. Válogatott írások*, ed. Lilla Krász, Budapest, 2005, pp. 247–50 (p. 250).

8 The most detailed study of the foreign connections of the Hungarian malcontents is Robert Gragger, *Preußen, Weimar und die ungarische Königskrone*, Berlin & Leipzig, 1923. This contains the full text of the crucial sources concerning Prussia. Other relevant documents can be found in Benda, *A magyar jakobinus mozgalom iratai*.

9 For details on this see Horst Haselsteiner, *Joseph II und die Komitate Ungarns. Herrscherrecht und ständischer Konstitutionalismus*, Wien–Köln–Graz, 1983.

simply as the victory of the conservative Hungarian nobility over a reforming ruler. Such a conclusion overlooks the fact that some of the leading Hungarian political figures were motivated not simply by stubborn conservatism but by hope of change. The most active in plotting against the Habsburgs, securing promises of support from Prussia, and even putting out feelers toward Great Britain, were not die-hard conservatives but former, disillusioned Josephists. These noblemen were all convinced that the Hungarian political, economic and social system was unsustainable. They hoped that moderate reforms, especially in the economic field, would defuse social tensions and bring prosperity. In 1789–90 they tried and failed. When Joseph II's successor, Leopold II restored calm in Hungary through international and domestic manoeuvres, the reformers of 1789–90 were silenced and temporarily bought off in 1791 with a general amnesty. On account of the terms of the amnesty, it has never been established who were the most involved, particularly in the anti-Habsburg negotiations with foreign powers. Only a few mediators were subsequently identified, such as Pál Beck, a nobleman and a minor bureaucrat in the Royal Lieutenancy Council who was the envoy of the discontented Hungarian nobles to the Prussian court in 1789.[10] Nevertheless, for Leopold II the prime suspects were administrators in key positions such as Baron József Podmaniczky, Councillor in the Royal Lieutenancy, another Councillor of the same, József Vay and his brothers, together with several other noblemen and aristocrats including the prominent Orczy brothers, László and József.[11] We will encounter their names again.

Dissatisfaction with Habsburg rule in Hungary did not disappear. It was a constant feature of the early reign of Francis I (II). Discontent was partly voiced through traditional channels, namely the petitions of the noble counties. Nevertheless, it also manifested itself in new forms such as in Masonic lodges and reading clubs. The latter were formed to discuss press coverage of the events of the French Revolution and the Revolutionary Wars, and were partly attended by the disillusioned Josephists who had been implicated in 1789–90.[12] Widespread but unorganized dissatisfaction was given a concrete form and programme in the spring of 1794 with the appearance of a talented but highly controversial figure, Ignác Martinovics. Martinovics started his colourful career as a Franciscan monk. Later, he was made professor at the University of Lemberg (Lviv) and finally made honorary abbot of Szászvár. In 1791, he became one of the

---

10 His name appears in Prussian documents together with the names of councillors Semsey and Ferenc Vécsey who worked at the Hungarian Royal Chancery in Vienna. For details see Gragger, *Preußen, Weimar*, passim. The involvement of Count János Pálffy was established by Éva H. Balázs in her 'Ki volt Rotenstein? Egy forrás azonosítása', *Ars Hungarica*, 15, 1987, no 2, pp. 133–38.

11 Leopold II compiled a list of the prime suspects for the benefit of his son, Alexander Leopold, on his becoming the Palatine of Hungary. The source was published in Elemér Mályusz, *Sándor Lipót főherceg nádor iratai, 1790–1795*, Budapest, 1926, pp. 440–45.

12 Éva H. Balázs examined the membership and the interests of the reading club that was established in Buda in December 1792, by amongst others Gergely Berzeviczy. From the point of view of the 'Jacobin' conspiracy the most important member was József Hajnóczy, who became one of the directors of the Society of Liberty and Equality. The club subscribed to French, German and the few existing Hungarian journals, but seven French journals headed the list of recommended readings. Amongst those seven, the following were accorded a special significance by the organizers: *Gazette de deux Ponts, Gazette Nationale ou le Moniteur* and *Mercure de France*. See Éva H. Balázs, *Berzeviczy Gergely, a reformpolitikus, 1763–1795*, Budapest, 1967, pp. 193–94.

many paid informers of Leopold II. Martinovics turned his attention to what was happening in Hungary only once he sensed that his services had gone unappreciated by the Habsburg court. The final blow was the accession of Francis I (II) to the throne, after which his services as an informant were no longer required and his pay was stopped. Nevertheless, his role in organizing the Hungarian 'Jacobin' conspiracy was pivotal.[13]

In 1794, just as in 1789–90, the international situation seemed to favour action. In May 1794, Martinovics managed to spur the discontented Hungarians into action by claiming that he enjoyed the financial support of the French Jacobin government and by pointing to the Polish uprising as the beginning of a general revolutionary movement that would engulf the region. He set in motion the organization of two parallel secret societies. The outer circle was the Society of Reformers, while the inner group, the Society of Liberty and Equality, was a more radical association, formed by the initiated members of the outer circle. The programmes of both societies are available.[14]

The programme of the radical Society of Liberty and Equality was tellingly written in French, although it also circulated in two different Hungarian translations.[15] It contained a description of the rights of man, drawn from Rousseau and contemporary French books that praised the early achievements of the French Revolution.[16] It continued with a call for the establishment of a democratic republic in Hungary that would be based on popular sovereignty and hence on the political representation of equal citizens. The main obstacles to this, according to the programme, were the king, the privileged orders of the nobility and the clergy, and the fact that the vast majority of the population was kept in serfdom. The serfs – so the programme put it – fared little better than slaves or even cattle. They were not consulted in decision-making processes but crushed by a heavy tax burden. The institution of the monarchy came under the fiercest and most verbose attack. It was deemed inherently corrupt and self-serving. Moreover, it was economically disastrous. The criticism levelled at the nobility was more concise, if not much less passionate. Nevertheless, the brunt of it was aimed at the aristocrats who were accordingly depicted as ignorant, immoral and parasitic. The untitled nobility got away with a sentence describing it as less ignorant but powerless and over-proud of its status, while the clergy was simply dismissed as a group that used religion for its own purposes: to gain access to power and wealth, and to keep people in ignorance.

The Society of Liberty's programme demanded the overhaul of the ignominious tyranny of monarchs and of the privileged orders. It regarded the situation as ripe for

---

13 Kálmán Benda, 'A magyar jakobinus mozgalom története', in Kálmán Benda, *Emberbarát vagy hazafi? Tanulmányok a felvilágosodás korának magyarországi történetéből*, Budapest, 1978, pp. 105–212 (pp. 155–69).

14 They were also published in English: see R. R. Palmer and P. Kenéz, 'Two Documents of the Hungarian Revolutionary Movement of 1794', *Journal of Central European Affairs*, 20, 1961, 4, pp. 423–442.

15 Benda published one of the two existing contemporary Hungarian translations of the French original. The original is attributed to Ignác Martinovics, while the translation is believed to have been written by Ferenc Szentmarjay. The other Hungarian translation was the work of János Laczkovics. See Benda, *A magyar jakobinus mozgalom iratai*, pp. 1015–36.

16 Kálmán Benda identified these sources in this source publication as Count Constantin François de Volney, *La loi naturelle ou Cathéchisme de citoyen français*, Paris, 1793; Collot d'Herbois, *Almanach du Père Gérard pour l'année 1792*, Paris, 1792; and Rabaut de St. Étienne, *Précis de l'histoire de la Révolution française*, in German translation: Strassburg, 1792.

such a revolution all over Europe, with the notable exception of France and some of the Swiss cantons. It claimed that it was the duty of the individuals to start such a revolution once circumstances were favourable. The text did not, however, contain an action plan and it was particularly fuzzy on when and how the revolution should take place. At one point, it argued that it should be bloodless. Nevertheless, it also stated that the fate of the king and of his supporters should be death, and at one point it excused the French terror by dismissing it as a teething problem of democracy.[17] For the purposes of my argument it is important to look at the ideal new leadership of the desired democratic republic. What we learn is that the new leaders should be strong, moral and talented persons whose individual merit naturally raises them above others and whose eyes had already been opened to the unhappiness of their fellow human beings by the ideas of the Enlightenment.

It seems that the Society of Liberty and Equality was to take over once the more limited aims of the Society of Reformers had been achieved. So what were these limited aims? First was the creation of an independent Hungarian republic. The programme of the Society of Reformers[18] is thus full of specific references to the reigns of four successive Habsburg monarchs, Maria Theresa, Joseph II, Leopold II and Francis I (II). There is a detailed discussion as to why each of these was harmful to the interests of Hungarians, from which it logically followed that Hungarians would be much better off in an independent state with a bi-cameral legislature. The representatives of the nobles would sit in one of the chambers and those of the non-noble population in the other. A noteworthy element of the programme is that there would be no need to pay taxes in the Hungarian republic since the confiscated royal and ecclesiastical estates would provide sufficient income to run the country. Further money was expected from the liberalization of trade that would take the place of the oppressive customs system of the Habsburg monarchy since, according to the programme, the customs regime introduced in 1754 had reduced Hungary to the status of a miserable colony. Apart from freedom of trade, there should be freedom of religion, freedom of the press, a national army and state support for national cultural institutions. The Society's programme was to be implemented following a rebellion that would dethrone the Habsburgs – a rebellion that was to be led by nobles. Such an uprising would be legal, the programme claimed, since Joseph II had broken the line of the Habsburg succession by ruling Hungary illegally, for he had not been crowned king of the country.

The demands of the Society of Reformers closely coincided with those of the reformist nobles who had set the tone in 1789–90. The idea that Joseph II had broken the contract between ruler and people (in this case the Hungarian estates), and that he and his successors ruled illegally, was already present in the pamphlet literature and the political discourse of the late 1780s;[19] calls for trade liberalization in Hungary even

---

17 For these contradictions, see in particular Benda, *A magyar jakobinus mozgalom iratai*, pp. 1028, 1032; for the new leadership p. 1027.

18 The original Latin text was published in Benda, *A magyar jakobinus mozgalom iratai*, pp. 1002–14. An early twentieth-century Hungarian translation is available in Fraknói, *Martinovics élete*, pp. 223–30.

19 This idea was popular amongst the Hungarian estates. It was developed, for example, by Gergely Berzeviczy in his pamphlet *De dominio Austriae in Hungaria* which he wrote in Buda in April 1790. The full text of this pamphlet is published in Benda, *A magyar jakobinus mozgalom iratai*, pp. 92–105.

predated Joseph II's reign[20] and there were tentative promises even to extend political representation down the social scale to include non-noble town dwellers. The formation of a national army and national cultural institutions were particularly dear to the reformist nobles' hearts.[21] The limitations of the programme of the Society of Reformers were also typical of the reformist nobility, as it was only willing to offer restricted property rights to the peasantry, who would be personally free but occupy the land not as full owners but simply as tenant farmers. Nevertheless, the programme of the Society of Reformers contained new ideas as well, such as the establishment of a republic and also the surprising suggestion that Hungary should be divided into provinces according to nationality and form a federative republic (*foederativa respublica*). Whether this reorganization would have only involved Croatia or whether it might have included other nationalities, is uncertain. The idea is said to have originated from Ignác Martinovics himself who was of Serbian origin although born in Pest. Otherwise, he seems to have taken over the reformist nobles' programme.

As mentioned above, the full extent of the Hungarian 'Jacobin' movement, including its membership, is not known. It is impossible to establish who belonged only to the Society of Reformers and who to both societies, since in the course of the investigation the police did not distinguish between the two. It seems that the Society of Reformers was more numerous, and politically and socially more influential. Many of the disillusioned former Josephists who had also been active in the political events of 1789–1790 were suspected of involvement but were ultimately not charged. Nevertheless, their membership in some cases has been later ascertained by historians. For example, Éva H. Balázs has proved that the well-known economist, Gergely Berzeviczy, who argued for the dethronement of the Habsburgs in 1790, was also a member of the 'Jacobin' movement.[22] Several others came under suspicion, although their membership was never proven. This was the case with Pál Beck, the Hungarian malcontents' envoy back in 1789–90, but also of Barons László and József Orczy, Baron József Podmaniczky and Baron Miklós Vay.[23]

Both programmes of the Hungarian 'Jacobin' movement remained just that – plans on paper. The movement's sympathizers had three months to organize and, according to estimates, they recruited around 2–300 members. In mid-August 1794, Ignác Martinovics was arrested in Vienna as part of a clamp-down on the Viennese 'Jacobin' conspiracy. During his interrogation he gave the full details of the Hungarian movement and boasted of his own role in its organization. Arrests soon followed in Hungary. During the trials that ensued, eighteen members of the so-called 'Martinovics conspiracy' were sentenced to death for treason and dozens of people received long prison sentences. Seven of the death sentences were carried out. On 20 May 1795, Martinovics was executed together with the director of the Society of the Reformers, Count Jakab Sigray and the three directors of the Society of Liberty and Equality, József

---

20 The most exhaustive exposure of this idea is to be found in the works of the contemporary economic expert, Miklós Skerlecz. *Skerlecz Miklós báró művei*, ed. Pál Berényi, Budapest, 1914.
21 For the various plans to establish a Hungarian Royal Society see Domokos Kosáry, *Művelődés a XVIII. századi Magyarországon*, 3rd edn, Budapest, 1996, pp. 562–71.
22 Balázs, *Berzeviczy Gergely*, pp. 181–216.
23 Benda, 'A magyar jakobinus mozgalom', p. 177 and footnote 61 on p. 210.

Hajnóczy, János Laczkovics and Ferenc Szentmarjay. Two more executions followed in early June. It is important to note here that those who were executed not only represented different social categories (for instance Sigray was an aristocrat, Laczkovics a nobleman and Hajnóczy a commoner) but were also of different political persuasions.

In his introduction to the 'Jacobin' source-publication and in his later works, Kálmán Benda argued that most noble members of the 'Jacobin' conspiracy were stooges. He claimed that they were privy only to the existence of the more moderate Society of Reformers and that they were manipulated by the members of the Society of Liberty and Equality. The latter, Benda argued, were also former Josephists, but commoners. They were non-noble intellectuals who felt betrayed by the nobles' willingness to compromise with the Habsburgs in 1790–91. In 1794 they saw their chance to use the nobles to instigate a rebellion which might later be turned into an anti-feudal revolution and hence lead to the establishment of a republic based on equality. Furthermore, Benda stated that discovery of the more radical wing of the 'Jacobin' movement so shocked even the reformist nobles that henceforward until the end of the French and Napoleonic Wars (and beyond), they would rally behind the Habsburg court.

A so far unknown political memorandum from 1790 sheds a different light on how the reformist nobles viewed social change. In his detailed biography of Sir Joseph Banks, Harold B. Carter recounts the story of a Hungarian baron, Miklós Vay.[24] Vay became a member of the Royal Society of London in 1787, at the end of an eighteen-month stay in Britain, before returning to Hungary. In late March 1790, Vay unexpectedly turned up at Banks's house. He came as the envoy of the Hungarian malcontents who tried to obtain British support for a Hungarian rebellion. Banks kept a record of Vay's activities. It is these notes that prove the earlier suspicion that Councillor József Podmaniczky was the mastermind behind the Hungarian malcontents' activities and that he worked in close cooperation with Miklós Vay's older brother and fellow councillor, József Vay, not to mention other influential aristocrats and noblemen who go unnamed. In the course of the following three months, Banks wrote several letters on Vay's behalf and arranged two private meetings between Vay and the British prime minister, William Pitt the Younger. On 31 March, Pitt heard Vay out in private and on 9 May he saw him again only to inform him that he could not be recognized officially as an envoy and to refuse any British help. Vay made one more attempt to change Pitt's mind. In late June, he wrote a lengthy memorandum which listed all the arguments in favour of British intervention in support of the Hungarians. This extensive document was not mentioned in Banks's biography. Nevertheless, it survives in two drafts in Banks's hand.[25] Vay probably produced a French or Latin version which Banks translated into English.

The memorandum emphasizes that the aim of the Hungarians was only to reinstate the ancient Hungarian constitution which had been consistently abused by successive Habsburg rulers and had been completely abolished by Joseph II. The bulk of Vay's arguments concern why it would be advantageous for Britain to support Hungary in its

---

24 Harold B. Carter, *Sir Joseph Banks, 1743–1820*, London, 1988, pp. 285–290.
25 Two undated manuscripts [written in June 1790] in a folder marked also in Banks's hand 'Matters relative to Hungary 1790': The Banks Collection of The Sutro Library, California State Library, HUN 1:17/a and b(1–6).

venture: it would gain a reliable ally in the region and it would also benefit commercially. Vay also attempted to counter possible British objections. The last of these concerned the effect of the re-establishment of the Hungarian constitution by the inclusion of non-nobles. Pitt must have raised this issue because Vay addressed it somewhat reluctantly. He considered it as an internal affair but then he added:

> If it is admitted that the Lower ranks of People in Hungary have not yet attaind a sufficient degree of Civilization, to be able to make a proper use of Compleat Liberty, it will follow, that it is better the part of the society that the Farther advanced in it, should enjoy some real superiority, over those who are still behindhand, & if considerd in the infancy of Civilization, should rather be Educated than abandond to their own Ideas & inclinations: add to this, that the Constitution of Hungary admits of many different ways of attaining nobility, all who in consequence of a liberal Education, have learnd the proper use & real value of their Freedom, or who have been so Fortunate as to render any sort of service to the state, may with the greatest Facility be Enobled, Whole Towns indeed by growing more industrious, cultivating the arts with more success, & Finaly becoming richer than their neighbors, have been made liberae regiaeque civitates, & gaind the Privileges of sending representatives to the Diet, & being considerd as noble. In short, the nobility of the Countrey are well disposd to grant to the people the right of being represented, & to allow them by gradual degrees a greater share of liberty, as they by their gradual improvement, may hereafter render themselves more capable of enjoying its blessings.[26]

In 1790 Vay thus portrayed the Hungarian nobility as an open elite which embraced the politically mature elements of society. From this it is not such a leap even to the radical programme of the Society of Liberty and Equality. Although the latter called for the eradication of feudal privileges (and hence that of the nobility as such), it still acknowledged that a select few towered above the population in talent, education and information. It was easy for the reformist nobles to believe that this meant them. The French Revolution might have influenced their rhetoric and even encouraged them to embrace certain limited reforms, but only on condition that they retained their dominant social, political and economic position. Some of them might well have been shocked by the discovery of the existence of a more radical wing of the 'Jacobin' movement, but others could reconcile their aspirations and the programme of the Society of Liberty and Equality, and become its members.

It is wrong, therefore, to believe that, had it not been nipped in the bud, the 'Jacobin' conspiracy would have ushered in a revolution, if by revolution we mean a new beginning in Hungarian politics. Considering its power-base it was just as likely, or even more likely, that the 'Jacobin' movement would have resulted in a re-run of the events of 1789–90. Thus it could have produced the last attempt at redressing the power-relations between the Habsburg dynasty and Hungary through the traditional path of rebellion without instituting great social change. This can, however, be no more than conjecture. The executions of 1795 – a stark demonstration of Habsburg power that carried a warning to all of those who were involved – cured the reformist nobles of their rebellious tendencies. The historic moment has passed and, in the face of French expansion, Habsburg rule and political immobility seemed the more favourable option.

---

26 Undated manuscript [June 1790]: HUN 1:17a(5–6).

Revolutionary Moments in Central Europe:
1846, 1848, 1918 and after

Benedek, Breinl and the 'Galician Horrors' of 1846

Alan Sked

The peasant response in Galicia in 1846 to the outbreak of revolution planned there by Polish patriots was not the one expected. Instead of backing the revolution, the peasants proclaimed their loyalty to the Austrian emperor and slaughtered the local nobility and gentry. A sort of bloodlust took over them with the result that between five hundred and two thousand people were killed, often in horrific circumstances.[1] In Tarnow county in particular the leading Austrian official, *Kreishauptmann* Breinl, gave travelling expenses to the peasants who brought in the dead and dying on carts, while Colonel Benedek, the Austrian officer in charge of dealing with the rebels, also paid out expenses. The result was that Austria was accused of deliberately bribing peasants to murder their masters. This canard has long survived historical research and even the latest German account states:

> There is no doubt that the Austrian occupation [sic] administration in Galicia was not overhasty to prevent the peasants from perpetrating atrocities, even though it is still not clear how much money they used in order to win the peasants over to their side.[2]

It does, however, add: '*There is not a single Austrian document or any other reliable evidence that can in the least demonstrate that the government paid out money for a dead or wounded insurgent or promised to do so.*'[3] (My emphasis)

This paper will take a close look at the roles of Breinl and Benedek during the 'massacres' to see what really happened. Although there is no proof that Austria started them, Metternich saw them as evidence of a 'new era' having dawned, of 'an extraordinarily significant event' which had in his eyes 'the full worth of an unparalleled phase in world history'. 'The democrats', he told Field Marshal Radetzky, 'have mistaken their base; a democracy without the people is a chimera.'[4] This had long been wishful

---

1 Estimates vary between 200 and 2000, but one Polish historian has listed 726 individuals. Another has listed 639 but estimated that over 1,000 were killed. It is extremely difficult to produce precise figures. For the latest discussion, see Arnon Gill, *Die Polnische Revolution, 1846. Zwischen nationalen Befreiungskampf des Landadels und antifeudaler Bauernerhebung*, Munich and Vienna, 1974, pp. 247–250.

2 Gill, *Die Polnische Revolution*, p. 352. Gill, however, has not used the Austrian archives or even important published sources such as Heinrich Friedjung (ed.), *Benedeks Nachgelassene Papiere*, Leipzig, 1901, (hereafter, *BNP*) and seems unaware of the key Austrian book on the topic, the endnotes of which contain a great deal of fascinating archival extracts, namely, Hans Schlitter, *Aus Österreichs Vormärz*, vol. 1, *Galizien und Krakow*, Zurich, Leipzig & Vienna, 1920. Benedek's role is simply ignored.

3 Gill, *Die Polnische Revolution*, p. 205.

4 Vienna, Haus-Hof-und Staatsarchiv, Staatskanzleiakten, Provinzen, Lombardei-Venezien, Karton 8, Metternich to Radetzky, Vienna, 16 March, 1846.

thinking among Metternich's circle. Count Ficquelmont, Austrian ambassador to Russia, for example, had told the tsar in 1837, 'It would take only a word to wipe out this (Hungarian noble) opposition by making the peasants think of an improvement to their lot, something the nobles have no wish to grant them.'[5] The fact that what had been predicted of Hungary came true in Galicia and had been actually welcomed by Metternich, convinced many foes of Austria that the massacres had indeed been planned.

(a) Benedek and the army

Benedek was to earn the reputation of a military hero after his expedition to West Galicia from Lemberg at the request of the Archduke Ferdinand d'Este and FML Retsey, the military and civil governor, and military commander of Galicia, respectively, both of whom wanted to know what was happening.[6] He soon discovered that he would have to act very much on his own and the actions taken on his own initiative led to the defeat of the insurrection. He had hoped to rely on others, particularly generals Csollich[7] and Collin[8], but this proved impossible. Collin, who rather amazingly had retreated from Cracow on 23 February, having given credence to false and unsubstantiated rumours of a massive Polish attack, withdrew so far – evacuating Podgorze and stopping only at Wadowice – and without sufficient ammunition, that he was of no help. Csollich, on the other hand, fearful of a second attack on Tarnow (the first had not in fact materialized having been frustrated by peasant opposition) would not budge from the town or send troops outside it.[9] In the words of the Archduke Ferdinand in his letter to Count Hardegg, the president of the *Hofkriegsrat* in Vienna, requesting the Maria Theresa Order for Benedek: 'The completely inactive FML Csollich had not moved from Tarnow during this whole time, nor had he ordered any troop movements. He had limited himself merely to an anxious occupation of Tarnow that was demoralizing for the troops. I must therefore conclude that his physical and moral reserves have sunk so low, that I now consider myself officially obliged to demand his immediate retirement.'[10] Csollich had been frightened ever since the previous winter when some Polish NCOs and soldiers had been won over by the conspirators. Thereafter his timidity had transferred itself to the *Kreishauptmann*, Breinl. Friedjung wrote of Csollich: 'It should have been the duty of General Csollich to send small raiding parties into the countryside to end the anarchy and to protect the fleeing landowners. He was so fearful, however, of an attack by the Polish insurgents on the town that he kept his troops concentrated in the town and even forbade his more humane and courageous officers to go and save their noble friends who had not taken part in the revolt.'[11]

---

5   Erzsébet Andics, 'Metternich és az 1830-as évek magyar reformmozgalma', *Századok*, 106, 1972, pp. 272–309, 304.
6   His story can be followed from his reports included in Vienna, Haus-Hof-und Staatsarchiv, Österreichischen Estensisches-Archiv, IV, Karton 108, (Henceforth Archduke Ferdinand Papers)
7   Military commander at Tarnow
8   The general sent to occupy Cracow and defeat the rebels there.
9   For a short overview of military events, see Friedjung's introduction to the *BNP* chapter on 1846, pp. 10–16.
10 Ferdinand to Hardegg, Lemberg, 1 March, 1846, *BNP*, pp., 22–23.
11 *BNP*, p. 12.

Benedek, therefore, was left to rely on his own resources together with those of whatever peasants he could persuade to help him. The revolution had been planned by the Polish insurgents to break out on the 21 February, but in Tarnow it was brought forward to 18 February on account of events in Cracow (General Collin's occupation of the city on 18 February). It was frustrated by the local peasants on the night of 18/19 February and according to Gill was effectively over by the 19th, although the peasant bloodlust now started in the west.[12] Most revolutionaries outside Tarnow who heard the call to take up arms on 21 February wisely abandoned the idea, although enraged peasant bands (often from Tarnow) still found some nobles to execute.[13] Collin's surprise retreat from Cracow on 23 February then brought back the threat from insurgents, but Benedek brought the uprising to an end on 26 February when he defeated the rebels at Gdow.[14] Before he was forced to confront the rebels, however, he had to make his way westwards through Galicia.

His first report was sent from Przmysl and was written at 4.00 PM, 18 February.[15] It recorded the views of the local authorities, who, according to Benedek were handling the situation 'calmly and intelligently'. These men, he reported, did not fear any trouble at present but he did predict unrest if the distress in their county – which was tangible – grew worse. He had provided them with troops as a precautionary measure, but added that 'up till now the inhabitants of the area [had] resisted all attempts to subvert them.'[16] He appeared, therefore, to endorse the view of the local mayor who 'place[d] no faith at all in the prospect of a common uprising among the people on the scale of a revolt or revolution.'[17] His views no doubt coloured the Archduke Ferdinand's thoughts when, on 20 February, he wrote to Hardegg for more artillery, nonetheless insisting that he would need it only 'if – contrary to reliable opinion – a political uprising should actually break out in this area.'[18]

The news from Rzeszow, on the other hand, was less encouraging. In a short note dated 20 February, Benedek reported the '*completely reliable and authentic news*' that the revolution was planned for 21 February. According to the colonel, all the nobles and the priesthood were involved, although the peasantry remained loyal. The local authorities, however, did not wish to declare martial law until clashes had already occurred. On the next day – supposedly that of the planned outbreak – Benedek submitted no less than three reports to Ferdinand.

His first report began with the words, 'Here everything is still peaceful.' Nevertheless, on the previous night he had received a report from Tarnow from a Colonel Moltke which stated that nine nobles had been killed by local peasants, that another fifty individuals had been wounded and that a hundred people had been 'brought in' to the

---

12 Gill, *Die Polnische Revolution*, p. 197: 'The defeat of the uprising was already visible on the morning of 19 February'. He then (p. 198) quotes M. von Sala, *Geschichte der polnischen Aufstandes des Jahres 1846 in Galizien*, Vienna, 1867, p. 193: 'Now the pursuit (of the rebels) on the part of the peasants really began in earnest.'
13 See below.
14 See below.
15 Archduke Ferdinand Papers, Benedek to Ferdinand, Przemysl, 18 February, 1846.
16 ibid.
17 ibid
18 Archduke Ferdinand Papers, Ferdinand to Hardegg, Lemberg, 20 February, 1846.

local authorities. Moltke had not said whether troops had been involved or not. He had merely complained that there had been some bureaucratic delay in arresting a priest and that the local officials had been lethargic. Despite this note, Benedek concluded that there was 'no real evidence' that Rzeszow was in any danger, writing that he personally would be 'very surprised if a revolt were to break out here today or tomorrow.' He would, however, visit Tarnow to see things there for himself.[19] His second report of 21 February confirmed this view.[20] He did not – and he underlined the 'not' – believe that there was any danger of revolution in Rzeszow county. 'I cannot prove with mathematical certainty that this country will remain peaceful', he wrote, 'but I have the innermost conviction that nothing significant will happen here'. If anything, events in Tarnow had paralysed any projected uprising in Rzeszow. And it was to these events in Tarnow, that Benedek devoted his third report of the day.

'The whole story,' he wrote, 'is assuming a totally peculiar shape, and it seems indeed that the peasantry who were summoned to give up their old ways and revolt are fighting with all the strength of an unleashed horde against the party of nobles and notaries which is revolting against the government. According to in part unconfirmed reports the tide of the misfortune is – in my view – flowing in favour of the government.' He then gave Ferdinand a few grizzly details of events, describing it as a 'sad fortune' that the two parties, nobles and peasants, should 'be committing and enduring atrocities.' But since they insisted on slaughtering each other, the government would succeed in controlling the uprising 'all the more easily'. Finally he declared that although he would be happy to oppose the rebels 'with fury' he would limit himself to the demands of 'justice and duty'. He added: 'Polishness (*Der Polinismus*) has summoned up a great misfortune for its homeland; I hope and am convinced within me however that justice and the government will retain the advantage.'[21]

On 22 February, Benedek sent in a further report from Rzeszow with details of events in Tarnow, a report which suggests the origins of the tales of imperial blood-money.[22] According to Benedek, assemblies of nobles and their officials had been threatening peasants and Jews who might betray them. The peasants, therefore, had sent a delegation to the prefect of Rzeszow, asking him what they should do. In fact they requested that an imperial official should be sent into the countryside to advise them. The prefect of Rzeszow, on the other hand, had informed him that they did not belong to his county and that he could not spare an official. He then, in Benedek's words '*went peacefully back to sleep without having properly bade farewell or comforted those needing advice, without even having given the poor peasants and the customs officer who had made their journey during the night a small allowance.*' He concluded: '*I felt sorry for these people (1 Jew, 1 customs official and 1 peasant) and, therefore, helped them out with a 20 (florin) piece.*' (My emphases). They then went on their way. But, according to Benedek, it would be quite understandable if they had conceived the idea that it was preferable to cut down nobles than to wait in vain for advice from officials. Meanwhile,

---

19 Archduke Ferdinand Papers, Benedek to Ferdinand, Rzeszow, 21 February, 1846.
20 ibid.
21 ibid.
22 ibid.

he had heard that the streets of Tarnow were full of murdering peasants, although 'nothing has been heard of any armed noble troops.' He was therefore 'curious' to discover what was happening in Tarnow since it was 'difficult to learn the truth from so many different rumours'. He had learned from Csollich, however, that there were 200 political prisoners in the town whom bands of people were trying to free; while there were reports that 300 dead and wounded noblemen had also been brought in by the peasants. Most serious of all, however, was a rumour that the town was to be attacked on 25 February by the revolutionaries. This was a threat which Benedek could only meet by being there.

His next report was sent on 22 February from Sediszow where county officials had had to allay peasant fears.[23] There had been rumours of noblemen disguised as cavalrymen and intent on murdering them. Allaying their fears, however, had been achieved quite easily. Yet, on account of the many other rumours which abounded, Benedek had decided to march his men in files through the villages en route to Tarnow. He had wished to take local officials from Rzeszow with him but the two who had accompanied him part of the way refused to leave their county, protesting that they had no written or verbal instructions to enter Tarnow county. He, therefore, had to let them go since he 'could not force them' to accompany him. Regarding Tarnow itself, he reported:

> It seems that in Tarnow county groups of raging peasants are continuing to select new victims, for the local inn here is full of wailing women who arrive clamouring for military assistance or the intervention of the county officials. I fear that the mayor of Tarnow has not yet made serious use of the conforming influence of the Church on the masses; in my opinion, however, it is high time that the religiosity of the peasants was powerfully appealed to, because only the priesthood can make a healthy impression which will quickly spread out everywhere.[24] This is what I shall urgently demand of the mayor the moment I arrive in Tarnow, and if necessary, from the bishop also.

Indeed, he had already instructed the two officials who were returning to Rzeszow to get the clergy there to do everything possible to put a stop to 'this outbreak of fanatical peasant rage'. He himself meanwhile would 'admonish' all the peasants he met on the road to Tarnow through an officer who spoke fluent Polish. He did not believe that he would encounter any resistance from them, but if he met any who suspected him of being a revolutionary in disguise he would have to act according to circumstances. Concerning the overall situation he had not yet decided what to say to Breinl. The following comment, however, clearly reveals the way his mind was working: 'If the completely fanatical influence of the peasantry which for the moment appears to be aiding the government is allowed, not merely in Tarnow county, to go too far, it may be as difficult for us in the end to combat this wildly raging communism as any armed uprising of the revolutionary party.'

The Archduke Ferdinand, meanwhile, had been keeping Count Hardegg, president of the Court War Council (*Hofkriegsrat*) in Vienna, in touch with events. On 21 February, for example, he reported Benedek's doubts about the prospects for an armed revolt in Rzeszow.[25] More interestingly, he also reported that he had received a letter

---

23 Archduke Ferdinand Papers, Benedek to Ferdinand, Sediszow, 22 February, 1846.
24 He did not yet know how the priesthood was behaving. He would soon, however, find out.
25 Archduke Ferdinand Papers, Ferdinand to Hardegg, Lemberg, 21 February, 1846.

dated 18 February from Breinl.[26] According to this, Breinl had been approached for military assistance by the peasants of the surrounding villages. They wanted troops to protect them from the nobles and their officials who were attempting to force them to take part in an attack on Tarnow. He in turn had told them that this was impossible, but he had exhorted them to remain loyal and 'if necessary, to seize the agitators and hold them.' This advice, according to Breinl, had led to clashes on the night of the 18/19 February in which both sides had suffered casualties. The next morning, peasants had entered the town with about a hundred prisoners (including a couple of known agitators) who had been handed over to the authorities for trial. All this, according to Ferdinand, was 'fresh proof' of the good spirit of the peasants and made him think that the 'planned' uprising in Rzeszow would never take place. That same day he ordered Benedek to proceed to Bochnia after Tarnow and thence return to Rzeszow to await orders before returning to Lemberg.[27]

The next day Ferdinand had even better news for Hardegg.[28] The feared uprising in Rzeszow had 'not merely not taken place but the probability of one [had] become more and more distant.' The lack of peasant support also made one unlikely, a factor which brought the Archduke back to Breinl. 'According to the latest report of the Tarnow *Kreishauptmann*,' wrote Ferdinand, 'the anxieties of the authorities there have in no way been allayed by events. They now fear that an attempt will be made to free those arrested and urgently request more troops.' The garrison there was already 'exhausted' from duty; but more important was the need to pacify the countryside. The Archduke, as a result, had ordered a squadron of *Kaiser chevaux légers* to proceed to Tarnow from Rzeszow. Like Benedek, however, Ferdinand was beginning to have doubts about the peasants' enthusiasm. Thus, although he was pleased to report that Tarnow was not the only town where clashes had occurred at the expense of the nobility, he added: '*However, it will soon become urgently necessary to adopt measures to stop the peasants from going too far in their enthusiasm for the good cause and from using it as an excuse to settle private scores and personal hatreds – of that there is no doubt.*'(My emphasis). On the other hand, he ordered Benedek to refrain from adopting a hostile attitude towards the peasants. '*The peasantry in these areas,*' he informed him, '*are not committing excesses wantonly but as loyal subjects who seize evil-doers and kill them [only] if they encounter armed resistance – under which circumstances any harsh or violent move against them would be inappropriate or even dangerous.*' (My emphasis). It was both 'remarkable and comforting that even in remote areas the peasants [were] showing the same good spirit both in word and deed.'

Benedek arrived in Tarnow in the evening of 23 February. The following day he wrote to Ferdinand.[29] He reported that an attack on the town was 'supposed' to have been planned for the 19th, but that this had been 'suddenly frustrated' by the peasant rage which had erupted against the insurgents. This mood had indeed spread so fast that, before long, anyone even suspected of supporting the nobles and their agents had been

26 Ibid.
27 Archduke Ferdinand Papers, Ferdinand to Benedek, Lemberg, 21 February, 1846.
28 ibid, 22 February, 1846.
29 Archduke Ferdinand Papers, Benedek to Ferdinand, Tarnow, 24 February, 1846.

attacked. On 20 February, for example, 16 people had been killed in the neighbourhood of Dembicie, while 'on the 21st the fanaticism or lust for blood and booty had grown to such an extent that nearly all the nobles with estates in Tarnow county had been slaughtered' – the innocent along with the guilty. When he himself entered Dembicie, the populace had shouted 'Viva Ferdinand' *but he had gathered magistrates and peasants together and had admonished them through an interpreter.*

Back in Tarnow, Benedek had taken the opportunity to read all of Csollich's reports and become 'thoroughly acquainted with the situation' in the town. As a result, he could candidly describe,

> how circumstances [had] changed, how, for the moment, every passion [was being] given vent in the whole west of the country, how the majority of priests [were] self-proclaimed traitors, who despised religion, how the rest of them [lacked] the courage to preach to the enraged populace, how all the local political authorities [were], so to speak, in dissolution, in short how complete anarchy must prevail if many troops did not occupy the countryside.

The rebels, he wrote, had to be crushed, but it was also necessary to '*contain the bloodlust of the peasants which [had] been unleashed, which (for the moment) [was] faithful to the dynasty but which might possibly take on a different hue, unless the caring hand of the emperor [was] made powerfully visible and tangible.*' (My emphasis). But the emperor was known to the peasants only through his soldiers and officials and according to Benedek he would need another 8–10,000 infantry, 1,500 cavalry and several artillery batteries before he could restore imperial authority. Breinl in the meantime had offered him the services of 900 'reliable' peasants. Regarding the record of the *Kreishauptmann* in Tarnow, however, Benedek reported as follows:

> *This county chief who was so resolute in the days of danger and who assumed such great responsibility must as a result of the unfortunate events in these parts be dismissed by the civil authorities. I do not consider myself empowered at this point, however, to give details of my private opinion of him. That I could state only to Your Imperial Highness and under your express command.* (My emphasis).

From Tarnow, Benedek was ordered to proceed to Bochnia, where, on 24 February, he found the local administration under the prefect, Bernd, in the process of packing up and preparing to evacuate the town, along with the local garrison of 185 badly trained and equipped infantry together with six weak columns of cavalry.[30] The rebels were on their way from Cracow, and the administration and the garrison were on their way to Tarnow. Benedek's appearance then changed everything and Bernd reported to Lemberg that he was a 'rescuing angel'.[31] Pickets were posted on all sides of the town and, inside, a citizen's militia of 120–130 men was quickly improvised. By 26 February, the rebels were reported in Gdow and ready to head for Bochnia. Benedek reckoned that a battle inside the open city would mean retreat and that retreat from Bochnia would cause panic in Tarnow. Thus, without orders and on his own initiative, he decided to head towards the rebels at Gdow. This would stop the rebels building up their strength, raise morale,

30 *BNP*, p. 14.
31 ibid.

restore honour, and help keep the peasants loyal.[32] Hence 'in agreement with the capable prefect Bernd',[33] he took the offensive. Bernd, meanwhile, in proclamations to the local peasants had offered salt to any volunteers and the prospect of five florins for each insurgent brought in '*alive and well*' (my emphasis).[34] Benedek set out, however, with only 327 infantry and 114 cavalry, but on the way he was joined by 3–400 peasants armed with scythes, pikes and pitchforks. They were afraid of the rebels' rifles and kept behind the troops. When the rebels fell back on the village of Gdow itself, however, they came into their own. According to Benedek: 'The village was stormed and all houses searched one by one. Behind us the peasants slew all who were wounded or who had laid down their arms. I could save the lives of a few young lads only with difficulty, good words and money, but there was little time to deal with it.'[35] Various officers and NCOs who had taken prisoners were overwhelmed by the peasants who then murdered the captives. Of 154 who were killed in the battle, which lasted only three-quarters of an hour, half were slain by the peasants. So, too, were those found accompanying a rebel baggage train: 'most corpses of the insurgents, which were scattered around as if on a battlefield, were mutilated by the peasants in the most grizzly way.'[36] Benedek concluded therefore: 'Our so-called auxiliary troops at Gdow, that is to say the peasants, rendered no help at all, apart from murdering our prisoners and plundering, and made off gradually with the booty they had acquired.'[37] Later on, when he arrived at Wieliczka, he reported: 'And so one succeeded with the help of some money here and there to bring order to the whole, wild, excited horde and gradually in an hour and a half, to direct it out of town, without plunder or excesses taking place, although the perjured town of Wieliczka would have completely deserved a few hours of plundering.'[38] (It had welcomed the rebels a few days before). Benedek, finally, was pleased to report that all his troops had behaved honourably – the Polish ones just as well and as loyally as any of the others.[39] Eventually, Benedek, who applied for the Maria Theresa Order, was awarded the distinctly less desirable Knight's Cross of the Leopold Order.[40] The same decoration was awarded to Major Fejerváry who had commanded the garrison at Neu Sandec. He had seen the behaviour of both sides there and had taken the initiative by sending patrols under officers to arrest 150 nobles. Many, indeed, had beseeched him to do so. Once the revolt was over, he simply let them go home.[41]

How then does one evaluate the behaviour of the Austrian officers on the ground? Benedek clearly abhorred what the peasants were doing and condemned Breinl's failure

---

32 ibid, p. 27. See Benedek's report on his expedition in support of his application to be awarded the Maria Theresa Order, ibid, pp. 25–36.

33 ibid, p. 27.

34 ibid.

35 ibid, p. 30. Cf. Friedjung's comment (ibid, p. 15) that a group of younger men were saved by the cry, 'Spare these children!'

36 *BNP*, pp. 30–31.

37 *BNP*, p. 31.

38 *BNP*, p. 32.

39 *BNP*, p. 34: 'The reliability of the Galician officers and soldiers in general and those of the Nugent regiment in particular, which unfortunately was called into question even by officials here, has been splendidly vindicated [...].'

40 For this dispute and the relevant correspondence, see *BNP*, pp. 18–9, 22–41.

41 *BNP*, pp. 12–13.

to control them (or at least that is what one deduces from his report to the Archduke Ferdinand). On the other hand, when he himself was forced to rely on peasant aid, he could control them no better. Like Breinl, he too had helplessly to witness murders and he, too, found himself having to use money to bribe the murderers. He did not offer blood money, but he used what funds he had to for military aid, transport, information and law and order. This did not make him a mass murderer. Benedek merely did his best in a tragic situation, provoked by rebels who had threatened death to those who did not join them and who had brutally murdered a local mayor. Major Fejerváry may have acted more astutely in retrospect, but he was not in the middle of a battlefield. As for General Csollich, he may have been timorous, but, on the other hand, on 19 February he did not know the revolution had definitely failed. Indeed, given the inflow of rebels from Cracow after Collin's retreat from that city, there might well have been an attack on the town had Benedek not chosen to attack the rebels first. Both the garrison and the civil administration of Bochnia were, after all, in the process of evacuating Bochnia for Tarnow when Benedek arrived. And what of the mobile columns in the countryside? They might have worked, but they might not have. Benedek found it impossible with 400 men to control the peasants at Gdow. Why should Csollich's 800 have been able to control the blood lust in Tarnow county as well as in the town itself? Controlling the peasants was clearly a hit-and-miss affair when there were few troops at hand. It cannot be taken for granted, as Gill and others seem to do, that all the Austrians needed to do in 1846 in West Galicia was to send in small mobile columns, give orders and wait for law and order to be restored. It did not work like that – as Benedek and others found out.

(b) Breinl

There were a variety of actions taken by a variety of prefects in Galicia during the uprising of 1846. Breinl's in Tarnow county were the most controversial. As has been seen, the revolution broke out there earlier than originally planned. Breinl had been fore-warned about it on the night of the 18 February by a deputation of village leaders, whom he had exhorted to support the government and to seize insurgents. He had no plans to send out troops, since, like General Csollich, he wanted to keep them in the town (where his wife and children were), nor had he any plans to arrest ring-leaders, something, which he had explained would be counter-productive.[42] The result was that he was dependent on the peasants. Like Breinl, the peasants themselves were in a state of fear as a result of what Kieniewicz has called,

> miscarried attempts by individual democratically-minded landowners to approach the people, vague rumours spread in the villages of war, knights from overseas who would bring freedom to the people, or, the other way around, rumours of bloodbaths, of attacks by landlords against the people [...] the priests founded village schools and hinted at the equality of all classes: here and there conspirators repeated the words from the book entitled *The Truths about the Questions of Life*, that death awaited everyone who would not join the revolution.[43]

---

42 See below, footnote 52.
43 Quoted by Gill, *Die Polnische Revolution*, pp. 190–191.

Their only hope was the Austrian administration. In Gill's words: 'The peasant, oppressed by his landlord or tenant farmer or estate manager, with the silent approval of the government, got used to seeing the person of the *k.-k. Landrat* [imperial-royal counsellor or administrator for the area] or his officials as his protectors against the landlords.'[44] Thus the peasants depended on the government and the government was now dependent on the peasants. The peasants reacted to the revolution by arresting or attacking all landowners who supported the revolution. They did this at once by attacking the groups of rebels on the night of the 18/19 February who were making their way to Tarnow, thus frustrating the planned attack on the own. They then brought in a hundred or so prisoners and a hundred or so corpses to the prefecture in the town and for this they received monetary compensation for time, effort and travel, just as they had previously been rewarded financially for information. No questions were asked as to how the victims had been captured, wounded or slaughtered – they were rebels, after all, killed or wounded in an act of revolution – although the peasants had to sign a protocol before they were paid.[45] One officer serving in the town later recorded: 'Had he [Breinl] not publicly distributed tips to the peasants, but promised by way of regulations to make payments later, after investigations had been made, the peasants would never have reached this conclusion [i.e. that they would be paid for murder].'[46]

Breinl and Csollich, to be fair, did issue a proclamation exhorting everyone to avoid breaking the law and 'to avoid all acts of violence'.[47] Yet they faced a number of problems. First, on 18 February, the rebels had brutally murdered the pro-Austrian mayor of Pilzno, Kasper Markl, to whom the peasants had been revealing information about them. According to von Sala:

> The news of this atrocity spread like lightning from village to village, from house to house and alarmed the whole neighbourhood. Now everyone who had remained loyal to the government and had shown himself opposed to the uprising, knew what to expect from the insurrection, if this should win the upper hand. If the peasants had trembled out of fear before the outbreak of the revolution lest they should be compelled by their landlords either to join it or be murdered, they now trembled after they had defeated the attack on Tarnow and experienced Markl's grisly murder, before the revenge of those insurgents who had been prevented from reaching their assembly points either by snowfalls or by the threatening attitude of the country folk or who had escaped.[48]

Thus, 'the peasants now began their pursuit in earnest'[49] motivated by a desire to kill off all the surviving landlords who might exact a grisly revenge on them. Besides, as Gill himself concedes, the booty that peasants, who were among the poorest in Europe, could expect to gain from plundering the estates – furniture, clothes, jewellery, linen, grain, horses, wine and so forth – was hugely more rewarding to them economically that

---

44 Gill, *Die Polnische Revolution*, p.191.
45 ibid, p. 206.
46 ibid.
47 Gill, *Die Polnische Revolution*, p. 204, ft. 40, quoting M. von Sala's *Geschichte des polnischen Aufstandes vom Jahre 1846 in Galizien*, Vienna, 1867, p. 291.
48 Von Sala, pp. 193–194, quoted by Gill, *Die Polnische Revolution*, p.198.
49 Von Sala, p.194, quoted in Gill, *Die Polnische Revolution*, p. 198.

Breinl's meagre tips.[50] And in any case, they hated the landlords. In this respect, the Polish Marxist historiographical tradition is correct: the peasant revolt was spontaneous.

Breinl's position was exactly the same as that of the peasants in one respect. He feared that the prisoners he held in Tarnow would make it the subject of a revenge attack. Moreover, Collin's retreat from Cracow on 23 February enabled an attack to come from that direction. On 20 February, therefore, he reported to Lemberg: 'The rebels will surely mount a stronger attack, since it will be a matter of freeing some hundreds of their own people.'[51] One day later he wrote: 'All measures are failing since the rebels do not intend to give up their plan of taking Tarnow as their main objective at any price.'[52] A day after that, he confirmed: 'Everyone in the countryside is trying to get here, many with evil intentions [...]. One is confronted on all sides by treason, everyone belonging to the nobility is against us.'[53] He simply had no alternative from his point of view but to rely on the peasants until military assistance arrived. And he used his funds to pay peasants instead of troops. If some noble rebels got killed in battle, that was hard luck, but it was a risk they took by committing treason. As the prefect of Bochnia was to put it, 'There is also no doubt that the dead and wounded brought their own fate on themselves by insubordination.'[54]

Breinl, however, has been accused (along with his deputy Count Lazansky) of lionizing Jacob Szela, the most notorious of the peasant leaders in 1846.[55] The prefect of Jasło accused him in a report of 22 February of leading his followers from Tarnow into his county and plundering fourteen estates in an act of 'unexampled vandalism.'[56] Certainly Szela had led, organized, controlled, and commanded many of the plundering bands in Tarnow in 1846. He had helped divide up the booty. He himself had taken part in many murders, most notoriously that of the Bogusz family, with whom he had a long-standing dispute. (He had told the weeping women on the estate, 'There's no need for you to feel sorry for the Bogusz clan, they have to die and we'll divide among ourselves what they owned and we'll be the better of it.')[57] On that occasion, it is estimated that between fourteen and twenty-two males died, although the family, albeit anti-Austrian, had not supported the uprising. Szela himself had previously been accused of inciting revolution and committing grievous bodily harm. He certainly advocated dividing up the estates among the peasants.

Did Breinl conspire with him? Since Szela had for thirty years been the official representative of two local villages (Smarzowa and Siedliska) involved in official disputes with the Bogusz family over labour services, he probably would have visited the prefecture regularly. He may well have had conversations with Breinl, as he later confessed, and the two almost certainly knew each other. But what were their conversations about?

---

50 ibid, p. 206.
51 ibid, p. 204.
52 ibid.
53 ibid.
54 ibid, p. 202.
55 On Szela, see Gill, *Die Polnische Revolution*, pp. 226–231.
56 ibid, p. 226.
57 ibid, p. 230, ft.112.

That we don't know. Certainly, according to Gill, Szela neither brought in corpses or prisoners, nor did he receive any compensation from Breinl.[58]

According to Kieniewicz, Breinl wrote in a report of 1 March:

> I have to strengthen the intentions of the citizens in every way possible to fight for the government and for public order. On the other hand, I have to use force against excesses and work against violations of the law through instruction, exhortation and confidential talks. A single, careless word could bring the greatest misfortune, namely that the peasants would turn against the government, in which case one could not see the government surviving in this country [...].[59]

Breinl was no hero, but given the circumstances in which he found himself, it is difficult to believe that he had many other options than to do what he did. Certainly, the ones that existed were neither easy nor bound to work. He certainly paid money to the peasants, but there is no evidence – however the peasants interpreted his actions –that he deliberately paid them to commit atrocities. This man was frightened almost out of his wits by what was going on, but there is no evidence to prove that he encouraged mass murder to save his skin.

Altogether, therefore, Austria can be cleared of organizing the 'Galician Horrors' of 1846.

---

58 ibid, p. 231.
59 Quoted by Gill, *Die Polnische Revolution*, p. 242.

'Revolutionary' Forces in a 'Traditional' Society:
The Place of the Peasantry in 1848

Robert Gray

The Revolution of 1848 resulted in the emancipation of the peasantry and the end to the feudal system of landownership in Hungary. Much can be made of the April Laws' significance in respect of Hungary's rebirth and modernization, and of their importance in establishing agrarian capitalism in the country. But how did the peasants themselves react to their new-found freedom? Did the national and political revolution lead to a revolution in the villages and in what was still an overwhelmingly traditional peasant society?

Of one thing we can be relatively certain, and it seems a useful point of departure for assessing the revolutionary potential of the peasantry in 1848. The fear of a peasant uprising played strongly on the minds of the nobility and made the issue of land reform one of the utmost urgency. Two violent jacqueries gave these fears weight: the cholera revolt of 1831 and the Galician uprising in 1846. Of these, the revolt of 1831 was of lesser significance, dying out with the epidemic itself and more memorable for the harsh reprisals that followed its suppression. Nevertheless, the two explosions yielded some important lessons for the Hungarian nobility. The 1846 uprising in particular became the disguised subject of Eötvös's novel, *Hungary in 1514*, which was set against the background of the Dózsa rebellion and first published in 1847. Eötvös used the novel to promote his own ideas, stressing the need for emancipation to be accompanied by education and enlightenment lest all too sudden freedom cause the peasantry to revolt once more. As he subsequently advocated in his works on the nationality question, on educational reform, and in his *Dominant Ideas of the Nineteenth Century*, Eötvös recognized the need to acknowledge a community's autonomy in matters of religion and language – important issues that had been ignored in the run-up to the 1846 uprising in Galicia.[1] On that occasion, the peasants had eschewed national loyalties and turned what had meant to be an anti-Habsburg rebellion into a bloody class-war directed against their lords. The lesson for Hungary was clear to Eötvös and to many others: if the peasants were to be won over to the cause of liberalism and the nation, their grievances had to be met first. The political consequences of the revolt in Galicia on Hungarian politics were

---

1   The condition of the Polish and Ruthenian peasants in Galicia differed, of course, from those obtaining in Hungary, but see Edit Fél and Tamás Hofer, *Proper Peasants: Traditional Life in a Hungarian Village*, Chicago, 1963, pp. 313–41, and Anthony Komjáthy, 'Hungarian *Jobbágyság* in the Fifteenth Century', *East European Quarterly*, 10, 1976, 1, pp. 75–111.

considerable. It forced the reformers to paper over their differences and establish the Unified Opposition as a party in 1847. This move elevated Kossuth, who advocated more radical policies than others, to leadership.

On the eve of the revolution it appeared that events were overtaking the nobility's attempts at gradual reform which had begun with the revised Urbarium of 1836. In March 1848 a rumour spread that a peasant army was marching on Pozsony to demand emancipation. Although the rumour proved false – it was merely peasants gathering to attend a fair – the fear was enough to ensure that the subsequent laws were more radical than the majority of the nobility wished.[2] Through Laws IX and XI of 1848 the diet abolished all urbarial obligations and the patrimonial authority of the landlord. Thus the *robot*, the tithe and all other dues payable to the lord were suppressed with the promise that the state would cover the cost of emancipation. This freed some nine million peasants in Hungary and Croatia from the feudal obligations owed under the terms of the Urbarium. But this was to be the limit of the April Laws. They did not, as yet, guarantee the peasantry ownership of their plot or *sessio*. Nor were the peasants to receive legal equality as part of their 'emancipation'.[3] In addition to all this, by restricting the laws to urbarial ('rustical') land almost a quarter of peasant-farmed land was left unaffected. The laws did not impact upon those peasants farming under leasehold arrangements their lords' private or dominical land, and their numbers had been increased dramatically from the mid-eighteenth century. It is almost certain, therefore, that many peasants – especially those farming the lords' dominical lands – must have expected more from emancipation than was actually granted. In view of this it is perhaps surprising that these peasants did not react with violence and rebellion. Much like the phantom peasant army, the events of 1848 would show that the threat of a peasant jacquerie and of a repetition of the Galician nightmare, no matter how strongly it played on the minds of the nobility, was not to be realized.

Before 1848 the Hungarian peasantry had means besides violence to redress any grievances against their lords. Through legal suits, non-compliance with landlords and their officials or, in some instances, pleading blind ignorance, many peasants had been able to stand up for their rights. Particularly after the first wave of urbarial reform in the 1830s and 1840s, many peasant villages opened suits against their lords whom they believed were not following the prescripts of the new laws. In 1837 the villagers of Poroszló in Heves county sent a petition to the county government complaining that their landlord continued to demand *robot* service despite their (incorrect) belief that it had been abolished. Seven other villages in Heves county submitted similar petitions in the first months of 1837.[4] At the town of Szentes in Csongrád county the peasantry resorted

---

2   Gábor Pajkossy, 'Kossuth and the Emancipation of the Serfs', in László Péter, Martyn Rady and Peter Sherwood (eds.), *'Lajos Kossuth Sent Word ... ': Papers Delivered on the Occasion of the Bicentenary of Kossuth's Birth*, London, 2003, p. 78–79. See also János Varga, *A jobbágyfelszabadítás kivívása 1848-ban*, Budapest, 1971, pp. 69–76.

3   László Péter, 'The Aristocracy, the Gentry and Their Parliamentary Tradition in Nineteenth-Century Hungary', *Slavonic and East European Review*, 70, 1992, 1, pp. 77–110 (pp. 82–84). It was not until Law LIII of 1871 that the peasants became true owners of their plots, and even this remained restricted to what had been urbarial land.

4   Imre Szántó, 'Parasztmozgalmok Heves és Külső-Szolnok megyében a 19. század első felében', in *Az egri pedagógiaia főiskola füzetek*, no. 16, 1955, pp. 320–347 (pp. 339–342).

to strikes in an attempt to force their landlord to consider the terms of a redemption contract and discuss the separation of pasture. In the summers of 1834 and 1835 the peasants refused to perform their *robot* obligation, leaving much of their lords' crops unharvested and the tithe uncollected.[5] Elsewhere a peasant could simply deny the performance of *robot* and other dues by claiming he believed it to be the local custom for payment to be made in cash, as was the case for one Mihály Petraj of Békés county. In his defence he pleaded that had he known otherwise he would not have taken on the plot.[6]

As these few examples show, the peasantry could resort to established means of protest prior to 1848 and it was to these that they turned to express their grievances in the early stages of the revolution. Of greatest concern to the peasantry was their access to land – to pasture, woodland, and, most importantly, plough-land. As noted above, a quarter of all land that the peasants had farmed before 1848 was open to dispute. In the course of 1848 many peasants sought the opportunity to submit or re-submit suits relating to such land. In Győr county, the peasants of Öttevénysziget and Győrság both lodged petitions to prove that their land was urbarial rather than dominical land which was held under contract and thus exempted from emancipation.[7] At Halogyközség in Vas county the peasants re-opened a dispute over the extent of urbarial pasture that they had first filed in 1846.[8] In other places some peasants took the opportunity of the April Laws to resolve such disputes for themselves, only occasionally resorting to minor acts of violence. For example, if they felt they were being deprived of pasture, they might drive their cattle onto the private lands of the lord – as was the case in Kiskomárom in Zala county, where troops had to be sent in to separate the parties. In other instances, peasants attacked the landlords' bailiffs, crops and property.[9] Győr county also had to bring in troops to restore order at Ravazd where the peasants had devastated the manorial forests and driven the lord's cattle from the communal pasture.[10] This issue of access had also been central to the cholera revolt in the previous decade. Rumours had then circulated that landowners were fuelling the epidemic as a chance to rid themselves of pesky tenants and to convert the peasants' plough-land to (the now more profitable) pasture.[11] It may be that such cases of unrest had occurred sporadically for years, and it certainly seems that some peasants took the opportunity to voice long-held grievances in the chaos and more sympathetic atmosphere of 1848. Elsewhere, moreover, acts of violence were plainly ritualized and probably intended to force a long-standing dispute to law.

Other grievances of the peasantry were expressed in a similar manner and again conformed to the pre-1848 methods. Upon hearing of their emancipation, groups of peasants across Hungary immediately downed tools and returned home, neglecting all

---

5 László Barta, *A szentesi örökváltság*, Szentes, 1966, pp. 43–44.
6 Pál Maday, *Szarvas története*, Szarvas, 1962, p. 62.
7 Péter Bálazs, 'Győr megyei parasztmozgalomnak 1848-ban', in *Arrabona*, 4, 1962, pp. 171–191, pp. 174–177.
8 Hungarian National Archive, P1313 Batthyány családi leveltár: úrbéri iratok, cs. 205: 3–5, 26.
9 Emil Simonffy, *A polgári földtulajdon kialakulása és a birtokmegoszlás Délnyugat-Dunántúlon*, Zalaegerszeg, 2002, pp. 17–22.
10 Balázs, 'Győr megyei parasztmozgalomnak', pp. 178–180.
11 István Deák, *The Lawful Revolution: Lajos Kossuth and the Hungarians, 1848–1849*, New York, 1979, pp. 21–2.

future *robot* duties.[12] In Zala county, peasants refused to pay the vineyard tithe; others openly violated the nobles' monopolies on brewing, access to woodland and hunting rights (all of these issues would be addressed, to a greater or lesser degree, by the government in 1849).[13] Similarly, peasants at Ladomér and Újfalu in Győr county refused to perform labour service for their parsons, while at Győrság the peasants prevented the landlord's official from making an assessment of the vineyard tithe.[14] It is significant, however, that such actions were, on the whole, peaceful and that they generally amounted to no more than non-compliance with landlords and officials. If peasants had eventually to concede that not all dues were abolished by the April Laws, they accepted revision of the same with an equal measure of good grace.

It should be stressed that violence between peasant and lord was rare in 1848, isolated and easily put down, either through the appearance of a county official (most often the deputy sheriff or *alispán*) or, as a last resort, troops. More usually, the peasants placed their faith in official means, filing petitions or suits against their lords, or coming to an agreement with the lord themselves. There is even an example where the peasants granted the lord as much pasture as he had reasonable need for – a sign of remarkably good relations between 'oppressor' and 'oppressed'.[15]

This is only a very brief overview of the peasants' reaction to the April Laws, yet it may shed some light on what they hoped for from their 'liberation'. The answer to what they wanted is relatively easy to answer, and may indeed seem obvious – they desired all the land they had hitherto made use of, or had previously made use of, to be theirs by right. When the April Laws did not grant this – for much of the land that the peasants had previously farmed comprised leaseholds on the lord's private or dominical property – the peasants simply took it for themselves. A similar situation developed with feudal dues. As soon as the *robot* was abolished, peasants (perhaps misunderstanding the laws, or even deliberately misinterpreting them to their own advantage) simply stopped performing all other duties. Thus it would seem relatively clear that for many peasants their 'liberation' meant the freedom to farm such land as they had always farmed and to do so without interference from, or obligations to, their lords.

It was the terms of access to land, and exactly what should be granted to the peasantry that remained the most problematic issue, both during 1848–49 and subsequently. Indeed, these issues were not to be fully resolved until 1896, when the issue of redemption of dues owed by cottars (landless peasants) living on their lords' private estates was finally addressed.[16] What land rightly 'belonged' to the peasantry and what should remain in the hands of the lords was never clear cut. In the early 1840s, it was believed by the nobility that only urbarial land (as stipulated by the Urbarium of 1767), over which the peasants enjoyed customary rights and on which they held hereditary tenures, would pass into the hands of the peasants after

12 Fél and Hofer, *Proper Peasants*, p. 32; Simonffy, *A polgári földtulajdon*, pp. 14–15.
13 Simonffy, *A polgári földtulajdon*, pp. 14–21, Győző Ember, *Iratok az 1848-i Magyarországi parasztmoz-galmok történetéhez*, Budapest, 1951, pp. 53–71.
14 Balázs, 'Győr megyei parasztmozgalomnak', pp. 182–183.
15 Simonffy, *A polgári földtulajdon*, pp. 22–3.
16 For the most detailed account of the legislation in 1848 and after, see István Orosz, 'Peasant Emancipation and After-effects' in Péter Gunst (ed.), *Hungarian Agrarian Society from the Emancipation of the Serfs (1848) to the Re-Privatization of Land (1998)*, New York, 1998, pp. 53–98.

emancipation.[17] This could not, however, meet the expectations of the peasantry, for they claimed use of more land than this and believed that they held customary rights to land in addition to what was defined as urbarial. For example, the Urbarium did not cover the use of cleared land, woodland, pasture and vineyards, nor those parts of the landlord's dominical land which the peasants farmed by separate leasehold arrangements. Sticking rigidly to the stipulations of the Urbarium, the lords might now challenge these claims, or at least seek to block them. The April Laws served to reinforce the sharp distinction between urbarial and non-urbarial land, as it was only the urbarial land that was emancipated – in the words of the law, all land 'which cannot be taken from the serf in an estate settlement or through regulations.'[18] All land was deemed to belong to the peasant if the lord could not produce written evidence that the tenancy was precarious and expired after a set time (which left therefore dominical land held under leasehold arrangements safely his own). Realizing the implications of this, peasants often sought to destroy the 'hated documents' and any such additional evidence that might have reduced the amount of land to which they were entitled. Given that leasehold tenancies were often passed from generation to generation, and renewed with little fuss, it is unsurprising that many peasants should have conceived their claim to this land to be as good in custom as it was to the plots which they farmed by hereditary right.

Even before 1848 the dominical peasants' land tenure was plagued by insecurity as landlords might interpret leasehold clauses in contrary fashion or refuse to renew leases upon expiry. The April Laws had suggested that this situation was about to change. Even if the cottars were not to be granted land outside the small cottage plot that they had previously farmed, a law of April 1849 granted them ownership of their home and garden and stipulated their right to own such land as was needed to support themselves and their families.[19] This was a vast improvement to their terms of their tenure, providing a security they had not known before, and enshrining their rights to the land in statute for the first time. This gain may have been enough to deter any attempts to demand more, for fear that it might be revoked (as it was after the fall of the revolution), or in the hope that further reforms might follow.

It is also possible that the majority of peasants were in no bad state before 1848, and thus that they saw no great benefit in challenging the rural status quo. If one considers certain aspects of the peasantry's lifestyle, such an attitude does not seem too unlikely. For example, we can look at the performance of the *robot*, so often described as the greatest burden to fall upon the peasantry. In the first case, it was regulated by the Urbarium in such a way that it should not be a heavy burden.[20] Rather than the terms of the Urbarium being circumvented by unscrupulous landlords, it instead appears that in many cases the stipulations of the Urbarium were followed almost exactly. Indeed some

17 Pajkossy, 'Kossuth and Emancipation', pp. 74–75.
18 Orosz, 'Peasant Emancipation', p. 65. The legal formulation given here presupposes the anterior rights of custom.
19 Orosz, 'Peasant Emancipation', pp. 71–73.
20 As one observer put it, Maria Theresa's Urbarium of 1767 proved 'no hard contract for the peasants': Robert Townson, *Travels in Hungary with a Short Account of Vienna in the Year 1793*, London, 1797, p. 131.

landlords had been able to increase *robot* service as it was rare for the full quota to be demanded.[21] Secondly, ways of reducing the burden of *robot* labour were manifold. Peasants were able to send their weakest animals, oldest tools, and any member of the family (or a hired hand if they could afford it) to perform this duty. And, of course, with the amount of *robot* stipulated by time rather than task, it was often performed in a slovenly manner – a common enough cause of complaint among the nobility. There was, then, little reason (except for the time it took away from working his own land) for *robot* to become a strong source of complaint for the peasant beyond its inherent injustice. Given the ineffectiveness of *robot* labour, it was unlikely that lords might obtain any great benefit from demanding more than the legal limit. Indeed, it was the lord rather than the peasant who was most hurt by the system of *robot* labour, for it deprived him of cash-rents, and thus not surprising that the impulse for reform came from above. Moreover, as has been stated above, the relative peace of the Hungarian countryside prior to 1848 speaks of content and comfort, not desperation and poverty: a picture reinforced by the accounts of travellers.[22] A similar portrait is painted by one of the most detailed accounts of the lives of the cottagers before 1848. In *People of the Puszta*, Illyés recounted the reminiscences of his grandfather, a former cottar, who looked back on the period before 1848 as one of happiness and plenty when the labourers' wives took lunch out to their menfolk 'in wooden bowls so immense they could scarcely keep their heads upright under their weight.' It was a time when no peasant was truly poor and even 'the beggars rode in carts.'[23]

Beyond all this, we may observe peasants across the world are notoriously hostile to changes in farming methods and lifestyle, and that the peasants of Hungary were no different. Both Miklós Wesselényi and István Széchenyi, for example, recorded problems when they tried to introduce new crops, machinery or field systems onto their estates. The former could find no peasants willing to work a new threshing machine, for it was believed to be the work of the devil. When Széchenyi wished to consolidate his dominical land so as to allow more intensive farming methods, he complained to John Paget that he had had to sacrifice much of his best land so that the peasants would agree to adjust their holdings. Much of this had to do with the peasantry's distrust of authority since, as Széchenyi himself admitted, they believed the landlord's interest to be constantly at odds with their own.[24] Moreover, the peasants were unwilling to experiment when innovation was perceived to threaten their subsistence. Such was the case in the village of Atány in Eger county after the reforms of 1848. Rather than consolidate their holdings when the opportunity arose, the majority of peasants preferred to maintain their land in strips and to stick with the safe, tried-and-tested method of three-crop rotation. This had as much to do with maintaining the village community as farming

21 Gyula Spira, 'Parasztsors Pest megyében a jobbágyfelszabadítás a forradalom külszőbén', in *Pest megye múltjából. Tanulmányok*, eds Ferenc Keleti, Ernő Lakatos and László Makkai, Budapest, 1965, pp. 204–05; Imre Wellmann, *A gödöllői Grassalkovich-uradalom gazdálkodása különös tekintettel az 1770–1815 esztendőkre*, Budapest, 1933, pp. 112–3.
22 See the various descriptions in Townson, *Travels*, pp. 106–31; John Paget, *Hungary and Transylvania, With Remarks on Their Condition, Social, Political and Economical*, London, 1839, vol 1, pp. 282–316; and A.J. Patterson, *The Magyars: Their Country and Institutions*, London, 1869, vol 1, pp. 159–60, 332–3.
23 Illyés, *People of the Puszta*, London, 1971, pp. 55–7.
24 Paget, *Hungary and Transylvania*, vol 1, pp. 282, 303.

methods, for it protected the importance of the village council which traditionally laid down how the fields should be rotated, and allowed for the sense of social cohesion engendered by farming alongside one's neighbour. As there was, as yet, little alternative to life outside the village for the peasant, it was important to maintain the entire established spectrum of village life. On the other hand, peasants would readily accept any change when the potential benefits were obvious. After the law of 1836 allowing for the separation of pastures was passed, the peasants of Atány immediately filed a suit to enact it, for their lord was dominating the communal pasture with a large flock of sheep.[25] The 'grab for land' that characterized much of 1848 may be viewed in a similar light. The peasants used the April Laws as an opportunity to improve their wealth the best way they knew how: by taking more land.

Many of the nobility who were present when the April Laws were passed believed that by granting the peasants ownership of urbarial land and freedom from their obligations to their lords they could stave off the threat of a violent 'revolution from below'. But far from meeting the demands of the peasantry, the April Laws left many issues unresolved and many peasants dissatisfied with the results. As I have sought to show, contrary to the fears of the nobility, this did not provide fuel for a peasant jacquerie. Indeed the threat of peasant violence appeared to be no more than noble paranoia. Rather than turn on their lords the peasants largely put their faith in the legal process and in peaceful means of protest that they had made use of in the time before 1848. For the most part the peasants accepted the limits of the reforms and, when the revolution was threatened by the invasion of Hungary with Habsburg troops, they chose to side with their former landlords in defence of the April Laws. Finally the attitude of most of the peasantry was not likely to spark a major rebellion. Many peasants, particularly those in a position to lead their fellows in revolt, were able to subsist comfortably – so often the limits of peasant ambitions – and had no great desire to challenge the status quo. These peasants did take the opportunity of 1848 to voice their grievances but they did so in a manner they had used before, and resort to violence was rare. Thus the nationalist revolution of 1848 did not become a class revolution in the countryside.

---

25 Fél and Hofer, *Proper Peasants*, pp. 46–7, 50–1.

Deserters or Freedom Fighters? A Hungarian Hussar Squadron in 1848

Róbert Hermann

The 1848–49 Revolution and War of Independence saw one of the most serious crises in the imperial army's efforts to preserve the unity of the Habsburg Empire. This crisis differed, however, from the wars fought against Prussia in the eighteenth century and those against the French Revolution and Napoleon. On this occasion, the army did not have to pit itself against a more powerful or better-led army from without; the danger of disintegration came from within. Until the Empire's collapse in 1918, 1848–49 was the only occasion when the army split into two (or, if Northern Italy is included, into three) parts on ethnic grounds, and the rank and file took, where it could, the side of its own national government. The situation was less the case in the multi-national officer core, if only because even in supposedly 'mono-ethnic' units it was not unusual to find the higher ranks composed of men drawn from eight or more different nationality groups. In the case of the officers, allegiance to the monarch and the unity of the empire often proved stronger than national feeling.[1]

It was accepted practice in the imperial army that soldiers stationed in a particular country or province should not be in units raised from that country or province. Nevertheless, in the spring of 1848, a little over half of the troops in the infantry regiments that included Hungarians and Transylvanians, and one-third of the hussars (cavalry) were stationed on home territory. The Hungarian government strove to have alien regiments moved out of the country and sought to have Hungarians brought home.[2]

Negotiations on these matters were still under way when, at the end of May/beginning of June 1848, astonishing news reached first Budapest, then Vienna: a squadron of the Sixth Hussars stationed at Mariampol (Mariupol, in present-day Ukraine) in Galicia had deserted and, after a day's march, reached Hungarian soil. This was an event unparalleled in the history of the imperial army. The desertion placed the Hungarian government in an awkward position, for public opinion supported the deserting hussars,

---

1   See István Deák, 'Where Loyalty and Where Rebellion? The Dilemma of the Habsburg Army Officers in 1848–1849', in Béla K. Király (ed.), *East European Society and War in the Era of Revolution, 1775–1856*, Boulder and New York, 1984, pp. 393–418.
2   See Zoltán Barcy, 'The Army of the 1848–1849 Hungarian War of Independence' in Király (ed.), *East European Society and War*, pp. 440–6; László Bencze, 'The Military System of the Habsburg Empire and the Hungarian Units of the Army on the Eve of the Revolution', in Gábor Bona (ed.), *The Hungarian Revolution and War of Independence, 1848–1849: A Military History*, New York, 1999, pp. 25–6.

but at the same time the government could not turn a blind eye to desertion, one of the gravest of military offences.[3]

The case did, however, help to accelerate the exchange of units. After the autumn of 1848 the possibility of an authorized return to the motherland came to an end, so the hussars came home in groups or even one at a time. The desertion of the hussars was also unparalleled in another sense: we do not know of any similar desertion taking place among, for instance, the Italian cavalry stationed elsewhere in the empire.

The desertion of these hussars differs, however, in many respects from later ones. For one thing, they did not rush home to defend a country at war, but one that was at peace. For another, the desertion took place not at the request of the Hungarian government but as the result of a message on an anonymous handbill. Finally, the desertion was planned by the rank and file, who not only failed to inform their officers, but even kept the junior ranks (sergeants, corporals, lance-corporals) in the dark. In contemporary terms, this was a spontaneous 'people's' initiative.

The case is also instructive in that its detailed investigation may perhaps enable us to understand the driving force behind those unsophisticated participants in the Hungarian War of Independence who, from the summer or autumn of 1848 onwards, were willing for several months to put their lives at risk for the abstract ideals of motherland, freedom and independence. What was it that persuaded peasant lads, serving far from home and untouched by the blessings of the end of serfdom, to challenge military discipline and overcome the subservience that had been literally beaten into them, to desert and even to risk serious punishment?

Before being ordered to Mariampol the squadron had spent some eight weeks in Stanislau (Stanislaw/Stanislawów, now Ivano-Frankivsk, Ukraine), where a local dignitary's night of revelry resulted in the summoning of an imperial infantry unit (raised in Galicia but consisting of Ukrainian rank and file) to restore order, in the course of which some soldiers shot dead a young Polish civilian. Since the hussars were on good terms with the Poles, several of them were present at the young man's funeral. The funeral was also attended by the captain of the squadron, János Lenkey.[4] As the coffin was borne in turn on the shoulders of 'all estates and orders', some citizens persuaded the hussars to act as pall-bearers for a while. When this happened, it was noticed by Lenkey, who intervened and forbade this as being tantamount to a demonstration.

---

3 On the desertion of Lenkey's squadron, see István Rédvay, *Huszáraink hazaterése 1848/49-ben*, Budapest, 1941, pp. 50–60; Benkő Samu, 'A história és a vers. Lenkei százada', in *Haladás és megmaradás. Művelődéstörténeti tanulmányok*, Budapest, 1979, pp. 514–30; Ildikó Rosonczy. 'Adalékok Lenkey huszárszázadának hazateréséhez', *Folia Historica*, 7, 1979, pp. 141–63; Aladár Urbán, 'értesitve valánk a Hazátul, hogy siessük védelmére...* Lenkey századának hazaterése 1848-ban', *Hadtörténelmi Közlemények*, 1992, no 3, pp. 3–36. Our study relies on these works as also on the investigation of the squadron in the Austrian Military Archive (Österreichisches Staatsarchiv, Kriegsarchiv), Alte Feldakten, Karton 1970 Sonderbestand. Generalkommando in Ungarn 1844–1848. Presidential Acts of the Generalkommando in Buda 1848. Nos 431, 447, 454, 483; ibid, Karton 1971. Sonderbestand. Akten des aufgelösten 1. Kavalleriekorps, 2. Armeekorps, 10. Armeekorps, 11. Armeekorps, Feldgenie-Direktion und Division-Ottinger (*Recte*: The Documents of the Generalkommando in Buda, 1848) P. 83/1. 5471 (these documents have not hitherto been consulted by historians).

4 On Lenkey, see T. László Ágoston, 'Három ismeretlen Lenkey-levél', *Honismeret*, 1983, no 5, pp. 31–5; Gábor Merényi-Metzger, 'A tizenhatodik aradi vértanú. Lenkey János tábornok emlékezete', *Hadtörténelmi Közlemények*, 1994, no 3, pp. 88–120.

When the incident became known, Lenkey was given six days in gaol for failing to prevent the hussars from participating in the funeral. The hussars also heard that Lenkey would not be returning to the squadron. The squadron itself was reprimanded in a brigade order for its behaviour, which stated that its members were not trustworthy as they had been consorting with Poles. The order allegedly also stated that should the squadron have to take action against the Poles, it was thought unlikely that it would use arms against them. Although the brigade commander, Major Mihály Répásy,[5] who read out the order, declared that he did not himself believe the hussars would take the side of the Poles, the rank and file were unhappy and annoyed not only at the reprimand and the rapid transfer to Mariampol, but also because of the jeering they had to endure from the squadron replacing them, and the news of the alleged departure of Lenkey. The reproof was also considered especially unjust because, although they were on good terms with the Poles, they were by no means sympathetic to their cause and would not have allowed them to try to persuade them from their duties.

Two corporals and two common soldiers from the squadron volunteered for interrogation by Captain Schimpf, who had taken over command of the squadron from Lenkey. They requested information as to what had happened to Lenkey and why they had been accused of siding with the Poles. To the first question, they received the response that it was none of their business and Lenkey could look after himself. To the second, the answer came that it was difficult to do anything about the matter because the news was already all over Stanislau. The annoyance of the squadron was intensified by the fact that in Mariampol they had been quartered in a field-encampment with irregular food supplies.

On 26 May, one of the common soldiers received a letter containing two handbills in Hungarian. These were headed by the first stanza of Sándor Petőfi's *National Song*. The handbill claimed that Hungary's hard-won constitution and freedom had brought it many enemies and that Hungary was in great danger. The handbill called upon all soldiers stationed outside Hungary (who, it claimed, were being deliberately prevented from returning) to go home and defend the motherland. The handbill urged the soldiers to persuade their Hungarian officers to do likewise and, if they would not do so voluntarily, to bring them back by force. Foreign officers should be allowed to flee.[6]

The soldier happened to be on the street when he read the handbill. He met a captain coming from the opposite direction who took one from him. The soldier intended to give the other copy to Lieutenant Pompeius Fiáth, but he did not find Fiáth at home and so proceeded to the encampment. There his fellow-soldiers asked him what was up, whereupon he showed them the handbill. Someone took it from him and read it out; meanwhile others approached and also had it read to them. They were all very much taken with its contents and wanted to be useful and helpful to their motherland.

---

5 Répásy commanded two squadrons, hence the designation 'division'. On Répásy, see now Gyula Kedves, *Répásy Mihály. A szabadságharc huszártábornoka*, Kemecse, 2007.

6 The original text of the handbill has not survived except in a German translation, but has been retranslated into Hungarian in Ildikó Rosonczy, 'A Lenkey kapitány százada megmuttata az utat. Dokumentok', in (eds) Sándor Csoóri and Sándor Sára, *80 huszár. Csoóri Sándor és Sára Sándor filmje. Ötlettől a filmig*, Budapest, 1980, pp. 47–9.

One soldier reported the handbill to Lieutenant Fiáth who sent two NCOs to retrieve the documents. They did so. Fiáth read it and, on 28 May, in the camp, in front of all the soldiers, tore both copies of the handbill into shreds saying that what they contained was not to be believed.

On Sunday, 28 May, the majority of the squadron's rank and file went to the Dniester to bathe. There they once more spoke of the summons and the needs of the country, and they all resolved to go to Hungary to assist the motherland in its time of need. They swore on the river bank that they would not abandon each other, or their motherland, even should it cost them their last drop of blood. They decided to set off at ten o' clock in the evening and to try to persuade the officers and junior ranks of Hungarian nationality. If they proved unamenable, they were to be taken by force. The soldiers then all returned to the camp and made preparations for their departure. As the junior officers returned in the evening, they were taken one at a time and informed that they should come with them and were to be kept under guard until later that night.

The resolve of the rank and file was communicated to one of the corporals, who rode off to Stanislau to report the matter. He met on the way an officer, Second Lieutenant Orsich, who happened to be travelling from Stanislau to Mariampol. The corporal reported the matter to him and continued with him to Stanislau, where they jointly reported to Major Répásy. Répásy accordingly went with Lenkey (who happened to be in his squadron) to General Kalliány. Kalliány's first thought was to send after them the squadron of hussars stationed in Stanislau, but since the deserters had quite a lead and because he feared that those sent in pursuit might be persuaded to join them, he decided instead to send Lenkey after them; perhaps their much-loved commander would be able to change their minds. Lenkey was amenable and was therefore entrusted by Kalliány with this task.

Meanwhile in Mariampol, another soldier had sought out Lieutenant Fiáth and Captain Schimpf in a restaurant and explained to them that the rank and file were saddling up and preparing to leave. Fiáth went to the encampment but was put under guard, despite his plea that they should desist from their intention or at least let him go. Schimpf sent a messenger to the divisional headquarters in Stanislau, and then went to the encampment himself. Here he tried to dissuade the hussars from their intention, but failed. (Schimpf was not detained, as he was not Hungarian).

The squadron proceeded to cross the Dniester with Fiáth and the junior officers still under guard. They met Captain Lenkey coming the other way and immediately surrounded his coach. Allegedly one hussar turned his rifle on him, while the others shouted that they were willing to lay down their lives. All he had to do was join them, because the motherland was in danger. Lenkey tried to talk them out of their intention, but in vain. Henceforth, they treated him and Lieutenant Fiáth as prisoners and marched them under armed guard across the town of Nadwórna (Nadvirna, Nadvornaya, now Ukraine). They reached the Hungarian border on 29 May. Here Lenkey once again tried to persuade them to return to Galicia, but in vain. Before they reached Kőrösmező (now Yasinya, Ukraine), two hussars called upon Lenkey to take over command and he accordingly did so. Later, under examination, he claimed that he wanted to prevent disorder among the troops and thought he could thus do sterling service for public order and security. Of the squadron's complement of 196, a total of 133 soldiers returned to Hungary.

Lenkey notified the administration of Máramaros County and the Hungarian government of their arrival. The matter was discussed by the government on 3 June: it was decided to order the Ministry of Defence to carry out an inquiry into the desertion, while at the same time requesting an amnesty for the rank and file.

The committee of inquiry met between 16 and 27 June and took evidence individually from the two officers, fifteen junior ranks and 27 common soldiers; on June 28 it heard nineteen men individually and, on 29 June, 70 members of the rank and file; that is, altogether 133 people were heard. In addition, the wife of a common soldier was also heard.

Those lower ranks (sergeants, corporals and lance-corporals) who were heard were all able to sign their own name. Of the first batch of common soldiers fifteen could not while, of the nineteen heard on 28 June, eleven, and of the 70 heard on 29 June, 49 were illiterate and signed with one or three crosses by their name. The wife interviewed was also illiterate. Of the 131 members of the 'non-officer corps', 74 (almost 57%) were illiterate; if we discount all officers, leaving 116 people, the proportion goes up to 65%. Of the 61 heard individually, the majority (48 people) had previously been unemployed and thirteen had been in employment. Of these, four had been students before they enlisted; the others included a smith, a butcher, a shoemaker, a barber, and a tailor. Both the students and those with a trade or craft were literate. Of the thirteen, four were officers.

The presiding judge-advocate and the members of the committee of inquiry were of course interested above all in the reasons behind the desertion. In this respect the statements were fairly uniform. Reasons given included the brigade document condemning participation in the funeral in Stanislau, bitterness at the removal of Lenkey, the relocation to Mariampol, and finally the handbill.

The depositions given led the members of the committee to decide on 29 June that further individual statements were superfluous, as the committee had no power to prevent the rank and file from discussing matters amongst themselves and in this way ensuring that their statements converged. They therefore summoned those soldiers who had not yet been heard and, warning them to repeat only the truth, took a statement from them en masse.

The statement delivered in this way said that the common soldiers had committed the crime of desertion only because they believed their motherland to be in danger and were anxious to hasten to its assistance. This was not a step that anyone suborned them into taking; they did it entirely of their own free will, although at the time they were not aware of the magnitude of their error. Now they all regretted their action and were prepared to submit themselves to whatever punishment was meted out, to obey every command, and they would try to make amends for their misdeeds by henceforward carrying out their duties to the letter. They had not spoken to civilians about their return to Hungary and not a single civilian had called upon them to do so.

On 30 June, the judge-advocate wrote a summary report on the results of the inquiry. In this he first stated that the unconditional loyalty of the common soldiers had already come into question on the occasion of their participation in the Stanislau funeral and in the subsequent inquiry, nor was there any doubt that they saw eye-to-eye with the Poles. Nonetheless, he went on, the primary cause of their return to Hungary was the appeal in the handbill. He added that there was no doubt that they must have heard of the changes in Hungary, the upheavals that followed, and the dangers threatening it, from their relatives' letters and the newspapers which were widely available. This news and especially its appeal to the rank and file had given rise to great enthusiasm and excitement, not least because there were many students among them, who were better able to pass judgement on and understand these circumstances, and so were able to fire up the 'less intelligent' members of the rank and file and win them over.

It was the judge-advocate's view that, since the act of desertion was so systematically and energetically executed, it had to be supposed that the rank and file were won over by someone who had not only great charisma but also the personal qualities and energy to carry the act through. It proved, however, impossible to identify such a person, although according to the judge-advocate that person must have been greatly assisted by the homesickness of the majority of the rank and file. To all this must be added their placement in the encampment at Mariampol, the lack of trust declared in them, and the dissatisfaction arising from the loss of Lenkey. According to his report, it was not impossible that the junior officers shared the convictions of the rank and file.

As has been seen, there were altogether four former students among those individually heard, two of them junior officers. (If we extrapolate from this proportion to those heard as a body, the number of students among them could not have exceeded five; that is, barely five per cent of the non-officer corps could have been former students). At the same time, the fact that those who were literate read out, and no doubt enlarged upon, what was in the handbill to the illiterate majority of the rank and file indicates that those with schooling really did influence the decision made by the rest.

The collective esprit of the body is indicated by the fact that no more than two of those interviewed mentioned people by name whom they said had encouraged them to join the deserters. But both of these stressed that they also considered it justified to return because the motherland was in danger. Lenkey and Fiáth, both of whom had been made captive by the rank and file, were also careful not to name names, as were the junior officers, although they must have known all the culprits by name and by sight. There were, naturally, some who claimed to have ended up among the deserters by mistake or through compulsion, but even these did not mention anyone by name.

The decisions could also have been influenced by the age of the participants. The majority of the individually-interviewed 61 rank and file were aged between nineteen and thirty; only eight were older than this and none was aged forty or older. It can therefore be stated that the majority were young men.

In sum, the judge-advocate probably hit the nail on the head when he wrote:

> The personal conviction of the rank and file seems to show that, while as soldiers they committed a serious offence against military law, on the other hand [no other way of proceeding was open to them] when they felt they had to choose between their duties as soldiers and their duties to the endangered motherland, than to follow their hearts, which powerfully called them back to the motherland; and so we must forget about the appropriate punishment because of their love of their motherland.

The squadron received as punishment that for which they had returned. In July 1848 they were ordered to the southern theatre of war and in the battle at Szenttamás (now Srbobran, Serbia), on 19 August, Lieutenant Pompeius Fiáth was mortally wounded. The squadron thus proved through its service on the battlefield that it had indeed hurried home in aid of the motherland.

The Birth of a Kossuth *nóta*

Ágnes Deák

During the course of the 1850s, the events of the Hungarian Revolution and of the War of Independence were vividly recalled in Hungary and they were commemorated in both public and private acts of memorialization. We should include among these popular and symbolic displays the preservation of relics of the revolution, such as necklaces and bracelets bearing the images or initials of the leaders of the War of Independence or the martyrs of Arad; bouquets imitating cockades; deployment of the national colours (red, white and green) in personal clothing or in the decoration of homes and public buildings; the sporting of the round Kossuth hat or the Kossuth beard; the celebration of Kossuth's name-day at family meals and events; dancing the *csárdas* at balls; and, above all, the clandestine distribution of manuscripts insulting the leading figures of the Vienna government and the ruler (and even, after some alcohol, the more public recitation of these manuscripts). Acts of memorialization such as these were carried out by people in all walks of Hungarian life and were not confined to the political elite.

Non-political forms of resistance waged by subaltern groups may be seen as the counterpart to the sort of 'illegal' actions described by Eric Hobsbawm as expressions of a larger, popular discontent.[1] Developing the notion of *Eigensinn*, advocates of the German *Alltagsgeschichte*, most notably Alf Lüdtke, have also sought to show the ways by which self-identity was preserved in Nazi Germany.[2] Nevertheless, it has been left to scholars of political anthropology to lead the way in the investigation of this phenomenon. James C. Scott has thus declared that:

> Formal, organized political activity, even if clandestine and revolutionary, is typically the preserve of the middle class and the intelligentsia [...] [for] most subordinate classes throughout most of history have rarely been afforded the luxury of open, organized, political activity [...]. Even when the option did exist, it is not clear that the same objectives might not also be pursued by other stratagems.[3]

Scott also emphasizes the simultaneous presence of opposition and cooperation: 'Most of the political life of subordinate groups is to be found neither in overt collective

---

1 Eric Hobsbawm, *Primitive Rebels: Studies in Archaic Forms of Social Movement in the 19th and 20th Centuries*, 3rd edition, Manchester, 1971, see also, Timothy Shakesheff, *Rural Conflicts, Crime, and Protest: Herefordshire 1800 to 1860*, Rochester, NY, 2003.
2 See thus Alf Lüdtke, *Eigen-Sinn. Fabrikalltag, Arbeitererfahrungen und Politik vom Kaiserreich bis in den Faschismus*, Hamburg, 1993.
3 James C. Scott, *Weapons of the Weak: Everyday Forms of Peasant Resistance*, New Haven & London, 1985, p. xv.

defiance of powerholders nor in complete hegemonic compliance, but in the vast territory between these two polar opposites.'[4] Scott has investigated the everyday-forms of peasant resistance, which he called the 'infrapolitics of subordinate groups', including for example, in one Malaysian village that he visited, foot-dragging, dissimulation, desertion, false compliance, pilfering, feigned ignorance, slander, arson and sabotage. The importance of folk culture, 'a politics of disguise and anonymity', has also been expounded in his works, as a public form of the 'ideological insubordination of subordinate groups'. Scott considers oral tradition an ideal vehicle for cultural resistance because it offers 'a kind of seclusion, control and even anonymity'. As a collective activity, 'the multiplicity of its authors provides its protective cover', and individual performers and composers can take refuge behind this anonymity.[5]

Folk culture in oral or written forms, most obviously in the underground distribution of manuscripts, was of particular importance in Hungary in the 1850s. As the 'everyday' of the 1850s became integrated into the centuries-old traditions of folk literature, we can speak of a particular variety of *folk poetry* flourishing from the autumn of 1848 onwards. Among the songs about Kossuth, the *Kossuth nóta* has a special role, as its semi-folk-song music is rooted in the traditions of the eighteenth-century *verbunkos* (recruitment song), and was often sung before 1848 with various types of text: as, for example, a love song.[6] These various strands of tradition came together, presumably in the autumn of 1848, as Kossuth went around the country recruiting men for the national *Honvéd* army.

In the period leading up to 1848, a new development in Hungarian literary life, and indeed in European literary life as a whole, was the (re-) discovery of folk poetry, with the aim of creating and/or reawakening national traditions.[7] Some items of artistic poetry had been folklorized, that is: become part and parcel of folk poetry tradition, and had often done so at striking speed through the printed *Trivialliteratur* of chapbooks and folk calendars.[8] Indeed, among village folk – especially those of the Great Hungarian Plain – the Kossuth cult of 1848–1849 ('Kossuth, the Magyars' Moses') was not a purely spontaneous development: in addition to the literary genres already mentioned, the lower clergy, supporting the War of Independence from the pulpit, also played a role here.[9] The Kossuth cult continued to live on in the years of neo-absolutism, supported by the conservative traditions of folk poetry.[10] Of course, there also existed after 1849 a

---

4 Scott, *Domination and the Arts of Resistance: Hidden Transcripts*, New Haven & London, 1990, p. 136.
5 ibid, pp. 157–161. See also, Gábor Benedek, 'A bürokratizáció történetéhez: az 1853–54. évi definitiv rendezés személyi következményei', in (ed.) György Kövér, *Zsombékok. Középposztélyok és iskolázatás Magyarországon a 19. századi elejétől a 20 század közepéig*, Budapest, 2006, pp. 240–52.
6 110 different melody-types of the Kossuth *nóta* with 600 variations can be distinguished. See Zoltán Ujváry, 'Kossuth Lajos a népdalokban', *Ethnographia – Népélet*, 106, 1995, pp. 31–37. See also Linda Dégh and H. Glassie (eds.), *Folklore Today*, Bloomington, 1976.
7 See Linda Dégh, 'Uses of Folklore as Expressions of Identity of Hungarians in the Old and New Country', *Journal of Folklore Research*, 21, 1984, nos 2–3, pp. 187–200, 189–191. On Europe in general, see Peter Burke, *Popular Culture in Early Modern Europe*, Aldershot, 1988 (reprint), pp. 3–22.
8 The 'Nemzetőrdal' written by János Arany had circulated as a folk song within weeks of its publication in 1848: Vilmos Voigt, '"Kossuth nem volt kormányzó, hanem király"! A szabadságharc népköltészetének utóélete napjainkig', *2000*, 10, 1998, no. 3. pp. 55–63 (p. 57).
9 Péter Zakar, '"Kossuth a magyarok Mózese" (Liberális egyházak Kossuth-képe 1848/49-ben)', *Aetas*, 18, 2003, nos 3–4, pp. 87–108.
10 Alice Freifeld, *Nationalism and the Crowd in Liberal Hungary, 1848–1914*, Washington, DC, Baltimore and London, 2000, pp. 109–112.

complex network of folk poetry, high-literary poetry and deliberate political agitation which, once they had become intertwined, helped to sustain revolutionary traditions. Much-loved items of forbidden manuscript literature included both artistic creations and folksongs. Conscious attempts were made by the political and intellectual elite to collect these revolutionary texts and to publish them abroad as well as at home, but the government strictly forbade the gathering and distribution of such material.[11] But even without any revolutionary content, the national folk tradition constituted of its own accord something that made it politically suspicious to the Habsburg government, which was at this time striving to build a unified empire that transcended national affiliations.[12] We should not, however, overlook the business aspects of book- and music-selling as factors promoting the circulation of literature that had been officially banned. Even before 1848, there existed distribution-networks for works published abroad which were forbidden in Austria, and these networks continued to function.

The distribution and promotion of such works was by no means limited to the village community, the traditional consumer of folk poetry. In so far as we may distinguish between popular culture and folk culture, we can safely say that these sung poems represented a form of popular culture. They were concealed and recited by virtually all strata of urban society and not only in a Hungarian-language milieu but also, for example, by those middle-class urban Germans who, in 1848–49, had been loyal to the Hungarian government. Yet in the way they came into existence, in their variant forms, and in the manner they were recorded, elements of popular culture and of elite culture were interwoven into them. This must be the reason they proved suitable bearers of the nation's collective sentiments and of its opposition to the status quo.

The story presented here offers an insight into the everyday village life of banned literature. It answers, in particular, the question as to by whom and how these revolutionary texts were disseminated.

In his study of the cult of the great Hungarian poet, Sándor Petőfi, which bears many similarities to that of Kossuth, the literary historian József Kiss sketches the breeding-ground of these literary products: '[...] social gatherings in a village or country town, spinning parlours, farm outbuildings, communal activities in the open, weaving, husking maize, plucking poultry: all these offer opportunities to pass on songs, poems, stories and memories.' Afternoons of Sundays and holy days, family gatherings and the seasonal events of economic life (fairs, harvests and so on) yielded opportunities for oral and written culture to come together, for on such occasions 'the participants [also]

---

11 'Gyüjtsük a népdalokat' by 'Apafi', in *Hölgyfutár*, vol. 2, no. 49, 28 August, 1850. Móric Kelemen (a 17 year-old, Calvinist university student) who had sent to 'Apafi' 'some subversive songs' published on leaflets in 1848–49 was sentenced to six weeks in iron shackles in November of 1850. Hadtörténelmi Levéltár (hereafter, HL), Abszolutizmus kori iratok, a pesti hadbíróság iratai, 1850–1/470. 'Apafi' announced in the newspapers at the end of September 1850 that his activity had been disapproved of by the authorities and the collected manuscripts had been officially seized. See *Pesti Napló*, vol. 1. no. 167, 28 September, 1850.

12 Simon Bánffay, the editor of the newspaper *Pesti Napló* who was at that time an enthusiastic propagandist of the modernizing endeavours of the Habsburg neo-absolutist government, received a formal severe reprimand in the summer of 1851 because he had published a leading article with the title: 'Let us collect our folk tradition', 'Gyüjtsük a hazai népszokásokat', *Pesti Napló*, vol. 2, no. 425, 7 August, 1851. For Bánffay's trial before a military tribunal, see HL, Abszolutizmus kori iratok, pesti hadbíróság, 1851–9/17.

include the upwardly-mobile, educated, literate, culture-transmitting representatives of the provincial intellectual strata.'[13]

The case below is linked to such an event, the Anna-Day *búcsú* at Lesencetomaj in Veszprém county. 'A *búcsú* is partly an outing, partly a meal out, partly a family occasion, and partly a social gathering of a religious nature,' according to the folklorist Ákos Szendrey. He goes on,

> The older the participant the more it assumes a religious character, and the younger the participant, the more the social aspect comes to the fore. Thus in the *búcsú* the morning is spent in church; there is a meal at noon with relatives and friends, while in the afternoon people meet and greet each other in the tents, and visit friends old and new. A *búcsú* is not something to which you are invited; but the door is open, the table is laid, and every visitor, whether friend or friend of a friend, is very welcome.[14]

Our story[15] begins at a *búcsú*, in the afternoon.

At the *búcsú* on 26 July 1850, at the house of the 28-year-old notary, Antal Varró of Lesencetomaj, a number of people were present: István Szívós, a schoolmaster, aged 28, from Vita; his assistant István Vitai, (21, unmarried); schoolteachers Mihály Hidasi from Balantonederics, Sándor Budai from Badacsonytomaj, István Vörös of Szigliget, and János Szabó of Köveskál, and Mária Fischer, wife of the watchmaker Antal Kovács from Sümeg. All were Roman Catholics. They sang as they played cards, and after several banned songs had been aired, István Vitai declared that he 'had a new Kossuth *nóta*' and at Mária Fischer's request he wrote it down from memory. The company began to sing the song quite loudly, but when their host returned from the tavern-store he tore up the piece of paper and prevented them from finishing the song because 'as host he did not want to be held responsible.' At this, the Badacsonytomaj schoolteacher launched into another mocking song. Vitai remarked that 'his new song' was widely known not just in Vita but throughout the area. This was backed up by a witness who had heard a group of peasants in the vineyards sing it, without of course (in his evidence to the court) being able to identify the singers. Another witness said he had heard the song one evening in the village street.

When the case came to court it was established that, around 21 July, the two-and-a-half-year-old daughter of Sidonai Kosár had found in the street a piece of paper with the song on it, which her mother and her uncle, József Kosár, a landowner and lawyer in Vita (and correspondent of the liberal newspaper *Pesti Hírlap* edited by Kossuth in the 1840s), had glanced at but, as they said, thinking it 'was of no importance', had given back to the little girl. From there it came into the hands of István Vita, who copied the text on the spot and showed it his boss before the *búcsú*, who returned it with the remark that 'he was wasting his time copying such trivial stuff.' But Vitai made several more copies 'at the request of a number of people', passing on the text and on occasion even receiving payment. At the bidding thus of Miksa Veisz, a 20-year-old local Jewish man,

---

13 József Kiss, 'A szibériai legenda mint a naiv népi Petőfi-kultusz terméke', in *Irodalomtörténeti Közlemények*, 94, 1990, no. 3, pp. 323–340. (p. 326.).

14 Ákos Szendrey, 'A népi élet társasösszejövetelei', in *Ethnographia – Népélet*, 49, 1938, nos 1–2, pp. 124–138 (p. 133).

15 The story has been reconstructed on the basis of the minutes of the ensuing judicial investigation: Hungarian National Archive (hereafter MOL), D 51 Der Bevollmächtige Kaiserliche Commissär für die Civilangelegenheiten in Ungarn Karl Freiherr von Geringer, elnöki iratok 1656/1850, and HL Abszolutizmus kori iratok, a pesti hadbíróság iratai, 1850–11/61.

he copied it down for three groschen. Veisz had subsequently been asked for the text by the Catholic priest of Vita, Gáspár Kranisz, who had, in return, promised to secure him exemption from being called up into the imperial army as a former *honvéd* recruit. It was the priest, however, who informed the gendarmerie that the song was being circulated and thus initiated the prosecution. Another witness, Antal Gosztonyi, also confessed at a later stage in the proceedings that he was visited by the priest while in pre-trial detention and convinced, 'partly by persuasion, partly by threats', that if he did not incriminate József Kosár, he would himself come under suspicion.

There were, however, other ways in which the text circulated in the village. The original was also shown by József Kosár's illiterate coachman to the above-mentioned Antal Gosztonyi 'to read and explain it' to him, but he responded by saying that 'we need hoes and scythes, not this sort of writing', and tore it up. The poem was also known beyond the confines of the village. József Kosár claimed to have heard it in Héviz, in July, being sung in a tavern by 'herdsmen and shepherds'. Records show that a close variant of the text was also found in November 1850 in a street in Szekszárd, seat of the adjacent county of Tolna, by someone from Nagygomba: that is, not a local man.[16]

It was widely held in Vita that the song had been brought into the village by the son of a cook in the service of one of the villagers, who was himself a wandering minstrel. The text was found on the same day that both cook and son had hurriedly left the village. No one knew where they were to be found. At all events, Vitai claimed that the writing on the piece of paper found by the little girl was that of an 'ordinary person', not highly educated, and not that of a local, since he knew and would have recognized a local man's handwriting. Interestingly, of those involved, the priest was not the only person to inform the authorities. Following his visit in early August to Héviz, József Kosár reported the circulation of the offensive song to the administrative leader of the county, József Bogyay, who ordered him to gather up all the copies he could find in Vita and send them to him. Kosár undertook only to find out who possessed copies and to report back. There was, however, no time for this during the gendarmerie's investigation, which had in the mean time begun.

The conclusion reached at the trial was that the author of the song could not be identified. But apart from István Vitai, József Kosár had also circulated the text that he had heard in Héviz. Vitai was sentenced to two years in irons in gaol, while János Szívós and Sándor Buday, who had distinguished themselves at the Anna-Day *búcsú* with their enthusiastic singing, each received one year in irons. The Kosárs received six months in irons for incitement and treason.[17] The three 'ringleaders' were sent to Olmütz (Olomouc) castle-prison in Moravia. Vitay and Buday served out their sentences, while Szívós volunteered after a few months for the gendarmerie and was thus set free.[18]

---

16 Baron Antal Augusz's district leader's report to Baron Karl von Geringer, chief of civil administration in Ungarn, Szekszárd, 22 November, 1850: MOL, D 51 1991/1850.
17 *Magyar Hírlap*, vol. 1, no. 302, 20 November, 1850. Imprisonment of several weeks was the usual punishment for concealment of such subversive texts, but those who presented such texts in public were sentenced more severely.
18 József Barsi, *Utazás ismeretlen állomás felé 1849–1856. Berzsenyi Lénárd rajzai. Az olmützi foglyok arcképsorozata*, Budapest, 1988, pp. 276–277, 249–250, 402–403.

The actors in our story are a notary, teachers, teaching assistants, lawyers, a priest and those not recorded by name in a village society: day-labourers and herdsmen. The role of catalyst – both those promoting the verses and those who drew the attention of the authorities to the misdeed – was no doubt played by the village intelligentsia, for although no light was shed on who brought the text into the village – Vitai (as we have seen) presumed that it was not an intellectual – and who first circulated it, the chief roles were played out by the village's more literate inhabitants. During the trial, the two leading figures admitted their motives, but both tried to present their actions as the thoughtless deeds of a scatterbrain. Vitai said, 'My youth and lack of experience means that I never suspected that with a song, which I did not write, I might be committing a punishable offence. [...] So, although in my youth and inexperience I did sing this song, I had nothing to do with its composition.' For his part, János Szívós declared: 'I thought the whole thing was a bit of a lark and I didn't think it so mattered as to have these sad consequences for me, who has always been loyal to my king [...].' A glance at the text of the song and those parts of it that cast doubt on the legitimacy of the ruler, will suffice to convince us that this part of his statement is not to be believed. The intelligentsia of the village which circulated the song were undoubtedly clear as to the subversive power of the text, and of its ability to undermine the loyalty of subjects and to stir up animosity.[19]

In the case, however, of the day-labourers and herdsmen who sang the song, along with other songs old and new, is it possible to speak of deliberate political resistance or opposition? The new textual variant of the familiar tune melded almost imperceptibly into the repertoire of those situations where songs were sung, and the lines of the verse comported in part with refrains with which they were familiar. And yet, was it not this ordinariness of habit that was the source of their power? As Scott puts it, '[...] such kinds of resistance are often the most significant and the most effective over the long run.'[20]

Appendix

Magyar Song

Lajos Kossuth's message came,
In our country it was the same.
He sent Uncle Bem, the commander of fame,
To battle for freedom.
Perish the Germans!

With 200,000 soldiers
And countless cannon
He came to the Danube at Orsova.
Soon the Germans will flee.
Long live the Magyars!

---

19 Geringer did not stop himself from drawing a generalized lesson from this case. On 20th November, he repeated his order to the district administrative leaders to dismiss politically suspicious people even from their 'lower' positions, as notaries, teachers and village headmen. Geringer to district administrative leaders, Buda, 20 November, 1850 (draft): MOL, D 51 1882/1850.
20 James C. Scott, *Weapons of the Weak*, p. xvi.

Muscovy's men will rue the day
They breached the borders of our land.
Make peace with Lajos Kossuth,
The apostle of freedom!
Long live our Kossuth!

Magyarland, Poland
Be not downhearted!
Your chains are shattered,
The chains that bound you.
Freedom's here.

Toppled is Franz Joseph,
The bastard German child.

Instead there was the Prince of Coburg,
A royal English child.
Long live the king!

Rejoice good Magyars,
That your star has risen
May God preserve our Kossuth,
The champion of our freedom!
Long live the Magyar![21]

---

21 A variant of the text (lacking the final two stanzas) appears in *Történeti énekek és katonadalok*, collected
    by Lajos Kálmány, edited by Linda Dégh, Budapest, 1952, p. 300. It was rumoured in Hungary that Queen
    Victoria's second son would ascend the Hungarian throne as King Béla V, while it was whispered that
    Franz Joseph's father was not Archduke Franz Karl but the Ban of Croatia, Count Josip Jelačić.

The Role of the Jews in the Hungarian Revolution of 1918

Thomas Lorman

The revolution of 30 October 1918 was a turning point in Hungary's history. A small group of radicals and socialists, headed by Count Mihály Károlyi, was swept to power promising an end to the war, social reform, democratization, and national independence. In power, however, the Károlyi regime ruled by decree and it presided over the economic, social and territorial disintegration of the country. This collapse was blamed not only on the incompetence of the Károlyi regime, but also on the revolution that had brought it to power, and on those sections of society which had carried out the revolution. The Jews in particular were singled out for blame.[1] As a result, the counter-revolutionary regime which took power in the autumn of 1919 criticized, punished and ostracized Jews from its ranks. A deep and lasting fissure between the 'Christian-conservative' right and the 'Jewish' left began, therefore, with the perception that the 1918 revolution was 'the work of the Jews'.

Some scholars have, however, also noted 'the enormously high Jewish participation' in the revolution.[2] The precise extent of, and reasons for, that participation have, nevertheless, not been established. This paper seeks to remedy that deficiency. It examines what role Jews played in the revolution, and the possible motives behind their involvement. It argues that any measure of Jewish participation is ultimately dependent on how Jews are defined. Nevertheless, it also concludes that because a large number of the revolution's leaders, and a significant proportion of the revolution's supporters were of Jewish background, and because there were specific factors encouraging the Jews to support the revolution, anti-Semites could with some plausibility hold the Jews responsible for having brought the disastrous Károlyi regime to power.

The path to the revolution was straightforward. On 18 October, 1918, the former prime minister, Count István Tisza, informed the Hungarian parliament that, 'we have lost the war.' The sharpest critics of the regime, Count Károlyi and his minuscule Independence and 48-er party (*Függetlenségi és 48-as Párt*), the even more unpopular National Citizens and Radical Party (*Országos Polgári Radikális Párt*),[3] and the Social Democratic Party (*Magyarországi Szocialdemokratikus Párt*), which had never won a

---

1 See, for example, Cecile Tormay, *An Outlaw's Diary*, New York, 1923, p. 9; Jenő Csaba, *A forradalom története Szegeden*, Szeged, undated, p. 113; Béla Kelemen, *Adatok a szegedi ellenforradalom és a szegedi kormány történetéhez*, Szeged, 1923, p. 62.
2 István Deák, 'Budapest and the Hungarian Revolution of 1918–1919', *Slavonic and East European Review*, 46, 1968, 1, pp. 109–120.
3 The National Citizens and Radical Party was formed by a small group of Budapest 'intellectuals' clustered around the 'progressive' journal, *Huszadik Század*; their acknowledged leader was Oszkár Jászi.

parliamentary seat, now felt sufficiently emboldened to demand not only an immediate ceasefire but also rapid democratization, Hungary's extrication from the defeated Dualist Monarchy, and the appointment of Károlyi as prime minister. To fulfil this programme, they formed, on 23 October, a National Council (*Nemzeti Tanács*) whose very existence was, as Károlyi himself admitted, technically a revolutionary act.[4] Increasingly large, aggressive and occasionally violent demonstrations in Budapest called for power to be handed over to the National Council, and added to the pressure on the government of Sándor Wekerle, who suffered a crisis of confidence and resigned. The authorities then lost control of the streets when the chief of the Budapest police, on 29 October, pledged allegiance to the National Council and his officers abandoned their duties.

When it became known on 30 October that the Emperor Charles I (Charles IV of Hungary) intended to appoint not Károlyi but the solidly unremarkable and decidedly conservative Count János Hadik as the new prime minister, soldiers supporting the National Council began seizing key buildings. It was a bloodless, ramshackle revolution. Károlyi, himself, went home to bed just as the revolution was gathering pace and returned to his office in the morning to find himself in charge of the country. On 31 October, the Emperor recognized reality and appointed Károlyi prime minister. Prominent Hungarians from across the political (and religious) spectrum were already lining up to swear loyalty to the National Council.[5]

Any discussion of the role that the Jews played in bringing this National Council to power must first tackle the thorny question of what constitutes a Jew. It appears difficult to lump together observant Jews with the growing number of converts to Christianity and the radicals and socialists who dismissed the very notion of a faith-based identity. As Béla Kun declared, 'my father was a Jew, but I am no longer one, for I became a socialist and a communist.'[6] For both anti-Semites and Zionists, however, religious observance had ceased to be the defining feature of a Jew. Instead Jews were defined by their parentage. Anti-Semites used descent to identify the Jewish 'race' and Zionists used the same to define the Jewish 'people'.[7]

Thus both contemporary observers and latter day scholars have repeatedly asserted that the National Council was dominated by Jews.[8] This is in spite of the fact that not one member of the Council attended synagogue, that the majority had magyarized their names, that several had formally converted to the Christian faith, and that they were all prepared to attack the perceived backwardness of the Jewish faith and 'ghetto life'.[9] One (Jewish) member of the council, Oszkár Jászi, had even been denounced as an anti-Semite.[10] One could also add that Count Károlyi, the undisputed leader of the Council

---

4   Mihály Károlyi, *Memoirs of Michael Karolyi, Faith Without Illusion*, London, 1956, p.107.

5   György Litván (ed.), *Károlyi Mihály. Az új Magyarországért*, Budapest, 1968, pp.371–402.

6   Ezra Mendelsohn, *The Jews of East Central Europe between the World Wars*, Bloomington, 1983, p. 95; The difficult of defining Jewishness is neatly summed up in William McCagg, *Jewish Nobles and Geniuses in Modern Hungary*, New York, 1972, pp. 19–20.

7   Victor Karady, *The Jews of Europe in the Modern Era*, Budapest, 2004, pp. 299–309

8   János Gyurgyák, *A zsidókérdés Magyarországon*, Budapest, 2001, p. 99

9   Andrew C. Janos, *The Politics of Backwardness in Hungary, 1825–1945*, Princeton, NJ, 1982, p. 181.

10 György Litván, *A Twentieth-Century prophet: Oscar Jászi 1875–1957*, Budapest, 2006, pp. 84–86; Janos, *The Politics of Backwardness*, pp. 176–177.

possessed impeccable Christian credentials, and that his deputy, János Hock, was a Catholic priest.[11]

We should recognize, however, that for anti-Semites the very fact that none of the National Council actually attended synagogue only underlined the threat posed by its Jewish majority. Since 'Jewishness' had been redefined from a religion to a race, and the implication accepted that races should be kept apart, the most dangerous Jews were now those who had abandoned their religious identity, had become Christians and/or Hungarians, and had thereby crossed and blurred the racial boundaries.

When we consider the Jewish presence among the supporters of the National Council who actually carried through the revolution, the same question of what constitutes a Jew is compounded by the limited and conflicting evidence on the identities of these revolutionaries.

Certainly some circumstantial evidence points to a significant Jewish presence among the crowds in the streets. First, the revolution was confined to Budapest. In the countryside even Marxist historians had difficulty finding a single case of revolutionary agitation among the peasants.[12] Indeed, the conservative *Budapesti Hírlap*, specifically contrasted the 'clamour' in Budapest with the 'quiet' in the countryside.[13] The fact, therefore, that the revolution was confined to Budapest increases the likelihood of Jewish involvement as Jews made up only 5% of the national population, but over 20% of the population of Budapest.

Secondly, the claim made by Marxist historians that the 'the industrial workforce was the spine of the October revolution' is not supported by the evidence.[14] There was only one factory that had a workers' council (*munkástanács*) in operation before 30 October, and the Budapest worker's council only held its first meeting after the revolution had taken place.[15] Moreover, when we look at the occupations of those injured in the disturbances of 28 October, (the so-called 'Battle of the Chain Bridge') when a crowd of supporters of the National Council made an abortive effort to storm the royal castle and were repulsed by the gendarmerie, only thirteen of the 55 casualties (three killed, 52 wounded) were in occupations associated with the industrial workforce. At the same time 26 of the 55 were in 'middle-class' occupations in which Jews predominated. (merchants, lawyers, bank employees, students, artists, small businessmen).[16]

Breakdown by occupation also disguises the fact that the majority of those involved in the Battle of the Chain Bridge were probably demobilized soldiers. It is estimated that there were 60–80 000 former soldiers in Budapest at this point, and they played a major role in the disturbances culminating in the revolution.[17] The first demonstration in support of the National Council on 24 October included an estimated 200 soldiers, while the violent demonstration the following day was led by some 3–400 soldiers.[18] A

---

11 One can, however, argue that Károlyi was, in part, a figurehead who owed his position to the Hungarian tradition of offering leadership roles to aristocrats to provide the necessary gravitas.

12 Tibor Hajdú, *Az őszirózsás forradalom*, Budapest, 1963, pp. 49, 101.

13 *Budapesti Hírlap*, 27 October, 1918.

14 Hajdu, *Az őszirózsás forradalom*, p.78.

15 Tibor Hajdú, *Tanácsok Magyarországon 1918–1919-ben*, Budapest, 1958, pp. 34–36.

16 *Budapesti Hírlap*, 30 October, 1918.

17 Hajdú, *Az őszirózsás forradalom*, pp. 80, 86, 89–91.

18 ibid, pp. 84, 91.

Soldiers Council (*Katona Tanács*) was established as the military wing of the National Council, and it was this Soldiers Council, (rather than the National Council) that actually took the initiative in launching the revolution of 30 October. Indeed, Jászi in his memoirs described the revolution as 'primarily a military one [...] the private venture of a few groups'.[19]

Certainly, the commanders of the Soldiers Council (József Pogány, Viktor Heltai) were of Jewish descent. One eyewitness noted that the revolutionary soldiers she saw on the streets were Jewish and a Jewish newspaper boasted that 'Jewish soldiers were the first to join' the Soldiers Council. A 'Zionist Guard' (*Cionista Gárda*) had also already been established by 3 November to defend the revolution.[20] It seems, nevertheless, probable that the radicalizing impact of four years of warfare and a fear of returning to the front lines were more important factors than religious or racial identity in encouraging these soldiers to support the National Council and carry through the revolution.

Although the evidence of widespread Jewish involvement in the revolution is inconclusive, scholars have nevertheless proffered a range of explanations to explain this involvement.[21] For Peter Pastor, the revolution's goal of reordering Hungarian society appealed to Hungary's 'best minds' and since many of these minds were Jewish they naturally assumed a leading role. Yet Pastor also recognizes that a section of the nobility could also be counted among Hungary's educated classes, yet they remained detached from the revolution.[22] Education was not, therefore, the defining feature of supporters of the revolution. This point is confirmed by the fact that there was not a single intellectual among the casualties at the Battle of the Chain bridge, which was actually inspired by the antics of a factory director (and future anti-Semitic Prime Minister), István Friedrich.[23]

István Deák offers a more detailed analysis of the revolution's appeal to Jews. He also stresses that the National Council's plan to reform and modernize Hungary had an appeal to Jewish intellectuals, but he also adds that there were 'other reasons – humanistic and messianic'. The Jewish intelligentsia, he has written, had a 'western, particularly German, orientation' that made them familiar with the 'latest German cultural trends, especially with expressionism' and led them to rebel against 'their assimilated and intensely patriotic families, and against their bourgeois background'.[24]

The problem with this argument is that, above all else, the revolution of 30 October 1918 was both in its immediate and long-term goals a nationalist revolution. The immediate trigger for the revolution was the rejection of the Habsburg emperor's right to choose Hungary's prime minister. Only seventeen days after the revolution, the new Károlyi regime had forced the Habsburg ruler to retire from public life and proclaimed Hungary's independence. Even the revolutionaries' contention that an independent Hungary offered the best guarantee of future social reforms (the Habsburg ruling family

---

19 *Déli Hírlap*, 1 November 1918; John Swanson, *The Remnants of the Habsburg Monarchy*, New York, 2001, p. 46; Jászi, *Revolution and Counter-Revolution*, p.43.
20 Tormay, *An Outlaw's Diary*, pp. 9, 70–71; *Egyenlőség*, 9 November, 1918.
21 For a more eccentric list of explanations for the attractiveness of left-wing politics to Jews, see Ezra Mendelsohn (ed.), *Essential Papers on Jews and the Left*, New York, 1997, pp. 15–16.
22 Peter Pastor, *Hungary Between Wilson and Lenin: The Hungarian Revolution of 1918–1919 and the Big Three*, Boulder & New York, 1976, p. 46
23 *Budapesti Hírlap*, 30 October, 1918.
24 Deák, 'Budapest and the Hungarian Revolution of 1918–1919', pp. 109–120.

and the entire constitutional framework was regarded as an impediment to reform) was an interlinking of nationalist and reformist rhetoric that harked all the way back to the nationalist, reformist revolution of 1848. It is not, therefore, the case that the Jewish revolutionaries were detached from Hungarian society by a 'cosmopolitan' enthusiasm for 'the latest cultural trends', but rather the reverse: it was their absorption of the Hungarian nationalist creed that ensured they ended up in the revolutionary camp.

János Gyurgyák puts forward a superficially more plausible explanation for the predominance of Jews in the revolution. He argues that the process of assimilation had obviously run out of steam by the turn of the century due to an upsurge of anti-Semitism and resistance to full equality for the Jewish faith.[25] As the contemporary commentator Robert Michels put it, 'even when they are rich, the Jews constitute [....] a category of persons who are excluded from the social advantages which the prevailing political, economic and intellectual system ensures for the corresponding portion of the gentile population.'[26] Thus, Jews embraced revolutionary change in order to create a new society in which they would not be treated as second-class citizens.

Certainly the pages of the Jewish community's leading newspaper, *Egyenlőség*, bear witness to a continuing sense of 'second class status'. Indeed that precise phrase was used by one writer to describe the position of the Jews in early 1918, adding that when the war ended, 'change' would be urgently needed.[27] The call to continue the 'struggle' for equality was frequently made in the paper, which greeted the success of the October revolution by declaring that 'the road has been opened for the long-felt, burningly necessary internal transformation' of the country and 'no one feels this more warmly than those Hungarians of the Jewish faith.'[28]

The thesis that Jews supported the revolution as the route to full assimilation can, however, be challenged on the grounds that the process of assimilation had not 'run out of steam' at the turn of the century but had actually continued to accelerate. While an explicitly anti-Semitic party had been formed in Hungary in the 1870s, it had disappeared by the 1890s, and while there had been resistance to equality for the Jewish faith, that equality had, in 1895, nevertheless been largely granted. Moreover, Jews were in larger numbers marrying into, or being elevated into, elite society. The number of baronial ennoblements for Jews, for example, continuously increased up to 1918, and Jews began to be appointed to senior cabinet posts.[29]

A more persuasive argument is, therefore, that Jews supported the revolution not to bring the assimilation process to fruition but to prevent that process being thrown into reverse. This argument was first put forward by Károlyi himself, who argued that the Jews supported the revolution in order to pre-empt the wave of anti-Semitic violence that would be launched following the cessation of hostilities.[30]

---

25 Gyurgyák, *A zsidókérdés*, pp. 88–90.
26 Arthur Liebman, *Jews and the Left*, New York, 1979, pp. 13–14.
27 *Egyenlőség*, 23 March, 1918.
28 *Egyenlőség*, 2 November, 1918.
29 See, in this regard, Andrew Janos's superb essay on the effectiveness of assimilation, 'The Decline of Oligarchy: Bureaucratic and Mass Politics in the Age of Dualism', in Andrew Janos, William Slottman (eds.), *Revolution in Perspective*, Los Angeles, 1971, pp. 1–60.
30 Károlyi Mihály, *Az új Magyarországért*, pp. 346–347.

Certainly, four years of warfare produced a noticeable upsurge in anti-Semitism, with Jews denounced for profiteering from the war, shirking military service, overrunning the country as refugees from Galicia and undermining the morale of the troops.[31] In 1915, for example, one Jewish newspaper claimed that twenty-three daily papers and ten weekly papers had published anti-Semitic articles, and in 1916, a new, explicitly anti-Semitic monthly journal, entitled *A Cél*, had been launched with the support of, among others, a senior Catholic bishop and the future prime minister, Count István Bethlen. By 1918, incidents of anti-Semitic violence were becoming a regular occurrence.[32]

Such incidents were regarded by *Egyenlőség*, and, no doubt, by a significant section of the wider Jewish community, as harbingers of worse to come. In March 1918, the paper warned that anti-Semites were planning new pogroms to be launched as soon as the war was over.[33] Then, in July, a leading rabbi warned readers that 'our enemies don't even wait for the end of the war but even now parade around with their bloody swords',[34] and the leading Jewish politician and former minister of justice, Vilmos Vázsonyi, declared, in September, that anti-Semites were actively preparing to make the Jews the 'scapegoats' for Hungary's loss in the war.[35] Meanwhile, the leading Zionist journal, *Zsidó Szemle*, informed its readers that there was now 'in Hungary a completely organized and strong anti-Semitic movement'.[36]

Anti-Semitic publications were able and willing to give credence to such concerns. *A Cél*, for example, announced in October 1918 that Christians had 'had enough of the liberalism, enough of the hospitality, enough of the gentleness' with which they had hitherto treated the Jews.[37]

Such was the fear among Jews that the end of the war would result in increased anti-Semitism, that in the autumn of 1918, they began to form a new 'League of Self-Defence' (*Önvédelmi Liga*). While the exact role that this league would play remained unclear, its formation was, nevertheless, endorsed by leading members from each religious congregation as well as the largely secular Zionist movement, and its first branches were established in early October.[38]

This fear of anti-Semitic pogroms gained concrete form on 29 October with the formation of an organization designed to rival the National Council, entitled the Association for National Defence (*Nemzetvédelmi Szövetség*, hereafter NVSZ). This organization formally denounced the demonstrations taking place in Budapest, Jászi's idea that Hungary should be turned into an eastern Switzerland and any notion that power should be handed over to Károlyi's National Council. Although the NVSZ's opening declaration concluded with an appeal for national unity irrespective of 'religious distinctions', its

---

31 Gyurgyák, *A zsidókérdés*, pp. 90–98. See also, Gábor Vermes, 'Hungarian Politics and Society on the Eve of Revolution' in Peter Pastor (ed.), *Revolutions and Interventions in Hungary and its Neighbor States, 1918–1919*, New York, 1998, pp. 116–117.
32 János Pelle, *Sowing the Seeds of Hatred: Anti-Jewish Laws and Hungarian Public Opinion, 1938–1944*, New York, 2004, pp. 8–10; *Egyenlőség*, 10 Aug, 1918.
33 *Egyenlőség*, 16 March 1918.
34 ibid, 6 July 1918.
35 ibid, 5 September, 1918.
36 *Zsidó Szemle*, 6 September, 1918.
37 *A Cél*, October 1918.
38 *Egyenlőség*, 12 October 1918

formation provoked immediate alarm among Jews because the founders included prominent anti-Semitic journalists and politicians (drawn largely from the strongly anti-Semitic Catholic People's Party and the *A Cél* monthly). Moreover, the Catholic People's Party's newspaper, *Alkotmány*, immediately confirmed that the new organization was anti-Semitic because its objective was to organize 'the Christian citizens of the country' and thereby 'stand in the way of the terror [...] of a minority'.[39]

In response, Jewish journalists immediately went on the attack. The *Az Est* newspaper described the NVSZ as a 'pogrom council' (*pogromtanács*)[40] while the *Egyenlőség* informed its readers that the notoriously anti-Semitic bishop, Ottokár Prohászka, had formed the NVSZ to ensure that Hungary would be run by 'Hungarians' not Jews. Moreover, the newspaper reported, the NVSZ had already set aside 14 million crowns for pogroms.[41]

Concern about the NVSZ can only have been enhanced by reports arriving in Budapest on the afternoon of 30 October that it had gained a positive reception across the country, and that it would be supported by all political parties which were outside the National Council.[42] While the emperor's appointment of János Hadik as Prime Minister spurred the revolutionaries into action, the threat posed by the anti-Semitic NVSZ, in an atmosphere in which the fear of pogroms was at fever pitch, is likely to have encouraged Jews to throw their support behind the National Council and press for the revolution to take place as quickly as possible.

We should also note that assimilated, urban, middle-class Jews were most likely to be concerned by the possibility that the process of assimilation was about to be thrown into reverse. They, of course, had the most to lose. This may explain why there is no evidence to suggest that orthodox and rural Jews played a role in the revolution. The irony, of course, is that the revolution produced precisely what it was intended to prevent. The perception, nevertheless, that assimilated Jews supported and participated in the revolution actually threw the process of assimilation into reverse. It supercharged Hungarian anti-Semitism by associating the Jews with both the disastrous Károlyi regime and the political 'left'. As a result anti-Semites found their natural allies among conservative critics of the revolution and thereby ensured that Jews would have to make their political home among the parties of the left.[43] By late 1919, the words 'Jewish' and 'left' had indeed become effectively synonymous while anti-Semitism became a defining feature of conservative and counter-revolutionary Hungarian thinking. This division was reinforced by the high level of 'Jewish' involvement in Béla Kun's 'Republic of Councils' and by the anti-Semitism that punctuated the counter-revolutionary 'white terror', but it was a division that can also be directly traced back to perceptions of Jewish involvement in the 1918 revolution.

---

39 *Budapesti Hírlap*, 30 October 1918; *Alkotmány*, 30 October 1918.
40 *Az Est*, 31 October 1918.
41 *Egyenlőség*, 2 November 1919.
42 *Alkotmány*, 31 October 1918
43 Throughout the inter-war period, not a single self-proclaimed Jew sat on the government's benches. In contrast, the leading liberal party was initially headed by a Jew, Vilmos Vázsonyi, while Jews persistently made up around a quarter of the MPs elected to represent the opposition Liberal and Social Democratic Parties.

Orthodox Rituals of Revolution and Rebirth in Interwar Romania

Rebecca Ann Haynes

The Romanian Legionary 'cult of death' has been frequently portrayed as the macabre side of the interwar Legionary movement and as evidence of its 'exceptionalism' within European fascism. This essay will argue, however, that far from being a gruesome feature of the Legionary movement, the 'cult of death' had its roots in popular conceptions of Orthodoxy which the Legion successfully incorporated into its nationalist ideology. The Legion further employed the Orthodox cult of martyrs and rituals of death and burial in its ceremonies as nationalist statements of revolution and rebirth. In this respect, the Legion was both a product, and exploiter, of the popular Orthodoxy that had long underpinned Romanian ethnic and national identity.

At the same time, however, participation in the Legion and its activity lent the individual a sense of personal rebirth and of 'palingenesis'.[1] Whereas this term has hitherto been largely applied to the fascist mission as a whole and to the transformative impact on society to which it aspired, we may observe that it also applied to the individual. By entering into the Legion and endorsing its goals, the individual himself was reborn as a 'New Man', but his being was rewritten and subsumed within broader categories of 'newness' and 'manhood'. Shrugging aside his own individuality, the new man now found his own measure of selfhood within the collective and was drawn by this to a larger awareness of the eternal and of the divine purpose which guided all human endeavour. As Brodie Richards has put it elsewhere in this volume in respect of Leveller and Jacobin belief, so may we aver for the Legionary movement that 'to love the community in service, in sacrifice, and in solidarity with his fellow citizens, was to be raised to a higher good, beyond personal interest [...].' Thereby, politics and the person took second place to the collective idea, and personal renewal was predicated on the prior death of the individual will. This notion of collective redemption and of the rebirth of the community of the faithful coincided with popular aspects of religious Orthodoxy and may go some way to explaining the Legionary movement's strong appeal in interwar Romania. Certainly, we may observe that all cults, and indeed all types of communal belonging, require the sacrifice of the person to some degree. In the context, however, of interwar Romania, this requirement demanded, and was indeed based upon, the subordination of not just the will but also the life. Only by this act of final sacrifice on the individual's part might the collective, alternatively written as the movement and

---

1   For the notion of 'palingenesis', see Roger Griffin, *The Nature of Fascism*, London, 1993, pp. 32–6.

the nation (for there was no obvious distinction between the two), be renewed, redeemed and reborn. Individual fates and sacrifices thus became talismans, around which the community measured itself and set itself new standards in the endless (and theologically hopeless) quest of rendering and bringing into being the divine purpose for this world.

* * *

Corneliu Zelea Codreanu founded the Legion of the Archangel Michael in 1927. As Codreanu subsequently wrote, the Legionary movement was not so much a political movement as 'a great spiritual movement [which] strives to transform and revolutionize the Romanian soul [...].'[2] Thus, despite the movement's ultra-nationalism and anti-Semitism, Codreanu originally had no political programme as such. The purpose of the Legion was, rather, to create and educate the so-called 'New Man': a spiritually and morally regenerated individual through whom the Romanian nation as a whole would eventually be renewed. This process, so Codreanu believed, would bring an end to the malaise and corruption endemic in Romanian political life. Although Codreanu won a seat as a parliamentary deputy in 1931 and the political wing of the movement, 'All for the Country', were to come third in the elections of 1937, the creation of the 'New Man' remained Codreanu's 'principal objective with regard to our people, because this man, once created, would be able to resolve all the problems of the nation.'[3]

From its inception the Legionary movement was marked by a strong Christian and spiritual character. Its internal structure was based around the so-called 'nest' system, the most basic Legionary unit, in which three to thirteen young people were to be taught the virtues of Christian faith and love, together with respect for work and discipline and a desire for social justice. All Legionary meetings began with a religious service. It was from within the Legionary 'nest' that the 'New Man' was to be created, and the 'New Man' himself was regarded by the Legionaries as indistinguishable from the Christian man.[4] Thus according to Mircea Eliade, writing in 1937, 'while all contemporary revolutions are political, the Iron Guard revolution is spiritual and Christian.'[5]

Strong links existed between the Legion and the Orthodox village clergy. Many of the Legionaries were themselves the sons of village priests, including Ion Moța, a co-founder of the Legion and effectively Codreanu's second-in-command until his own death in 1937. Thirty-three of the 103 candidates put forward by the Legion in the elections of December 1937 were Orthodox priests,[6] while 218 priests were later charged with participation in the Legion's revolt against General Antonescu in January 1941.[7]

---

2 Corneliu Codreanu, *Cărticica șefului de cuib*, Munich, 1987 (originally published in Bucharest in 1933), p. 111.

3 Horia Sima, *Istoria mișcării legionare*, Timișoara, 1995, p. 143.

4 Interview with Horia Sima in 1984, see, Gh. Buzatu, Corneliu Ciucanu, Cristian Sandache, *Radiografia dreptei românești*, Bucharest, 1996, pp. 319–332 (p. 321).

5 Z. Ornea, (translated by Eugenia Maria Popescu), *The Romanian Extreme Right: The Nineteen Thirties*, Boulder & New York, 1999, p. 187.

6 Radu Ioanid, *The Sword of the Archangel: Fascist Ideology in Romania*, Boulder & New York, 1990, p. 142.

7 *Pe marginea prăpastiei. 21–23 ianuarie 1941*, 2 vols, Bucharest, 1992 (originally published in 1941), vol. 2, p. 56.

Indeed, popular Orthodox Christianity had long underpinned the sense of Romanian national identity both in the Danubian Principalities as well as Transylvania. Consequently, the Legion's mystical nationalism was virtually inseparable from Orthodoxy.[8] As Henry Roberts writes, 'The employment of religious symbolism and mysticism was not merely a tactical device of the Legion, but was an integral part of its ideology.'[9] Moreover, members of the clergy frequently shared the Legion's strong anti-Semitism.

The Legion's close cooperation with the Orthodox lower clergy and its assimilation of popular Orthodoxy into its rhetoric and rituals, which will be discussed below, was reinforced by intellectual currents prevalent in Romania. Since the nineteenth century, many traditionalists had argued that certain features of modern life, such as liberal democracy, urbanization and industrialization, were alien imports into Romania. As such, these elements of Western 'modernity' were unsuitable for the Romanians whose 'spiritual essence' was deemed to be rural and Orthodox. For some inter-war intellectuals, such as Nichifor Crainic, Orthodox Christianity was virtually a hereditary, genetically-determined characteristic of the Romanians. Crainic, as well as other prominent intellectuals from this school of thought, were connected to the Legionary movement.[10]

The Legion ultimately aimed, therefore, at the spiritual regeneration of the Romanian nation and its peasantry, which constituted the vast majority of the country's population. Since peasant values were more or less synonymous with popular Orthodoxy, it was through religious imagery that Codreanu put forward his message of moral and national renewal. The Legion's message was transmitted through the Legion's regular expeditions into the Romanian villages, which had a markedly religious flavour.

The religious and nationalist aspects of Legionary expeditions into the countryside is brought out by a contemporary who witnessed such processions. 'Nobody who lived in Rumania during this period can forget the eerie and anachronistic character of a Legionary demonstration. It was something between a political protest, a religious procession and a historical *cortège*. The [...] core of the demonstration consisted of a well-organized body of young people in uniform – the 'green shirts'. It was normally headed by a group of priests carrying icons and religious flags. Finally, all this was followed and surrounded by men and women in national traditional dress. [...] the Captain [i.e. Codreanu] normally appeared in traditional Moldavian dress [...].' [11] Such processions must have had a highly dramatic effect within the relatively 'primitive' villages of rural Romania, which lacking electricity and paved roads were largely cut off from the outside world.

A number of historians, including Norman Cohn and, more recently, Eugen Weber, have pointed out that modern revolutionary movements, (even those of a secular nature), have inevitably drawn upon time-honoured religious symbols, myths and

---

8   Nicholas M. Nagy-Talavera, *The Green-Shirts and the Others: A History of Fascism in Hungary and Rumania,* Stanford, CA, 1970, p. 270.
9   Henry Roberts, *Rumania: Political Problems of an Agrarian State*, New Haven, 1951, p. 229.
10 Keith Hitchins, *Rumania, 1866–1947*, Oxford, 1994, pp. 54–78, 298–319.
11 Zev Barbu, 'Rumania', in S. J. Woolf (ed.), *Fascism in Europe*, London, 1968, pp. 151–70, (pp. 168–9).

rituals, especially those of *The Revelation of John*.[12] The latter includes descriptions of the Apocalypse, the destruction of the 'whore of Babylon', the resurrection of the oppressed and their entry into the New Jerusalem, while the 'perverts, sorcerers and fornicators' remain outside. *The Revelation of John* has thus provided a known framework in which revolutionary movements have announced their own brands of apocalypse and regeneration. The Legion, with its appropriation of Christianity, was no exception to this. Moreover, since the forces of secularization had barely begun to scratch the surface of Romanian society, the Legion was able to appeal to religious sentiments and imagery that were still very much alive.

A contemporary has written of the entry of the Legion into a Transylvanian village, with Codreanu resplendent in white and mounted on a white horse.[13] As Eugen Weber argues, this may have been a conscious mimicry of the following passage in the *The Revelation of John*: 'I saw heaven wide open, and a white horse appeared; its rider's name was Faithful and True [...]. The armed of heaven followed him, riding on white horses and clothed in fine linen, white and clean.'[14] According to Weber, 'not the least influential of John's prophecies was his vision of Christ's Second Coming as a warrior on a white horse, [...] sword in his hand to smite Antichrist.'[15]

Moreover, Codreanu's speeches were shot through with biblical imagery and allusions to the Resurrection and Christ's Second Coming drawn directly from *The Revelation of John*. Through these, Codreanu sought to put forward his own analogous message of Romania's ultimate spiritual and national regeneration. His speech from the first large-scale Legionary expedition to Bessarabia in January 1930 is typical of his style: 'The hour of the redemption and of the resurrection of our people is drawing nigh! [...] New times are knocking at our doors! A world with a soul which dried up long ago is dying, and a new world is being born – the world of those who are strong and have faith [...].' Codreanu went on to describe the final aim of the nation as, 'Resurrection [...] in the name of the Saviour Jesus Christ [...]. There will come a time when all the peoples of the earth shall be resurrected, with all their dead and all their kings and emperors, each people having its place before God's throne.'[16]

It was fitting, therefore, that the symbol of the Legion should have been the Archangel Michael, rescuer of the souls of the faithful at the hour of their death, and leader of the Heavenly army against the forces of hell in *The Revelation of John*. Moreover, it is the Archangel Michael who is responsible for binding down Satan and thereby inaugurating Christ's thousand-year reign of bliss. The Legionaries carried icons of the Archangel Michael, together with Codreanu's portrait in icon form, when they travelled into the countryside. They thereby exploited the ubiquity of icons in Orthodox churches and homes, and their mystical associations. According to the Orthodox bishop Kallistos Ware, '[...] icons act as a point of meeting between the living members of the Church

12 Norman Cohn, *The Pursuit of the Millennium: Revolutionary Millenarians and Mystical Anarchists of the Middle Ages*, New York, 1970; Eugen Weber, *Apocalypses: Prophecies, Cults and Millennial Beliefs through the Ages*, London, 1999.
13 Nagy-Talavera, *The Green Shirts and the Others*, p. 247.
14 Revelation of John, 19: 11.
15 Weber, *Apocalypses: Prophecies, Cults and Millennial Beliefs throughout the Ages*, p. 30.
16 Nagy-Talavera, *The Green Shirts and the Others*, p. 281; Corneliu Zelea Codreanu, *For My Legionaries (The Iron Guard)*, Madrid, 1976, p. 315.

and those who have gone before. Icons help the Orthodox to look on the saints not as remote and legendary figures from the past, but as contemporaries and personal friends.'[17]

This sense that the dead are somehow still alive amongst the living was given expression in Codreanu's concept of the collective nation. According to Codreanu, the nation included not only the living members of the Romanian community, but also Romanians as yet unborn and, as Codreanu put it, 'all the souls of our dead and the tombs of our ancestors'. The nation, Codreanu believed, 'is an entity which prolongs her existence even beyond this world. Peoples are realities even in the nether world, not only in this one.'[18]

As an extension of this idea, Codreanu also believed that the power of dead, ancestral Romanians could be transmitted to the living through prayer. This was invoked by Codreanu as an essential element in the Legion's struggle and ultimate victory over its enemies: 'Wars were won by those who knew how to summon the mysterious powers of the unseen world [...]. These mysterious powers are the souls of the dead, the souls of our ancestors who too were once attached to this land [...].' Prayers invoking the power of the ancestors were thus to take place during 'nest' meetings on Saturday evenings, and at church on Sundays.[19] This sense of a community in which the dead inter-acted with the living was given expression during Legionary 'nest' meetings when the names of fallen comrades were read out and one of their living fellows would pronounce them as 'Present!' Following the deaths of the two senior Legionaries, Ion Moța and Vasile Marin, in the Spanish Civil War in January 1937, their names were also added to the top of the list of all fallen Legionaries to be read out at Legionary meetings and declared to be 'Present!' Members of the movement were also exhorted to hold services and requiems for deceased Legionaries.[20]

The Legionary ideology of the nation as an inter-dependent and, indeed, inter-active community of the living and ancestral Romanians had its counterpart, and drew upon, the Orthodox Church's concept of the church as a collectivity of the living and the dead. As Bishop Kallistos Ware has written in his study of the Orthodox church: 'In God and His Church there is no division between the living and the departed, but all are one in the love of the Father. Whether we are alive or whether we are dead, as members of the Church we still belong to the same family and still have a duty to bear one another's burdens. Therefore, just as Orthodox Christians here on earth pray for one another [...] so they pray also for the faithful departed and ask the faithful departed to pray for them. Death cannot sever the bond of mutual love which links the members of the Church together.'[21] In Orthodox belief, therefore, the church is regarded as a collectivity in which all its members, dead or alive, are saved together rather than as individuals. The sense that the dead are somehow still part of the community of the living church is also apparent in Orthodoxy's rejection of the notion of Purgatory. The

---

17 Venetia Newall, 'Icons as Symbols of Power', in H. R. Ellis Davidson (ed.), *Symbols of Power*, Cambridge, 1977, pp. 61–100 (p. 91); Timothy Ware, *The Orthodox Church*, London, 1963, p. 261.
18 Codreanu, *For My Legionaries*, pp. 313, 315.
19 Codreanu, *Cărticica șefului de cuib*, pp. 55–6.
20 *Ion I. Moța. Prezent!*, Bucharest, 1937, pp. 1, 7.
21 Ware, *The Orthodox Church*, p. 258.

dead are held to be in a sense neither dead nor alive. Their souls are said rather to 'sleep' until their resurrection on the Day of Judgement. The living have a duty to pray for the souls of the dead to ensure their ultimate entry into Heaven.[22] Services for the commemoration of the dead remain an important and frequent feature of the Orthodox calendar. Saturday is the day of the week consecrated for prayers to the dead and services of commemoration (hence Codreanu's injunction to the Legionaries to pray to the dead at Saturday evening 'nest' meetings), while the Saturdays before Shrove Tuesday, Whitsunday and Saint Michael's Day are, amongst others, regarded of special importance.[23]

The belief in the power of the ancestral dead for the Legion's victory also found expression in the Legionaries' first vow-taking ceremony held on St Michael's Day, 8 November 1927. As the Legionary periodical, *The Ancestral Land*, explained: 'This solemnity began by mixing the earth brought from the tomb of Michael the Brave from Turda, with that from Moldavia [...] where Stefan the Great fought his greatest battles, and from every other place where our ancestors' blood was soaked by the earth in ferocious battles, thus blessing it.'[24] As Codreanu continued in his memoirs: 'Small leather sacks were then filled with [the soil] and tightly tied with laces. These were to be received by Legionaries as they took their vow [to the Legion] and were to be worn close to their hearts.' He described the bags of soil as 'a symbol which could be a faithful expression of the character of our movement, of our union with the earth of our ancestors, our dead and the heavens.'[25]

These bags of soil were also carried by the so-called 'Death Teams'. The first of these was set up in 1933 and its members were dedicated to defending the movement, as the representative of the Romanian nation, even unto death. Ten 'Death Teams' were set up at the student congress of Târgu Mureş in April 1936 to seek vengeance on politicians and other individuals responsible for the persecution of the Legion and to protect Codreanu. Members of the 'Death Teams' took a vow over the bags of soil to this effect.[26]

The Legion's 'cult of death' and creation of the 'Death Teams' inevitably led to a glorification of violence and murder. In December 1933, three Legionaries, thereafter known as the *Nicadori* within the Legionary martyrology, murdered the Liberal premier Ion Duca. One of the most grotesque expressions of the Legionary death cult, however, was the murder of the former Legionary Mihail Stelescu in 1936 by one of the teams set up at the Târgu Mureş congress. Stelescu was deemed to have betrayed

22 Adrian Fortescue, *The Orthodox Eastern Church*, London, 1907, pp. 389, 408–9.
23 Vasile Răducă, *Ghidul creştinului ortodox de azi*, Bucharest, 1998, pp. 201–3.
24 Codreanu, *For My Legionaries*, pp. 249–50.
25 ibid. Emily Gerard, who investigated Romanian folk beliefs regarding the dead in the late-nineteenth century, found evidence that the bodies of the deceased and the soil surrounding their graves were held to have medicinal powers. Apparently, pleasant dreams would result from laying earth from a fresh grave-mound behind the neck at night, while the following cure for fever is reminiscent of the Legionary *penchant* for bags of ancestral soil: 'Having gone to the grave of a beloved relative and taken from the grave a handful of earth, which he is careful to tie up tightly and place inside his shirt, the sick man goes away, and for three days and three nights he carries this talisman about with him wherever he goes'. See Emily Gerard, *The Land beyond the Forest: Facts, Figures and Fancies from Transylvania*, Edinburgh, 1888, p. 316.
26 Nagy-Talavera, *The Green Shirts and the Others*, pp. 291–2.

the movement by leaving the Legion and founding a rival organization. While recovering in hospital from an illness ten members of his former Legionary 'nest' broke into his room. They apparently shot him 120 times, after which they chopped his body into little pieces and 'danced around it and kissed each other.'[27] These ten Legionaries were subsequently arrested and mythologized by the movement as the *Decemviri*. In September 1939, a group of Legionaries murdered the minister president, Armand Călinescu, King Carol II's right-hand man and architect of Codreanu's downfall and subsequent murder in 1938. The Legion's most spectacular political murders, however, took place during the period of the National Legionary State. On 27 November 1940, the exhumation of Codreanu, together with the bodies of the *Decemviri* and *Nicadori* took place at Jilava prison outside Bucharest. The exhumations were accompanied by the murder by Legionaries of sixty-four political prisoners held at Jilava in connection with persecution of the Legion during King Carol II's royal dictatorship. On the following day, Legionaries murdered the historian Nicolae Iorga, who had been implicated in Codreanu's arrest in April 1938, together with the National Peasant Party economist Virgil Madgearu, who had long been an adversary of the movement. The violence which marked the government of the National Legionary State culminated in a pogrom against Bucharest's Jewish community during the January 1941 rebellion.

Without denying the Legion's potential for violence, we should, however, note the brutality of the Romanian government in its handling of its political opponents in this era. Between 1924 and 1937 the Legion committed a total of eleven known murders (together with a great deal of thuggery and damage to property), but over five hundred Legionaries were condemned to death and the movement was frequently outlawed.[28] Between Codreanu's murder in 1938 and the establishment of the National Legionary State in September 1940, some three thousand Legionaries were executed or 'disappeared'.[29] Clearly, however, for a movement which believed in the Christian concept of resurrection, death was not something to be feared. Moreover, a willingness to die made members of the movement, and of the 'Death Teams' in particular, believe themselves invulnerable in the face of mounting government persecution. As one Legionary maxim put it, 'Whoever knows how to die, will never be a slave', or, as Codreanu explained, 'Not being able to win while alive, we will win dying [...].'[30]

Members of the Death Teams additionally faced likely death as a result of the Legion's doctrine of expiation. This had been developed by Constantin Papanace in order to reconcile the apparent Christian nature of the movement with its frequent acts of violence. According to Papanace, an act of violence or even murder was justified in terms of the greater good of the nation but must be paid for by the perpetrator of the act. As Codreanu insisted, the Legionary's 'breast must be of iron, but lily-white his soul'. Any Legionary who committed an act of murder was expected to turn himself into the

27 Barbu, 'Rumania', in Woolf (ed.), *The Nature of Fascism*, p. 163.
28 ibid, p. 162.
29 Politisches Archiv des Auswärtigen Amtes, Berlin, Deutsche Gesandschaft, Bukarest, 1A5, Rumänien, Innenpolitisch, vol. 9, 4. 1939–1. 1940, Bucharest, 24 December 1939, Tgb. Nr. 7819, To the Foreign Ministry, Berlin, from Fabricius.
30 Codreanu, *For My Legionaries*, pp. 218, 226.

authorities who were more than likely to condemn him to a life of hard labour or to death.[31] It is not surprising, therefore, that Legionary writings were infused with images of death and resurrection. As the newspaper, *Dacia*, explained in December 1940: 'The finest aspect of Legionary life is death [...] by death the Legionary becomes engaged to eternity'.[32] In December 1940, in keeping with a concept of the nation in which the dead mingle with the living, the newspaper *Cuvântul* simply declared that 'the dead are the living'.[33] The form of greeting for members of the 'Death Teams' was 'Long live Death!' and the principal song of the Death Teams expressed a sense of ultimate transcendence over death by comparing death with a wedding:

> Legionary do not fear
> That you will die young
>
> For you die to be reborn
> And are born to die
>
> For we are the death team
> That must win or die
>
> Death, only the legionary-death
> Is a gladsome wedding for us.[34]

The death of any Legionary in the service of the movement was regarded as the ultimate act of sacrifice and martyrdom for the nation. The Legion was thus strongly influenced by the Christian concepts of martyrdom and the *Imitatio Christi*. The Legionary path was often compared to that of Christ in as much as it lay through suffering, sacrifice and death to resurrection.[35] Legionary supporters frequently likened Ion Moța, and later Codreanu, to Christ, as sacrificial victims for the good of the Romanian nation. Following Moța's death in the Spanish Civil War, Professor Nae Ionescu, declared that 'for the salvation of our nation, God had to accept Moța's sacrifice, as for the salvation of the human race he accepted that of the lamb.'[36] Indeed, the creation of a Legionary martyrology must have done much to increase the movement's appeal amongst the Orthodox peasantry, long accustomed to the saints and martyrs of the church. Pictures of these new Legionary 'martyrs' appeared regularly in Legionary publications. A booklet published to mark Moța's death included a full page photo of the deceased leader and compared his presence amongst his living Legionary comrades with that of the risen Christ amongst his disciples.[37]

---

31 Eugen Weber, 'Romania', in Hans Rogger and Eugen Weber (eds.), *The European Right: A Historical Profile*, Berkeley, 1965, pp. 501–74, (p. 533); Constantin Papanace, *Stilul legionar de luptă. Concepția tactică a Căpitanului*, Bucharest, 2004, pp. 78–9.

32 Quoted in Martyn Rady, *Romania in Turmoil: A Contemporary History*, London & New York, 1992, p. 25.

33 Quoted in Ioanid, *The Sword of the Archangel*, p. 148.

34 Quoted in Zeev Barbu, 'Psycho-Historical and Sociological Perspectives on the Iron Guard, the Fascist Movement of Romania', in Stein Ugelvik Larsen, et al (eds.), *Who were the Fascists? Social Roots of European Fascism*, Bergen, 1980, pp. 379–94 (p. 389).

35 Nagy-Talavera, *The Green Shirts and the Others*, p. 266.

36 Quoted in Weber, 'Romania', in Rogger and Weber (eds), *The European Right*, p. 525.

37 *Ion I. Moța. Prezent!*, p. 1.

As an extension of the cult of the Legionary martyrs, the rites of burial were success-fully utilized by the Legion as important political statements and as a focus for national consolidation under Legionary auspices. Of particular importance in this respect was the funeral of Ion Moța and Vasile Marin held in Bucharest on 13 February, 1937. Their bodies had been returned to Romania from Spain by train and in Berlin the coffins were honoured by detachments of the SS. As the train proceeded through Romania, it stopped at stations for the coffins to be blessed by Orthodox priests and acknowledged by the public. The large and ostentatious funeral in Bucharest included a heavy clerical pres-ence, including the Patriarch Miron Cristea, and was attended by vast crowds of ordinary Romanians. Significantly, members of the diplomatic corps of Germany, Italy and Spain also attended the funeral. The coffins were buried at a mausoleum in the Green House, the movement's Bucharest headquarters, and were permanently guarded by Legionaries. Reports of miracles quickly began to circulate.[38]

King Carol was greatly affected by the signs of massive public support for the move-ment, as well as the apparent foreign support for the Legion accorded by the presence of the diplomats at the funeral.[39] Carol now feared that the level of support for the move-ment was a very real threat to the monarchy. Carol's fears were by no means unfounded. In his memoirs, the Legionary Horațiu Comaniciu describes how the deaths of the two Legionaries, who had given their lives on foreign soil to protect Romania and Europe from Soviet-backed bolshevism and anti-clericalism, had 'sent an electric current through the country.' The death of Moța and Marin was the decisive event that had drawn him, and many other young people, to join the Legionary movement.[40] Indeed, the 12,000 Legionary 'nests' which existed at the start of the year, had risen to some 34,000 by December 1937.[41] In the elections of that month, the Legion officially won sixteen percent of the popular vote. This was no mean achievement in a country in which the incumbent government regularly indulged in massive electoral malpractice. The Moța and Marin funeral undoubtedly did much to raise the profile of the Legion throughout the country and to consolidate the Legion's claim to be the foremost protector of the Romanian nation.

The funeral was, however, only the starting point of the Moța and Marin cult. As we have seen, the names of the two Legionaries were incorporated into the 'roll-call' of the dead to be read out at Legionary meetings. In May 1937, the decision was made to construct a monastery and mausoleum on land near Predeal in the Carpathian mountains to be dedicated to Moța and Marin and to come under the authority of the archbishopric

---

38 Francisco Veiga, *Istoria Gărzii de Fier 1919–1941. Mistica ultranaționalismului*, Bucharest, 1993, p. 231. The Ministry of the Interior reported that on 18 June 1937 a fire had broken out at the Moța and Marin mausoleum at the Green House. Although the canopy had burned, the fact that the wooden cross emerged unscathed was regarded as a miracle by the movement's supporters. See Arhivele Naționale (Bucharest), Fond Ministerul de interne. Diverse, dosar nr. 9/1937, Secția I-a, Nr 3, 21 June 1937.

39 Politisches Archiv des Auswärtigen Amtes, Berlin, Politische Abteilung IV: Po 5, vol. 1, 5.36–8.37, German Legation in Bucharest to the Foreign Ministry, daily report nr 669/37, 11 March 1937, signed Fabricius.

40 Horatiu Comaniciu, *In lupta neamului (Amintiri), Consiliul National Roman*, no place of publication, no date, pp. 28–9, 297.

41 Nagy-Talavera, *The Green Shirts and the Others*, p. 293.

of Alba Iulia and Sibiu.[42] In January 1938, Codreanu set up the Moța-Marin corps, an elite body of around 10,000 Legionaries ready to die for the nation in the manner of the two martyrs. The corps' members were to be under the age of thirty, to be of high moral character and willing to dedicate themselves to a life of austerity. Members of the corps were, moreover, to 'love suffering', since suffering was believed to strengthen the soul. All members of the corps swore an oath, based upon Moța's writings, acknowledging their willingness to die.[43]

The Moța and Marin funeral was not the final example of the Legion's cult of 'worship of the corpse' as a vehicle of political and national consolidation. In early February 1938, the Ministry of the Interior reported that a deceased Legionary was effectively 'lying in state' at the movement's headquarters in Bucharest in the presence of a number of Orthodox priests. Around 600 Legionaries had already filed past the catafalque and groups of Legionaries were posted on surrounding streets, presumably to check the great flow of people still paying their respects to the deceased.[44] The Legionary had almost certainly died in the violent government repression which marked the opening of the new campaign for the elections scheduled for March 1938. The above ceremony doubtless reminded the public of the government's persecution and 'martyrdom' of the Legion.

The Legionary cult of martyrdom received its greatest boost with the murder of Codreanu himself. On the night of 29/30 November 1938, Codreanu, together with the *Decemviri* and *Nicadori*, the murderers of Mihai Stelescu and Ion Duca respectively, was taken in a truck from Jilava prison to the woods outside Bucharest. The prisoners were fettered and chained and then garrotted. Their bodies were shot in the back of the head to make it look as though they had been 'shot trying to escape', as the official explanation later put it. After having acid poured on them to disguise their identities, the corpses were hastily buried in the grounds of Jilava prison.

We have already noted that Codreanu's picture was carried, like that of a saint, in icon form while Codreanu was still living. During the government of the National Legionary State, Codreanu's followers attempted to have their deceased leader canonized and to found a new Romanian capital to be named 'Codreni' in his honour.[45] Although they were unsuccessful, the National Legionary State did not fail to exploit Codreanu's genuine popularity even beyond the grave. A notable feature of the important Legionary demonstration held on 6 October 1940 was the use of enormous pictures of Codreanu on which were daubed the words 'Corneliu Zelea Codreanu – Present!', a reminder, as if one were needed, that the spirit of the dead Captain continued to preside over Legionary affairs.[46] Moreover, his presence amid the living was often likened to that of Christ. As one intellectual noted: 'With the exception of Jesus, no dead man has

42 Arhivele Naționale (Bucharest), Fond Casa regală, dosar nr. 33/1937, Letter from the archbishop and metropolitan of Alba Iulia and Sibiu, nr 4785 of 18 May 1937 to the mayor of the Municipality of Brașov.

43 Arhivele Naționale, (Bucharest), Fond Ministerul de Interne, Diverse, dosar 10/1938, Note, 25 January 1938, pp. 12–19 (p. 17).

44 Arivele Naționale, (Bucharest), Fond Ministerul de Interne, Diverse, dosar nr 19/1938, Corpul Detectivilor, Secția I-a, D.Of., 6 February 1938, p. 5.

45 Nagy-Talavera, *The Green Shirts and the Others*, p. 322.

46 ibid, p. 313.

been more present amidst the living [...]. From now on, the country will be led by a dead man [...]. This dead man has spread the perfume of eternity over our human dregs [...].'[47]

The use of funerals, as well as commemorations and requiems for the dead, as a focus for political and national consolidation reached its height during the period of the National Legionary State. Indeed, the regime was apparently dubbed the 'regime of funeral processions' owing to the frequency and pomp with which the many Legionaries who had been murdered by the royal regime between 1938 and 1940 were exhumed and reburied.[48] Thus, only three days after the establishment of the National Legionary State on 14 September 1940, the Legionary newspaper *Buna Vestire* announced the compilation of an album to commemorate the fallen Legionaries. Families and friends of the deceased were exhorted to send in photos, together with the place and date of death, and any information to illustrate 'the history of Legionary suffering'.[49] On 22 September, Horia Sima, Codreanu's successor as leader of the movement, declared the day to be dedicated to the heroes and martyrs of the Legion. On this date, prayers were to be said for them in all churches throughout the country.[50] Amongst the interminable requiems which marked the National Legionary State was one held on 27 September for Alexandru Cantacuzino, commander of the Moța-Marin corps, who had been murdered by King Carol II's regime in 1939. Spanish representatives were present to hear an oration delivered extolling Cantacuzino's role as a soldier in the Spanish Civil War.[51]

The most important of the exhumations and reburials conducted during the National Legionary State was, of course, that of Codreanu himself. Indeed, those of Codreanu's followers who resented Horia Sima's leadership of the movement had already founded a 'black shirts' cohort to signify mourning for Codreanu and the 'real Legionaries' whom they believed had been supplanted by Horia Sima and his supporters.[52] The exhumation of the corpses of Codreanu and those of the *Decemviri* and *Nicadori* took place on 27 November, 1940, at Jilava prison and was accompanied by the murder of the 64 political prisoners to whom we have already referred. Prince Michel Sturdza, Foreign Minister in the National Legionary State, described the exhumation of the bodies: 'They found them hidden under several tons of concrete, corroded by the vitriol that had been poured on them, the ropes still twisted about their throats, with fettered feet and arms. The Captain's body was recognized by its size and by the little crucifix Codreanu always wore around his neck.'[53] The funeral itself was held on 30 November – the second anniversary of Codreanu's death – and the procession which wound its way from Jilava to the Green House in Bucharest was apparently several miles long. The funeral, as well as being an expression of Legionary and, by extension, national solidarity, was also the opportunity for the consolidation of political alliances. It was attended by senior representatives of Romania's German ally and, in a gesture of

---

47 Ornea, *The Romanian Extreme Right*, p. 179.
48 Nagy-Talavera, *The Green Shirts and the Others*, p. 318.
49 *Buna Vestire*, 17 September 1940.
50 ibid, 20 September 1940.
51 ibid, 28 September 1940.
52 Arhivele Naționale, (Bucharest), Fond Președinția consiliului de ministri, Cabinet militar 1940–1944, dosar nr. 199/1940, p. 30, unmarked note dated 22 November 1940.
53 Prince Michel Sturdza, *The Suicide of Europe: Memoirs of Prince Michel Sturdza, former Foreign Minister of Rumania*, Belmont, MA, 1968, p. 205.

nationalist fraternity, German planes dropped wreaths over the open graves.[54] Such was the national significance accorded to the funeral, that all shops were ordered to be shut for the day and public services and factories throughout the country came to a standstill.[55]

Since the death of Moța and Marin in January 1937, the Legion had commemorated the anniversary of their deaths. The commemoration service held during the government of the National Legionary State was, naturally, an important occasion, used to further cement links with Romania's Axis allies. Thus, the service held on 14 January 1941 in Bucharest was attended by representatives of Germany, Italy and Spain.[56] Similar services were organized by Legionaries in Berlin and Italy.[57]

If the Legion often exploited the rituals of burial and exhumation and commemoration as national and political statements, the rites themselves drew upon popular Orthodox funeral customs and upon beliefs regarding death and the hereafter. We have already noted the importance of commemoration of the collective and ancestral dead in the Orthodox calendar and the importance of the prayers of the living in mediating for the dead and their eventual entry into Heaven. Likewise, it is considered extremely important for the correct funeral rites to be observed if the soul of the deceased is to reach the hereafter safely. Agnes Murcogi, writing at the end of the Great War on burial customs amongst the Romanians, noted that to the peasants, the great number of war casualties and the consequent lack of opportunity to perform the necessary burial rites was 'one of the greatest tragedies of the war'. Murgoci added that, 'There is amongst the Roumanians a great deal of enjoyment of the death rites even of strangers.'[58] Moreover, Murgoci's researches indicate that the ritual of exhumation was widespread in the aftermath of the war amongst Romanians, presumably in order to ensure that the correct burial rites had been performed for the deceased.[59] In Orthodox ritual, exhumation and reburial of the corpse after seven years followed by a requiem mass, was clearly not uncommon in some areas of inter-war Romania, especially in Moldavia. This was accompanied by a final funeral feast (*pomană*) next to the grave to which the deceased would also be called. Such funeral feasts were traditionally held on the day of burial and at intervals thereafter.[60] It is clear, therefore, that the exhumations carried out by the Legion were a manifestation of the religious and cultural norms of their day – a fact over looked by those historians anxious to stress the macabre side of the movement.

---

54 Nagy-Talavera, *The Green Shirts and the Others*, p. 321.
55 Arhivele Naționale, Fond Președinția consiliului de miniștri, dosar nr 310/1940, p. 24, note, 29 November 1940.
56 *Buna Vestire*, 14 January 1941.
57 *Universul*, 16 January 1941.
58 Agnes Murcogi, 'Customs connected with Death and Burial amongst the Roumanians', *Folk-Lore*, 30, no. 2, 1919, pp. 89–102 (pp. 89, 94).
59 Murcogi refers to 'an orgy of burials and re-burials in the years 1919 and 1920' in the Bukovina. See Agnes Murgoci, 'The Vampire in Roumania', *Folk-Lore*, 37, 1926, pp. 320–49 (320). For similar information regarding Bessarabia, see Murgoci, 'Customs connected with Death and Burial amongst the Roumanians', p. 99.
60 Răducă, *Ghidul creștinului ortodox de azi*, pp. 201–3; Murcogi, 'Customs connected with Death and Burial among the Roumanians', p. 99.

Conclusion

The success of the Legionary movement during the 1930s was partly due to its ability to draw upon the popular religious beliefs of Romania's largely peasant masses and to employ these within the framework of a revolutionary, nationalist ideology. The 'cult of death' itself originated in Orthodox teachings regarding death and the hereafter and was a major feature of the movement. In particular, the Legion's ideology of the nation as a collective of the unborn, living and ancestral Romanians drew upon the Orthodox belief in the church as an interactive community of the living and the dead. Legionary ceremonials were closely interwoven with those of the Orthodox church and reinforced a sense of Romanian nationhood based on common ancestry and religion. In the same way, the grandiose burials and exhumations carried out by the Legionaries acted as political statements of the unity of the Romanian nation even in death and of the Legion's role as the nation's protector.

Something should be added here, however, regarding the apparent 'exceptionalism' of the Legion's strong cult of death and adherence to Christianity within European fascism. Despite their more ambivalent attitudes towards Christianity, both Nazism and Italian Fascism were deeply marked by the language of millenarianism, the Christian symbolism of death and resurrection, the Christian cult of martyrdom, the veneration of fallen comrades and the 'worship of the corpse'.[61] Moreover, it should be noted that the 'worship of the corpse' to reinforce national or group solidarity was not unique to the right-wing in inter-war Europe. Quite apart from the display of Lenin's corpse in Bolshevik Russia, the anarchists of Barcelona, who only a few months previously had displayed the long-dead corpses of monks and nuns in the streets of Barcelona to the jeers of their anticlerical supporters, had their fallen leader embalmed and placed on display in a glass coffin in November 1936.[62]

Furthermore, the 'cult of death', with its Christian symbolism, invocations of the fallen, martyrs' cults and elaborate funerals was not confined simply to the more popular fascist movements in inter-war Europe. It marked, for example, the Spanish Falange: a movement that never achieved anything like the popularity of the Legion. The execution of José Antonio in 1936 resulted in his becoming the object of a 'massive martyr's cult without precedent in the history of modern Western European politics'. José Antonio's cult culminated in a huge ceremony in which his remains were transferred for reburial at the high altar of the Church of San Lorenzo at the El Escorial (the traditional burial place of the Spanish kings).[63] Likewise, the Croatian Ustasha movement was pervaded by a 'cult of death' of 'chiliastic intensity' which 'mimicked the rites and beliefs of Roman Catholicism'.[64] The Legion's 'cult of death' and

---

61 See, for example, James M. Rhodes, *The Hitler Movement: A Modern Millenarian Revolution*, Stanford, 1980 and Emilio Gentile, *The Sacralization of Politics in Fascist Italy*, Cambridge, MA, 1996.

62 Bruce Lincoln, 'Revolutionary Exhumations in Spain, July 1936', *Comparative Studies in Society and History*, 27, 1985, 2, pp. 241–60 (p. 258).

63 Stanley G. Payne, *Fascism in Spain 1923–1977*, Wisconsin, 1999, pp. 232–3 (p. 233).

64 Rory Yeomans, 'Cults of Death and Fantasies of Annihilation: The Croatian Ustasha Movement in Power, 1941–45', *Central Europe*, 3, no. 2, 2005, pp. 121–42 (p. 121).

recourse to Christian symbolism was thus no bizarre aberration, but well within the mainstream of European fascism.[65]

In its eschatology, and in the centrality that it gave to the life after death and therewith to a higher vocation in human existence, the Legion like fascism as a whole built upon older traditions that rested not only upon romanticism but also upon the conviction that the centre of the universe and the heart of creation represented unattainable goals but ones that were still worth striving for. George Steiner's summary of De Maistre's political philosophy and of a persuasive trend in European thought now eclipsed by Marxian and bourgeois materialism may stand as an epitaph for the Legion and for the position it sought to assume in the larger dynamic of world-history:

> The only true revolution will be that of the messianic, of the apocalyptic in the light prefigured by the Book of Revelation. At that day of judgement, the inhumanities, the absurdities, the injustices wrought by man on man, will be resolved in a finality of punishment and of recompense. The endeavour of mundane revolutions, of revolutionary tribunals, to anticipate that last judgement, to enforce upon history and social relations some man-made code of equity are, in the strictest and most concrete connotations, blasphemy.[66]

---

65 It should be added that exhumation and reburial has not been uncommon amongst Catholics. It was practised in parts of rural Poland in the 1930s and in remote parts of Portugal as recently as the 1970s. See, Lincoln, 'Revolutionary Exhumations in Spain, July 1936', pp. 249–50; João de Pina-Cabral, 'Cults of Death in Northwestern Portugal', *Journal of the Anthropological Society of Oxford*, 11, no. 1, 1980, pp. 1–14.

66 George Steiner, 'Aspects of Counter-Revolution' in (ed.) Geoffrey Best, *The Permanent Revolution: The French Revolution and its Legacy 1798–1989*, London, 1989, pp. 129–53 (p. 148).

War, Stalinism and Disillusionment

Setting Europe Ablaze? The SOE, Central Europe and the Czechoslovak Government-in-exile, 1940–1945

Martin D. Brown

Close to midnight on 16 July 1940, Winston Churchill called for one of his cabinet ministers, Hugh Dalton, and asked him to take command of a new clandestine organization called the Special Operations Executive (SOE), tasked with stimulating resistance across Nazi-occupied Europe. 'I accepted the Prime Minister's invitation with great eagerness and satisfaction,' remembered Dalton in his memoirs. ' "And now," he exhorted me, "set Europe ablaze." '[1]

It is a nice story, but an examination of Dalton's original diary entries reveals that it is not entirely accurate.[2] Nor do we have any independent verification of Churchill's comments; the meeting does not appear in his own multi-volume history of the war.[3] Nevertheless, these three words – 'set Europe ablaze' – have since come to dominate academic, official, and popular understanding of SOE's activities. Indeed, it is difficult to find books or articles on the subject that do not cite them.[4] If SOE's only aim was to ignite all-out mayhem across occupied Europe, then it failed. But, as we shall see, it was not. The organization's tasks during the six years it operated were far more complex, contradictory and politicized than Dalton's dramatic recollections suggest.

---

1 Hugh Dalton, *The Fateful Years: Memoirs 1931–1945,* London, 1957, p. 366.
2 Ben Pimlott (ed.), *The Second World War Diary of Hugh Dalton, 1940–45,* London, 1986, pp. 60, 62.
3 David Reynolds, *In Command of History: Churchill Fighting and Writing the Second World War,* London, 2004, pp. 175–176.
4 In chronological order: Maurice James Buckmaster, *Specially Employed. The Story of British Aid to French Patriots of the Resistance,* London, 1952, p. 15; Bickham Sweet Escott, *Baker Street Irregular,* London, 1965, p. 40; Edward Henry Cookridge, *Inside SOE: The Inside Story of the Special Operations Executive in Western Europe 1940–45,* London, 1966, p. 3; D. Stafford, 'The Detonator Concept: British Strategy, SOE and European Resistance after the Fall of the France', *Journal of Contemporary History,* 10, April 1975, 2, pp. 185–217 (p. 199); Douglas Dodds-Parker, *Setting Europe Ablaze: Some Account of Ungentlemanly Warfare,* London, 1983; Callum MacDonald, *The Killing of Obergruppenführer Reinhard Heydrich,* London, 1989, p. 73; Ian Dear, *Sabotage and Subversion: Stories from the Files of the SOE and OSS,* London, 1996, p.9; Norman Davies, *Rising '44: The Battle for Warsaw,* London, 2003, p. 51; G. Bennett, 'British Intelligence Services during the Second World War', in Tessa Stirling, D. Nałęcz, T. Dubicki (eds), *Intelligence Co-operation between Poland and Great Britain during World War II. The Report of the Anglo-Polish Historical Committee,* vol 1, London, 2005, pp. 127–132 (p. 129); The Cabinet Office, 'The UK Government's Official History Programme, SOE Histories', <http://www.cabinetoffice.gov.uk/publicationscheme/published_information/1/officialhistory.asp#soe>; The Foreign and Commonwealth Office, 'SOE Offical Histories', <http://www.fco.gov.uk/servlet/Front?pagename=OpenMarket/Xcelerate/ShowPage&c=Page&cid=1050510206588> [both sites accessed 20 December 2006].

Since the end of the Second World War, SOE's work with the French *maquis*, its involvement with the audacious attacks on Norway's heavy water industry, and its support for Tito's partisans in Yugoslavia[5] have been thoroughly integrated into Britain's 'collective memory' of the conflict.[6] For nearly sixty years, the executive's missions behind enemy lines have been repeatedly portrayed and fictionalized in numerous books, television series and feature films.[7] These high-profile operations have come to dominate understanding of the term 'resistance', which the public all too often associates simplistically with heroic acts of derring-do, ignoring the more nuanced realities on the ground.

Moreover, resistance in all its forms, whether active or passive, was the pre-eminent wartime experience for the majority of peoples in Nazi-occupied Europe, and SOE was the organization that took the lead in promoting these activities.[8] It should also be recognized that Europe's – as opposed to Britain's – collective memories of the war remain a controversial subject.[9] As Tony Judt has noted, '[...] to be innocent a nation had to have resisted, and to have done so in its overwhelming majority, a claim that was perforce made and pedagogically enforced all over Europe.'[10] An explicit link has therefore long existed between demonstrating that active, violent resistance existed and a nation's supposed 'innocence' – a process that has frequently taken liberties with the historical record. As a result, British and European recollections of this period remain markedly different, as do their attitudes towards the legacy of resistance.[11] Jean Monnet, the architect of postwar European integration, gave a persuasive explanation for the persistence of these divergent perspectives when he stated, 'L'Angleterre n'avait pas été vaincue, elle n'avait pas connu l'invasion. Elle ne se sentait pas obligée d'exorciser l'histoire.'[12]

Equally, the respective contributions made to the defeat of the Third Reich by American, British and Soviet-backed irregular forces became the focus for long-running

5   F. W. Deakin, *The Embattled Mountain,* London, 1971; Fitzroy Maclean, *Eastern Approaches*, London, 1949, pp. 303–532; R. Mears, *The Real Heroes of Telemark*, London, 2003; David Stafford, *Secret Agent: The True Story of the Special Operations Executive*, London, 2000.

6   The term 'collective memory' is a complex one, for an overview of the current status of this subject see, Jim House and Neil Macmaster, *Paris 1961: Algerians, State Terror, and Memory*, Oxford, 2006, pp. 186–189; Jay Winter and Emmanuel Sivan, 'Setting the Framework', in Jay Winter and E. Sivan (eds.), *War and Remembrance in the Twentieth Century*, Cambridge, 1999, pp. 6–39.

7   M. Connelly and D. R. Willcox, 'Are You Tough Enough? The Image of the Special Forces in British Popular Culture, 1939–2004', *Historical Journal of Film, Radio and Television*, 25, March 2005, 1, pp. 1–25; G. Eley, 'Finding the People's War: Film, British Collective Memory, and World War II', *The American Historical Review*, 106, 2001, 3, <http://www.historycooperative.org/journals/ahr/106.3/ah000818.html> [Accessed 20 October 2006].

8   From July 1940 until the invasion of the Soviet Union in June 1941, SOE was the only organization responsible for promoting resistance across occupied Europe.

9   Michael Howard, *The Causes of Wars and Other Essays*, London, 1983, p. 166.

10 Tony Judt, 'The Past is Another Country: Myth and Memory in Postwar Europe' *Daedalus*, 121, Fall 1992, 4, pp. 83–118 (pp.89–90).

11 István Deák, Jan T. Gross, Tony Judt (eds), *The Politics of Retribution in Europe: World War II and its Aftermath*, Princeton, 2000; Pieter Lagrou, *The Legacy of Nazi Occupation: Patriotic Memory and National Recovery in Western Europe, 1945–1965*, Cambridge, 2000, pp. 19–78, 262–306; M. Nolan, 'Germans as Victims During the Second World War: Air Wars, Memory Wars', *Central European History*, 38, 2005, no 1, pp. 7–40; Henry Rousso, *Le Syndrome de Vichy: De 1944 à nos jours*, Paris, 1987, pp. 28–30, 318–321.

12 Jean Monnet, *Mémoires*, Paris, 1976, p. 362.

acrimonious disputes during the Cold War.[13] Since the fall of communism in 1989, many states across Central and Eastern Europe have tried to compensate for these influences and reclaim their own histories of the war, with varying degrees of success.[14] Any analysis of SOE and its work thus carries implications that extend far beyond the military history of the Second World War.

While British historians have documented the executive's work in France and Yugoslavia extensively, they have given its actions elsewhere in Europe less attention. It has often been presumed, for example, that active resistance was negligible in the former Czechoslovakia.[15] On the contrary, the Czechoslovak government-in-exile, based in London after 1939 and led by the former President Dr Edvard Beneš, cooperated closely with SOE from its inception, with mixed results. It was in Prague, on 27 May 1942, that a joint operation succeeded in mortally wounding *Reichsprotektor* Reinhard Heydrich. Two years later, an SOE team was on the ground in Slovakia during its abortive national uprising (*Slovenské národné povstanie*, *SNP*). And, as the war ended in May 1945, the head of SOE's 'Czech'[16] section bluffed his way past the Soviet Army's front lines to reach Prague, where he briefly performed the duties of the official British representative to the newly liberated state.[17]

It is about time this geographical imbalance of coverage was rectified, not least to highlight some of the difficulties that the executive confronted in trying to foster resistance in Central Europe, and, moreover, to explore the ways in which Cold War debates have distorted our understanding of these activities. In this essay, I want to examine three aspects of SOE's work and of its relations with the Czechoslovaks. I shall begin by problematizing the historiography of SOE. Next, I will detail, based on the available evidence, its strategic objectives and the obstacles it faced in achieving them. Then I will consider, as a brief case study, SOE's relations with the Czechoslovak government-in-exile. I will also argue that, notwithstanding its continued popularity, the phrase 'set Europe ablaze' sheds very little light on the history of the executive or on our understanding of the term 'resistance' more generally.

At a rough estimate, well over two hundred books and articles have been published about SOE since 1945.[18] These range from the memoirs of former officers and agents, to popular accounts, official histories and academic studies. We are primarily interested

---

13 *Proceedings of the Second International Conference on the History of the Resistance Movements*, London, 1964 (hereafter, *Second International Conference*), pp. 639–646; see also notes 43 and 57 below.

14 R. S. Esbenshade 'Remembering to Forget: Memory, History, National Identity in Postwar East-Central Europe', *Representations*, (Special Issue: Identifying Histories: Eastern Europe Before and After 1989), 49, 1995, pp. 72–96; Judt, 'The Past is Another Country', pp. 108–112; Jan Rupnik, 'Politika vyrovnávání s komunistickou minulostí: Česká zkušenost', *Soudobé dějiny*, 9, 2002, no 1, pp. 9–26.

15 In particular see Detlef Brandes, *Die Tschechen unter deutschem Protektorat. Besatzungs-politik, Kollaboration und Widerstand im Protektorat Böhmen und Mähren bis Heydrichs Tod 1939–1942*, vol 1, Munich, 1969; Vojtech Mastny, *The Czechs under Nazi Rule: The Failure of National Resistance, 1939–1942*, New York, 1971.

16 In its internal correspondence SOE referred to its 'Czech' section, rather than its Czechoslovak section. Technically, Slovakia was an enemy state, allied to Nazi Germany.

17 For a detailed examination of these relations see, Martin D. Brown, *Dealing with Democrats: The British Foreign Office and the Czechoslovak Émigrés in Great Britain, 1939 to 1945*, Frankfurt aM, 2006, pp. 307–354.

18 Mark Wheeler, 'The SOE phenomenon', *Journal of Contemporary History*, 16, July 1981, 3, pp. 513–519 (p. 515).

here in English-language texts; the relevant foreign-language sources understandably tend to focus on their own localized resistance movements rather than on SOE's role in supporting them.[19]

In addition, Czech, Polish and Slovak accounts have been distorted by the political imperatives of the Cold War, not least by the relevant communist parties' attempts to inflate their own contributions to the war effort.[20] This situation has changed since 1989, but recent texts continue to focus on the domestic resistance, and the material on SOE is largely based on British sources.[21] Equally, texts produced by anti-communist émigrés in the west must be treated with caution, as they have tended to take ideologically motivated positions, not always supported by the available evidence, and are often diametrically opposed to those expressed by the communist authorities.[22]

One further factor, related to the fate of SOE's archives, necessitates our reliance on English-language sources. When the executive was quietly disbanded in January 1946, the British Secret Intelligence Service (SIS or MI6) retained its files. SIS also absorbed some of its personnel and resources and duly pressed them into service against a new enemy, Soviet communism.[23] Access to SOE's papers was strictly regulated by the Foreign Office and a series of 'Advisers', beginning with Lieutenant-Colonel Edwin Boxshall, who was appointed in 1958.[24] The files were withheld even after the wartime Cabinet and Foreign Office papers were released in 1972.[25] On one level, such behaviour was entirely consistent with the British state's long tradition of secrecy (SIS's own archives remain sealed[26]).[27] On another, such reticence may have been connected to the fact that SOE's techniques were still being employed in Europe during the immediate post-war period.

When SOE's records began to be declassified in June 1993, a result of the 'Waldegrave Initiative on Open Government', it was revealed that only thirteen percent of the

---

19 E. Maresch, 'SOE and Polish Aspirations', in Stirling et al., *Intelligence Co-operation*, pp. 198–215 (p. 198).

20 Bradley F. Abrams, *The Struggle for the Soul of the Nation: Czech Culture and the Rise of Communism*, Oxford and Lanham, MD, 2004, pp. 9–38, 104–117; K. Bartošek, 'Czechoslovakia: The State of Historiography', in D. Cameron Watt (ed.), *Contemporary History in Europe*, London, 1969, pp. 206–218; Czechoslovak delegation, 'Les Alliés et la résistance tchécoslovaque', in *Second International Conference*, pp. 224–247.

21 S. Kokoška, *Praha v květnu 1945: Historie jednoho povstání*, Prague, 2005; V. Smetena, 'Mise plukovníka Perkinse v kontextu britské politiky vůči Českoslovsensku a pomoci jeho odbojovému na sklonku 2. svetové války', *Historie a vojenství*, 2001, 3, pp. 692–736; J. Šolc, *Podpalte Československo! Kapitoly z historie Československého zahraničního a domáciho odboje, 1939–1945*, Prague, 2005.

22 Brown, *Dealing with Democrats*, pp. 10–23.

23 Richard J. Aldrich, 'Secret Intelligence for a Post-war World: Reshaping the British Intelligence Community, 1944–51', in R. J. Aldrich (ed.), *British Intelligence, Strategy and the Cold War, 1945–51*, London 1992, pp. 15–49 (pp. 26–27); P. H. J. Davies, 'From Special Operations to Special Political Action: The 'Rump SOE' and SIS Post-war Covert Action Capability, 1945–1977', *Intelligence and National Security*, 15, Autumn 2000, no 3, pp. 55–76.

24 House of Commons Debates (hereafter, HC Deb.), 5th Series, Vol. 579, Cols. 757–758, 15 December, 1958.

25 See, David Stafford, *Britain and European Resistance, 1940–1945: A Survey of the Special Operations Executive, with Documents*, London, 1980; Phyllis Auty and Richard Clogg (eds), *British Policy towards Wartime Resistance in Yugoslavia and Greece*, London, 1975.

26 HC Deb., 6th Series, Vol. 306, Col. 324, 12 February, 1998.

27 Peter Hennessy, *Whitehall*, London, 1989, pp. 344–368.

originals had survived. There is nothing particularly suspicious about these losses; they were simply the result of deficient office management by SOE itself (which lacked a central registry) and over-enthusiastic 'weeding' by subsequent custodians.[28] Neverthe-less, this means that the bulk of the literature produced prior to the mid-1990s – except for the British official histories – was written with limited or no access to these primary sources (although other archives were accessible[29]). This is a crucial point, as lack of access meant that some interpretations of SOE's work could not be definitively substan-tiated or refuted.

During the Second World War, SOE's existence was a closely guarded secret. No reference could be made to its existence, least of all by governments-in-exile.[30] Only after the conflict ended did information about its work begin to appear in the media.[31] Around the same time, former officers and agents, such as George Millar and Maurice Buckmaster, began to write up their experiences.[32] These authors were obliged to submit their manuscripts prior to publication for official clearance by the Foreign Office. This was a somewhat arbitrary process,[33] but permission was granted early in 1948 for the former head of SOE, Major-General Sir Colin Gubbins, to give a public lecture in London – the first public remarks made about the organization by a senior officer.[34] The only reference to SOE's activities in Czechoslovakia to emerge from this period is to be found in a short essay by another former member of the organisation, the historian Hugh Seton-Watson.[35]

By the late 1950s, a critical period in the formation of Britain's collective memory of the war, SOE's activities were regularly being portrayed in books and films. They provided a factual basis for the fictional exploits of 'Commander James Bond', for example, and the phrase 'Set Europe ablaze!' became well established.[36] Most of these accounts dealt with SOE's activities in France ('F-section' having been led by the afore-mentioned Buckmaster), and an increasingly ill-tempered controversy arose regarding

---

28 London, The National Archives [TNA] of the United Kingdom, Foreign and Commonwealth Office, FCO 77/90 HM Treasury Organisation and Methods Division: 'Historical Review of SOE Records', September 1967, pp.1–15; D. Stuart, ' "Of Historical Interest Only": The Origins and Vicissitudes of the SOE Archives', in Neville Wylie (ed.), *Intelligence and National Security*, Special Issue on Special Operations Executive – New Approaches and Perspectives, 20, March 2005, 1, pp. 14–26.

29 Cookridge, *Inside SOE*, pp. xiii-xvi, 610–614.

30 See, Czechoslovak Ministry of Foreign Affairs, *On the Reign of Terror in Bohemia and Moravia under the Regime of Reinhard Heydrich*, London, 1942; Jan Masaryk (ed.), *The Sixth Column: Inside the Nazi-Occu-pied Countries*, New York, 1942.

31 *Daily Telegraph*, 2 June, 1945; *The Times*, 19 January, 1948; ibid, 15 July 1950.

32 Buckmaster, *Specially Employed*; George Millar, *Maquis*, London, 1945.

33 M. Seaman, 'Good Thrillers, but Bad History: A Review of Published Works on the Special Operations Executive's Work in France during the Second World War', in K. G. Robertson (ed.), *War, Resistance and Intelligence: Essays in Honour of M. R. D. Foot*, Barnsley, 1999, pp. 119–133.

34 C. Gubbins, 'Resistance Movements in the War' (hereafter, 'Resistance Movements in the War'), *The Journal of the Royal United Service Institute*, 93, May 1948, 570, pp. 210–223; *The Times*, 29 January 1948.

35 Hugh Seton-Watson, 'Resistance in Eastern Europe', in Patrick Howarth (ed.), *Special Operations*, London, 1955, pp. 88–113 (pp.109–112).

36 David Cannadine, *In Churchill's Shadow: Confronting the Past in Modern Britain*, London, 2002, pp. 279–311; Mark Connelly, *We Can Take It! Britain and the Memory of the Second World War*, Harlow, 2004, pp. 1–15, 267–297.

the alleged penetration of these networks by German counter-intelligence.[37] One veteran argued that collectively these accounts presented 'a distorted and exaggerated picture' of the resistance, and that a considered resolution to this dispute could be achieved only through access to SOE's own files.[38]

The British Government's position was unambiguous: the archives were and would remain sealed. As Lord John Hope announced in the House of Commons on 22 February, 1956, '[The] Special Operations Executive was a secret wartime organization much of whose activity must, in the public interest, remain secret. For this reason the organization's files cannot be made available to the public [...].'[39] Undaunted, a Member of Parliament, Dame Irene Ward, persisted in tabling questions regarding the penetration of SOE's French networks and argued that an inquiry was required to settle the matter once and for all.[40]

Further calls for SOE's files to be released emanated from the British participants who attended two international conferences on European resistance, convened in Liège in 1958 and in Milan in 1961. These meetings marked the beginnings of academic research into SOE.[41] Participants such as William Deakin, another veteran of the executive, were especially concerned that the lack of British transparency over this issue was giving communist historians the upper hand in the debate.[42] He had a point; the history of the Second World War, and the question of who had supported which resistance movements, had already become a contested issue in the Cold War's *Kulturkampf.*[43]

These dual pressures encouraged Harold Macmillan's Government to commission an official study into SOE's 'F-section'. A further inducement, as the relevant records now reveal, was the opportunity to help undermine anti-British propaganda from communist governments.[44] Whitehall began looking for a suitable historian early in 1959. The process was chaired by Burke Trend at the Treasury, and overseen by the Cabinet Secretary, Norman Brook, assisted by the former head of SOE's 'Czech' Section, Peter

---

37 Buckmaster, *Specially Employed*; Cookridge, *Inside SOE*, pp. 600–609; Elizabeth Nicholas, *Death be not Proud: On Seven Women who Served with the French Section of the Special Operations Executive during World War II*, London, 1958; Jean Overton Fuller, *The Starr Affair*, London, 1954; Jean Overton Fuller, *The German Penetration of SOE: France 1941–44*, London, 1975, pp. 170–178; *The Times*, 1 December, 1958.

38 C. M. Woodhouse, 'The Greek Resistance, 1942–44', in *European Resistance Movements, 1939–1945: First International Conference on the History of the European Resistance Movements,* London, 1960 (hereafter, *First International Conference*), pp. 374–390 (p. 375).

39 HC Deb., 5th Series, Vol. 549, Col. 364, 22 February 1956.

40 TNA, Prime Minister's Office, PREM 11/5084 'Official history of activities of SOE: correspondence from Dame Irene Ward to P.M.', October 1958 to June 1964; HC Deb., 5th Series, Vol. 549, Cols. 363–366, 22 February, 1956; Vol. 553, Cols. 1070–1071, 6 June 1956; Vol. 559, Col. 121, 11 December, 1958, Cols. 757–758, 15 December, 1958; Vol. 617, Cols. 1258–1260, 17 February, 1960; *The Times*, 23 February, 1956; ibid, 14 November, 1958.

41 *First International Conference*; *Second International Conference* (for full details of these conference-proceedings, see above, notes 13 and 38.

42 TNA, Cabinet Office, CAB 103/566, R. W. J. Hooper to F. A. Bishop, Cabinet Office, 20 January, 1960; TNA, FCO 12/75 'Study of the Pros & Cons of Publication of Further Histories of SOE in the Light of Experience Gained since the Decision to Publish *SOE in France*' (hereafter, 'Study of the Pros & Cons'), July 1969, pp. 1–30 (p. 4).

43 Davies, *Rising '44*, pp. 509–615; Reynolds, *In Command of History*, pp. 407–411, 434–440; Frances Stonor-Saunders, *Who Pays the Piper? The CIA and the Cultural Cold War*, London, 2000, pp. 1–44.

44 TNA, FCO 12/75 'Study of the Pros & Cons', pp. 3–5, p. 28.

Wilkinson, then employed by the Foreign Office.[45] After some discussion, Wilkinson offered the position to an Oxford historian and war veteran, M. R. D. Foot, who was duly appointed in November 1960.[46]

Foot was granted wide-ranging access to the remaining files but was allowed only limited access to veterans, and his remit was restricted to French affairs. His study finally appeared in April 1966, with Prime Minister Harold Wilson's consent, and became the first text to be wholly based on the primary sources.[47] (Revealingly, Foot made no reference to 'setting Europe ablaze' in his work). Although the book was judged a success, senior civil servants proved reluctant to repeat the exercise, not least as the final expenditure was nearly £43,000 and had involved some unwelcome publicity.[48] Foot concluded that SOE's 'F-section' had indeed been compromised, as had its networks in the Low Countries, but that the organization had not deliberately endangered its agents, and that its work in France had been largely successful.

The second volume in this series did not appear until 1983, and further studies are still in production.[49] To date, no official histories have been produced about SOE's relations with the Poles or the Czechoslovaks. An Anglo-Polish Historical Committee has, however, recently published its findings into intelligence cooperation during the war.[50] These official studies have been supplemented by continued scholarly research into the previously 'missing dimensions' of the Second World War, including further work by Professor M.R.D. Foot. This process intensified after the release of a tranche of wartime files in the mid-1970s and by the continued publication of veterans' memoirs.[51]

When SOE's archives were finally opened, one set of files in particular attracted much attention. These contained the executive's original 'secret in-house' history, written by Professor William Mackenzie between 1945 and 1947.[52] (No mention of the words 'set Europe ablaze' is to be found in Mackenzie's text either!). Arguably, Mackenzie's history remains the most lucid, comprehensive and authoritative account

---

45 TNA, CAB 103/566, unsigned and undated letter to Sir N. Brook regarding the history of SOE, pp. 1–7, minutes of meetings held on 2 April, 7 May and 11 May, 1959; ibid, 103/571, minutes of meeting held on 13 October, 1960; TNA, Treasury, T 220/1388 'History of Special Operations Executive', 11 May, 1959 to 31 July, 1959; R. J. Aldrich, 'Policing the Past: Offical History, Secrecy and British Intelligence since 1945', *English Historical Review*, 119, 2004, pp. 922- 953 (pp. 935–944).

46 Author's conversation with Professor M. R. D Foot, 9 August, 2006; TNA, CAB 103/157, P. Wilkinson, FCO, to Foot, 7 November, 1960, Foot's reply, 8 November, 1960.

47 TNA, PREM 13/949 Prime Minister's minute, 8 September, 1965; M. R. D. Foot, *SOE in France: An Account of the Work of the British Special Operations Executive in France, 1940–44*, London, 1st ed., 1966, 2nd, 1968, 3rd, 2004; *The Times*, 28 April, 1966.

48 TNA, CAB 103/572, 573, 576 '*SOE in France* post-publication developments, 1966–1969'; TNA, FCO 12/75 'Study of the Pros & Cons', pp.12–13, appendix B; *The Times*, 14 April, 1964, and editions of 25 April, 28 April, 29 April, 30 April, 11 July, 15 July 1966, 28 January 1969.

49 The Cabinet Office, <http://www.cabinetoffice.gov.uk/publicationscheme/published_information/1/officialhistory.asp#soe> [Accessed 25 October, 2006]; *The Times*, 24 December, 1980; ibid, 3 January, 1981; ibid, 9 January, 1981.

50 Stirling et al., *Intelligence Co-operation*.

51 *Proceedings of a Conference on Britain and European Resistance, 1939–1945: Organised by St. Antony's College, Oxford*, Oxford, 1963; Mark Seaman (ed.), *Special Operations Executive: A New Instrument of War*, London, 2005; Peter Wilkinson, *Foreign Fields: the Story of an SOE Operative*, London, 1997.

52 TNA, CAB 102/649–653, Cabinet Office Historical Section, W. J. M. Mackenzie, 'History of the Special Operations Executive', 4 vols.

we have of the organization's activities in Europe.[53] Furthermore, within its pages we may at last find a fairly detailed account of SOE's relations with the Czechoslovak government-in-exile, which can now be compared against the surviving documentation.[54]

The lack of access to SOE's archives from 1945 to 1993 undoubtedly intensified and prolonged various disputes regarding SOE's effectiveness, professionalism, political orientation, and the extent to which it helped win the war.[55] This situation has also allowed politicized Cold War misrepresentations of the organization to remain unchallenged for decades, not least in respect of its support for the Warsaw Uprising of 1944 and its decision to back Tito's partisans in Yugoslavia.[56] As of December 2006, the majority of SOE's remaining files have been released.[57]

So what can we say about SOE's strategy in Central Europe based on the available evidence? First and foremost, SOE was established because of the desperate military situation Britain found herself in by the summer of 1940. Some way, no matter how unorthodox, had to be found to continue the war and undermine the Third Reich. Gubbins and Colonel Joe Holland, SOE's founding fathers, had already developed plans for just such an enterprise, and the guerrilla techniques they proposed were drawn from British imperial experiences as well as, interestingly enough, from lessons learnt combating the Irish Republican Army (IRA).[58] Crucially in this context, SOE's methods were not only completely novel but they had also emerged from entirely different origins to those forms of resistance familiar to the peoples of Central Europe.

SOE was originally designed to be an autonomous organization, a fourth armed service, with its own Minister, the Labour MP Hugh Dalton. Somewhat predictably, the existing military and intelligence services, especially the Army, the Royal Air Force (RAF), and SIS, proved reluctant to assist what they regarded as a rival for scarce resources. Dalton also proposed to unleash 'permanent revolution' across occupied Europe through the mobilization of 'leftist' forces.[59] Consequently, many British officials viewed the new organization with barely concealed scepticism. As Gubbins later recalled,

> [...] The creation of a new and secret organization with such an all-embracing charter aroused suspicions and fear in Whitehall. SOE was looked upon as an organization of harmless backroom lunatics which, it was hoped, would not develop into an active nuisance [...]. In fact SOE was not taken seriously; neither its existence nor its potential.[60]

---

53 M. R. D. Foot, 'Foreword', in W. J. M. Mackenzie *The Secret History of SOE: The Special Operations Executive, 1940–45*, London, 2000, pp. xi–xxvii.

54 Mackenzie, *The Secret History of SOE*, pp. 309–311, 317–320, 527–530.

55 John Keegan, *The Battle for History: Re-fighting World War II*, London, 1997, pp. 92–93, 102–112; Mark Seaman, 'A Glass Half Full – Some Thoughts on the Evolution of the Study of the Special Operations Executive', *Intelligence and National Security*, 20, March 2005, 1, pp. 27–43.

56 E. D. R Harrison, 'The British Special Operations Executive and Poland,' *The Historical Journal*, 43, 2000, 4, pp. 1071–1091 (pp. 1081–1090); Ralph Bennett, Sir William Deakin, Sir David Hunt and Sir Peter Wilkinson, 'Mihailovic and Tito', *Intelligence and National Security*, 10, July 1995, 3, pp. 527–529.

57 A few files are still retained; one or two have gone missing. Foot, letter to author, 26 December 2006.

58 M. R. D. Foot, 'The IRA and the Origins of SOE', in Foot (ed.), *Historical Essays in Honour and Memory of J. R. Western, 1928–1971*, London, 1973, pp. 57–69.

59 Dalton, *The Fateful Years*, pp. 367–371; Stafford, 'The Detonator Concept', pp. 199–200.

60 C. Gubbins, 'SOE and the Co-ordination of Regular and Irregular War', in Michael Elliott-Bateman (ed.), *The Fourth Dimension of Warfare: Intelligence, Subversion, Resistance*, vol 1, Manchester, 1970, pp. 83–101 (p. 85).

Thus SOE's first battles were fought not against the forces of the Third Reich, but against the bureaucracy and vested interests of the British wartime state.[61]

From its inception the executive was constantly under-resourced and repeatedly side-lined in favour of more traditional, and supposedly proven, methods of warfare, such as the aerial bombardment of Germany. As the war progressed, SOE's independence was gradually eroded. It was eventually brought under centralized Allied military control and made subservient to wider British strategic objectives and to prevailing foreign policy. Finally, in 1946, the executive was disbanded and its assets reallocated.

What then was SOE's primary goal, if not to 'set Europe ablaze'? Here we must return to the lecture Gubbins gave in February 1948. He argued that it was

> [...] To encourage and enable the peoples of the occupied countries to harass the German war effort [...] and at the same time to build up secret forces therein, organized, armed and trained to take their part only when the final assault began. These two objects are, in fact, fundamentally incompatible: to divert attention from the creation of the secret armies meant avoiding any activity which would attract German attention and the efforts of the Gestapo and the SS [...].[62]

SOE's purpose was not simply to train agents to blow things up or to garrotte unsuspecting *Wehrmacht* sentries, but rather to establish secret armies behind enemy lines ready to stage uprisings in support of the advancing Allied forces.[63] These plans required detailed, long-term preparations, not arbitrary acts of random violence. When Dalton presented his first report to the British Chiefs of Staff, on 20 August 1940, he identified two countries where these preparations could commence: Czechoslovakia and Poland.[64]

This brings us to SOE's relations with the Czechoslovak government-in-exile, which were dominated by three key considerations: politics, geography, and logistics. By the late summer of 1940, as SOE was being formed, a growing number of European politicians, servicemen and refugees had sought sanctuary in Britain. It was from this disparate and often fractious community that SOE had to identify partners willing to help further its plans. While the executive's officers proved themselves to be relatively adept at negotiating the corridors of power in Whitehall, they were to find the Byzantine complexities of émigré politics far more challenging.

Difficulties soon arose with the French, with the Poles, with the competing resistance movements in Yugoslavia and, after June 1941, with Europe's communists.[65] All these factors hindered the executive's ability to operate effectively. As an SOE agent dispatched to Albania, Julian Amery, later noted,

---

61 Mackenzie, *The Secret History of SOE*, pp. 3–102, 337–388.
62 Gubbins, 'Resistance Movements in the War', p. 211.
63 TNA, CAB 80/56, COS (40)27(0) Chiefs of Staff Committee, 'Subversive Activities in Relation to Strategy', 25 November 1940, pp. 1–5 (p. 2).
64 TNA, CAB 80/16, COS(40) Chiefs of Staff Committee, 'Future Strategy', appendix 1, 'Probable State of Readiness and Ability of Certain Countries to Rise against the Nazi Regime', 20 August 1940, pp. 52–54; HS 4/31 meeting between F. Moravec, Joe Holland and Peter Wilkinson, 5 January, 1940.
65 Tony Judt (ed.) *Resistance and Revolution in Mediterranean Europe, 1939–1948*, London, 1989.

[Resistance] is not a military formation but an armed political movement [...] Resistance movements, like the States to which they are embryonic successors, wage war for political ends. Now those ends are not, despite all propaganda, 'Victory' or 'Liberation', but the recovery or the gaining of political power.[66]

This maxim was equally apposite to the Czechoslovak émigrés based in London, led by Beneš, who during the war tenaciously pursued his own political objectives, principally the restoration of Czechoslovakia within her pre-Munich frontiers.[67] Czechoslovakia had ceased to exist on 15 March 1939, when Nazi Germany occupied the western portion of the truncated, post-Munich state and established a Protectorate of Bohemia and Moravia complete with its own 'quisling' Government. Slovakia had by then declared its independence and joined the Axis powers. Once war was declared, some six months later, all available resources and assets, including the domestic resistance, were mobilized to help realize Beneš's objectives. But this was no easy task, and success for governments-in-exile was by no means assured, as the Greek, Polish and Yugoslav émigrés in London were to discover.

Beneš was assisted in these endeavours by the head of Czechoslovak military intelligence, Colonel František Moravec, whom SIS had spirited out of Prague on the morning of the German invasion.[68] By the time SOE was operational, Moravec's team had already built up a formidable reputation as the 'doyen' of the Allied intelligence services and were in radio contact with the resistance in the Protectorate.[69]

Joint relations therefore began with high hopes, coordinated by the head of SOE's 'Czech' section, Peter Wilkinson, and his successor, Harold Perkins; but they never quite lived up to expectations. SOE managed to send a total of 75 agents and some 59 tons[70] of material to the former territory of Czechoslovakia by 1945.[71] These figures may sound impressive, until one compares them to the 1800 agents and 10,000 tons of equipment delivered to France.[72] The problem was not the Czechoslovaks' willingness to fight, Soviet intransigence, or Beneš's supposed predilection for communism, as has been suggested, but rather the prosaic realities of European geography.[73] It simply

66 J. Amery, 'Of Resistance', *Nineteenth Century and After*, 125 (March 1949), pp. 138–149 (p. 140).
67 TNA, FO 371 22899 C13303/7/12 E. Beneš to N. Chamberlain, 3 September 1939; Edvard Beneš, *Paměti, Od Mnichova k nové válce a k novému vítězství*, Prague, 1947, pp. 156–157.
68 František Moravec, *Master of Spies*, London, 1975, p. 159; Šolc, *Podpalte Československo!*, pp.9–16; *Daily Telegraph,* 15 March, 1939.
69 London, Imperial War Museum's archives, P. Wilkinson's private papers, Wilkinson to Colonel J. Holland, 4 June, 1940; Wilkinson's talk given to the Special Forces Club on the 'Anthropoid' mission, 1982; V. Modrák, 'Radio Contact', in Lewis M. White (ed.), *On All Fronts: Czechoslovaks in World War II*, vol 3, New York, 2000, pp.133–146.
70 The British imperial unit of weight.
71 TNA, HS 7/9 'History of the Special Duties Operations in Europe (Airforce), 1939–1945', parts II & III, appendix H8, p. xxvii, appendix I.1, p. xxxiv; a complete list of all the missions sent to the Protectorate by SOE from 1941 to 1945 can be found in HS 7/108, F.E. Keary, P. W. Auster and G. I. Klauber, 'SOE Country History, Czechoslovakia, 1940–1945' (Hereafter, 'SOE Country History: Czechoslovakia'), pp. 1–35, appendixes A and B.
72 Foot, *SOE in France*, pp. 421–426.
73 V. Mastny, *Russia's Road to the Cold War: Diplomacy, Warfare, and the politics of Communism, 1941–1945*, New York, 1979 (hereafter, Russia's Road to the Cold War), pp. 133–144; Condoleezza Rice, *The Soviet Union and the Czechoslovak Army, 1948–1983. Uncertain Allegiance*, Princeton, NJ, 1984, pp. 32–33; Zbynek Zeman and Antonin Klimek, *The Life of Edvard Beneš 1884–1948: Czechoslovakia in Peace and War*, Oxford, 1997, pp. 176–178, 180–182, 217–220.

proved impossible for SOE to dispatch regular flights to the former Czechoslovakia, due to distance and to a chronic lack of available long-range aircraft.[74]

Furthermore, we now know that neither Beneš nor Moravec had any intention of allowing SOE to 'set the Protectorate ablaze'. Beneš was far too experienced an operator to let an unproven and radical foreign organization interfere in the region's political affairs.[75] Nor were these fears of internal conflict entirely groundless, as the situation in Slovakia in 1944 and the civil war in Greece were to demonstrate.[76] In addition, Moravec had little inclination to allow unregulated sabotage to hinder his intelligence-gathering operations – a point he conceded in an interview with Josef Korbel in 1962. (An essay containing this interview was later deposited in SOE's archives by an unknown hand).[77]

These contacts did result in one well-known success: on 27 May, 1942, Reinhard Heydrich, one of Nazi Germany's leading figures, was attacked in Prague by two SOE-trained operatives and died from his wounds soon after.[78] The motives behind Heydrich's assassination were unquestionably political and designed to promote Beneš's agenda, not SOE's. The attack's timing also proved fortuitous, occurring as it did (probably by chance) the day after an Anglo-Soviet Treaty had been signed in London.[79] From the Czechoslovak perspective the mission was a success, if a costly one, and this dramatic example of active resistance helped aid the reestablishment of Czechoslovakia in 1945. SOE willingly supported this operation, not least because it helped rid Europe of one of Germany's leading counter-insurgency experts.[80]

But the resulting German retribution eviscerated resistance in the Protectorate and, due to serious concerns about Moravec's security procedures, SOE and SIS collaborated to strip him of his operational autonomy.[81] To all intents and purposes, the assassination marked the end of SOE's attempts to foster active resistance in the Protectorate. Henceforth the partnership foundered, and the Czechoslovaks increasingly turned to the Soviet Union for military assistance.[82]

74 TNA, HS 7/108 Keary et al., 'SOE Country History: Czechoslovakia', p. 34.

75 L. Otáhalová and M. Červinková (eds.), *Dokumenty z historie československé politiky, 1939–1943. Vztahy mezinárodní diplomacie k politice československé emigrace na západě*, vol 1, Prague, 1966, pp. 297–298; vol 2, pp. 701–702.

76 Bradley Abrams, 'The Politics of Retribution: The Trial of Jozef Tiso in the Czechoslovak Environment', and Mark Mazower, 'The Cold War and the Appropriation of Memory: Greece after Liberation', both in Deák et al., *The Politics of Retribution*, pp. 252–289, 212–232.

77 TNA, HS 7/108 Draft essay by Josef Korbel 'Political Aspects of the Resistance Movement in Czechoslovakia during World War II', November 1962, pp. 1–47 (p. 33). This work includes extracts of Korbel's interview with Moravec conducted on 11 September 1962.

78 TNA, HS 4/39 'Detailed Report on Operation Anthropoid' by P. Wilkinson, 30 May 1942, pp. 1–12.

79 Margaret Carlyle (ed.), *Documents on International Affairs, 1939–1946*, vol 2, London, 1954, pp. 316–317.

80 TNA, HS 8/250 SOE's quarterly report to the Prime Minister, June 1942, p. 7; Brown, *Dealing with Democrats*, pp. 293–300, 318–323.

81 TNA, HS 4/39 Intercepted German radio transmission, 26 May, 1942; HS 4/1 Record of a luncheon given by Lord Selborne for Beneš, General S. Ingr and Moravec, 24 September, 1942.

82 TNA, HS 4/277 'Detailed Outline of Operational Activities in the Protectorate after the Summer of 1942'; HS 4/4 SOE internal minute, 1 May, 1943, briefing paper for Gubbins, 5 January, 1944; HS 8/278 'Summary of SOE's work in Czechoslovakia up to 30 November 1944'.

SOE reached its apogee with the massed rising by the French resistance in support of the Allied landings in Normandy in June 1944. The Slovak National Uprising, which began three months later, should have been equally successful, but it was not. Western commentators have long argued that the executive's inability to resupply the Slovak insurgents was the result of Soviet machinations, as was the case with the uprising in Warsaw, but there is little evidence to substantiate this argument.[83] As we have already seen, the executive's resources were finite, and by 1944 its ability to resupply large resistance forces by air was restricted to France and Yugoslavia. In any case, in March 1943 the British Chiefs of Staff had issued SOE with a new directive that had effectively ended its support for 'secret armies' in Central Europe, leaving these activities to be supported by the Soviets.[84] Indeed, SOE's transport problems were so acute that when the uprising in Slovakia began to falter, the organization was unable to rescue its own agents working on the ground with the insurgents. They were later caught and executed.[85]

SOE's attempts to resupply the Prague Uprising in May 1945 proved no more successful, although once again the files clearly demonstrate that this was the result of logistical constraints, not Soviet scheming.[86] Within days of the war's end and soon after the Soviet Army had liberated the city, the head of SOE's Czech section, Harold Perkins, had reached Prague. In his dispatches he quickly linked what he perceived as the failure of Czechoslovak anti-Nazi resistance to the then as yet undeclared Cold War:

> Resistance throughout the country has been exceedingly weak, almost negligible [...] The Czechs are now quite openly speaking of their dislike and disappointment regarding Eastern liberation, but I do not think that we should blind ourselves for one moment with the thought that they will do anything about it. The same psychology which prevented them from taking action against the Boches will come to the fore again and weak submission will be the answer [...].[87]

This was at best a one-dimensional analysis, as Perkins should have known, but one that has had a lasting effect. It also reveals far more about Perkins's British perspective of the war than about the realities of Czechoslovak resistance.

Now that we have access to SOE's remaining archives, we know that it could not deliver what it promised to the Protectorate, and that the Czechoslovak government-in-exile preferred to rely, as did the British Government, on more traditional forms of military activity to win the war and liberate their homeland. For Beneš, this increasingly

---

83 M. R. D. Foot, *Resistance: An Analysis of European Resistance to Nazism, 1940–1945*, London, 1976, p. 208; Abby Innes, *Czechoslovakia: The Short Goodbye*, London, 2001, pp. 18–19; Josef Lettrich, *History of Modern Slovakia*, London, 1956, p. 213; Mastny, *Russia's Road to the Cold War*, p. 192; Moravec, *Master of Spies*, p. 243; V. Prečan, 'The 1944 Slovak Uprising', in William Deakin, Elisabeth Barker and Jonathan Chadwick (eds), *British Political and Military Strategy in Central, Eastern and Southern Europe in 1944*, London, 1988, pp. 223–234 (pp. 225, 231–232); Rice, *The Soviet Union and the Czechoslovak Army*, p. 35; Seton-Watson, 'Resistance in Eastern Europe', p. 110.

84 TNA, CAB 80/68 COS(43) 142(0) Chiefs of Staff Committee, 'Special Operations Executive Directive for 1943', 20 March, 1943, pp. 1–7 (p. 6).

85 Martin D. Brown, 'The S.O.E. and the Failure of the Slovak National Uprising', *History Today*, 43, December 2004, 12, pp. 39–45.

86 Brown, *Dealing with Democrats*, pp. 347–354.

87 TNA, HS 4/51 Perkins to P. Boughey, 21 May 1945, pp. 1–6 (p. 6). 'Boches' is a pejorative term for Germans.

meant preparing for the arrival of the Red Army in Central Europe: not a scenario anyone had envisaged back in 1940. These divergent perspectives hindered effective cooperation between Beneš and SOE, while geographical and logistical constraints meant the executive had little choice but to concentrate its limited resources elsewhere. Ultimately Beneš did manage to reconstruct Czechoslovakia, but because of the Soviet Union's military efforts, rather than because of his relations with SOE.

SOE undeniably had its successes during the war, but it had its fair share of failures too – exactly the sort of result we might expect from a novel, experimental, and often under-resourced organisation. The lack of access to the SOE's files since 1945 has sometimes distorted our understanding of the multi-faceted and politicized nature of the executive's work. So have the reductive debates of the Cold War and Europe's complicated relationship with its collective memories of the conflict. Nevertheless, we can now assert, with some confidence, that SOE's attempts to promote resistance were far more involved than merely trying to 'set Europe ablaze', if indeed those ever were Churchill's words.

The Hungarian Opposition and Resistance to Stalinism in the early 1950s

Gábor Bátonyi

Since 1989, anti-communist resistance has been one of the most enduring themes of Central and East European historical writing. The memory of 1956 made the study of political dissent highly topical in Hungary. The Hungarian revolution started as a rare mass protest against a Stalinist regime; only because of two Soviet interventions did it escalate into a crisis in international affairs, coming to represent a critical juncture in the history of communism. Hungarian historians accordingly cherish not only the political and military achievements but also the very 'ideas of the revolution'.[1] They view the 'Magyar October' as the 'greatest challenge to the Soviet empire', one that shattered the myth of Moscow's total control over Eastern Europe and signalled the 'failure of Soviet-style socialism'.[2] In the main, western historians tend to go along with this assessment. A recent American monograph has even suggested that Hungary was the 'first domino' in the collapse of communism.[3] And yet, when it comes to the study of resistance in the first half of the 1950s, there appears to be a yawning gap in the understanding of Hungarian and Anglo-Saxon historians. The legacy of the opposition and political dissent during the final years of Stalin's life is especially contentious.

At the heart of the debate lie some fundamental disagreements as to the strength and resilience of Hungarian civil society during the years of unfettered dictatorship. The role and importance of the middle-class opposition has been identified by western historians as a subject of particular controversy. In addition, there are question-marks over the engagement of both individuals and social

Despite the official rhetoric of class discrimination and class warfare, the Hungarian communists were constrained even in their treatment of the traditionally hostile, educated middle class.[4] As late as 1953, the chief theorist of the Hungarian Workers' Party (MDP) was at pains to explain why Hungary, unlike the Soviet Union, was still in possession of a fairly strong middle class with its own intellectual baggage and national and cultural

1   Béla Király and Lee W. Congdon (eds.), *A magyar forradalom eszméi*, Budapest, 2001.
2   János M. Rainer, '1956 a XX. század történelmében', in Miklós Horváth (ed.), *'Tizenhárom nap amely...'*, Budapest, 2003, p. 9.
3   Johanna C. Granville, *The First Domino: International Decision Making during the Hungarian Crisis of 1956*, College Station, TX, 2004.
4   James Mark, 'Discrimination, Opportunity, and Middle-Class Success in Early Communist Hungary', *The Historical Journal*, 48, 2005, no. 2, pp. 499–521 (p. 499).

identity.[5] In a private conversation with Andropov, *chargé d'affaires* and later head of the Soviet embassy in Budapest, Rákosi bluntly admitted that a large proportion of the technical experts in heavy industry and coal mining were intellectuals of the old school, imbued with nationalist ideas and with antipathy to the communist system.[6] Arguably, the political survival of this class was indicative of the weakness of the Rákosi regime. For some British scholars, though, the survival of the educated elite was, at least in part, due to the malleability and adaptability of this class. When, in December 1949, the organizational department of the MDP reported that the introduction of the 'Stalin shift' (supposedly voluntary overtime in the workplace) had inspired a 'wave of enthusiasm even amongst the technical intelligentsia', there was some truth in this blatantly official lie. Most members of the old elite were learning to play by the new rules. In the era of high Stalinism, pragmatic considerations, such as the need for engineers, doctors, and teachers, might have weighed against the dogmatism of the communist leaders, but such considerations could not have outweighed the leaders' security concerns. It seems that, despite its unpopularity, the Hungarian communist state apparatus had little to fear from old enemies among the educated middle class. Consequently, a British historian has gone so far as to question whether there was any concerted resistance in Hungary, save the 'remarkable exception', the revolution of 1956.[7]

The essentially justified attempt to counterbalance the 'resistance-obsessed historiography'[8] of the region has, plainly, led some Anglo-Saxon historians to the opposite extreme. Instead of overplaying the importance of resistance, they make too much of the bargaining power and popular appeal of communist regimes. In particular, recent works have focused on the deep pre-war roots of communism, the general appeal of left-wing ideology in the post-war era, and the engagement of wide sections of the population in the 'inherently social project of reconstruction'.[9] Following the same logic, resistance stories have been dismissed out of hand as distortions of the historical memory of communism. Breaking with the western Cold War tradition, even the depiction of 1956 'as a gallant (if tragic) first step in the fight against Communism'[10] has been scorned. In the scathing words of an American scholar, in the post-socialist states the forty years of communism have been 'excised from the national narrative as aberrant.'[11] In line with this damning approach, even such emotive issues as the rape of some 50,000 Hungarian women by Soviet soldiers have been revisited, only to explode the myth of all-pervading anti-Soviet sentiments amongst the urban population.[12] According to James Mark, the

---

5 Note by József Révai, 26 February, 1953, Rákosi Papers, Hungarian National Archive (hereafter MOL), M KS-276 f. 65 cs. 16 ő.e.
6 Memorandum of a conversation between Mátyás Rákosi and Yuri Andropov, 24 September, 1953, in Magdolna Baráth, *Szovjet nagyköveti iratok Magyarországról 1953–1956, Kiszeljov és Andropov titkos jelentései*, Budapest, 2002, p. 91.
7 James Mark, 'Society, Resistance and Revolution: The Budapest Middle Class and the Hungarian Communist State 1948–56', *English Historical Review*, 120, 2005, no. 488, pp. 963–86 (p. 963).
8 Mark, 'Society, Resistance and Revolution', p. 979.
9 Bradley F. Abrams, 'The Second World War and the East European Revolution', *Eastern European Politics and Societies*, 16, 2002, no. 3, pp. 623–64 (pp. 623–4, 642).
10 Mark, 'Society, Resistance and Revolution', p. 981.
11 Abrams, 'The Second World War and the East European Revolution', p. 624.
12 James Mark, 'Remembering Rape: Divided Social Memory and the Red Army in Hungary 1944–1945', *Past and Present*, 188, 2005, pp. 133–61.

stories of rape have been retold by nationalist historians time and again since 1989 in order to legitimize 'the historical reading of Communism which characterizes ordinary Hungarians as victims of a foreign ideology violently imposed from outside the country.'[13] In two other articles, the same author cites the controversial example of the Hungarian middle class to drive home the point that 'post-communist estimation of resistance has developed beyond its actual historical scale.'[14] He argues that the opposition was 'politically fractured' and weak.[15] Mark takes a particularly dim view of the political role of the conservative opponents of the regime, who were allegedly the 'least likely to engage in acts of resistance'.[16] But, in Mark's view, the 'left-liberal opposition' did not fare very well either. He concludes:

> Only by removing ourselves from the demands of the post-Communist celebration of dissent, by accepting the overwhelming absence of open protest against Communist states, and by addressing the variety of valid ways in which people chose to live in opposition, can we hope to create a sophisticated history of resistance in central-eastern Europe [...]. [17]

For all this harsh criticism of political bias, western scholars have followed a strikingly similar research agenda to that of the native historians of Central and Eastern Europe. In spite of the general scepticism over the scale of resistance, there has been a steady stream of articles in major English historical journals examining 'the limits of dictatorship' in the former Soviet satellite states.[18] Political opposition in Hungary during the early Cold War, ranging from the discontent fomented by listening to the Voice of Free Hungary[19] to 'labour indiscipline',[20] has received unusually comprehensive treatment. This research focus is startling enough, given the normally limited appeal of Hungarian history in the West. The upsurge of interest in political dissent is more remarkable still in view of the generally negative assessment of the prevalence and historical significance of resistance. Nevertheless, when it comes to the appraisal of dictatorial rule, British and Hungarian historians are not a world apart. There is an emerging consensus that pre-war identities proved far too strong to be successfully undermined by Stalinist social engineering. While the relative strength of the state and the opposition remains a moot point, British historians concede that the Hungarian Stalinists did face, at the very least, some low-level and indirect 'infra-political' resistance.[21] Thus, the 'state's failure to strip society of its autonomy' was capitalized on by individuals and social groups alike. Those who demonstratively withdrew from active political life, even if they were persecuted and marginalized, did not necessarily become 'passive victims of socialist despotism'.[22]

---

13 ibid.
14 Mark, 'Discrimination, Opportunity, and Middle-Class Success', p. 501; Mark, 'Society, Resistance and Revolution', p. 963.
15 ibid.
16 Mark, 'Society, Resistance and Revolution', p. 966.
17 ibid, p. 986.
18 Pittaway, 'The Reproduction of Hierarchy', p.739.
19 Mark Pittaway, 'The Education of Dissent: The Reception of the Voice of Free Hungary, 1951–56', *Cold War History*, 4, 2003, no. 1, pp. 97–116.
20 Mark Pittaway, 'The Reproduction of Hierarchy: Skill, Working-Class Culture and the State in Early Socialist Hungary', *Journal of Modern History*, 74, 2002, 2, pp. 737–69 (p. 739).
21 Mark, 'Society, Resistance and Revolution', p. 972.
22 Pittaway, 'The Reproduction of Hierarchy', p. 738.

The most paradoxical aspect of this new research on Hungarian resistance is that it focuses on the early 1950s, a period when the repressive apparatus of the state allowed hardly any scope for manifestations of dissent. After all, how much opposition was possible in a police state where a slight misspelling in a birthday telegram to the Soviet leader might lead to suspicions of sabotage and very nearly landed a translator in prison?[23] To what extent could resistance be expected in a country where queuing for bread, meat, or sugar was construed as the work of the enemy, warranting police intervention and arrest?[24] What was the chance of home-grown revolt against a regime that was looking for 'unreliable' and 'hostile elements' even among the thoroughly 'vetted' employees of Soviet companies?[25] What latitude was there publicly to criticize an administration that tried to ensure that even priests 'preach socialism'?[26]

Given the surreal environment, in which the ruling elite relentlessly and deliberately fabricated, falsified, and reinvented the very image of the enemy, it is well-nigh impossible to assess retrospectively either the actual strength or the exact nature of the dissent with any certainty. Clearly, none of the avowed assumptions of the communist security services can be taken at face value today, even though state records certainly provide some glimpses of the 'real', as well as the 'imagined', enemies of the state. Undoubtedly, similar doubts and obstacles have never really stopped western scholars from studying resistance in such extremely oppressive environments as Hitler's Germany or Stalin's Soviet Union. On the contrary, historians of totalitarian regimes have sometimes expressly chosen to measure the strength of civil society by its resilience in the face of the most brutal and explicit forms of oppression. The study of Hungary between 1949 and 1953 fits perfectly into this pattern.

Nevertheless, the researcher faces some peculiar difficulties in studying Stalinist Hungary. The problem is not just the inflated self-assessment of former dissidents, but the gross exaggeration and blatant distortion inherent in state records. The collective 'conspiracy obsession' of the Hungarian communist leadership, coupled with the 'paranoid style of politics' at every level of the state bureaucracy, is truly reminiscent of the conspiratorial culture of the French, Russian, and Chinese revolutions.[27] Rákosi may have been a far cry from Robespierre, but his blend of ruthlessness, fear, cynical demagogy and conviction politics was indeed, to adopt a famous phrase of a French historian, 'the figment of a frenzied preoccupation with power'.[28] Hence, the regime's assessment of its enemies was, predictably, flawed from the outset: factual accounts and realistic observations were mixed with irrational fears, miscalculations, and obfuscations, not to mention the lies inherent in Stalinist propaganda. This explains why some British historians have opted to rely solely on the accounts of dissidents, rather than on the readily

23 Report by the ÁVH on the misspelling and crossing-out of Stalin's name, 8 December, 1949, Rákosi Papers, MOL, M KS-276 f. 65 cs. 76 ő.e.

24 Erzsébet Kajári, 'Egy házkutatás története 1950-ből', *Múltunk*, 46, 2001, no. 1, pp. 285–97.

25 László Borhi, 'Empire by Coercion: The Soviet Union and Hungary in the 1950s', *Cold War History*, 1, 2001, no. 2, pp. 47–72 (p. 54).

26 Memorandum by the Office of Church Affairs on the religious opposition, 31 October, 1953, MOL, M KS-276 f. 65 cs. 41 ő.e.

27 Timothy Tackett, 'Conspiracy Obsession in a Time of Revolution: French elites and the origin of the Terror, 1789–1792', *American Historical Review*, 105, 2006, no. 3, pp. 569–78.

28 François Furet, *Interpreting the Revolution*, Cambridge, 1981, p. 54; see also Tackett, 'Conspiracy obsession in a time of revolution'.

accessible documents of the state, and have used oral archives, instead of written records, in estimating the strength of the opposition. Regardless of the merits and demerits of focusing on high politics and official documents alone, I mainly fall back here on a varied batch of files relating to state security in the archive of Rákosi's secretariat in order to examine how far the regime succeeded in locating and sizing up its opponents. My assumption is that, despite the 'institutional system of public falsehood',[29] the official records tell us much about society's varied response to dictatorship. They also show how the fabrication and distortion of the image of the enemy contributed to the growth of anti-communist feeling and its violent outburst in 1956.

Arguably, the Hungarian communist apparatus was deluded both about the mood of the public and its own strength, even by the standards of the early Cold War. Characteristically, when a Hungarian diplomat reported from Prague that Clement Gottwald had become isolated from working people and no longer shared their company, Ernő Gerő's response was brief but biting: 'Ez megpistult!'[30] (He's got a screw loose!). The Hungarian communist leaders' isolation from the masses does not, however, sufficiently explain their fear of society. It could be held that the memory of rejection at the ballot box, combined with the failure to legitimize political and social change after the war, predisposed Rákosi to distrust his ex-enemies, former coalition partners, and fellow travellers alike. Mark Pittaway has gone so far as to claim that the electoral humiliation in 1945 'set in train the logic that created the social roots of dictatorship'.[31]

Be that as it may, the uncritical acceptance and adoption of the Soviet style of branding the enemy as 'Trotskyists', 'imperialist agents', 'kulaks', and so on greatly compounded the existing state of confusion by the end of the 1940s. Despite Rákosi's surprisingly candid admission to Molotov in 1947 that 'Yugoslavia was more popular than the Soviet Union in Hungary', even the Titoist label had more to do with international politics than the Hungarian reality.[32] The pro-Yugoslav sentiments of the Hungarian communists rapidly gave way to an insane level of hostility. Anton Rob, general secretary of the Democratic Association of Southern Slavs in Hungary, was issued a virtual ultimatum on 29 June 1948 to renounce Tito:

> Comrade Farkas summoned me for 9 a.m. in the morning [...]. In the polished manner of a drill sergeant he ordered me to study some Cominform documents on Yugoslavia. He gave me one hour to make up my mind and declare whether I agreed with the damning verdict on the Yugoslav Communist Party [...]. When I expressed reservation about this treatment and refused to endorse his views under the circumstances, he demanded my immediate resignation. I pointed out that I was not only a member of the Hungarian Communist Party but a representative of a national minority, which gave me my mandate. He ordered me to give up my parliamentary mandate without more ado [...].[33]

29 János Kenedi, *Kis állambiztonsági olvasókönyv. Október 23 – március 15 – június 16 a Kádár korszakban*, Budapest, 1996, vol. 1, p. v; János M. Rainer, 'Submerging or clinging on again? József Antall, father and son, in Hungary after 1956', *Contemporary European History*, 14, 2005, 1, pp. 65–105 (p. 70).
30 Comment by Ernő Gerő on a report of János Boldoczky from Prague, 26 December, 1951, MOL, M KS-276 f. 65 cs. 102 ő.e.
31 Mark Pittaway, 'The Politics of Legitimacy and Hungary's Postwar Transition', *Contemporary European History*, 13, 2004, no. 4, pp. 435–75 (p. 474).
32 Zsoltán Ripp, 'Példaképből ellenség, a magyar kommunisták viszonya Jugoszláviához, 1947–1948', in Éva Standeisky et al. (eds.), *A fordulat évei 1947–1949*, Budapest, 1998, p. 46.
33 Anton Rob to the Hungarian Communist Party's secretariat, 30 June, 1948, Rákosi Papers, documents relating to Yugoslavia, MOL, M KS-276 f. 65 cs. 103 ő.e.

By the time of the Rajk trial in 1949, not only the Yugoslav communists but also the representatives of the Serb and Croat minorities in Hungary were regarded as Tito's 'storm-troopers'.[34] Meanwhile, the same charge was levelled against Hungarians who had precious little to do with Yugoslavia and had never accepted the Titoist label. As late as 1955, Gerő used in Moscow the bogey of Yugoslav-style 'national communism' to discredit Imre Nagy and his followers. With no little venom, he told the Soviet ambassador that Imre Nagy was 'yearning for Tito's laurels'.[35] The animosity between the Hungarian Muscovite leaders proved more enduring than the campaign against the Yugoslav 'enemy'. Paradoxically, in July 1956, it was Gerő himself who issued a written apology to Tito in the name of the MDP's Central Committee for all the false allegations and personal insults.[36]

Similarly, the campaign against Zionism was primarily a knee-jerk reaction to Soviet events. The case against Gábor Péter in many ways mirrored the preparations for a show trial in Moscow, although the head of the Office of State Security (ÁVH) was undeniably a convenient scapegoat for Rákosi. In any case, the charge of political dissent was used to justify anti-Semitic measures. In a top-secret memorandum, Major Sándor Rajnai of the ÁVH claimed that at least ten per cent of Hungary's Orthodox Jews were strongly opposed to the regime and wished to leave the country:

> Their hostility is stirred by the Zionist propaganda of Israel's diplomatic mission [...]. It could be said that there are at least 10,000 Jews in Hungary who are toying with the thought of emigrating. Considering their professional background, dissident political views, limited involvement in industrial production, and above all their capacity to keep a large section of society in a constant state of agitation, one can see no reason why their wish should not be granted [...].[37]

The historical debate in Hungary in recent years has focused on the ethnic background and identity of Hungarian Stalinists. But the ambivalence in the official attitude towards the surviving Hungarian Jewry was scarcely based on personal factors. As Rákosi pointed out at a politburo meeting in February 1953, Holocaust survivors and their relatives had been welcomed into the ranks of the party, even though a large proportion of the Jewish middle class was in fact hostile to communism. The 'sympathetic'[38] attitude of the regime changed virtually overnight, as the news of the planned trial of nine Jewish doctors in Moscow reached the MDP leaders. Rákosi could not explain away the sudden shift:

> Of course, our stand against Zionism is not anti-Semitism, although the enemy will label it as such. They will say that the communists have turned on the Jews. But when we moved against the American agent Cardinal Mindszenty, they claimed that there was a pogrom against Christians in Hungary [...].[39]

---

34 Unsigned memorandum entitled 'Javaslat a kémbanda perével kapcsolatos propagandára', 7 September, 1949, papers of the MDP secretariat, MOL, 276. f. 54. 46–54 ő.e.
35 Memorandum by Yuri Andropov, 15 March, 1955, in Baráth, *Szovjet nagyköveti iratok Magyarországról*, p. 223.
36 Ernő Gerő to Josip Broz Tito, 29 July, 1956, Rákosi Papers, MOL, M KS-276 f. 65 cs. 103 ő.e.
37 Report by János Boldoczky, 17 November, 1953, MOL, M KS-276 f. 65 cs. 184 ő.e.
38 Draft of Mátyás Rákosi's speech to the MDP politburo on 19 February, 1953, MOL, M KS-276 f. 65 cs. 30 ő.e.
39 ibid.

The distinctly anti-communist 'cosmopolitan' values of the Budapest bourgeoisie were attacked from the outset by Révai, the MDP's chief theorist. Yet Jewish opposition or resistance to communism had nothing to do with the anti-Zionist campaign in Budapest.

By contrast, the severity of the witch-hunt against 'kulaks' had some domestic causes. After all, the political legacy of the Smallholders was still alive in rural Hungary, even if their party had ceased to function. Once again, the brutal campaign was not about pleasing the landless peasants or combating anti-communist sentiment, but about earning the gratitude of Moscow. Ironically, the staggering number of nearly 80,000 court cases was regarded as excessive, even by Soviet advisers. Ultimately, however, propaganda against the 'kulaks' came to serve a clearly defined economic purpose. In July 1951, Gerő sent one of his characteristically blunt notes to Rákosi:

> In the Sunday intelligence reports, I have come across the case of a Mrs Molnár, a peasant woman who has hidden large piles of goods in her flat. I find this an excellent opportunity to make a lot of noise [...]. The woman has plenty of money and four houses. Her husband is already sentenced to two years in prison for a similar offence. Now that the peasants are expected to increase their purchase of consumer goods, we could really do with a few meaty cases and all the publicity surrounding the appropriate punishment. In this case, the woman should be sentenced to at least ten years in prison, and all her possessions should be sold to the public at the lower, official price. This might be well received by the neediest section of the populace. In the following few weeks, we should keep our eyes peeled for similar cases [...].[40]

Gerő appended a solemn warning not to overdo this rural campaign in view of the country's increasingly scarce food reserves. This showed that the communist leadership was not entirely unaware of the economic consequences of its militancy. Conversely, the growing intimidation by the state was not triggered by any signs of political opposition, but by the Hungarian economy's perilous state and the acute shortage of consumer goods. All the same, the use of the police and the courts in controlling supply and demand was a reflection of the Hungarian communist leaders' siege mentality. By passing the buck to the consumer for all the shortages, the regime tried to maintain the illusion of law and order, but this only fuelled resentment. Even Yuri Andropov noted the mind-boggling insensitivity of the Hungarian communists to the population's growing misery.[41]

The deteriorating economy rapidly became the communist administration's Achilles heel in the early 1950s. The ÁVH was given the task of putting a stop to the appalling levels of waste in industry by clamping down on any 'spontaneous or organized sabotage'.[42] But concerns about production, or the shortage of goods, hardly explain such fiascos as the police raid and arrest of a leading actress for the grave 'crime' of owning two French gold medallions.[43] The propaganda battle over the economy induced bureaucratic madness, which often turned into propaganda disaster and farce. Thus, it is difficult to study opposition and resistance in this period without considering the links

40 Ernő Gerő to M. Rákosi, 23 July, 1951, Rákosi Papers, MOL, M KS-276 f. 65 cs. 184 ő.e.
41 M. Baráth, *Szovjet nagyköveti iratok Magyarországról*, p. 90.
42 Unsigned ÁVH document on a reported sabotage in Diósgyőr, 2 February, 1950, Rákosi Papers, MOL, M KS-276 f. 65 cs. 184 ő.e.
43 Memorandum by Lt-Col. György Sós, 19 December, 1950; see Kajári, 'Egy házkutatás története 1950-ből', pp. 290–7.

between economics and state terror. According to a memorandum written in June 1953 by Colonel Rudolf Garasin of the ÁVH, the planned rehabilitation and release of 13,820 prisoners raised the spectre of huge losses in state revenue from the captive labour force. The size of the working prison population was more than 40,000 at the time, the size of a major industrial enterprise. In the same vein, the reinstatement of the pensions of up to 25,000 politically unreliable people was blocked, in July 1953, by the sly economic reasoning of Ernő Gerő:

> We would incur the expenditure of some 50–70 million forints, which we can't allow. In any case, we would reap no political benefit whatsoever. We may, however, make a few exceptions in some deserving cases, and give back pensions to a few hundred people [...]. [44]

In short, the freeing or compensating of the victims of persecution was delayed and complicated by economic considerations as much as by the power struggle between Imre Nagy and Mátyás Rákosi. The continued oppression had a compelling economic, as well as political, logic.

Conversely, opposition to the regime came in various economic guises, from 'informal wage bargaining', through sabotage and black-marketeering, to deliberately shoddy workmanship.[45] Consequently, state statistics provide little help in quantifying resistance. Zoltán Biró, deputy head of the Central Committee's Department of Agitation and Propaganda, reckoned in 1953 that there were still around 500,000 'hostile elements',[46] but this estimate was probably no less crude than his definition of the 'enemy'. The statistics only tell us how many people were investigated and condemned by the courts. Indeed, the label 'hostile element' was frequently used against ardent communists, the very supporters and most loyal servants of the regime. The example of János Kádár is a case in point. Recalling his prison experience in 1954, he wrote to Rákosi:

> I have been struck by fear many times over the years [...]. But I have been scared out of my wits only once in my life. It was an August evening, when, quoting the confession of Szakasits, you implied that I had been an informer of the Horthyist police and a provocateur. I could never recover from this [...].[47]

As a former minister of the interior, Kádár knew more than most how forced confessions and unfounded suspicions might lead to arrest and persecution. He was clearly broken by his experience, both physically and psychologically:

> What I went through over the past four years would be too much for any human being. I would have swapped twelve months in our prisons with twelve years in any capitalist state. Unfortunately, I have experienced incarceration in both systems. There is no meaningful comparison![48]

---

44 Ernő Gerő to Mátyás Rákosi and Imre Nagy, 18 July, 1953, MOL, M KS-276 f. 65 cs. 41 ő.e.
45 Pittaway, 'The Reproduction of Hierarchy', p. 739.
46 Borhi, 'Empire by Coercion', p. 54.
47 Personal letter by János Kádár to Mátyás Rákosi, 21 July, 1954, Rákosi Papers, MOL, M KS-276 f. 65 cs. 44 ő.e.
48 ibid.

Yet, he declared to Rákosi, 'If I were in your position, I would have done the same.'[49] As it happened, he was more exercised by criminality in the ÁVH: a prison guard had stolen his watch! The fear of the invisible enemy afflicted communist leaders, including those with first-hand experience of miscarriages of justice. They were not cured of this illusion, in spite of their own mistreatment. Thus, the number of court cases and sentences against the perceived enemy remained hugely inflated, even after 1953. This became a cause for concern in Moscow, too, where the terror had been initiated. According to Soviet sources, 362,000 people were taken to court in 1951, and the police investigated another 500,000.[50] An ÁVH report, sent by the deputy minister of the interior, László Piros, in November 1953 to Rákosi's secretariat, mentions four different categories of legal proceedings against 758,611 people, although in 640,534 cases, prosecutions were halted, sentences were overturned, or prisoners were amnestied.[51] Most Hungarian secondary sources put these figures even higher, and suggest that, between 1950 and 1953, the courts tried 650,000 people and sentenced nearly 390,000, while the police imposed fines in 850,000 cases.[52]

The statistics tell a tale of repression, but what do they tell us about the nature, composition, and comparative strength of the identified enemy groups in society? How far do the documents bear out the thesis, for example, that the Hungarian middle class was 'forced into exile' by the Stalinist state? Playing the devil's advocate, James Mark maintains that a large proportion of those who escaped the purges had in fact 'benefited from Communism'. According to Mark, aspiring members of the pre-war bourgeoisie 'were given the opportunity to achieve a limited amount of social mobility' even during the worst period of 'high Stalinism'.[53] How far is this thesis substantiated by official documents? Admittedly, by the 1950s, the state security services were less concerned about ex-officials of the Horthy era than about former left-wing coalition partners or any enemies within the ruling party. Manifestations of resentment amongst the working class were taken more seriously than any criticism by the old elite. Still, the communist leadership was fairly unrelenting in its use of intimidation against the middle class. As early as June 1948, Mátyás Rákosi issued an ominous warning: 'The patience of our democratic regime has run out [...]. Those who resist democracy will cry out in pain [...].'[54]

Savage rhetoric of this kind was not unusual from prominent Hungarian communists in the immediate post-war years. As early as September 1946, Rákosi and Révai forecast a bloody and distinctly 'painful' transition to socialism in Hungary.[55] They sent a series of threatening messages to political opponents, notably the Smallholders' Party. More to the point, from January 1947, the political police and the courts played a central role in eliminating some of the most vocal political opponents. Yet, true to Soviet advice, Rákosi usually took great care not to frighten the general public. His change of tack in

---

49 ibid.
50 Borhi, 'Empire by Coercion', p. 54.
51 László Piros to Mátyás Rákosi, 23 November, 1953, Rákosi Papers, MOL, M KS-276 f. 65 cs. 184 ő.e.
52 György Gyarmati, 'Hungary in the Second Half of the Twentieth Century', in (ed.) István György Tóth, *A Concise History of Hungary*, Budapest, 2005, pp. 579–80; Borhi, 'Empire by Coercion', p. 54.
53 Mark, 'Discrimination, Opportunity, and Middle-Class Success', p. 500.
54 Mátyás Rákosi's speech in Budapest, 12 June, 1948, Rákosi Papers, MOL, M KS-276 f. 65 cs. 4 ő.e.
55 *Szabad Nép*, 29 September 1946; ibid, 1 October 1946.

the summer of 1948, in the wake of the 'merger' of the two workers' parties, was a sign of rapidly growing confidence. The constant references to the 'fist' of the state apparatus, not to mention some abusive comments about Cardinal Mindszenty, Smallholder exiles, and the liquidated Social Democrat leadership, ushered in a new combative style.

The speech at Budapest's Heroes Square can be interpreted as a declaration of class war. The middle class was designated as the main source of opposition to the political changes. Although Ernő Gerő conceded as late as 1950 that the country was reliant on non-party intellectuals 'at least for five or six years',[56] the Rákosi regime launched such a frenzied attack on intellectuals that even the Soviets anticipated a backlash. Already in April 1947, Rákosi had turned to Molotov for support in respect of a series of show trials against the former political and intellectual elite:

> We need some dramatic momentum. We need to find another conspiracy, even though we have to be careful. People are getting tired of this [...]. We know of more than 1,500 non-Jewish fascists. These are racists, professors, and intellectuals. We have to get rid of them [...].[57]

Such ranting was too much even for Molotov, who emphatically warned against antagonizing the entire Hungarian middle class. Four years later, at the height of the Cold War, the Soviet ambassador, Kiselov, repeated the same warning and singled out for criticism the MDP's deplorable attitude towards the technical intelligentsia. The historical claim, therefore, that the technocratic elite was entirely pacified in the early 1950s is hardly borne out by the documents. In 1949, at the time of the Rajk trial, the main concern of propagandists was not the attitude of workers, but the hostility and scepticism of the intelligentsia. A 'mood report' by the Department of Agitation and Propaganda concluded: 'The majority of intellectuals appear to be fairly passive. According to our intelligence, they are rather surprised and baffled by events. In several cases, the police were called on to suppress manifestations of dissent [...].'[58]

Quite apart from the passing reference to unspecified 'manifestations of dissent', the passivity of the urban population was a serious concern in itself. It flew in the face of any attempts to use the Rajk trial 'to incite patriotic hatred against the imperialists and their agents in the general public.'[59] For the show trial was certainly meant to be the 'greatest victory'[60] of the MDP, and the crowning achievement of Rákosi, who regarded the Slanský and Kostov trials as pale imitations of the Rajk case.[61] Thus, the stunned silence of Hungarian intellectuals was scarcely the expected result. In the 1950s, this passive stance was generally regarded by the regime as a form of resistance. In May 1954, an ÁVH document quoted the only former Social Democrat member of the MDP leadership as saying: 'It is typical of the political indifference of "the majority" that

---

56 Draft of Ernő Gerő's speech at the second party congress, 27 December 1950, Rákosi Papers, MOL, M KS-276 f. 65 cs. 6. ő.e.

57 Memorandum of 7 May 1947 by G. J. Korotkevich on the Molotov–Rákosi talks of 29 April, 1947, in István Vida (ed.), *Iratok a Magyar-szovjet kapcsolatok történetéhez, 1944 október-1948 június*, Budapest, 2005, p. 261.

58 Documents on communist propaganda, Rákosi Papers, MOL, M KS-276 f. 65 cs. 61 ő.e.

59 Minutes of the meeting of the MDP secretariat, 30 May, 1949, MOL, M KS-276. f. 54 cs. 46 ő.e.

60 ibid.

61 Report by Oszkár Bethlen on the Slanský trial, 28 November, 1952, MOL, M KS-276 f. 65 cs. 102 ő.e.; see also Mária Schmidt, *Diktatúrák ördögszekerén*, Budapest, 1998, p. 251.

even at the party congress, the main subject of discussion was the England–Hungary football game [...].'[62]

These observations went down no better in the Ministry of the Interior than incisive comments by the same individual about police brutality and 'family rule' in communist Hungary. Having failed to engineer a new class, the MDP mandarins wished to secure the active participation of the educated elite, and not just their silent tolerance. Consequently, in June 1953, Gerő initiated the promotion of university-educated young and middle-aged cadres in both the party and the state apparatus: 'Even though there may be some risks involved, all new positions should go to intellectuals, no older than forty-five years of age. In Budapest, I think of engineers, economists, and perhaps teachers [...].'[63]

Leaving aside the slogans about its working-class identity, the MDP was consciously trying to secure a support base amongst intellectuals. This approach bore some fruit. In August 1948, in the capital's twelfth district, eighty-four per cent of party members were not of working-class origin.[64] Official documents clearly bear out the claim that the Budapest intelligentsia enjoyed some social mobility.[65] For every individual removed from an important position, the regime had to find a replacement. Gerő noted in 1952 that it would take at least a couple of years 'to quietly get rid of' the president of the Hungarian Academy.[66] Appointments were quicker, despite an acute shortage of qualified and reliable personnel. The most loyal section of the teaching profession, dedicated to teaching Marxism-Leninism, was expected to indoctrinate a new generation of intellectuals in double-quick time. Characteristically, their reliability and the importance of their mission did not spare them from petty persecution.[67]

In any case, there is no evidence of the emergence of 'specifically communist middle-class identities'[68] in the 1950s. The transformation of the intelligentsia along socialist lines was no more successful than the attempts to create a 'new working class'.[69] After 1953, the belligerence of the hitherto more or less 'quarantined'[70] section of the urban population only increased and became more vocal. Although the debates of the Petőfi circle primarily attracted the party intelligentsia, communist writers and journalists, and the internal opposition of the Stalinist leadership, according to Gerő 'some 30–40 people',[71] the New Course ushered in by Imre Nagy certainly had a liberating impact on society at large. Whilst it was feared by many, and not without foundation, that the terror had only temporarily abated,[72] 'Imre Nagy's seventeen months', according to János Rainer's analysis, 'significantly changed the social and

62 Lt Col. Sándor Rajki to László Piros, 29 May, 1954, MOL, M KS-276 f. 65 cs. 54 ő.e.
63 Ernő Gerő to Mátyás Rákosi, 8 June, 1953, MOL, M KS-276 f. 65 cs. 41 ő.e.
64 Mátyás Rákosi to Mihály Farkas, 27 August, 1948, MOL, M KS-276 f. 65 cs. 41 ő.e.
65 Mark, 'Discrimination, Opportunity, and Middle-Class Success', p. 500.
66 Ernő Gerő to Mátyás Rákosi, 12 September, 1952, MOL, M KS-276 f. 65 cs. 52 ő.e.
67 Mátyás Rákosi's memorandum on personal matters for Ernő Gerő, József Révai, and Mihály Farkas, 2 December, 1952 , MOL, M KS-276 f. 65 cs. 52 ő.e.
68 ibid.
69 Pittaway, 'The Reproduction of Hierarchy', p. 766.
70 Rainer, 'Submerging or clinging on again?', p. 67.
71 Minutes of the conversations of Yuri Andropov, Ernő Gerő, and András Hegedűs, 19 June, 1956, in Baráth, *Szovjet nagyköveti iratok Magyarországról*, p. 309.
72 Lt Col. Sándor Rajki to László Piros, 29 May, 1954, MOL, M KS-276 f. 65 cs. 54 ő.e.

psychological environment.'[73] By the summer of 1956, the growing opposition of 'national-minded intellectuals' and students was becoming a mantra frequently repeated at the meetings of Gerő with the Soviet ambassador.[74]

It is reasonable to assume that the threat, as perceived by the Hungarian Stalinists, was much stronger than the actual strength of the opposition. Nevertheless, it is an inescapable conclusion that the revolution of 1956 was not just a unique exception to the rule of passivity and indifference, but a culmination of various strands of dissent, brought together by an unexpected and violent turn of events.

---

73 János M. Rainer, *Nagy Imre, 1953–1958*, Budapest, 1999, p. 138.
74 See, for example, Yuri Andropov's report of his conversation with András Hegedűs, 18 September 1956, in Baráth, *Szovjet nagyköveti iratok Magyarországról*, p. 348.

Disillusioned Revolutionaries: Jewish-Communist Activists in Poland 1945–1956

Grzegorz Berendt

From the very beginning of the Marxist revolutionary movement in Poland, people of Jewish descent played an important role in the ranks of the various socialist organizations. Hundreds and then thousands of them joined the Communist Party of Poland (founded in December 1918) and structures affiliated to it and to the Comintern.[1] They dreamed of creating a new world and of overcoming pressing economic, social and ethnic problems. Before 1918 and to a great extent also in the years 1918–1939, many people who became members or sympathizers of the communist movement in Poland adopted highly idealistic approaches to the most important public issues. Many of the first communists came from wealthy families, and their political activity was sometimes scornfully called 'salon-communism'.[2] On the other hand, these people were often better prepared to take charge of the organizational structures than poor illiterate artisans or labourers. One remark must be added, though, in respect of the cultural diversity of Jewish communists. There were those who could easily work with non-Jewish comrades on account of their good knowledge of Polish, but there were others who were only able to exist in the so-called 'Jewish street' as their mother tongue was still Yiddish. Nonetheless, for all of them revolution carried only positive connotations.

The exact number of Jews who joined the communist movement in Poland before 1939 is unknown. It could have been about 5–10,000 persons or a little more.[3] At the time, they constituted only a very small fraction of Polish Jewry, but they assumed a significant place in communist organizational structures, especially in large cities, like Warsaw and Łódź, and in the eastern Polish borderlands. Jewish professionals also dominated the editorial staff of the party organs.

Many Polish-Jewish communists died in the 1930s in the Stalinist purges, and the majority perished shortly afterwards in the Shoah. The number of those who found shelter in the Soviet Union has been estimated by Jaff Schatz at about 2000 and there were also some others who survived in the area occupied by the Nazis.[4] According to

---

1 Henryk Cimek, *Komunisci – Polska – Stalin 1918–1939*, Bialystok, 1990, pp. 77–78; Marian Mushkat, *Philo-Semitic and anti-Jewish attitudes in post-Holocaust Poland*, New York, 1992, p. 237; Jaff Schatz, *The Generation: The Rise and Fall of the Jewish Communists of Poland*, Berkeley, Los Angeles, Oxford, pp. 96–97; Zbigniew Szczygielski, *Czlonkowie KPP 1918–1938 w swietle badan ankietowych*, Warsaw, 1989, pp. 82–92.
2 Henryk Grynberg, *Memorbuch*, Warsaw, 2000, pp. 26–27, 35–39, 52, 66–67.
3 Schatz, *The Generation*, pp. 96–97.
4 ibid, p. 209.

statistics prepared by the Jewish committees in Poland in 1947, among the 110,000 or so persons that they registered, about 7000 were members of the communist Polish Workers Party.[5] The number of those who remained unregistered has not yet been established. In the years 1944–1951, the majority of the 270,000 or so survivors registered in the country decided to emigrate. Only about 75–80,000 were still living in Poland in 1955. We do not know even the approximate number of those who joined the Polish United Workers Party and the affiliated Association of Polish Youth. A hand-written note placed at the margin of a report of the Social and Cultural Association of Jews in Poland mentions 3000 party members in that organization in 1953. The total number of the members of the Association was at the time about 11,000 persons.

One significant feature of the consciousness of communists of Jewish origin in Poland was their attitude to their own ethnicity. We can safely assume that all of them had lost most of their family-members during the war. Consciousness of the fact that they had miraculously missed death acted as a link between those who were deeply rooted in the Polish cultural environment and those who moved in a still Yiddish-speaking milieu. Repatriates from the USSR and former partisans or persons that had hidden on the 'Aryan side' often attributed the fact that they were still alive to the Red Army. For these, the role played by the Soviets in defeating the Third Reich and its allies was one more argument for communism and for the fatherland of socialism and its leader. Although the overwhelming majority did not want to live in the Soviet Union longer than was necessary,[6] once returned to Poland they stressed many times in public their gratitude to the Soviets. In the late 1940s, Jewish communists still hoped that communism might ensure a dignified life for the overwhelming majority of society, notwithstanding in many cases their first-hand experience and knowledge of what was actually going on in the Soviet Union.

Many Jews were also alarmed by the activities of the anti-communist underground and opposition and interpreted the violence of anti-communist resistance as acts of terror aimed at the survivors of the Shoah.[7] By contrast, the new regime seemed to offer them protection and to stand up for order and forbearance. Their support for the new regime was strengthened by other considerations. For the first time in Polish history, Jews had open access to all posts in public institutions and, thus, or so it might seem, unlimited possibilities for social advancement.[8] Of course, they had in return to toe the party-line and, if this was unwelcome to them, the option of leaving for the democratic

---

5 Grzegorz Berendt, *Zycie zydowskie w Polsce w latach 1950–1956. Z dziejow Towarzystwa Spoleczno-Kulturalnego Zydow w Polsce*, Gdańsk, 2006, p. 133.

6 David Sfard, *Mit zikh un mit andere*, Jerusalem 1984, p. 154–155; Pesakh Novik, *Eyrope – Tsvishn milchome un shalom*, New York 1948, p. 144–148.

7 P. Novik, *Eyrope*, pp. 94–99, 154–157; D. Sfard, *Mit zikh un mit andere*, pp. 155, 203–203; Hersh Smolar, *Oyf der letster pozicje mit der letster hofenung*, Tel Aviv 1982, pp. 50–52.

8 Józef Adelson, 'W Polsce zwanej ludowa,' in *Najnowsze dzieje Zydow w Polsce w zarysie (do 1950 roku)*, ed. J. Tomaszewski, Warsaw, 1993, pp. 387–477; Leszek Olejnik, *Polityka narodowosciowa Polski w latach 1944–1960*, Łodz, 2003, pp. 361–380.

countries.[9] Representatives of the poorer strata of Jewish society had stable work, health insurance and medical help and could see their children entering education at all levels.

By degrees, however, Jewish communists realized that the People's Poland was not, after all, a secular paradise and that they were still marked out in a negative fashion. Some were advised by their superiors to give up their Jewish family- and second-names and even their patronymics in order to be seen as persons of Polish and Aryan origin.[10] Many were also persuaded to change their statement in the periodic censuses in regard to national and religious affiliation. A special colloquial term was created for such people: POP – *pełniący obowiązki Polaka* – 'acting as a Pole'. Officials in the higher branches of the state and party hierarchy took part in discussions as to the 'over-representation of the Jews in some branches of the public service', for example in the ministries of Foreign Trade and Public Security, or in Military Counter-Intelligence. In 1947–1948, General Secretary of the Polish Workers Party, Władysław Gomułka, repeated several times during closed sessions of party meetings, that 'Jewish over-representation' should be addressed.[11] This attitude persisted even after Gomułka's dismissal in September 1948.

Such influential party functionaries as Jakub Berman learnt immediately of the renewed 'anti-Zionist tones in the Soviet Union' in the second half of the 1940s. Communist Hersh Smolar, chairman of the communist caucus in the Central Committee of Jews in Poland, mentioned in his memoirs that he and his comrades had already known in November 1948 of the liquidation of Jewish institutions in Moscow[12]. They later lost contact with almost all the Jewish cultural activists that they knew. It was clear that an anti-Jewish policy was being implemented in the East and that it would probably soon come to Poland. An atmosphere of fear gradually spread among Polish Jews. Most of the communist veterans had started their political activity when still in their mid-teens. Those who came from Yiddish-speaking homes had generally first joined Jewish socialist organizations and only later gone over to communist ones. In 1949, when filling out personal-questionnaires, they omitted any reference to these non-communist Jewish organizations so as to avoid the accusation of being previously attached to Jewish nationalist circles.

For unknown reasons, Stalin failed to support the campaign in Poland aimed against well-known communists of Jewish descent. He must have been persuaded by Bolesław Bierut, First Secretary of the Central Committee of the party, who until his death protected potential victims of the political anti-Semitic purge within the party ranks.[13] Nevertheless, Bierut did not try, or else failed to stop, the anti-Jewish action in the

9 In the years 1944–1951, about 180,000 Jews and their relatives decided to leave Poland, and some 30,000 in the years 1949–1951. See thus, A. Stankowski, 'Nowe spojrzenie na statystyki dotyczace emigracji Zydow z Polski po 1944 roku', in Grzegorz Berendt, August Grabski, Albert Stankowski (eds.), *Studia z historii Zydow w Polsce po 1945 roku*, Warsaw, 2000, pp. 103–117.
10 Feliks Mantel, *Stosunki polsko-zydowskie*, Paris, 1986, p. 12; Michał Rudawski, *Moj obcy kraj?*, Warsaw, 1996, pp. 136–144.
11 Adam Schaff, *Moje spotkania z nauka polska*, Warsaw, 1997, pp. 106–107; Dariusz Stola, *Kampania antysyjonistyczna w Polsce 1967–1968*, Warsaw, 2000, p. 127; Andrzej Werblan, 'Przyczynek do dziejow odchylenia prawicowo-nacjonalistycznego', *Dzis*, 1994, no 10, p. 18; Leszek W. Gluchowski, 'Gomulka writes to Stalin in 1948', *Polin*, 17, 2004, pp. 365–382.
12 Smolar, *Oyf der letster pozicje*, pp. 163–164.
13 *Sovietskiy faktor v Vostochnoy Yevropye 1944–1953*, vol. 2 (1949–1953, *Dokumienty*), Moscow, 2002, pp. 321, 324, 696, 835–836, 859, 863–864, 871–872.

Polish People's Army (*Ludowe Wojsko Polskie*) carried out by Soviet officers in charge of counter-intelligence operations. That action must surely have been backed by the Soviet marshal, Konstantin Rokossowski. It started in October 1950 and went on for at least three years.

At the turn of 1952–1953, the communist bloc learnt of Rudolf Slanský's notorious trial and of the so-called 'Kremlin Doctors Plot'. At that time, many Jewish officers in the army and political police were fired, having been accused of backing reactionary and nationalistic opinions or of being influenced by such reactionary elements as their religiously observant Jewish relatives. The anti-Semitic campaign in Russia and Czechoslovakia frightened many Polish Jews and Jewish communists. Many Jewish communists, like their comrades abroad, were astonished that such events could happen in communist countries. They did not sever their links with the party all of a sudden, because such an act was still too dangerous, but for many people the events of the early 1950s marked what Bernard Wasserstein has called 'the end of the revolutionary Jew'.[14]

The process of loosening ties with communism, especially its Soviet version, stretched in many cases over several years, and Soviet anti-Semitism strongly influenced its course. In 1956, French and other foreign guests to Moscow came back home with reports of the scandalous anti-Semitic opinions expressed by Nikita Khrushchev who propagated his theory of the 'national regulation of cadres', that is, the introduction of a *numerus clausus*.[15] For many Jews, this amounted to blocking their career in much of public life. The first time that this term was used in Poland occurred in 1956 during the course of conversations between Jewish communists and high-ranking communist apparatchiks (among others, Wladyslaw Matwin, Zenon Nowak and Edward Ochab).[16]

The death of Bierut in Moscow about two weeks after the final session of the Twentieth Soviet Party Congress and the heated exchanges over the political and legal responsibility for the events of the previous years had negative consequences for Polish Jews. A group of Polish communist leaders came to the conclusion that political responsibility for previous excesses might best be attributed to several of Bierut's closest collaborators, most of all to Jakub Berman, Hilary Minc and Roman Zambrowski. From the first half of 1956, the group representing this viewpoint had been referred to as the 'Natolin' faction.[17] In their opinion, communists of Jewish descent were primarily guilty of creating distrust of the Party among ordinary people and, later on, of attacking the principles of communism and of the political system itself in Poland.[18] The Natolinists mainly directed their attack against the intellectuals and the new intelligentsia affiliated with the party. The idea of associating the Polish political crisis with the Jews was fervently supported by the Soviets.

Jakub Berman was fired in May from all his party and state posts. Several months later, Minc experienced the same fate. Although no official person publicly mentioned the Jewish origin of either, their situation was interpreted by some as the signal for other Jews to be removed from their posts. Week after week, there were a growing number of

---

14 Bernard Wasserstein, *Vanishing Diaspora: The Jews in Europe since 1945*, London 1996, p. 56.
15 Haim Sloves, *Sovetishe yiddishe meluchishkayt*, Paris 1979, pp. 332–334.
16 Sfard, *Mit zikh un mit andere*, pp. 208, 272–273; Smolar, *Oyf der letster pozicje*, pp. 222–223.
17 So called after the Natolin Palace in Warsaw where the faction usually held its meetings.
18 Michael Chęciński, *Poland: Communism – Nationalism – Anti-Semitism*, New York 1982, pp. 104–22.

press reports of anti-Semitic events in factories, institutions, at schools and in the street. Hooligans, often drunk and sometimes party members, attacked Jews beating them up and humiliating them.[19]

The Jewish response to the situation was varied. Probably most of them expected a rapid crack-down by the political leaders of the country on these excesses. Nevertheless, there was no explicit statement condemning anti-Semitism by any first-rank politician until early 1957. No representative of the Politburo or even Central Committee of the Party attended the extraordinary meeting of the Main Board of the Social and Cultural Association of Jews in Poland that was called in November 1956 to discuss current issues of importance to Jews. Members of the Board wandered in vain through the long corridors of the Central Committee building in Warsaw endeavouring to find somebody ready to address the despairing and frustrated delegates of the Association's local branches.[20]

The long silence maintained by the first secretaries of the Central Committee and prime minister regarding the situation of Polish Jewry made many Jews think that the party wanted them to leave the country, that they had been left alone with their problems, and that they had been betrayed. Such opinions were expressed during meetings organized in Jewish institutions and during the open conferences eventually called by the party in the spring and summer of 1957. But the reaction of the political leadership was belated. Party members and individuals of non-communist affiliation had already started registering for emigration. In their meetings with the communist activists of the Social and Cultural Association, people had for months been requesting just two things: physical protection and help in emigration. Between 1956 and 1959, 52,000 Jews emigrated. The number of communists who left the country with them is not known, although we do know that only a few joined the pro-Soviet, Communist Party of Israel. Many more decided to work within the established Israeli Zionist-socialist parties.[21] For them communism was no longer a solution either to the larger human condition or to specific Jewish issues.

Despite the large exodus, communists of the Jewish descent remained in Poland, determined to continue their life and work there. But many of them now had a changed attitude towards the Soviet Union and were sceptical of the possibility of any real Jewish emancipation in the communist bloc as such. Several dozens of them and their children later joined the various circles of political dissidents, helping to undermine the political system of the Polish People's Republic.[22] Many others became sympathizers and silent supporters of the dissident movements. On the other hand, one could still find examples of the ultra-orthodox, old-style communist for whom the 'Solidarność' movement was proof of the counter-revolutionary work of the imperialists, and who considered that the only solution was to smash the movement to pieces with truncheons.

---

19 Berendt, *Zycie zydowskie w Polsce w latach 1950–1956*, pp. 305–312.
20 Smolar, *Oyf der letster pozicje*, pp. 235–236; Sfard, *Mit zikh un mit andere*, pp. 200, 221–222, 270–271.
21 Od Nowa, 1959, no 39.
22 One can name here for example such important Polish-Jewish dissidents as Adam Michnik, Seweryn Blumsztajn, Aleksander and Eugeniusz Smolar. See also A. Friszke, *Opozycja polityczna w PRL 1945–1980*, London 1994, pp. 155–550.

After 1956 one could also observe in Poland the rebirth of Jewish consciousness in the families of Communist-party members. In some of these families, children were brought up in comparative isolation from the gentile environment and warned about its strong anti-Semitic prejudices. This prompted the emigration of many young Poles of the Jewish origin who saw for them no future in the 'Polin', the homeland of their fore-fathers.[23] This was a further consequence of the disillusionment experienced by these former supporters of the communism.

---

23 G. Berendt, 'Emigracja ludności zydowskiej z Polski w latach 1945–1967', in *Polska 1944/45–1989. Studia i materialy*, vol. 7, Warsaw, 2006, pp. 52–58.

Ira populi: Targets of Popular Hatred and Scapegoats in Hungary, 1944–1956

Attila Pók

Az élet a történelem tanítómestere (Vita est magistra historiae)
(Tibor Hajdú, *Világosság*, March, 1999, p. 5)
We did not have enough evidence to prove the role of the imperialist powers in the preparation, in the sparking off and in support of the counter-revolution. Due to the weakness of operative work we did not have documents to prove that the counter-revolution, as it started on 23 October, was the result of the coordinated action of internal and external forces and not a spontaneous action. (Report of Colonel László Mátyás, head of the Department of Political Investigation of the Hungarian Ministry of the Interior on the period from November 8, 1956 to February 1, 1957. Cited by Gábor Kiszely, *Állambiztonság 1956–1990*, Budapest, 2001, pp. 29–30.)

Love and hatred, sentiment, passions, feelings: how do they shape history? The theme of this volume is the relevance of resistance, rebellion and revolution to Central European history. My own contribution raises the question of the role of feelings and passions, and of popular hatreds, both manipulated and 'spontaneous', in shaping the emergence and course of the revolutionary breakthrough in Hungary in 1956. In other words, it seeks to examine forms of personal and popular hatred among the forerunners, makers and during the course of the 1956 rebellion. The argument is highly abstract, but I prefer to present new ideas in an unrefined, rough form rather than to reproduce conventional wisdoms. My contribution is part of a larger work on scapegoating in twentieth-century Hungary. This is why it deals more with putting the hatreds of 1956 within a contemporary European and longer twentieth-century Hungarian context than with 1956 itself.

Conceptual framework; historiographical background

In 1927, a few years before national socialism became a key issue on the European political and intellectual agenda, a most influential French intellectual of Jewish origin, whose views had a great impact on his European contemporaries, wrote the following: 'Our age is indeed the age of the *intellectual organization of political hatreds*.'[1] Julien Benda argued that there was a fundamental difference between pre-nineteenth-century and nineteenth- to twentieth-century political passions. Up to the time of the Napoleonic wars, these 'consisted of purely passionate impulses, natural explosions of instinct [...]

---

1 Julien Benda, *The Betrayal of Intellectuals*, Boston, 1959, p. 21. (Originally published as *Le Traison des Clercs*, 1927)

[but] today I notice that every political passion is furnished with a whole network of strongly woven doctrines [...].'[2] According to Benda, this situation came about in the aftermath of the Napoleonic wars and the decisive element in its composition was the blending of national and political passions: '[...] very powerful political passions, which were originally independent of nationalist feeling, have now become incorporated with it.'[3] The 60-year-old philosopher gave a list of these major passions: the movement against the Jews, the movement of the possessing classes against the proletariat, and the movement of the champions of authority against the democrats.

One of the foremost experts of twentieth-century European conservative thought, an American of German descent, Fritz Stern, author of what is perhaps still the most important work on the intellectual roots of national socialist ideology,[4] wrote when starting his work on the politics of cultural despair, ' I hope to show that ours is the age of the *political organization of cultural hatreds and personal resentments.*'[5] Aware of the disastrous practical consequences of national socialism, Stern argued for a different approach to the origins of extreme political hatreds by putting these into a broader context. He indicated how nationalists attacked modern (i.e. liberal, secular, industrial-urban) culture and how essentially non-political grievances intruded into politics. He defined this aspect of nationalism as a conservative revolution and traced its origins to romanticism. Its followers 'sought to destroy the despised present in order to recapture an idealized past in an imaginary future.'[6] Among the representatives of this European intellectual trend, Dostoevskii and Nietzsche[7] came up with the most pervasive pessimism (God is dead!) in respect of the future of the West. According to Stern, the next stage in this process was the transformation of cultural criticism into political ideology. The combination of cultural criticism with extreme nationalism could be observed in almost every continental country (Barrès in France, D'Annunzio in Italy, and Lueger in Austria). This 'ideology of resentment' first arose in the 1890s, was powerful in the aftermath of World War One, surfaced again during the Great Depression, reached a peak in Hitler's Germany, and also shaped the international political climate in the form of the East-West confrontation during the Cold War. Stern thus considers hatred as a central issue of the twentieth century. Nevertheless, he believes that it is not political issues that awaken culturally expressed and 'intellectually organized' passions but instead an opposite causal relationship: the deeper-lying cultural hatreds and resentments are *politically* manifested.

Two other authors helped me formulate the points of this essay. The first was Peter Gay who has succeeded most originally in combining social, cultural and intellectual history in his comprehensive survey of Victorian Europe. In his *The Cultivation of Hatred* (New York, 1993), he calls upon Freud and argues that the major events of the 'long' nineteenth and the 'short' twentieth centuries can be described as a series of attempts aimed at curbing the eruptions of individual and collective aggressions. The

---

2　ibid.
3　ibid, p. 18.
4　Fritz Stern, *The Politics of Cultural Despair*, New York, 1961.
5　ibid, p. 6.
6　ibid, p. 7.
7　See also Peter Bergmann, *Nietzsche: The Last Antipolitical German*, Bloomington and Indianapolis, 1987.

great challenge for a historian venturing into the realm of social psychology is to try to contribute, through the analysis of numerous case-studies, to the debate on the relationship of 'nature to nurture' in respect of the causes of aggression. The second is the classic essay by Richard Hofstadter on 'The Paranoid Style in American Politics' (1963),[8] which explains how extreme radical nationalism shows the signs of clinical paranoia. This political paranoia differs from its individual psychological counterpart in referring to the sense of persecution felt by the whole of the national community. Paranoid politicians are mighty advocates of conspiracy theories and they seek to explain complex social, economic and political situations by 'enforced attribution': that is, by 'presenting oversimplified, unicausal clarifications', most often treason or high treason by leading political figures.

Beyond these two, I have also used Charles Tilly's works, especially his book on half a millennium of European revolutions, in the series edited by Le Goff, 'The Making of Europe'. Tilly defines a revolutionary situation as having three consecutive aspects: first, contenders appear and advance claims that they should control the state; secondly, a 'significant segment of the population' endorses these claims; and, thirdly, the state proves itself incapable of accommodating these claims. His main points are that revolutionary explosions, resulting from such situations, can be located in the mainstream of state-building; they are not, therefore, aberrations. His other, related point is that only movements that have a real chance of seriously contending for power, are revolutions worth studying.[9]

When analysing the various manifestations of cultural and political hatred, the concept of scapegoating, as defined in its socio-psychological sense, can be of great help. A careful examination of selected scapegoats shows that the scapegoat-victim incorporates the most hated elements of the scapegoaters' own personalities. The members of the scapegoating group project their internal tensions, worries, and fears onto the scapegoat. For example, in smaller groups of adolescent children, those with a mature physical appearance and sexual attraction frequently become scapegoats. Namely, the group punishes the member who deviates from traditionally determined norms of behaviour or appearance. They punish the scapegoat for what they secretly long to be themselves and in this way they disown their own desires. It is also an important psychological observation that 'blame allocation' means not only the evasion of responsibility but also the obscuring of the original problem. This is far from intending to suggest that the scapegoater is always aware of the true causes of the problem, that he consciously wants to hide them and to divert attention from his own responsibility. Indeed, the reverse is the case. The scapegoater is often also prisoner of enforced attribution, and seeks by a single act to rise above the complexities of his own situation.[10]

There are three aspects to this social psychological phenomenon that are essential. First, contrary to the original Old Testament interpretation that considered scapegoating as a process of atonement by consciously transferring guilt onto the innocent goat,

---

8   Republished in *The Paranoid Style in American Politics and other essays*, Cambridge, MA, 1965.
9   Charles Tilly, *European Revolutions: 1492–1992*, Oxford and Cambridge, MA. See also the review by Michael Richards in the *Journal of Social History*, Summer 1995.
10 Thomas Douglas, *The Scapegoat*, London, 1995, chapter 8.

modern scapegoaters are convinced that the scapegoats are actually guilty. Secondly, scapegoating serves the interest of enforced attribution: that is, easing social tensions by giving simplified monocausal explanations to more complicated phenomena or processes. Thirdly, scapegoating is essential in creating social cohesion and can well mobilize social groups or complete societies, especially in post-crisis situations. Scapegoating is thus a form of systematic hatred that frequently results in an aggression that is also driven by fear. For a historian tracing the origins of aggression, the concept of scapegoating can be most helpful. Following Peter Gay, it can help in *shifting the focus of research from looking at the spreading ground of freedom in modern societies towards the causes behind eruptions of individual and collective aggression.*

The Hungarian Historical Context

From the perspective of the history of modern hatreds in Hungary as driving forces of aggressive mass behaviour, I would like to place Hungary's 1956 revolution in the process starting with the 1905–6 political crisis in the eastern half of the Dual Monarchy.

It is quite remarkable that one of the greatest thinkers of twentieth-century Hungary, László Németh, in his famous article, published on 2 November, 1956, 'Emelkedő nemzet' (Nation on the Rise) which came out in the weekly *Irodalmi Újság*, wrote as follows: 'Hungarian intellectual development over the last fifty years clearly defined the aims that we must strive for in a Hungarian revolution.'[11] Fifty years back from 1956 is 1906. It is unlikely that Németh's statement, written in the revolutionary turmoil of 1956, could have been based on a scholarly analysis, but the spontaneous insights of creative writers can occasionally be much more enlightening than academic discourses. For it was the 1905 political crisis that helped bring to the surface the decisive antagonisms of early twentieth century Hungary that – *mutatis mutandis* – have been with us ever since. It was Tibor Hajdú who recently pointed out the significance of the political crisis that followed the defeat at the January 1905 elections of the Hungarian Liberal Party after thirty years in power.[12] These old dilemmas included national interest versus social progress, and debates concerning the actual meaning of sovereignty and independence. According to Hajdú's argument, until 1905 there was always some hope that Hungarian democracy could emerge out of Hungarian liberalism. This hope was lost when the emperor allowed the nationalist coalition led by the 1848-ers to take over government, in return for which the coalition gave up its demands for an enhanced measure of Hungarian self-government. Thus the opportunity was lost in which there might emerge a national radicalism combining a programme of national sovereignty with far-reaching social and political reforms. The majority of society increasingly identified programmes of radical social and political change with unpatriotic 'cosmopolitanism'. For eight decades, national liberalism had dominated Hungarian politics (both in its '1867-er' and '1848-er' forms). The 1905–6 controversies initiated a process that broke the national liberal platform apart.

---

11 *Irodalmi Újság*, 2 November, 1956, p. 1.
12 Tibor Hajdú, '1905 – az utak szétválnak', *Világosság*, 1999, no 3, pp. 5–10.

Henceforward, liberals, democrats, and the exponents of 'bourgeois' radicalism parted ways. Splits and cleavages also arose within the group of radical democrats. In the expression of these differences, mutual hatreds played an important role. From about this time on, in political and cultural debates, the image of destructive feudalism and of reaction was frequently contrasted with the concept of rootless, alien, western-courting cosmopolitans. The best example of this type of excessive hatred on a personal level is that between two of the most outstanding figures of early-twentieth century Hungary: Endre Ady, the great poet and writer, a radical critic of the Hungarian establishment, and István Tisza, prime minister from 1903 to 1905, and, again, from 1913 to 1917. Tisza did his best to promote the industrial modernization of the country but was opposed to any substantial political or social reforms.[13] Ady described Tisza as a wild fool and fire-raiser, while, for Tisza, Ady was a louse on the tree of Hungarian culture.[14]

Universal, equal suffrage was one of the big issues on the early twentieth-century Hungarian political agenda, prompting extra-parliamentary struggles loaded with hatred. A hundred thousand socialists and their supporters rallied in front of the recently-opened parliament on 'Red Friday' (16 September 1905) demanding full adult suffrage and hailing the recent royal initiative in this regard. An anti-Socialist, anti-Vienna demonstration of about the same size was staged very soon after, on 6 October, which was also the day marking the execution in 1849 of the 'Arad martyrs'. In tandem with the conflicts on the street, intra-parliamentary struggles so intensified that nationalist MPs had to be evicted from the parliament by military force on 19 February, 1906. Confrontations among hatred-filled intra- and extra-parliamentary forces continued on an even more intense level after the national coalition lost power and István Tisza returned to office. 'Bloody Thursday' (23 May, 1912) was the result of Tisza's attempt at removing obstructionist deputies from parliament. Contemporary reports write of 192 people seriously wounded and six dead, and of about eight hundred arrests in street demonstrations. This is considered to have been the biggest riot in Budapest after August 1883 when anti-Semitic crowds had responded violently to the acquittal of the accused in the Tiszaeszlár 'ritual murder' trial.[15]

In the decade preceding the First World War, passionate hatreds erupted in connection with two other issues. The first related to the political and social status of the national minorities and is exemplified by the infamous example of the 'Černová massacre' of 27 October, 1907, when gendarmes shot into a crowd of Slovak peasants gathered for a church dedication, killing eleven. On this occasion, the number of victims was smaller than at Élesd in April 1904, when 37 poor Romanian peasants were killed by gendarmes, but the incident at Černová was internationally much better known on account of European interest in the political crisis in the Hungarian half of the Habsburg Monarchy.[16] Finally, the agrarian problem fed the potential for hatred in early twentieth-

---

13 Gábor Vermes, *István Tisza: The Liberal Vision and Conservative Statecraft of a Magyar Nationalist*, Boulder & New York, 1986.
14 László Tőkéczki, *Tisza István eszmei, politikai arca*, Budapest, 2000, p. 205.
15 See Alice Freifeld, *Nationalism and the Crowd in Liberal Hungary, 1848–1914*, Baltimore & London, 2000, p. 247.
16 László Péter, 'Az 1905. évi alkotmányválság, a "magyarkérdés" az angol sajtóban és Scotus Viator pélfordulása', in Péter, *Az Elbától keletre*, Budapest, 1998; Géza Jeszenszky, *Az elveszett presztizs. Magyarország megítélésének megváltozása Nagy Britanniában 1894–1918*, Budapest, 1986.

century Hungarian society. Under the spell of the 1907 Romanian peasant uprising, the government made serious attempts to deal with these issues but numerous agrarian movements unleashed an aggressive hatred towards the peasantry which the peasantry returned: 'The soldiers of György Dózsa are getting together. Their soul is inspired by the spirit of the great peasant leader [...] And if these shared feelings are ever connected by an indissoluble chain, a great reckoning will follow', wrote an agrarian paper in January 1910.[17]

The Trianon Syndrome

The aftermath of the First World War introduced a new chapter in the history of hatred in Hungary. There were two types of hatred that – although they had certainly existed before – now rose to prominence. The first hatred was directed at the victorious entente powers, which, as contemporary political rhetoric put it, had in the course of their imperialist expansion destroyed historic Hungary, which as part of the Austro- Hungarian Monarchy had been a bulwark of peace and security in the centre of Europe. The peacemakers 'created two mutilated countries that are cut off from the most elementary conditions of their survival and also created three other countries that are unfit for life; their internal national contradictions and tensions carry the potential for explosion at any moment.'[18] This idea had been a recurring part of Hungarian political thought ever since the sixteenth and seventeenth centuries. It defined Hungary's position as a guarantor of peace and balance in the centre of Europe, standing up to both Ottoman Turks and Habsburg Germans. With the eclipse of Turkey as a power, its mantle was assumed by Russia. The Turks had given asylum to several generations of Hungarian patriots in exile, and following the Paris Peace Treaties they were transformed in the popular imagination into heroic resisters to the imperialist great powers. By contrast, Russia was perceived as a new and greedy imperial power, especially after its intervention in Hungary in 1849, its Balkan adventures of the 1870s, and its decision to make a world war in 1914. In the interwar period, Russia was also viewed as the disseminator of the bolshevism that had contributed to Hungary's destruction in 1918–1919.

The other target of hatred were Jews. Why was the ire of Hungary's interwar political leaders primarily directed at Hungarian Jewry and how did their anti-Semitism permeate large segments of contemporary Hungarian society? This was first of all because the dimensions of national disaster in 1918–20 were beyond imagination. Who or what could bring about such a fundamental change in the life of a nation and a state, unless a force of inconceivable and yet hidden, malign influence and one, moreover, which, despite cloaking itself in the mantle of the nation, was yet opposed in its very essence to the Hungarian state-building project? That part of the Hungarian self which was judged to have become executioner of the Hungarian state was the 'familiar foreigner', the Hungarian Jew. Hungarian Jewry was sufficiently familiar to be seen as part of the self,

---

17 Péter Hanák (ed.), *Magyarország története 1890–1918*, Budapest, 1978, vol 2, p. 717.
18 István Bethlen, cited by Ignác Romsics, 'A kereszténység védőpajzsától az uniós tagságig. Helyzetértékelés és szerepfelfogás a magyar politikai gondolkodásban', in Ignác Romsics & Mihály Szegedy-Maszák (eds.), *Mi a magyar?*, Budapest, 2005, p. 222.

and yet sufficiently foreign to be excluded from the new conception of what Hungarian meant. This separation unfortunately turned out to be most rapidly concretized, as not very long after the Red Terror of the Hungarian Soviet Republic (which also had Jewish victims), hundreds of Jews were killed during the White Terror. This was a completely new phenomenon in Hungary, as politically motivated pogroms carrying a high death toll of Jews were not historically part of Jewish and non-Jewish relations in Hungary.[19]

The social acceptance of anti-Jewish legislation in Hungary (both in 1920[20] and under completely new circumstances in 1938–41[21]) correlates, in terms of the history of hatred, with popular attitudes towards Germans. The idea of a large scale-expulsion or resettlement of Germans in Hungary had already come up in the 1920s and the call for a 'cleansing' of interwar Hungarian society targeted Germans as well as Jews. Let us here recall Dezső Szabó's most influential ideas: Germans are as threatening to Hungarian purity and to the Hungarian national interest as Jews.[22] From the perspective of the accumulation of hatred, the scapegoating of Germans, as manifested in their post-1945 expulsion, was part of the same process that made possible the deportation and destruction of two-thirds of Hungarian Jewry.

Both Germans and Jews were important agents of Hungary's modernization. Hatred against them had been part and parcel of the great dilemma that has escorted Hungary since at least the early eighteenth century: how do national sovereignty and social emancipation and modernization relate one to another? Do these automatically go together or can they come into conflict? This was a quandary faced by intellectuals and political leaders not only in the interwar period but also in the years between 1945 and 1956.

The bipolar world of the Cold War did not encourage self-critical reflection but initiated new waves of hatred. To put it simply, one might say that fear-driven hatred was a major force of great-power policies and that similar paranoias – as described by Richard Hofstadter – also shaped domestic politics on both sides. Paranoid politicians, when sensing any problem, search for – and always find – evil enemies who conspire against nation, class, or the issue of the day. The defining element of a paranoid politician's identity is hatred towards his or her supposed enemies. I think that one more point is essential in this analysis. As the above short survey shows, hatred can be best examined together with two other individual psychological and social psychological phenomena: aggression and fear. In addition to the call for freedom, rebels as individuals and rebellions as social and political movements have also been driven by these states of mind.

This point takes us to the actual subject of this paper: a cursory analysis of hatreds in Hungary during the decade preceding 1956. I suggest that if we want to organize and arrange systematically the hatreds at work during the decade before 1956, they may be roughly divided into four groups: first, 'officially' and centrally incited hatred that

---

19 László Karsai, *Holokauszt*, Budapest, 2001, p. 215.
20 The Hungarian parliament passed the so called *numerus clausus* law (that limited the number of Jews in Hungarian higher education) in September 1920.
21 Act 1938: XV (passed on May 29, 1938, limiting the proportion of Jews in professional chambers and among business employees to 20 %); Act 1939: IV (passed on May 5, 1939, imposing further limitations on the employment, business and social activities of Jews); Act 1941: XV (passed on August 8, 1941, forbidding marriage between Jews and non-Jews). See also Nathaniel Katzburg, *Hungary and the Jews 1920–1943*, Ramat-Gan (Israel), 1981.
22 János Gyurgyák, *A zsidókérdés Magyarországon*, Budapest, 2001, pp. 554–559.

targeted internal enemies; secondly, 'official' hatreds targeting external foes; thirdly, 'popular' and 'spontaneous' hatreds aimed at internal adversaries; and, fourthly, 'popular' and 'spontaneous' hatreds focusing on external antagonists. The hatred targeting internal enemies was partly fed by traditional ('old wine in new bottle') elements, as determined by contemporary circumstances. The hatred targeting external enemies was also partly traditional and partly also rooted in the contemporary circumstances of the Cold War. What these hatreds had in common was their radical bipolarism. This is, of course, far from being uniquely Hungarian – it was part and parcel of the overall Cold War climate of international relations that permeated not only domestic politics but also the intellectual and cultural climate. So before looking at these types of hatreds, let me move outside Hungary.

The International Context After the Second World War

Tony Judt has argued that the major intellectual and political frontline in post-war Europe was not simply between East and West but between communists and anti-communists and that this opposition was played out on both sides of the Iron Curtain.[23] After the Munich conference of 1938, fine shades, compromise and a 'third way' were deemed politically useless and morally discredited. Henceforward, the platforms were clearly defined: Good versus Evil, Freedom versus Slavery, and Resistance versus Collaboration. One of the political expressions of this cultural climate came at the end of September 1947 when the Information Bureau of the East European Soviet vassal parties declared that the world had been split into two camps (imperialist and anti-imperialist) and that a new war could not be avoided.

Political developments, including Churchill's Fulton speech in March, 1946, and Stalin's comparison of the mastermind of the anti-Hitler coalition with Hitler himself, had clear intellectual parallels. They may serve as a basis of comparison for the Hungarian case.

It was especially France, however, that showed a longstanding tradition of bipolarism, cherishing the great revolution's myth and worshipping violence as a tool of public policy. The famous Radical Party politician, Edouard Herriot, argued after the war that without a bloodbath normal political life in France could not be restored.[24] Let me refer to just a few further French examples. The leader of existentialism, Jean-Paul Sartre, argued at the time of the East European show trials that one had to choose between the Soviet Union and the Anglo-Saxon bloc.[25] As editor of the *Temps Modernes*, he published Marcel Peju's approving comments on the Slanský trial. Paul Eluard wrote in Bucharest in October 1948, 'I come from a country where no one laughs any more, where no one sings. France is in shadow. But you have discovered the sunshine of Happiness.'[26] Anti-communism was considered to be pro-fascism by a great number of influential intellectuals (as, for instance, the writers Louis Aragon or Jean

---

23 Tony Judt, *Postwar: A History of Europe since 1945*, New York, 2005, p. 197.
24 ibid, p. 211.
25 ibid, p. 214.
26 ibid, p. 212.

Bruller Vercors; the 1935 Nobel prize-winner, Fréderic Joliot Curie; and the great painters Léger and Picasso). Tony Judt's point is not properly supported with empirical data but it is certainly worth considering: 'Western intellectual enthusiasm for Communism tended to peak not in times of "Goulash communism" or "socialism with a human face" but rather at the moments of the regime's worst cruelties: 1935 and 1944–1956.'[27] Or, as Abbé Boulier explained to Ferenc Fejtő at the time of the Rajk trial, 'Drawing attention to communist sins is to play the imperialists' game.'[28]

On the communist side in Eastern Europe, discourse rested on the same underlying suppositions as on the communist side in the West: 'youthful enthusiasm for a Communist future was widespread among middle-class intellectuals, in East and West alike!'[29] These suppositions included the following. First, that terror was a necessary means of historical progress, for in the anti-fascist coalition the Soviet Union has sacrificed the most for the victory against Hitler. Accordingly, all means for the implementation of socialism and communism under the leadership of the Soviet Union were legitimate. And, secondly, that America's sins both in terms of its system of values and in respect of its domestic and foreign policy outweighed the incidental mistakes committed by the Soviet Union. To illustrate the longevity of the last motif, let me quote Claude Roy's editorial from the December 1956 (!) issue of *Esprit* under the title, *Les Flammes de Budapest*: 'We reproach Socialist ideology with idealizing man and being blind to his fallibility, but the average American is blinder still. What can one expect from this civilization that mocks and caricatures Western spiritual traditions and is propelling mankind into a horizontal existence, shorn of transcendence and depth?'[30]

Bipolarism

We seek to demonstrate by reference to the above that the sort of radical bipolarism which we associate with twentieth-century Hungary was also part of the post-1945 international intellectual and political climate. The Hungarian intellectual landscape after the Second World War was thus not very different to the larger European one. Post-crisis situations call for unambigous, clear definitions of guilt and responsibility. In this respect, Milovan Djilas's point conveys a larger truth: 'Totalitarianism at the outset is enthusiasm and conviction; only later does it become organizations, authority, careerism.'[31]

One can come up with a long list of influential twentieth-century Hungarian politicians, either in power or in opposition, as well as prestigious social scientists, political thinkers, writers or other leading intellectuals (a random list might include Oszkár Jászi, Ignác Darányi, Dezső Szilágyi, Mihály Károlyi, István Tisza, Gyula Szekfű, Dezső Szabó, István Bethlen, Ernő Garami, Vilmos Vázsonyi, Kálmán Darányi, Gyula Gömbös, László Németh and István Bibó) who, when trying to come up with 'national

---

27 ibid, p. 216.
28 ibid, p. 217.
29 ibid, p. 199.
30 Tony Judt, *Past Imperfect: French Intellectuals. 1944–1956*, Berkeley, Los Angeles, London, 1992, p. 196.
31 Cited by Tony Judt, *Postwar*, p. 200.

salvation programmes' of all kinds, generally thought in terms of dichotomies and of basic cleavages. The most frequently counter-posed concepts included revolution versus counter-revolution, progressive versus conservative, democratic versus reactionary, 'deep Hungarian' versus 'shallow Hungarian', 'kuruc' versus 'labanc',[32] 'small Hungarian' versus 'big Hungarian', Eastern orientation versus Western orientation, 'Realpolitiker' versus prophet, 'false realist' versus 'romantic essentialist',[33] 'emulating Europe' versus 'national egotist', a healthy Hungarian instinct versus a distorting foreign influence, 'gentlemanly' versus 'ungentlemanly',[34] 'urban' versus populist.[35] The exponents of the one frequently attached as much or more significance to discrediting the other, alternative programme as to formulating their own agenda. There have certainly been alternatives to this dichotomizing and even schizophrenic way of thinking: the idea of a 'third way' and the search for a 'middle way' have been a conspicuous trend in Hungarian intellectual history from the reform generations in the 1830s and 1840s through the 'Hungarian Victorians' and the 'bourgeois radicals' of the early twentieth century to the populists, reform socialists and reform communists of all shades.[36] These views were, however, generally expressed by individuals who lacked influence within the state or party administrations, were bereft of political power, and had a restricted scope for political action. One may observe, however, that in the political thought of those individuals who were closer to political power, bipolarism frequently gained ground.

'Official' and 'spontaneous' hatreds on the eve of 1956

According to a widespread view in the literature on the origins of the 1956 Hungarian revolution, as for instance argued by István Vida, 'Rákosi's authoritarian regime was overthrown by popular wrath. On 23 October an armed uprising emerged that was followed by a popular movement including almost all layers of Hungarian society and involving a large part of the country's territory.'[37] Let me try to modify this statement by arguing that a series of officially-excited angers, combined with popular, 'spontaneous' hatreds, played a decisive role in bringing about the so-called 'revolutionary situation'.

'Official' *external* enemies were certainly the imperialists and their allies. The major target was, of course, the US, but the deepest hatred was reserved for the 'German

---

32 *Kuruc* meaning anti-Habsburg, radical Hungarian nationalist; *labanc* pro-Habsburg, traitor to the Hungarian national cause.
33 In Hungarian, 'túlfeszült lényeglátók'. See Iván Zoltán Dénes, *A 'realitás' illúziója. A historikus Szekfű Gyula pályafordulója*, Budapest, 1976.
34 In Hungarian, *Úri és nem úri*.
35 In Hungarian, *Urbánus* versus *népies*.
36 See an interesting article by one of the most influential politicians in Hungary between 1920 and 1944, István Bethlen, on tradition and revolution in politics: 'Hagyomány és forradalom a politikában', *Magyar Szemle*, 20, 1934 (February), 2, pp. 105–118, republished in Ignác Romsics (ed.), *Bethlen István. Válogatott politikai írások és beszédek*, Budapest, 2000, pp. 158–173. For a survey from a reform socialist perspective, see Tibor Huszár, 'Az értelmiségszociológia és -szociográfia hazai történetéhez', in Huszár, *Nemzetlét – nemzettudat – értelmiség*, Budapest, 1984, pp. 109–311.
37 István Vida, 'Kedves Lóránt!', *Élet és Irodalom*, 2 June, 2006, p. 2.

conquerors' (in their contemporary reincarnation as West German imperialists) who had been presented as a threat to the Hungarian people ever since the foundation of the Hungarian state. A very special hatred was also generated against Tito's Yugoslavia; at military shooting exercises Tito-heads were frequently used as targets. As to the 'official' *internal* enemies, the leading party elite considered about 20–25% of the population as a real or potential enemy of the regime. An Interior Ministry document, dated September 1953, listed 28 categories of registered enemies. They included former aristocrats, capitalists, landowners, members of the army, police and gendarmerie of the Horthy-period, members of fascist parties, leaders of churches, monks, nuns, members or followers of post-1945 'rightist' parties, rightist social democrats, Trotskyites, people expelled from the party, family members of 'political criminals', and the Hungarian employees of the embassies of capitalist states as well as all those who were in touch with those embassies.[38] There was also a very broad category of all persons with evidence of present or past hostile activities against the people's democratic regime, the communist party or the working class. Kulaks and other kinds of 'traitor' were easily put into this category. By the summer of 1954, about 666,000 persons had been removed from this register but the numbers had increased again by 1955. The tendency of 'increasing vigilance' is most noticeable if we study the prison population. Between 1952 and 1954, it dropped from 35,000 to 23,000, but then shot up to reach 37,000 by the end of 1955.[39]

The communist regime devoted much attention to ways of exciting hatred. Let me here limit myself to a very few examples. On the occasion of the thirtieth anniversary of the death of one of the greatest twentieth-century Hungarian poets, Endre Ady (1877–1919), who in his poetry (and journalism) was a passionate critic of the political and social establishment of his time, József Révai (one of the four top-level communist leaders and responsible for ideological issues) raised the issue of the politics of hatred. He asked rhetorically: how can Ady's legendary hatred of István Tisza, symbol of the 'reactionary', 'retrograde, early twentieth-century Hungarian political establishment, together with his pathetic call for revolution, address the needs of today's workers? How can his powerful passion help the realization of day-to-day and longer-term plans for peaceful construction? Révai's answer was: '[…] let us not believe that we have finally defeated the forces of the Hungarian Hell and that we can dispose of Ady's passionate, democratic hatred. It is not our merit but our weakness that we cannot hate the same way as Ady did. We are building socialism, but the forces of the Middle Ages are still with us and, if Ady's great hatred is yet alien to us, that only means that our being is defenceless against Hunnia's former […] insidious and dangerous lords.'[40] It was this powerful, 'constructive' hatred that appealed to numerous contemporaries who believed in the feasibility of a fast and sweeping rebuilding of Hungarian society. In much the same vein, a performance given in 1951 of the classic masterpiece of Hungarian literature,

---

38 *Az állambiztonsági szervek célszemélyei 1956 előtt és után.* Unattributed manuscript on the homepage of the Historical Archive of the State Security Services: <www.abtl.hu> .
39 Ignác Romsics, *Magyarország története a XX. században,* Budapest, 1999, p. 381.
40 József Révai, *Élni tudtunk a szabadsággal,* Budapest, 1949, p. 679.

'Bánk bán',[41] was praised because it succeeded in 'exciting legitimate hatred against tyranny'.[42] In similar fashion, the Hungarian National Association of Journalists made the point in 1951 that the satirical weekly *Ludas Matyi*, 'does not exhaust all the possibilities inherent in satire and cannot awaken enough hatred of the enemy. Battle against the internal and external enemy must precede criticism of the shortcomings of the socialist establishment.'[43]

This propaganda, however, backfired. The hate-loaded, centrally manipulated scapegoat-myths did not ease social tensions (as is generally the case with 'regular' scapegoats) but, on the contrary, contributed to the revolutionary ferment. This takes us to the 'popular hatreds' which are well reflected in the extensive police-record and to official criticisms of party and state functionaries who, in the remarkable terminology of Stalinist Hungary, 'were swept away by the demagogy or evil influence of the masses' (*a tömegek uszályába kerültek*). The police records of reactions to Stalin's death give some insight into the hate-loaded views of Stalin. Many people expressed delight on hearing of the death of the dictator. For instance, a prostitute from Gyöngyös said, 'there will be a great crop in the Soviet Union as the biggest dung enriches the soil.' Many of the 219 people who were arrested for subversive agitation against the state in March and April, 1956, cursed Stalin as the worst criminal. Another aspect of these criminal cases is a good source on hate-driven official scapegoating. A report of the Special Case Department of the Supreme Attorney's Office of 15 March, 1954 (thus well after Imre Nagy's appointment as prime minister on 4 July, 1953) records that 78 of the 219 people arrested were still in prison. Most of them, the prosecutor in charge argued, were 'kulaks', former state officials of the Horthy regime, or petit-bourgeois elements. A small number comprised, however, toiling peasants and workers who had received sentences of undue severity. The report recommended that, whereas cases should be reopened only in very exceptional cases, an exception should be made in respect of those involving peasants and workers.[44]

Popular hatred of the ruling communist elite was deeply rooted in the systematic humiliation of most members of the society, and was not confined to those who belonged to the twenty-eight categories of enemy or to those who were the beneficiaries or erstwhile supporters of the regime. Reference to the fate of enthusiastic young communists in the National Alliance of Peoples Colleges (NÉKOSZ) or the harsh official public criticism of such outstanding communist intellectuals as the world famous Marxist philosopher, Georg Lukács, or the prestigious novelist, Tibor Déry, sufficed in this respect. The disregard and frequently very hostile approach to professional standards of conduct served to alienate some of the most ardent supporters of the regime

---

41 József Katona wrote 'Bánk bán' in 1815 and it was first published in 1820. It is one of the best known Hungarian dramas and still mandatory reading for all schoolchildren. Set in the Middle Ages, it tells a story of heroic, national resistance to foreign tyrants.
42 Gábor Bóta, András Gervai & Gábor Szigethy, *Kállai Ferenc*, Budapest, 2004, p. 48.
43 Róbert Takács, 'Education and Inspiring Hatred', in István Feitl and Balázs Sípos (eds.), *Regimes and Transformations: Hungary in the Twentieth Century*, Budapest, 2005, p. 332.
44 Árpád Pünkösti, 'Súlyosbító körülmények', *Népszabadság*, 5 March, 2003, p. 8.

The major external target of popular hatred was the Soviet Union. This was felt not only by the 6–700,000 people[45] who along with their family members were victims of the aggression meted out by Soviet soldiers or KGB employees, or had been deported to the Soviet Union, but also by many of those who had been truly liberated by the Soviets. As a reaction to presenting everything Soviet as utmost perfection, the Soviets more and more appeared as a universal scapegoat. Despite the very bad experiences of the Slovak-Hungarian population exchange or the difficulties of maintaining ties to the Hungarians of Transylvania, anti-Soviet feelings were more powerful or at least more visible than hatred directed against Hungary's other neighbours.

It might be thought surprising that I have not so far mentioned anti-Semitism, as this was a part of both 'official' and 'popular' hatreds. The Rákosi-Gerő group was fully aware of the suspicion and fear expressed in the identification of Jews with communists and did everything possible to sweep the issue under the carpet. In the aftermath of the Second World War, a strong anti-Semitism survived from the period before the Communist take-over, and we know of numerous spontaneous pogroms or attempts at them both in Budapest and many other cities.[46] Both the police and the law courts were indecisive in dealing with these issues. After the communist take-over, the highly centralized dictatorship cautiously sought to channel these feelings. 'Bourgeois' was often a codeword for Jewish, and personnel files after 1949 registered membership in the Zionist movement in the same rubric where former membership of the Arrow Cross party appeared.[47] This attitude of the Rákosi regime had the consequence that – as Victor Kárády put it – the first army of those disappointed in socialism was recruited from Jewish activists and supporters of the regime: 'Their disappointment was just as bitter as their feverish enthusiasm when they had first engaged themselves with the movement.'[48] Ferenc Fejtő even argues that, 'Thanks to these Jewish writers, the conflict between Rákosi's party machine and the Petőfi Circle was transformed into a battle between good and evil – a theological and metaphysical dispute which the entire nation followed with baited breath.'[49] From the perspective of the history of hatred this demonstrates that the targets of hatred can easily change, but whatever the poles of bipolarism may be, the total lack of any empathy felt by the one for the other can easily lead to the eruption of aggression.

Let me by way of a conclusion refer to a looming contradiction. As I have tried to show, aggression driven by hate and fear was an important element of the political and intellectual climate in Hungary during late October and early November 1956. Nevertheless, the civil upheaval, followed by a war of independence, that is a real war, was limited to Budapest. In the other large cities, violence was a generally a single, short and bloody (though certainly most tragic) event. Nevertheless, in most of the country, there was no fighting. If we want to give an overall picture of the country, János Rainer's statement (based on a large amount of source material) is convincing: '[...] most places in the country did not experience the violent character of the revolution nor its aspect as

---

45 See the research of Ágnes Gereben, Tamás Stark, Ágnes and Béla Várdy.
46 See Andrea Pető, 'Népbíróság és vérvád az 1945 utáni Budapesten', *Múltunk*, 2006, no 1, pp. 41–71.
47 Róbert Győri Szabó, *A kommunista párt és a zsidóság*, Budapest, 1997.
48 *Világosság*, 1989, no 6, pp. 453–459. Cited by Róbert Győri Szabó.
49 Ferenc Fejtő, *Behind the Rape of Hungary*, New York, 1957, p. 209.

a fight for freedom. The most important element of the revolution in the country was not armed resistance but a manifold organizing activity. Its outstanding figures were not demonstrators and freedom fighters but revolutionaries struggling to set things right and to restore public order.'[50] Despite the accumulation of a huge potential for hatred, the majority of society showed sober cohesion rather than radical bipolarization. Just as much as during the power vacuums in the final phase of the Second World War or during the spectacular transition of 1989–90, both of these being occasions when the state was temporarily far from being able to fully control society, peaceful cooperation and planning for the future became the guiding norm. And this is just as much part of the Hungarian political and intellectual heritage as the terrible ethnic and social hatreds of the twentieth century.

---

50 János Rainer, 'A Progress of Ideas: The Hungarian Revolution of 1956' in Lee W. Congdon & Béla K. Király (eds.), *The Ideas of the Hungarian Revolution, Suppressed and Victorious, 1956–1999*, Boulder & New York, 2002, pp. 29–30.

Violence and Resistance in Hungary before 1956

János Rainer

The starting point of this discussion is the 1956 Hungarian Revolution, which was the largest and most radical rebellion against the Soviet-type system to take place in Europe. My first question concerns the period in which this system was introduced, built up, and operated until 1957. If violence and coercion were a prominent feature of the Soviet-type system, did they assume greater dimensions in Hungary? Can '56 be explained, therefore, in terms of the extreme terror which preceded it? This calls for consideration of the characteristics of the Hungarian system and whether or not it preserved special features of its own. My second question is as follows. What was the character of resistance to the Soviet-type system up to 1956, and on what scale did it operate? Only my final question concerns '56 more closely: were the active participants in the revolution drawn from those who had previously resisted communism, or, to put it another way, what proportion of those participants who participated in '56 had resisted before?

* * *

Violence and coercion under Soviet-type systems took on a wide variety of forms. They ranged from various degrees of open repression for political reasons (death sentences, imprisonment, internment, deportation), to surveillance by the secret police, confiscation of property and the depriving of a livelihood, and the broad field of direct and indirect restrictions (on freedom of worship, assembly, education, information and so on.) The scale of these is difficult to measure within a single country, and the opportunity to undertake thorough research in the field was denied until 1989. No comparative study of the matter has appeared so far.

Using the data given in a relatively recent work,[1] the numbers of those arrested in 1951–3 for political reasons in certain East-Central European countries were as follows:

Bulgaria	15,992
Czechoslovakia	48,715
Poland	35,627
Romania	48,792
Hungary	26,507.[2]

---

1 Krzysztof Persak, and Lukasz Kaminski (eds) *A Handbook of the Communist Security Apparatus in East Central Europe 1944–1989*, Warsaw, 2005.
2 As the source given in note 1 has no chapter on Hungary, information has been taken from the report of the 1989 'Fact-Finding Commission': *Törvénytelen szocializmus. A Tényfeltáró Bizottság jelentése*, Budapest, 1991, p. 317.

Taking these figures in conjunction with national populations at the time, the Hungarian system *cannot* be considered outstandingly repressive.[3] The scale was the same as in the other authoritarian systems of the time which were likewise, strongly repressive. The introduction of the Soviet system in Poland temporarily met with strong resistance, and similar violence occurred as the Soviet system was re-imposed in Western Ukraine and the Baltic. No such resistance occurred in Hungary. So in the light of '56, the early period of the Soviet system in Hungary can be described as a strongly repressive, authoritarian system, eliciting weak resistance in the longer term, but with a strong, one-off potential for rebellion or revolution. This is a unique picture. Poland can be described as showing strong, lasting resistance (albeit in various forms) with a strong, enduring potential for rebellion. In Romania and Bulgaria, resistance and the capacity for rebellion both appear weak – even weaker in Bulgaria than in Romania. The potential for resistance and rebellion in Czechoslovakia seems to have been of only medium intensity.

There are, however, no conspicuous differences between countries in respect of the scale of repression. The differences in propensity to resist or rebel must be explained in terms of different social situations, cultures, traditions and histories. Even today, the Soviet system is often seen in the familiar terms of the totalitarian paradigm.[4] Its opponents, historical revisionists and believers in the new cultural history have all shown, first, that the system was never capable of truly total rule, and, secondly, that it enjoyed a measure of legitimacy in certain historical periods and among certain social strata.[5] According to these approaches, it was a matter of Soviet-Bolshevik *civilization* being imposed on Central Europe, as a kind of colonization.

Outside coercion was certainly a decisive factor in the transformation of Hungary after 1945. But László Péter warned more than twenty years ago that 'the people's democracies did not fall out of the sky onto the countryside beyond the Elbe; it was not only alien bayonets that forced this upon a resisting population, for everywhere without exception, the people's democracies came into being through the active (and how active) cooperation of tens and even hundreds of thousands of the local population.'[6] Such cooperation obviously presupposes that the Soviet-type system possessed a measure of legitimacy for many groups, at least at some point in its history. Behind this, Péter sees in the longer term the specific features of social development in Eastern Europe, and as a direct antecedent, the institutions and political traditions that had grown up in the nineteenth century. These included, for instance, the system of large landed estates, the unequally developed industrial system, the tradition of étatism, the weak constitutional forms, the discretionary nature of government, and the narrow and ever narrowing scope for autonomous social action.[7]

---

3 This is borne out by other comparisons, of numbers deported, sentenced to death, executed and so on.
4 Hannah Arendt, *The Origins of Totalitarianism*, Revised ed., New York, 1973.
5 Sheila Fitzpatrick, *Everyday Stalinism: Ordinary Life in Extraordinary Times, Soviet Russia in the 1930s*, Oxford, 1999, pp. 225–226.
6 László Péter, 'Miért éppen az Elbánál hasadt szét Európa? (A népi demokratikus rendszer társadalmi gyökerei)' in Miklós Tóth and Lóránt Czigány (eds.) *Önarcképünk sorsunk tükrében 1945–1949*, Amsterdam, 1984, p. 21.
7 ibid, pp. 21–43.

Two important differences emerge if Hungary's Soviet system is examined in the conceptual framework devised by Charles Tilly for European democratic development. In terms of political participation, Hungary's Soviet system set a very wide prescribed zone and a wide forbidden zone as well, as indeed did the regimes of the other countries.[8] Nor did the prescribed zone in Hungary preclude a degree of demonstration of national feeling, although the degree was largely set from above, by the central authorities. Since Hungary's national grievances were stronger and livelier and less susceptible to expression than those of the other countries, the manifestation of national feeling split apart, with some parts entering the prescribed zone and some the forbidden zone. This led to special tensions.

Elsewhere, Tilly speaks of the regimes being 'seen from the perspective of relations between governmental agents and other political actors. Three variable elements of regimes' social environments strongly affect their organizations: coercion, capital and commitment.'[9] In respect of the elements of coercion, the Hungarian version accumulated and centralized to the same extent (or possibly a slightly lesser extent) the means of application as the other states of the East bloc. But Hungary was probably distinctive in the state of its social commitments and of the informal networks which serve to bind society. These social commitments had been weakened by the Jewish laws, the part played by the country in the Second World War, the passage of the front across the country, the changes of system in 1945 and in 1947–9, and the many rapid, nervous and conflicting changes in property relations, religious toleration and social mobility. 'A fragmented population faces high costs of communications and resistance on a large scale but also presents formidable coordination costs to its government.'[10] To this it must be added that even an extremely coercive regime creates social commitments, networks of trusts, and spheres of cooperation of its own.

* * *

The second question calls above all for a definition of the concept of resistance. Earlier use of this concept naturally differed strongly depending on which side of the Iron Curtain the speaker was. American intelligence-gathering agencies in the mid-1950s used the following definitions:

> Dissidence is a state of mind involving discontent [...] Resistance: dissidence translated into action [...] Organized resistance: group of individuals accepted common purpose [...] Unorganized resistance: carried out by individually or loosely associated groups, may have been formed spontaneously [...] Active resistance: intelligence collection, psychological warfare, sabotage, guerrilla actions [...] Passive resistance: conducted within the framework of the resisters' normal life and duties, involves deliberate non-performance, or malperformance of acts.[11]

---

8 Charles Tilly, *Contention and Democracy in Europe, 1650–2000*, Cambridge, 2004, p. 29.
9 ibid, p. 45.
10 ibid, p. 47.
11 'Hungary: Resistance Activities and Potentials. Study Prepared for the U. S. Army Intelligence by the Georgetown University', in *The 1956 Hungarian Revolution: A History in Documents*, edited and introduced by Csaba Békés, Malcolm Byrne, János M. Rainer, Budapest & New York, 2002, pp. 86–105. According to the original footnotes, the definitions were drawn from an analysis of Poland conducted two years before.

The obvious assumption behind these definitions was that the ideology and praxis of the totalitarian system were alike unbearable for those living under them. The fact of resistance thus becomes self-evident, questionable only in its form and grade.

On the other hand, there was no concept of resistance *from within*. Communist political ideology started from the assumption that the whole society of working people, apart from a small group of former exploiters, would strive *objectively* to realize the communist project. There were differences at most in degrees of awareness. Those opposing the communist project were categorized as the enemy and were divided into the external and the internal enemy, although these were essentially the same, since the weaker, internal enemy acted according to the intentions or under the direct orders of the huge external enemy: America or the imperialists in general. This concept of the enemy suggests a handful of committed activists, but its bounds can in fact be extended at will. The image of the enemy expressed verbally by Hungarian state-security organizations largely corresponded with the categories of active resistance advanced by American intelligence. But in practice, any kind of action, or even inaction, could transmute into enemy activity.[12]

Those considered to be resisters (enemy) in that period were not necessarily so. Likewise, five decades later, we do not necessarily have to describe as such those who defined themselves at the time – or *later* – as resisters or *enemies* of the system. The editors of one book on dissent and opposition in Eastern Europe, Detlef Pollack and Jan Wielgohs, tried to distinguish the categories of 'resistance', 'dissidence' and 'opposition' in their introduction. They described resistance as 'individual or collective action directed at the removal of the Communist regime. It encompasses both conspiratorial and public activities, militant as well as non-violent, spontaneous and organized action.'[13] They grouped here not only the post-war Baltic, Polish and Ukrainian armed resistance movements, but the East German workers' uprising of 1953 and the 1956 Hungarian Revolution, calling the latter an uprising as well. Dissidence was labelled in general as 'questioning the official ideological doctrine of the state party', but distinguished from other forms of criticism. True dissidence constituted, or sought to constitute, 'an autonomous sphere of public, political and cultural communication outside of the official institutions of the party state and [...] in so doing openly denied the claim of the regime to full control of public life.'[14] The term 'opposition' was confined to post-1945 anti-communist political parties and to 'political formations' of the late 1980s. Throughout the discussion on definitions runs a concern to avoid confusing dissidents with critical groups of reform-communist ideology, whether inside or outside the communist party. A very similar position is taken by Tamás Meszerics in his study of political resistance in Hungary: 'For us to consider a type of action to be resistance, there must be a system-weakening effect perceptible also to outsiders, political intention pointing beyond individual ambitions for

---

12 Letter of A. E. Bogomolov to Y. D. Kiselev, Oct. 5, 1951, in T.V. Volokitina, T. M. Islamov and G. P. Murashko (eds.), *Vostochnaya Yevropa v dokumentakh rossyskikh arkhivov 1944–1953*, vol. 2 (1949–1953), Moscow & Novosibirsk, 1998, pp. 625–6; see also Kartashov's report to State Security Minister Abakumov on the work of the Hungarian state-security organizations, Feb. 10, 1950, in T.V. Volokitina (intr. and ed.), *Sovietsky faktor v Vostochnoy Yevrope 1944–1953*, vol. 2. (1949–1953 Dokumenti), Moscow, 1999, pp. 258–72.

13 Detlef Pollack and Jan Wielgohs (eds.), *Dissent and Opposition in Communist Eastern Europe: Origins of Civil Society and Democratic Transition*, Aldershot & Burlington, VT, 2004, p. xii.

14 ibid, p. xiii.

power, and questioning of the legitimacy of those in power.'[15] James C. Scott, on the other hand, places in the foreground the everyday forms of resistance, irrespective of systems, speaking above all of a constant, stubborn, covert, yet fruitful struggle waged mainly by the peasantry, but also by all working groups engaged in a class struggle against expropriation. Answering the objection that this kind of resistance was self-interested, aimed simply at survival, and tantamount to bargaining with the repressive regime, Scott points to all the steps taken against expropriation as manifestations of resistance of a kind. The class war in all its forms was connected with selfish material needs and conflicts. Resisters, he argued, seldom sought to instigate a revolution and their actions did not amount to an open challenge to the prevailing conditions of power.[16]

Consideration of the spectrum of resistance in Hungary in 1945–56 reveals the following:

a. Very sporadic attempts at active armed resistance were confined almost entirely to attacks in 1945–6 on Soviet occupation forces. There are no historical traditions of armed resistance in Hungary. The country is geographically unsuitable for partisan warfare. The fractured social ties and networks of confidence left hardly any scope for organized sabotage units or an illegal press.[17]

b. Instances of anti-communist organization occurred infrequently before 1956. They were usually detected in their initial stages by the state-security organizations, infiltrated and eliminated. Elimination usually extended to the organizers' system of connections, so that the repressive activity presumably covered a far wider sphere than just the actual resisters.[18] Almost all these instances, before and after the communist assumption of power, can be considered as *preparations* – non-public discourse among small groups of people, concerned with the consequences of some historic turn of events that would bring down the Soviet system in Hungary. The participants were diametrically opposed to the system. They were drawn partly from those who had lost as a result of the change of system in 1945, above all the old Christian middle class and those on the fringes of the national political and prestige elite,[19] and partly from local leaders of anti-communist parties excluded from politics in 1947–8. The collectivization and anti-kulak campaign of the early 1950s drew many rich peasants and young people from such families into their organizations. Only in rare cases did preparations extend to drawing up real *plans*. Where these were outlined, they tended towards simplification rather than differentiation, their features being the idea of national independence and an undifferentiated anti-communism.[20]

---

15 Tamás Mesznerics, 'Politikai ellenállás 1945–56', *Beszélő*, 2000, nos 9–10.
16 James C. Scott, *Everyday Forms of Resistance* (Occasional Papers Service, no. 15), Yokohama, 1993. Scott's views have significantly influenced a younger generation of researchers into Stalinism. See Fitzpatrick, Sheila (ed.), *Stalinism: New Directions*, London & New York, 2000, p. 17.
17 The analysts of Georgetown University reached the same conclusion in their study of Hungarian resistance in January 1956. See above, note 11.
18 See István Fehérváry Kő-Nagy, 'A hazáért éltek-haltak, Zsitnyányi Ildikó', *Hadtörténelmi Közlemények*, 2002, nos 3–4.
19 The top members of the elite had usually been condemned as war criminals or had left the country.
20 See the recollections of survivors in Kő-Nagy, 'A hazáért éltek-haltak', and Meszerics, 'Politikai ellenállás 1945–56'.

c. Special mention must be made of the seemingly most active form of resistance: the action of those who sought and found contacts with the Western secret services. They were mainly regular army officers of the pre-1945 regime, often using émigré organizations as intermediaries. Almost all of them were ill-prepared and untrained for special tasks and they were soon discovered.

d. As for the number of active resisters, data drawn from the regime's state-security organizations is as misleading as later recollections. Both sought to exaggerate the numbers and the quality of the resistance. Almost 43,000 people were convicted of political crimes in Hungary between 1946 and 1956, of whom about 500 were sentenced to death.[21] However, the total includes those who tried to make an illegal frontier crossing, for instance, or 'agitated' against the system (by telling a joke in the pub, for instance). According to a 1953 estimate by the Interior Ministry, about 30 per cent of those arrested in 1951–3 on political charges were accused of *the most serious* political crimes: 'espionage, diversion, terror, sabotage, conspiracy'.[22] That meant an average of 860 persons a year during that period. A cautious estimate would be that half of those were real resisters, so that the number of participants in Hungary involved in active, conscious resistance between 1945 and 1956 was at most about 4–5,000. Active collaboration with the regime was more widespread than that. In the early 1950s, there were no less than 40,000 non-professional agents and informers assisting with state security work.

e. The extent of 'day-to-day', unorganized resistance is even harder to measure. The documents that the system itself produced *criminalize* and exaggerate the phenomenon, most often by attributing a false context and suppressing other parts in the telling. The commonest and most basic case was as follows: a peasant farming on his own account concealed some of his output to escape having to deliver it compulsorily to the state, and consumed it himself instead or had an urban relative sell it on the black barter market. If he managed to conceal his act, no sign is left of it ever having happened, or, if it emerges at all decades later, does so as an oral tradition. If the peasant did not get away with it, he was convicted of the crime of endangering public supplies and could expect a fine, brief incarceration in police cells, or even a prison sentence. In this case, a criminal record of the case survives as a classic example of the borderline between political and common crime.[23]

Still, there are one or two pieces of information that convey the scale of this type of resistance. In December 1952, Moscow's attention was drawn by its ambassador in Budapest, Yevgeny Kiselev, to the way the Hungarian authorities were harassing the public on a massive scale. During 1951, he wrote, the prosecutors brought charges against 362,000 people and administrative (police) proceedings were taken in over half

---

21 *Törvénytelen szocializmus* (see above, note 2), p. 317.
22 Erzsébet Kajári (ed.), *A Belügyminisztérium Kollégiumának ülései 1953–1956*, vol. 1, Budapest, 2001, p. 148.
23 On this, see István Rév, 'The Advantages of Being Atomized: How Hungarian Peasants Coped with Collectivization', *Dissent*, Summer 1987, pp. 335–49. In the 1996 re-publication of this study, Rév, in dispute with James C. Scott, additionally warned against classing the day-to-day resistance of the peasantry as some kind of politically conscious, system-changing struggle for freedom.

a million cases.[24] If common crime is taken to account for half that ghastly number, it is clear that there were probably several hundred thousand to a million people engaging in 'day-to-day resistance'. This is supported by a report from the end of 1953 on the amnesty declared in that year by Prime Minister Imre Nagy: 'The measures affected about 748,000 people.' Of these, only about 40,000 were freed from prison, internment camp, or resettlement, but the number of fines for minor offences pardoned was almost 660,000.[25]

* * *

There was no active, organized resistance preparing for the Hungarian Revolution. On the whole, the day-to-day resisters were more interested in surviving the difficulties than in working to overturn the regime, although what they did was still very risky, because the system took what they did to constitute *resistance* and even enemy activity.

The Americans concluded early in 1956 that although there was no active resistance in Hungary, Hungarian society had one of the greatest potentials for resistance in Eastern Europe. They saw this potential mainly in the peasantry and church, and in the *youth and the industrial working class*. With the youth, they mentioned mainly its cynicism and apathy. Yet they certainly managed to identify two of the main participants in the explosion that would ensue in the autumn of 1956, even if cynicism and apathy were hardly what the university youth of Budapest displayed on 23 October, 1956.

The Soviet leadership since 1945 had mainly sought the enemy within the Hungarian communist elite. This effort lessened in 1956, at the very time when the Hungarian communist elite really was splitting and alternative groups forming on its peripheries,[26] and at the very time when the Hungarian regime turned even more unusual. Specific to Hungary (apart from the circumstances outlined above) was that it took broader corrective measures after Stalin's death than the other satellite countries did. Also specific to Hungary was the exceptional strength of a movement critical of the regime, yet remaining within communist ideology. This arose out of a combination of three factors. The Hungarian anti-Stalinist communism of 1955–6 was embraced by the majority of the young communist intelligentsia. The majority of politically conscious society appreciated and understood the anti-Stalinist critique and adopted it as a common platform at a single historical moment. Finally, the critical movement possessed within itself, in Imre Nagy, a leader of charismatic force. The Hungarian Revolution did not arise out of frontal opposition to the concept of totalitarianism when at its most tyrannical. Instead it confirms the proposition advanced by Alexis de Tocqueville in relation to the French Revolution. The evil that people bear patiently suddenly becomes unbearable when the idea flashes before them that they have a chance of breaking out of it. This happens

---

24 Kiselev's report to A. Y. Vishinsky, Dec. 25, 1952, in *Vostochnaya Yevropa*, vol. 2, pp. 852–3.
25 Report by László Piros and Kálmán Czakó on the repeal of the decree with legislative force on the exercise of general amnesty and the institution of police-authority custody, and implementation of the Council of Ministers resolution on lifting deportations, in Pál Solt et al, (eds.), *Iratok az igazságszolgáltatás történetéhez*, vol. 2, Budapest, 1993, pp. 586–7.
26 After the revolution had been crushed, Hungarian state security compiled a special report to show it had foreseen and warned of 'activity during the counter-revolution by inimical elements activated' during 1956. See Rolf Müller, 'A politikai rendőrség tájékoztató szolgálata 1945–1962', in György Gyarmati (ed.), *Trezor 2. A Történeti Hivatal Évkönyve 2000–2001*, Budapest, pp. 126–35.

when attempts begin to alleviate the tyrannical force through reforms, as occurred in Hungary in 1953–4.

Not a few surviving, active resisters from before 1956 took part in the '56 revolution. Cardinal József Mindszenty, in a radio speech on 3 November, expressed the feelings of many of them about the pre-'56 regime, the revolution, and the new system that was emerging out of the revolution. And Mindszenty was a figure suited to resistance. In his speech, he rejected the term revolution in favour of *war of liberation*. Roughly speaking, he sought a return to 1945, adjusted at most to give greater importance to the church. He had nothing to say of communists or socialism, about which the other participants in the revolution spoke so much. He called the Soviet Union the Russian Empire, returning to the terminology of a vanished world. But there were a few brave and committed resisters then and earlier, who thought in Mindszenty's terms. It was not, however, they but students and workers who formed the vanguard of the revolution, and the most active participants were not drawn from their ranks.

In its early stages, the Soviet system in Hungary managed to blunt active resistance, but it elicited day-to-day resistance on a vast scale. The criticism that drew on the internal split became reinforced by the dissatisfied masses. The impotence of the intelligentsia led to collapse; practically no one stood up for the regime.

1956 and Beyond: Participants and Interpretations

Crossing the 'Moral Threshold': The Rejection of Communist Systems in Hungary and Eastern Europe

Paul Hollander

There is no shortage of explanations – political, economic or cultural – as to why communist systems were unpopular in Eastern Europe and why uprisings erupted as they did in 1953 (East Germany), 1956 (Hungary and Poland) and 1968 (Czechoslovakia). Of these uprisings the Hungarian was the most significant, its demands the most far reaching, its popular support the most widespread, and its human toll the greatest. There were numerous well-founded grievances against the communist regimes in Eastern Europe. Under these regimes the standard of living declined due to rapid, forced industrialization, the collectivization of agriculture, mismanagement and a decline of the work ethic. Nationalistic sentiments were deeply offended by the slavish imitation of everything Soviet. The populations were terrorized by the political police modelled on the KGB. Grotesque, compulsory cults of Stalin and his local emissaries flourished. Cultural life was homogenized and politicized while political indoctrination became part of formal education and daily life. Religious institutions were crushed and religious practices discouraged. Meaningless but time-consuming political participation was demanded and extracted from the population, such as voting in one-party elections, attending demonstrations and endless meetings. Freedom of movement was severely curtailed: the Iron Curtain was not just a figure of speech. Last but not least, political propaganda was as ubiquitous, pervasive and irksome as commercial advertising in capitalist countries (but far more monolithic) and, unlike advertising, its propositions and commands could not be questioned or ridiculed. Not all these grievances were equally strongly felt but there was a continuity and convergence which led to the uprisings noted above and to the final extinction of communist rule in Eastern Europe at the end of the 1980s. Needless to say, the events of 1989 could not have occurred without unmistakeable indications that the Soviet Union was no longer prepared to impose its will and control over this area and shore up the local governments by military force.

There is an important aspect to the discontent which all these developments and policies generated that has not received adequate attention: namely, the subjective perceptions and evaluations of ordinary people and the moral indignation and outrage they created. This essay will seek to comprehend these more subjective undercurrents beneath the widespread political disaffection which pervaded these countries, and especially the part played by, what I will call, the 'moral threshold' of their citizens. Much of the discontent, I suggest, had as much to do with matters subjective and socio-psychological than with objective social-political conditions and deprivations. This is not to diminish the importance of the objective conditions. People can tolerate a wide range of deprivations if they are legitimated or justified in some fashion, or made meaningful. This can be accomplished by custom, communal solidarity, religious belief, law, or charismatic leaders. In traditional societies, most people were impoverished but widespread poverty was considered normal and hence not conducive to much, if any, indignation. Likewise, time-honoured social inequalities were readily accepted as inescapable and justifiable. This was in part the case because alternative social arrangements were unknown and unthinkable, and partly because the deprivations of life here and now were widely believed to be temporary, to be compensated for in some kind of other-worldly existence – in short, because people were sustained by supernatural religious beliefs which helped to diminish the importance of the material (and other) difficulties of life in the here and now. The restrictive, repressive aspects of traditional societies were likewise readily accepted because they were longstanding and part of deeply-rooted and often religiously-sanctioned social arrangements. Traditional societies were successful (up to a point) in controlling and stabilizing personal expectations; stable expectations in turn stabilized social and political institutions and practices. By contrast, communist systems, (and indeed all revolutionary societies) rapidly and abruptly raised a wide range of expectations. As Raymond Aron wrote half century ago, 'A revolution seems capable of changing everything [...] [it] provides a welcome break with the everyday course of events and encourages the belief that all things are possible.'[1] In addition to these elusive promises and expectations, communist systems were quite specific in their (unfulfilled) promises. These included vast material improvements, freedom from various social restraints (such as traditional societies maintained), a sense of personal liberation that was to be combined with new, sustaining communal ties (a new, improved and enlightened sense of community), rational, scientific ways of organizing and perfecting society, ample opportunity for participation in public life and political decision-making, the eventual attainment of social equality (to be preceded by modest, temporary inequalities based on indisputable merit), and, most crucially (and implausibly), the elimination of the conflict between personal and public interest, or between the individual and society. Last but not least, these systems also promised to create a new, greatly improved human being, 'the new socialist man', a secular version of the saintly heroes and protagonists of organized religion. The attributes of this new socialist man were most readily and meticulously revealed and elaborated in the figure of the so-called 'positive hero' who was an integral part of the socialist-realist literature produced in these countries. Vasily Grossman, the Soviet writer, observed:

> Writers dreamed up out of whole cloth people and their feelings and thoughts[...]. The literature which called itself 'realistic' was just as formalized and imaginary as the bucolic romances of the eighteenth century. The collective farmers, workers and rural women of Soviet literature seemed [...] to be close kin to those beautifully built villages and those curly headed shepherdesses who played on pipes and danced in the meadows among pure-white lambs [...]. In novels and poems [...] the Soviet people were depicted like people in medieval art, who had represented the Church's ideal, the idea of divinity [...].[2]

---

1   Raymond Aron, *The Opium of Intellectuals*, London, 1957, p. 42.
2   Vasily Grossman, *Forever Flowing*, New York, 1972, pp. 102–3.

Socialist-realist literature was another ambitious attempt to obliterate the dividing line between actual, perceptible realities and the way things were supposed to be according to the official, ideological blueprints and aims. Arguably, socialist-realism was the most far-reaching, grotesque and elaborate denial of the realities to which the inhabitants of the communist states were exposed.

The promises made by these systems were not limited to their early, idealistic, revolutionary stages; they persisted well after the revolutionary objectives were abandoned. The propagandists and ideologues insisted that these promises had been fulfilled or were in the process of fulfilment, that a historically unprecedented, just and gratifying social system was being built. These claims were put forward and repeated by the enormous, comprehensive agit-prop apparatus that encompassed the mass media, door-to-door verbal 'agitation' and the entire system of education. At places of work, special seminars were organized with compulsory attendance requirements which would elaborate and regurgitate the same messages. Slogans were particularly offensive in their brazen defiance of reality. For example in Hungary the slogan *Tiéd a gyár, magadnak dolgozol!* ('The factory is yours, you are working for yourself!') was plastered all over factory buildings. These were the same places of work where at the end of the shift workers were searched as they exited (to make sure they did not steal), where their earnings were determined by distant authorities, where they had no say in their working conditions and no autonomous unions to represent and protect their interests. To be confronted day after day with such reality-defying slogans in every walk of life was a slap in the face, a daily humiliation. Understating the case, one of the fighters in the 1956 Revolution wrote, 'The workers did not feel that they owned the factory, the land, the fruits of their labour.'

Given the comprehensiveness and relentlessness of the propaganda campaigns, the public in communist states was well acquainted with, on the one hand, the official claims of rectitude and accomplishment and, on the other, their lack of fulfilment which they knew only too well from daily experience. This led to the sentiments and attitudes here discussed. A specific kind of outrage was generated by the routine misrepresentations of reality which culminated in the crossing of the moral threshold. The latter refers to internalized moral norms and sensibilities which define in a compelling way what kinds of behaviour, policies or events are morally acceptable or unacceptable, and what can or cannot be tolerated. Communist systems created a specific and intense moral outrage by institutionalizing and perpetuating these discrepancies between theory and practice, ideal and actual, promises and the realities. This became their particular weakness, at any rate in the long run. György Litván, a Hungarian historian (and former supporter, later opponent of the system) wrote:

> [I]t was the moral cynicism, or moralizing cynicism, that became the Achilles heel of Stalinism. The latter was only effective as long as the edifice of faith was intact, but its nakedness was revealed as soon as the edifice began to shake and fall apart. It was obligatory to moralize because of the redemptive claims, but it was precisely the moralizing that made the system vulnerable.[3]

The mendaciousness of the rulers was widely recognized. People came to resent being lied to and compelled to lie in turn, pressured as they were to participate in hollow

---

3 György Litván, *Októberi üzenetek*, Budapest, 1996, p. 335.

displays of loyalty to a system they despised. During their earlier phases, these systems were not content with passive acceptance on the part of the population; they were determined to extract displays of approval, a semblance of supporting, enthusiastic participation in the political-public life the authorities created and permitted. Such compulsory participation took several forms. On official holidays (and some other special political occasions) virtually the entire working population as well as schoolchildren and university students had to take part in huge mass rallies. People were routinely obliged to vote in elections which provided no choice, only the opportunity to endorse the official candidates. Workers had to attend at their place of work political seminars while students at every level in the education-system had to imbibe the official messages in the framework of courses in humanities and social sciences as well as in newly-created courses on Marxism-Leninism. Special boarding party-schools were also created for those already in elite positions and others groomed for such positions.

While no political system lives up completely up to its own ideals or idealized self-conception, communist systems excelled in creating an unprecedented gulf between their policies, promises and claims on the one hand and their performance on the other. The ceaseless exposure to reality-defying propaganda stimulated a reflexive comparison with the daily reality experienced by the citizens and with its official representation and misrepresentation. The political jokes of the period remain a highly informative repository of popular awareness and responses to these manifold discrepancies and misrepresentations. Alexander Wat, the Polish author, memorably summed up the phenomenon here discussed: 'The loss of freedom, tyranny, abuse, hunger would all have been easier to bear if not for the compulsion to call them freedom, justice and the good of the people.'[4] Two Hungarian writers, Tamás Aczél and Tibor Méray, made the same point: '[...] most intolerable was the simulation of virtue, the endless proclamation of good intentions: everything was taking place on behalf of "the people", in the name of the workers' power [...].' It should be noted here that for the deeply committed, idealistic supporters of the system (including those belonging to the political elite) the journey to disillusionment, to the crossing of the moral threshold, was much more prolonged, painful and halting than for ordinary people. This was a result of their long-standing commitment to the system and the techniques they developed to avert or delay a drastic moral awakening. It was possible to avoid or postpone the crossing of the moral threshold (or face up to the abyss between theory and practice) by refusing to generalize from particular experiences as long as the internalized beliefs of a distinctly religious character were in place. This mindset is revealed by incantations such as those of Georg Lukács who averred that 'the worst socialism is better than the best capitalism.' His former disciple, Ágnes Heller, an early supporter of the regime (later émigrée) observed that Lukács was led to communism by 'a search for redemption. He wished to be the new St Augustine of a universalistic movement such as Christianity used to be. The communist St Augustine. He longed for a movement that would transform the world [...]. If there was anything he took from his Jewish background it was

---

4   Alexander Wat, *My Century*, Berkeley, CA, 1990, p. 173; Tamás Aczél and Tibor Meray, *Tisztító Vihar*, Munich, 1978, p. 276.

messianism.'[5] For these believers, the experience of the specific flaws and shortcomings of the system could be neutralized by their faith and commitment, and by the attendant capacity to defer to the future the benefits that the system was going to deliver; in the absence of such faith, personal experience was devastating. The most widely used technique or defence mechanism was what Arthur Koestler called 'the doctrine of unshaken foundations'[6] – the conviction that, notwithstanding apparent problems and deficiencies, the system was headed in the right direction, and that its positive aspects outweighed its questionable ones. Or, to put it more simply, that the ends justified the means. A Hungarian writer, István Eörsi, who moved from sincere devotion to equally sincere opposition to the regime, also used this defence-mechanism and a similar terminology: 'On the rare occasion when we were stung by the pricks of doubt, we instantly applied the balm of magic incantations to the wound. They included "essentially" and "in the final analysis". Certain aspects of the confession of the "traitors" [in the show trials] perhaps were not entirely true, but in their "essentials" and "in the final analysis" the charges were well founded.'[7] Likewise Ágnes Heller clung to the sentiment that under difficult conditions 'the essentials are OK.'[8]

Another defence mechanism was described by Miklós Gimes, a dedicated Hungarian communist functionary who became a revolutionary in 1956 and paid with his life for his changed convictions:

> Gradually we came to believe [...] that there are two kinds of truth, that the truth of the Party [...] could possibly be different and more important than objective, factual truth, that truth and momentary political expediency are identical [...] if there is a truth higher than factual truth [...] then lies can be 'true' since lies can be useful in the short run; a fabricated political trial can also be 'true' since it may yield political benefits. Suddenly we are transported to the outlook which infected not only those who devised the show trials [...] which poisoned our public life [...] paralysed our critical thinking and finally prevented us from perceiving basic facts of life.[9]

Wolfgang Leonhard, a communist functionary in East Germany after the Second World War, had a traumatic and tangible encounter with the abyss between theory and practice when he found out that there was a hierarchy of food services at the party headquarters entailing several classes of meals for different groups of staff members depending on their position. András Hegedűs, former prime minister of Hungary, also recalls the special, high quality meals he was served in his office; he was uneasy about them but allowed himself to be persuaded (at the time) that they were justifiable given his devotion and the value of his services to the Party.[10]

As an adolescent supporter of the communist regime in Hungary (around the same time Leonhard met his moral threshold, after World War II), I made my own troubling discoveries of what struck me as a serious conflict between theory and practice. These

---

5   Cited in Rudolf L. Tökés, *Hungary's Negotiated Revolution*, New York, 1996, p. 469; Ágnes Heller, *Bicik- lizó majom*, Budapest, 1999, pp. 86, 136.
6   Arthur Koestler, *The Yogi and the Commissar*, New York, 1961, p. 123.
7   István Eörsi, *Versdokumentok magyarázatokkal 1949–1956*, Budapest, 2001, p. 8.
8   Heller, *Biciklizó majom*, p. 81.
9   Cited in Sándor Révész, *Egyetlen élet. Gimes Miklós története*, Budapest, 1999, p. 291.
10 Wolfgang Leonhard, *Child of the Revolution*, Chicago, 1958; András Hegedűs, *Történelem és hatalom igezetében*, Budapest, 1988.

doubts arose from my daily contemplation of the luxurious American automobiles used by members of the nomenklatura. On my way to school every day, I walked by a stream-lined Hudson parked by the pavement with the chauffeur waiting for his passenger (a minister) and I wondered why a much smaller Škoda, VW or Opel would not be suffi-cient. I wondered what it meant that under conditions of scarcity when private automobiles were mostly unheard of, these functionaries were provided with large, luxurious vehicles (Packards and Chryslers too were popular along with smaller British Vauxhalls and sleek Czech Tatras for the political police). I was well aware of the egal-itarian rhetoric and proclaimed policies of the regime and was under the impression that they were being implemented. I also believed that discrepancies between luxury and deprivation (as exemplified by the different modes of transportation for high-ranking officials and the 'masses') were only accepted and prevalent in capitalist systems. The bad impression created by these luxury vehicles was deepened by the curtains on the windows hiding the faces of the occupants in the back, symbolizing their inaccessibility, or perhaps an embarrassed preference for anonymity.

This kind of moral revulsion was an unintended consequence of the extraordinary claims of the official propaganda (and its distant connections with the utopian aspects of the official ideology) that were designed not only to make these systems acceptable but also to convince the citizen of their unprecedented superiority in a comparative and historical sense. It may, nevertheless, be asked how we know that there was a popular awareness of these manifold moral transgressions, and how it was manifested? Which forms of the discrepancy between theory and practice were the most unacceptable or outright intolerable? The most obvious evidence of these perceptions and feelings comes from the rapid unravelling and, indeed, collapse of these systems at the end of the 1980s and early 1990s. Once it became clear (under Gorbachev) that Soviet troops would no longer guarantee the survival of the governments in Eastern Europe, these systems rapidly fell apart with surprisingly little effort on the part of the rulers to hang on to power. It was as if they themselves realized and admitted their own unpopularity and illegitimacy. Inside the Soviet Union, the long-simmering crisis of legitimacy (that began with Khrushchev's 1956 Speech at the 20th Party Congress) intensified during the years of glasnost (which brought to the surface much that had been hidden) culmi-nating in a corresponding loss of political will to cling to power on the part of the Soviet ruling elites. Earlier evidence of popular discontent also comes from the uprisings noted above which were put down by force. The dissident literature of the entire post-Stalin period is another important source of information on discontent and especially the moral indignation that permeated it.

While it is difficult in retrospect to assess or classify different moral thresholds in various groups or strata of the population, it is possible to speculate about some of its determinants. It is likely that those who held strongly internalized traditional and espe-cially religious values, as well as those who believed in some kind of secular, humanistic values were more deeply offended than others. Not surprisingly, those who suffered at the hands of these regimes also looked for and easily found additional, larger moral causes for their own rejection of these systems.

At last, an effort should at last be made to comprehend the likely motives and mentality of those who devised the counter-productive propaganda campaigns which directly contributed to the discrediting and moral rejection of these systems. The propaganda directed at the populations in communist systems was remarkably heavy-handed, humourless, self-righteous and repetitive. Little effort was made at anything resembling a more sophisticated type of persuasion. Instead the population was inundated with unqualified assertions and claims reflecting a totally polarized and oversimplified view of the world and human beings. Whether or not, and to what degree, the power-holders themselves believed the propaganda they disseminated or presided over is debatable. They certainly believed in its overall necessity, as something that made a contribution to the survival of the system and to keeping them in power. Many citizens of the communist states were convinced that the rulers themselves did not believe their own propaganda, that it was all put forward and disseminated in a totally cynical fashion. If so, this provided further reasons for rejecting the system. As the literary incarnation of a Czech political refugee put it:

> [...] what is so debilitating, so spiritually debilitating, is that no one believes in the Party line, least of all those who are charged with enforcing it. At least in the past, at the time of the Inquisition [...] or in the early days of the Russian Revolution, those who imposed an ideology believed in it, but in Czechoslovakia, since 1968, no one believes in Marxism or Leninism, and so what they impose upon us is what they themselves know to be a lie.[11]

The key to understanding the nature of the communist propaganda that was used in communist systems (as distinct from the propaganda of the communist parties in the West or communist state-propaganda directed at the West, or other parts of the world) is that it was inspired and pervaded by a totalitarian mentality and was integrated with the possession of power. Just as the communist attitude to power was uncompromising, so was the communist attitude to the battle of ideas. No quarter was given and no concessions were made in presenting the case for the official world-view and policies. As György Litván put it, those in power feared that 'if only one brick is pulled out, the whole edifice would collapse.'[12] This also applied to their propaganda.

The qualities of this propaganda were further determined by the monopoly on power exercised by those dispensing it. The communist systems kept up the propaganda barrage in the manner here described since their power rested far more decisively on coercion and intimidation than on persuasion. The possession of power obviously reduces the need for propaganda. Consequently, the survival of these regimes did not depend on persuading their citizens as to the righteousness of their objectives and policies; obedience was instead exacted by coercive measures, or their threat. Nonetheless, it is likely that the rulers would have preferred to govern on the basis of a genuine popular acceptance of their policies.

Another major stimulant of communist propaganda was the mirage of the new socialist or communist man which these systems sought to create. Appropriate models of behaviour had to be created, promoted and disseminated in various ways and settings and this too became a task of propaganda. Finally, it is also likely that another major source of communist propaganda (as a compensatory device) was the unacknowledged

---

11 Piers Paul Read, *A Season in the West*, New York, 1988, p. 27.
12 Litván, *Októberi üzenetek*, p. 336.

awareness of the leaders of their own questionable legitimacy and lack of genuine or wide popular support.

I have argued in this essay that communist systems in Eastern Europe and Hungary in particular, lost their legitimacy not merely because they created repressive police states which imposed a wide range of material, social and cultural deprivations on their people but also because they violated, basic, elementary moral precepts which had been internalized by the populations of these countries. The intense moral revulsion followed from the feeling that these systems engaged in prolonged and determined attempts to drastically redefine and deny the validity of the personal experiences of their citizens: that is to say that they sought to deceive them without the least hesitation. If so, one of the many lessons of 1956 may well be that ordinary human beings are capable of moral judgement and that these judgements can have profound political and historical consequences.

Potentials for Unrest: Some Peculiarities of Hungary's History

Gábor Gyáni

Hungary's successive efforts to gain independence and the varied forms of uprising and of revolutionary movement that have characterized its history suggest a potential for unrest in the country that has lasted over several or more centuries. Examining these upheavals more closely, two major factors appear to coincide, for, in almost every case, resistance to imperial expansion and rule has coincided with efforts to alter the social and political structure. The exception is the Rákóczi War of Independence, where social and political modernization played a lesser role.

The close relationship between the emergence of a modern, sovereign nation and the processes of modernization was especially clear in 1848. Although the revolution of 15 March was not intended to bring about a total break with the Habsburg empire, as time passed events easily moved in that direction. In 1918, when Hungary's independent statehood was already an accomplished fact, revolution seemed again a necessary corollary, and the attempt to defend the new-found state's territorial integrity precipitated the establishment of a Bolshevik-type political regime in 1919. Finally, there is again evidence in 1956 of a symbiosis between national ferment and a no less important wish to change the political and social order.

Still, it has to be admitted that alongside the successive insurrections there has historically been another kind of tradition, one of negotiation and compromise, which exerted an impact of its own on the course of Hungary's history and of the way it may be read. According to this alternative reading, the various outbursts of unrest prepared the way for compacts aimed at resolving the recurrent tensions and conflicts in the country. It is often argued that the main outcome of the Rákóczi War of Independence, the 1711 Treaty of Szatmár, decided the place of Hungary within the framework of the Habsburg Monarchy. This ostensibly allowed some modest development aimed at reconstructing the country after the devastation of the wars of liberation from the Ottoman empire. The same has also been assumed of the 1848–9 Revolution and War of Independence which culminated in the Compromise of 1867. The dual monarchy, several historians have affirmed, provided a favourable framework for modernizing the country as well as the political preconditions for subsequent development. Furthermore, several contemporary authors have seen the Kádár regime as reviving and continuing that historical tradition of concession, allowing greater scope to a subdued nation and society, and thereby stabilizing the communist dictatorship. This reading both of Hungary's history and of the Kádár 'consensus' turns attention to the often negative consequences of negotiation – to the cynicism (at least according to István

Bibó) that stood behind 1867 Compromise and the way the whole construction of the Dual Monarchy was based on a falsehood.[1]

Over the last three centuries, unrest has often proved a decisive method of resolving critical issues in Hungary's history, and there seem to have been some constantly recurring elements that were crucial to the way events turned out. One has been the constant imperial challenge, threatening the country itself; the other, the composition of the country's social structure, characterized by a local elite at the centre that has been able to exercise direct influence on the form of reaction to external challenges.

The most important factor to mention here is the continuous existence of a more or less autonomous ruling group, whose authority has always been strengthened by stable economic conditions. Although Hungary, having been an independent kingdom in the Middle Ages, was almost permanently subject in modern times to the direct or indirect rule or dominating influence of one or another imperial power, the country was never without a domestic ruling elite of its own. This contrasts sharply with the peripheral elite-formations usually found in the state machinery of empires.[2] The ruling elite obtained its legitimacy not only by being co-opted into the core state, as happened with the Hungarian 'court aristocracy', but also by their dominance within the operation of the state at a local level through the control exerted by the land-owning, *bene possessionati* nobles over the county administration. The relative autonomy assigned to the counties within the state hierarchy of the Habsburg Monarchy, meant that the *bene possessionati*, as representatives of the periphery, could easily engage in resistance and revolt.

Despite critical assessments of this social group, mainly by historians associated with a pro-Habsburg intellectual and political orientation, it cannot be seriously disputed that the potential for unrest would have been far less in Hungary had the *bene possessionati* been absent. Furthermore, the possibility of successfully negotiating with the Habsburg rulers would have been the less, as this elite was, through its control of the local administration, in a position to enforce the results of such negotiations and to act thereby as a brake on imperial rule.

The claims of social history, however, demand an additional ideological and intellectual argument, resting on psychology, to explain the incessant, inexhaustible sources of unrest. I have already touched on this in relation to the critique of the 1867 Compromise and the differences that have arisen in respect of how efforts at independence since Rákóczi should be evaluated. An ideology and collective mentality of independence was established in Hungary in the early modern period and was closely interwoven with the Calvinist Reformed Church. This widely-shared emotional and intellectual tradition became the solid basis of modern national identity during the course of the nineteenth century but had over several centuries (starting with Bocskai in the early 1600s)

---

1 István Bibó, *Democracy, Revolution, Self-Determination. Selected Writings*, ed. Károly Nagy, Highland Lakes, NJ, 1991. On the dual traditions of the discourse on Hungary's historical path, see Gábor Gyáni, 'Ungarische Erinnerungkamnones zur Österreichisch-Ungarischen Monarchie, in Amália Kerekes et al. (eds), *Leitha und Lethe. Symbolische Räume und Zeiten in der Kultur Österreich-Ungarns*, Tübingen und Basel, 2004, pp. 263–271.

2 Alexander J. Motyl, 'How Empires Rise and Fall: Nation, Nationalism, and Imperial Elites', in Justo G. Beramendi et al. (eds), *Nationalism in Europe Past and Present*, vol. 1, Santiago de Compostela, 1994, pp. 383–405.

provided a major cause of unrest. The true cult of independence and the revolts associated with it were cherished not only by a narrow elite (the landed nobility in particular), but, from the time of the Rákóczi war of independence onwards, by the common people as well. Rákóczi's movement succeeded in mobilizing masses of serfs who were promised emancipation (vainly, as it turned out). This created a collective memory of the event, even among the lower segments of contemporary and later society, as is abundantly shown in peasant folklore. So the memory of Rákóczi and his struggle for independence found easy access to the national collective memory when the time came to construct a nationalist ideology and sentiment.[3]

This historical pattern repeated itself in the events of 1848–9, when 'the people', embracing almost every segment of society, including the newly-emancipated serfs, shared the same experience of events. The response of the imperial centre was both to oppose the revolution and to preserve as much of the old social order as was possible. In this way, 1848–49 further shaped collective mentalities, reinforcing memory of the Rákóczi revolt, and establishing an indissoluble association between political revolution and (thwarted) social change.

These associations had a cumulative character, urging the importance of collective action, and even violence, over negotiation, and this provided the pattern which emerged again in 1956. The association of revolution with social change also accounts in part for the ambiguity in the conceptual definition of '56. The most frequently-applied term is revolution, but that does not seem wholly adequate for an event the social content of which is hard to reconcile with the what is regularly meant by revolution.[4] So qualifications are often added or other words used to describe what took place in 1956. It is thus sometimes called a revolt or uprising, with the implication that '56 has to be placed more in a national than a trans-historical perspective. As alternatives to revolution, terms such as '*national* revolt' or '*national* uprising' are intended to express the defining character of the Hungarian October. A good example is the historical narrative of Ferenc A. Váli, produced as early as 1961. The title, *Rift and Revolt in Hungary*, and still more the subtitle, *Nationalism versus Communism*, clearly reflect the author's view that nationalism impelled the events of 1956. At the end of the book, Váli devotes a chapter to the idea that national and nationalist resentment was the main motor. He discusses the resentments, generally felt in the satellite states, that might result in a revolt like the Hungarian '56, assuring us of the central contribution of nationalism: 'Soviet Russian *nationalism* and Marxist-Leninist *internationalism* act upon *local nationalism*. They also act upon local aspirations for individual freedom.'[5] While not denying altogether the revolutionary character of the basically national(ist) events of '56, as eloquently indicated by his own inconsistent terminology, it is clear that Váli restricts his perspective to the disintegration of the communist elite, caused by the forces of nationalism erupting beneath them. Only after conscious or unconscious national sentiment, 'the most powerful motivation leading to a rift within the Communist Party

3　László Kósa, *Megjártam a hadak útját. A magyar nép történeti emlékezete*, Budapest, 1980.
4　The term 'revolution' has been analysed through the method of *Begriffsgeschichte*. See Tamás Ungvári, 'Revolution: A Textual Analysis', *Nineteenth-Century French Studies*, 19, 1990, no 1, pp. 1–22.
5　Ferenc A. Váli, *Rift and Revolt in Hungary: Nationalism versus Communism*, Cambridge, MA, 1961, pp. 505–6.

of Hungary', had unleashed itself, did 'an impulse for revolutionary aggressiveness [... forming] the molten core of collective hatred' follow as a 'secondary, but still outstanding, motivation [...], the aspiration for *freedom* and *democracy*.'[6] Váli thus dissects the revolution as being in the first place a nationalist revolt, to which demands of a political and social nature were only later added.

We are more concerned here with the lessons for social history that may be drawn from the events of October 1956. The main question is which of the classes led the revolution in the direction of realizing its own social interests and power ambitions. The relevance of this follows from a Marxist interpretation, focusing on the class content of an event worthy to be called a revolution. Such an action is, according to Marxist theory, always moved by the will of a single social force, embodied in modern times in the bourgeoisie, the proletariat or even the peasantry. But what can be said of the Hungarian '56, which seems not to include such a single revolutionary social force, despite the efforts by some theorists (Hannah Arendt) and historians (Bill Lomax) to make it seem so?[7] This insight led some neo-Marxist theoreticians to admit that the main protagonists of the dramatic events of '56 were 'the political elite, which was disintegrating into antagonistic factions, *and the people*' (my emphasis).[8]

In attempting to identify the concrete social groups that took an active (or even outstanding) role in the revolutionary mobilization of 1956, one has to deconstruct the highly obscure term, 'the people'. Three broadly defined macro-social groups seem to occupy a dominant place either in preparing the insurrection, or 'managing' the events both locally and nationally: left-wing intellectuals, university students and the industrial working classes. I do not deny the possibly considerable role that several members and sections of the rural peasantry or other parts of the intelligentsia played at the time. Still, the three groups outlined here look to be the most important forces generating and representing the revolutionary spirit and behaviour. The forces driving each of these social groups were certainly varied while their aims and the ideals they acknowledged were by no means uniform.[9]

I do not wish to dwell overmuch upon the question of revolutionary programmes and ideals, but to pay more attention to potentials for unrest. As Ferenc Váli observed, one of the most important sources of unrest, common to almost everybody, was national resentment. This came about not only on account of Hungary's subjugation to the Soviet imperial power but also, and cumulatively, as a consequence of the Trianon syndrome and of the still vital memory of defeat in the Second World War.

Another crucial factor facilitating revolutionary mobilization was the obvious discontinuity occurring in Hungary in 1953 when, after Stalin's death, a political alternative, albeit modest, emerged within the rigid Stalinist dictatorship. That was the moment when Imre Nagy came to power as prime minister. Nagy's short-lived rule contributed enormously to the creation of a niche in the fabric of Hungary's communist

---

6 ibid, p. 494.
7 Hannah Arendt, *On Revolution*, Harmondsworth, Middlesex, 1984; Bill Lomax, *Hungary 1956*, London, 1976.
8 Marc Rakowski [György Bencze and János Kis], *Towards an East European Marxism*, London, 1978, p. 31.
9 The problem is discussed more fully in Gábor Gyáni, 'Socio-psychological roots of discontent: paradoxes of 1956', *Hungarian Studies*, 20, no 2, 2006, pp. 65–73.

power structure which widened the sphere of autonomy even within the subdued society. Revisionist intellectuals, our first macro-social group, were pioneering in advancing the process of thaw. Building on the traditional role of the intellectual in shaping and even defining the realm of politics, their special identity was feared by the communist political elite.

'Status insecurity', which was equally felt by everybody who had moved up or down the social ladder during the previous decade may also be indicated as an important factor adding to the sources of unrest. Due to the enormous and enforced social mobility that characterized so much of Hungarian society in the wake of the Second World War, no social group could see itself any longer as a stable entity, provided with a specific and unambiguous group identity that coincided with its own self-image. This widely shared social experience seems as much to be characteristic of university students, who had mostly come out of the ranks of lower social groups (poor peasants and the urban workers), as of factory employees (manual workers, technicians, engineers, and those in the lower echelons of management). They were all moved by anxiety and frustration. University students experienced it when confronted by the restrictions imposed on their development of an autonomous youth subculture (universal in most European countries and North America). The same was true even for the industrial employers, who suffering from insufficient and declining wage-levels and the bad supply of goods, also found their own social advancement constrained. Unfavourable social experiences and the prospect of further uncertainty drove these two other macro-social groups, university students and the industrial working classes, into the arms of the revolution and contributed to its mass character.

The interpretation given here on the potentials for unrest lying behind '56 is as much concerned with the 'reality' as with a narrative image of the past. In seeking to identify and understand the forces and motives behind events, two rival historical traditions shaping the course of Hungary's past in the last two or three centuries have to be reckoned with, the 'revolutionary-type' and the 'negotiation type'. These 'inverse narratives'[10] which provide stable although contrasting collective identities, supply us with alternative discursive contexts. They also find expression in the changing use of the terms, 'revolution' and 'revolt', as descriptions of the conceptual meaning of the Hungarian '56.

---

10 See Jan Assmann, 'Narrative Inversion. Erzählte Gegenidentität am Beispiel biblischer und ausserbiblischer Exodusberichte' in Michael Neumann (ed.), *Erzählte Identitäten*, Munich, 2000, pp. 119–33.

Forward into the Past: Some Thoughts on Historical References in the 1956 Hungarian Revolution

János M. Bak

Fifty years after the event, it is almost impossible to reconstruct what people really wanted to achieve by rising against totalitarianism, even though many of them risked their lives in the process. Nevertheless, it may be worth looking at the explicit and implicit historical references in the form and content of manifestos and other expressions of the time, as they may give us a glimpse of the ideas in people's minds.[1]

Let me start with two obvious points. First, most revolutions are 'staged' in a historical garb, essentially for their legitimization. By doing so, the revolutionaries argue (mainly symbolically) that they have historical antecedents and that they cannot therefore be dismissed as vain 'novelty-seekers'.[2] It has often been pointed out that the French Revolution 'played' Roman Republic, that the Bolsheviks imitated Jacobins, and so on. Secondly, since revolts against tyrannical regimes imply that the rejected form of government was the result of the deformation (or destruction) of a previously good state of affairs, they set as their aim the reconstruction of this past. The 'good past' may be as far back as Paradise (the 'When Adam delved and Eve spun...' of the Peasants' Revolt of 1381); or, in a more sophisticated version, a sort of primeval communism where alienation and private property were unknown and which may be achieved on a higher level after the elimination of capitalism; or, yet, some closer past, such as the early church for the Reformation, and so on. It has been pointed out many times, and may now count as proven, that in Central Europe references to history in the political discourse are more typical than elsewhere.[3]

In respect of 1956, the Hungarian Revolution and War of Independence of 1848–49 provided the obvious historical examples and for several reasons. 1848, Kossuth, Petőfi and Bem were icons built up through many decades; they were initially used by the Communists as well, although, at the time of complete bolshevization, the commemoration of the revolution, 15 March, was abolished as national holiday. And so was the

---

1 This essay was going into print when I occasioned upon Éva Standeiszky's 'Követett és elvetett múlt az 1956-os forradalomban', *Történelmi Szemle*, 2006, pp. 91–119, in which this subject is treated in more sophistication and detail than here. Standeiszky's essay is now reprinted in (eds) Gábor Gyáni & János Rainer, *Ezerkilencszázötvenhat az újabb történeti irodalomban*, Budapest, 2007, pp. 222–53.
2 Cf. Sallust, *Catilina*, 28, 4 and elsewhere.
3 See thus, J. M. Bak, 'Politisierung des Mittelalters in Ungarn', in Petra Bock and Edgar Wolfrum (eds), *Umkämpfte Vergangenheit. Geschichtsbilder, Erinnerung und Vergangenheitspolitik im internationalen Vergleich*, Göttingen, 1999.

national day of mourning on 6 October, the day when thirteen Honvéd generals were hanged and Prime Minister Batthyány shot by the victorious Habsburg authorities in 1849. No wonder that the restoration of these two holidays – for the detached observer only marginal matters – appeared among the demands of the student-meeting at the Technical University held on 22 October. General Bem, the Polish freedom fighter in command of the Honvéd regiments opposing the Russian intervention in 1849, was a self-evident icon symbolizing solidarity with the Polish anti-Muscovite reforms; and recollection of his role provided the actual trigger for the demonstration planned for 23 October at his (and Petőfi's) statue. Moreover, 6 October had already been 'brought back' by the festive funeral on that day in 1956 of László Rajk and the other executed and finally rehabilitated Communists.

Once Soviet ('Russian') tanks appeared in the night of 23/24 October, the parallel became tragically apposite. On 25 October, a reporter asked a 16-year-old freedom fighter why he took to the streets with weapon in hand; his answer was typical: 'Just as our freedom fighters of 1848 rebelled against foreign repression, so we cannot allow an alien oppressor to do as he pleases in our homeland.' Obviously, he had learned in school about 1848 and, if he had perhaps had a somewhat oppositionally-minded teacher, quite a lot about the 1849 fight against the interventionist army of Prince Pashkievich. If he had been (as he most likely was) a Young Pioneer, he would also have learned the traditional battle cry of the 1849 Honvéd: *Előre!* ('Forward!').[4] The parallel was not illusory: Gerő's call to Khrushchev for troops in the late evening of 23 October was close enough to the one that the young Franz Joseph made to Tsar Nicholas I on 1 May, 1849.

Among the original Fourteen/Sixteen Points of the students featured the restoration of the national coat-of-arms (and the traditional army uniform). The demand referred to the 'Kossuth coat-of-arms', a traditional Hungarian crest with the red-and-white bands on the right and the double cross on three mounds on the left, blazoned on a so-called Renaissance (or 'elegant') shield. This was in contrast to the same surmounted by the so-called Holy Crown that had been used not only by the Habsburgs as kings of Hungary but also by the interwar kingless monarchy of Admiral Horthy.[5] But there was usually not enough time to replace the torn-out Soviet-style coat of arms from the middle of national flags. With the round hole in the centre, these became the symbol of 1956.

One may add a few semantic references to 1848, some of which may not have been consciously so chosen, but which nevertheless emerged from the 'similarity' of situations. To begin with, in imitation of 1848, 'National Guard' (*Nemzetőrség*) was the name given to the planned law-enforcement organization uniting freedom fighters and ordinary armed forces loyal to the revolutionary government. The governing body of this organization called itself the *Forradalmi Karhatalmi Bizottmány* (Revolutionary Committee of Executive Power), deploying thereby a nineteenth-century word, not used

---

4 This word, taken from a famous patriotic poem by Károly Tóth (1831–81), was chosen as the greeting of the Hungarian blue- or red-kerchiefed youngsters. It was thus of substantially greater vintage than the *Smrt fashizmu – sloboda narodu!* ('Death to Fascism – Liberty to the People!') used by the Yugoslav Pioneers.
5 Now also by the renewed Hungarian Republic of 1990.

since 1849, but clearly harking back to Kossuth's emergency government, the *Honvédelmi Bizottmány*. There were other such borrowings.

Thus, in brief, the legitimization of the revolution – beginning with the students' demands and their demonstration, and reinforced by the armed struggle against 'Russian' intervention – was based to a very great extent on referents which looked back to the events of more than a century earlier. And since the events of 1848–49 and the programme of 15 March 1848 – the original twelve points of Petőfi and his friends, including the basic civic liberties – had been unquestionably raised into the Hungarian pantheon, no revolutionary who paid homage to them could be charged with deviation from the holiest traditions of the nation.

In a strictly scholastic fashion one might ask why other revolts and rebellions, such as Bocskai's in the seventeenth century, Rákóczi's in the eighteenth, or the 'Chrysanthemum Revolution' of October 1918 could not offer an example for '56. Certainly, the older rebellions were not as vivid in the collective memory as 1848. (Although, in the late nineteenth century, Rákóczi and his *kurucok* may very well have served as an example for revolt). Károlyi's Octobrists, however, had been successfully denigrated by the interwar counter-revolutionary system as harbingers of the 1919 communists and thus excluded from the national pantheon. But so much for explicit historical references employed for the purpose of legitimization.

The different programmes that emerged in the few days of freedom, written up in manifestos or just adumbrated in speeches and articles, were neatly categorized by György Litván several years ago.[6] He distinguished at least three major tendencies: first, the adherents of a 'better socialism'; secondly, the socialist-oriented democrats (often labelled 'third roaders'); and, thirdly, the conservatives who, although the least articulate, were clearly significant. Even less developed were the rather diffuse ideas of unreflective (and often outright right-wing) anti-Communists and the aims of the politically unsophisticated but heroic street-fighters. One could rephrase all this in terms of implicit historical references: to what points in history did the protagonists of the various programmes want to return – when did they want their 'new start' to begin?

Embarking on a reverse chronology we may imagine that Imre Nagy wanted to go the least far back, essentially only to 1953 and the programme of the 'New Course' launched the next year. In his (later published) writings and in his submissions to MDP party organs in the year preceding the revolution, Nagy had pleaded for a resumption of that policy and direction. From what he said from the window of the Parliament on the evening of 23 October, one may imply that even then he still envisaged such a solution.[7]

Many of his 'like-minded friends' (*elvbarátok*) would probably have wanted to go further back, to the years before complete Stalinization, say 1948. Most (though not all) of them imagined a communist socialism without the ruthless dictatorship and with a 'human face' (as it was to be called twelve years later in Czechoslovakia). There were some in Nagy's circle (for example Miklós Gimes) who embraced the programme of true

---

6 For instance in György Litván, *Az 1956-os magyar forradalom hagyománya és irodalma*, Budapest, 1992.
7 He certainly realized during the following days that the revolution needed to go 'further back'. Nevertheless, to include here the dates of the Warsaw Pact, which Hungary left on 2 November, and Austria's declaration of neutrality – both 1955 – would, I believe, be inconsistent with my scheme.

parliamentary democracy and thus would have gone back to the years 1945–6 (doubtless, with reservations as to the limited freedom permitted under Soviet occupation). These would have been close to those democratic politicians (e.g. of the Smallholders' Party), who certainly approved of the radical land reform of 1945, some of them even of the first round of nationalization in 1946 (at that time quite widespread all over Europe). If one reads the programmes of the workers' councils, they surely advocated the retention of basic 'socialist measures' (thus the point reached in 1948), but with the added demand of workers' self-management. They thus looked back to 1945–6, when 'factory committees'(*üzemi bizottságok*) had de facto organized the reconstruction of Hungary's ruined industry. Certainly, 1946–7 would have been a point of departure for such non-socialist democrats as Béla Kovács of the Smallholders' Party, just recently back from the Gulag, when on 30 October he said in Pécs: 'No one should dream of the old order. The world of counts, bankers, and capitalists is gone for good; anyone who sees things now as if it were 1939 or 1945, is no authentic Smallholder.'[8]

But we also meet 1945–6 (implicitly) among the earliest student demands: the name MEFESZ (given to their newly-founded independent association in opposition to the party-controlled youth organization, DISZ) harks back to the end of the war. While using a much earlier date (to which I will come back), the highly influential writer and thinker, László Németh, meant in fact also a return to nothing earlier than 1946: 'We must be vigilant, while the people in arms are focused on the withdrawal of Soviet forces, to ensure that new opportunists do not make a Counter-Revolution out of the Revolution and set the Hungarian struggle for freedom on the course of 1920.'[9]

What would have been the date for Cardinal Mindszenty and his circle? From one passage of his speech delivered on 3 November – 'We live under the rule of law in a classless society; we are developing further our democratic accomplishments; and we hold to the principle of private property limited by social concerns' – one might imply that 1945 (of course, with appropriate compensation for ecclesiastical property) would also have been acceptable for Mindszenty's circle.[10] On the other hand, the implicit claim of the conservatives for continuity with the pre-war (or possibly even monarchical) constitution, would place them in 1944 or even earlier.

1944, of course, conjures up the date of radical right-wing Arrow Cross terror and the issue of anti-Semitism. The most recent research has shown that there were several anti-Jewish acts and (often absurd) anti-Semitic slogans around in 1956, but that no serious political force stood on an anti-Semitic platform.[11] Doubtless (and as I heard in Budapest's Second District), just as there were some cries of 'Standards aloft with the Virgin Mary!' (*Szűzmáriás lobogót!*: a seventeenth-century rallying-call), so there was some equally anachronistic sloganeering about Jews. Nevertheless, in respect of the sort of 'counter-revolutionary' sentiments feared by Németh, even the most outspoken national programmes did not advocate the restoration of Horthy nor even a return to Hungary's historic frontiers. Considering the importance since the late 1980s of the issue of the

8   Reported in all dailies. See thus the organ of the Smallholders' Party, *Kis Újság*, 31 October, 1956.
9   László Németh, 'Emelkedő nemzet', *Irodalmi Újság*, 1 November, 1956, p. 1.
10 The Roman Catholic newspaper, *Új Ember* (2 November 1956, p. 3), spelled it out in so many words that the church did not demand the return of its landed properties.
11 See Éva Standeiszky, 'Antiszemitizmus 1956-ban', *Évkönyv 1956-os Intézet*, 12, 2004, pp. 147–86.

Hungarian minorities in the neighbouring countries, this constitutes a remarkable omission.

While it is difficult to reconstruct the aims of the (mostly young) freedom fighters, without whose intransigence the uprising would surely have ended in some kind of compromise, their 'dates of reference' may have been very divergent. There were a few, like István Angyal – and perhaps some of his comrades in Tűzoltó utca – with ideas about a communism 'cleared from Stalinist aberration', who clearly belonged to the '1948-ers' or were even close to Nagy's '1954'. But the wide variety of their possible points of reference cannot now be established. Certainly, the older ones, some of whom may have served in the Hungarian army during the Second World War, may have had positive memories of pre-war Hungary. Others, forced to be menial labourers by Communist expropriations, may have wished to return to some 'good old times', in 1946 or even 1939. But what kind of historical 'peg' could have been in the minds of officers of the 'Peoples' Army', who joined the armed fight? And could the great number of the young, 16- to 20-year-old boys and girls, who grew up in post-war Hungary, have had any memory even of the 'New Course' or, indeed, any image of a historical moment worth returning to? Perhaps they, in an almost subconscious way, were not looking back to the past but rather towards a more up-to-date 'liberation' from regimentation and daily oppression by their elders, and towards freedom of daily life, dress, music, hair-style, and so on. Were they, indeed, 1968-ers *avant soixante-huit*?

So much for the 'dates-game'! What I have sought to demonstrate is simply the wide variety of aims and ideas – as far as one can reconstruct them at a distance of half a century – almost all of which were far from what the Kádár-regime was later to characterize as a restoration of capitalism and of the political system of pre-war Hungary. Trying to speculate on how the political spectrum may have developed had the revolution succeeded in establishing parliamentary democracy and national independence would be another 'guessing game', and one which is usually prohibited to historians.

1956 and the British Legation

Éva Figder

In what follows, I will examine the British endeavours in Budapest, London and New York, to make a difference to Hungary's future in late 1956. These endeavours, however, were (and to some degree still are) misunderstood by the general Hungarian public. Some thought that the West would actually commit itself to armed intervention and help Hungary become a neutral country – along the Austrian and Finnish models. The other, similarly persistent, misconception is that because of the Suez crisis, Hungary failed to receive the help it desired and deserved. As we shall see, Sir Leslie Fry, then British minister in Budapest, extended aid and succour to the revolutionaries by sheltering them and generally did everything within his remit to further the Hungarian cause in London. At the same time, the Foreign Office (FO) exerted considerable pressure with the same purpose through its ambassador to the United Nations (UN) in New York. Yet, neither of these agencies contemplated armed intervention on Britain's part at any stage of these proceedings. My examination of the British endeavours to assist Hungary during these crucial weeks is based on official British documents and the recollections of British diplomats.

The year of 1956 opened with Mátyás Rákosi – to all appearances – as firmly as ever in power: the ease with which he expelled Imre Nagy from the Hungarian Workers' Party and quashed the 'Writers' Revolt' in November 1955 suggested to British observers that he had little to fear.[1] The fact that British Legation staff were under close surveillance by the secret service and several dozen visitors to the Legation were detained, suggested to the British minister that some sort of a spy trial was about to be staged by the authorities. In February 1956, the new policies introduced by the Twentieth Congress of the Communist Party of the Soviet Union, coupled with the denigration of Stalin and denunciation of the cult of personality, gave powerful encouragement to all those who opposed Rákosi and the anachronisms he embodied. Rákosi had to reckon with a growing opposition within his party. Attacks on him showed very few results at first. Then, grudgingly, he had to make some concessions, such as releasing non-communist politicians (Béla Kovács) and re-starting talks with the Yugoslavs. He also admitted some of his errors. In the view of the British Minister, Sir Leslie Fry, the climax was reached with the outspoken debate at the Petőfi Circle on 27 June.

---

1   The National Archives (Public Record Office) FO371/128662.

From then on, the minister believed that Rákosi had become a liability from Moscow's point of view.[2] His view was further buttressed by the arrival of Mikoyan in Budapest and Rákosi's replacement by ⬚rnő Gerő. Nevertheless , this was just a small change. It was also clear to Fry that the Soviet leaders were not inclined to offer any concessions to Hungarian aspirations. Whatever hopes the national communists may have had were quickly dashed. Communist parties in the satellite countries were warned by the Kremlin early in September that the idea of separate roads to socialism must not be taken too far. By 23 October, when Gerő was due to arrive from Moscow, 'the national Communists had come to realise that no share in power would be theirs unless fate took – or was helped to take – an unexpected turn.'[3]

On 23 October, Fry and his wife went to visit a scientific laboratory outside Budapest. Hardly had they begun their tour than the director was called away and his deputy took over. It was apparent to Fry that something extraordinary must have happened as their presence, although very welcome at first, had suddenly become inconvenient. On their way back to the city they saw large numbers of people, many carrying Hungarian flags with the communist emblem cut out of the middle.[4] The telephone at the Legation rang incessantly, with callers conveying one report after the other of developments. Mark Russell, the third secretary, recalls events:

> The lights in the Legation burned late that night. By the time that most of us went home at about midnight the demonstrations were out of control. Soviet intervention in the early hours of 24 October did not come as a surprise. What followed most certainly did. After the lifting of the curfew at 9.00 that morning all the staff, British and Hungarian, managed to get to work. The presence of Russian armour on the Danube bridges and in the main streets suggested that all would be swiftly over. However fierce firing broke out again. Movement became dangerous. The bridges were blocked. We were forced to stay in Harmincad utca [the address of the Legation] for a week while our families were marooned in their houses and flats widely scattered over Buda and Pest.[5]

On 25 October Leslie Fry sent a report to Selwyn-Lloyd, the British Foreign Secretary, informing him that a crowd of about 2000 people had congregated outside the legation; fifty of them actually gained entry so Fry went to talk to them. They expressed their wish for independence and an end to Russian domination. Fry told them that '[I] was doing my utmost to keep HMG fully informed of events here and of their causes as they appeared to me. I could not say what decision would be taken; I could undertake only to act as a faithful reporter. Meanwhile the Hungarian people could be certain of the sympathy of the British people.'[6]

It now proved fortunate that the Legation building was as big and well equipped as it was. Over next few tumultuous days, families were brought into the Legation. The consul, Joan Fish, with considerable courage, gathered in the British community. One of these was a journalist, Sefton Delmer, working for the *Daily Express*. He persuaded the

---

2   FO371/128662.

3   FO371/128662.

4   Sir Leslie Fry, *As Luck Would Have It*, London, 1978, cited in Éva Figder, 'The 1956 Revolution', in Nigel Thorpe and Petra Matyisin (eds), *Harmincad utca 6 – A Twentieth Century History*, Foreign and Commonwealth Office, London, 1999, pp. 45–51. (An internet version is also available on the FCO website <www.fco.gov.uk>).

5   Figder, 'The 1956 Revolution', pp. 45–51.

6   FO77/10.

minister to allow him to use the Legation's wireless link to transmit messages to his paper in London. The Legation shop operating in the old bank vaults supplied essential foodstuffs. Sleeping accommodation was arranged on the top two floors and rotas were prepared for use of the bathrooms. [7]

According to a confidential telegram, as early as 27 October Fry was considering what practical steps the British might take to demonstrate sympathy for the Hungarian people and to exploit propaganda opportunities:

(a) we must do nothing to encourage the idea that military support might be forthcoming,
(b) anything we do must be done at once, while resistance continues.[8]

To this end, Fry suggested the immediate dispatch of a convoy of food and medical supplies from Austria to Budapest.

Downing Street acted accordingly. On 28 October, it issued a statement in which the British Government assured the Hungarians of their sympathy and admiration. They also offered immediate practical help by way of a donation of £25,000 to the International Red Cross 'to alleviate the suffering by provision of medical and other supplies.'[9] But on 1 November, reports were received of Soviet forces pouring into the country from the east. It was therefore decided that the wives and children of Legation staff and of the British community should be evacuated. On 2 November, Mark Russell led the convoy all the way to Vienna.

As the situation further deteriorated after 4 November, Leslie Fry decided to offer refuge to Commonwealth citizens, the families of the Legation's Hungarian staff, and the domestic staff of the British members of the Legation. He also decided to attend to any wounded person who approached the Legation. On instructions from London, he refused to grant asylum to any other Hungarians except for two small children.[10]

The evacuated members of the Legation returned from Vienna on 13 November. The building had been relatively unscathed in the fighting. There were two broken windows and several bullet marks in the walls. But the staff knew it would not be all. They had burnt confidential papers and prepared for the worst, and they had remained in the Legation for several days after the revolution had been finally broken following the general strike in December. One of the Legation drivers, László Régeczy-Nagy, was arrested and imprisoned. He was charged with being an intermediary between István Bibó, Árpád Göncz and Kit Cope, the first secretary at the Legation. Other Hungarian staff members were also arrested but released after some days or months respectively.

Even after János Kádár's take-over, the British did not give up on the Hungarian cause. There is a confidential memo on Hungary, or rather, a series of memos, produced by the Northern Department of the Foreign Office and dating from the beginning of December 1956. They thought the situation in Hungary remained grave and therefore:

---

7 Figder, 'The 1956 Revolution', pp. 45–51.
8 FO477/10.
9 ibid.
10 Figder, 'The 1956 Revolution', pp. 45–51.

It is for consideration whether, apart from action in the UN, there is anything to be done to prevent the Soviet liquidation of Hungary or the development of an even more explosive situation which might threaten more immediately the peace of ⬜urope. [...] If the Russians are determined to liquidate Hungary there is probably little we can do to stop them. But we cannot be sure that the Kremlin are united in such a purpose. The suggestion has been made recently by at least two Soviet officials, in conversation with foreign diplomats, that an Austrian solution might be found for Hungary. [...] The reason why the Soviet Union will not let Hungary go is partly political and partly strategic."[11]

The memorandum predicted that regardless of the outcome of the revolution, Hungary would never be considered as reliable by the Russians; international communism had suffered and there was the possibility that 'rot' would set in and spread in communist ⬜astern ⬜urope. Consequently the 'prolongation of Soviet violence in Hungary is defeating its own object.'[12] Strategically, the quickest overland route to Italy (and hence to the Mediterranean) was through Hungary. Moreover, Hungary was part of the Soviet Union's *cordon sanitaire* that now had been dented by events and by the unreliability of Hungarians.

The memorandum also suggested a possible form of action. Because the British, Americans and French were considered to be the main enemies of the Russians, a neutral intermediary was considered best. The obvious choice was India. First, therefore, the British should approach the Indian government without American or French cooperation. Nehru should ask Soviet opinion of the following British proposal: the Soviet Union, USA, India, France and the UK would make a joint declaration with binding force, guaranteeing the Hungarian borders from armed intervention. A free and independent Hungarian government would be established that would be allowed to pursue a policy on the neutral Austrian model. The above five powers would guarantee that neither the Arrow Cross nor the Horthy regime would be re-established and that the socialist achievements, which the majority of the people wished to preserve, be retained. Soviet troops should be withdrawn in stages, and free elections held under UN auspices.

The document warned that '[t]here is a very slender chance of the Russians accepting such a solution', but that Nehru was well placed to point out the advantages to them.[13] In terms of advantages for the West, the officials indicated that a mutually acceptable solution would immediately reduce international tension' 'which would indirectly facilitate a solution of the major problems in other parts of the world (e.g. the Middle ⬜ast).' This is the only document I have seen where 'Middle ⬜ast' was added when otherwise discussing the Hungarian revolution.

As the days went by and the original memo was passed from one official to the other, the officials' views became correspondingly less optimistic. One of them thought that the Soviet government would not agree to free elections in Hungary or anywhere else because they could not risk a communist regime being swept away by a genuine free vote. Then it was suggested that the Hungarian people be persuaded to accept a Gomułka regime which would be acceptable to the Russians. Other officials thought that they could not possibly urge the Hungarians to accept the Kádár government if it moved towards 'Gomułka-ism' because this would mean condoning its previous acts. Sir Thomas Brimelow argued that the possible effectiveness of Nehru's intervention

---

11 FO371/12866.
12 ibid.
13 ibid.

depended on how the Russians saw their own situation, and/or whether they thought they were in an impasse.[14]

In the end, K.P.S. Menon, the Indian Ambassador to Moscow, went to Budapest in mid-December. He was very much disturbed by what he saw in Hungary, especially what had happened to the workers in December. His suggestion that the UN Secretary General should visit Hungary was refused by Kádár.

The British delegation worked tirelessly both in the General Assembly and on the Security Council. They endorsed Imre Nagy's request to the Secretary General to call on the Great Powers to recognize Hungary's neutrality. They produced a hefty document on Hungary, submitted to the UN Special Committee on Hungary in February 1957. Sir Pierson Dixon, ambassador to the UN, often enough expressed HMG's hope that the UN would be able to help the Hungarians achieve their natural aspirations. Dixon was a most ardent supporter of the Hungarians' cause.[15]

As early as 3 January 1957, Leslie Fry elaborated on the 'Causes and Likely Conse-quences of the Hungarian Revolution'. In his opinion, the events that had taken place in October and November 1956 were a revolt by a nation. This revolt was led by workers and students, two segments of society that the communist regime might have thought to have done its best to win over. There was no sign of a conspiracy. Nor had there been any western help. The causes of the revolt lay in the pent-up hatred and despair engen-dered by ten years of tyranny. Its genesis was also to be found in the Hungarian Communist Party itself – the revolution was the end-product of a process that had started with Stalin's death, followed by Imre Nagy's experiment with a more national and liberal communism, and with the Writers' Revolt.

Fry clearly saw that with the ascendancy of the Nagy Government, the country's path was to be that towards a type of socialism which the Soviet leaders might have been expected to recognize because there was no inclination to disturb the twin bases of 'socialist achievement': land reform and the public ownership of all mines, industrial concerns and businesses. But, by announcing Hungary's withdrawal from the Warsaw Pact on 1 November, Nagy had gone too far too fast.

> It seems more probable however that the Soviet leaders had never intended to relinquish their grip on Hungary, the withdrawal of their armour from Budapest being no more than tactical. [...] It is possible that this concentration of might was occasioned either by desire to teach Hungary and the other satel-lites a resounding lesson, out of proportion to the imminent misdemeanour, or – as seems more probable – by anxiety over the repercussions of possibly serious impending difficulties with Poland.[16]

To sum up, we can see that the British did everything they could, both in Budapest and London, to help the Hungarians – in the physical sense, by distributing food to mothers with babies, and through diplomatic channels. Nevertheless, they never made any promise of armed intervention either directly or indirectly. Ideally, they would have liked to have seen a free and independent Hungary. Nevertheless, they always had doubts as to its feasibility, possibly because their long-term diplomatic memory was so good. Foreign Office officials still remembered Anthony Eden's visit to Moscow in

---

14 FO371/12866.
15 FO477/10 and 11.
16 FO477/11.

December 1941. Stalin had told ☐den expressly that the Soviet counter-attack on Germany would not stop at the Soviet Union's existing borders, as it was clear to him that no diplomatic guarantee would actually physically guarantee his country's existing borders. It was thus clear that the Soviet Union needed a territorial buffer zone along its frontiers. Then, in October 1944, when Churchill and ☐den went to Moscow, they negotiated the details with Stalin. We all know of the 'naughty document' and the percentages listed in it. Therefore, I think that from the end of 1941, reinforced by the 1944 meeting, the fate of much of eastern ☐urope was a foregone conclusion. The British knew only too well that if they respected the Soviet wishes, they might expect something in return in other places which were much more important from the point of view of British interests. At this juncture, the Middle ☐ast and the Suez crisis came into the picture. Naturally, Suez overshadowed everything else that was happening at the same time elsewhere and it did have an effect on the Hungarian cause in so far as the Middle ☐ast was more geo-strategically important than ☐astern ☐urope. ☐gypt was dealt with by the Middle ☐astern Department at the Foreign Office, and Hungarian affairs were dealt with by the Northern Department at the time. British military intervention in Hungary was unlikely because of the agreements of 1941 and 1944, and the documents I have seen expressly state that they would not make any such intervention.

'Saints of the Streets': The Participants in 1956[1]

Zsuzsanna Vajda and László Eörsi

Introduction: Individuals and history

The 'great men' view of history has endured even into this century. As early as the nine-teenth century, however, attention was directed to the masses who, along with the so-called 'great men', were also the shapers of history: those who conducted trade and commerce, who served as soldiers, and who rose up against their rulers. The reason that this happened at this time had only a little to do with any advance of knowledge, but largely arose from the fact that the masses had finally taken to the 'historical stage'. We must limit ourselves to a brief summary of the causes: from capitalist mass-production through rapid urbanization to the enormous advances in literacy. Beyond all this, however, the coming to prominence of the masses – and their acknowledgment in historical writing and in the emerging social sciences – derived from the fact that indi-viduals now began to examine their own fate with an ever-increasing awareness and, in order to take their destinies into their own hands, to form various social aggregations which then became political agents. In the developed countries, it is clear that an eman-cipation of the masses took place in the course of the late-nineteenth and twentieth centuries. 'The little man' in his hundreds of thousands, emerged from history's undif-ferentiated narrative to become a member of political parties, a voter, a customer and a consumer. Students of the emerging social sciences, from Le Bon to Ortega y Gasset, were full of foreboding at this process, while others clearly appreciated that the 'pariahs of history' were a reality that had to be reckoned with. Thus were born those emancipa-tory approaches – above all, Marxism – which ascribed to the masses a positive role and, indeed, a historical mission.

A well-known exponent of political psychology, Jon Elster, has recently proposed a new hypothesis in respect of the link between the individual and the masses, which he has called 'methodological individualism'.[2] In his view, the basic building blocks of social phenomena are individual actions undertaken by rational, individual actors. Elster regards social class as illusory, claiming that the participants in historical movements are neither classes nor groups. At first sight, Elster's claims appear diametrically opposed to those of Marx and his followers, who have consistently regarded classes as

---

1   The term 'saints of the streets' or, more properly, 'holy youngsters' (*szent suhancok*) was coined by Tibor Déry. In the 2 November 1956 issue of *Irodalmi Újság*, Déry wrote, 'It is said that this is the revolution of youngsters. From today, youngsters are saints for me.'
2   Jon Elster, *Political Psychology*, Cambridge, 1993.

history's chief actors. Closer scrutiny, however, suggests that both approaches are reductive, although from opposite directions. Marx claimed that the interests of the masses of wage-workers were so uniform that individual intentions and motives could be safely ignored – the community created on the basis of shared interests necessarily forms a united front against oppression and exploitation. The limitations of this theory have been frequently pointed out, for, as Marx's critics have indicated, globalized, multi-national wage-workers are plainly incapable of uniting and of communally protecting their interests, not least because of their religious and linguistic differences. By this measure, cultural difference trumps class solidarity. It may well be that in political discourses quite unrelated to Marxism, in today's 'pop social sciences', there is often talk of 'population', 'public' and 'masses' in an anthropomorphized sense, as if each of these possessed its own thoughts, taste, and ability to take decisions. Nevertheless, Elster bridges the dichotomy between individual and group only at the rhetorical level. It may be true that at the materialistic level at which rational agents operate, the actors are individuals, but the essence of revolutions and social earthquakes is precisely the repetition of unitary, singular actions which coalesce and lend the group collective influence on events affecting (and effecting) the broader community. As we hope to show in what follows, the memories and statements of those who took an active part in the 1956 Revolution confirm that this is what they experienced in joining the Revolution.

The purpose of our essay is to present the participants in the 1956 Hungarian Revolution. There are special reasons for selecting this event. A feature of the 1956 Revolution was that it had goals and slogans that were essentially identical in several segments of society, yet the activity of the various segments was not integrated, and indeed, on occasions, efforts and actions came into conflict. Gyula Kozák goes so far as to speak of three revolutions: (1) a political movement of intellectuals, (2) organized actions by organized workers, and (3) an uprising on the streets.[3] While it is not our intention to argue for or against this schematization, it is beyond doubt that on 23 October 1956, at the moment that general dissatisfaction erupted both in Budapest and elsewhere, a genuinely mass uprising took place spontaneously on the streets.

Another special feature that marks out the history of the 1956 Revolution as suiting the micro-historical approach is its nearness to us in time: a large number of documents and many witnesses are still accessible. Over the last few years, we have documented the history of the various rebel groups in Budapest, recording biographies and memoirs. We have published the biographies of over 400 participants in some detail: 158 from Széna Square, 261 from the Józsefváros, 57 from Ferencváros, as well as information on over 1000 active participants. Our work has antecedents, especially in the publications of Gyula Kozák, who in an article published in 1999 certainly tries to bring the participants to life. If the reader knew nothing of 1956 but this, he would probably condemn the Revolution and its participants. In Kozák's view, the most important psychological precondition of those who took part in the uprising was anomie, in the sense developed

---

3   Gyula Kozák, 'Szent csőcselék', in É. Standeisky and J.M. Rainer (eds.), *Évkönyv 1999*, Budapest (1956 Institute), 1999, pp. 255–282. On-line version: <http://www.rev.hu/html/hu/kiadvanyok/evkonyv99/kozak.html> [accessed 19 April, 2007].

by Robert K. Merton.[4] We agree with György Forintos[5] who does not consider the anomie model used by Kozák appropriate either for Hungarian society in the 1950s or for those who rose against the political system. Forintos raises basic issues which are difficult to handle within a psychological framework, and which arise from the elevation of conformism to a social aspiration of a general and positive kind. Forintos has a more nuanced view of Kozák's three, parallel revolutions: he is convinced that all three movements were the consequence of a general dissatisfaction that forged a national unity in the face of intolerable political circumstances.[6]

The descriptions used by Kozák in his psychological profile of the freedom fighters are also unfortunate. 'A casualty of intergenerational mobility', 'his primary socialization was stunted', 'unsuccessful', 'deeply frustrated', 'an unbalanced personality', 'chaotic family life' – to mention only a few. (For Forintos these labels are 'troubling'). The fundamental weakness of Kozák's study is the application of a typical intellectual preconception concerning the motives and behaviour of the 'holy mob' which are widely found in such classic texts as those of Le Bon and Ortega y Gasset. By this measure, the masses participating in revolutions and movements act 'instinctively', emotionally, while being hardly aware of (and being certainly incapable of understanding the complexity of) the values and goals articulated by political leaders and the more educated participants. This stereotype also provides the lens through which the masses and the freedom fighters may be viewed as a homogeneous mass and as some sort of anthropomorphic 'monster'.

Here we are concerned with unravelling the circumstances that led people to take part in the Revolution. In what follows we attempt a more nuanced and accurate portrait of the personal world of the freedom fighters and of their motives, using biographies, analyses of the dynamics of group-formation, and the events of the uprising. The chief questions to which we seek answers are: what were the true motives of the people who risked, and often gave, their lives in the Revolution? What factors made it impossible for them to conform and give in?

The events in brief

In the international easing of tensions that followed the death of Stalin, the Soviet party leadership removed the by now unpopular Stalinist party leader Rákosi. The new leader, Imre Nagy, radically cut back major investment and the forced collectivization of agriculture, and took significant steps to restore legality. By the end of 1954 the international atmosphere had cooled significantly and this helped Rákosi back to power. The Stalinists were not, however, able to restore earlier methods, and an opposition of writers, journalists and teachers supporting Imre Nagy continued to gain ground. A

---

4 See thus Robert Merton's seminal 'Social Structure and Anomie', *American Sociological Review*, 3, 1938, pp. 672–82.
5 György Forintos, 'Modell és valóság. Észrevételek Kozák Gyula "Szent csőcselék" c. esszéjéhez', in Zs. Kőrösi et al, *Évkönyv 2000*, Budapest (1956 Institute), 2000, pp. 338–369.
6 Forintos, 'Modell és valóság', p. 359.

turning point came with Khrushchev's anti-Stalinist 'secret speech' in February 1956, and the Poznan workers' rising. The final death rattle of the weakened dictatorial state, which had been riven by internal conflict for many years, came in October 1956, when the victims of the most prominent show-trials, László Rajk and his colleagues, were ceremonially re-buried.

The crowd of 100,000 that attended amounted to a silent protest against Stalinism. On 22 October news came of political struggle in Poland and the defeat of the Stalinists. The students at the Technical University of Budapest now formulated demands under sixteen headings which were considerably more radical than earlier ones (removal of Russian troops, free elections, economic independence) and the following day they initiated a protest march in support of their demands and to express solidarity with the Poles. The students' march on 23 October was joined by large segments of the population, now demanding independence and democracy. Imre Nagy's speech in parliament proved ineffective, and the radicalizing throng pulled down the statue of Stalin and demanded that the students' points be broadcast on the airwaves. The secret police defending the radio building reached for their weapons and the protesters rapidly turned into freedom fighters. The Stalinist wing of the party sought military assistance from the Soviet Union, which gladly obliged. Armed Soviet units appeared on the streets in the early hours. Imre Nagy, who was concerned about further radicalization of the masses, accepted the prime-ministership he was offered. In the course of these days the party-state crumbled away throughout Hungary and, after the protests, the organs of the old apparatus were replaced by revolutionary and national committees and workers' councils. In the cities and villages every organized body agreed with the main goals of the Revolution, with independence and democratization, while preserving social achievements. As 24 October dawned, (mainly) small groups of freedom fighters were formed under the direction of commanders, using arms and petrol taken from the police, the army, as well as barracks and stores, predominantly in working-class districts past which the Soviet forces had marched. The majority of the population supported the groups, membership of which changed almost by the hour. The total number of freedom fighters must have been about 15,000. Its members were mainly young workers, and unskilled men, whose sufferings under the Stalinist system had left them embittered and humiliated. Of the older ones, many were returnees from the Soviet labour camps. Most of them supported the revolutionary demands. Having endured eight years of terror, they took arms to bring an end to dictatorship and to fight for the independence of the country. The vast majority wanted a rather hazily defined 'true socialism' and rejected any kind of restoration of Stalinism. Others joined the freedom fighters out of a sense of adventure, to own a weapon, perhaps with an eye to a future career. Their activity – especially in the first days of the Revolution – was largely spontaneous, for those who took part in the fighting were by no means the most aware and best informed strata of society.

The Soviet forces were surprised that the spontaneous recruits, often teenagers, not only dared confront them but even inflicted serious damage on the armed soldiers who ventured into houses. The most effective weapon of the freedom fighters was the petrol bomb known as the 'Molotov cocktail' with which they blew up, one after the other, armoured vehicles and tanks. A number of centres of resistance sprang up in the capital consisting of workers, unskilled men and apprentices and trainees. Of course, there was no shortage of 'daredevils' but faith in the truth and the heroic struggle for liberty proved irresistible to virtually everyone. Even threats of martial law failed to get them to put down their weapons. Their resolution and stamina proved vital to the temporary victory of the Revolution.

In the early hours of 4 November, Russian forces launched a massive attack on Hungary. In Budapest it took them just a week to overwhelm the heroic freedom fighters. Imre Nagy and his supporters sought refuge in the Yugoslav embassy. Although the Revolution had failed, throughout the country, mainly thanks to the workers' councils, political resistance held out until the beginning of 1957. Almost 200,000 people left the country and severe reprisals began.

The Budapest freedom fighters of 1956

Understandably, not everyone is able or willing to fight, weapon in hand, even for the most noble of causes. Important differences exist as far as risk-taking is concerned in terms of people's personalities, gender, and age. As in every historical upheaval, in the 1956 Revolution too, those most willing to take their chances in dangerous situations were those with relatively less to lose: young people and those on the periphery of society. None of this, however, affects anything of importance. At turning points in history, roles present themselves and are filled largely by those able to reconcile the role with their personalities. While we hope that the extensive sources at our disposal will give us a better understanding of those who took part in the Revolution, we should say at once that it is not our intention to sketch the personality of the 'typical freedom fighter'. We are certain that active participation in progressive movements and revolutions, the willingness to take risks, is a personal, moral decision by each individual, the particular ethical value of which derives from this fact.

First we should like to offer some statistics. Taking the total number of participants to be some 15,000, data is available on some 1,500 people, that is, about ten percent. While this 'sampling' is less than systematic, we have no reason to think that it is distorted, for much of the data that has survived is random. (The amount of data on each person varies: sometimes nothing more than the 'codename' is known and some dates of birth are uncertain, so the totals in the various columns do not always correspond). Since we have brief biographies of 435 freedom fighters, as well as the record of the interrogations in the trials and more recent, in-depth interviews, this amount of data is at least enough to give a picture of some essential features and the social background of the participants.

It is often said of those who took part in the Revolution that an *unusually high proportion were young people*. Almost every participant mentioned this as of importance. From the interviews and the trials we know that this was a matter of concern to the adult participants: during the revolution it frequently came up in the freedom fighters' discussions with the representatives of the government that it was essential to disarm those under the age of eighteen.

Table 1: The age of those documented as participants (reliable data only for 1113 people)

Year of birth	before 1910	1910–1920	1920–1930	1930–1937	1938 and after
Ferencváros	6	14	49	64	40
Széna Square	13	39	65	95	71
Józsefváros	18	41	179	254	165
Total	37	94	293	413	276

A separate column shows those who were eighteen or younger in 1956. As can be seen, at the time of the Revolution the bulk of the participants, some 689 people in all, were 26 or younger, and more than a third of these were eighteen or younger. (The youngest cohort was born in 1942; there are about ten of these fourteen-year-olds.)

The relationship of minors to war and politics is a sensitive issue both for political history and for psychology, though unfortunately the conjunction is by no means rare. The willingness of young boys to take part in mass movements is also linked to their sexual and personal development. Young people who have acquired the ability to follow rules and reached the fullness of their intellectual abilities tend to be more sensitive to injustice and unfairness. Furthermore they are significantly less afraid of death and more willing to take risks. This attitude is clearly mirrored in the memories of our interviewees:

> I was young, not much given to reflection. In the sense that, as I said, I didn't consciously consider that I might die. Although before I said I wouldn't go in case they shot me dead. And from the moment I got there, I simply never gave it a thought, that I might get killed. As if I had complete immunity from the guns. So, that's how I was. And from beginning to end, from 23 October to 7 November, I had not the slightest sense of fear. Why that should have been so, I have no idea. (interview with Pál Kabelács)

It must be remembered that it was only a decade or so since the end of the Second World War. The experience of war makes the use of arms seem more natural, more acceptable, relativizing the value of life. Witnessing the terror of the postwar years, experience of the internal exile system and the forced labour units, had a similar effect on children and young people:

> Look, these kids lived through the siege of Budapest [in 1945] and the 1950s. So it was not because I was only sixteen. We grew up in this, we got used to it, used to people dying around us. How many died at Galánta in the War? This was a generation that [...] there was shooting. Well, there had been shooting before. It never crossed our minds that it might be dangerous. (interview with Péter Czajlik)

In reality, however, beyond these general points, the most important factors influencing the willingness of young people to take part was a sense of frustration and the attempt to find a political identity, factors to which we shall shortly turn.

The majority of the participants were *men*. Of the 267 participants registered from Ferencváros, there are 23 names of women; in Széna Square they are 31 out of a total of 384, while in the Eighth District women amount to 100 out of a total of 1,202. It is well known that women are notably less willing to participate actively in acute, weapon-ridden conflicts. From the description of events and from the more detailed life-stories, it is evident that women carried out mainly auxiliary tasks, patching up the wounded and preparing food. Mention of younger women actively taking part in armed fighting is most unusual. An exception is Mária Wittner, although there was at least one other woman, Katalin Sticker (Mrs Béla Havrilla), whose statement suggests she actively joined the struggle because she was impressed by Mária Wittner's bravery. Indeed, at the trial where she received a death sentence, she claimed she had fought mainly because of her close friendship with Mária Wittner and not because of her political convictions. Erzsébet Márton, another active female participant, informally headed a fighting unit and in this capacity took part in the capture of György Marosán, although we are not aware if she actually took part in the armed fighting.

Important information is provided by the *place of birth and origins* of the participants. Although this information is unfortunately lacking for one-third of the sample, it is striking that less than half were Budapest-born. Even in the 8th District, the out-of-towners are in a slight majority, even if we treat the (then still autonomous) areas of Újpest, Soroksár and Pesterzsébet as part of the capital, while in Széna Square only one third of the people were locals (here a significant role was played by miners from the provinces). We have little information on when individual families moved to the capital and whether close relationships had been formed among the young people before the Revolution, which might have encouraged them to join in. The regions from which the families of the freedom fighters moved to the capital reflect aspects of Hungarian life that are still important today. While few came from Transdanubia (western Hungary), many came from parts of historic Hungary that had been absorbed by the neighbouring states. For example, the well-known Gergely Pongrátz came with five of his siblings from Szamosújvár/Gherla (Romania), but there were others born in Nagyvárad/Oradea, Kolozsvár/Cluj (Romania), or Beregszász/Beregovo (Ukraine), while some were born as far afield as Brussels, Barnaul (southern Russia), Plzeň and Skopje. The Greek immigrants form a distinct group, many of them having settled in Hungary as children while the parents ended up elsewhere. Between three and five percent of the freedom fighters were Roma and differed little socially from the majority. Almost a third of the non-Roma participants were from large families of poor peasants and were employed as labourers or in other manual work. Of course, half a century ago the majority of those in employment carried out physical work, and manual labour, particularly if it involved special skills, enjoyed much higher social prestige than today.

Our research has already registered the *education and employment* data of the freedom fighters. Looking only at those of whom we have at least a biographical sketch, the various districts show broadly similar distributions. Of the 235 participants from the 8th district, about forty, of the 118 in Széna Square twenty-three, and of the 57 in Ferencváros nine had graduated from high school. As the eight-grade primary school system was introduced only in 1945, those born before 1932 had generally completed only six years of primary schooling, though the younger ones had mostly completed eight years. On the other hand, the figures on schooling from half a century ago must, like that on occupations, be seen in the context of the time. Although compared with the period immediately before World War II people were generally better educated and the percentage of those completing secondary and tertiary education went up, the total number of the latter was still rather small. The table below shows the major changes in the levels of education in the two decades before 1956.

Table 2

Year	Percentage of those of school age (6 to 14) attending school	Percentage of the population aged 15 or over completing 8 grades	Percentage of the population aged 18 or over who completed either secondary school or apprenticeship/ training	Percentage of the population aged 25 or over with a degree or degree-level qualification)
1938 (1941)*	78.8	15	5.1	1.8
1955/56 (1960)	97.6	32	9.1	2.8

*Some of the data refers to the years in brackets.
(based on J. Kardos & M. Kornidesz, *Dokumentumok a magyar oktatáspolitika történetéből, 1950–72*, Budapest, 1990).

The goal of those striving to reach the middle class was still the securing of a trade or craft, and almost a third of those in the Revolution had obtained, or were in the course of obtaining, such qualifications. That is to say, it is not necessarily correct to assume that the freedom fighters were recruited from the lowest strata of society. They had set out on the road to the middle class in significant numbers, expanding their horizons by exploiting opportunities to obtain skills and acquire crafts through study, and their attitudes to ways of life and political relations were significantly more self-conscious and critical.

The biographies and the origins of the freedom fighters suggest that those taking part in the Revolution came from the more *frustrated and disillusioned* strata of society. Nevertheless, even if in respect of the extent or effects of their frustration they formed a special group, as far as the sense of frustration is concerned they were far from unique. In the society of the 1950s, there was hardly a social group, stratum, or even family which had not endured a great deal of suffering in the course of the century. Apart from the human and political tragedy of the two world wars, in the interwar years many ordinary Hungarians, both the peasantry and the factory workers, had to endure the poverty and hopelessness of the Horthy regime. Hundreds of thousands of families mourned soldiers killed in fighting, while very many Jewish families were almost entirely destroyed by labour service and extermination. Witnesses and documents alike suggest that liberation in 1945 brought genuine optimism. Nor can there be any doubt that the long-suffering, seriously-deprived peasantry and workers welcomed the emancipatory slogans and the Left, which promised to eliminate poverty and inequality. Nevertheless, disillusionment set in quite quickly, as the 'buzz-words' were replaced by political terror and an unsustainable economy. Rapid industrialization and the serious crisis that developed in agriculture forced large masses to migrate to the cities and towns, where, though they might have found work, they encountered shortages of accommodation and goods.

The political and economic difficulties, the backwardness of the 1940s and its poor public health record naturally took their toll on lives and on relationships within families. Family planning was virtually unknown, many grew up in hopeless squalor in large families, and many children were born out of wedlock. Parents died in wars and through illness, or families were torn apart. Thus, although today the numbers of revolutionaries who were brought up in hostels, by foster parents or other relatives may seem to us rather high, such circumstances were much less exceptional fifty years ago. Nonetheless a difficult childhood full of problems and uncertainties still left its mark on the development and the identity of these individuals. The revolutionary movement, offering the experience of a multi-faceted community, served in many ways as a balm for these personal ills.

A few quotations by way of illustration from the childhood of the participants:

> I was born in 1930, in Pécs. My parents had Yugoslav nationality [...] I tried to find my parents, but without success. I haven't seen them since I was a child, I really don't remember them. I was fostered out and lived in Paks until 1945, as a servant in a peasant household. I don't want to go into it. (interview with László Schmidt)

> I was born on 23 March 1940, in Székesfehervár. My father worked for the state railways, he was an engineer in the MÁV Repair Workshop. My mother kept house. My father died in 1943, and a year later mother married A.R., who brought me up until 1948, when my mother died. She died of TB, which she caught when we were escaping [...] Escaping? We were getting out of the Russians' way [...] My mother was quite young, we had to hide for the obvious reasons. And she got TB. In those days they didn't have the medicines they have now, and she got ill. She died on 6 May 1948.' (interview with István Szigetvári)

Those whose families were seriously aggrieved were especially frustrated, though several biographies show that when a situation is utterly beyond hope, those who have been damaged prefer to withdraw and even become pro-actively conformist. But this places a heavy psychological burden on the young and when tensions explode things can easily swing over to the other extreme.

A typical example is András Kovács, who tells how his father, an army officer in the Horthy regime, was executed. As his father's trial was in progress, 'I joined the board of DISZ, the students' union, hoping I could influence the decision of the hooded executioner.'[7] Later he became a member of the Communist Freedom Fighters Association, and took part in the 1949 World Youth Jamboree. The Association gave him the opportunity to do target-practice. 'That was the main thing, to perfect my skills,' he explained, stressing that he was driven solely by thoughts of revenge.

Factors such as the prevailing social and political conditions and the sense of frustration felt by the population, as well as the role played by the conditions of the dictatorship, must also be considered when looking at the rather high number of those among the freedom fighters who had already clashed with the law and committed minor (or even major) criminal acts. Nonetheless, in the areas of education, culture and health important steps had been taken in the direction of modernization: there was compulsory schooling, kindergartens and nurseries, and the basic institutions of child protection and health were in place. The children's homes of the 1950s appear in a positive light in the memories of the freedom fighters. István Szigetvári, mentioned above, was so unhappy living with his relatives that he himself sought out the social services. Although he had a left-wing education in the children's home and before 1956 accepted without question

---

7   A reference to Zoltán Tildy.

all he had been taught, it was his meeting with the legendary hero of 1956, István Angyal, that made him join the armed uprising.

It is important to note that by this time there were media such as wireless and film which made it difficult to seal borders hermetically and thus restrict the influence of other cultures. It may be surprising that some young people were unhappy with their isolation from western cultural influences even as early as the 1950s:

> We young people did not, in fact, talk politics all the time; we were more upset that we couldn't watch western films, which were important to young people. And we couldn't dance the way we wanted to, we couldn't listen to western music, these were all taboo [...] all these stupid restrictions turned us against communism. Just because we were banned from there and the police took me in. We went to see films at the British and US Embassies. (interview with Gyula Táky)

The processes of modernization, which often precede critical movements and mass upheavals, are typically uneven. The horizons and cultural perspectives of the man in the street expand as improvements in demographic conditions favour processes of individualization, while individuals' living standards and participation in political decision making not only fail to improve but make it worse: being educated makes tyranny less tolerable and injustice more outrageous.

Aux armes!

We have tried in our earlier publications to draw attention to the fact that the armed groups, the freedom fighters, and their leaders all had their own special ambitions and goals.[8] Some made the demands of the students their own, some took arms because of their family's grievances, and there were undoubtedly people who were simply swept along by events:

> I was at home, late in the afternoon, in the flat, having something to eat in the kitchen and the lads all came in [...] On the estate, with the lads [...] One says: there's shooting in the city centre. Give over, you're having me on [...] But they really are. And then I heard the ambulance sirens. I didn't think anything. I saw in the dark that there was light flashing in town. Then they came and said he's going and so is he, they said come, and I said: no way, I'm not going to get myself killed. Then they went off. We went out to the edge of the estate, I keep hearing shooting. I could hear each round, the rattle of pistol shot – Good grief, I thought, I have to take a look. (interview with Pál Kalebács)

The many different human fates, a variety of aims and motives, suddenly, like the instruments in an orchestra, united in striking up a single harmony:

> It was the sound of the crowd, not of individual voices, everyone felt that his fellow man's thoughts were his own, added his own thoughts to it, and passed it on. It dawned on us, the people of the streets, that what each one of us thought separately was just what the other fellow was thinking, and this was a marvellous realization, that the complete stranger I have just met was thinking the same way as me. It was the realization that I was not alone, that I was not an isolated phenomenon. Then someone came up with the cry that we should get over to the Stalin statue. (interview with Mihály Nagy)

> The schedule for the afternoon of 23 October looked interesting. With Mara and Orsi, two of my friends, we agreed to meet at Calvin Square and attend the meeting of the Petőfi Circle. So I asked for

8   László Eörsi, *Ferencváros 1956*, Budapest, 1997; Eörsi, *Corvinisták, 1956*, Budapest, 2001; Eörsi, *A Széna tériek*, Budapest, no date.

a day off work. I turned up as agreed but there was no trace of my friends, though an unexpectedly large crowd had gathered in the square. In the middle of a knot of people there were speakers openly, loudly abusing the system, logically pointing out its failings and faults, of which there were certainly many. By the entrance to the Museum they were giving out ribbons in the national colours. Well, I no longer cared whether my friends were coming or not, as the temperature seemed to rise and the situation turned more and more serious. I asked for some ribbons and so did every other passer-by. Money was collected on the spot for more ribbons, so everyone could have some. (Recollections of Zsuzsanna Vízi [Mrs Alpár Bujdosó]).

Speaking out after long years of lies and enforced silence demolishes the walls erected between individuals by fear and tension, the community of fate becomes plain, as does the necessity and, finally, the possibility of joint action. For a historic moment the crowd is galvanized into a community which fulfils the desires and goals of the individuals comprising it and turns its members into a political fact. It is not instinct but the meaningfulness of joint action, now obvious to all concerned, that turns a mass movement into an uprising. It is this cross-over that results in the heroic taking to arms by the people, with its decisive influence on the course of the Revolution and the subsequent political ramifications.

Cautious Dissent, Reluctant Conformity: Young East Germans and the 1956 Revolution in Hungary

Alan McDougall

During the Hungarian Revolution, young people were at the forefront of protests against the hated Stalinist regime – and they paid a heavy price when Soviet tanks invaded and crushed all hopes of liberation from communist dictatorship. It was Hungarian students who first turned inner-party opposition into a more radical programme for change, via the Petőfi Circle, the re-creation of an independent student association, and the publication of detailed reform manifestos. It was, overwhelmingly, the working-class youth of Budapest who – hopelessly outmatched – led the armed struggle against Soviet military might in late October and early November 1956.

Elsewhere in the Soviet bloc, with the obvious exception of Poland, the political situation appeared much calmer – and youthful protests against Stalinism largely absent from the political radar. For a long time, this was the conventional view of the situation in East Germany in 1956.[1] Archival evidence released since 1989, however, shows that the reality was rather different. Neither the East German population in general nor its young people were as politically disengaged as was once believed.[2] Indeed, particularly in places of education, the East German communists faced substantial levels of youth dissent in 1956 – inspired in no small part by events elsewhere in the Soviet bloc, beginning with Nikita Khrushchev's 'secret speech' denouncing Stalin in February and culminating in the tragic events in Hungary during the autumn.

This essay examines the scope and intentions of youth protest in the GDR in 1956 within the wider framework of the Hungarian Revolution, paying particular attention to the ways in which events in Hungary impacted, and failed to impact, upon events in East

---

1   In fact, pre-*Wende* (i.e. pre-1989) studies written in the West tended to focus less on popular unrest in 1956 (widely considered to have been limited at best) than on the 'elite' opposition to Ulbricht led by reform-minded intellectuals such as Wolfgang Harich, Ernst Bloch, and Fritz Behrens during this period. See for example Karl-Wilhelm Fricke, *Opposition und Widerstand in der DDR. Ein politischer Report*, Cologne, 1984, pp. 117–28; Martin Jänicke, *Der Dritte Weg. Die antistalinistischer Opposition gegen Ulbricht seit 1953*, Cologne, 1964, pp. 104–19; and Martin McCauley, *The German Democratic Republic since 1945*, 2nd edn, London, 1986, pp. 78–87.

2   See for example the new insights on East Germany during 1956 contained in Mary Fulbrook, *Anatomy of a Dictatorship: Inside the GDR 1949–1989*, Oxford, 1995, pp. 187–90; Alan McDougall, *Youth Politics in East Germany: The Free German Youth Movement, 1946–1968*, Oxford, 2004, pp. 68–109; and Armin Mitter and Stefan Wolle, *Untergang auf Raten: Unbekannte Kapitel der DDR-Geschichte*, Munich, 1993, pp. 165–295. For a post-*Wende* work that still emphasizes the limits of 1956 as a crisis year (especially in smaller towns and rural areas), see Mark Allinson, *Politics and Popular Opinion in East Germany 1945–68*, Manchester, 2000, pp. 67–78.

Germany. A complex picture emerges, revealing that youth dissent in East Germany during the autumn of 1956 was both more extensive than previously imagined but also, for a variety of reasons, limited in its ultimate aims and achievements. Youthful rebellion did not come close to reaching the levels that it attained in Hungary at this time. But it was sufficient to trigger an existential crisis within the East German communist youth organization, the Free German Youth (FDJ), and to highlight the quiet but ongoing dissatisfaction of large sections of GDR youth with communist rule.

Though not to the same degree as in Poland or Hungary, 1956 can be considered a crisis year in the GDR. The economic situation – a major factor in the June 1953 uprising, the first major anti-Stalinist uprising in the Soviet bloc after the Second World War[3] – remained poor, with shortages of basic foodstuffs such as eggs, meat, milk, and butter still common. This was reflected in the large numbers of East Germans, especially the young, committing the treasonable act of 'flight from the Republic' (*Republikflucht*) and quitting the GDR for the 'golden West' during the mid-50s.[4] In political terms, particularly after Soviet tanks ensured the defeat of the predominantly working-class protests in June 1953, there was little room for manoeuvre. The ruling Socialist Unity Party (SED), led by the obdurate Stalinist Walter Ulbricht, did its level best to avoid any public discussion of Stalinism – or a possible programme of de-Stalinization – following Khrushchev's secret speech at the 20th Soviet party congress in February, during which the Soviet leader attacked his predecessor's 'cult of personality' and renounced some of his key ideological precepts (including the ideas that the class struggle intensified as socialism was being built and that the only road to socialism was the Soviet one).[5] 'So far as Stalin is concerned, dear friends,' Ulbricht's Politburo colleague Otto Grotewohl told students at Berlin's Humboldt University in April, 'the best thing is to pack everything into a big chest and drop it to the bottom of the sea.'[6]

Young people had particular cause to feel disillusioned with life in the GDR. The FDJ, the 'united youth organization' founded in 1946 to ostensibly represent their interests, was – like its Hungarian counterpart, the Union of Working Youth (DISZ) – authoritarian, ineffective, and widely unpopular, especially in schools and universities, where high membership levels generally signified no more than reluctant lip-service to an unloved creation. Pressures to conform to the increasing demands of the socialist state came not only from the FDJ, but also from a new secular 'confirmation' ceremony (the *Jugendweihe*), introduced in 1954 to further undermine church influence on the

---

3   For various interpretations of the June 1953 uprising, see for example Gary Bruce, *Resistance with the People: Repression and Resistance in Eastern Germany 1945–1955*, Lanham, MD, 2005; Torsten Diedrich, *Der 17. Juni 1953 in der DDR. Bewaffnete Gewalt gegen das Volk*, Berlin, 1991; and Gareth Pritchard, *The Making of the GDR 1945–53: From Antifascism to Stalinism*, Manchester, 2000, pp. 206–24. On the role of young East Germans in the uprising, see Alan McDougall, 'Young workers, the Free German Youth (FDJ) and the June 1953 uprising', in Eleonore Breuning, Jill Lewis and Gareth Pritchard (eds), *Power and the People: A Social History of Central European Politics 1945–1956*, Manchester, 2005, pp. 29–41.

4   Approximately 184,000 East Germans left the GDR in 1954, with the number rising to 253,000 in 1955 and again to 279,000 in 1956. See Hermann Weber, *DDR. Grundriß der Geschichte 1945–1990*, Hannover, 1991, pp. 296–9.

5   See Nikita Khrushchev, *The 'Secret' Speech of Nikita Khrushchev*, Nottingham, 1976, pp. 19–81.

6   Interview with Kurt Turba, 26 October 2000. Turba was the editor of the FDJ's student newspaper *FORUM* between 1953 and 1963 and a prominent supporter of reform in the GDR.

young, and in particular from the renewed, and deeply unpopular, campaign to increase 'volunteer' recruitment to the nascent East German army in 1955 and 1956.[7]

A sharper edge to these ongoing domestic problems in the relationship between regime and young was provided at this time by external events, beginning with Khrushchev's secret speech. As mentioned above, the SED leadership attempted to bury this speech as best as it could, arguing unconvincingly – just as the Rákosi-led hardliners in Hungary did – that de-Stalinization was unnecessary in the GDR, as Stalinism and its 'excesses' had never taken root there. All of the available evidence suggests the hopeless inadequacy of this head-in-the-sand approach and the powerful impact that Khrushchev's speech had on many young East Germans, who had been taught for years 'to stand up for the cause of Comrade Stalin' – as one FDJ secretary in the Berlin district of Prenzlauer Berg proudly declared – and were now suddenly being sung a different tune. There was widespread confusion, disbelief, and even anger at the turn of events, encapsulated in such remarks – made by young East Berliners – as 'we just cannot believe what is being said about Stalin' and 'now we don't believe anything at all any more'.[8] Evidently there was some truth in the SED education secretary Kurt Hager's observation that Khrushchev's revelations created 'a psychological crisis' among GDR youth.[9] They brought sharply into focus a number of issues – from Ulbricht's dictatorial style of leadership to the resurrection of a possible 'German road to socialism'[10] – that would remain on the agenda for much of the rest of the year and beyond.

Khrushchev's speech had more profound ramifications in Poland and especially in Hungary. It was events in these countries that dominated political discussion in the GDR during the second half of 1956. For the floundering FDJ, the sight of 'united youth organizations' in two fraternal countries – the DISZ and the Union of Polish Youth (ZMP) – dissolving themselves in the face of popular unrest (unrest often led by the very youth that they were trying to educate and control) was highly disturbing. For young East Germans the contradictory reports that they were receiving from the East German state media and the western media (especially about the 'counter-revolutionary machinations' in Hungary) were hard to reconcile and led to widespread criticism of the former's secrecy and outright lies. Indeed, inadequate domestic coverage of the dramatic events of 1956 did much to establish western radio stations as the primary source of information for GDR citizens during times of crisis.[11] The behaviour of Hungarian youths – prominent in the Petőfi Circle, in overturning the Soviet system of higher education in Hungarian universities, and in the street-fighting against Soviet forces that began in Budapest in late October – was meanwhile being greeted with a mixture of admiration, fear, and cautious criticism. Reports filed by the party and the

---

7   On the *Jugendweihe*, see Allinson, *Politics and Popular Opinion*, pp. 101–9 and Corey Ross, *Constructing Socialism at the Grass Roots: The Transformation of East Germany, 1945–65*, Basingstoke, 2000, pp. 136–8.On the unpopularity of the army recruitment drive, see Ross, *Constructing Socialism*, pp. 126–30 and McDougall, *Youth Politics*, pp. 71–2, 79.

8   McDougall, *Youth Politics*, p. 83.

9   Helmut Müller, *Wendejahre 1949–1989*, Berlin, 1999, p. 103.

10 The idea of a 'German road to socialism' had been first advanced by the communist party theoretician, Anton Ackermann, in 1946. For an eyewitness account of its content and impact, see Wolfgang Leonhard, *Die Revolution entläßt ihre Kinder*, Cologne, 1990, pp. 518–21, 546–8.

11 Allinson, *Politics and Popular Opinion*, p. 77.

FDJ from across the GDR in October 1956 repeatedly emphasized that 'in connection with the events in Hungary [...] great uncertainties exist especially among young people' ('great uncertainties' being an SED euphemism for 'unrest' or at the very least dissent).[12] Widespread and often openly stated youth sympathy for the Hungarian uprising reflected the strong sense of disillusionment and anger triggered by Khrushchev's secret speech earlier in the year.

Let us now examine in a little more detail the character and scale of youth unrest in the GDR during the autumn of 1956, focusing on three main issues. First, who was involved? Secondly, what sort of protest actions were undertaken? Thirdly and finally, what were the aims of the protestors? What limitations did they place upon themselves – and what limitations did they face from outside circumstances?

One former leading FDJ functionary, interviewed by the author in 1999, was adamant that the FDJ's only difficulties in 1956 were with the students.[13] But it might be more accurate to say that the regime's major, rather than only, problems were to be found on the GDR's university and college campuses. In contrast to the June 1953 uprising, when young workers were to the fore in industrial centres such as Berlin, Leipzig, Halle, Magdeburg, Bitterfeld and Görlitz, students took centre stage three years later. Khrushchev's secret speech – allied to domestic issues such as the ongoing restrictions on student travel to (and contact with) the West and the FDJ's continued unpopularity – had already encouraged student calls for reform during the early months of 1956. It was thus no surprise that the party line on events in Poland and Hungary was widely disputed when the new academic year began in the autumn. Particular attention was paid to the briefly successful efforts of Hungarian students to break with the DISZ – reforming their own independent student association, the Association of Hungarian University and College Unions (MEFESZ), which had been shut down in 1950 when the DISZ was founded – and challenge the Stalinist system of higher education, especially via the abolition of compulsory social science and Russian lessons in Hungarian universities.[14] The major points of the various Hungarian students' reform programmes (numbering 10, 14, or 16 from place to place)[15] – which included the withdrawal of Soviet troops from Hungary, freedom of the press, self-management in the factories, and democratization of the Hungarian youth movement – were apparently widely known and much discussed among students even in the distant north-eastern university cities of Rostock and Greifswald.[16]

Youth unrest was not, however, confined to the campuses, even if it found its main voice there. Party and FDJ reports recounted widespread incidents of dissent and misbehaviour in the GDR's schools during the autumn of 1956. Many young workers also baulked against the party line about 'counter-revolution' and 'White Terror' in Hungary, arguing that the unrest there was 'no putsch but a workers' uprising'. With

---

12 McDougall, *Youth Politics*, p. 89.
13 Interview with Helmut Müller, 12 May 1999. Müller was a member of the FDJ's most powerful leadership body, the Central Council (ZR) secretariat, between 1955 and 1966.
14 See György Litván, *The Hungarian Revolution of 1956: Reform, Revolt and Repression 1953–1963*, London, 1996, pp. 51–2. The MEFESZ was officially (re-) founded on 16 October by students in Szeged.
15 ibid, p. 53.
16 McDougall, *Youth Politics*, p. 96. This SED report in fact refers to the 'fifteen points' of the Hungarian students' reform programme.

memories of June 1953 fresh in many minds, Soviet intervention in Hungary was seen not as proof of 'the principles of proletarian internationalism' (as SED propaganda put it) but as unwarranted and illegal intervention in the internal affairs of another state. Or, as young workers in one Berlin factory put it, 'the Russians are nice friends. They are shooting Budapest to pieces.'[17]

What sort of protests were undertaken by young students, pupils, and workers during the autumn of 1956? Most commonly recorded was verbal dissent – particularly about the brutal Soviet invasion itself (unfavourable comparisons to the concomitant act of Franco-British imperialism in the Suez were common), about the biased and quickly outdated East German media coverage of events in Hungary, and about the implications of events in Poland and Hungary for the GDR itself (manifested especially in a slew of 'negative' comments about 'the second Stalin', Ulbricht).[18] Anti-regime graffiti – anonymous, easily visible, and relatively risk-free – was also widespread. Particularly in schools, young people frequently refused to donate any money to officially organized 'solidarity actions' for socialist Hungary. Twelfth-class pupils at the Johannisthal secondary school (*Oberschule*), for example, stated simply: 'solidarity action for Egypt yes, but for Hungary no'. Another, somewhat less common form of expressing dissent – one that carried strong echoes of protests undertaken following the defeat of the June 1953 uprising – was the holding of 'minute's silences' for the victims of the Soviet invasion by pupils at schools in towns such as Zittau, Freital, and Dresden.[19]

The lengths to which a minority of young East Germans took their protests against the crushing of the Hungarian uprising – and their dissatisfaction with life in the GDR – can be seen in some of the more striking examples of what the SED regime termed 'special incidents' (*besondere Vorkommnisse*). These occurred in schools, factories, and universities, reiterating the fact that unrest in the GDR in 1956 embraced a wide cross-section of the youth population.

With studies of the East German education system during 1956 focusing primarily on the unrest in the universities, dissent in the schools has been somewhat under-reported. Yet during the Hungarian Revolution – as, to an even greater extent, during the crisis that followed the construction of the Berlin Wall five years later[20] – they constituted a thorn in the side of the communist regime. At the Salzwedel secondary school on 6 November, two days after Soviet tanks invaded Budapest, the all-female Class 12a undertook a minute's silence during a lesson. The class had come to school that day dressed in Hungarian national colours and had sat during lessons in three rows of green, red, and white respectively. A similar example – on the same day – came from a school in Leipzig, where all but three of the pupils in Class 12c came to school dressed in black, as an expression of solidarity with the defeated Hungarian uprising.[21]

In comparison to three years earlier, youthful working-class protests were largely subdued during the autumn of 1956, but they were not silenced entirely. This could be seen particularly in Magdeburg, one of the centres of unrest during the June 1953

17 ibid, p. 90.
18 ibid., pp. 90, 93.
19 ibid, p. 91.
20 ibid, pp. 145–6.
21 ibid, pp. 91–2.

uprising and the scene once again of widespread discontent in the autumn of 1956.[22] At the Dimitrov factory in the city, for example, approximately 25 or 30 young workers went on strike on 30 October in protest against the publication in the local SED newspaper of a statement by the factory's FDJ organization about events in Hungary. They only went back to work after a two-hour discussion with the FDJ secretary, during which they called for free elections throughout Germany and 'a change in the government' in the GDR and stated that 'in reality the counter-revolution has triumphed in Hungary.'[23]

At universities across the GDR, reform programmes circulated widely during October and November 1956. Common themes – following the Hungarian example – included the abolition of Russian and social science classes, reduced restrictions on travel to, and contact with, the West, and calls either to democratically reform the FDJ or to replace it with a students' organization. Things went furthest, arguably, in the medicine and veterinary medicine faculties at the Humboldt University, a particularly sensitive institution given its close proximity to the open border with West Berlin and student organizations there. Here democratically-elected student councils had replaced the FDJ leadership organizations in late October and the authorities were complaining of an atmosphere smacking of western 'parliamentary liberalism'. A clash between student protestors, among whom plans existed to carry out an anti-regime rally at the Brandenburg Gate on 1 November, and the state authorities was only narrowly averted – in part because of the threatened deployment of pro-regime workers' militias against the students ('then they can put their bones together again in their own hospitals', as one party report starkly warned) and in part because of the arrests of 'ringleaders' that followed the final defeat of the Hungarian Revolution in early November.[24]

We have now seen various examples – among various sections of the GDR's youth population – of the dissent that was inspired, or at the very least heightened, by events in Hungary during October and November 1956. It is important to recognize that even the relatively small-scale cases outlined above entailed great risk in an authoritarian dictatorship such as the GDR – despite the fact that, in the mid-1950s, the East German secret police (*Stasi*) still fell some way short of the grim ubiquity of spying and surveillance that it was to achieve during the 70s and 80s. The young protestors in the schools in Leipzig and Salzwedel or the dissenting medical students at the Humboldt University, for example, risked expulsion from educational institutions that would cause irreparable damage to subsequent study and career prospects in the GDR. The young workers at the Dimitrov factory in Magdeburg risked losing their jobs. They – and others like them – offered proof that a dissenting civil society had not yet withered entirely on the vine in the Soviet bloc's westernmost outpost.

What can we conclude as to the character and aims of these protests? Perhaps their limitations rather than their extent are ultimately most striking. Many of the forms of protest undertaken in autumn 1956, especially in schools and factories, were either relatively low-risk (such as verbal dissent or graffiti), passive (such as the observing of

---

22 See Fulbrook, *Anatomy*, pp. 188–9.
23 McDougall, *Youth Politics*, p. 92.
24 ibid, pp. 97–102.

minute's silences for Hungarian 'counter-revolutionaries'), or involved *not* doing something (such as refusing to donate money to socialist Hungary). Even in the universities, where protests were more pro-active, there were limitations that were both self-imposed and conditioned by outside factors.

In regard to outside factors, and in contrast to their counterparts in both Poland and Hungary, East German students were unable to tap into a wider pool of discontent in 1956. There was no anti-regime alliance of the intelligentsia and students with the workers in the GDR – and the party leadership did not implode as it did so spectacularly in Hungary.[25] This naturally limited the effectiveness of any sort of nationwide student protest 'movement': indeed, none emerged. In terms of self-imposed limitations, it is interesting to note that the widespread demand for the creation of a new student organization in October was often couched in consciously non-confrontational terms. Dissenting students at Greifswald University stated explicitly that their proposed 'socialist student association' was not directed against the FDJ, while their peers at the architecture college in Weimar justified their similar proposal with the comment that the FDJ was not in a position 'to guarantee the socialist education of the students'. History students at both Jena University and the Humboldt University did not even go this far, eschewing the idea of a separate student organization entirely and confining themselves to calls for leading FDJ functionaries to be directly elected by the students.[26]

The conciliatory nature of these demands stemmed from a combination of wariness about pushing the regime too far and genuine belief among many students in the continued viability of the (albeit reformed) socialist model – a 'Third Way' between Soviet-style communism and western capitalism that was also being advocated by Hungarian reformers at this time.[27] It is interesting to note that, for a brief time at least in late October, the SED Politburo gave serious consideration to the idea of creating a 'student council of the GDR', thereby ending the FDJ's monopoly hold on the organization and political education of young East Germans.[28] Though the plan was quickly shelved in the volatile climate of those days, it reveals how the events of 1956 triggered an existential crisis within the FDJ, at least in higher education. Unlike the ZMP or the DISZ, however, the East German youth organization survived the crisis unscathed and continued – despite renewed, and indeed more extensive, restructuring attempts in the mid-60s[29] – on its unreformed path until 1989.

In 1956, as in other crisis years of the Ulbricht era (such as 1953 and 1961, and to a lesser extent 1968), there was widespread dissent among various sections of the GDR's

---

25 Tensions certainly existed in the SED Politburo, primarily between Ulbricht and the somewhat more reform-minded Karl Schirdewan. But they were kept behind closed doors and there was nothing to compare to the schisms that so bitterly divided the Hungarian communist party during 1956. On the Ulbricht-Schirdewan rivalry, see Peter Grieder, *The East German Leadership 1946–1973: Conflict and Crisis*, Manchester, 1999, pp. 108–59 and (for its impact on youth policy during the mid-50s) McDougall, *Youth Politics*, pp. 73–5.

26 McDougall, *Youth Politics*, pp. 99–100.

27 On 'Third Way' ideas in the GDR during 1956 (particularly those of Wolfgang Harich), see Grieder, *The East German Leadership*, pp. 109–10. On the 'Third Road' in Hungary, see Litván, *The Hungarian Revolution*, pp. 128–9.

28 McDougall, *Youth Politics*, pp. 100–1.

29 ibid, pp. 153–63. See also Alan McDougall, 'The liberal interlude: SED youth policy and the Free German Youth (FDJ), 1963–65', *Debatte: Review of Contemporary German Affairs*, 9, no. 2, 2001, pp. 123–55.

youth population, undermining older assumptions on both sides of the Iron Curtain about the political conformity of young East Germans (and the GDR population more generally). But ultimately this dissent was, even among the students, localized and fragmented. The majority of young malcontents – in the shadow of the crushing of the June 1953 uprising and with fresh evidence of Soviet brutality in Hungary now at hand – self-consciously limited the scope of their 'anti-state' behaviour, avoiding offences upon which the SED regime was likely to come down most heavily (such as strikes, protest rallies, or any sort of political activism on the scale of that undertaken, briefly, by the Petőfi Circle in Hungary) and contenting themselves with less dangerously provocative actions such as verbal dissent, graffiti, and moderate reform demands. Here we see the mixture of cautious dissent and reluctant conformity that coloured much of youth life in the GDR, where a pattern of 'conformity and grumbling' (*Anpassung und Meckern*) was clearly emerging among large sections of the population by the mid-50s.[30]

Youthful protest against the Soviet invasion of Hungary – and youthful solidarity with the Hungarian Revolution – was relatively widespread in the GDR during 1956. But the unmistakeable air of tension and expectancy was offset in many places by resignation and scepticism about the real prospects for change, both at home and abroad. A frequently posed question by young people was 'why have Poland and Hungary drawn no lessons from our 17 June...?'[31] It serves as a salutary reminder of both the limited scope for protest at this time in East Germany and the extent to which events in Hungary unfolded in a manner unthinkable in the GDR, where Stalinism had been imposed with less brutality, where Ulbricht (though widely unpopular) was not the hated figure that Rákosi was, and where young people – in contrast to their Hungarian peers – ultimately felt unwilling or unable to turn undercurrents of dissent into a serious challenge to the communist status quo.

---

30 See Fulbrook, *Anatomy*, p. 139.
31 McDougall, *Youth Politics*, p. 94.

Revolution in Hungary 1956: Failure and Success

György Schöpflin

Revolutions are extraordinarily difficult to define consistently. We sort of know what they are, but all comparative work on revolutions tends to flounder when attempting to find their common structural features. We agree that revolutions include: (1) regime change, (2) discontinuity, (3) new modes of legitimation and legality, and (4) relatively rapid change, but it is unclear when a revolution can be said to be finished.

Then, must a revolution be successful to count as one? The French Revolution was followed eventually by the Restoration, including that of the monarchy, but it enrooted a very deep republican tradition that could not be undone, as well as a certain acceptance of the role of the crowd in politics – this was visible even in 2005. Restoration was even slower in the case of the Russian revolution, though by now the difference between Putin and Rasputin seems to be narrowing. So what we can say is that a revolution that is more than a putsch must involve the following: radical change and spontaneity; a political project and a legacy; (some) irreversible consequences; and mass mobilization

The Hungarian events of 1956 are all the more interesting because a large number of non-Hungarian commentators deny their status as a revolution and call what happened an uprising, something they would clearly never do with the French revolution – 'the French uprising of 1789' sounds distinctly idiosyncratic. Why this should be so in the case of 1956 is not at all clear at first sight, but it could be explained by the interaction of several factors. In the first place, there is ignorance, which is never to be underestimated: the inability or unwillingness to consider the distinction between revolutions and uprisings. Then, there is denial, because in western thinking, especially left-wing thinking, revolutions are positive, progressive and morally good. Yet the Hungarian revolution took place against a left-wing regime and was ignored by many – although not all – on the left as an uncomfortable anomaly. A.J.P. Taylor's analysis that the choice was between 'clerico-fascism' and the Soviet invasion was not that unusual.[1] Next, there is a residual guilt felt by western commentators at having abandoned Central and South-Eastern Europe to the Soviet Union. The western left was always ready for this, as witness its distaste for Solidarity in 1981. Ultimately, though, 1956 has been neglected because it does not fit pre-determined categories of thought. It was, or could

---

1 See thus A.J.P. Taylor, *A Personal History*, London, 1983, p. 214: 'It seemed to me that the movement for liberty was falling into the hands of the Hungarian reactionaries who had supported Horthy. Better a Communist regime supported by Soviet Russia, I thought, than an anti-Communist regime led by Cardinal Mindszenty. Hence my conscience was not troubled by the Soviet intervention. Everything I have seen in Hungary since then confirms my belief that I was right.'

be so characterized, as both left-wing and right-wing, as both national and European in its implications. It raised tacit questions of national liberation in Europe at a time when de-colonization was in the air outside Europe. It was both democratic and egalitarian. It was also to an extent a factor of major inconvenience for both the Soviet Union and the United States, because it disturbed the post-Yalta dispensation and took the US's roll-back rhetoric at its word. This was, as we now know, a major error. And on top of all this, Hungary 1956 appeared to have no palpable consequences. The Cold War persisted, the Russians were shown to be beastly, the Hungarians were heroic (or irre-sponsible, take your pick!) and not to mention Hungary having to redeem itself for having been Hitler's last satellite. In any case, the West considered itself to have fulfilled its obligations by giving to shelter to around 200,000 refugees.

In Hungary, of course, 1956 was always understood to have been a revolution or a counter-revolution, but a 'counter-revolution' still recognizes the revolutionary quali-ties of what happened. The collapse of the Kádár regime in 1989 turned precisely on this point.

What are the reasons why, fifty years later, the events of 1956 can still be seen as having a revolutionary significance. A number of special features may be identified. First, the events had the quality of both speed and acceleration. What was unthinkable one day became the norm two days later. There was an extraordinarily rapid shift in perspectives. Secondly, there was the element of spontaneity: no one set out to make a revolution; there was no plan, and there was great fluidity in which none of the actors could see the consequences of their actions. Thirdly, the revolution completely elimi-nated the ancien regime. If a *tabula rasa* is ever possible, then Hungary 1956 came close to it. The communists lost all their legitimacy and had no means of regaining it, other than re-establishing their power by force. Fourthly, the programme of the revolution was radical and innovative. Bill Lomax has stressed the workers councils as the core of the project,[2] but that is not the whole story. A variety of new institutions was thrown up by the revolution, the central feature of which was extensive popular participation, which was unsurprising given the total exclusion of the population from all political action during Stalinism. These institutions included street demonstrations, self-manage-ment (territorial as well as work-place), a voice given to all who sought it, and the return of the multi-party system, ie. representative democracy. How direct and representative democracy would have worked in practice, how they would have fitted together, we just do not know, because there was never a chance to make it work (I am sceptical myself). Fifthly, national, social and civic unity was remarkably far-reaching. Class differences were (briefly) forgotten, likewise urban-rural, old-young and other cleavages. Beneath this was a striking concept of social harmony, which would not have lasted. Note that something similar underlay Czechoslovakia 1968 and Poland 1980–81. Finally, the European significance of 1956 was to demonstrate that communism was not what it claimed to be; it was neither consensual nor democratic, but rested instead on violence. At the same time, it could be overthrown – this was a message that Europe found diffi-

---

2   Bill Lomax, *Hungary 1956*, London & New York, 1976; Lomax (ed.), *Hungarian Workers' Councils in 1956*, Boulder & New York, 1990.

cult to accept and understand. For many, communism was there for ever and, even in 1989, they were reluctant to accept the proposition that it could disappear.

The Hungarian revolution was put down by force and in this sense it was widely seen as having failed, but that did not mean that it had no long term effects. 1956 deeply traumatized both rulers and ruled. They both tacitly recognized certain boundaries with respect to each other in consequence. The Kádár regime, once it had begun to mature in the 1960s and had recovered from the initially devastating shock of the revolution, was designed in such a way as to ensure that the population would accept the inevitability of communist rule, would stay out of politics for good, and would remain demoralized. The population, reluctantly at first, accepted that its high hopes of 1956 would have to be abandoned in exchange for relative economic well-being and for some retraction of coercion from everyday life. By the late 1960s, the Kádár system was ready to make a distinction between political crime and political error, that there would be a right not to identify oneself publicly with the regime, but to stay silent, though this 'right' was not to be understood in any legal sense.

The underlying deal was that the party would retain its monopoly of political initiative and action, for fear of a resurgence of revolutionary aims, that 1956 itself would be removed from the public sphere (the euphemism 'the unfortunate events of 56' was devised), that there could be no question of press freedom or questioning the leading role of the party or of Hungary's connection with Moscow. The system worked well for a time in its own terms. It substituted political stability for political legitimacy – shadow for substance – and functioned as long as all involved were prepared to accept this. The sociological outcome, a partially intended consequence of the original design, was the emergence of a sizeable section of society with a vested interest in the system or at least in something that would continue to guarantee the benefits of the system.

In this sense, the depoliticization pursued by the regime brought into being a depoliticized barrier that one could breach only at some risk to the system itself. Since change is always destabilizing and has unforeseeable consequences, so the Kádár system's quest for stability became conservative and, over time, even stagnant, with narrowing perspectives. Yet society changed and the world around Hungary changed too – most significantly, with the arrival of Gorbachev, whose perestroika was a seriously unwelcome development for the ageing rulers of the later Kádár years.

These rulers, furthermore, were incapable of renewing their legitimacy, not least because they could not even see the problem. Equally, renewed activism to relaunch an ideological party would breach the barriers set thirty years before, disturbing the stability of the regime. The Moscow connection also proved to be broken reed once the Soviet leadership embarked on a renewal process, for that necessarily removed the so-called Soviet pretext, to the effect that 'we would love to reform, but the Soviet comrades would look askance at that.'

The rulers of the Kádár system were in a political and ideological trap from which they could only escape by writing themselves out of the script. Stability no longer counted because it was taken for granted; communism as an ideology had decayed – few people took it seriously; and the Soviet Union was no longer a source of support. Equally, by the late 1980s, the elite, sensing that change was in the air, began to manoeuvre to acquire state property for itself.

Logically, therefore, from 1988 onwards, the system began to crumble, leaving behind a society that had become accustomed to a stability which looked more like changelessness, and which was politically very inexperienced, had no real knowledge of market conditions and only the vaguest sense of the relationship between democracy and freedom. The memory of 1956, then, was the central focal point as a symbolic event around which all could organize against the communist regime, and that included the reform communists. It is important to stress that this was exclusively symbolic. The trauma of remembered violence and devastation was alive and well in 1989 and it acted as a severe constraint on action. There was a kind of fearful determination that there would be no revolution in the sense of 1956. This also had the result that, as so often with a struggle for symbols, once the initial aim was gained, unity disintegrated and thereafter 1956 was contested between left and right.

In conclusion, failed revolutions never fail completely, but invariably have unintended consequences. In the case of Hungary, it resulted in a 'Sleeping Beauty society' that actually came to like its somnolence. It is from this perspective that 1956 had and has delayed effects that have shaped both rulers and ruled in the years of post-communism. The particular way of leaving communism, and it really was more like a quiet farewell than anything more dramatic, had virtually no popular input, quite unlike Czechoslovakia, for instance, or Estonia. The re-interment of Imre Nagy on the 16 June 1989, the nearest to a popular event, was carefully monitored, supervised and choreographed.

There existed a politically rather inexperienced counter-elite and a society that had very little understanding either of power or of governance. I suspect that many believed at the time that the end of communism as a system and mode of legitimation would bring with it a thorough-going transformation, in which those who had been excluded from power would now be able to exercise it. This assessment failed to reckon with the far greater political experience of the beneficiaries of the previous system, with their determination to preserve their privileges and to make their grab for state property, to maintain their networks, resources and so on, as well as their complete unwillingness to accept any form of democratic self-limitation or ethical constraints on action. They accepted only the minimum – the results of elections, the Constitutional Court and, to some extent, European disapproval.

From this perspective, it becomes understandable why 1956 is contested and why both left and right seek to own it. The left would like to derive its legitimacy from it for the present, as the heirs of a social revolution, and the right sees it as a democratic, national and anti-communist revolution. Though the 1956 revolution was put down by force – and it failed only in that sense – it lives on in various complex, indirect and sometimes distorted ways.

1956: Aftermath

The Afterlife of 1956 in the Open and the Silent Opposition: Some Personal Notes

Géza Jeszenszky

It is difficult to arrive at a general understanding on any country's recent history, but it is next to impossible to have consensus in Hungary in respect of its extremely turbulent twentieth century. The 'Revolution and Fight for Independence' of 1956 look like an exception, as since 1990 there seems to be unanimity about its heroism, significance and noble character. There is no agreement, however, as to whether it was basically socialist, syndicalist, liberal, or anti-communist.[1] On the personality of Kádár, strong disagreement is likely to continue for a long time.[2] As to the 33 years of the so-called 'Kádárera', most accounts agree that after about four years of brutal repression a 'thaw' set in and that Kádár successfully consolidated his rule by cautious liberalization, and especially by allowing more economic activity, so as to turn attention away from politics by filling the stomachs and encouraging consumption. When economic growth slowed down and the standard of living stagnated, the usual grumbling gave way to more open criticism. Most western observers (then and now) acclaimed what they called the 'dissidents' or the 'democratic opposition', consisting mainly of disillusioned Marxist philosophers, sociologists and a few released political prisoners, who published clandestine samizdat literature and critical writings duplicated for a rather small circle of intellectuals. The increasingly loud protests and worries of writers, poets, teachers and artists, who had hardly more illusions about the regime than the writers of samizdat, but

---

1   The 'Yearbooks' of the Institute on the History of the 1956 Revolution were the first to publish the results of unhindered scholarship on '56 in Hungary. The first definitive work on 1956 is B. András Hegedűs (ed.), *1956 kézikönyve*, 3 vols, Budapest, 1996. On the character of the revolution, see several writings by György Litván and János M. Rainer (the author of a two-volume biography on Imre Nagy), especially Litván, 'Mítoszok és legendák 1956-ról', in *Évkönyv 2000*, Budapest (1956 Institute), 2000, pp. 205–218. Cf. Frigyes Kahler & M. Sándor Kiss, *Kinek a forradalma?* Budapest, 1997. There is a short survey of post-1990 writings: Sándor Horváth, '1956 történetírása a rendszerváltás óta' in *Évkönyv 2002*, pp. 215–224, The number of books, articles, conferences, even films marking the 50th anniversary is impressive. A massive collection of documents edited by Attila Szakolczai, *1956*, Budapest, 2006, completes his authoritative work published in 2001. In the UK alone at least four books came out on the subject last year. Cf. Tibor Fischer, 'In the Goulash', *The Times Literary Supplement*, December 6, 2006; see also Eric Hobsbawm, 'Could it have been different?' *London Review of Books*, vol 28, no 22, 16 November, 2006.

2   What a contrast exists between the adulatory and deliberately provocative two-volume biography of Kádár by György Moldova, published in 2006, the serious and more balanced, but still sympathetic, work of Tibor Huszár (the second volume, covering the years 1956–89, also came out in 2006), and the thorough and impartial judgement by Roger Gough, *A Good Comrade: János Kádár. Communism and Hungary*, London, 2006!

did not want to risk losing their job or to jeopardize the possibility of publishing in officially approved organs, were seldom recognized as an opposition, and were lumped together under the term 'populists', a somewhat misleading translation of the word 'népi', i.e. one coming from the ranks of the ordinary people, most often from the peasantry. This categorization derives from differences in background, family and personal history, and looks even more valid in view of the years following the great transformation of 1988–90, when the first formed the nucleus of the Alliance of Free Democrats, and the latter that of the Hungarian Democratic Forum, which were the two main contenders at the free elections held in 1990.

Without questioning the duality of the emerging opposition to Kádár's version of communism (euphemistically called 'real' or 'existing' socialism) or the pre-eminence of the producers of the samizdats, I propose another approach, which takes into account the close relationship of the two groups throughout most of the 1980s, and gives a better explanation both for the unexpectedly rapid growth of the opposition movements in 1989, and the victory of the Centre-Right in 1990. My thesis is that after the extremely brutal suppression of the revolution, the spirit of 1956 did not entirely disappear to surface again only in the 1980s. Throughout the decades of Kádár's *counter*-revolution, I witnessed the existence of a silent, sullen opposition, and also, following the amnesty in 1963, a small, but growing open opposition. When, towards the beginning of the 1980s, in the wake of permanent economic crises, the dictatorship weakened and became disoriented, when internal and external developments removed some of the obvious barriers and the silence was broken, the two types of opposition came to the surface and naturally coalesced. In order to ensure, however, the victory of this united opposition a third internal factor was needed: the emergence of a reformist wing within the communist party. The banner which all the various versions of opposition raised was that of 1956.

I belong to a fortunate generation, unlike my forebears. One of my great-grandfathers fought in 1848/49 as a *honvéd* colonel against the Habsburgs and was sentenced to sixteen-years imprisonment, serving more than ten. My grandfather died in action in one of the first battles of World War I, and left his widow, a talented pianist, with two little girls to be raised on a music teacher's salary. I know of no one in the family history who did not detest the experiment with bolshevism, or who approved the 'white' reprisals. All were dismayed by the 1920 peace treaty and the legal dismemberment of Hungary; it ceded the birthplace of three of my grandparents to Romania. My parents and my wife's parents told me how their families lost their savings in war loans and in the post-war inflation, and the Great Depression also affected them seriously. My father was an Anglophile opposed to the Nazis and their Hungarian supporters; fortunately, he was too old to be sent to the front. My wife's grandfather risked his life in saving tens of thousands of Poles and allied prisoners-of-war. He was arrested by the Gestapo when in March, 1944, Germany occupied its reluctant satellite in order to prevent its defection. Many family friends were affected by the anti-Jewish laws and the deportations. I and my parents (like most inhabitants of Budapest) spent the six-week siege in the 'cellar'; our flat was hit and partly destroyed by a grenade. The Russian liberators took my father for a 'malenky robot', but took pity on his little boy, myself, and allowed him back. When the bank which employed my father was nationalized, he was sent into retirement.

In the 1947 elections my parents were unlawfully deprived of their right to vote. During the cruellest version of Stalinism under the dictator Rákosi, they lived in constant fear of arrest as a 'class enemy', or of being turned out of our flat and deported to a remote village. This did not, however, prevent my father committing the crime of listening to the BBC, Voice of America and Radio Free Europe.

I, the fortunate offspring, was just three during the siege, not realizing how close I was to death due to an illness. By the time I turned ten, I fully understood that I had to keep silent in school about many things I heard at home, and that the world around us was not friendly at all. Nevertheless, I still enjoyed playing with my friends among the ruins of the royal castle and in the bomb-craters of the huge Tabán Park nearby. And then I came of age on 23 October, 1956. At my gymnasium we had already been following with great interest the intellectual ferment of the previous months, and we were among the first at the Bem statue to express our sympathy with the Poles, who demanded an end to Stalinism. When I marched with the crowds to the building of Parliament and heard people demanding that the Soviet occupiers should return home, I knew that events had reached a point of no return. At the parliament building we waited for Imre Nagy for, it seemed, far too long, so my friends and I went on to the radio building to demand the reading of the sixteen-points of the students. And at nine in the evening I went home, knowing that I had failed to turn up for my private English lesson and that my parents must be very worried as to where their fourteen-year-old son was. So I missed the first shots. But in the following days I went around the town. I faced the machine-gun of a Russian tanker, but the young soldier spared my life. By sheer luck I did not happen to be at Kossuth Square during the massacre on the 25th. In the days following, I stepped over dead bodies sprinkled with chloride of lime, which lay in front of burnt-out cars and tanks, saw many buildings with all the floors on the ground, while the paintings remained on the walls. And then on 4 November, I woke up to the sound of Soviet guns taking away that liberty of ours which had made us so exuberant just a few days earlier. With such experiences it must have been natural that when everything was over and my class met again (for lack of heating) in the basement of the school, we unanimously adopted a motion refusing to recognize Kádár's puppet government. On the first anniversary of the Revolution my whole school staged a so-called 'silent demonstration', standing still and in dead silence during the breaks. Yes, one of my classmates cut the cord of the school radio, which tried to break the silence with loud music. A few weeks later, somebody betrayed him and he was expelled and not permitted to attend any school after that. Such a crowd of young 'counter-revolution-aries' was naturally banned from receiving higher education, by special order of the minister, Mrs. Benke. We had an additional crime: our history teacher and form master was a young man named József Antall. Antall was the head of the Revolutionary Committee of the Eötvös Gymnasium, was a member of the National Guard, and he had helped his father in reorganizing and running the Independent Smallholders' Party. He was also much involved in various rear-guard actions after 4 November. He was to be elected prime minister in 1990.

It is relatively well-known that passive resistance in the form of a general strike lasted almost until the end of 1956. Nevertheless, the brutal repression, involving hundreds being executed and thousands imprisoned, eventually seemed to have broken the back of the nation. On the following May Day, an apparently impressive crowd turned out at Kádár's mass-meeting at Heroes Square. It has become a widely accepted view that a kind of collective amnesia eventually overtook the nation. With most people conveniently forgetting how they felt during the October days, the memory of 1956 was kept alive only abroad, by and among the Hungarians who had escaped.[3] This thesis was challenged by a noted social historian, initiating a debate in a weekly periodical.[4] I can personally testify that the spirit of '56 did not die and it did not go into exile, but lived on in many minds and hearts in the Carpathian Basin. It was rather like magma, apparently frozen after a volcanic eruption, but smouldering under the crust, and bound to break out again, when the inscrutable interplay of forces allowed it to resurface.

Since 1990 and the restoration of freedom, there have been many, often heated, debates about who initiated the Revolution, what its aims were, and who may be entitled to claim its legacy. The basic debate is whether in 1956 Hungarians wanted to improve the socialist system, to make it democratic and genuinely representative of the interests of the common people, or whether it was an uprising against communism in favour of the restoration of multi-party democracy, and, by implication for the restoration of the market economy and private property. It is quite easy to cut through this debate. The 1956 Revolution had many different aims and factions, but in the short time allowed to it, these differences were blurred by one common aim: to replace the dictatorial system personified by Rákosi and Gerő. In 1956, the demand for change could only come from such institutions as existed, from the ranks of the Party and the youth movement, and the 'Petőfi Circle' and Writers' Association. Some of the speakers, the most outspoken critics, were former communists who had lost their illusions after the purges. But most still believed in the Marxist utopia, and thought that the problem lay not in the principle but in the practice and in the 'mistakes' made by Stalin and Rákosi. Both the disillusioned intellectuals and the students deserve credit for starting the Revolution and for steadfastly supporting Imre Nagy, not only in the glorious days of apparent victory, but also in the death-cell, or in the prison, and they preserved his memory for decades, even when Kádár's conduct appeared to have been justified. The non-communist, genuine Social Democrats (Anna Kéthly and her followers) as well as the Smallholders, Christian Democrats, Peasant (Petőfi) Party people and Radicals could speak out only after October 28–30, with the restoration of the multi-party system. The unity of all these factions, represented in the last government of Nagy, would not have survived the planned free elections, but they would have made up a good parliament, united in their opposition to the system embodied by Rákosi, Gerő, Révai and Farkas. Talking about the 'anti-Rákosism' of 1956 may be a more accurate term than 'anti-Communism', but we may agree that the spirit of '56 meant and still means opposition to totalitarian dictatorship, dedication to a multi-party democratic system and to a grass-roots democracy represented by revolutionary committees, the rejection of intolerance and anti-

---

3   Péter György, *Néma hagyomány. Kollektív felejtés és a kései múltértelmezés. 1956 1989-ben*, Budapest, 2000.
4   Gábor Gyáni, '1956 elfelejtésének régi-új mítosza', *Élet és Irodalom*, 45, no. 6, 9 February, 2001; György Litván, 'Az elnémult hagyomány', *Élet és Irodalom*, 45, no 15, 13 April, 2001; K. Zsolt Horváth, 'Ami személyes és ami kollektív', *Élet és Irodalom*, ibid.

Semitism, and, very emphatically, the desire for social justice and a decent life for every citizen.

Like St Peter in the Garden of Gethsemane renouncing Christ three times, millions of Hungarians felt compelled to renounce the Revolution and to repeatedly call it a counter-revolution. Some tried to avoid so doing by using ingenious terms like 'the unfortunate events of October' or 'the tragic days of 1956', but for the common people 1956 remained a landmark, and they kept talking of 'before the revolution', 'after the revolution', and so on. In much the same way few people ever used the term 'liberation' for 1945, but only spoke of 'the war' and 'the siege'. More importantly, society was intimidated into silence by the political trials and the harsh sentences imposed, as also by the knowledge that the host of informers, bugging devices and surveillance enabled the authorities to penetrate even one's thoughts. Many families refrained from talking about political questions even at home. The apolitical society was the deliberate creation of Kádár and his accomplices. But their 'success' was more apparent than real. In many families parents kept talking to their children, and there was open and often devastating criticism of Kádár and his policies at the workplace, and even more during parties, excursions, in the pubs, and not least in a large number of jokes. That was the only way of resistance – almost.

Historians have not yet done much work studying the political trials of the Kádár era after 'the great repression', 1957–61. The few exceptions are the publications of Frigyes Kahler,[5] Tibor Zinner,[6] and some local, amateur historians.

The personal account of László Vaczkó, the 'ringleader' of an 'armed conspiracy' in 1965, explains that the population of the villages and small towns[7] around the famous Somló winegrowing region were strongly opposed to communism after 1945, showed much enthusiasm in 1956, and suffered immediate retaliation.[8] They continued to denounce Kádár and his regime in their conversations in the wine-cellars and cottages on Somló Hill and also in the bauxite mines around the town of Ajka. Vaczkó, a young teacher at Devecser (born in 1933), and his friends met every year on 23 October in his vineyard to remember the Revolution. They gave themselves the name 'October Front', and hoped that international developments would soon bring communism in Hungary to an end. Their written programme called for a 'free, independent, democratic and neutral Hungary', where social justice would prevail. As the tenth anniversary of 1956 was approaching, they decided to remind their compatriots of the martyrs by sending out leaflets prepared on a toy printing press. Vaczkó also kept two pistols (one without ammunition) acquired in 1956, hidden in his vineyard. Starting with these postcards, investigators of the political police found and arrested the senders in early 1966. They were charged with 'armed conspiracy' and given very harsh sentences.[9] Miners at nearby Ajka, organized by János Hamusics, also hoped for international complications

5 Frigyes Kahler, *Joghalál Magyarországon, 1945–1989*, Budapest, 1993.
6 Tibor Zinner, *XX. századi politikai perek*, Budapest, 1999; idem, *A kádári megtorlás rendszere*, Budapest, 2001.
7 Particularly Devecser, the scene of one of the worst atrocities committed by Tibor Szamuely and his 'Lenin Boys' in 1919.
8 László Vaczkó, *Lángbaborult idő. Somló-vidék, 1956*, 2006.
9 László Vaczkó, *Virrasztótűz. Egy ellenálló mozgalom története*, 2002.

that would lead to a new revolution in Hungary. By blowing up the statues of Lenin in Budapest and Szombathely they hoped to raise the political awareness of the public, but found that carrying out their plan was practically impossible. As an alternative they blew up the railway-line at Városlőd, derailing a freight-train.

Kahler shows that the two cases were not isolated:

> The fourth statutory regulation of 1963, which brought to a legal end the greatest political retaliation in Hungarian history [...] granted amnesty to those who had participated in the revolution and had been imprisoned because of it. The Kádárian politics that followed did its best to try to obliterate memory of the revolution, and it did so successfully. Still there remained a small number of people who not only failed to forget the event but wanted to keep its memory alive and even continued the fight. *In the year of the tenth anniversary of the revolution, 991 persons were prosecuted on charges of (political) attempts against the state. This figure was 594 in the previous and 529 in the following year.* In 1966, political police discovered six so-called armed conspiracies. With one exception, all of these covered such acts as the printing of leaflets, while in one case miners with an anti-Soviet intent blew up a railroad. Papers describe two cases tried at the County Court of Veszprém. In the Vaczkó case, an 'armed conspiracy' of a number of village intellectuals who had distributed leaflets, the first defendant was sentenced to eight years imprisonment. In the Hamusics case, the death sentence was passed and carried out, while many of the miners who had been ready for an armed fight against the Soviet army got severe prison terms.[10]

Kahler's figures demonstrate that despite the very obvious dangers involved in any public criticism of the regime, the silence was occasionally broken, and that '56 was not conveniently forgotten. On the other hand the failure of the 'conspirators' to enlist more than a handful people in their small groups shows how successful the intimidation was, and the message of the extremely severe sentences (violating even the laws actually in force) was certainly understood.

These two trials (and less serious but similar cases) did not receive any publicity. On the whole, the 1960s (until the invasion of Czechoslovakia) were characterized by gradual improvements. In 1961 Kádár announced that 'whoever is not against us, is with us', thus reversing Rákosi's earlier threat. The amnesty announced in March 1963, set all the better-known political prisoners free, although many non-intellectual participants, mainly workers, who had been convicted as common criminals, were not released. But if one behaved in a 'reasonable way' and did not make any trouble, one was left alone, and reports on his or her activities and thoughts, collected by a host of informers (sometimes close friends or relatives), were just stockpiled. From the mid-1960s foreign travel was made possible – requiring however an exit visa, which was not issued automatically, but had to be applied for and supported by local communist officials. Intellectual restrictions were also eased, and the much publicized reform of the economic management system really raised expectations.[11] This was the time when many people who had been involved in 1956 but had escaped serious repercussions – professionals, especially those working in the technical professions (*műszaki értelmiség*) – felt entitled to make their own compromise with the apparently progressing regime, and joined the party. But for the *par excellence* intellectuals, those

---

10 Frigyes Kahler, '1956 szellemének megtorlása tíz év után. Vaczkó László és Hamusics János ügye', *Aetas*, 2006, no 1, 38–56 (my italics).
11 András Veres, 'Kis magyar értelmiségtörténet', *SzocHáló. Társadalomtudomány Online* <http://www.szochalo.hu/hireink/article/102035/1333/>.

engaged in the humanities, the suppression of the Prague Spring was a great disappointment and marked the end of the hope that a socialist utopia might still be attained. For
the rest, for the technical people and for the economists, who were growing both in
number and influence, the loss of illusions came a little later, in the early 1970s, when
Moscow ordered Hungary to scale down and cut back on its reformist mood. But the
Soviet model of arresting protesters, sending them into exile or into mental institutions,
was not followed in Hungary. A few trials and mild sentences were sufficient to indicate
that there were limits not to be ignored.

My classmates and I all started 'to build socialism' as manual workers, but after a
few years we were allowed to continue our studies, to acquire a degree, and to achieve
professional advancement. Most of the sons and daughters of the old middle class,
including those who had been turned out from their home and deported to remote
villages, became respected engineers, physicians and teachers. The modest economic
concessions allowed people to have second jobs and so to have a little extra income, or
to build a week-end cottage and thus escape from the dreary atmosphere of the workplace. Hungary acquired the reputation of being 'the happiest barracks in the communist
bloc'. The regime was so successful that eventually almost a tenth of the adult population joined the Hungarian Socialist Workers' Party. They did so, however, not out of
belief but out of opportunism, in the knowledge that membership was rewarded by
better pay, quicker advancement and higher positions. All this was a clever way of
corrupting society. The press, the film industry and many writers became accomplices.

The western media and politicians readily swallowed the bait and the despised Kádár
became an object of admiration. In Hungary itself knowledge of the growing prosperity in
the West spread; its affluence was much envied, leading to an incredible craving for
western goods, which became available at extraordinary prices in special shops or on the
black market – or by purchases while abroad. The only way to increase one's income was
by working overtime, having a second job, often moonlighting. One could save money by
stealing from public (that is state-owned) property: paper, clips, ribbon for type-writers
from the office; tools and petrol from the factory; and feed for the animals kept at the
household plot from the collective farm. The standard of living was growing slowly, but
steadily. 'Kicsi vagy kocsi', a baby or a car: that was choice in the 1970s, and most opted
for the latter. Few noticed that Hungary, like all the 'socialist' countries, was rapidly
falling behind in the race with the west. The general public lived in a fool's paradise.

I think there is consensus in the above picture, and since the 'system change' the
details have been diligently supplied by a younger generation of historians. It is a widely
held view that opposition to the Kádár regime was restricted to a few brave intellectuals:
the 'dissidents' of the western media, who became active in the wake of the Helsinki
Final Act, testing and challenging the conduct of the communist system mainly in the
field of human rights. I would be the last to question or underrate the activities of the
Hungarian samizdat writers. The fact that most of them came from communist families,
that they gradually lost their Marxist illusions,[12] and rebelled against the system which

---

12 The best examples are the writings of György Bence and János Kis, the most profound authors of samizdat
in the 1970s. Marc Rakovski (= György Bence and János Kis), *A szovjet típusú társadalom marxista
szemmel*, Paris (Magyar Füzetek 5), 1983.

their parents and relatives helped to build, went in my eyes only to their credit. The son of Rajk, the victim of Rákosi's purges, could certainly afford a far more critical attitude towards the regime than the descendents of the old middle class, but it still required great moral courage for the 'cadre-children' to denounce the crimes and follies of Kádár and his accomplices.

Most members of this emerging opposition were still children during '56, but old enough to have been influenced by it. Because of their family background they were, nevertheless, somewhat ambiguous in their interpretation of it. Although sympathetic to the revolution, they had misgivings about the crowd controlling the street.[13] They were enthusiastic about the Prague Spring, as it held out the hope of a democratic version of socialism. The conduct of the Soviet leadership, though unexpected, could not have come as a total surprise to the honest socialist, leftist advocates of 'socialism with a human face', but the participation of Hungary in the suppression was a great disappointment to them. Then in 1972–73, on the orders of Moscow, economic reform was curtailed, accompanied by a mildly anti-Semitic turn, and the disciples of Georg Lukács, as well as their students, the last believers of the socialist utopia, made their final break with 'Kádárism'. For a while, they still looked to Marx as a guiding spirit and a rallying-figure against the bureaucratic and authoritarian 'real socialism', and they looked down upon those writers and other public figures who played some role in '56 but eventually made their compromise with Kádár. The negotiations in Helsinki leading to the signing of the Final Act and the campaign for human rights were an important milestone in the emancipation of Central Europe. The example of Charter '77 in neighbouring Czecho-slovakia gave another push, and by the end of the decade the Hungarian dissident movement was born.

The progress of the young, idealist Marxist pilgrims to identify with 1956 and their gradual endorsement of 'bourgeois democracy' is well documented, as their writings (the later ones published only in samizdat) show.[14] On the other hand, it is next to impossible to give documentary evidence for the continuous survival of an anti-communist, non-Marxist, pro-western opposition in Hungary, with origins lying in the pre-war opposition (Smallholders, Social Democrats, liberals), and in the non-communist elements of the 1945–47 coalition government. In the last government of Imre Nagy they formed the majority, and it is most likely that if the Soviet intervention had not taken place, they would have become the majority in a free election. Unlike the disillusioned communist followers of Nagy, they (Tildy, Bibó, Göncz) received 'only' long prison terms, while the younger, less prominent ones either fled the country or escaped with internment, short-term arrests, regular police surveillance, and bad marks on their CVs. The attitude of those who remained at large was most probably as in the anecdote told by Ferenc Fehér, one of the most distinguished members of the 'Budapest School' of unorthodox Marxist philosophers. In a much quoted recollection he mentioned that his fellow-student and friend in the 1950s, József Antall, who had been an outspoken non-communist as a student during Rákosi's time (he even wrote a kind of samizdat

---

13 Ferenc Kőszeg, '1956: a magunk képére formált forradalom', *Beszélő*, 1997, no 7.
14 See esecially E. Csizmadia, 'A szamizdat szubkultúrája', *Budapesti negyed 22* , 1998, no 4.

criticism of Marxism),[15] told him after the Soviet invasion: 'Now I'll submerge and survive them' (*most alámerülök és kibekkelem őket*).[16] I do not believe that Antall used exactly those words, but what he meant was clearly a determination to survive the hard times, not to give in or give up, and to be prepared for a new round when the circumstances were conducive to success. That at any rate was the advice he gave us, his students.

In May, 1957, after the arrest of Bibó, it became obvious that the new phase of communism would be long, but the vast majority of the population did not join the communist party. Many kept hoping for a turn for the better, expecting the United States eventually to win the Cold War. Numerically, they may not have been a majority, but they formed the majority of the politically conscious part of the population. They had learned the hard lesson that they had to keep silent; their opposition to the regime was restricted to listening to Radio Free Europe and other western radio stations, grumbling at the workplace, telling anti-government jokes, exchanging news and views in the closer circle of family and friends, sympathizing with all the foes of the Soviet Union (from Israel to South Vietnam and the guerrillas in Angola), and heartily hating the party apparatchiks. A smaller number, but still many, kept going to church, and educated their children in an anti-communist spirit.

The 'liberalizing' features of the last two decades of the Kádár-era were not expected to cover intellectual life. They were accompanied by exhortations to maintain a socialist-communist mentality, an 'internationalist' (i.e. pro-Soviet) attitude in questions of foreign policy, and (at least until the mid-1980s) a neutral, passive attitude towards the fate of the millions of Hungarians who had been incorporated in 1920 in the neighbouring countries. Most Hungarian citizens (including the rank and file of the Party) were not too happy with these requirements; in fact, they deplored them. The possibility of travelling beyond the Iron Curtain exposed visiting Hungarians to unimaginable prosperity and enviable commodities, also to books and newspapers which were full of material banned at home. Honest history (including on the Soviet Union and its satellites), sensible political analysis, and of course relatives or old friends (mostly '56 refugees) waited for the visiting Hungarians who temporarily escaped from tyranny. Most of those travellers were more (or at least as) interested in the museums and the bookstores than the department stores. Fortunately the 'cold warriors' of the US and the UK realized the importance of breaking through the information blackout that covered the eastern half of Europe. Starting in the late 1950s, scientific and scholarly books, encyclopaedias, and journals were sent to selected individuals beyond the Iron Curtain. The letters acknowledging them (unless stopped by the censors) were so enthusiastic that a campaign soon gathered great speed.[17] A small bookshop near St Paul's Cathedral offered for a small amount (my recollection is five pounds in the 1970s) an unlimited number of books published in languages used in the Eastern Bloc. (The visitor's responsibility was more than just carrying the weighty volumes; the problem was how to

---

15 Entitled 'The Irony of History – Marx as the Saviour of Capitalism'. Written in 1951–52, it was first published in József Antall, *Modell és valóság*, Budapest, 2006, pp. 373–378.
16 Ágnes Heller, 'Biciklifő majom. Kőbányai János interjúregénye', *Kortárs*, vol 47, no 12, 1997.
17 John P.C. Matthews, 'The West's Secret Marshall Plan for the Mind', *International Journal of Intelligence and CounterIntelligence*, 16, 2003, pp. 409–427.

smuggle them over the border, as the selected publications were usually politically sensitive.) Many young Poles and Hungarians availed themselves eagerly of the opportunity to learn the truth, to receive uncensored information, and they readily shared the publications with friends and colleagues. The 'forbidden fruit' had considerable impact, literally liberating the 'captive minds'.

Travel in Western Europe had an additional advantage for the non-communist Hungarian intellectuals, for they might meet there prominent Hungarian political exiles, whether '56-ers or those who escaped earlier. Their discussions and the ties formed as a result were extremely important for both sides, building a bridge between the refugees who were cut off from the homeland, and the representatives of Hungarian cultural life who had been very much isolated from western thought. The various Hungarian clubs and associations in the western hemisphere were all united in upholding the memory and principles of 1956, and many visitors from Hungary were eager to meet both famous and less well-known compatriots. My own visits might serve as a typical example. During two private visits to Britain (1964 and 1971) and a five-month scholarship for historical research in 1975, I met, among others, László Péter, László Cs. Szabó, Zoltán Szabó, Lóránt Czigány, István Siklós, Tibor Zsuppán and Mátyás Sárközi; in Paris, Pál Tar; in Munich, the staff of *Új Látóhatár*; in Vienna, István Szépfalusi and Ernő Deák, just to mention the few that are better known. From them, I learned much about the West and also about the history and culture of a virtual, hoped-for Hungary, the democratic, anti-Nazi and anti-Communist one. Many other younger Hungarians had similar experiences in the capitals of Western Europe. Our knowledge of Hungarian history, particularly about 1956, the origins of the Cold War and the crimes of communism owe a great deal to these encounters and to the books and journals we acquired on those trips. On my very first trip, in 1964, I bought a collection of István Bibó's writings, *A harmadik út* (The Third Way), in a bookstore in Vienna. I digested every letter of that book, which also contained Bibó's practical proposal for a political compromise, drawn up immediately after the Soviet intervention. At home, many friends of mine borrowed this and other publications, which were officially termed 'hostile to the Soviet Union and the people's democracies' and, therefore, banned and confiscated if found. (My first consignment of such sensitive literature, including also Robert Conquest's works on the crimes of Stalinism, was left in Vienna and later smuggled in by an American friend of mine.)[18]

Towards the end of the 1970s, the 'dissident' authors started, albeit still hesitantly, to turn away from an idealized Marx and criticizing social conditions in Kádár's Hungary from a leftist, sometimes even Maoist angle. It was then that they 'discovered' 1956 as a forerunner. Péter Kende, a Hungarian political exile in France, told György Bence and János Kis, meeting them in Cluj/Kolozsvár in 1979: 'An intellectual opposition in Hungary can only start from 1956.'[19] Heeding this advice, the dissidents soon realized that 1956 was the very opposite of a reactionary counter-revolution. Having

---

18 My copy of Bibó's book disappeared into somebody else's collection. While I miss it to this very day, in the case of many other books and papers smuggled home we did not mind their eventual loss, knowing that the more hands they went through, the better.

19 Quoted by E. Csizmadia, 'A szamizdat szubkultúrája', p. 46. Kőszeg's essay, quoted above, explains in some detail the endorsement of 1956 as a starting point.

endorsed Charter '77, and with a few even signing it, it was a logical concomitant to discover a flagrant abuse of human rights: the systematic oppression and mistreatment of the Hungarians in Romania and Czechoslovakia. My friends and I, as well as so many other Hungarians, were pleased to see that turn of the honest leftist intellectuals, and to find that they also endorsed liberal ('bourgeois') democracy, our old model. We welcomed their conversion, seeing them as the prodigal son of the Scriptures. Throughout the greater part of the 1980s, there was a kind of long spiritual honeymoon between the anti-communist, older middle class (many in exile in the West, but most of them still living in a kind of internal exile, in silent opposition to 'the system' at home), and the disillusioned former Marxists. They were joined by another, intellectually influential group, the successors of the 'village explorers' of the 1930s: writers and poets, later also filmmakers and other artists, whose roots were in the countryside, in the villages, and who in many cases came from peasant families. Most of them had received a higher education in the late 1940s, and they were grateful for that rapid social rise, but by 1956 they, too, had discarded their illusions about communism. Their spiritual leader and patron was Gyula Illyés, whose poem, 'A Sentence on Tyranny' is a world-ranking classic. First published during the days of the Revolution, it will be forever associated with '56. The alliance and collaboration of the three groups resulted in an upsurge of publications and circulation, both abroad and at home. *Irodalmi Újság* (Literary Journal, published first in London, later in Paris), *Bécsi Napló* (Viennese Diary), *Új Látóhatár* (New Horizon) and *Nemzetőr* (National Guard), both published in Munich, and *Katolikus Szemle* (Catholic Review, Rome) were joined by the handy, easy-to-smuggle series *Magyar Füzetek* (Hungarian Pamphlets, edited by Péter Kende in Paris) which started in the late 1970s. The European Protestant Hungarian Free University, based in Switzerland, published the four volumes of Bibó's selected writings in the early 1980s, while the Kelemen Mikes Circle in the Netherlands as well as the Márton Szepsi Csombor Circle in London held conferences attended also by guests from Hungary, and carried out some publishing activity. Several organizations in the Federal Republic of Germany, Switzerland and Sweden, and also the Hungarian Society of Friends in the United States started regularly to invite writers, poets and scholars from Hungary, taking them round to meet other Hungarian circles. In this way, what the writer Sándor Csoóri called a large 'Hungarian Archipelago' was created, spanning many countries and even continents, whose members knew each other at least through their correspondence and writings. The twentieth, twenty-fifth and thirtieth anniversaries of the 1956 Revolution presented welcome opportunities for meetings and publications, ensuring also the attention of the western media and the general public. Simultaneously a few monthly periodicals in Hungary (notably *Tiszatáj* of Szeged, *Alföld* of Debrecen, *Forrás* of Kecskemét, *Új Forrás* of Tatabánya, *Életünk* in Szombathely, and *Jelenkor* in Pécs) published essays and poems which often troubled the authorities, resulting in various disciplinary actions, including the removal of pages from the publication or even the confiscation of whole issues. The first 'scandal' was the suppression in 1978 of a book of essays by Gyula Illyés, *Szellem és erőszak* (Spirit and Violence), just for calling attention to the plight of Hungarians in Romania.

Naturally, the foremost aim of the underground publications in Hungary and the writings and talks outside the country was primarily not the discussion of the past and particularly 1956, but the analysis of the present, thinking how to influence events beyond the Iron Curtain, and how to ease conditions both in Hungary and for the oppressed Hungarian minorities in the Carpathian Basin. The persecution of religion and opposition to the 'fellow traveller' church leaders was also a theme. It was reinforced by Cardinal Mindszenty emerging from his asylum in the US Embassy in Budapest, and by his touring the West and reminding people of the dark side of Kádár's 'goulash communism'.

Undoubtedly, the most important symptom and product of the meeting of the three social and intellectual tendencies was the memorial volume dedicated to István Bibó, whose burial in 1979 was a kind of demonstration, attended by a large 'coalition' from Illyés and Csoóri on the one side, through a large number of professional historians and social scientists to János Kenedi, a courageous dissident, on the other, and also by Antall and myself. Why did Bibó become the rallying point for all those Hungarians who did not acquiesce in the 'mild' version of Kádár's dictatorship and who were ready to test its limits? One answer is the intellectual strength of Bibó, the silenced political thinker.[20] But the other is that he became a legend even during his lifetime, as the lonely member of the Nagy government who remained literally in his position, in his chair, after the Soviet invasion, and drew up a plan for saving the most basic aim of the '56 revolution: pluralism, even under the puppet imposed upon the nation. In short, after the execution of Nagy and his closest associates, Bibó became the living symbol of 1956. The disillusioned Marxists (both of '56 and of the 1970s) appreciated the fact that this political philosopher was very much aware of the social problems of pre-war Hungary, and always advocated the collaboration of the left and the centre as a means for the creation and maintenance of democracy. The surviving Smallholders and Peasant Party adherents (coming either from the middle class or from the peasantry) saw in him their colleague in 1945–48. People with Christian Democratic proclivities knew that Bibó was a practising Calvinist and married to the daughter of the famous Bishop Ravasz. Freedom fighters released from prison saw in him the fellow-prisoner and respected him for his courage during and after the Revolution. The younger generation of non-communist intellectuals, my own generation, now forming a growing section of the silent opposition, who were just beginning to cast away their fears and to abandon their silence, looked up at him as a moral and political leader and as a guiding spirit. The 75 authors of the Memorial Volume represented all those categories. A third of them – 24 – were born after 1940, so they had not witnessed Bibó's active years first hand, but they were familiar with his writings, and most of them had met him.[21] When a publisher – as expected – turned down this collection of essays, the pioneer document of the emerging opposition, it was circulated in a typed and duplicated version.[22] Several sessions of the

---

20 István Bibó, *Democracy, Revolution, Self-Determination. Selected Writings*, ed. Károly Nagy, Boulder, 1991.
21 I should have been the 25th younger contributor, but being a slow writer, I missed the deadline – to my great regret then and even more now. Bibó was naturally pleased to find followers in the younger generation, but took pains to protect them from the wrath of the authorities. A typical example: he was kind enough to sign for me his last book, *The Paralysis of International Institutions and the Remedies*, Hassocks (Sussex, UK), 1976, but did not want to 'compromise' me by signing the politically far more dangerous *Harmadik út*.
22 It was properly published only after the change of system: *Bibó-emlékkönyv*, Budapest & Bern, 1991.

powerful Political Committee of the Communist Party discussed its implications. They considered it especially 'dangerous' because the 75 authors represented such a wide cross-section of Hungarian intellectual life, and brought together typical 'urban' (*urbánus*) and populist (*népi*) personalities, thus creating a most important 'bridge' between the two traditions. The Party was of course worried mainly because of the clearly 'oppositional' character of the whole enterprise (according to a confidential report seventeen authors fell into this category), but it was also troubled by the way the authors regarded 1956. Two notorious apparatchiks, Knopp and Kornidesz, summarized the Party position as follows:

> [...] the authors restore [*rehabilitálják*] 1956 as a revolution, 'an uprising of elemental strength by a people deeply hurt in its self-respect'. According to them in 1956 there was an attempt to go back to the position before 1948, to democratic institutions and a multi-party system. This democratic and revolutionary attempt was bloodily crushed by Soviet troops; the result of their intervention was the Kádár-regime, which was just a continuation of the illegal exercise of power.[23]

This was not an inaccurate description of what 1956 stood for, but it was anathema to those in power. The most direct writing on 1956 in the volume was by Ferenc Donáth, a close associate of Imre Nagy, who had been sentenced to twelve years imprisonment in 1958. He saw three major tendencies in 1956: those who wanted to restore pre-1945 Hungary with some democratic glaze, those who wanted to go back to the genuinely democratic system which existed between 1945 and 1947, and social forces (mainly workers) who hoped to improve parliamentary democracy with modalities of direct democracy. Donáth expressed his conviction that without the Soviet intervention this 'socialist' character of the revolution would have been preserved, and might even have become the paramount political force. That is questionable but irrelevant to my story.

The breadth and depth of the anti-system opposition was also shown in the far less well-known collection of essays and poems, *Független Fórum*, published in Munich in 1985.[24] It contained 59 samizdat or confiscated pieces from thirty-two authors living in Hungary, and also twenty documents. This was the result of the concerted efforts of 68 Hungarian organizations in North America and in Western Europe, joined by 153 individuals or couples that were named and 31 unnamed (three from Hungary), while fourteen contributed in the memory of deceased persons. The list of authors included Illyés, Konrád, Solt, István Kovács, Utassy, Bali, Miklós Szabó, Csoóri, Zsille, Hervay, Lezsák, T. Pákh, Demszky, Dalos, András Nagy, Petri, Krassó, Bulányi, Kőszeg, Pál Szalay, Gáspár Nagy, Csurka, Duray and T. Zalán. The majority of the themes dealt with contemporary issues in Hungary, the fate of the Hungarian minorities, and ten were related to the 1956 revolution. Never before and since has there been such an impressive mustering of Hungarians united to a common cause and all showing their opposition to what went on in 'the happiest barrack.' It coincided with elections in Hungary, which gave the customary strong support for the list of the 'Patriotic People's Front', and which

---

23 The strictly confidential report was leaked and appeared in samizdat. Recently it was found that the report was based on an earlier critical and hostile analysis drawn up by the noted author Tibor Huszár. See Gábor Murányi, 'A (Huszár-)Knopp-Kornidesz-jelentés', *Élet és Irodalom*, 49, 21 Oct., 2005.
24 Zoltán Zsille (ed.), *Független Fórum. Kéziratos tiltott magyar irodalom a Kárpát-medencében*, Munich, 1985.

provoked adulatory comments from some parts of the Western media, including the foolish statement that in a free election the result would not have been much different.[25]

True, repression in Hungary in the 1980s was nothing like the brutal measures against the open or semi-open opposition in the Soviet Union, Romania and Czechoslovakia. Moving one from a politically more exposed job to another, where 'less harm' could be done, was the most common punishment, apart from taking away one's passport and thus preventing travel abroad. In 1982, the editors of *Tiszatáj* and *Mozgó Világ* were called upon to resign, and when F. Kulin of *Mozgó Világ* refused, the whole editorial board was removed and replaced by party hacks.[26] The spirit of resistance, however, could no longer be contained. In the October 1984 issue of the little-know periodical *Új Forrás*, Gáspár Nagy's legendary 'political-system changing' poem, 'Öröknyár, elmúltam kilenc éves' (Eternal Summer, I'm Over Nine), was published. The courageous verse was about the unmarked grave of Imre Nagy and Nagy's unnamed murderers.

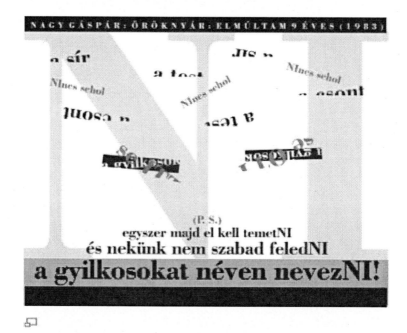

Gáspár Nagy: Eternal Summer (typographic transcription by István Orosz)

'One day he must be INterred
and we must not be forgettINg
the murderers' namINg by name!'

---

25 An indication of the real mood of the electorate was that – unlike at previous formal elections – about 15 % of the voters had the courage to stay at home, and the number of invalid votes (in effect showing opposition to the official candidates) reached 20 % in many places: Károly Szerencsés at the conference organized by the Institute on the Twentieth Century, 18–19 November, 2004.

26 *Mozgó Világ* was boycotted by all decent people then, but today it continues to have the very same boycotted editor.

The scarcely hidden initials of the martyred prime minister appeared in the last two letters of each line in the original Hungarian. This second meaning escaped the notice of the censors, but not that of the vigilant party leadership. The young author was dismissed from his post as secretary to the Hungarian Writers Union, and the remaining copies of the paper were destroyed. Although photocopying was at that time under strict control, the poem soon circulated in many duplicated, typed or hand-written copies.

The thirteenth congress of the Hungarian Socialist Workers' Party met in March, 1985. Its proceedings showed no sign of any serious trouble; indeed, the congress promised substantial growth and improvements. Three months later, 45 well-known writers and 'dissidents' met at a camping place near the town of Monor, not far from Budapest, and discussed the most serious political and social problems facing Hungary. It was indeed a milestone in the history of the post-1956 opposition, for it brought together the leading figures of both the post-Marxists (Ferenc Donáth, Miklós Vásárhelyi, János Kis, Miklós Szabó, János Kenedi) on the one hand, and the 'populists', Sándor Csoóri, István Csurka and Dénes Csengey on the other. From now on at the various manifestations of the opposition (in connection with the Cultural Forum of the CSCE in Budapest, an anti-forum in October 1985; the proliferation of samizdat periodicals; the revolt in the Writers' Union in 1986 replacing all the party favourites; and the gathering of close to 200 intellectuals in the home of the poet Sándor Lezsák under a big tent at Lakitelek in September, 1987 that called for regular public discussions – 'Democratic Forums' – on the most urgent problems of the country) there was not much talk about '56, but rather of preparing seriously to challenge 'the system' itself. But after the thirtieth anniversary, in December 1986, a conference was held in the home of the poet István Eörsi (himself imprisoned after 1956), attended by 60 guests from the open opposition, which refuted the extremely rigid line taken in the official media on '56.

The present paper does not aim at giving a summary of the Hungarian road to the collapse of communism; nor will it try to explain how and why the split occurred within the opposition between the 'urbanist' Free Democrats and the 'populist' Hungarian Democratic Forum, with the Alliance of Young Democrats in between (but then much closer to the former). What is important here to emphasize is that the three new parties, as well as the reviving 'old' parties, like the Independent Smallholders, the Social Democrats, and the Christian Democrats, drew their increasing membership from what I have called the silent opposition, people who had lived through the days of '56 and recalled its aims and atmosphere. Now they felt that the time was right to come out from mental hiding and that a chance had presented itself for reviving the fight for the restoration of a multi-party democracy in an independent Hungary.

József Antall, one of the hundred or so founding members of the Hungarian Democratic Forum in 1988, personified this large body. After several short-term arrests and interrogations in 1959, he was banned from the teaching profession, and for a few years earned his living as an assistant in a lending library. Eventually, he joined the Semmelweis Museum for the History of Medicine and built it up into an internationally recognized scholarly institution. It provided jobs for many ill-treated men and women (including the widow of Pál Maléter, the minister of defence in 1956, hanged in 1958), and became a gathering place for many opponents of the Kádár-regime, including Árpád Göncz, who in 1990 was elected President of the Republic. In October 1989, Antall was elected chairman (or president) of the MDF, the Hungarian Democratic Forum. This soon grew into the largest new political organization, having more than 13,000 members in March 1989 on the occasion of its first national convention. The early membership consisted mainly of people who were students or young professionals in 1956, had taken an active political part in the revolution, and had often through various forms of harassment and punishment faced the consequences. The 'dissidents' (the so-called democratic opposition) formed their own party in November 1988, the Alliance of Free Democrats, while a small group, consisting mainly of law students, set up the Alliance of Young Democrats (Fidesz), originally for people under 35. By 1989, a strong reformist group, led by Imre Pozsgay, emerged within the ruling communist party. His statement delivered in February 1989, that 1956 was not a counter-revolution but a popular uprising, proved a sensation both at home and abroad. It shattered the basis of the system set up and maintained by Kádár and his followers. The anti-communist opposition still appeared to keep together: they organized a large demonstration on 15 March, and, most importantly, the re-burial of Imre Nagy and his fellow-martyrs on 16 June, the anniversary of their execution. That was much more than a traditional communist 'rehabilitation'. Watched by the whole world, and attended by many foreign dignitaries, it was a unique expression of national unity. The reform-leaning government of Miklós Németh stood the costs and also provided security, and several prominent members of the communist party were included in the rotating guard-of-honour standing by the six coffins. The planning and organization of the ceremony itself was in the hands of people who were close to the former dissidents, the Free Democrats. Order in the crowd (approaching half a million) was maintained by hundreds of volunteers from the Democratic Forum. And the most stunning speech was given by the young leader of Fidesz, Viktor Orbán. The burial was more then an act of homage to the heroes and martyrs of 1956; it was a call for radical change. It was also a call for Kádár, the traitor of 1956, to face his responsibility. He died less than three weeks later, haunted by his crimes.

Following the example of Poland, the anti-communist parties and organizations formed the 'Opposition Roundtable' in order to coordinate their aims and tactics at the proposed 'National Roundtable.' It was there, after weeks of tense discussions, strengthened by the very noticeable support of the population, that an agreement was reached in September on changing the basic laws of the country and on the peaceful winding down of the communist system. In the following weeks, the last communist parliament passed a series of cardinal laws, and to all intents and purposes adopted a new constitution. With this negotiated, peaceful revolution, all the aims of 1956 were met or were put on the right course to be realized.

In subsequent weeks a rather serious rift occurred within the opposition and between the parties that were to contest the free elections, but its causes and consequences fall outside the scope the present essay. By that time, when on 23 October, 1989, a democratic republic was proclaimed on the thirty-third anniversary of the outbreak of the 1956 Revolution, all the parties, including the revamped communist party (now called the Socialist Party) swore by '56 and claimed to represent its legacy. Several people convicted after 1956 (Á. Göncz, Gy. Litván and I. Mécs being the best known) became prominent Free Democrats, while about a quarter of the MPs elected on the ticket of the Democratic Forum (including Prime Minister Antall, Speaker of the House Szabad, cabinet ministers Lajos Für and I. Szabó, and at least three former political prisoners) were active participants in the revolution, who had never betrayed it even by speaking or writing disparagingly about it.[27] With the free elections held five months later the process was completed and Hungary became a western-type, parliamentary democracy. One may regret that the survivors of the Revolution today belong to very different political factions, that the memory of 1956 does not trump political differences, and that the fiftieth anniversary of the Revolution was marred by violence and mutual recriminations. But is not this division of the Hungarian body politic a sign of the victory of that pluralistic democracy which the freedom fighters had all along advocated?

---

27 Letter of Imre Kónya, leader of the parliamentary party of the MDF (1990–94) to the author, 22 January, 2007. Cf. *Parlamenti Almanach 1990.*

Informing or Information? Scholars Targeted by the Hungarian Security Services Under Kádár

Krisztián Ungváry

Those embroiled by the recent scandals involving informers for the Kádár regime have generally claimed that they had little or no choice: anyone who wanted any sort of life under Kádár is bound to admit that he lived and acted under some constraints. Nevertheless, evidence from the documentation on informers suggests that even within the perceived constraints there was considerable individual room for manoeuvre. Several of those involved subsequently claimed that they had to do no more than file a report on their trip abroad – something that does not in principle amount to informing on people: even today everyone travelling abroad on official business is obliged to file a report on their trip. Nevertheless, the 'overseas reports' under the Kádár regime were often of a quite different order. The 'organs' certainly knew how to sort the wheat from the chaff and those who gave even the slightest indications of enthusiasm in their reporting were sooner or later recruited. Very often recruitment was predicated on the fact that a report on the trip was obligatory, or systematic guidance was offered prior to departure abroad. In what follows the approaches made by the state security services to a number of people fairly, or very, well known in public life are outlined.

The first case is that of the person codenamed 'Historian', i.e. György Ránki, one of the best-known historians during the Kádár regime, who enjoyed international renown. His career progressed at an extraordinary pace, for by 1965 he was already deputy head of the Institute of History of the Hungarian Academy of Sciences. In that year, too, he obtained a Ford Foundation scholarship to study in the United States and the security service attempted to recruit him in an 'advisory' capacity prior to his departure. What this meant was that they wanted him to collect the basic information for drawing up background briefings on those he considered 'suitable' for later recruitment as informers. The first exploratory discussions with him were held at his place of work on 26 November 1965. The official of the Ministry of the Interior spoke only in very general terms, which must have struck Ránki because, according to the record of the conversion, 'targeted person received me in a cordial manner, but from the way he reacted to the questions it was clear he wanted to know unambiguously what we wanted from him.' The first impressions of Captain Pál Viczián of Section III/I-1-a were at all events not negative, because barely two months later, on 17 January, 1966, in his assessment of 'Historian', he recorded that 'it is my view that he will, as he has already indicated in general terms, be prepared to let us entrust him with work of an advisory, research kind and with tasks involving the obtaining of intelligence.' His superior officer must have known a little more, because he altered the words 'entrust him with' to 'ask him to perform'. This suggests that the higher-ranking officers at the Ministry of the Interior did not think it a good idea to recruit people under coercion, at least in the field of intelligence-gathering – which is understandable, as anyone recruited in this way in principle regains his freedom of action as soon as he is abroad.

But Ránki proved a disappointment. On his return in November 1966 the information he offered was worthless. Viczián commented on his report as follows: 'We attempted to maintain our clandestine relationship with our contact "Historian" upon his return, but he declined. He expressed his wish to meet us only at an official venue, so I conducted his debriefing in the complaints office of the Ministry of the Interior. In the course of the conversation he claimed that what he was telling us could be told to any of his friends.'

According to a document dated 25 November, 1966, the Ministry of Interior officer wanted to meet Ránki in the safe flat codenamed Mátra, but

> [...] some hours later 'Historian' rang me to say he would prefer to conduct the conversation in the official venue of the Ministry of the Interior, or in his office in the Institute of History. [....] On this occasion I wanted to discuss with him the form of his written report. 'Historian' demurred, saying he did not like writing[1] and even at work he preferred to dictate to his secretary. He suggested therefore that I put questions to him and he would reply. I asked him directly why he did no want to meet me outside the Ministry of the Interior, to which he replied that he preferred to do things by the book.

Subsequently they met on two occasions, on the second of which Ránki

> [...] spelled out that he preferred not to enter into a conspiratorial relationship with us, which would involve certain kinds of obligation. To this I explained at length that it was in the nature of the work of the Ministry of the Interior that a degree of 'conspiracy' was inevitable. Additionally, the questions we were discussing were classified and secrets of state. He replied that he could not tell me about any matters that were secret, state secrets or otherwise, as what he was telling me he could say just as well to any of his friends.

The editor of the document, Captain Viczián, added the following comment to the report:

> At a recent meeting of the heads of Section III/III, I met its deputy head Comrade Lieutenant-Colonel Szilveszter Harangozó, who remarked jokily 'What are you doing making the leaders of the intelligentsia nervous?' On my inquiry he said someone from the Party HQ had told him that the Ministry of the Interior was making certain leading members of the intelligentsia feel nervous. By way of reply he had said that anyone having trouble with their nerves generally sees a doctor, not the Ministry of the Interior. He said his reply had been well taken and there was no problem in this respect.

> Assessment: In my view 'Historian' is not prepared to maintain conspiratorial relations with us and to thus enter into certain kinds of obligations. This is evident from the way in which he has hitherto avoided meetings of a conspiratorial nature.

We can only surmise that Ránki lodged a complaint at the Party HQ through one of his high-ranking acquaintances. Nonetheless, the Ministry of the Interior was in no hurry to get off the back of a target it had carefully identified, because Ránki, by virtue of his position and membership of the party, counted as a trustworthy supporter of the regime,

---

1	Ránki was already widely known for his prodigious written output.

and so it was odd and unusual of him not to undertake work that it expected. Viczián's report dated 28 November 1966 sketches his renewed efforts:

> At the beginning of the conversion I suggested to 'Historian', after he had said he could say little about the scholarship students here, that it was time for him to decide whether or not he was prepared to give us information unconditionally in connection with American scholarship students here and with his contacts in the USA.
>
> For it is in my view, and indeed that of my superiors, that this is a political issue: whether a member of the Hungarian Socialist Workers' Party (HSWP) in a leading position supports the work of the Ministry of the Interior in the battle against the No. 1 enemy, and I told him that if he had a problem in this respect, he should tell me to my face.
>
> To this 'Historian' reacted by saying that, naturally, he would gladly supply us with the necessary information, but his work and other duties prevented him from spending any length of time with the scholarship students. Nevertheless, at my repeated insistence, he promised he would talk to them. In the end we agreed to meet in three weeks' time, by when he will have met the scholarship students.
>
> In my view 'Historian' is not being entirely frank with us and is prepared to discuss only those issues he regards as being part of his 'official duties'. He appears to treat our relationship as a necessary evil arising out of his position.[2]

Gutsy behaviour like Ránki's was not, at this time, risk-free. Many of his colleagues behaved quite otherwise. A contemporary example might be Gizella Kocztur (Mrs Aladár Kis). This case is also noteworthy because it shows that even higher-ranking HSWP members were not exempt from recruitment. Gizella Kocztur worked in the English Department of the Eötvös Loránd University of Budapest (ELTE) and in 1964 obtained a ten-month scholarship to study in the UK. She had already cooperated with the state security services as a 'social contact' (her husband was also a party member and a teacher at ELTE. After 1956, he carried a pistol at the university). Major Pados put the following proposal forward on 8 October 1964: 'I propose that under order no. 04 of the comrade at the Ministry of the Interior, bearing in mind the possibilities of her ten-month stay in England, we should orient her towards the execution of information-gathering tasks.' It is instructive to read Major László Szabó's marginal comment: 'Comrade Major Pados! I will personally take part in the orientation. I agree that Mrs Kis can be recruited; in her case it is but a formality! I request permission to do this.'[3] Nevertheless, a further note in the margin indicates that Captain Pados did not (as yet) consider this necessary.

The interest of this case is that Mrs Kis was given information-gathering tasks without being assigned a codename or the usual 'card-6', which indicated recruitment; her handlers were content to keep her on the record as a 'social contact' in an informal manner. It would be little more than presumptuous to imagine this was connected to the fact that Mr and Mrs Kis were both well-known activists in the ELTE branch of the party. 'Budai' sent the following telegram on 13 October, 1964, to the information-gathering London 'resident', 'comrade' Pusztai: 'In the light of all the circumstances, she was not formally recruited and we shall not attach her to the resident, but will debrief her

---

2   Állambiztonsági Szolgálatok Történeti Levéltára (Historical Archive of the State Security Services, hereafter ÁSZTL), K-2086, social contact codename 'Történész'.

3   ÁSZTL, British Council 0–8-103/1, part II, p. 86.

thoroughly upon her return. Bearing in mind the above, comrades are at liberty to make such regular use of Comrade Mrs Kis as they wish.'[4]

It is not clear what use, if any, was made of Mrs Kis in London by the 'organs', but on her return she gave a lengthy account of her experiences, writing about Pál (Paul) Ignotus and other Hungarian émigrés. A year later she again applied for a visa, having obtained another scholarship. The intelligence-gatherers were, however, somewhat embarrassed, as Major Szabó, who had been present at Mrs Kis's previous orientation, had in the interim defected to the UK and identified all the Hungarian agents known to him, whereupon the British Council had warned the Hungarian Foreign Ministry that it was unwilling to finance the language studies of communist agents and would therefore be denying them entry visas. Mrs Kis thus could not travel to the UK, but her handlers praised her qualities in handing her over to Madame Comrade Földvári of Section III/III-2 in the Keringő (Waltz) coffee bar on 27 June 1966. The report notes: 'They hit it off at once.' Typically, Mrs Kis characterized the students of ELTE: 'She was very bitter about the effect of western propaganda in intellectual circles [...] the KISZ [Communist Youth League] at the university was weak, practically little more than a travel bureau, with very little political dynamism.'[5] Her new boss, Major Emil Zalai, head of Section III/III-2b (then an activist for the Workers' Party, Óbuda branch), gave the following assessment of her merits:

> Madam Comrade Kis gladly supported our work from the outset, regarding it her duty as a communist. She strove to carry out the duties assigned to her, though the English tried to isolate her and her modus operandi was restricted, but the account she gave of her visit is valuable. She has a good feel for how to operate. On her return she supplied interesting data on citizens of western nationality visiting ELTE, assisted the new operational officer, and kept us informed of events at the Department.[6]

Mrs Kis's supplying of intelligence was not motivated by any necessity to do so. Decent people were able, even at this time, to get around having to act as informers, for example by simply not accepting the carrots dangled before them. This may be illustrated by the case of the scholar of literature, Mihály Szegedy-Maszák. Very promising though his recruitment might have appeared to the secret services, at the exploratory discussion in the guise of an orientation meeting on 7 October 1966, the people of the Ministry of the Interior were disappointed to note that 'his artistic-scholarly personality does not make him suitable even at the operational level. He took a passive role in the conversation and although attending to our advice, he became more animated only when the conversation turned to literary topics.'[7] As a result of this report, the Ministry of the Interior did not pursue the attempt to recruit Szegedy-Maszák.

In the 1970s, the state security forces attempted the recruitment of two well-known historians. The method was the usual, tried and tested one: 'preventive instruction' prior to travel abroad in order to assess responses and to dangle the usual carrots. Even at this time the thinking of the state security forces was rooted in the Stalinist notion that the West European research institutes were spy-centres for the CIA and the *Bundesnach-richtendienst* and hotbeds of subversive politics. Accordingly, they continued to spare

---

4   ibid, part II, p. 100.
5   ibid, report dated 25 November 1965, p. 104.
6   ibid, part II, p. 117.
7   ibid, p. 190.

neither money nor effort in attempting to penetrate these institutions and identify the modus operandi of the individual institutes. Their interests extended to such practical details as to how it might be possible to enter, for instance, the South-East European Institute in Munich, the location of the director's room, and so forth..

On 15 November, 1973, Police Captain Béla Kalota met Ferenc Glatz, then an associate of the Institute of History of the Hungarian Academy. The notes made of this meeting are heavy with disappointment and reproof:

> I conducted a conversation with historian Ferenc Glatz in a public place. In 1972 he spent twelve months in the Federal Republic of Germany on a Humboldt Scholarship. Before he left, our section 2 gave him instruction. Also present at the meeting was Comrade Police Lieutenant János Szecsődi, who conducted Glatz's orientation and briefing [....]. After the meeting Comrade Szecsődi explained that Glatz was not being entirely frank with us: he had been to the Institute several times, he was well acquainted with [Karl] Nehring [a researcher at the South-East European Institute in Munich], as he had met Nehring many times while the latter was here this year, and had indeed invited him to his home. Glatz simply does not want to help us and explore topics that are for him perhaps delicate; he is prepared to help us only superficially. Mutual assistance is not in his interests, as he has a family relative in the Central Committee [of the Party].[8] Despite knowing at least two people in the target institution, Glatz is unusable, not straight; he recalls 'nothing'.[9]

It is clear from the report that Glatz found a way to disarm those that approached him and revealed nothing of his professional or personal relations that could have been disadvantageous to any of them. Thanks to this, the state security apparatus abandoned its attempt to recruit him.

Glatz was not the only one approached at this time. On 17 August, 1973, Kalota recorded the following:

> On the 9th inst. between 10 and 11.30 AM, I had a conversation in the passport department with Dr Jenő Szűcs [...], of the Institute of History, who from October of this year will be spending three months in the Federal Republic of Germany on a DAAD scholarship. [....] In the course of the conversation, Szűcs showed readiness, but is limited to what was due to an 'official organ' when certain of our affairs are dependent on that state organ. There is in him no genuine preparedness to help. He knows the institutions, which are important to us, and has a positive view of them: it is not possible to decide whether he really does not see, or simply does not want to see, the nature of their true activities. On his return I shall have him called in again and interrogate him with specific questions about the institutions and their employees.

Kalota returned to the issue on Szűcs's return, but to no avail. According to a report dated 4 March:

> On 17 February 1974 we had a conversation with Dr Jenő Szűcs in the passport department of the Ministry of the Interior, reviewing his three-month visit to the FRG at the instance of the South-East European Institute in Munich on a DAAD scholarship. The conversation was arranged and conducted by Police Captain Béla Kalota [...]. Dr Szűcs showed himself to be as willing as on the occasion of the previous conversation, but there were repeated indications that he was not genuinely willing to assist us and that he knew more than he was prepared to tell us.

A handwritten note on the document by head of section Tamás Kiss added: 'It is my view that he knows more about a number of things. [...] No need to concern ourselves with him in the future or to assist him on any future trips.'

---

8 The identity of the person alluded to is unknown.
9 ÁSZTL 0–8–448/1 'Tömjén' (Incense), Südost-Institut, Munich.

Those just mentioned were left in peace despite their passive attitude. None of them was disadvantaged thereby and all were free to travel to Western Europe. As party secretary at the Institute of History, Glatz was later even able to offer a degree of protection to those working in his Institute.

A response of quite a different order to the organs seeking him out was registered by 'Borkuti', otherwise Dr László Szita, director of the Baranya County Archives. Szita's first dealings with the state security services went back to the end of the 1970s. He was employed first as a 'social contact' and then, when it was realized that his volubility and lack of inhibition made him an excellent agent, as a 'secret employee'. For the state security services Szita was of interest because he had direct links with the South-East European Institute in Munich, which the main Section III regarded (erroneously) as a cover organization for the *Bundesnachrichtendienst*. In the image of the enemy enshrined by the state security services, the capitalist countries were conspiring together against socialism, and their latest weapon in this struggle was the politics of subversion, namely: an ideological battle disguised as an East-West dialogue maintained through cultural contacts. It should be noted that this image of the enemy had been preserved quite unchanged from the Stalinist period; only the means of its expression had been refined. Of his contact in the Institute, referred to as 'Broder', Szita gave expressly negative reports, despite the fact that 'Broder' was Szita's friend, guide, host and financial supporter. An officer in the Pécs branch of III/I stated at Szita's orientation:

Our social contact was right to note how on any particular occasion 'Broder' spoke or reacted in the course of their conversation.

When he was entirely sober, he spoke with great care, but more openly and in a more friendly way than before about general matters. When he became tipsy, his real character was revealed: he spoke uninhibitedly but coherently about the Institute, his political views and the information he had available. In fact, it was in this state that he gave us material that we can make best use of. But when he got drunk, and this happened several times, he spoke incoherently, mostly about his family problems [...].

It emerged unequivocally that his attitude to our regime is hostile, but his anti-Soviet attitude is – if possible – even more so.

'Borkuti' had become an informer in order to obtain foreign currency. While he was also willing to accept money from 'Broder', whom he had betrayed, he also managed to get the state security services to finance him. According to Lieutenant Béla Dudás of Section III/I-3,

We have for some time been employing 'Borkuti' as a social contact in the Broder case jointly with Section III/I in Pécs [then headed by Captain Péter Lusztig, who between 1994 and 1998 was an MSZP MP and since 2002 chief adviser to Mónika Lamperth], in the course of which he always carried out his tasks conscientiously. He never accepted any expenses for work arising out of his activities here at home. In line with earlier practice, we hereby apply for permission to reimburse Borkuti for operational costs and expenses on his present trip to the sum of 500 DM, to be signed for.

'Borkuti' rapidly climbed up the state security services ladder, for by 1980 he was a 'tmb', a secret agent. In the course of that summer, however, doubts began to circulate as to whether or not he actually was in the employ of the German secret service, as he did not admit to having received 1100 DM and 600 Austrian schillings from 'Brader' (sic) for personal purposes. A further cause for suspicion was the fact that 'Borkuti' supplied 'Broder' with 'materials relating to the nationalities [i.e. national minorities] that might also be used for incitement.' By this was meant the details of the pre-1956 census of Germans in Hungary, which in the post-ÁVH paranoia was regarded as a state secret. For this reason his handler, Major Lajos Huszár, arranged a meeting on 2 September 1980, in a safe flat liberally stocked with drink, with Dr YX, a psychiatric army major pretending to be a detective [he currently specializes in the treatment of addicts in County Somogy], and another official from the Ministry of the Interior. In the course of this 'Borkuti' was subjected to the 'Star' treatment-regime, which consisted of a psychological interrogation. As this progressed, with liberal interpolations of the 'I'm fucking telling you!' and 'Why the fuck didn't I say?', he expounded intimate aspects of his own and his friends' lives. Extracts from the recorded conversation are as follows:

Handler (H): Excuse me, what can I get you? There's beer, wine, soft drinks, Pepsi, Hungarian Cola.

B: [speaking of a colleague at the South-East Europe Institute in Munich]: A classy woman. Intelligent, stylish, I was the only one she didn't fuck, because it wasn't possible.

H: That reminds me, [....] How did she react? Tell Feri here, when you said, 'Well, that's subversion.'

B: [...] Well, I thought that it was as much me subverting them as them subverting me [...].

H: You couldn't get shot of your wife?

B: Dear God, how I wanted to find a Munich brothel! [...] Do you know how fantastic brothels can be?

Unfortunately the outcome of the conversation is not known, because the report of the psychologist cannot currently be made public for legal reasons. 'Borkuti''s dossier was destroyed at the time of the regime change, and 'Borkuti' himself died recently. But it is known that his information contributed to the security services being able to clarify the relationships between his colleagues, to assisting or preventing people in the obtaining of overseas visas, and to instigating the recruitment of others.

From the mid-1960s, the recruitment of people into the network was increasingly a voluntary activity. This was especially true of those who were used to obtain intelligence. The state security services always made their first approach in some disguise, using a storyline, and would generally back away at the slightest sign of resistance. It is significant that no punishment of those who expressed open opposition was even contemplated. An example of this is the case of János Géresi, who first appeared on the intelligence-seekers' horizon on 26 January 1979. The organization carefully documented every step in the process of his attempted recruitment. Lieutenant Gábor Sike of Section III/I-2 wrote on this day:

János Géresi has come to our attention as a result of our research among company representatives regularly visiting the FRG. He is a scientist at the SZKI Computer Laboratory, employed there since 1 July 1971, currently as group leader in the developmental work of RPG Computer, a project of SIEMENS-METRIMPEX-SZKI.

In the preparatory discussions with the other services we established that no direct approach should be made to János Géresi: calling him in to the passport section of the Ministry of the Interior was not indicated for other reasons, so I suggested contact be made with him by telephone, inviting him to a public venue ['somewhere official' – a handwritten interpolation from the head of the department]. The apropos would be his trip abroad, scheduled to begin in two weeks' time. The invitation would be an open one, from the Ministry of the Interior, and should Géresi accept the suggested format, following the discussion of mutual signs of recognition, the conversation could be set in motion. [...] In the event of a positive response I propose a repeat encounter following his return from abroad. If negative impressions are noted, I will remind him of the need to observe secrecy and draw his attention to his general duties as a citizen and the obligation to file a report in any event.[10]

The document also carried the salutary observations of the deputy head of department, Major Galla: 'I agree in the matter of the method of invitation as discussed at the meeting. Very important at the first encounter is the official character of the meeting. By ensuring that we appear, and are respected, in an official framework, we ensure that the target has a different attitude to the proceedings. In this case there is plenty to discuss.'[11]

For reasons unknown, the projected meeting took place only some months later, so the Ministry of the Interior officials used aliases. The report on this is dated 16 June 1976:

> The meeting took place in the official premises of the passport department under the guise of verification [...]. In thanking Géresi for the meeting I requested another meeting on his return – he would be again in Vienna between 17 and 29 June. He did not dismiss the suggestion but stated that 'he did not wish regularly to discuss the above issues.' He felt adequately briefed from the security angle, that is, he did not consider himself or his group to be under personal threat. In any event, should he experience the kind of provocation I had outlined earlier, he would – in accordance with his duties as a citizen – duly inform the Embassy or the Ministry of the Interior. Before concluding the session, I informed Géresi that I did not have in mind any 'regular consultations' with him. Nevertheless, in our capacity as the passport authority, we needed to know the situation and the nature of the activities of those of our experts travelling abroad, so that we can take appropriate decisions in the matter of the worthiness of issuing 'unrestricted exit' permits.
>
> I drew his attention to the fact that while the purpose of our meeting was the verification of data, none of the matters raised could not be discussed with other persons.
>
> Assessment:
>
> - János Géresi is not appropriate, by virtue of his character and proclivities, for further consideration.
>
> - The nature of his personality is such that he is neither prepared nor inclined to consult with representatives of the Ministry of the Interior; in particular, he rejected my suggestions to this effect somewhat high-handedly. He claimed to have acquired his security knowledge while he was a soldier, when he had taken part in a number of activities where the security officer detailed what it was necessary to know and this was enough for him to recognize enemy activity when he was overseas.[12]

It would be a mistake to imagine that the most damaging type of agent activity was cooperation with the state security services. There were those prepared to inform on their colleagues without being recruited. An example of this is the historian Károly Vigh, after 1989 president of the Endre Bajcsy-Zsilinszky Friendship Society and later active in the Teleki Statue Committee. Vigh worked as a historian and as party secretary in the Institute of History in 1950 and, like many of his colleagues, informed on them to the ÁVH. Having been unsuccessful in his first attempt to report on the distinguished historian Domokos Kosáry – who was merely sacked as head of the Institute but not jailed – he made a second attempt a year later, on 29 June:

---

10 ÁSZTL 0–8-130/15 Gehlen intelligence network, p. 173, Gábor Sike's report.
11 ibid.
12 ibid, p. 182, Gábor Sike's report.

I wish to report Domokos Kosáry, formerly head of the Institute of History, who has very close ties with England and the USA and is behaving in a hostile manner towards the democratic people's republic of Hungary. [....] In 1937 [*recte* 1936] he wrote a book about Görgey which I have myself read and noted that in this he supports Görgei [sic] and the treacherous pro-Habsburg policies of the Peace party [sic]. In the given political circumstances this was essentially historical support and justification for the deferential pro-German policies of Gömbös and his associates [....]. [In his English-language book on Hungarian history] he uses the language of the gutter to vilify the Great October Revolution and the Hungarian Soviet Republic of 1919, and adulates the triumph of the counter-revolutionary Horthy regime, Gömbös [....]. The tea-time meetings at the Revue, a monthly event in the Institute, was [sic] a gathering-place for every kind of enemy of the people's democracy. The low-level representatives of the various western embassies were regulars at these gatherings, thus e.g. leading officials of the Britis [sic] Council, and István Csicsery-Rónay, convicted in the Hungarian Community conspiracy.

The only possible thing that might be brought up in mitigation of Vigh is that the grammatical howlers in his report were contributed by the ÁVH official transcribing the minutes. The informer must have known very well what it meant to say at this time that someone had 'very close ties with England and the USA'. It was Kosáry's good fortune that his projected show trial was, for unknown reasons, shelved in 1951, though thanks to the industrious Vigh and his colleagues all the preparations were in place for a major show trial. The fact that Kosáry had in 1944 hidden an English parachutist from the Gestapo and the Hungarian fascist police was presented by the historian Zsigmond Pál Pach in his 'report' to the ÁVH, somewhat tendentiously, as evidence that Kosáry was a member of the Secret Service. It was sheer luck that the informing activities of Pach and Vigh did not have consequences of the utmost seriousness.

The cases mentioned here are but the tip of the iceberg. There are very many stories buried in the archives which can provide evidence that in dictatorships there were not only traitors, but also many brave people. No regime in Hungarian history has left as detailed a record of its operations as the secret services of the Kádár regime. Sooner or later everything will come to light. It is in the interests of Hungarian society that we get to know the perpetrators and the victims of these stories. It is something that the perpetrators deserve, and something that we owe to the victims.

Negotiated Mythopoeia: A New Model for Art in Hungary After 1956

Rachel Beckles-Willson

In recent years research strategies for East Central Europe have become more self reflexive, benefiting from the challenge of Edward W. Said's *Orientalism* by attempting to overcome simplistic dualisms of 'East' and 'West', and taking note of the relationship between knowledge and power. Larry Wolff's *Inventing Eastern Europe* (1996) and Maria Todorova's *Imagining the Balkans* (1997) in particular offer insights into ways by which the West has appropriated its geo-political 'other', and more recent work has expanded on their research, seeking to create less static, more inter-actional theoretical frameworks, as well as more nuanced and variegated images of both sides.[1]

Notwithstanding these developments, there is still a bald binarism at play in writing on music under communism. Richard Taruskin, for instance, constructs Soviet composer Alfred Schnittke's work entitled *Pianissimo* (1969) as pure and simple opposition: 'Soviet composers were expected to make affirmative public statements, *fortissimo*', he writes, '[t]o speak in atonal whispers was *genuinely countercultural*.'[2] Elsewhere writers speculate vaguely: Paul Griffiths writes of Schnittke's restoration of Orthodox music into his symphonic work in 1979 that '[p]art of the point may have been to make a protest against the persecution of religion in the Soviet Union, but equally the music laments the loss of divine community, of the social order that sustained the individuality which all Schnittke's music pursues.'[3] Griffiths' idealization of oppressed religiosity is frustratingly romantic.

The aim of this paper is to analyse the context for Eastern Europe's artistic production in the 1960s and beyond in order to gain a richer and securer context in which to position apparently oppositional and/or religious musical statements. Within that broad sweep, my main attention will be honed on how individual artists may become the focus of oppositional longing and quasi-religious worship. As Taruskin has observed, there

---

1 Two research projects in particular illustrate this new approach. The project 'East Looks West: East European Travel Writing on European Identities and Divisions, 1600–2000', led by Wendy Bracewell, at the Centre for South-East European Studies at London's UCL School of Slavonic and East European Studies (<www.ssees.ac.uk/seecent.htm>); and the project led by György Péteri, 'Imagining the West: Perceptions of the Western Other in Modern and Contemporary Eastern Europe' at the Program for East European Cultures and Societies of Trondheim's Norwegian University of Science and Technology (<http://www.hf.ntnu.no/peecs>).

2 Richard Taruskin, *The Oxford History of Western Music*, New York & Oxford, vol 5, 2004, p. 464. My italics.

3 Paul Griffiths, *Modern Music and after*, Oxford, 1995, p. 254.

was a 'romantic aura of martyrdom' surrounding commentary about Schnittke, and this is congruent with the 'mythification of the artist' that is widely recognized as a phenomenon in Eastern Europe. Indeed I will be presenting a parallel case from Hungary in this article. But here I will examine how this mythopoeia coexisted with the apparently conflicting demands of the regime. Was not mystic aura out of line with government policy?

In the first part of the article I present three oppositions in order to explore their shifting relations after 1956: the state versus the church, the state versus the western avant-garde, and the state-sponsored discourse versus silence. I then offer a reading of a work by composer György Kurtág (b.1926), positioning it within the shifting discourses and suggesting the ways in which it could contribute to precisely these discourses. As I hope to make clear, it is a model of reciprocity, rather than suppression and resistance, which is appropriate for this time and place.

1. Shifting positions and negotiations of power

1.1. The state and the Catholic Church

The uprising and its bloody repression in October-November 1956 was a profoundly destructive and dispiriting event for the Hungarian nation. It proved the ruthlessness of the Soviet Union despite de-Stalinization, the unwillingness of Western powers to intercede, and the apparently hopeless national cause. One voice from the West made a notable protest nonetheless, namely the Vatican, which condemned the brutal Soviet tactics.

The Catholic church inside Hungary had attempted to oppose the communist takeover after the Second World War, but its most vociferous campaigner, Primate of Hungary and Archbishop of Esztergom (the seat of the head of the Roman Catholic Church in Hungary) Cardinal Mindszenty, was sentenced to life imprisonment in 1948 on charges of conspiracy and treason. All the churches were forced to give way in the ensuing years. Calvinist and Lutheran bishops succumbed to pressure and took an oath of loyalty to the new People's Republic and constitution in 1950, and, after Archbishop Grósz was imprisoned in 1951, Catholic prelates did the same.[4]

The thaw led to reform in many areas and, very briefly in 1956, to a restoration of multi-party politics. Cardinal Mindszenty was released from prison on 31 October. His public activity was, however, short-lived. When in November the Soviets re-entered the country to reverse the political process and stamp out the uprising, Mindszenty took political asylum in the US Embassy where he remained for fifteen years, opposed to any form of dialogue with the new government and refusing to leave the country until his conviction was revoked. Only in 1971 did the government revoke his conviction, but even from outside the country he fought against the appointment of his successor until his death in 1975. Finally a successor was appointed in 1976. After nearly thirty years without a participating leader, the Hungarian Catholic Church was newly intact.

---

4   Ignác Romsics, *Hungary in the Twentieth Century*, trans. Tim Wilkinson, Budapest, 1999, pp. 257–9, 281–3. Hungary's religious communities suffered less than those in other Soviet satellites. Although their outreach activities were curtailed, they were able to conduct services throughout the regime.

While on a symbolic level Mindszenty's resistance was forceful, directly after 1956 the new government leader, János Kádár, entered a dialogue with the operative members of the Catholic Church, striving to disperse their hostility. He succeeded in engineering a tense but ultimately productive relationship. The state was to provide the church's main income and support religious instruction in schools, and an agreement with the Vatican in 1959 ensured that priests newly appointed by Rome swore allegiance to the Hungarian constitution. Kádár's strategy was guarded watchfulness and forceful penetration: as recent research has revealed, many priests (and bishops too) would be coerced into becoming secret agents.

This snapshot of negotiations makes clear that the period following 1956 allows no clean separation between the institutions of the church and the government. It also offers a way of grasping some of the cultural formations that may otherwise seem bafflingly paradoxical. Whereas in 1948 the study of church music had been abolished, during the late 1960s the Catholic church began to expand its use of music in services, and seminarists were able to study plainchant at a summer school set up in 1967. This event recurred annually and led subsequently to the establishment of parish scholas and choirs; by 1972, the study of plainchant had been introduced to the curriculum at the Liszt Academy of Music.[5] Even more obviously, from 1957 onwards, the Catholic Church was allowed to publish its own periodical, *Új Ember* (New Man). Acknowledging such reciprocal acknowledgments emerging between church and state begins to shift our perspective onto the work of one regular contributor to *Új Ember*, the religious and metaphysical poet János Pilinszky. It is generally argued that the publication of his book *Harmadnapon* (On the Third Day) in 1959 was an anomalous event, because writers who were understood as subversive were denied opportunities to publish their work until the mid-1960s or beyond. In fact, however, this publication was in line with the government's policy of rapprochement.

1.2. The state and the Western avant-garde

Although Kádár's initial task following 1956 was to take vicious retribution against those who had been part of the political reforms and the uprising, he combined terror action with enticements. He arranged pay rises and tax cuts, for example, and made promises that his government would not return to Stalinism. Taming the intelligentsia with new journals and Kossuth Prizes, with the contributions of György Aczél in particular, deputy minister for cultural affairs (1957–67), Kádár also implemented a new arts policy according to which cultural diversity was a crucial part of socialism. Although the government would still favour 'socialist realism', it would, from then on, also tolerate other arts so long as they did not undermine party principles. Two well-known catchphrases sum up this new situation: first, Kádár's remark that 'Those who are not against us are with us' (a reversal of the slogan of the pre-1956 regime), and, secondly,

---

5 László Dobszay, 'Thirty Years of the Gregorian Movement in Hungary', *Hungarian Musical Quarterly*, 9, 1998, nos 3–4, pp. 4, 7–8. The circumstances of this new movement need to be fully evaluated within the context of the shifting relations between the USSR and the Vatican. Dobszay, who led it, plays down the explicitly political problems he encountered in his publications, arguing that there were plenty of other ones to deal with first.

the categorization of art into what was to be 'boosted', 'bearable' or 'banned' (*támoga-tott*, *tűrt*, and *tiltott* – the 'Three Ts').[6]

From this perspective the 1960s emerge as years of experiment, for as new works of art emerged, criteria for categorizing them and mechanisms for banning them were less than clear or efficient. In the musical sphere the polity that embraced 'diversity' paved the way for apparently provocatively 'Western' avant-gardist music to be tolerated in concert. When a work that blatantly drew on the Western modernist style of musical pointillism was premièred in January 1960 – Endre Szervánszky's *Six Orchestral Pieces* – nobody in the press denied that it deserved to be heard (once) and considered along with everything else.[7] The 'Three Ts' allowed for works to be claimed for their 'humanist' qualities where justification on the grounds of socialist realism would have been impossible. One writer attempted to legitimate the *Six Orchestral Pieces* in just such terms: in spite of the work's unmelodic, splintery and fractured character (it could easily have been categorized as 'formalist'), he contrived to attribute its style to the composer's 'inner voice'.[8]

Notwithstanding the discourses of legitimation, events such as this première were eruptive for some years. In 1961 György Kurtág's String Quartet Op. 1, a work that had previously been banned from public performance, finally saw the light of day in an exceptional concert organized by Kurtág's former professor, Ferenc Farkas. The single reviewer complained that the concert had become a political event that created what he sourly called a 'sensation'. Indeed it transformed the hitherto unremarkable Kurtág into a symbol: for those daring to desire an end to the regime he was a vessel of forbidden fruits, while for official rhetoricians he was irritatingly incendiary. Even one year later, in 1962, establishment writers claimed that his music was both dated and socially irresponsible. Kurtág's Eight Piano Pieces Op. 3 succeeded in portraying only loneliness and despair, they wrote. Kurtág neglected his duty to make the world a better place: he was stuck in darkness, unable to move to the light.[9]

But the rules were changing by that time, and the framework for this performance was a state-sponsored series of modern chamber music called 'Chamber Music of Our Time' that had already programmed several modernist works from the West. Indeed the tone taken by critics had shifted substantially in the series' second year in 1963. Writers

---

6   See Paul Ignotus, *Hungary*, London, 1972, pp. 263–64, and Romsics, *Hungary in the Twentieth Century*, p. 389. Révész argues in more detail that the boosted category was reserved for socialist realism (understood as the most 'modern' art), the bearable was 'humanist' and non-oppositional, while the banned was art that was understood to be damaging to the People's Democracy: Sándor Révész, *Aczél és Korunk*, Budapest, 1997, pp. 101–02.

7   Sándor Kovács, 'Szervánszky hat zenekari darabjáról', *Muzsika*, 3, 1960 (March), no 3, pp. 40–42; Sándor Jemnitz, 'Modern művek zenekari estje (január 14.)', *Filharmónia Műsorfüzet*, 7, 1960, pp. 34–35; András Pernye, 'Egy hét Budapest hangversenytermeiben', *Magyar Nemzet*, 16 January, 1960.

8   This is particularly clear in Jemnitz 'Modern művek', p. 34; but see also Kovács 'Szervánszky' and Pernye 'Egy hét'.

9   János Breuer, 'A korunk kamarazenéje', *Muzsika*, 5, 1962 (July), no 7, pp. 43–44; András Pernye, 'Egy hét Budapest hangversenytermeiben', *Magyar Nemzet*, May 12, 1962. The fact that the work in question, Eight Piano Pieces Op. 3, had already been performed at the avant-garde hub *Internationale Ferienkurse für Neue Musik* in Darmstadt, surely heightened its political significance. According to Kurtág's recollections in April 1998 (private conversation with the author), when dissident Andor Losonczy performed these pieces there, the organizers requested more of his scores. The ministry in Hungary refused to allow scores to be sent; and they called Kurtág up for two months' military service that effectively prevented him from going to Darmstadt that year. Documentation to confirm this has not been traced.

accounted for Kurtág's Wind Quintet Op. 2 and Eight Duos for violin and cimbalom Op. 4 by arguing that the composer was now evoking not only suffering but also joy, and demonstrating a desire to reach out to people.[10]

Their shift reflected a broad trend towards tacit rapprochement between the government position and the activities of composers. Increasingly, music that had been understood as oppositional was subsumed into justification of the post-Stalin (Kádár) regime. Thus the fact that Kurtág's Opus 1 was so different from his earlier work was no longer constructed as a problem, but as a metaphor for broad political change. Rather as the Kádár regime was justified as a crucial rejection of Stalinism, Kurtág's new style emerged from an uncontrollable 'inner need' to make a radical break from his earlier path.[11] Kurtág was appropriated for this discourse but he was not the only one: all music that could be absorbed into it was defined in terms of the progressive humanism that was ostensibly a principle of the new 'diversified' regime.[12] The emerging 'corpus' of works that were celebrated in this way was increasingly defined in terms of its relation to the Hungarian nation, and it was not long before composers themselves participated overtly in the same project. Zsolt Durkó's work, for instance, drawing explicitly on Hungarian styles in *Una rhapsodia ungherese* for two clarinets and orchestra (1965) and *Fioriture ungherese* for chamber choir and orchestra (1966), is emblematic of the resurging national tolerance of (and even confidence under) the new government.

Once the national project began to solidify in this way, what had been eruptive was absorbed into myth. Thus in 1968 a constellation of events that would have been explosive ten years earlier (indeed they would not have been allowed to occur) was grasped as a milestone in the history of Hungarian music. The year saw the formation of a new music group (the Budapest Chamber Ensemble), the first new work by Kurtág for some years (*The Sayings of Péter Bornemisza* Op. 7), the new ensemble's visit to the *Internationale Ferienkurse für Neue Musik* in Darmstadt in Germany for a concert at which *The Sayings* was premièred, and a repeat concert in Budapest. A substantial number of critics regarded the Budapest concert not only as a turning point, but also as a moment of redemption for the nation. Kurtág's *The Sayings of Bornemisza* was understood as metonymic of that redemption, either because of its reported success in Darmstadt, or because of its extension of the musical tradition from Schütz to Bartók.[13] Just as Kurtág's composition represented a rough ride into light (the programme note for the concert described it with the Latin motto 'per aspera ad astra'), so too could be under-

---

10 András Pernye, 'Egy hét Budapest hangversenytermeiben', *Magyar Nemzet*, 1963, March 30; János Breuer, 'Modern kamarazene', *Muzsika*, 6, 1963 (July), no 7, p. 38; András Pernye, 'Egy hét Budapest hangversenytermeiben', *Magyar Nemzet*, November 23, 1963.

11 András Pernye, 'Egy hét Budapest hangversenytermeiben', *Magyar Nemzet*, November 23, 1963.

12 Thus, in a free variation on progressive humanism, Rudolf Maros was soon acknowledged for drawing techniques learned from Polish sonorists (revealed in his *Euphonia I-III*), and celebrated because his 'striving for sonorous beauty speaks of the desire for the *psyche's deep and honest* statements': István Raics, 'Maros Rudolf: Eufónia 64', *Muzsika*, 3, 1966, no 4, p. 6 (my italics). Zsolt Durkó (1934–1997) made a particular impact with his Violin Concerto *Organismi* (1964) that was regarded as path-breaking but also – in the words of one leading establishment critic János Breuer – 'filling apparently speculative forms with *true emotions and content*': Breuer, 'Magyar bemutatók', *Muzsika*, 8, 1965, no 12, pp. 6–7 (p. 6). (My italics).

13 See Rachel Beckles Willson, *György Kurtág's The Sayings of Péter Bornemisza Op. 7*, Aldershot, 2004, pp. 129–146.

stood both Kurtág's own development, and the development of the nation.[14] Most importantly, *The Sayings* was grasped as a herald of Hungary's re-integration with the western world. As one writer expressed it, *The Sayings* contained a quality that since Homer had been known as 'European'.[15]

Clearly the establishment of such an ensemble was only possible because the state supported it, just as its trip to Darmstadt reveals the state's permission to travel out to the avant-garde hub of the West. Six years later in 1974 when the government established an annual festival for contemporary music, the tension between Soviet-style aesthetic dogma and Western-style avant-gardism had effectively imploded. This so-called 'Music of our Time' festival (*Korunk zenéje*) cannot be understood as residing on either side of an artistic-cum-political dichotomy split between 'East' and 'West'.

1.3. The power of speech, and the power of silence

One off-shoot of the recovery in national self-esteem during the latter half of the 1960s was a book of interviews conducted with composers. Almost all the composers interviewed were born in the 1930s, and each gave an account of his compositional history and aspirations. This was a significant moment for the discursive construction of a generation, for it marked a moment in which composers could construct themselves as individuals. But perhaps the most significant aspect of the volume is that although Kurtág did not take part, he was nonetheless brought within its pages. Indeed from the tone taken by the performers interviewed in his place, he patently could not be excluded: he was simply '*our* composer of the time'.[16]

At core this notion stemmed from his stylistic change after 1956. One pianist proposed that Kurtág had practised the 'strictest honesty' and a 'self-reproaching statement of truth', and the interviewer suggested that because Kurtág had such a 'responsible' attitude to musical materials and a 'merciless search for truth', he spoke directly to 'the Hungarian person today'.[17] And that he chose not to take part in a public interview actually fed precisely this sentiment: within a few years a journalist would explain that Kurtág could not introduce audiences to his music because of 'an ethical stance that makes it imperative for [him] to communicate everything that can be said in

---

14 Péter Várnai, 'Kurtág: Bornemisza Péter mondásai – concerto zongorára és szopránhangra, Op. 7', *Filharmónia Műsorfüzet*, 1968, no 37, pp. 20–21 (p. 21).

15 István Homolya, 'A budapesti kamaraegyüttes hangversenye (okt.4)', *Filharmónia Műsorfüzet*, 1968, no 40, pp. 20–22 (p. 22).

16 Ádám Fellegi, in Imre Földes, *Harmincasok. Beszélgetések magyar zeneszerzőkkel*, Budapest, 1969, p. 193. Italics original.

17 Ádám Fellegi, in *Harmincasok. Beszélgetések magyar zeneszerzőkkel*, p. 194. It is not actually clear that Kurtág would have had a blossoming public career had he continued to write in the styles of his *Korean Cantata* and Viola Concerto, but he was indeed sidelined by official organizations subsequently: his music was never featured in a 'composer portrait', for instance. It might be argued that he had not composed enough to warrant such exposure, and that there was no reason for his exclusion from the series other than that. Many such portraits were divided between several composers, however, and whether or not people ever stood in its way, the very fact that such a composer portrait never did take place is representative of Kurtág's situation on the edge. In other words, he was not celebrated 'as Kurtág' – unlike older composers such as Farkas, Kadosa and Ránki, or the younger ones such as Bozay and Durkó. It was not until 1978 that he would have a LP recording dedicated to his works, whereas Balassa, Bozay, Durkó, Petrovics and Láng each had one rather earlier on.

music, and only that when he has found the appropriate form for it.'[18] In other words, the idea that he had rejected public success in favour of inner truth after 1956 had been mapped onto his unwillingness to speak publicly. His refusal to build conceptual bridges between music and the outside world was argued as being emblematic of his ethical superiority.

It is not difficult to detect a deeply romantic view of artistic loftiness emerging in this discourse. Kurtág apparently occupied a space – and had recourse to messages – that would be reduced, perhaps even besmirched, by concepts. But in order to grasp how this eminence had developed, it is instructive to look beyond discourses and view Kurtág's position sociologically. Three factors seem particularly significant, namely timing, networking, and use of language. And the first is relatively straightforward. Kurtág's change of compositional style and his symbolic gesture of writing an Opus 1 coincided with a moment in which people were eager for both musical and political change. He 'came of age' at an opportune moment: Opus 1 was banned, but then rescued and performed, in an environment of exceptionally overheated political dissatisfaction.

The second factor is more complicated to establish, for the society was not one in which people developed documentary records of their activities – far from it. There is nonetheless ample evidence to argue that Kurtág had three types of influential contacts. One is symbolic: his association with figures of artistic importance such as the poet János Pilinszky and painter Lili Ország endowed him with cultural respect in intellectual and artistic circles.[19] Another group of contacts was professional, of whom the most important was composer and 'cellist András Mihály. Mihály had several guises: illegal communist during the Second World War, defender of Bartók in 1949, apparatchik on trial in 1951, instrumental coach of players for the première of Kurtág's String Quartet Op. 1 in 1961, Hungarian symphonist in 1962, founder of the Budapest Chamber Ensemble in 1968, and organizer of the Darmstadt concert programme that presented Kurtág's *The Sayings of Péter Bornemisza*. Given how the reception of his String Quartet and *The Sayings* shaped Kurtág's reputation, it is transparently clear that he benefited considerably from Mihály's support.[20]

---

18 According to a concert review of an event in the bi-annual series of 'composer audience encounters', László Somfai announced this about Kurtág, and proceeded to introduce the composer's music himself. It is revealing to note that after the performance, Kurtág was available for informal discussion with those who wished, and was rapidly surrounded by people talking to him: András Székely, 'A zenei könyvtár és közönsége', *Muzsika*, 17, 1975 (February), 2, pp. 15–16.

19 The nature of their contact is of less importance than the fact that they were understood as a group. Lili Ország's turn to a highly spiritual semi-abstract modernism and public recognition occurred in the early 1960s, parallel with Kurtág's own shift, and her work is referred to by art historian Katalin S. Nagy as 'lonely but not without companions [...] distant from the period's official, supported art, but close to the true representative creations of the 1960s spirit: Pilinszky, Kurtág, Béla Kondor': Katalin S. Nagy, *Ország Lili*, Budapest, 1993, p. 26.

20 A further network of contacts that contributed to his renown consisted of performers and students. From 1959 Kurtág worked as an accompanist at the Bartók Conservatory, but was subsequently, and more significantly, employed as pianist at the state concert agency, the National Philharmonia. There he accompanied a range of professional singers and instrumentalists and helped them prepare for concerts. Already in touch with a large number of performers as a result, when he began teaching piano at the Liszt Academy

In the second section of the article I will consider ways that these observations enable us to engage with Kurtág's music, but first of all I will trace a little further through the idealist discourse in which he was enveloped. For by the early 1980s Kurtág had been claimed on all sides as *the* leading Hungarian composer. One critic observed that even in the context of new music *internationally*, Kurtág's music simply provided more and 'other' qualities; another presented him in the English-language *The New Hungarian Quarterly* as 'clearly [...] the most important living Hungarian composer'. Even more expansively, the editor of the music magazine *Muzsika* made an extended list of the foreign promoters of his music in 1987, arguing that Kurtág, the 'taciturn creator of our tiny homeland', was now regarded by a range of notable figures as one of '*the world's best living composers*'.[21] And the critic who had represented the voice of the regime since 1956 wrote in 1983 that it would have been worth organizing the annual 'Music of our Time' festival simply to hear Kurtág's latest piece.[22]

The irony is that Kurtág had been claimed as a symbol for the nation, and had moved into the centre of the state-sponsored concert life, and yet he still functioned as a living legend of autonomy and ethical purity. The contradiction emerged particularly overtly in 1981, when he changed policy towards public statement and made himself available in Paris and London for interview, and in the following year agreed to contribute to a new book of interviews in Hungary.[23] The resultant text is a cipher for his position in Budapest life: hesitant and somewhat meandering, it portrays an uncertain composer who cannot understand quite how he composes, and who is simply grateful when he manages to write at all (especially after escaping one of his regularly paralysing depressions). As we have seen, in Budapest there was a scenario in place within which the struggles described could be not merely appreciated, but even admired as part of his commitment to exploring the most searching questions of existence. Even for those not persuaded by his candour, it would have seemed obscene in this climate to attack. For Kurtág presented himself as weakness itself: 'the fact that I can write anything at all is, in itself, a great joy. [...] Sometimes, I manage to make something good out of nothing quite by accident. But more often than not I don't.'[24]

At the close of this first section, then, we have arrived at a moment in which Kurtág is actively inscribing himself into the institutionalized space that he occupies and

---

of Music in 1967 he encountered more of the younger generation. He clearly developed thereby a wider reputation as pedagogue than would have been possible had he worked only in a composition faculty or with new music enthusiasts. And when he left the piano faculty, taking up the post of professor in the Department of Chamber Music (where Mihály was chair), he was in touch with a wider range of students. And at the same moment – as mentioned above – a book was published that included a discussion about his national, moral and musical supremacy.

21 János Maróthy, '22. Festival Pontino di Musica', *Muzsika*, 29, 1986 (October), 10, pp. 22–23 (p. 23); György Kroó, 'Egyetlen énekhangra', *Élet és Irodalom*, 3 December 1982, p. 51; Mária Feuer, 'Megint Kurtág', *Muzsika*, 30, 1987 (July), 7, pp. 5–6 (p. 5). My italics.

22 János Breuer, 'Zenei krónika', *Népszabadság*, 2 November, 1983.

23 Hungarian journalists covering the Paris and London concerts at which he spoke (premières of *Messages of the Late Miss R. V. Troussova* Op. 17) expressed astonishment: Mária Feuer, 'Szabálytalan beszámoló Londonból', *Muzsika*, 24, 1981 (April), 4, pp. 11–15 (p. 11); Márta Grabócz, 'Kurtág-bemutató Párizsban', *Muzsika*, 24, 1981 (March), 3, pp. 34–37 (p. 34).

24 György Kurtág and Bálint András Varga, 'It's Not My Ears That Do My Hearing', *New Hungarian Quarterly*, vol 42, 2003 (Spring), pp. 126–134 (p. 134). These are the last words.

shapes. And this situation is particularly well illuminated by a comment made by musi-cologist and critic György Kroó in 1981. Kroó was confronted by a new work by Kurtág, one that broke away from progressive musical trends to take recourse to Gregorian chant and folksong (*Attila József Fragments* Op. 20 for solo soprano). His commentary fell straight into mystification: Kurtág's move, he said, could only be the result of 'inner necessity' and 'melodic genius'.[25] State socialism, we realize, supported both the concept, and the practical existence, of the archetypical romantic genius.

2. Reading Kurtág through Pilinszky

In attempting to locate Kurtág's works within this emerging discourse one immediate starting point is the poetry that he chose to set, and his choice of the work of Pilinszky was highly significant. *Four Songs to Poems by János Pilinszky* Op. 11 (1975) enacted his alliance with a modernist poet who had been banned from publishing his work in the Stalinist years, but whose writing, as observed earlier, was licensed by the Kádár government despite Pilinszky's emphatically spiritual approach and lack of engagement with party rhetoric. Pilinszky was thus a channel for exploring ideas that differed considerably from the mainstream political policy and discourse, but that were nonethe-less tolerated by the state.

The political provenance of the first poem, 'Alcohol', is resolutely opaque: its text is inscrutable. In the song, moreover, the singer seems barely able to enunciate it. Rather than singing or even intoning the poem, he opens with an extended 'Ey' sound (the first syllable) that is to be produced first on the palate, then with a 'pressed sound', and then *molto vibrato*. His unsettling contortions to vocal timbre finally give way to an intona-tion – on the same monotone D – of the first line of the poem. 'Ey' follows again, this time ushering in an intonation of line 2, broken only by an extended 'Ey' that passes through other vowels before settling on the last words of the line. The voice then takes on a quieter, 'guttural' tone, then hums, before intoning the last, weird, lines. The whole poem is as follows:

I conjure up the impossible,	Előhívom a lehetetlent,
a house stands on it, a bush,	egy ház áll rajta s egy bokor,
a silent, silent creature and	egy néma, néma állat és
a trouser leg in falling darkness.[26]	egy nadrágszár a szürkületben.

The vocal cavity itself seems throughout to be painfully pinioned on a line, yet at precisely the moment of the poem's 'falling darkness' the voice sinks one semitone onto C sharp; dropping one further to C natural, for a final, sustained thin vowel, 'üü'. A sustained bass zither D underpins the entire incantation.[27]

25 Kroó, 'Egyetlen énekhangra'.
26 Translation by L.T. András, as printed in the score, Editio Musica Budapest Z.7939. Original: János Pilin-szky, *Pilinszky János összes versei*, Budapest, 1997, p. 133. The collection sets two songs each from Pilinszky's *Dénouement* ('Végkifejlet', 1974) and *Crater* ('Kráter', 1975). As was the case with all poems in these volumes, all four were previously published individually in literary journals, the first two in 1973, the second two in 1974.
27 The score indicates bass 'citara' (presumably zither), viola da gamba or double bass *con sordino sul pont*. This accompaniment is optional.

The last two songs of the collection also engage explicitly with corporeal struggle. In the third, 'Hölderlin', lurching rhythms created by the thick texture of strings are reminiscent of the *aksak* 'limping' dance patterns Bartók associated with Bulgaria. The explicitly mimetic sounds of the instruments seem to scratch and gnaw at themselves too, viola and 'cello playing partly *sul ponticello*, partly *col legno*, partly *battuto*, partly *tratto*. The voice rages above, until the moment at which it renounces life, when a 'resolution' surfaces in triple *piano* tremolo string playing (partly on harmonics); and a whispered last sentence.

December heat, the hails of summers,	December hőse, nyarak jégverése,
a bird knotted to a piece of wire,	drótvégre csomózott madár,
what was I not? Gladly I die.[28]	mi nem voltam én? Boldogan halok.

The title of the last song, 'Beating', implies blows, and the musical setting is unmistakably physical. In between groups of strikes and strike-like gestures in the instrumental group (two cimbaloms, string trio, zither, horn and clarinet), the voice gasps bits of the text, as if it is this singer, here on the stage, who is being beaten. The musical and textual focus is unremittingly in the present.

Now it's endurable.	Most elviselhető.
Now I think of something else.	Most másra gondolok.
Now there's nothing.	Most semmi sincs.
Now I am myself.	Most én vagyok.
Now there's everything.	Most minden van.
Now it's unbearable.	Most tűrhetetlen.
Now, though, now and alone,	Most pedig, most és egyedül,
here and now, alone for good	itt és most, végképp egyedül
only you and me.[29]	csak te meg én.

Patently, then, and despite their reference to Hölderlin, these songs do not project the image of Kurtág's ethical elevation that one might expect from the way in which his public verbal reticence was discussed. They are earthy and visceral. But the second song, 'In memoriam F. M. Dostoevsky', provides a larger and very suggestive context for both their physical torments and Kurtág's discursively-constructed moral loftiness. Its title invokes the revered and deeply religious novelist of nineteenth-century Russia; meanwhile, however, the poem itself alludes to Russia's arbitrary cruelty by presenting a humiliating unclothing:

Bend down. (Bends to the ground.)	Hajoljon le. (Földig hajol).
Stand erect. (Rises up slowly.)	Álljon fel. (Fölemelkedik).
Take off your shirt and underpants.	Vegye le az ingét, gatyáját).
(Takes them off one by one.)	(Mindkettőt leveszi).
Turn and face me. (Turns away. Faces him.)	Nézzen szembe. (Elfordúl.
	Szembenéz).
Put on your clothes.	Öltözzön fel.
(Puts them back on.)[30]	(Fölöltözik.)

28 When he published it in 1974, he dedicated it to Kurtág: *Kortárs*, 10 (September, 1974), p. 1349. Translated here by Peter Jay: Pilinszky, *Crater*, London, 1978, p. 32. Original: *Pilinszky János összes versei*, p. 146.

29 Translated by Peter Jay in Pilinszky, *Crater*, p. 31. Original: *Pilinszky János összes versei*, p. 146.

30 Translation by L.T. András, taken from the score (Editio Musica Budapest Z.7939). Original: *Pilinszky János összes versei*, p. 133.

The performers articulate a confrontation between interrogator and interrogated: the bass-baritone speaks the text (to approximate pitches) in paired sections, and violin and double bass, *meno forte*, accompany each descriptive statement. This grows into a mini-narrative. Whilst the violin's dissonant double-stops and the plucked bass pizzicato initially follow the vocal line, they diverge increasingly from it, generating greater motion and variation, a process that reaches its climax on '(Turns away. Faces him.)'. The substantial pause that ensues invites reflection on the suggestion of the text: a naked man (powerless) stands in front of a clothed one (in command). Yet this pause is followed by sounds that transform the imaginary scenario. As if conjuring up the fairy-tale magic of a harp, a spread triple-stop on the violin introduces open fifths, *piano, quasi dolce*, and the double bass plays *arco*. The next command, 'Put on your clothes' is intoned *quasi falsetto*. The final bar provides consonant closure, in the form of the four open strings of the violin, partially supported by the open C on the double bass. The condemned man was saved.

As a group of four, then, these songs present not only distorted vision and physical cruelty (with a specific political resonance), but also the hope of redemption (Dosto-evsky's own death sentence was revoked at the last moment).[31] The music of 'In memoriam F. M. Dostoevsky', moreover, enacts a process of salvation through unin-hibited corporeality: the moment of nakedness is a turning point of the intoned text. For if it seems initially that the power is in the hands of the one uttering the commands, then by the end it appears that the one stripped naked gains strength from his very nakedness, triggering a loss of voice in the commander, and a harmonic resolution to the entire episode. The song is thus metaphorical. It moves beyond the specifics of a prison interrogation (where an unclothing would not result in any such transformation in a real sense) to a level of intimating – while not describing – some of the powers of nakedness.

The songs could, consequently, contribute to the idealized image of Kurtág that was emerging in the press. For writer Gábor Thurzó, lines 5 and 6 of 'Beating' touched on precisely the need to be searching – but never finding – Truth. 'Now there's everything' followed immediately by 'Now it's unbearable' encapsulated Thurzó's philosophy for life, according to which life itself would be over once everything was known and under-stood. He also found that the music *touched* him, physically: the sounds became more and more homely as he listened repeatedly so that finally he felt that they came from within him.[32]

We can, however, explore this physicalized idealism further by comparing the songs with Kurtág's *Szálkák* (Splinters) Op. 6c. When the so-named four pieces for solo cimbalom were first performed in Budapest, not all writers were aware of the prove-nance of the title, which was a volume of Pilinszky's poetry published in 1973. Leading critic János Breuer knew, however, and celebrated Kurtág himself as a 'true poet' when

---

31 The volume in which this poem was published, *Dénouement*, contains two other explicit references to Dostoevsky, two poems about the character Stavrogin from *The Devils*, 'Stavrogin takes his leave' and 'Stavrogin returns'. Stavrogin's name being Greek for 'cross', this unfortunate character was an entirely appropriate focus for Pilinszky's obsessions, as will become clearer below.

32 Gábor Thurzó, 'Pilinszky és Kurtág', *Élet és Irodalom*, 22 October, 1977, p. 12.

he heard it, a claim that is worth examining.[33] He quoted from 'Metronome', one of the poems published in Pilinszky's own *Splinters*, as an analogy for Kurtág's own mastery of silence and musical time:

Measure time	Mérd az időt,
but not our time,	de ne a mi időnket,
the motionless present of splinters,	a szálkák mozdulatlan jelenét,
the angles of the drawbridge,	a fölvonóhíd fokait,
the white winter of our execution,	a téli vesztőhely havát,
the silence of paths and clearings[34]	ösvények és tisztások csöndjét

This claim for the poem's relevance to Kurtág was actually an amazing obfuscation, for Breuer had omitted its last two lines, precisely the lines that reveal the poet's primary source of inspiration:

in the setting of the fragmented jewel	a töredék foglalatában
the promise of God the Father.	az Atyaisten ígéretét.

At one blow, in fact, Breuer had erased the single most significant element of Pilinszky's new volume (and, by extension, of the title of Kurtág's new work). Although metaphysics had been a crucial part of Pilinszky's poetry from his very earliest work, *Splinters* had been understood at the time as a particular milestone in his spiritual development. Not only had it made a break with conventional forms, pared down poetic means and shifted into an almost fragmenting texture, it had also transformed death from being a source of terror and horror to something that might be welcome.[35] Pilinszky's adherence to profoundly violent imagery remained unbroken, but now physical suffering was rediscovered as a vital force, and the poems drew repetitively on the ultimate Christian symbol for such suffering, the cross. Most importantly, one of the words he used for the crucifix was nothing other than 'splinter'. Thus the very title of his new volume bore the weight of the spiritual symbol, as indeed did Kurtág's own pieces. As the poem 'Before', for instance, suggests, the poet sees the day of judgement before him and:

... The Father, as if it were a splinter,	... Az Atya, mint egy szálkát
withdraws the cross...[36]	visszaveszi a keresztet, ...

---

33 János Breuer, 'Zenei krónika' (review including Kurtág's *Szálkák* Op. 6c), *Népszabadság*, 9 October, 1974.
34 Translated by William Jay Smith. Miklós Vajda (ed.), *Modern Hungarian Poetry*, includes an introduction by Miklós Vajda and a foreword by William Jay Smith, Budapest, 1977, p. 152. Original: 'Metronóm', *Pilinszky János összes versei*, p. 99.
35 András Diószeghi, 'P.J.: Szálkák', *Kortárs*, 1973, 10, pp. 1676–1679 (pp. 1676–77); László Fülöp, 'Pilinszky János: Szálkák', *Alföld. Irodalmi és Művészeti Folyóirat*, 24, 1973, 3, pp. 78–81 (p. 78); Miklós Béládi, 'P.J.: Szálkák', *Kritika*, 1973, 2, p. 22. This ability to face the future may have been a response to the new political situation as much as an internal shift within Pilinszky himself. At least one writer argued this was a response to general trends in Catholicism within the Eastern Bloc, where an effort was made to look beyond suffering and to offer a vision for life (or afterlife) beyond it (Diószeghi, 'P.J.: Szálkák', pp. 1678–79).
36 'Mielőtt' in *Pilinszky János összes versei*, p. 95. My translation.

Withdrawing the splinter of life leads here to salvation later on in the poem, represented by weeping at the Lord's Table with angels in attendance.

If we examine this transformative moment more fully, we gain a telling perspective for reading Kurtág. Pilinszky's splinter (crucifix) represents a universal human besmirchment: humanity, in its inherent evil, is as a whole deservedly and permanently nailed to a cross – we may even 'be' the nail in the flesh of humanity. Sheer physical mutilation thus shaped a number of poems, including 'Cattle Brand', in which:

A nail driven into the world's palm,	A világ tenyerébe kalapált szeg,
pale as death,	holtsápadt,
I flow with blood.[37]	csurom vér vagyok.

But the crucifix was also a representation of a cross-section of death with life. Its two physical dimensions were a constant reminder that human life was not a straight line from birth to death, thus it could remain a symbol of hope, evoking a repetitive encounter with Truth through which one could forget oneself (a sort of death), only to rediscover oneself.[38] The constant pain of being nailed to the cross was thus something to celebrate, just as was its echo, the piercing pain caused by splinters. As the second poem in the volume, 'To Jutta', concludes:

'Like thieves – in the lovely words of Simone Weil	„Latrokként – Simone Weil gyönyörű szavával
– we are nailed to the cross of time and space.'	– tér és idő keresztjére
I faint, and the splinters arouse me.	vagyunk mi verve emberek."
At such times I see the world with piercing clarity,	Elalélok, és a szálkák fölriasztanak.
and try to turn my head towards you.[39]	Ilyenkor metsző élességgel látom a világot,
	és megpróbálom feléd fordítani a fejemet.

Here splinters are the fragments of a great crucifix borne by mankind as a whole, and they trigger a painful vision of truth. Thus physical suffering evolves into a means to superior understanding.[40]

Even on a superficial level, such an understanding of 'splinters' is a potent context, for Kurtág's Op. 6c. Movement 2, marked 'Sostenuto', is composed of three sweeping 'blows' to the strings, and their resonant aftermaths. During the dying resonances, lightly touched gestural fragments seem to make 'comments', the last one of which anticipates the lament motive of movement 4. We might imagine these three explicitly physical strikes as references to Pilinszky's crucifix, each percussive blow to the

---

37 Translated by William Jay Smith, adjusted by Peter Sherwood: Vajda, *Modern Hungarian Poetry*, p. 154. Original: 'Marhabélyeg', in *Pilinszky János összes versei*, p. 110.

38 Such 'deaths' or moments of revelation became for Pilinszky more consequential than physical death, which could never be truly experienced in itself. These sentiments – differentiating his ideas dramatically from those of Beckett – are characteristic of Pilinszky's writings over the early 1970s, but are particularly clearly summarized in his 'Egy lírikus naplójából', *Új Ember*, 25 February, 1973, reprinted in Pilinszky, *Publicisztikai írások*, Budapest, 1999, pp. 694–95.

39 Juttának', in *Pilinszky János összes versei*, p. 94. My translation.

40 Reference to the nature of the splinters crops up throughout the literature. For example, in a 1973 interview with the poet (Endre Török, (ed.), *Beszélgetések Pilinszky Jánossal*, Budapest, 1983, p. 83), in commentary (Fülöp, 'Pilinszky János: Szálkák'; Béládi, 'P.J.: Szálkák'), and in Ted Hughes' visionary essay on his work first published in 1976: Hughes, 'Introduction', in János Pilinszky, *The Desert of Love*, trans. János Csokits and Ted Hughes, London, 1989, pp. 7–16.

instrument a nail driven through flesh into the cross, and the fragments stirring after them are as if splinters under the skin.

Movement 4 labels itself as a reflection on death, not only subtitled *in memoriam Ştefan Romaşcanu,* but also drawing on musical weeping figures typical of folk laments and the *pianto* topic of the Baroque. And – as if an echo of Pilinszky's consoling and optimistic reflections on mortality – while this first section evokes the sadness in death and loss, the second may evoke liberation from such pain. Above a 'tolling' bass note (D) in a continuous decrescendo from *fortissimo to quasi niente,* the widely displaced chromatic descent (from C sharp thirteen steps to C natural) creates a broken melody of fragmentary musical shapes allowing the performer to create a sense of resolution and release.

Yet it is even more rewarding to bring this frame of reference to *Four Songs* Op. 11. The nail through the palm hovers in the background there too ('a bird knotted to a piece of wire'); and a martyr's death is suggested immediately thereafter: '... (Gladly I die)'. Pilinszky's poems, as Ted Hughes argued, 'reveal a place where every cultural support has been torn away, where the ultimate brutality of total war has become natural law, and where man has been reduced to the mere mechanism of his mutilated body.'[41] Yet such anti-aesthetic, 'primal' moments in *Four Songs* are striking for the way that they stage extreme indignity and pain in order to transform it – such as in the moment of nakedness – into calm resolution. Degrading reduction, perversely, becomes a moment of transcendence in musical expression.

As already mentioned, not all critics were aware of the provenance of the title 'splinters', and none of the texts of *Four Poems* prompted them to mention the broader spiritual frame within which their poet existed.[42] Unsurprisingly they also made no reference to the ways in which either work might be positioned within the current political reality. Silence in that area does not alter the fact that references to Dostoevsky's near-execution and being 'knotted to wire' could have been understood as an allusion to the suffering caused by the Soviet oppression, and perhaps human culpability more generally as well. The moments of resolution and salvation could even have been grasped as projections of martyrdom for a greater good.

Narratives of tragedy and redemption have a history in Hungarian mythology, and recent events – the crushed uprising of 1956 in particular – fitted into the mould of Hungary's role as tragic 'witness'. The songs touched on precisely this set of ideas, even if only tangentially. Once presented on the musical stage, moreover, they publicly drew Kurtág into the sphere of Pilinszky's sacrificial religiosity, and they implicitly

---

41 Hughes, p. 11.
42 Reviewers uniformly praised the immediacy of Op. 11 and focused on its exposure of the 'greatest secrets' of the composer's workshop along with the 'primal' connection it created between speech and song. János Breuer, 'Zenei krónika', *Népszabadság,* 7 October, 1975; Péter Várnai, 'Zenei levél' *Magyar Hírlap,* 4 October, 1975; Tibor Tallián, 'Korunk zenéje a hangversenyeken', *Muzsika,* 16, 1974, 12, pp. 3–12. For András Wilheim ('Kurtág György: *Szálkák*', *Filharmónia műsorfüzet,* 1975, no. 15, p. 37) *Splinters* was an 'unbroken whole' developing in an 'uninterrupted line', Dominic Gill ('Reviews – A Collage' (published originally in *The Financial Times*)), in Bálint András Varga, (ed.), *Contemporary Hungarian Music in the International Press,* Budapest, 1982, pp. 43–60 at p. 43) heard a single '*piece* in four sections', while Várnai (Péter Várnai, 'Zenei levél', *Magyar Hírlap,* 5 October, 1974) openly puzzled about the strange title, for the music wasn't, he said, 'splintery' at all.

constructed the two artists in terms of a struggle to speak the truth through physical torment and anguish. And yet the première of *Four Poems* took place in a particularly prominent and prestigious (state-supported) concert, a composer 'portrait concert' in the Music of Our Time festival. Confused and contradictory government policy led it to participate in an exploration of guilt and incarceration, and celebrate spiritual revelation through suffering.

The Importance of Reading the Actual Lines and not in between them: Ferenc Juhász's Poem *Évszakok* (1957) in the Shadow of its English Versions[1]

Peter Sherwood

It is a truism to say that there is an intimate link between literature and politics in Hungary, and verging on a truism to point out that there (and probably in many other countries) literary ferment often precedes political explosion and, often, revolution: 1848–49 and 1956 are excellent examples. In both these cases the failure of the revolt was followed by repression in every sphere, but I should like to show, in relation to 1956, how the personal and the political remained intertwined in an interesting way in at least some native poetry, even in the immediate aftermath of the Revolution.

Ferenc Juhász was born in 1928, the son of a stonemason and a housemaid, in Bia, a village south-west of Budapest, and educated there and in nearby Bicske. He married Erzsébet Szeverényi in 1948; her family were declared kulaks and his father-in-law spent seven years in jail for this; as the daughter of kulaks, Erzsébet was not allowed to take a job at the university in 1951, which led or contributed to her depressive illness. Juhász's first poems appeared at the end of 1947 and his progress up the poetic ladder was startling: he won the József Attila prize at 22 and the most prestigious Hungarian literary prize, the Kossuth (silver grade), a year later, in 1951. To many at the time he seemed to embody the spirit of Petőfi: a fluent, sweeping talent, a poet-shaman of the Hungarian people drawing deep from the well of the literature of the folk. In the late 1950s and during the 60s he was feted, particularly by the all-powerful Writers' Union, as the greatest living Hungarian poet. His poem *The Boy Changed into a Stag Cries Out at the Gate of Secrets*, an ambitious attempt to match verbally Bartók's *Cantata Profana,* won the admiration of no less an authority than W. H. Auden.[2] As his poetry darkened over the years, it filled with a world of biological terror: prehistoric creatures, mythical birds, overwhelming proliferations of flora and fauna. The poems expanded to hundreds and even thousands of lines in length – for example, *Halott feketerigó* (Dead Blackbird, 1985) consists of 25,747 lines – and became uneven in quality. I believe his poetry draws on two main sources: Hungarian tradition in (as mentioned) its folk aspect

---

1 I should like to express my thanks to Richard Benson (BA Hungarian and East European Studies, UCL-SSEES, 2006), whose excellent coursework on this poem inspired me to finally pull together my thoughts on it.

2 He called it 'one of the greatest poems written in my time.' (Cited from the inside cover of the McRobbie/Duczynska volume.)

but also Hungarian history and literature more broadly, and his reading of Ob-Ugric literature in Hungarian translation (the Ob-Ugrians, comprising the Voguls or Mansi and the Ostyaks or Khanty, whose languages are the nearest relatives of Hungarian) and particularly Bernát Munkácsi's translations of Vogul folk poetry, published mainly between the 1890s and the 1930s. I have tried to show elsewhere[3] that Munkácsi's translations have influenced several twentieth-century poets; here I will just mention that, for instance, the title of the Juhász volume *A szent tűzözön regéi* (Legends of the Holy Flood of Fire, 1969) is taken directly from Munkácsi.[4] In fact, he does not, to the best of my knowledge, read any foreign language with ease, and has never translated any poetry into Hungarian, which is unusual among Hungarian poets.

The poem I shall be considering was written in 1957[5] and was first collected in Juhász's first post-1956 volume *Harc a fehér báránnyal* (Battling the White Lamb, 1965). The volume contains two major poems and therefore the shorter pieces in it, such as *Seasons*, are rarely given much attention. Even in his monograph on Juhász, Bodnár devotes only one short sentence to it: 'In *Seasons* it is the (hi)story of crisis and hope that is embedded in the description of the changes in Nature.'[6] Yet, despite its characteristically difficult vocabulary and typical Juhászian Niagara of biological imagery, it is in fact a poem of considerable formal discipline, with rich assonances, very interesting rhymes, and a distinct metrical structure, only certain aspects of which will be explored here. Its brevity also makes it suitable for a short essay such as this. And it is not, as I hope to show, only about nature, and does not offer a great deal of hope.

The innocuous classical title and theme is immediately undermined (lines 1) by the sequence in which the seasons are presented: they begin in what was the previous autumn.

1 Elmúlt *az ősz*
1 S elmúlt *a tél* is
1 Ó, ez *a tavasz!*
1 Majd jön *a nyár*

Amid all the baroque and/or surrealistic flora and fauna, there are quite startlingly straightforward statements, when, for example, the author goes begging for bread in the freezing and starving winter months. So the poem begins with the autumn of 1956, and the *elbomlás* (dictionary equivalent: 'disintegration, decomposition') that has passed with it is not, or not simply, 'the leaves turning to mould' or a Victorian-sounding

---

3 Peter Sherwood, 'Ob-Ugric literature in English: A case study in indirect contacts', in R. Blokland, C. Hasselblatt (eds), *Finno-Ugrians and Indo-Europeans: Linguistic and Literary Contacts*, Studia Fenno-Ugrica Groningiana 2, Maastricht, 2002, p. 345.
4 *Vogul Népköltési Gyűjtemény*, vol 1. Regék és énekek a világ teremtéséről, Fascicle 1, Budapest, 1892, p. 68. NB This is Munkácsi's own 'cover term' and does not correspond exactly to any Vogul phrase found on this page.
5 György Bodnár gives 1958 as the date of composition (Bodnár György *Juhász Ferenc*, Budapest, 1993. p. 53), which (if true), makes the poem even more remarkable. The poem is often printed with a question-mark at the end, but I do not believe this to be in the manuscript; in any case it makes little difference to the analysis offered here.
6 'Az *Évszakok*ban (1958) a változó természet leírása foglalja magában a válság és remény történetét', in Bodnár, p. 53.

'decay' that is 'sped', as in the two English translations appended below. The stem *boml-* is much more to do with falling or coming apart, of some unifying force not, or no longer, holding things together, and it is also a frequent euphemism for loss of sanity. There is certainly a tragic personal story told in the poem: in particular, each stanza ends with a reference to an attribute of a 'you' that is female. Juhász's wife, Erzsébet Szevérenyi, had suffered a breakdown and was in hospital.

Autumn/	line 8	bolyongó szem-ed-be.#1/s2→	(23[?] syllables)
Winter/	line 8	lángfehér ének-ed-re.#2/s2→	(23 syllables)
Spring/	line 8	szagos-sírkövű mell-ei-d-re.#3/s2→	(23 syllables)
Summer/	line 6!	szív-ed-re.#4/s2→	
	line 8!	a szív-ed-be#4/s2→*temetve*	(25 syllables).

There is no question of the supreme importance of this very personal dimension. However, there is more to this poem than what one of its translators, David Wevill, says about it: 'a personal lament written during his wife's illness', in which there is 'despair.' (Sándor Weöres [and] Ferenc Juhász, *Selected Poems*, Penguin Books, Harmondsworth. 1970. p. 77). His other translator, Kenneth McRobbie, who visited Hungary a number of times and was (and may still be) married to a Hungarian, hints that there might be more to the poem, writing in the Introduction to his volume that it 'tells of [his wife's] tragic breakdown amid personal and indeed social crisis in 1957.' (Ferenc Juhász *The Boy Changed into a Stag: Selected Poems 1949–1967*. Translated by Kenneth McRobbie and Ilona Ducyznska. Oxford University Press (Canada) 1970. p. 17). It is difficult to know how much McRobbie understood of the poem, partly because his comment may reflect a reluctance to upset his official sponsors by being more explicit about 1956 and its aftermath. But even if he was aware of something more, his appreciation of the work was hindered by the serious handicap of not knowing Hungarian (Wevill freely admits that he knows none; McRobbie is coy). Both English versions, published the same year, 1970, are examples of the 'double translation' technique, whereby the foreign poet relies on rough versions and commentaries from native speakers considered fluent in the foreign poet's native tongue. This approach enjoyed especial popularity, notably in North America, at the time these versions were made. When both the foreign poet and the native informant(s) are gifted and able to appreciate the intellectual level of the original work, and there is (preferably) some spark between the two poets, the results can be powerful and memorable (even if they do not please everyone), as the example of Ted Hughes's versions of János Pilinszky, or Edwin Morgan's of Weöres and Attila József, strikingly demonstrate. But, as will become apparent, this is not the scenario in this case.

Returning to the actual rhymes, a subgroup of these are of the type known as *ragrím* in Hungarian: grammatical suffix morphemes where the rhyme is given by the grammar and therefore not highly valued. Here, however, they bring together the four stanzas in an interesting way and gain additional prominence thereby. These lative (dynamic, 'movement towards') suffixes in *–re, -be*, in the rhyme position are counterpointed by another set of formally identical grammatical suffixes in this position: those in the front-vowel version, *-ve*, of the supine (an adverbial form, sometimes called a gerund), the meaning of which is approximately 'in a state of x-ing or of having x-ed', where x is a verb:

Autumn/line 6 kicsüng-ve	*approximately*	'hanging out'
Winter/ line 6 tipeg-ve		'tip-toeing'
Spring/ line 6 sistereg-ve		'sizzling'
Summer/line 8! temet-ve		'buried'

If we now bring together the suffixes of lines 6 and 8, we see something of considerable interest: in the final stanza, which refers to the Summer still to come, the supine normally in line 6 is found in line 8, while the lative normally in line 8 is found in line 6 – although there is still a 'matching' lative form in the 'correct' line, line 8, of this stanza, whose dynamic positional finality is usurped by the stasis of the final supine form, *temetve* ('in a state of being, or having been, buried'), which is placed at the end of the line, the end of the stanza, and the end of the poem. That is, the phrase *a szívedbe temetve* 'buried in your heart' ends the poem on a note of enormous, cumulated personal helplessness.

However, there is another striking set of lines in the poem, which I believe confirm that its context is even broader. I refer to the form of line 5 in each of the four stanzas, where the repetitions and the identity of syntactic structure attest to the utmost importance accorded to these lines:[7]

5 Hulla-viola árnyékot csurgattak a bálnaszájú rácsok,
5 Jácint-kék árnyékot gondoltak a tündérország-rácsok,
5 Epezöld árnyékot öklendeznek a foltos-bőrű rácsok,
5 Savas árnyékot sziszegnek a foszló hüllőtestű rácsok,

5 ADJ árnyékot [TOPIC] csurgattak	a ADJ rácsok,	[SUBJECT]
5 ADJ árnyékot [TOPIC] gondoltak	a tündérország-rácsok,	[SUBJECT]
5 ADJ árnyékot [TOPIC] öklendeznek	a ADJ rácsok,	[SUBJECT]
5 ADJ árnyékot [TOPIC] sziszegnek	a ADJ rácsok,	[SUBJECT]

↕	↕		
SHADOW	DRIBBLE	*past tense*	rácsok
	THINK	*past tense*	
	VOMIT	*non-past tense*	
	HISS	*non-past tense*	

As mentioned, an important point about these lines is their four-times-repeated, rock rigid syntactic structure (weakened to the point of almost total loss in the translations). Moreover, the four-fold repetition or self-rhyme in the four lines consists of their subject, *a rácsok*, the nature of Hungarian syntax making it possible to place the grammatical subject at the end of the line, i.e. in the highlighted, rhyming position. At the same time, the grammatical object *árnyék* 'shadow' is placed in the topic slot, 'topic' being the term used in the pragmatic-informational strand of syntactic analysis to refer to what the sentence is about. This double-anchoring could perhaps be expressed, in a

---

7 I first referred, briefly, to the inaccurate translation of these particular lines by McRobbie and Duczynska in my paper 'Nyelvtipológia és a modern magyar költészet angolra fordítása' in M. Béládi, J. Jankovics, J. Nyerges (eds), *A magyar vers*, Budapest, 1985, p. 439.

temporary *Mischsprache*, as 'x SHADOW – DRIBBLED(etc.) – BY THE y *RÁCSOK*'. This suggests a degree of intense unity between the four stanzas/seasons, both through the repeated topic and especially through the prominent position of the repeated subject at the line-ends. The latter point to, or point up, the other, similarly not-truly-rhyming four-fold repetition, that of the supine ending –*ve*, especially of the –*ve* that ends the final stanza of the poem.

This – we may now add – is given extra prominence: the final line of the poem is extra-metrical, two syllables longer than the other stanzas' final lines, locating *temetve* simultaneously inside the poem and in the 'real' world outside it.

The reason I have not yet suggested a translation for *a rácsok,* the only grammatical subject repeated four times and in the same place in every stanza, is that while the word might be, as the translators think, rendered as 'railing' or 'railings', another sense – perhaps, even lexicographically, its primary translation – is certainly invoked: '(prison) bars'. The hospital may well have been a bleak place fenced about with railings, but the poem is equally about the bleakness of the country as a whole: it was a prison.

Any lingering doubts about the scope of the poem will be dispelled if we consider, finally, the only 'bars' in it attached to a noun: the compound in the Winter stanza, *tündérország-rácsok*. McRobbie's 'shadows from [!] fairyland [?], behind [!] that [!] railing' are as wide of the mark as Wevill's 'frosted [!] railings'. *Tündérország* is indeed something like Faërie the 'land of the fays or faeries', or perhaps as in Spenser, with additional attributes of magic and wonder and ineffability. Possibly 'Wonderland' would better convey here the combination of the magically special and ironically/tragically unattainable. For Hungarians *tündérország* here recalls the roots of Hungarian folk literature and its implicit continuation in the *tündérország* of the national poet Petőfi's *János Vitéz,* as well as, in post-Trianon Hungary, Zsigmond Móricz's *Tündérkert* (Faerie's Garden), the title of the first part of his tableau of 'Golden Age' Transylvania, which remains for many the historical heartland of Hungarianness.

'…I, in your heart buried', as McRobbie has it, certainly; but also, in the Spring of 1957, buried in the prison of the Magyar lands.

Évszakok
Elmúlt az ősz. Az elbomlás is elmúlt.
Rothadt növényeken gázoltam tehozzád.
Árva szemem halottak elhagyott szemhéjába bújt,
mint gyöngy-kérgű csigaházba magányos, meztelen rák.
Hulla-viola árnyékot csurgattak a bálnaszájú rácsok,
korhadt csecsemők és szutykos őszirózsák nyögtek ajkukból kicsüngve.
Kék gerlét vezettek hozzám, kis lábán viselt csengettyűs aranyláncot:
Atom-hasító mosolyodban áztam, s beleőszültem bolyongó szemedbe.

S elmúlt a tél is. Nem úgy, mint a többi.
A vedlett ég ropog a harangok fogsorában.
Gépfegyver-fogvacogásban indultam neked kenyeret könyörögni.
Csendből-bogozott erdő szikrázik a tél anyagában.
Jácint-kék árnyékot gondoltak a tündérország-rácsok,
csöndernyős bánat alól a vadak az ablakhoz tolongtak tipegve.

Ágyad szélén, mint öreg ház jázminbokrot, hallgattam gondtalan csacsogásod
és szarvas, nyúl, fácán, rigó figyelt a lecsülkölt hóban lángfehér énekedre.

Ó, ez a tavasz! Zöld, húsos tajték tódul,
s ráforr a falakra repedezett zománccal,
gombos kocsányán virág-hullák foszlánya bódul,
s benyúl a szemekért az űr gomolygó tapogató-halállal.
Epezöld árnyékot öklendeznek a foltos-bőrű rácsok,
hova emberhúsevő halak, nagyfogú csillagok gyűlnek sisteregve,
mert odacsalják burjánzó vágyak, beteg imák, átkok és boldog makogások.
Itt borulok én, tetszhalott sírra bodzabokor, szagos-sírkövű melleidre.

Majd jön a nyár. Népet arany-éremmé ver!
S a holdban fölágaskodik kék vigyorral az egyszarvú csődör
és jajgat a világ a szenvedés rátekeredő idegzetével.
S ibolyántúli habban a rovar álmodozva dőzsöl.
Savas árnyékot sziszegnek a foszló hüllőtestű rácsok,
s rásül üszkösen sok lepke a gyíkkézből kidagadt szívedre.
S hártyásodó lombok alatt hallgatom akkor is virágnőstény-zokogásod,
míg itt hörgök én, piros cseppkőbarlangkertben, fekete párduc, a szívedbe temetve.

Four Seasons

Autumn is gone. The leaves have turned to
        mould.
I trampled over the mush of plants on my way to
        you.
My orphaned eyes skulked in holes the dead had
        abandoned
like hermit crabs in the dead shells they crawl to.
The whale-mouthed iron railings dribbled violet
        shadows of the dead,
spongy babies, stale chrysanthemums, hung from their
        lips, moaning and crying.
They brought me a blue turtle dove, a gold chain and
        a bell on its tiny leg.
I drowned in your atom-splitting smile, your moongaze
        turned my hair grey.

And winter's over. Not like the winters we knew.
A sky of bone crackles in the jaws of the church
        bells.
Teeth chattering like machine-guns I went out
        begging crumbs for you.
The still forest glittered like broken glass.
Shadows blue as hyacinth blurred from the frosted
        railings,
And grieving, hooded in quiet, the animals, tip-toeing
        circled your window.

By the bed I listened to your breezy chatter, like a
    jasmine rustling,
and red deer, hare, pheasant, thrush, heard the white
    flame of your song in the churned snow.

    And now it is spring. A soft mould-flush
oozes and sticks to the walls in a thin green glaze.
Dead flower-heads drift and soak in the jelly mush,
and death circles in from the void, misting the eyes.
    The blotchy railings vomit bile-green shadows
where maneating fish and stars with shark's teeth swirl
    home to the feast,
    Bought by sick lusts and stale prayers, mad gibberings
    and curses.
And I, an elder tree on year deadalive grave, throw my-
    self on the stelae of your breasts.

    Summer will come, minting us gold with light.
On the moon the magic unicorn rears with his
    blue grin.
And the wailing world remembers its griefs, the
    nerves tensing around it.
In its ultraviolet scum, the insect breeds to dis-
    traction;
Acid shadows drip from the peeling railings,
and butterflies burn to ash on your heart, as the lizard's
    fist squeezes it.
    In this garden of ferns I hear your girl-flower
    weeping.
In this cave of blood-red stones I moan to you, a black
    leopard buried alive in your heart.

Translated by David Wevill [+ Flora Papastavrou (+ István Siklós), p. 80]. From *Selected Poems: Sándor Weöres/Ferenc Juhász*. Penguin Modern European Poets. Penguin Books, Harmondsworth, 1970. pp. 114–5. Layout as printed.

Seasons

    Sped is Autumn! And decay is sped.
  I tore towards you across the rotting plants.
My helpless eyes hid behind the vacant lids of the dead,
like solitary naked crabs in pearl-rimmed shells.
Dead men's shadows run purple from the whale-tooth railings.
Mouldering babies hang from their maw, and moaning
                soiled chrysanthemums.
A blue dove they led towards me, her feet belled silver
             chains trailing.
I slumped before your atom-splitting smile, turned grey
             under your wandering glance.

And Winter's gone! Unlike others we knew.
   The city jaw of bells gnaws the bald heavens.
My teeth machine-gun the cold streets, where I begged bread for you.
Winter ties up the woods in silence, knotting the white ends.
Hyacinth-blue the shadows from fairyland, behind that railing,
  up to your silent window lope animals in a sorrowing throng.
Grey ruin hugging the lilac, at your bedside I listen to
                      your heedless babbling,
deer, hare, and thrush in the marked snow follow you flame-white song.

    Pitiless Spring! Foam encrusts the walls,
     organic green flesh has dried in a cracked glaze,
    shreds of dead flowers shrivel beside spooled tendrils,
     death's whirling arms for the bright seed grains reach from outer space.
    Shadows vomit up green bile beside the railing,
cannibal sharks and saw-tooth starfish thrash hungry in swarms,
lust sprouts at your dribbled prayers, chuckles, and happy gabbling.
I throw myself here, grass on living grave, covering breasts
                  fragrant as tombs.
     And in time Summer! Into a gold medal it mints a people.
     The moon's randy stallion flashes his badge with a blue grin,
    beneath ropes of nerves, cries of pain rise from the world.
    In ultra-violet froth the insect slavers in its daydream.
    Acid shadows are licking from the snake-fang railing,
    lizard fingers grasp at your bulging heart, where many moths
              to red ash burned.
Under the hardening leaves, I listen to your female flower's
             husky moaning,
groaning by the red cave's dripstone garden, great panther, I,
           in your heart buried.

Translated by Kenneth McRobbie and Ilona Duczynska. From: Ferenc Juhász *The Boy Changed into a Stag. Selected Poems 1949–1967*. Oxford University Press (Canada), 1970. pp. 73–4. Layout as printed.

1956: Recollections

Speaking Up: The History of a Comment

György Litván

The comment in question was addressed to Mátyás Rákosi, in his presence, in 1956, but before describing that encounter in detail, I should like to explain how I became a communist in 1947 and how I subsequently turned against communism.

My social background and upbringing did not predispose me towards communism. I came from a well-established Jewish middle-class family. My father and his circle of friends were progressive liberals and belonged to what was known as the 'bourgeois democratic' movement in the interwar period. My generation, after the horrors of the Second World War, faced a different world.

There is no question that the imposing and coherent theoretical framework of Marxism proved extremely attractive to the young generation of intellectuals who came on the scene in 1945 or soon afterwards and who had been up to that time exposed to an array of different influences and pressures. For them Marxism had the answer to any question, whether about society or economics or art or, indeed, life in general. Nevertheless, experience suggests that in the majority of cases the main driving force behind Marxism was not intellectual. The process did not begin, even for a György Lukács, with the blinding truth of Marxism-Leninism holding us spellbound and obliterating every other theory and world view. Its chief attraction tended to be a composite of motifs of other kinds. Of these, the following four would seem to be the most important, but the list is not intended to be exhaustive: first, rebellion against the social injustices of the old order, reinforced by bourgeois 'class guilt'; secondly, the desire by those who led an intellectual, essentially isolated, existence to form an integral part of the community; thirdly, the possibility of taking real action by those who until then had been condemned to look merely on as spectators; and last, but not least, the thirst for power or, more precisely, the desire to identify with those in power who because of their social status, Jewish origins, or both, were historically the outcasts of society.

These factors may serve to account for people joining up and identifying both intellectually and aesthetically, but fall short of explaining why a communist intelligentsia that had once been trained to think did not wake up to reality, even when they witnessed the most outrageously evil deeds and lies. The force that kept them within the party and blindly loyal to it was obviously fear and dread; yet that fear was strikingly different from the entirely rational fear of the non-communists at this time, for what we were terrified of was the power of a party we supported – indeed, deified – as well as of our own suppressed thoughts and feelings. As long as monolithic Stalinism existed, the recognition of reality, and the learning of lessons from it, was tantamount to taking a leap into the void, to moral and physical annihilation. This was true even beyond the physical boundaries of Stalin's empire.

A cornerstone of our view was that we were on the threshold of a new era in world history. Both the victors of the war and the defeated fascist countries and their satellites were undergoing fundamental changes. There were a number of indications of this: the apparent strength of the French and Italian communist parties, the nationalizations in Britain, the popularity of Sartre and other trenchant critics of the bourgeois lifestyle, and so forth. These irrefutable signs of crisis led us to think that traditional western values were in decline and had indeed already lost their validity. The teachings of György Lukács recognized this. From time to time we attended his lectures at the university and although our reaction to his ideas tended to be either critical or ironical, we certainly fell under his spell and ended up sharing his delusions. We had believed that the bourgeois world and so-called bourgeois democracy with its rights to liberty, art, philosophy and so on, could not be rescued or defended. From this we drew the painful – and erroneous – conclusion that the barbarism that was coming from the East to destroy these values and glories, intellectually inferior though it might be, could still bring a healthy breath of fresh air and a much-needed rejuvenation. With these beliefs in our heads we innocently walked into the trap laid by the communist party and unwittingly made ourselves ready and willing to receive Marxism-Leninism, that is to say, Stalinism.

What we did not give any consideration to in those days is something that cannot be dismissed today: our relationship to Hungarian realities, or to put it simply, the Hungarian nation. One might ask why we did not feel guilty, or at least have scruples, about assisting a transparently violent regime to bully the Hungarian people in a most anti-democratic way. Although of bourgeois origin, we had a strong 'class guilt-complex' in relation to the poor, who had throughout Hungarian history been down-trodden, yet we had no 'national guilt-complex', despite the fact that we considered ourselves to be fully-fledged Hungarians. In my opinion this can be put down to the times we were living in, to our experiences of 1944, and to the immediate postwar atmosphere. I can honestly say that in the company to which I belonged, no one felt vengeful towards the country and the nation for what we had suffered. Neither, however, did we feel indebted to the nation, nor obliged to take it into account. This came later, after 1953, following our awakening as we began to examine our position. In the period around 1945–47, although we did not reflect on the matter that time, we felt that Hungarian public opinion, which had not behaved particularly well in previous years, was not morally entitled to protest about the way the world was going and about the sentence imposed by the moral and military victors in the war. This was especially so because to us the 1945 elections were proof that 'old Hungary' had not learnt her lesson, had not changed, and still wanted to re-establish the pre-war status quo.

So this 'national inhibition' did not work with us. It might be said in mitigation that it did not work either for our contemporaries of 'national' origin. By 1947, the year of what is known as the turning point, the situation had obviously become acute and polarized. In February there came the unconstitutional arrest of Béla Kovács, prime minister Ferenc Nagy was driven into exile, the Smallholders' Party was decimated, and the elections were brought forward. At the same time, the forces of 'reaction' started to crystallize around the parties of Zoltán Pfeiffer and István Barankovics (these were the most courageous and committed democrats). This was the time when we felt we had to make up our minds and join the communist party. In the spring and early summer of 1947 I had plans to go to Paris to attend a summer course at the Sorbonne. I shall never know what the heady atmosphere of Paris might have tempted me to do, as the French refused me a visa.

The death of Stalin in 1953 jolted us back to reality. The most important factor behind the change must be that after the death of Stalin it became clear that there did indeed exist an alternative within (or apparently within) communism; that an alternative was possible; and to think that once a few bricks had been eased out of the wall of lies and coercion, the whole edifice would begin to collapse.

Initially, we received the new course of 1953, when Mátyás Rákosi was replaced as prime minister by Imre Nagy, with a great deal of trepidation, precisely because we felt that if you pulled an important brick from the wall, it would start to crumble, and our confidence would crumble along with it. By 1954, however, we had begun to understand – and not merely because of the rehabilitations but thanks to the enlightenment offered by some of our older friends, particularly Miklós Vásárhelyi – just what it was that was happening. And after the meeting of the central leadership in October we became unconditional disciples of Imre Nagy. This was more or less the turning point: so much so that we were resolutely opposed to the March 1955 resolution of the MDP's [Hungarian Workers Party's] central leadership that criticized Nagy for 'right-wing deviation', after which he was ousted as prime minister and later expelled from the party. We considered this a disgraceful act of coercion. About this time I had a conversation that proved to be important for us with my old friend Gábor Tánczos, with whom it had not previously been possible to speak so openly. I loathed Rákosi especially because of the illegal acts with which he compromised us, simple party members, and I was quite clear in my own mind that without his removal there was no hope of reform. I put to Tánczos my view that Rákosi and co were gangsters and murderers, and this proved to be a turning point in our relationship, as he turned out to be in full agreement with me on this. No great issues of ideology were on the table, only whether that statement was acceptable to someone who was a party member. I also suggested that we should start organizing (illegally, of course), but he quite rightly rejected this as pointless at that stage.

But we achieved one or two things, unspectacular though they might appear. It was necessary to work on the communist intellectuals one by one. Each had his circle of friends, the five or six people he regarded as decent and worthwhile, and each had to be convinced, step by step: first what this party leadership was about, and who Rákosi and his people really were. If that was accepted, the next step was to grasp the real role of Stalin. This in fact laid the groundwork for what was to become, at a more favourable juncture, the substance of the intellectual debate in the Petőfi Circle. I remember Tánczos saying: 'We can move hundreds!' and we mocked him for what we thought was a wild exaggeration. But later, in the late spring and early summer of 1956, when the moment came, it was clear that the Petőfi Circle could indeed stir hundreds, and eventually even thousands.

But by the spring of 1956 we were no longer content to work at this level. By this time I had been waiting for two years for the opportunity to attack Rákosi and his supporters and policies, although an ordinary party member in his little grass-roots organization could hurt only himself and not Rákosi. But the opportunity presented itself one fine day, in an unexpectedly ideal form. A great tension and longing grew in us to actually do something concrete. I say this to explain why, when I happened to find myself in the appropriate situation, I did not fight shy of action. That situation arose when, following the 20th Party Congress [of the CPSU], Khrushchev's secret speech was debated at the various local party committees: not the whole six-hour speech, but a substantial, 90-minute-long summary. At that time I was a party pedagogue in District XIII of Budapest, Angyalföld, and I was invited to a meeting of the local branch of the party on 23 March 1956, unaware of what was on the agenda. I was simply telephoned and asked to make a contribution to the debate, because it was thought István Kovács, the first secretary of the Budapest party, would be there and they wanted a few quality contributions. I was unwilling, but in the course of the afternoon I happened to hear from a friend that the secret speech would be on the agenda – in fact, by then we were aware of the contents of the speech, more or less, having heard about it from western broadcasts on the wireless and from other sources – but I was most interested to see how it would be presented and received by the membership. So I hurried out to Angyalföld at the last minute.

The meeting was in an industrial training school on the Váci Road, and as I entered I could see a shining ball rolling up to the podium, amid loud clapping. I was rather shaken, because I could see even from the back of the hall that it was Rákosi himself: I was in a position to shoot a goal and could not miss. It was a quite exceptional opportunity to speak relatively freely in the presence of Rákosi, for normally only carefully-vetted contributions could be made in his presence. At these district meetings of the Party, however, it was customary for anyone with something to say to simply put his hand up and say it.

A woman read out the 90-minute summary of Khrushchev's speech and Rákosi sat on the podium with an expression that suggested it was virtually his own views being presented and no indication that he himself always concluded every speech with extravagant tributes to the great Stalin. I need hardly say that the few hundred people sitting there were petrified as they listened to the hitherto unheard-of list of Stalin's crimes. Then, to my great surprise, people spoke not from their seats, but according to some previously compiled list – obviously these were loyalist comments, as if nothing had happened. I wrote my name on a piece of paper and took it out to the front to indicate that I wanted to speak. My name was duly called a few minutes later. Basically I said that the Twentieth Party Congress gave rise to new hopes and created the opportunity for a genuine, major renewal, but in Hungary there had already been changes of direction, and that the party had carried out 180 degree turns in the last three years, still under the same leadership. This led me to conclude that public opinion simply would not believe that this was now not some tactical change of direction, as hitherto, but a genuine, major renewal. I then came to my carefully prepared sentence: 'I declare, in full cognizance of my responsibilities, that the membership of the Party and the majority of the Hungarian people no longer trusts the current leadership and has, in particular, no trust in comrade Mátyás Rákosi.' I fully intended this to be a bloodless coup, calculating that his presence would increase both the impact of my words and the effectiveness of my protection, as public opinion would clearly hold him responsible for whatever happened to me. And I calculated, coolly, that while every course of action would be bad for him, whether he had me arrested or not, it would be worse for him if he had me locked up, as this would fan unrest.

Rákosi received the comments in a very measured manner, and indeed called off one his lieutenants who was about to stop me in my tracks. Then he rounded on the various folk who had inveighed against the rootless intelligentsia. In the end he took almost an hour to respond to the criticisms, coming round to me by name only in the last ten minutes or so. He took up the piece of paper, slowly picked out the name (as if it were not already etched in his memory) and said: 'I have never met the comrade and he may well be a very decent man, a communist, but what he said, that I should go, that the party should give up power – and he regards these two things as one – this is something that the Voice of America rants about constantly. These voices must be rejected, unmasked, smashed to pieces', and so he went on. The air by then was beginning to thicken, for in his dictionary expressions such as these had over the years acquired meanings that were quite clearly understood..

As always, Rákosi spoke these words in a measured way. He was a consummate politician. I could see this from the composure with which he received these remarks, made to his face by a young man – for this could be seen as the symbolic end of his power. Indeed, he later allegedly ordered the district party leadership – who were purple with agitation and embarrassment – to ensure that no harm should come to me (the district party head at that time was Béla Biszku, later a notorious minister of the interior). Recently, I heard an alternative scenario from a young historian of the party working on a biography of Imre Mező (then second secretary of the Greater Budapest district), who claims Rákosi wanted me expelled from the party but that Mező and Biszku intervened on my behalf. I don't know about the role of Mező as I have never spoken to him in my life, but Biszku behaved very decently afterwards, because there were certainly knock-on effects.

One such was a vicious, denunciatory leader in the daily *Szabad Nép*, by Tivadar Matusek, but the local branch took no disciplinary action. It would indeed have been difficult for them to do so, as I had calculated that mine had been a wholly party-loyal statement, which could not really be faulted: it was made at a party activists' meeting, in the party spirit, even though I was no longer a party man inside – I have to say this because the charges against us were justified to the extent that we did indeed support a party faction. We no longer felt bound by an inner communist discipline, and had not for some time; what we were bound by was what we heard from the Imre Nagy group, which determined our affiliation unambiguously. I composed a vigorous response to the *Szabad Nép* article, and Biszku, to whom I showed the letter, gave the piece his unqualified approval. So in the end the affair had no consequences for me at all. Though my counterblast was not printed, I was offered the chance to write for the daily under my own name on other issues, for example, party education (I was then in charge of the local party seminar). I wrote the article, exploiting to the utmost the framework it offered, and it was said that it was spiked only because of the events in Poznań.

At the meeting itself, my contribution had a mixed reception. About one-third of those present burst into applause, one-third remained silent, and the remaining one-third gave vent to their outrage and anger. The effect of the statement was more or less as I had calculated. Within forty-eight hours it had done the rounds of the capital. To check, I did not say anything about it to our best friends, the Vásárhelyis, and the next day they rang to ask 'Was it you?' And I remember lamenting to Miklós my sins of omission, that I should also have said this and also have said that, but predicted that all that would be recalled about the whole thing would be two sentences: what I had said (that Rákosi should resign) and how Rákosi had responded (that's the Voice of America speaking).

Ferenc Donáth (a co-defendant with Imre Nagy) said of the effect of this statement that it was like saying 'The Emperor has no clothes!' So it had a liberating influence. This means more than people might think, for it must not be forgotten in looking at all the events of 1956 that as a matter of historical fact it was within the party that the thaw began. And within the party it was primarily the intellectuals that played a significant role, and the effect of this remark was truly historical in changing their role, because people had this incredible fear and uncertainty, so characteristic of the Rákosi period, that even good friends were unable to tell each other their thoughts, lest they were made public – my statement brought this to an end and critical voices were reinforced. This event completely changed, for example, the atmosphere at the Institute of Economics, where Donáth was employed at the time. All this was received with such enthusiasm at the Institute that, as I recall, every party meeting turned into a lively political forum, of a kind that did not previously exist. This process, which began at the end of February 1956, was the true beginning of the thaw in the intellectuals' party organizations. And that is why it deserves attention in the context of all that happened in 1956.

(The author does not mention here one additional outcome of his intervention – Rákosi's own spirited attack on Stalin, Beria and Gábor Péter, delivered on 29 March. *Eds*).

1956: The Diary of a University Student

Thomas Kabdebo

At dawn of 4 November I woke with a jolt: the window panes shook, and loudly rattled, as if they were to cave in – boom, boom, boom, the heavy sound of gunfire filled in the half darkness. My aunt sat up, then stood up in her bed, her white, uncombed hair flying, the lamp hanging from the ceiling swayed slowly. I switched on the lights. I turned on the radio, and the familiar, countryish accent of prime minister Nagy announced solemnly: ... our troops are engaged in combat... the government is holding out...

We lived in Madách Square, my aunt and I. I was her guest or lodger, someone paying no rent but otherwise earning his keep. I was a fourth year university student at the Faculty of Arts in Budapest University, in my final year. I had a small grant, and a little extra from my swimming club, supplemented by earning from casual work. My father had been imprisoned for imaginary political reasons so I got no support from home in the south. Now it took me no time to dress, to get my national guard rifle from the wardrobe, pocket my revolver, and to run down the smaller boulevard to the University. There I climbed up straight to the second floor rapidly, where the military department was located, and boosted my armoury with a submachine gun. I had to sign for it (the lieutenant was spick and span as if he was going to a party) just as I had signed for the rifle and the revolver the week before...

The 'arsenal' was buzzing with activity. Many of the assembling students had been enlisted in the National Guard, like myself, a week before, others were coming back from compulsory national service in the country. I soon spotted the boys of my tutorial group, all seven of them were there, sampling weapons. Only the five girls of our group were missing. One of them, Liz, my girlfriend, active in the first phase of the revolution, stayed with her relatives near the Eastern Railway station – I had accompanied her there, the night before. Two others had returned to their parents, outside Budapest, the remaining two – whose home village was on the shore of Lake Balaton – stayed in the student hostel for girls. That two-storey building stood at the crossroads of Rákóczi Road and Museum Boulevard. Out of the seven boys I knew particularly well: Oliver from Bácska County, Anti from Eger, 'Z. the poet' from Transdanubia, and Bankó from the Tisza region. 'What are we going to do?' asked one of them. 'Thousands of tanks are coming in to put us down,' said Oliver. Anti remarked: 'My dad was at the Don bend facing an army of millions.' 'And what happened to him?' quipped Bankó, usually a silent mug. 'He died in the POW camp.'

I knew all that, since Anti was my friend. Then a dark vision loomed large in front of my half closed eyes. In 1945 when the Soviets took my home town they raped dozens of local women, and shot dead one protesting husband. I said: 'Let us go to the girls' hostel, and defend them. We shall avoid all provocations but if the soldiers break in we will be ready for them, armed.'

They all agreed. The hostel was ten minutes walk from the university. At about 6 a.m. the roads were empty – the sky was grey – but the distant sound of arms was constant. Not knowing how much food we were going to find in the hostel I filled my rucksack with bread, cheese and smoked sausages.

There were eleven girls left in the hostel, out of an original forty, all country lasses, all from the first and second year except our classmates Joli and Teri, daughters of a blacksmith and a locksmith, respectively. They embraced and kissed us. Joli was dark with short hair, Teri was blonde with long hair, both were well dressed. Amidst cheers and muted ovations the others introduced themselves, then went into the kitchen to prepare breakfast for all of us. 'There is no milk, just milk powder,' said Menci, a pleasant but bossy girl, who seemed to be ordering the others around. The kitchen could seat about ten people, the adjoining dining room another twenty. We ate like wolves except one girl called Panka, who had placed herself next to me and inspected my weapons, one by one. She was a well build peasant girl, with strong limbs, a generous chest and buttocks, and a very regular round face. She wore her long black hair in a tail which I was to call the 'Turkish Flag'.

The breakfast was interrupted by a frantic exchange of fire right outside, on the road. Then came repeated loud bangings on our heavy oak door. 'The Russians,' squealed Oliver. 'I'll go and see,' said Z. the poet. 'Who are you?', he shouted from inside. 'It's me, Steve,' bellowed a voice from outside, 'and my mate, Zoltán. He is badly wounded, open the door!' We did. Zoltán was lying there in blood, he was shot in the back. He had lost consciousness but still breathed. There was a sickroom in the hostel, and a stretcher in there. We placed Zoltán on it and the three of us, Steve, Z. and me carried him to the next street's makeshift clinic. In peaceful days it was a gym where I used to go for fitness training before my water polo matches. We waited an hour for a doctor, coming from Rókus Hospital. During that time Steve related that the two of them were going to join us in the hostel but crossing Museum Boulevard Zoltán was shot in the back. They were both unarmed. The doctor came, tried to extract the bullet, but Zoltán died on the operating table, in a pool of blood. The afternoon was relatively inactive. There was no working radio in the hostel but, miraculously, the telephone wires were alive. I phoned my aunt, my two best friends, my water polo trainer, and my girlfriend, Liz. I wanted to know whether she would attempt to escape with me from Hungary if I came out of the present quagmire alive. After much hesitation, sobbing, and heart searching she said she would not.

There were plenty of empty beds in the hostel. I am a light sleeper so I chose the single room with the single bed of the absent warden. The night was relatively silent but there was a tremendous explosion at dawn. I sat up. Panka burst into my room her great brown eyes glistening and embraced my knees. 'Do you want to come to my bed?' I asked. She shook her Turkish flag. 'Let us carry down mattresses to the cellar and sleep there. It is safer.' We did. And so did all the others, coming out of the dormitories.

In the morning Menci surveyed the food situation. 'There are eighteen of us here', she said, 'The food we have couldn't last for more than two days.' Oliver said: 'We have sardines. I've never eaten sardines. May I?' 'At the last resort', she said.

I took my rucksack and ran to the university on the double. The streets were deserted apart from two Soviet armoured cars driving up and down, monitoring the situation. I had to wait until they disappeared. In the university food store – which was full of goods, partly with Anglo-American food supplies – I filled my backpack and returned safely. Menci baked flat, yeastless bread. Prunes were for dessert.

The night was quiet apart from the occasional barking of a submachine gun. Panka lay beside me in her blue tracksuit. I caressed her face. 'Take your tracksuit off.' 'I am an old fashioned girl.' 'But the circumstances are not old fashioned. What if a Soviet soldier forced it off you?'

Joli had a gramophone and three 78 discs. She played her favourite more often than the other two. It started like this: 'I want to be immortal so that I can love you, forever.' She said she was thinking of her fiancé.

On the third day I nipped out for food – American butter, English cheese and sardines, a bag of flour and twenty eggs were with me, on the way back. There was a skirmish at the crossroads (around a large hole in the asphalt) between stray ÁVH troops and revolutionaries. Although the ÁVH was officially disbanded on 28 October pockets of them had obviously remained and reawakened. I was coming up on the pavement of Kossuth Street, and tried to make myself as flat as a pancake at a doorway, with the result that on eventual arrival in the hostel the eggs appeared to have been scrambled in my backpack.

In the afternoon Bankó furtively crossed the street, walked into a broken shop-window across the way, and emerged with a heavy overcoat on his shoulders.

This was the only piece of looting I witnessed in the fortnight of the revolution. We shunned him. Yet he was there with us.

My third journey for food was eventful. On the way back, running with the loaded backpack on Kossuth Street, I became aware of the approaching rattle of a T34 tank behind me. Instinctively I sought refuge in a gateway. In the next second, four young kids, perhaps fifteen years old, sprung across the street finding the same gateway instantly. They divested themselves of their submachine guns and picked up petrol filled bottles from inside the gateway. (The term *Molotov Cocktail* was invented by Western journalists.) The tank was level with us now in the middle of the street. It had stopped for some reason and its turret moved. My companions lit the paper wicks in the bottles and hurled them at the tank. Flying candles. I followed suit. The T34 had its petrol tank in the back. 'Aim at that!' shouted one of the kids. Indeed, in peaceful days I was a water polo player. I imagined now the target being the goal of the opposition. In a couple of seconds the tank was in flames and trundled away first slowly, then picked up speed on the Rákóczi Road.

I got back to the hostel safely. Joli and Teri were kneading noodles, the rest of the girls were changing the bed clothes, Anti, my friend, sat in a corner and read a bilingual book of Horace's poems. Just after lunch a group of young men filed in through our kitchen door. They had climbed through the back fence, weapons and all. The leader, whom the others called *Boss*, explained that they were the Petőfi brigade from Csepel and came to fight. Anti and I pleaded with him. 'The safety of the girls... the overwhelming force of the Soviets...'. The Boss listened to us, said nothing, beckoned his group of seven lads and occupied window positions on the second floor.

The brigade brought two large cans of petrol with them and filled up about three dozen glass bottles, opened the windows and waited. Three of us, Anti, Z. the poet and

I joined them. (If you can't beat them, join them.) In half an hour, not more, a tank appeared, crawling slowly on Rákóczi Road. It stopped in front of our building, perhaps because of the large hole in the road which was covered by a dish or large plate. It looked like a mine. There was an already naked plain tree in front of our building, between us and the tank, which caught many of the bottles we hurled at the mammoth, but not all. Many of the little flames got extinguished in flight, but not all. Like all the others I did my best at throwing. The drum of the tank exploded. Amidst smoke and flames a soldier appeared in the turret. A rifle shot – Z. the poet got him. The soldier somersaulted and ended up flat on the pavement, beside his burning vehicle. Then a second soldier appeared, in the turret, he was already out to the waist, I could see his white face and flaxen hair. I aimed, but not at him. I aimed at the body of the tank. Releasing the bullet I was thinking of not hitting a sitting duck. How can one shoot at a human being? The steel mammoth, the tank is different. Then this second soldier jumped off, unharmed, and made his escape to the broken shop window across the street. The Boss, himself a twenty-two year old worker, blond and athletic, raced down the stairs, out to the street where he encountered new gunfire from an unknown source. He crawled towards the shop window. A hand grenade thrown by one of his own lads from our second floor, stopped him. He ended up with a heavily damaged right arm in the makeshift clinic. The members of his group disappeared from sight.

Soon the damaged T34 was towed away. Its space was filled by another two giants. Rounds and rounds of tank cannon shots, ripple fire. We were all down in the cellar, registering the shouts above us. Was the hostel still standing? Three of the girls – their names are clouded up in my memory – prayed the rosary all evening, all night. There was no more central heating or electricity, still we had water. The building – as I was able to survey it in a lull next morning – was like a Swiss cheese. Apart from occasional distant sounds of small arms, the street, the neighbourhood was quiet. Teri's dad came up from his Balaton village and took the two girls with him. I hid my weapons in the loft, bade goodbye to Panka and made my way to the south, stealthily.

Z. the poet, showed me his notebook before he too took his leave

> 'There was a student demonstration on 23rd October which grew
> into the wingbeats of revolution,
> but that was trampled in blood.
> (I had been super active before. Now I don't wish to live any more.)'

The poem was dated 11th November 1956.

On 29 November I reached Austria on foot, safely. In March 1957 Z. the poet was arrested, he was tried in May. Bankó was witness for the prosecution. Z. the poet was executed in June 1957. He was one of the hundreds of young and middle-aged men and three women who were hanged or shot or died in prison.

Note: the above is an abbreviated version of my book: *A Time for Everything*, Maynooth: Cardinal Press, 1996. (In Hungarian: *Minden idők*, 4th edition, Budapest: Mundus, 2006).

Budapest in 1956

Gabriel Ronay

The fiftieth anniversary of the Hungarian Revolution has been marked with fitting cele-brations all around the world. The solemn words of praise only help to emphasize that we, the participants in the Revolution, are becoming history. But before we fade away, we can go once more in search of the remembrance of things past. This Central Euro-pean 'A La Recherche du temps perdu' must, however, focus on loss, not on deliverance from time. My personal memories, centred on unmapped events, may perhaps help explain to rising generations how a peaceful demonstration could turn into a rebellion and national revolution.

In the run-up to October 1956, I followed the political ferment with excitement, but I stayed detached. The fate of Imre Nagy's 1953 'New Course' was reason enough for not trusting the party's own attempt at de-Stalinisation. As an alienated, middle-class student, I did not want to get involved. I felt that I had no role to play in the reform communists' challenge to their party's terror-based power; nor did I wish to breathe new life into that murderous regime. I attended, nevertheless, the thrilling debates of the reformist intellectuals' Petőfi Circle, read with joy the Writers' Union's challenges to the party state, and cheered the attacks on 'Comrade Kutchera' and his ilk in the pages of *Irodalmi Újság*. Even after the reburial of László Rajk and the other victims of show trials, I was still determined to concentrate on my own personal survival and my forth-coming exams.

For me the 'moral Rubicon' was crossed following our jubilant march across the city, at the Budapest radio building at 9.00 pm on 23 October. Thousands of us were there to demand that our 14-points of reform and democratic renewal be read over the radio. In response, the communist state set upon us the police and the People's Army. When neither would fire on us, the Radio's ÁVH guards came charging out of the building, their submachine-guns blazing. People lay dead and dying around me. Outrage and defencelessness turned me, a peaceful philology student, into an insurgent.

In the battle for the radio building, we found ourselves pinned down by ÁVH fire in the Museum Gardens. Casualties were mounting. Yet instead of trying to save our skins and run, we stood our ground. Although some conscripts handed over their weapons and joined our ranks, halfway through the battle for the radio building it became clear to me that, without reinforcements, we would soon be overwhelmed. A desperate situation required a desperate solution. Using a friend's 'borrowed' office car, we drove to the Athenaeum Printing Plant, ran off hundreds of leaflets with our 14-point demands and took a car-load to the industrial heartland of Csepel Island. Standing outside the main gate of the Csepel Arms Factory, I urged the nightshift ~~to come~~ out on sympathy strike and to join us, armed with Kalashnikovs off the assembly lines, at the radio building. They did so.

To organize a strike against the workers' state and to convince the Csepel workers, the mythical vanguard of the proletariat, to join the battle for the Budapest radio building were capital offences in the book of the party-state. My academic career was dead. I was now a 'counter-revolutionary' with nothing to lose but my chains, to paraphrase Marx. But there was no going back. The dynamic of the Revolution carried us along a precipitous path at the end of which independence and multi-party democracy beckoned.

During the thrilling days of the victorious Revolution, I was drawn to the 'Revolutionary Party of Youth', a new forum for Budapest's pro-democracy young. It was a middle-of-the-road group, backed and financed by Pál Maléter, the Nagy government's charismatic defence minister. The former partisan and hero of the recent battle for the Killián Barracks, sought a power-base among the country's young. Anyone intending to skip the tainted older generation had my support.

The youth party needed a newspaper to put over its views and ideological goals. On 3 November, I was invited to the founding meeting of the daily 'Október 23' in a villa on Andrássy Boulevard. Those selected to join the editorial team stayed behind. As I spoke foreign languages and had had some journalistic experience, I was asked to cover foreign news. The editor-designate made the point that the pen was now mightier than the sword. Street-fighting experience alone, he said, was not going to win hearts or the battle of ideas facing us.

We then turned to the task of thrashing out the paper's orientation. Formulating our ideological platform was hard. We were full of illusions, naïve even, but had our fingers on the city's pulse. In heated debates, the seven of us seated around an oval table agreed that the paper would fight for multi-party democracy, economic pluralism and national independence. 'We will return factories and enterprises with up to 100 employees to their owners, and the peasant should own his land up to a 100 hectares,' we decided. Private enterprise must be given encouragement, but the great estates, banks, mines and utilities would, for the time being, stay in public ownership. Given the hitherto immutable state-ownership structures, our idea of a mixed economy of public-private ownership, was revolutionary. We were reinventing social democracy.

Maléter was to have taken part in the debate but, we were told that he was delayed on account of a hitch in negotiations at Soviet Army HQ on 'Russian withdrawal with honour'. Unknown to us, he was already a prisoner of KGB General Serov, his safe-conduct notwithstanding.

We were asked to start work the next day, 4 November, but, at dawn, the Soviets attacked Budapest with overwhelming force. The leaders of the Revolution and the government were arrested, or forced to shelter in the Yugoslav Embassy. The voices of freedom were silenced. The Red Army and the ÁVH were having their revenge. There were reports of terrible atrocities.

I was sickened by the carnage and wanted to tell the world of Hungary's agony. There were, however, no easy ways to make the West heed our cry. Facts were needed, but how to gather proof of atrocities under the barrels of Soviet tanks? And through what channels could one get such a dossier out of curfew-bound Budapest to New York? To find a way seemed vital to me, as the UN Security Council was even then discussing the 'Hungarian Question' there. Unfortunately, I was an ordinary student with no funds, no connections, no organization behind me, and no standing. And even if I were to succeed, there was no reason why the UN should take note of my dossier. Nevertheless, I wanted to give it a try.

A perilous incident at the Grand Hotel on Margaret Island gave me a chance. The hotel was full of stranded visitors and foreign diplomats sheltering from the Soviet shelling. As a freelance interpreter working for the Institute of Cultural Relations, I used to go there to help marooned guests. One day I arrived at the hotel as the first Soviet foot patrol drew up outside the all-glass entrance. Diplomats lined up on the inside watched in horror as a Russian soldier got stuck in the revolving door by his submachine-gun. His screams unnerved the patrol and they trained their guns on the diplomats. I spoke calmly in Russian to the trapped soldier and told him that he could release himself by lowering his gun. He got out of the revolving door. Then I reassured the patrol that the door was not a '*burzhoaznaya zabratyelnaya mashina*'. The soldier stepped out and the crisis was over.

The relieved diplomats showed their appreciation. The incident established my bona fides with them and provided the introduction I needed to open channels of communication to the West. The hope that the world would raise its voice in our defence depended, I felt, on receiving reliable reports from Budapest. But who should speak up for us? The British and the French were engrossed with Suez and the Americans feared that helping Hungary could trigger a nuclear war. Non-aligned India, then chairing the Security Council talks on Hungary, retained, however, high credibility both in Moscow and Washington. M.A. Rahman, the new Indian envoy to Budapest, would, I felt, be the best channel to the UN. As a non-aligned diplomat, his words would carry weight. Following the revolving door incident, Rahman invited me to be his Hungarian-Russian interpreter and 'curfew guide'. Herr Drechsler, a West German concert pianist also stranded in the Grand Hotel, offered to act as our driver. The team to verify reports of Soviet Army atrocities was in place.

Friends and acquaintances telephoned me about acts of terror that they had witnessed or heard of. If an incident was still verifiable, we would drive to the spot and gather eyewitness-accounts for inclusion in Rahman's despatches. The dossier of atrocities grew. The problem was how to get it out of Budapest. As the Indian Embassy had no radio link to the outside world, the only way round this was to take the dossier to the Austrian border and hand it over to India's ambassador in Vienna to be passed on to higher authority. But with Hungary in the stranglehold of the Soviet Army, a road journey was a hazardous undertaking.

Although we had artfully obtained a Soviet laissez-passer, our journey to the Austrian border was a surreal experience. The embassy car was stopped time and again at gun-point. Starving soldiers begged for bread; their officers for cigarettes. Most did not even know in what country they were. North of Budapest, officers of a newly arrived tank division said, 'we're on our way to Berlin to put down a fascist revolt.' Near Győr, Khirgiz and Khazakh soldiers asked to be guided to 'the Canal'. They had come, so they averred, 'to aid our Muslim brethren at Suez'. We eventually reached the Austrian border after yet more bizarre adventures. At Hegyeshalom, a troublesome KGB officer tried to stop Rahman from crossing to Austria, but my routine threat of reporting him to Moscow worked wonders. The dossier was eventually passed to Rahman's colleague in Vienna. The rest was now up to the West.

A couple of days after our hazardous journey, two Soviet GRU military intelligence officers called at the Grand Hotel. They were looking for Rahman and me. After crude warnings to Rahman about 'getting involved' and threatening 'to deal' with me later, the situation was defused with vodka. Litres of it. When one drunken officer challenged Rahman to arm-wrestling and forced his arm flat on the table, Rahman said, 'That's what you want to do to Hungary.' The officers, too drunk to carry out their muttered threats, were eventually dragged away by their driver. But the writing was on the wall. Without a chance to say goodbye to family and friends, I fled to Austria.

The work with and through Rahman was taken up by people of political weight, like István Bibó, a minister in the Nagy government, and his circle. Their contact man was Árpád Göncz, a writer. Eventually, they were arrested and only Nehru's personal intercession with Khrushchev saved their lives. But the Kádár regime could not forgive my involvement and I was barred from Hungary for thirty years. Our struggle had not, however, been in vain.

On 23 October, 1991, communism was dead, Hungary was free and Árpád Göncz was its president. In the Hungarian parliament, Rahman, Göncz and I met up for the first time in thirty-five years. Rahman told me of a newly uncovered twist to our mission. Late in 1956, Krishna Menon, India's communist defence minister, had sent Rahman's superior a secret cable, 'I have had enough of these reports from Budapest.' Nevertheless, as Göncz said in Parliament, 'in those months, the Indian embassy in Budapest became the embassy of the Revolution.'

My (abbreviated) Career in the Interior Ministry[1]

László Péter

The record of this interview is mainly concerned with the Central Building of the ÁVH. It gives evidence as to its organization and the daily operations of the ÁVH, a general description of the documentary material found there, together with a more exact description of some specific documents.[2]

I spent five days in the building[3] from Tuesday, 30 October, to Saturday, 3 November inclusive. On the morning of 30 October, I joined a small *ad hoc* committee with three other young historians charged with the duty of sifting through the documentary material to be found in the building.[4]

The ÁVH evacuated the building without fighting on the evening of 29 October and it was occupied by a platoon of police and about twenty students from the Budapest Technical University. Most of the policemen drifted off on 30 October, only half a dozen or so remaining together with the NCO in charge, as well as a fair number of armed students who slept there and who amused themselves with the equipment in the building.

The Building

The Central Office of the Ministry of Interior, which of course was at the same time the headquarters of the ÁVH, was housed in the Gresham Palace and the adjoining buildings, constituting a block facing the Danube and bordering Roosevelt Square, József Attila Street, Mérleg Street, and Nádor Street. The front gate to the Square was normally closed and the entrance on József Attila Street used. In the same block, on the north side, there were also the premises of a state architectural office, to which access was impossible from the rest of the bulk of the block occupied by the ÁVH. This complex of buildings is the main headquarters of the ÁVH, and is not to be confused

I am grateful to Angus Walker for the preparation of this text.

1   This text is an edited and corrected version of an English translation of a tape-recorded interview I gave in Hungarian to Anthony de Jasay, probably in June 1957, at Nuffield College, Oxford, for a Columbia University project.
2   Anthony Jasay's notice.
3   The ÁVH (*Államvédelmi Hatóság*), the Secret Police, was an integral part of the Ministry of the Interior.
4   János Varga, together with István Pozsár, leader of the Revolutionary Student Committee of the University, enlisted László Benczédi, István Purjesz, Jenő Szűcs, Antal Vörös and myself 'to render safe the documents of the Interior Ministry' (the letter of appointment is in my possession). The five of us and Varga, all historians, were close friends for many years.

with the operational headquarters of the Budapest ÁVH on Jászai Mari Square further along the Danube.

One of two boilermen who stayed behind after the ÁVH evacuated the building (referred to below as boilerman number one and boilerman number two) told me that, after moving into the Gresham Palace, the Ministry of Interior endeavoured to get the whole block for itself and over a period of time they moved out the other tenants of the block so that by the time the Revolution broke out only the architectural office on the corner of Mérleg and Nádor Streets was not occupied by them. The block is a labyrinth of inner courtyards; I believe I counted sixteen of them. Nevertheless, although I know that there used to be an arcade running right along the whole of the Gresham Palace, today the south end of the former arcade is built in as a result of internal additions to the Gresham Palace and transformed into a courtyard. The south end of the arcade is now an ordinary gate leading to a double staircase, the left-hand side of which, on the first floor, leads to the offices of László Piros (the last Minister of the Interior before the Revolution). I only used the József Attila Street entrance – in wandering through the complex I found other gates but they were barred from the inside.

The building contained a large number of rooms and I saw at most one-sixth of them. On the first floor, at the south end, is the József Attila Street side: the staircase and corridor were maintained in neo-baroque luxury: huge rooms with chandeliers were lavishly fitted out. Piros and the three or four deputy ministers had their offices at this end. In the rest of the complex, there were roughly three types of layout to be found which I will call corridor type one, type two and type three.

Type one was like a rabbit warren. Rooms were about four by four-and-a-half metres. Three or four rooms were interconnected and access to the next set of interconnected rooms was provided by a short section of corridor. The staircases had not been repositioned and continued to go right through all the floors. The rabbit warren system was clearly of recent origin: all the partitions were new or not more than a few years old. The vertical layout was clear because of the system of staircases but, horizontally, it was much more difficult to follow. I lost my way several times and had to find a street window to get my bearings. The internal fittings were comfortable but not luxurious, with good modern carpets and desks.

On the type-two corridors, there were old-fashioned dusty third-rate offices, rather fewer of them than in the case of type one. The rooms were large and long with rows of desks and the function of these offices seems to be mostly the keeping of police personnel files. I found three large rooms full of the personnel files of the post-1945 police while in another two rooms were the current personnel files of the ÁVH. It should be noted that the ÁVH did not exist as a body separate from the Ministry of the Interior, but was an integral part of it and the differences between Interior Ministry personnel and ÁVH employees were only differences of degree. A separate ÁVH existed only in the sense that any department might be said to have a separate existence.

The type-three corridors were probably the most unusual. They were packed with a mass of electrical apparatus. These corridors were mainly on the third floor of the central part of the building. The type-three premises consisted in part of very large and long halls with a row of machines running down the centre and about twenty to twenty five seats on either side. On the top storey, in a remote part of the building, were two long halls which turned out to be a telephone exchange. To these halls I shall return below.

The attic was even more of a labyrinth than the main storeys and I never had time to search it. Some of our team believed that ÁVH personnel were still hiding there. The basement had several levels with circular tunnels containing the utility mains – from the tunnels, trolley rails led to furnaces, a big coal store and at the lowest level, to the safes.

First Impressions of the Building

On the morning of 30 October, I happened to visit the University Revolutionary Committee where the chairman was instructing a friend of mine and someone whom I did not know to go and inspect the ÁVH building that had been occupied the previous night. On seeing me, he told me to join them and also told me that he wanted a fourth person, a friend of mine who was also a historian, to come with us. He gave us three armed students as an escort.[5] We found the building occupied by police and students. The police NCO would only admit us after referring by telephone to Kopácsi's deputy. (Kopácsi was head of the civil police). On the following day, our search was formally authorized. (Apart from myself the other members of the group were present only on the first day.)[6]

When we started looking the place over, we found that some students from the Technical University and others who were unidentified were already in the building but apparently they had only examined the rooms nearest to the József Attila Street entrance. In going through the previously unexplored areas of the building we at first carried sub-machine guns but felt rather ridiculous in doing so and soon discarded them.

The first thing to attract attention was the frantic disorder in the ministerial rooms on the József Attila Street side. Everything was undamaged as there had been no fighting inside the building but there were obvious signs of the collapse of order. The ÁVH had apparently made preparations to defend the building against attack. In most of the rooms overlooking the street there were machine guns fixed on top of the polished desks and a lot of ammunition lying about in open cases. There was also a large quantity of small arms and pistols strewn around that were eventually collected by the twenty students who were in the building when we arrived and who continued to remain there for some time. Civil police uniforms were lying all over the floor, as well as police boots. There were more jackets than trousers. The ÁVH changed their clothes twice. First they replaced ÁVH uniforms with civil police uniforms. Nevertheless, they were issued with brand new uniforms and boots and it was almost as dangerous for them to wear these as it was to wear the ÁVH uniform. The discarded ÁVH uniforms were probably left in the store where the civil police uniforms were issued and put on. When the ÁVH personnel came back to the ÁVH building they apparently changed into civilian clothes but so hurriedly that they had only time to discard their jackets and had no time to change their trousers.

Discarded uniforms and weapons were scattered throughout the building. In the well-appointed rooms and in the 'rabbit warren' parts, I saw very large numbers of used

---

5   See note 4.
6   Purjesz was with me in the building on the evening of 3 November.

champagne and wine glasses together with gin and rum bottles. These I took to be visible signs of demoralization. The ÁVH personnel had been without sleep for 36 hours, fortifying themselves with drink and behaving in an entirely undisciplined way. It was curious to see pictures of Lenin, Stalin and Dzerzhinsky looking down upon heaps of pornographic pictures and books, American magazine pin-ups and so on. The contrast between the magnificence of the building with its banqueting halls on the one hand and the disorder of discarded clothing and pictures of nudes powerfully illustrated the extent of the collapse of an organization that had once been all-powerful.

It is perhaps significant that apart from the standard pictures of Marx, Engels and Lenin, pictures of Stalin and of Dzerzhinsky (the spiritual father of all communist secret police) were prominently displayed while Rákosi's picture could also be found in many rooms. The Twentieth Congress seems to have left few traces here. The students removed only the pictures of Stalin and Rákosi, leaving Marx and Lenin in peace.

Boilerman number one was the only member of the building service personnel who actually lived in the building. Curiously enough, he used to be the pre-war janitor of the building. Boilerman number two was a young man, the assistant to boilerman number one. They tried to be helpful and I agreed on 3 November that they should get hold of an electrician who was familiar with the wiring of the building who could explain the use of the puzzling electrical apparatus. But by the next day, of course, it was too late for that.

The József Attila Street staircase was made of marble and the corridors and rooms were covered with inlaid baroque parquet. On the first floor landing there was a magnificent gallery still in its pre-war state. Two long corridors led left and right from the gallery. Onto these opened the rooms of Piros, his staff, two conference rooms and the offices of the two or three deputy ministers and their staffs. The rooms had enormous Persian rugs and fin-de-siècle furniture.

Piros's office was on the first floor on the corner of the Square and József Attila Street, a huge semi-circular room with large numbers of small arms lying about. By the time we arrived Piros's desk had been rifled – it was not clear by whom. What remained was absolutely inconsequential administrative material, routine memos and so on. Stalin's picture was still on the wall. Boilerman number two's friend, a cabinet maker in the building, told him that after the Twentieth Congress a great deal was spent in improving the offices of the deputy ministers. Since there was oak panelling in Piros's office, the offices of the deputy ministers had had to be panelled with oak too in the name of the fight against the cult of personality.

From 31 October onwards, the Technical University students were dissuaded from any further interference with papers and were told to confine their attentions to the electrical equipment. Up to 2 November, I was concerned that no one should touch or remove anything. On 2 and 3 November, beginning to feel uncertain about our ability to maintain the occupation of the building and apprehensive about the prospects for the revolution in general, I no longer opposed the removal of material, including documentary material, from the building. There was some talk of removing the documentary material in an organized way to one particular place,[7] but the staff of the National Archives became anxious, feeling that anything connected with the ÁVH was too

---

7   The dry cellars of the Roman Catholic Basilica were practically next door to the Ministry.

dangerous to handle and they refused to organize the removal of papers. Most of the documents were accordingly left in the building.

The 'rabbit warrens' had one significant feature: as described, the line of corridors was very frequently broken and one had to go through a set of rooms to reach the next segment of the same corridor. There was another difference from ordinary offices: there were many more telephones here, there being a switchboard in each room with a variety of telephone sets, four or five on most of the desks. In each room there were one or more big safes, some closed and some opened, containing papers or tapes. West German-made tape recorders were strewn about, at least two, and sometimes half a dozen in each room. As was later discovered, the main reason for this was that here much more material was recorded than typed. In the corridors, steel partitions, electric bells and lamps abounded. Boilerman number two described how, on the second and sixteenth of each month, he had to go for his pay. He had to report at a definite hour, not being supposed to go anywhere without special permission. As he went along the corridor he had to check the lamps and if certain lamps were lit up, he had to turn back. Boilerman number one said that the electricians had greater freedom of movement. His electrician friend told him that his section of the building was subdivided and he was allowed to do his routine maintenance jobs at particular hours of the week in each subdivision. If he was called to an emergency job he too had to check the lamps. If the bell went, everybody had to return to the room from which he had just come, clearing the corridor. I came across other small curiosities in the 'rabbit warrens'. For instance, the police NCO brought to me a perfectly normal book with the ten first and ten last pages untouched, but the middle pages having their centre cut out so that there was a cavity in the middle containing what was probably a miniature recorder with battery. I found the same book (with the same title) in several of the rooms in the 'rabbit warrens' standing on bookshelves. I checked and found them to have the same concealed apparatus. In this rabbit warren section, for each dozen or so rooms there was one with more elaborate furnishings, presumably belonging to the section chief. The standard equipment of the rooms seemed to be one safe, two cupboards with clothes, boxes of tapes, two tape recorders, a battery of films, a couch, a desk, a bookshelf and a picture of Dzerzhinsky. I numbered the staircases with chalk and made chalk marks on the corridors to enable me to find my way about.

The type-three premises on the third floor rather resembled a radio factory. In the centre of the large, low-ceilinged halls there were long tables with rows of steel cabinets on them or in some cases one long steel cabinet standing on the floor running down the centre of the hall. There was a smell of plastic and a constant humming noise, and coloured lamps constantly went on and off. Astonishingly enough, once one of the telephones started ringing. Every bit of apparatus seemed to have been left on. It gave us the feeling that 'they' were still in control. We recalled the story of the Germans occupying Kiev whose building blew up as one of them picked up a ringing telephone and we left this one strictly alone.[8] Later, however, I was no longer so apprehensive and used the phones that were connected to the local exchange. Against one of the walls there was a row of tall steel cabinets with a ventilation grill near the top. At the central tables there were stools with earphones and mobile plugs. On 2 and 3 November, a committee of

---

8 Szűcs and I warned the others about this.

Technical University students and engineers arrived to examine and dismantle the equipment in these rooms but I had no opportunity to learn of the results. The areas of responsibility for my team and for the engineers were clearly delineated: we looked after papers and tapes and they concerned themselves with the electrical equipment. Alongside these long halls there were rooms of a rather better quality than those in the rabbit warren with piles of recording tapes and tape recorders. They also contained a few more mysterious pieces of equipment: among even less comprehensible items there was, for example, a box on which small models of aeroplanes could be positioned and moved with the aid of a number of levers. On the top floor, which I think was the fifth floor, there were two long rooms about 20 yards long overlooking the courtyards with bare walls and steel cabinets in the centre emitting a humming noise. As it turned out, this was the telephone exchange for the whole building. On opening the door of the cabinets, long cylindrical columns could be seen, six in each cabinet and in each column there were 30 or so tapes one above another, continually recording conversations on each telephone line.

Documentary Material

Needless to say, there was written material in every room. But the great bulk of the documents was in the cellar, in the vaults used as safes by the previous occupier of the building, which was a bank or an insurance company. In one corner of the vaults I actually found some banking documents. The vaults were very tidy. There were about 800 yards of shelves. They used a good cataloguing system, the old 'basic numbers' system. In 1949, a new cataloguing system was introduced for the state administration, the so-called 'decimal system'. This system required the division of cases into ten main groups according to the nature (character) of the case. But since an individual case could fall into one or more of three or four groups and could be filed under each of the three or four decimal numbers, confusion reigned and documents could often not be retrieved. The ÁVH sensibly did not feel bound to use this system, compulsory for all other branches of state administration. Current dossiers were, of course, up in the rooms and in certain sections of the ÁVH. Apparently, even settled cases were not always sent down to the central filing store in the cellar. In one room, for example, I found a pile of dossiers dealing with economic crimes dating back without interruption to 1949. In addition to the central file in the vault and to the individual dossiers in the rooms, I found a third group of papers. Just prior to or during the evacuation, a great deal of material was apparently dumped in the cellar in two huge heaps, each about five feet high. The second heap was wet and had obviously been dumped from the coal trolleys. These two heaps will be referred to as miscellaneous papers No. 1 and No. 2.

Boilerman number one said that from 21 October onwards, the ÁVH men were frequently to be found working in the cellars; on 26 and 27 October, men brought down files apparently for destruction. He believed they had less time to evacuate the building than they expected, as suddenly there was a general exodus and within half an hour the whole building was abandoned. This may explain the uniforms thrown on the floor of the offices and the failure to destroy the documents. However, one heap had been sprinkled with paraffin. The boilerman claimed that he had frightened off two men who were supposed to soak and light the heap by telling them that insurgents had already entered the building and that they must run for their lives. It is strange that they did not complete their task. Either the ÁVH did not expect to have to abandon Budapest or they thought they might have to leave the building for only a couple of days. They could not have destroyed very much. In each of the larger rooms in the upper storeys there was a small paper shredder, a machine about three feet high with two cylinders turning in opposite directions with teeth driven by a small electric motor which cut up paper into thin strips like fine straw. These machines seemed to be standard equipment. The ÁVH constantly destroyed redundant or obsolete documents. But apparently in the last few days rather more paper was shredded than usual because the wire baskets that received the shredded material were overflowing and in some cases shredded paper covered the floor of the room. I assume that on 24 and 25 October they must have received an order to speed up the shredding of paper already due for destruction or for destruction by the end of the year.

(Intermission: On 9 November I risked a walk past the building and saw that it was still closed. I wondered what had happened to the former occupants of the building and to the whole organization. Psychologically, it is hard to imagine a simple resumption of activity where they had left off at the outbreak of the revolution. It is quite possible that the same rooms were reoccupied by the same people. But after seeing the signs of the disorganization and disintegration of this central nerve system of the regime, I suspected that this was unlikely. It is, of course, known that on 16 November Kádár had a row with Grebenyik, the Soviet commander of Budapest, who threatened him with the reinstatement of Piros. Of course, after the decisive turn in January 1957, presumably everything was restored but I rather believe that until that time the ÁVH was dormant and inactive.)

Contents

In looking through the material found in the building, it became clear that the work of the ÁVH was a comprehensive reflection of the social, economic and political life of the country. The ÁVH was the central controlling agent; each operative arm of the state had, as its counterpart within the ÁVH, a corresponding controlling and supervising unit. There was an elaborate division of labour – e.g. the documentary material on economic frauds disclosed that the state office overseeing the 'maszek' petty private businesses, had an ÁVH section supervising it (e.g. materials procurement, theft and so on). Needless to say, the major branches of state industry had their own controlling sections within the building. The operative arms of the state contained large numbers of informers whose reports to the ÁVH were cross-referenced. A dossier in connection with a planned fraud in an enterprise disclosed the presence in the enterprise of at least four informers. Perhaps surprisingly, both the informers and those to be informed upon were referred to in the written material by pseudonyms and yet the keys (lists of real names set against cover names) were to be found in the same dossiers. For instance, a chronological file on one particular enterprise contained a list of names and pseudonyms renewed every six months. The reason for using pseudonyms even in such confidential material is perhaps explained by an exaggerated 'internal vigilance'. A manager would have to conceal the identity of his informers even from his colleagues. This requirement for 'vigilance' is not entirely ridiculous: it is no doubt based on the principle that if you 'ask for the moon, you will get the earth'; if you require absurdly rigid vigilance you will probably get at least reasonable caution. Nevertheless, this sort of vigilance, the concealment from the left hand of what the right hand is doing, was enforced in non-sensitive fields as well. For instance, a friend of mine who was assistant prosecutor at a district court, was transferred to the supreme court after a successful case for a trial period.[9] He returned in despair because utter secrecy was demanded even in perfectly ordinary, non-political economic criminal cases and he could not discuss legal problems attending these totally harmless cases with his colleagues in the prosecutor's office.

In one of the miscellaneous heaps in the cellar, I found a great deal of material relating to foreign trade, particularly to foreign traders visiting Budapest. The ÁVH section dealing with these people seemed to have the closest possible contact with Budapest night-life. Typical documents in this regard were weekly summaries of reports of informers employed in night clubs, including taxi girls, waiters, singers and the more distinguished prostitutes. The reports were in a rather primitive vein. Comrade Szabó, reporting on a Swedish merchant visiting Budapest, would note that contact with the Swede was made by 'Red Lily' and the latter would report that friendship was established. Comrade Szabó would then report that he had instructed 'Red Lily' to keep him sweet and so on. There were statistical reports, drawn up every three months, covering all foreign visitors to Hungary, showing purpose of visit, place of residence and other details. The intention seems to have been not so much counter-espionage as simply to keep a record of everybody who was coming and going between Hungary and the West.

On my first morning in the building, the police NCO mumbled something about an ÁVH roll or roll of informers having been found, but then, the same afternoon, denied having said so. I am told, however, that he probably forwarded it to his own superior authorities. Certain groups of material have remained reasonably fresh in memory.

1. Summary report, found in a filing cabinet in an upstairs room describing the planning activity etc. of the leaders of former bourgeois parties, covering the period between March and August 1956. This was extremely well written, logical and intelligently phrased. The report was divided into two parts, one dealing with the Smallholders' and Peasant Party and the other dealing with the Social Democrats. There was a detailed description of the meetings that took place giving the location, time, attendees and purpose. For instance, a meeting between Szakasits and three other former Social Democrats was described where Szakasits stated that the regime was bankrupt and would collapse within months, that a system with several parties was in the making and warned against any co-operation with Marosán.[10] The very next item described a meeting between Marosán and some of his friends, where Marosán declared that Social Democracy would be called upon to play a key part very soon and that in any future Social Democratic Party there would be no room for Szakasits. Nevertheless, the sources of this information were not given. It was also stressed that neither Marosán nor Szakasits would have anything to do with either

---

9   József Makranczy, a schoolmate.
10 György Marosán, leading left-wing Social Democrat.

Kéthly[11] or with any of the émigré Social Democrats. The plan of campaign of the Social Democratic Party was said to be the restoration of the former rights of the trade unions and the re-establishment of contacts with workers in the factories. In the report on the Smallholders' and Peasant Parties, such names as Tildy, Béla Kovács, Ortutay, Dobi, Ferenc Erdei, Mihályfi and a large number of lesser names were treated as a group.[12] Much mention was made of their frequent mutual contacts. I quote verbatim from the report: 'Smallholder opinion is in general that the regime is living its last days.'

According to this document the Smallholders discussed the question of cooperation with those former Smallholders who worked with the regime after the dissolution of the party. In working out their programme they concentrated on the problems of how to restore the position as it was after the land reform and before the spreading of collectives. At one meeting, Dobi was reported to have said that it had been a 'fatal step' to organize the collectives by force. I found it most illuminating that István Dobi, the President of the People's Republic, was put in the same category as declared class enemies.

2. Although the phrasing of most reports was very poor, ungrammatical and infested with party jargon, there were a few items, such as the one described in the previous paragraph, which were well written. A huge decorated album found on the desk of one of the deputy minister's rooms, contained two photographs of every western employee of western missions in Budapest together with their family background, schools, life history, presumed weaknesses (e.g. 'passionate angler', or 'likes high life') as well as their political views (e.g. 'leans towards Bevanism'). This album seems to have been the play-thing of the deputy minister.

3. *The B-29 Subsection.* As a rule, documents bore a letter and a number and it seems probable that the letter denoted the department or section and the number, the subsection. B-29 need not mean that there were 29 or more subsections in Department B. The numbering was probably discontinuous, the first digit denoting the subject and the second digit denoting the branch of subject. From the material found in this section, it seems that the duty of section or subsection B-29 was the observation of Hungarian émigré political organizations and the undermining of these organizations through 'diversions' and so on. It must have been a fairly new section struggling to establish itself.

The written material relating to this subsection was found in one of the rooms in the rabbit warren. It ran into 5 or 6 foolscap pages. There were quarterly plans submitted for approval and quarterly reports on plan-fulfilment relating to 1954 and 1955 (two years). The plan submissions were suggestions by subsection, paragraph by paragraph for its own activity in the following quarter. In each quarter, the first main heading was usually 'network development.' A typical item would be: 'In connection with such-and-such a diversion, recruitment abroad of three informers,

---

11 Anna Kéthly, right-wing Social Democrat.
12 In fact these politicians were miles apart. See below.

the sending out (the technical term used was 'agent-expatriation') of two new informers, improvement of work methods of the existing staff of informers.' Curiously, no financial details were ever mentioned. Then, in the plan fulfilment report for the same quarter, the same items reappeared with a summary explanation if the original plan submitted had not been fulfilled. For instance, they would state that contrary to the plan, only one new informer was sent abroad 'because of the unavailability of suitable recruits'.

These reports were, however, of a fairly general character and very specific details were usually not included. The second main heading of the 'network development' was usually: 'Operations'. There was usually paragraphs on: 'repatriation' with two subheadings, 'forced'(*presszio̧s*) and 'voluntary'; 'diversions against émigré military organizations'; 'propaganda activities among groups close to émigré political organizations', and so on. It is characteristic of the extreme care for discretion that I never found any names or any description of methods employed under the subheading 'forced repatriation'. But for 'voluntary repatriation', appendices were often enclosed. For example, in one of the plan submissions relating to a quarter of 1954, I found a list of pseudonyms and a remark that the voluntary repatriation of these people was desirable. On the very next sheet there was the key to the names. Among them was the opera singer, Járay, who actually returned in 1955. It seems the persons concerned never realized that they had returned because the ÁVH had decided to persuade them to do so. Nevertheless, it transpired from the papers that in the Járay case, two agents, both old friends of his, were furnished with valid passports and sent out to him, as these were people he trusted. The promises made to him in the name of the 'authorities' were indeed fulfilled; the state opera gave him an excellent contract. In the last quarter of 1954, or the first quarter of 1955, a new list of names appeared, about ten in all, including, as transpired from the key, Antal Páger. I will have more to say about this in a moment. Typical remarks in the plan fulfilment reports ran like this: 'Out of ten candidates for repatriation, we have had agents working for three months on four, for two months on two, for one month on three. No agent as yet on one.' The decision to repatriate Páger appears to have been of particular significance. As is well known, internal party opposition gathered strength after 1953, and started to collaborate with the non-communist intelligentsia. It was important for the regime to disrupt this alliance by reminding the internal party opposition of events immediately before 1945. The internal party opposition consisted to a large extent of Jews who had been persecuted in 1943 and 1944. The intention was to make them feel their vulnerability. This was the reason for the decision to repatriate the notorious Arrow-Crossist Páger, who upon arriving back in Hungary, made a (probably officially inspired) statement of great arrogance, infuriating Jews. They were indignant and began to ask whether 1944 was to be repeated. It was hoped the Jewish opposition would turn back to the Party and to the radical communist sentiments of 1945–46. The decision to repatriate Páger was taken either in late 1954 or early 1955, and it is an open question whether this precipitated his return in early 1956 or whether it was a shrewd anticipation of Páger's own intentions.

Under the main heading 'Operations', there was also an item entitled 'Disruption of émigré military organizations.' This item stuck in my mind accidentally because I spotted the name Ferenc Kisbarnaki Farkas, who was Chief Scout when I was a boy scout at school. It appeared from the submissions and reports relating to this item that the aim was to establish some contact with him so that his activities could be kept under surveillance. More specifically, they wanted to acquire the co-operation of one of his aides. There were pencilled remarks and queries on several of these papers, apparently by a departmental chief, such as 'Why no progress yet?' Then followed a supplementary plan report on this item alone, explaining Kisbarnaki's precautions, stating, 'We could not even put into effect the basic rule of gaining the co-operation of at least two relatives or friends still in Hungary.' This apparently was a basic rule in regard to all leading émigrés. Eventually, a close friend of his living in Hungary was found but in the words of the report, 'no good purpose would be served by mere correspondence, she should be enabled to meet FKF.' Then there was a memo, apparently from the section or departmental chief, asking for a detailed proposal. In the plan for the next quarter, under the main heading 'Network Development', there is mention of the despatch of an agent, giving the cover name used for the friend mentioned above. She was given a position in a state trading firm and sent abroad, if my memory serves me right, to a Swiss town where Kisbarnaki happened to be staying for a couple of weeks. This friend was not, however, a businesswoman and her appointment to such a job must have aroused the suspicions of an intelligent observer. In the next plan fulfilment report there was a cryptic statement saying that the agent had succeeded in establishing permanent liaison with FKF. This may not have amounted to very much for their purposes, however. Another interesting case in the B-29 papers related to Monsignor Béla Varga. There was, in a plan submission, a suggestion for a 'diversion' to compromise him. The referent proposed to exploit the pathological suspicions typical among the émigrés by suggesting, through a double-agent of the ÁVH, that the regime was interested in Varga giving the pseudonym by which he was known. The double-agent was believed by the ÁVH to be working both for them and for the CIA or some other western intelligence agency, his double allegiance being known to both sides. The plan provided for a telegraphic message in code which was known to have been broken by the western intelligence agencies (such telegrams were sent on an open telephone line – such a line was referred to as a 'residential line'). The telegram was to have been sent to a Hungarian legation informing them that our agent is meeting so-and-so (giving the cover-name chosen for Varga) at such-and-such a time. The western side, of course, was assumed to have learned the identity of the person covered by that name through the double-agent. A week later another telegram was to be sent confirming that the meeting had taken place. A 'blown' agent (i.e. one whose identity was already known to foreign agencies) was to call on Varga and the western intelligence services, keeping an eye on Varga, would notice that this man, known to be working for the ÁVH, had in fact met him. The call was to be on a harmless pretext, an inquiry about the whereabouts of a supposedly mutual friend. Then another telegram was to be sent on an open telephone line to the legation stating that the negotiations with Varga had yielded no definite results so far but that they were continuing to progress the case. Then yet another blown agent was to be sent. As these calls on empty pretexts could become suspicious, there was to be no more actual visits paid to Varga, and further contacts were to be restricted to a few more telegrams purporting to relate to negotiations with him, expressing impatience with him for making many promises but fulfilling few. Eventually a telegram was to confirm the receipt of 'material' furnished by him. The final act was to be a last telegram to the mission stating that Varga (the cover name leaked to western intelligence) had requested a temporary suspension of co-operation because of difficulties at his end. This plan submission went before the head of Department B. There was no further evidence of its being carried out, except a paragraph of the plan submission for the subsequent quarter stating 'with regard to [cover name], we suggest the same plan as that carried out in connection with [Varga's cover name].'

Yet another characteristic item related to a planned 'diversion' against Radio Free Europe in Munich. Exceptionally, this was an entirely separate item and not part of any quarterly plan submission. Inside a covering sheet, there was a memo from department to sub-department, of which more presently. The plan was to transport 'materials necessary for diversion' to Munich 'by plane' (whatever that may have meant). Three agents were to be sent to Munich as state foreign trade representatives. There then followed a fairly incomprehensible text, with a large number of letters and figures, apparently symbols in some kind of code. Next came further details describing the personal qualifications and identity of the proposed three agents. The departmental head noted on the plan that it betrayed dilettantism, a lack of even elementary competence and ordered those responsible for the plan to stop dreaming up adventure stories. The relevant quarterly plan fulfilment report contains some paragraphs of self-criticism; it confesses that the staff of the subsection were still untried and lacked technical education and personal experience; the subsections's performance was unsatisfactory and displayed naiveté and dilettantism; 'much further development is needed [...] in view of the early stage of our rapid development and in view of the importance of the more complex tasks that it will need to be undertaken in the future.' The more experienced comrades were to look after the less experienced ones. The time devoted to professional seminars within the subsection (apparently four hours a week) was to be doubled, translations of Soviet technical literature on 'our subjects' were to be promoted, and there was a suggestion that 'despite our basic rules, it seems desirable in this subsection to enlist the help of more experienced comrades working in other sections.' This part of the self-criticism was full of pencilled explanation marks, queries and disapproving remarks, particularly in relation to the last suggestion.

My general impression after reading through some of this material was that despite some realism, there was a good deal of naiveté and that what was done was of poor quality, while the slavish adoption of the 'planning and plan fulfilment technique', utterly unsuitable for intelligence work even if it were appropriate in productive industry, demonstrates little independence of mind. Nevertheless, it was obvious that the staff at section level were superior in quality to those at subsection level.

4. Informers. There were two types of informers: 'voluntary informer' and 'forced informer'. The first type did not appear to have given much trouble. With regard to the second, there were apparently many 'objective difficulties'; whenever in a plan fulfilment report an excuse was required for some failure or poor quality work, reference was made to the ratio of 'voluntary informers' to 'forced informers'; if the ratio was low this was presented as a self-evident excuse. There were several ways of finding forced informers. Somebody caught stealing state property might be offered freedom from prosecution in return for enrolling as a 'forced informer'. If someone was unexpectedly arrested and subsequently released by the ÁVH, the inference could usually be drawn that he had become a 'pressed informer'. Such people did not always or even usually report regularly. Instead, on specific occasions they were interviewed about matters they were presumed to know of. Even a man called in and cross-examined for a few hours on his acquaintances was classed as a 'forced informer'. Nowhere did I come across their reports. Although they appeared normally to have written the reports down, these were apparently not preserved. Nevertheless, documents often stated that 'we interrogated so-and-so, but were unsuccessful in getting useful information.' Occasionally, I saw references to 'unsatisfactory work' and even 'deletion of so-and-so from our list of "forced informers" '. It is an error to believe that they could extract everything they wanted from everybody. They did not always, nor perhaps in the majority of cases, use torture. Often, people were bribed into co-operation. Old people whose pensions had been cancelled were, for instance, recruited as informers in return for 'help' with their pension claim. The ÁVH could, of course, settle matters with a ministry in a way impossible for a private individual.

5. Coordination. I found no evidence of collaboration between subsections. B-18 might have informers and material relevant to a case dealt with by A-11 but it appears that A-11 was unlikely to hear of this or be able to call on the help of B-18's informers. Its own 'vigilance' must have been a severe handicap to the ÁVH. The recurrent use of the term 'vertical organization' strongly suggests that contact between sections was only through the deputy ministers in charge of them.

6. Melinda Ottrubay. This was a folder about eight inches thick relating to the wife of Prince Pál Eszterházy. It appears that she was being pressed by the ÁVH to furnish or sign some deed enabling the Hungarian state to claim the ownership of certain Eszterházy estates in Burgenland (Eastern Austria).

7. Paper and tape recordings. I was struck by the fact that in the recording of the operation of the internal administration of the state, only the formal framework (plan submissions and plan fulfilment reports, staff, pay, statistics) was recorded on paper; operational activity was recorded on tapes. In other words, the objects of activity, the actual cases, were very seldom put on paper (the Ottrubay-case and a very few others I came across were the exceptions), but were recorded on tape. I did not then know how to handle tape recorders and was too pressed for time to start to learn how to do so. I thought there would be ample time for that later. But a member of the engineers' committee put on one tape for me just to see what it was like. This particular tape was a record of quite inconsequential office conversation – apparently everyday talk in the office was automatically recorded; the recording machine being presumably operated by some automatic mechanism.

Thus there is a fundamental difference from the historian's point of view between the study of the administration of this kind of state and of old-style states. Here, on tape, is a vivid and absolutely detailed record of what went on, if only of a limited period of time. No earlier state administration could be observed in this manner – only written records were made and such records must be more formal and less revealing. On the other hand, this new-style state does not preserve records of settled business but destroys most of it as it goes along, keeping a record of the immediate past only. This, however, is recorded in great detail. (For instance, cross-examinations are recorded verbatim on tapes). Moreover, what was recorded was not confined to records of the dealing of the ÁVH with the objects of its surveillance; it also included internal records. Had we succeeded in salvaging this material we would have faced enormously difficult methodological questions. For history based on this kind of material would start to be a natural science rather than an art. (Nevertheless, apart from this one trivial occasion neither I nor my colleagues listened to the tapes – we did not realize that we only had five days and we only got as far of making a quick visual stock of what there was in the building).

8. The Exile of Ferenc Nagy (Prime Minister of Hungary, 1946–47). Some of the tapes, however, seemed to have been translated by a typist pool, where, as I learned indirectly, music was relayed from loudspeakers during work. I must stress that these transcripts do not have the same authenticity as signed documents since there is greater chance of their being fabricated.

In one open safe of five drawers, four were empty, while in one I found half-a-dozen dossiers. The very first piece in the top dossier purported to be the transcript of telephone conversations between Mátyás Rákosi and Ferenc Gordon, Hungarian minister in Berne, dated and timed 1 June, 1947. The transcript looked like the manuscript of a play, and since it impressed me considerably, I believe I can render it now accurately.

First day (May 30?)
    G: Hello, Mátyás.
    R: Hello, how are you? What is the form? Ha-ha-ha! How about that crazy Feri?[13]
    G: He is plodding on. Worse luck, there is nothing up with him.
    R: Is he still going to your place?
    G: Of course, he is hanging about the whole day.
    R: What is he doing?
    G: He is crying on our shoulders.
    R: What do you mean, crying? Couldn't he make up his mind yet?
    G: As far as I can see, not.
    R: What is he saying?

---

13 Ferenc Nagy, Prime Minister on a visit to Switzerland.

G: Well, the same old stuff. He is complaining about his own difficult position.

R: What do you think? How could he be impressed?

G: Well, I don't know. I just don't know. I am trying to talk to him. I am trying all the time.

R: By what time do you expect some result?

G: Perhaps this afternoon.

R: Well, all right, tonight we will talk some more.

(Then follows some humorous personal exchanges).

Evening:

R: Well, my little old Gordon?

G: Alas, Mátyás, I still cannot say anything.

R: What do you mean? Was he in this afternoon?

G: Yes, he was in, ruminating.

R: What sort of worries does he have?

G: Well, his son and…er, er…

R: Financial?

G: That too.

R: What is he saying?

G: Nothing worth speaking of. He is talking about the country.

R: It beats me to see why Feri is kicking up such a fuss. To be frank, I can't see why you can't bring him to his senses.

G: Please Mátyás. I did what was humanly possible.

R: Why do you have no results then?

G: Don't argue with me, Mátyás. I am only an agent of yours.

Gordon then expressed his hope that he may be able to report progress tomorrow.

Second day. Conversation opens without polite exchanges, annoyed tone.

R: The whole country is anxiously awaiting developments. You must realize, my little Gordon, I am saying this as Deputy Premier of Hungary. I must say it in that way as this matter must be settled before the day is out. Is or is not Feri willing to settle with us?

G: Well, he is talking about it.

R: Well, if he is talking about it, why can't you report to me officially to that effect?

G: Because he has not said anything substantive yet.

R: Couldn't one speed this up somehow?

G: How do you mean speed it up?

R: Well, simply by reporting it officially to us.

G: But I can't report it officially until he has said yes!

R: But my dear man, if you so report it, that means that he has so decided!

G: No, Mátyás, I couldn't possibly do that.

R: Look here, I don't want to argue about this now but realize that it is important for me to get this report today. Do you get me?

Second day, afternoon. Very short conversation. R inquiring about results. G reports no progress. Promises for tomorrow. R bursts out and G says the whole leadership of the Smallholders' Party is incensed. The whole action stands or falls on this. If we can't get results quickly the political consequences may be immeasurable. We must carry out our own plan of political development. Merely because Feri is hysterical, we cannot deviate from, we cannot give up our road of development. On the night of the second day, probably 31 May, another brief, inconclusive conversation was recorded.

Third day.

    R: Well, what's up?

    G: Er…I mean…

    R: Have you got it or haven't you?

    G: Er…yes but…I take it Mátyás that in affairs of this sort you used to be magnanimous…

    R: How much?

    G: Three hundred thousand.

    R: Ours or yours? (This is untranslatable: the term refers to home currency versus Swiss currency).

    G: Ours.

    R: How much is that in forints?

    G: About eight hundred thousand.

    R: All right, all right. This at last is settled. Now a few technical details. We need three bits of paper from you. One signed by him, that is for the Party (Smallholders' Party). One from you through the residential line. And one you must send direct to me, so that I should be covered. [This sounded cryptic to me.] Will that be all right?

    G: All right. You shall have these.

    R: Bye-bye.

    G: One moment. How about the kid?

    R: Of course. He is on the way. Bye-bye.

I wish again to stress that this transcript has, strictly speaking, no value as documentary evidence, for it bore no signature and it could have been prepared by anyone. The fact, however, that I found it in the place I did, lends it some significance . Nevertheless, there was another significant feature. This conversation appeared to have taken place about nine years earlier. Nevertheless, it was clear from the freshness of the paper and the type that the transcript had been prepared very recently. One possible interpretation of this is that the authorities had recently been thinking about preparing a Rákosi trial and were gathering evidence that might be of use. It would then be natural that they should refer to old tape-recorded telephone conversations of Rákosi's. I have a very vague recollection of having seen in the same pile of dossiers a transcript of Imre Nagy's telephone conversations.

    On Saturday, 3 November, I noticed several unidentified people coming and going in the building. I was on the third floor looking through some papers and I came across the engineers' committee locking up the machine rooms, saying they would be back the next morning. I then went down to look at the miscellaneous papers in the cellar and after some time there I had to leave in order to attend a revolutionary council meeting in my own office. Late in the afternoon, I went back to the ÁVH building with a historian friend.[14] We went to the cellar to continue sifting through the miscellaneous papers, lost our way and while making our way through the cellar could hear slow footsteps. This was rather unsettling. We left the cellar around 10.00 p.m. and in the corridor leading towards the main exit, we saw a stranger who was neither a student nor a policeman pacing up and down (with his

---

14 István Purjesz.

right hand in his pocket).[15] We did not dare challenge him as we had by then a particular reason not to draw attention to ourselves.[16] Another unarmed civilian unknown to us, was standing behind the main staircase as we left.

Summary of Findings

As suggested before, the disordered state of the building and the condition of the rooms made me feel that this huge Byzantine organization was already decaying and falling apart, the revolution furnishing the last push needed for its disintegration.

The written material, of which I only read a negligible fraction, suggested a more sober and down-to-earth picture. The documents indicate that the ÁVH was a straightforward state authority, not a *grand guignol* from a cheap film. Moreover, the stereotyped, stale phraseology of a people's democracy was missing. The tone was more realistic and level-headed than the style of most of the other institutions of the Hungarian state. It was a reasonably factual and dispassionate voice compared to the tone of the party administration's communications. The description of the activities of the bourgeois parties lacked the coloured language and vituperation to be found in press reports. Nonetheless the material was not entirely objective.

It would be a mistake to interpret the realism of these papers as a sign of cynical intelligence. The work on which these people were engaged could, of course, be expected to make them cynical. But this was not reflected in the way they drafted their reports. It is quite possible that the fabrication of false charges and the manufacture of evidence left those involved with clear consciences. They may well have felt that such procedures were necessary for the defence and progress of the system. On the other hand, objectivity and realism must be understood in a relative sense, i.e. as compared to the manifestations of other Hungarian state agencies. By the standards of commonsense, the ÁVH reports still presented a distorted picture of reality, albeit less distorted than that projected by the party proper. I cannot claim to offer a definitive overall picture, but on the strength of the small sample that I had a chance to see, it would seems that the ÁVH apparatus was not homogenous but one where several levels of operational methods were to be found. At the top, there was factual and intelligently written material, but at the lower levels one found appalling pieces of quite stupid and muddled writing, where the style of the lower party seminars was fully preserved with all its nauseatingly meaningless phrases and the standard adjectives.

Their organizational methods reveal considerable naïveté and the slavish application of patterns of centrally planned industrial organization to a totally different field of intellectual endeavour. It is surely farcical to apply quarterly plans and percentage plan fulfilments to the production of confidential information, diversion and counter-intelligence. In a sense, however, the ÁVH was a factory producing reports and destroying ('consuming') them as it went along. It was simultaneously recording by means of tapes virtually its own whole life and much of that of the nation. The ÁVH seems still to have been in a phase of rapid growth. Several of its sections were still in their infancy.

---

15 In facing him at a distance I also kept my hand in my pocket, although there was no pistol in it.
16 I was carrying under my overcoat a pile of documents.

Although it was big, it still had growing pains. It must not be conceived of as a smoothly functioning organization, nor even as one complacent and unconscious of its own incompetence. It was anything but an omniscient and wise apparatus.

Its two main shortcomings appeared to be, first, the generally poor quality of its staff. They seem to be totally devoid of subtlety. During their ten or twelve years in power they produced many well-trained people but these were only sufficient to fill the managerial positions in an organization constantly inflated by over-ambitious tasks. For operations, they had to use second-rate people. There was thus a gap in quality between the executive and the operative personnel. A second main shortcoming is implied by the rapidity of its development, as well as by the idiosyncrasies of communist organizational principles. This principally shows itself in the lack of co-ordination. The left hand went about its work, not knowing that the right hand has already done much of it. The result of 'vertical organization' is frequently apparent and the ÁVH was itself very conscious of it.

Undoubtedly the effectiveness of the ÁVH apparatus was greatly overrated by the Hungarian population. It was, nonetheless in its interest to foster public belief in its competence and infallibility.

Provocation by Gerő?

At about seven p.m. on 23 October, I was in Parliament Square[17] and near me on top of a motor car a young man was standing and describing to the crowd what was happening in front of the radio building. As he got to the phrase 'the ÁVH did not let them in', a voice from the crowd shouted 'Why didn't you take away their guns?' Scores of voices from the crowd protested 'Shut up, that is *their* method not ours...', 'We want to do this by lawful means,' and so on. This does not fit with the assertion that the crowd was 'counter-revolutionary'[18] in mood. It was essentially a *bien pensant* crowd, leaning over backwards to remain within the bounds of existing law. In this connection, serious attention should be paid to the question of what role was played in the events of 23 October by deliberate provocation. The facts partly speak for themselves. Gerő first permitted the demonstration at the Bem statue, then prohibited it over the radio, then permitted it again. The changes not only infuriated the population but also created confusion, probably deliberately, as to whether the government had a consistent policy. This was followed by the unnecessary opening of fire in front of the radio building.[19] That event should be seen in conjunction with attempts at provocation in Parliament Square between about 8 and 9 PM. At about that time, many motor cars began to arrive in the square, and I saw at least two with mounted loudspeakers shouting 'Hungarians are being slaughtered.' (*Ölik a magyart!*) 'Everybody to the radio building.' Their

---

17 I joined the demonstration with my students outside the University in Váci Street in early afternoon. As happened to many other people, I lost the people I started with and teamed up with others. I crossed over to Buda but could not get to the Bem statue because the adjoining streets were already jammed. With the crowd I moved back to Pest, to Parliament Square and was waiting for Imre Nagy to address the crowd.
18 Repeated by the organs of the Kádár regime after the event.
19 I was not there but in Parliament Square.

occupants looked as if they had been especially recruited for the purpose. These two cars moved slowly through the crowd. I became curious and walked beside one of the cars asking everybody as I went along whether they knew who the people in the car were. Nobody knew them and nobody knew where they came from. Their rhythmical shouting had a trained and professional quality. They kept up this shouting for quite some time. They began while Imre Nagy was still speaking and they were still circling about well after he left the balcony. As the crowd began to disperse, part of it moving towards the radio building, half a dozen or so men who were known to belong to Imre Nagy's circle of followers made their appearance. These people were well-informed and some of them were known to me. They implored the crowd not to go to the radio building, shouting, 'the whole thing is a provocation.' The people whom I took to be provocateurs were equipped with cars and loudspeakers while those belonging to the Imre Nagy group had neither. It is also known that Imre Nagy was warned as early as August 1956 that the Gerő-clique[20] were planning a provocation in order to save themselves from being replaced by Moscow.[21] This, of course, comports with the way in which Imre Nagy's people clung to the phraseology of the *bien pensant* and mildly revisionist programme of June 1953 and their evident fear of any political radicalism in the early stage of the revolution.

It is also known that during the Spanish Civil War in Barcelona, Gerő used the same technique of provoking a 'rightist' demonstration in the streets, so as to strengthen the left faction on whose behalf he was working.[22] Gerő was a distinguished NKVD man and it is not improbable that he (or some people in the disintegrating ÁVH) attempted to create what they thought might turn into another Poznań or East Berlin, deliberately allowing the ferment to go on during the summer and making no attempt to get it under control as he could have done in August. Would the Soviet Union not wish to have a 'stable' Hungarian government wedged in between an unstable Poland and unreliable Yugoslavia? Gerő (or somebody else) may have supposed that any action of his designed to bring this about would be looked upon at least with benevolent neutrality by Moscow, despite the Twentieth Congress. An outbreak on an East German scale would have finished off the 'revisionists' and Moscow might have given full powers to Gerő.[23]

---

20 Our group of historians were aware of this through Szűcs's contacts.
21 I learnt years later from Gyula Juhász that around noon on 23 October about a dozen ambulances were lined up on the lower embankment under the parliament building.
22 I learnt in Oxford in 1957 about this background of Gerő and discussed the subject at length with Miklós Krassó. History is full of cock-ups and not many conspiracies. Yet it would not be worthless to inquire into whether what happened on 23 October 1956 in Hungary had elements of conspiracy in addition to being a cock-up of the regime.
23 Because of what I saw in Parliament Square I was despondent about the chances of Imre Nagy replacing Gerő, which we had all hoped. Around 11.30 at night I rang Benczédi. He was not at home, but I remember telling his sister: 'Everything is lost!' That was after I had been to the radio building and before I was arrested, about 1 AM, and thrown into a cellar by ÁVH men outside the Party Headquarters in Akadémia Street.

Incident at the Party Headquarters[24]

Zoltán E. Tóth, Dean of the Faculty of History of Budapest University and Péter Hanák, on behalf of the University Party Committee, as well as a number of others acting as spokesmen of the Faculty and students of Eötvös Lóránd University, after telephone agreement with the Party headquarters, went to call at Akadémia Street on the morning of 25 October. When they arrived at one of the Akadémia Street entrances, the blood-bath in Parliament Square was already in progress. Only three members of the group were admitted. E. Tóth, Hanák and a few others were left standing at the entrance. The shooting drew nearer, whereupon the gate was locked from the inside. Those of the group left outside sought cover from the flying bullets and moved behind a tank standing in the gate. After a few minutes a tank turned in from Parliament Square into Akadémia Street and opened fire on the tank behind which they were sheltering. Their tank began to move forward and they ran to the gate, pushing it in. By the time they got in, Tóth was already dead and Hanák was wounded. They moved down into the base-ment and Hanák lay there bleeding. The basement had high windows opening onto an inside corridor with potted palms. Along this corridor, after a few minutes, a procession of men walked away from the wing most exposed to fire. They were wreathed in cigar smoke and moved unhurriedly and without any apparent concern about the situation. Among them were Gerő, Piros and Apró as well as several Russians among whom Hanák recognized Mikoyan. Imre Nagy, with Losonczy, followed in a separate group a few paces behind. As Imre Nagy drew level with Hanák, who was sitting propped up on the other side of the bay window, he recognized him: 'Comrade Hanák, how do you come to be here?' On hearing him speak, the Gerő group who had already passed the window, turned back and listened. Hanák explained why they had come and stressed that the only chance of a solution of the present crisis was the disbandment of the ÁVH, a cessation of the machine-gunning and a firm promise of elections. As he spoke, there were several interruptions of 'This is absurd' and, on his uttering the word 'elections,' there were scandalized shouts: 'This is pure counter-revolution, what else?' Thereupon, Imre Nagy turned back from Hanák and facing the group said gravely, 'Comrades, it is far from being as simple as all that.' Then he turned to Hanák again, bowed and they all moved on.

---

24 I was not there. The account is from Péter Hanák and I heard it from members of the Historical Institute in November 1956. Meeting Hanák in London years later he confirmed the account.

Life as a British Diplomat in Hungary, 1961–63

I. W. Roberts

On 17 July 1961, my wife and I arrived in Budapest to begin my posting as second secretary in chancery of the British mission in Hungary. The previous six months had been spent learning Hungarian at the School of Slavonic and East European Studies which had accepted a grant of £350 from the Hungarian government in 1937 to introduce the study of Hungarian into the curriculum. My tuition was supervised by the late Professor George Cushing, a Cambridge classicist, who had learned Hungarian at the School during the Second World War and subsequently served with the British forces in the Middle East. The late Professor Hugh Seton-Watson, the younger son of one of the founders of the School, an acknowledged expert, like his father, on East-Central Europe and Professor of Russian History, also assisted me in my studies. I was able to supplement my language instruction with conversation lessons at the home of a Hungarian family that had left Hungary in 1956 where they were later to be joined by the elderly mother of the husband. I learned much about Hungary and its history from all these people and was well briefed before my arrival in Budapest. I should also mention that one of the two undergraduates learning Hungarian at that time was Michael Branch, later to become professor of Finnish and director of the School.

The 'English Legation' (Az Angol Követség) had, like the other British missions in Eastern Europe, not yet been upgraded to an Embassy. As a Scot from Edinburgh, I had always been fascinated by the oldest building in the city, Queen Margaret's Chapel, built on the rock of Edinburgh Castle, and by the queen's link with Hungary. This connection has been disputed by historians and it remains a subject of controversy.[1] My efforts to persuade the Protocol Department of the Hungarian Ministry of Foreign Affairs to change the Hungarian title of the mission from 'English' to 'British' met with no success. However, after my own service in Hungary, the Legation was upgraded, together with the other missions in Eastern Europe, to an Embassy and it thus became 'A Brit Nagykövetség' (The British Embassy).

During my service in Hungary, the mission was headed by a minister who was supported by nine diplomatic staff. Besides these people, the mission included a number of UK-based, non-diplomatic staff engaged in secretarial and administrative duties. The Legation also had the support of Hungarian local staff whose assistance was essential, mainly for linguistic reasons. Inevitably, members of the local staff lived in a world of

---

1 See thus, Gabriel Ronay, 'Margaret of Scotland: Queen, Saint and Legend', *The Hungarian Quarterly*, 34, 1993, pp. 92–8.

divided loyalties because of the constant attentions of the secret police. Two of them, the late István Gál and József Molnár were given obituaries in *The Times* after their deaths on, respectively, 7 July, 1982, and 29 January, 1996.

The Legation was housed in a former bank building in Harmincad utca in Pest, its original premises in Buda having been destroyed in the fighting that took place between German and Soviet forces at the close of the Second world War. It was able to play a leading role in the life of the relatively small non-communist diplomatic corps, largely because the US mission was in the care of a chargé d'affaires and had been drastically reduced in size as a result of President Eisenhower's decision to grant asylum in the building to Cardinal Mindszenty. Mindszenty remained there until 1971 when he reluctantly left Hungary at the request of the Pope and President Nixon who wished to improve US diplomatic relations with Hungary.

One of my main duties in chancery was to supervise the production of a daily English-language summary of the Hungarian press. It was the work of a small team of local staff and was sold to most of the western missions, as well as to subsequent new arrivals in the early 1960s, such as Ghana and Indonesia. It did so indeed at a small profit, much to the satisfaction of the Foreign and Commonwealth Office. The press summary was supplemented by a fortnightly review of Hungarian periodicals, such as *Társadalmi Szemle* and others of a similar nature. Occasionally, the press summary included items from the Hungarian provincial press. I also deputized for the commercial secretary and information officer during their absences on leave. My wife, a former FCO employee, worked part-time in the visa section which, besides dealing with travel to Great Britain, undertook the necessary formalities for Hungarian citizens, mainly elderly, who had been given passports so that they could leave the country and join relatives living in Australia, Canada and New Zealand. As a Russian speaker, I also acted as interpreter for the Minister at National Day parties and on other occasions: for, example, when the FCO instructed the mission to establish diplomatic relations with the Embassy of Outer Mongolia, whose deputy chief spoke excellent Russian. Shortly after my arrival, while my wife and I were still living in the Duna Hotel, I was soon made aware of the extent of Soviet influence in Hungary,

The minister, the late Sir Nicholas Cheetham, instructed me to accompany to the Soviet Embassy a visiting British MP with business interests, who was travelling by car through Eastern Europe and the Soviet Union. After his visit to Hungary he intended to travel to Uzhgorod (Ungvár) in Ukraine via the railway junction of Csap. The minister was uneasy about this plan and persuaded the MP to pay a visit to the Soviet Embassy in order to make sure that he would not encounter any problem in crossing to Ukraine. Ensconced in the minister's official car, the MP and I were driven to the embassy where we were introduced to the consul. Speaking in Russian, he informed me that the proposed itinerary was 'quite impossible because there is no road'.

In response to the MP's protest that he had already cleared the route with the Soviet ambassador in London, the consul then informed us that 'the bridge is down for repairs'. Nevertheless, in order not to be unhelpful, he would now ask the Czechoslovak Embassy to issue the MP with a transit visa so that he could reach Uzhgorod via Czechoslovakia. A telephone conversation in Hungarian then took place, in the course of which the consul made it clear to his interlocutor that he had banned the MP from travelling via Csap and that, for this reason, a Czechoslovak transit visa should now be issued.

At the conclusion of this conversation, the consul informed us in Russian that we were now free to go to the Czechoslovak Embassy to collect the transit visa as he had arranged. I quickly decided that further argument was pointless, but, on leaving the Soviet Embassy, I was unable to resist remarking to the consul, to whom I was, as a new arrival, a complete stranger: 'Nagyon érdekes volt ez a beszélgetés, konzul úr. Do svidaniya.' (That was a very interesting conversation, Mr Consul, Goodbye). His face was a study, but he remained silent. Upon our return to the Legation, we explained to the minister what had happened. My action was approved and the minister commented to the MP that he was glad that there would now be no risk of an incident during the continuation of his journey.

Not long after this, my wife and I left the Duna Hotel and moved into our permanent accommodation in Budapest. Unlike the Soviet Union and other countries, foreign diplomats in Hungary did not live in diplomatic ghettoes guarded day and night by policemen. The Diplomatic Service of the Ministry of Foreign affairs allocated accommodation to foreign missions. Ours proved to be the ground floor of a large villa in the Second District in Buda. The house had originally belonged to a banker who had left Hungary for Canada shortly after the communist take-over. All the furniture and many of the family's other possessions had been left on the premises, including photo albums and a well-stocked, multi-lingual library. Rent was paid quarterly to a representative of the family still living in Budapest. We had the use of one bedroom (with adjoining bathroom), a sitting room, a dining room, kitchen and maid's room. Two other Hungarian families lived in the upper storey of the villa, while the basement was occupied by a *házmester* (concierge) and his family, originally from Transylvania, who tended the garden, of which we had exclusive use. We were also fortunate to secure the services of an excellent cook who had worked for the previous British consul before his departure. She was the daughter of a former rich peasant who had acquired a knowledge of English. We eventually discovered that she had hoped to study at university but because of her background had been classified as *osztályidegen* (class-alien). After a brief period working in a factory in Budapest, she had found employment as a cook to members of the western diplomatic corps. An unabashed anti-communist and great lover of Hungarian poetry, she was regularly interviewed by the secret police and she kept me informed in out-of-doors conversations about items that she thought might interest me. I shall never forget her outburst of rage during a journey made with her to an ordinary *csemegekereskedés* (grocery shop) in Pest where access via a secret door at the rear admitted us to an Aladdin's Cave of items, unavailable to the Hungarian public, which included choice cuts of meat, normally delivered by order to the Legation, which was the purpose of our visit.

My wife and I were able to travel freely throughout the country with the exception of a thirty-kilometre zone bordering Austria and Yugoslavia in which stopping the car was forbidden. We travelled the length and breadth of Hungary, sometimes staying for weekends at places such as Pécs and Szeged. I asked several times for permission to visit Fertőd (the former Eszterháza) in the thirty-kilometre zone, but to no avail. I was, however, able to compensate for this by visiting Eisenstadt (Vasvár), Haydn's other place of residence in the Burgenland, in the course of our visits to Vienna. I had come to know that city well during the years 1949–50 while serving as a National Service officer in the Royal Air Force at Schwechat airfield which, during the years of the Allied occupation of Austria, we shared with the French air force.

I have many memories from our travels. I recall a 'Szuper' petrol-station attendant in Debrecen supplying me, while filling up my car, with the registration number of a secret police car that had anticipated our arrival. During one of our outings to places nearer Budapest, such as Tihany, Eger and Gödöllö, we visited Esztergom. On entering the cathedral, I found, to my surprise, the young Russian driver of a military vehicle gazing in wonder at the interior of the cathedral, who was interested to find someone willing to talk to him in his own language. During one of the absences of the information officer, I made an official visit with other members of the Legation local staff to Pannonhalma monastery to deliver copies of English magazines that were gratefully received. I also accompanied a delegation from the Federation of British Industries to the steelworks at Dunaújváros and had one or two brief conversations with the workers, much to the vexation of the accompanying officials from the Ministry of Foreign Trade. In 1963, Sir Nicholas Henderson, then head of the FCO's Northern Department, paid a visit to Budapest. At his request, I took him to Ráckeve on Csepel Island so that he could inspect the ruined summer palace of Prince Eugen of Savoy, the central hall of which was being used as a grain store. Sir Nicholas was researching a book about the prince, which was published the next year and was the first English-language biography of Eugen of Savoy. One Whit Sunday my wife and I drove to Hollókő where we were able to photograph women and girls wearing their traditional, colourful costumes, as well as talking to the priest after the service. Nor can I forget a visit to the college of Sárospatak, famous for its links with my native Presbyterian Church of Scotland, as well as the neighbouring vineyards of Tokaj.

In 1961 János Kádár made his historic statement, endorsed by the Eighth Party Congress in November the following year, that 'whoever is not against us, is with us'. One of the results of this declaration of policy was that it became possible for members of the Hungarian professional and intellectual community to attend Legation functions and accept invitations to meals and parties given by members of the diplomatic staff. István Gál, who knew many members of the Hungarian intellectual community, was indefatigable in fostering such contacts. After the expulsion of the British Council from Hungary during the Rákosi regime, the Legation continued to maintain on its ground floor a library of English books and periodicals in a reading room which was frequented by elderly Hungarians who were permitted entrance to the building by the secret policeman on duty outside. The Information Department also distributed a bulletin about events and life in Britain and assisted those Hungarians who sought information about such matters.

Because of this relaxation in the atmosphere of Anglo-Hungarian relations, the decision was taken by the FCO to post another first secretary to the Legation who was to concentrate on cultural relations in the absence of the British Council. I myself was promoted to first secretary at the same time. My wife and I, who are both fond of music and the theatre, much enjoyed our visits to Budapest's two opera houses, the Operetta Theatre, as well as concerts. It gave us the opportunity to see and hear several works seldom performed in Britain and meet some of the performers. We came to know the ballet dancer Gabriella Lakatos, the pianist Annie Fischer, as well as making the acquaintance of Zoltán Kodály and his young ward. We enjoyed listening to Sir John Barbirolli, a former cellist, playing on the instrument with the small orchestra in the 'Kis Royal' restaurant during his visit. When Lord Harewood came to Budapest to negotiate the participation of the Hungarian opera and ballet in the annual Edinburgh Festival, I had a long discussion with him about the Festival as I had attended the first post-war Festival in August 1947 while still a Cambridge undergraduate. My wife also agreed to accompany me to a production of Agatha Christie's *Az Egérfogó* (The Mousetrap), the setting of which had been transferred to a hunting lodge. We were also fortunate to visit the studio of Margit Kovács and still possess one of her charming statuettes of a young lady. It was also most interesting on another occasion to talk to Professor László Országh about his Hungarian-English dictionary. Országh was made an Honorary OBE and also received an obituary in *The Times* on 24 February, 1984.

Throughout my service in Hungary I was naturally involved in the Legation's reporting to the FCO on the political situation in Hungary. I made the first draft of several despatches, such as the Eighth Party Congress and the strengthening of party control over the secret police, of which Kádár himself had been a victim during the Rákosi regime. The late Sir Ivor Pink, who replaced Nicholas Cheetham as minister, regularly issued invitations to senior party officials to official functions, such as the Queen's Birthday Party. Nevertheless, such invitations, unlike those to government ministers, were refused. I remember accompanying him to the Diplomatic Gallery of the Hungarian parliament on 3 July, 1963, to a session of the house, but found it, as he did, a somewhat uninspiring occasion. I also recall reporting on the February 1963 elections which resulted in a vote of 98.9% in favour of the Patriotic People's Front.

Before leaving Hungary in August 1963, I wrote a short biography of János Kádár which was forwarded by the minister to London where it met with a favourable reception. After retirement, I was able to re-read it as a member of the team of senior officials reviewing old FCO papers before release to the National Archives. I was gratified to find that it stood the test of time and I shall now give extracts from the final paragraph, as the whole document is too long to quote in full:

> Kádár can never have the real confidence of the Hungarian people but, in present circumstances, he seems to be accepted by many Hungarians as the best Prime Minister they are likely to get [...]. He is essentially a mediocrity who has risen to the top because of events and [...] has adopted the realistic policy of "la mesure du possible". Compromise seems to be Kádár's motto and so long as he enjoys the support of his Soviet masters, there seems little doubt that he will be allowed to develop a Hungarian brand of communism similar to that of Gomulka in Poland.

It will be recalled that, nine years later, in his birthday speech of 25 May, 1972, published in *Társadalmi Szemle* in June, 1972, Kádár himself stated, 'I might divulge here [...] that life is in many ways a compromise. Nothing ever comes about in the way one believes it will at the beginning.'

I must now conclude this brief account of my two years in Hungary by stating that it was a rewarding experience since it left me with a lifelong interest in the country. In retirement I have been fortunate enough to be associated with the School of Slavonic and East European Studies as its official historian. In addition, I have written a book under the School's auspices on the Russian intervention in Hungary in 1849 that was published in 1991. Three years later I was invited by the FCO to give a lecture to some of its members as part of a series entitled 'Nationality and Nationalism in East-Central Europe'. I entitled my contribution 'The Hungarian Nation: the Persistence of Nationalism 1848–1958', since as a Scot I have been much impressed by this feature of the Hungarian character. Finally, I must add that my wife and I have made a return visit to Budapest since the collapse of communism and were delighted to view the Crown of St Stephen in its rightful home, instead of in Fort Knox in the United States, as well as the rebuilt Vár which was still in ruins during our posting.

Conclusory Essay: Hungary's War of Independence in 1956

Martyn Rady

Hungary's war of independence in 1956 claimed the lives of 2500 Hungarians and over 700 Soviet troops.[1] A further 20,000 Hungarians and more than 1500 Soviet soldiers were wounded. In the wake of Hungary's military defeat, 200,000 of its citizens fled abroad. Of those that remained, over 20,000 were gaoled or interned for having participated in Hungary's struggle, and 341 were hanged.[2] Doubtless, the number of those murdered by the communists would have been more had not one or two of the contributors to this volume joined the emigration.

The impact of 1956 was larger than its casualty list. 1956 demonstrated that the Soviet bloc was no longer impregnable and it aroused in equal measure admiration for Hungary and contempt for the Soviets, who were now seen in their true light as military occupiers. Even schoolchildren in the GDR did not conceal their sympathy for Hungary.[3] For others in Eastern Europe, the example of Hungary led their first steps in dissidence. In Western Europe, the ruthlessness of the Soviet action had a devastating effect upon left-wing morale and fellow-travellers. After 1956 it was no longer possible to equate Soviet communism with liberation. Like the French poet, Claude Roy, many now sought to escape the 'stink of Stalinism' and turned their 'nostrils towards other horizons',[4] to a 'third way', Castro, 'non-alignment' and the Trotskyist 'International'. Already confused by Khrushchev's 'secret speech', communist-party members left the party in droves. Between 1956 and 1958 the Communist Party of Great Britain lost around nine thousand members, over a quarter of its total.[5] In Italy, as many as 400,000 communists quit the party, prompting Togliatti, even at the height of the crisis of 1956, to explain with characteristic circumlocution to the Soviet leaders: 'Hungarian events have developed in a way that renders our clarifying action in the party very difficult; it also makes it difficult to obtain consensus in favour of the leadership.'[6] As in France, the

---

1 The figure for Soviet deaths comes from the latest research in the Russian archives. See Johanna C. Granville, *The First Domino: International Decision Making during the Hungarian Crisis of 1956*, College Station, TX, 2004, p. 99.

2 *The Hungarian Revolution: A History in Documents*, eds Csaba Békés, Malcolm Byrne, János M. Rainer, Budapest & New York, 2002, p. 375.

3 See Alan McDougall's essay here, pp. 239–46.

4 Cited in Tony Judt, *Postwar: A History of Europe Since 1945*, London, 2005, p. 322. As Attila Pók reminds us, however, Claude Roy's loyalty to Soviet communism meant that it took him some time to reach this position. See here p. 185.

5 Robert Service, *Comrades: A World History of Communism*, London, 2007, p. 315.

6 Judt, *Postwar*, p. 321.

'difficulty' identified by Togliatti would by degrees lead his party away from Moscow in the direction of 'Euro-communism'.

* * *

The effect on Hungary of its war of independence after 1956 has been compared with that of Hungary's earlier war fought against the Habsburgs in 1848–49. It is maintained that in both cases the wars that were fought led directly to a compromise with the imperial power.[7] In 1867, therefore, Hungary acquired home-rule within the Habsburg Monarchy; a century later, it received 'goulash socialism'.[8] Certainly, the Kádárist 'compromise' gave a degree of artistic latitude even to the extent of offering 'a model of reciprocity'.[9] It permitted a small measure of dissidence, and rewarded compliance – either individually through state-preferment or, collectively, with decent *Téli* salami in the shops in 1979, scented West German soap the next year, and so on. Moreover, the regime made only half-hearted, almost comical attempts to enlist intellectuals to its side, even permitting a sort of coded criticism – although sometimes the code left the message opaque both for western readers and even for the official censors.[10] The success of the compromise so obtained may be measured both by the sense of moral repugnance which it engendered and by Kádár's posthumous reputation which, according to a poll conducted in 1999, acquitted him as the third greatest figure of Hungarian history.[11]

In reflecting upon historical parallels, we may however observe that it was not so much 1848 that led to 1867 as the resistance mounted by Hungarians after the formal conclusion of hostilities. Throughout the 1850s and 60s, Hungary refused to be pacified. Its political leaders, at both national and local levels, were drawn neither to the side of the unconstitutional Bach regime nor to the centralizing 'Schmerling theatre'.[12] Daily instances of minor protests, even the singing of a patriotic song, were sufficient to convince Vienna of a deep well of unrest that might all too easily spill into rebellion.[13] Rumours of Hungarian armies waiting in the countryside or massing in Italy, and of their generals' collusion with Prussia, eventually forced Franz Joseph's hand and led to the Settlement of 1867. The same pattern may be discerned after 1956. Certainly, Kádár was delighted that Hungary's renewed communist party could on May Day 1957 bring 100,000 workers into the streets – ' a success beyond the leadership's expectations'.[14] Nevertheless, the party which he headed was in complete disarray, with its pro-Soviet

---

7   The same point is made here by István Szijártó in respect of the consequences of the Rákóczi Revolt, pp. 67–76.

8   Discussed here by Gábor Gyáni, pp. 209–10.

9   See here, Rachel Beckles-Willson's discussion of Kurtág's reception, p. 282.

10 See the essays here by Krisztián Ungváry (pp. 271–9), Peter Sherwood (pp. 297–304), Géza Jeszenszky (pp. 266–7) and István Szijártó (pp. 67–8, on the writing of Jenő Szűcs).

11 After St Stephen and István Széchenyi; Kossuth came tenth. See Roger Gough, *A Good Comrade: János Kádár, Communism and Hungary*, London & New York, 2006, p. xi; further details of the poll are given on <http://hirek.prim.hu/cikk/5698> [accessed 8 July, 2007].

12 See László Péter's essay here, pp. 51–3.

13 See the essay by Ágnes Deák here, pp. 113–9. The Rákosi regime was equally convinced in the existence of a widespread opposition. See the essays here by Gábor Bátonyi (pp. 159–70) and Attila Pók (pp. 177–90).

14 Gough, *A Good Comrade*, p. 110.

members harried even in the higher echelons.[15] Workers' councils maintained a shadowy life for at least a year after November 1956, while attempts to arrest 'trouble-makers' were met by wildcat strikes and sabotage. As in 1956,[16] moreover, the principal agents of resistance were young workers – members of precisely that group in whose name the party claimed to stand. Moreover, by the end of 1956, the old ÁVH security apparatus had all but dissolved and it proved impossible to restore. The work therefore of repression had necessarily to be undertaken by KGB and Soviet MVD units. On 9 November 1956, the young László Péter did indeed discern correctly that the 'central nerve system of the regime' had been shattered and that the rooms in the Ministry of the Interior building through which he had walked were unlikely to be reoccupied by their former staff.[17]

Rather than the independence war, it was the impossibility of restoring communist power in anything like its previous form that compelled the Kádárist compromise. As Johanna Granville has put it elsewhere, in the making of this compromise 'passive resistance is key.'[18]

* * *

Discussion of the interrelationship between 1848 and 1956 and their respective after-maths indicates one of the aims of this volume and of the conference upon which it draws. It was the intention of the conference's organizers, who are also this volume's editors, to put 1956 into the larger context of resistance, rebellion and revolution in the history not only of Hungary but also of Central Europe and, indeed, of Europe as a whole. In such an enterprise, coverage must necessarily be patchy and selective, and much be passed over. The editors are conscious that, although there are essays here on the English Civil War, interwar Romania and Jacobin France, neither the Prague Spring nor Polish Solidarity are included. Moreover, the editors have not sought to impose a single view on 1956, nor to interfere with individual author's preferred terminology – revolution, uprising, and so on.[19]

It nevertheless soon became clear that contexts, parallels and common-denominators were more elusive than the organizers had hitherto imagined. Certainly, behind the explosion of events in 1956 lay much the same disillusionment as afflicted a section of contemporary Polish communists.[20] Within the context of Hungarian history, we may also observe along with Hannah Arendt that successive upheavals threw up institutions of local democracy – *soviets* and other councils which, both in 1918 and in 1956, moved smartly to fill gaps in authority.[21] Likewise, all revolutions, uprisings and rebellions have at their heart the mystery of individual and group psychology that forces people

---

15 Granville, *The First Domino*, p. 146.
16 See thus the essay here by Zsuzsanna Vajda and László Eörsi, pp. 227–37.
17 See László Péter's essay here, p. 327.
18 Granville, *The First Domino*, p. 157.
19 One Stalinist reviewer criticized our failure in an earlier volume that we edited to force all our contributors to use a single term in respect of the Compromise/Settlement of 1867!
20 See the essays here by Grzegorz Berendt and the late György Litván, pp. 171–6, 307–12.
21 Hannah Arendt, 'Reflections on the Hungarian Revolution', in Arendt, *The Origins of Totalitarianism*, 2nd edition, London, 1958, pp. 480–510 (p. 497).

across the 'moral threshold'[22] – just what is it that compels a student to grasp a Kalash-nikov or, as in 1848, a squadron of hussars to defect?[23] For much of Hungary's history, however, a guiding principle behind its periodic confrontations with the Habsburgs was the conviction that the political community had the right to resist. Belief in a historic *ius resistendi*, first expounded in the Golden Bull of 1222 and then reworked and revived in Stephen Werbőczy's *Tripartitum* of 1517, provided the constitutional underpinning for a succession of rebellions. In the Bocskai Revolt of 1604, the *ius resistendi* provided a critical justification, noised abroad for the benefit of foreign audiences.[24] A putative right of resistance was likewise invoked in support of Thököly's rebellion of 1684 and the Rákóczi Revolt of 1703–11. It even resurfaced in discussions in the 1840s over Hungary's new penal code.[25] Thereafter, however, recollection of the *ius resistendi* languished. It was invoked neither in 1848, nor in 1918, nor in 1956. (Ironically, however, it resurfaced at the very moment when the conference upon which this volume is based was in the midst of its discussions. In September 2006, hooligans seeking to justify their assault on the Hungarian police and the symbols of the socialist Gyurcsányi government invoked no less an authority than the resistance clause in the Golden Bull of 1222!)[26]

The eclipse of the resistance clause was directly due to the new concepts of political sovereignty and legitimacy which emerged over the nineteenth century. The rights of a feudal elite structured around the bipolarity of king and community (*ország*) were superseded by rights that were held to adhere to the nation.[27] It was in the name of the Hungarian nation that Kossuth challenged the Habsburg rulers and it was also in its name that successive Hungarian governments sought to broaden the powers allowed them by the terms of the 1867 Settlement. By the second half of the nineteenth century, concepts of nation, statehood and independence had become inextricably linked, and the connection between all three persevered throughout the twentieth century. In their resistance to Soviet rule in 1956, Hungarians thus had no need of such constitutional rights as were afforded them in the Golden Bull or *Tripartitum*. The prerogatives already belonging to the nation, as a subject of right, were sufficient of themselves to justify and explain opposition to Soviet rule. Accordingly, it was with reference to the united nation of workers, peasants and intellectuals and in the name of the Hungarian people and their *national* government that Imre Nagy announced both the end of one-party rule in Hungary and his country's exit from the Warsaw Pact.[28]

Quite how these declarations should be understood remains controversial. Did the events of 1956 constitute a rebellion, revolt or revolution? The Hungarian contributors to this volume are much exercised by terminology – others noticeably less so. For Michael Braddick, therefore, revolt and revolution should be understood simply as

---

22 The term is Paul Hollander's. See his essay here, pp. 201–8.
23 See the essay here by Róbert Hermann, pp. 107–12, and Tamás Kabdebo's own recollections on pp. 313–6.
24 See thus Martyn Rady's essay here, pp. 57–66.
25 See László Péter's essay here, p. 50.
26 Reported in *Népszava online*, 19 September, 2006. See <http://www.nepszava.hu/default.asp?cCenter= article.asp&nID=824759> [accessed 20 September 2006].
27 On the structural dualism that sustained the resistance clause, see László Péter's essay here, pp. 53–4.
28 *The Hungarian Revolution: A History in Documents*, pp. 290–1, 334.

extra- or non-institutional means to political ends, and further distinctions are otiose.[29] Here, Braddick echoes Arthur Hatto's famous line: 'A revolution is simply a recognised extra-legal method of changing a government.'[30] We may moreover note that other violent episodes in European history retain a lack of certainty in their descriptions: English Revolution versus the Great Rebellion, or as in the case of Galicia in 1846, *Aufstand* versus *Revolution*.[31] And yet Hungarian concerns are not just a question of semantics. The description of 'revolution' is meritorious. It conveys esteem and Hungary's history in the twentieth century is singularly lacking in moments of merit. Moreover, the name of Revolution lends salience to events and accords a short episode in Hungary's history the same monumental quality as 1789, 1848 and 1917. Nevertheless, there are certain reasons for believing that what happened in Hungary in 1956 was not a revolution in many of the accepted senses of the word.

The seminal work on revolution and the meanings that have attached to it was published by Eugen Rosenstock in 1930.[32] Rosenstock's analysis was made available in English by Arthur Hatto and has subsequently passed, usually without acknowledgement, into the leading literature on the vocabulary of politics.[33] Rosenstock argues that for long in its history, revolution implied restoration or, as Clarendon understood it, a return of the wheel of fortune to its original point of equilibrium. During the seventeenth and eighteenth centuries, however, revolution acquired the meaning of a new ordering of things, as Montaigne's 'Mutation d'Estat'. Indeed, Rosenstock finds the earliest use of this meaning in 1593 with the conversion of Henri IV of Navarre and in an exchange between the Duc de Guise and his followers. It was one of these that pointed out in respect of the political consequences that must follow Navarre's act, 'C'est la révolution': the exact phrase that the Comte de Liancourt used in reply to Louis XVI almost two centuries later.[34] As Rosenstock observes, however, the events of 1789 were to bring 'revolution' into common parlance, to its modern meaning of a *Totalumwälzung*, and to introduce for the first time the term 'revolutionary' as an adjective. It was only with the adjective, applied either to persons or acts, that the modern idea of a revolution came of age. From this point onwards, however, revolutions would stand on the acts of revolutionaries. After 1789, Rosenstock argues, spontaneous revolutions ceased to take place and were replaced by 'made revolutions' (*gemachte Revolutionen*), and all revolutions hereafter depended upon the prior work and leadership of revolutionaries. 1830, 1848, 1870 and 1917 were thus all 'made revolutions', crafted and led by revolutionaries.[35] So, might we add, were the Hungarian Chrysanthemum and Soviet revolutions

---

29 See Michael Braddick's essay here, p. 3.
30 Arthur Hatto, ' "Revolution": An Enquiry into the Usefulness of a Historical Term', *Mind: A Quarterly Review of Psychology and Philosophy*, 58, no 232, 1949, pp. 495–517 (p. 515).
31 See Alan Sked's essay here and, in particular, the titles in the literature on which he draws, pp. 87–98.
32 Eugen Rosenstock, 'Revolution als politischer Begriff in der Neuzeit', in *Festgabe Robert Heilborn*, Breslau, 1931, pp. 83–124.
33 Hatto, ' "Revolution": An Enquiry', *passim*; László Péter's essay here (xiii–xix) picks up many of the points made originally by Rosenstock and communicated by Hatto.
34 Rosenstock, 'Revolution als politischer Begriff', pp. 92, 104.
35 ibid, p. 116. Rosenstock begins his list of 'made revolutions' with 1830, although we might go further back and start with Hungary's abortive Jacobin revolution of 1794. See Orsolya Szakály's essay here, pp. 77–84.

of 1918, even though their revolutionary character would later be eclipsed by the accusation that both were essentially Jewish in their inspiration and leadership.[36]

1956 fits uneasily into this pattern. The events of October may have been preceded by much urgent discussion among party-members, students and intellectuals, but there were no revolutionaries until 23 October. What happened thereafter was spontaneous and too fast-moving to qualify as a 'made revolution'.[37] In its uncertainty, lack of leadership, equivocation and pace, 1956 belongs more to 1789, although in a highly compressed form, than to the period between 1830 and 1917. And this brings us to the larger point. The speed of the insurrection, its rapid crushing, and the very fact that it was not 'made', renders it impossible to determine whether or not it aimed at a *Totalumwälzung*. Certainly, there are good grounds for arguing that those who participated in it had no intention of bringing about radical change. After 1944, Hungary had experienced colossal alterations in its social composition, its economic organization and all aspects of its political life. In just half a dozen years, Hungary went through a double socialist revolution, the first introduced by fascist rule, the second by Stalin and his agents.[38] But none of the programmes pronounced in 1956 by students, the Nagy government, workers' councils and even Cardinal Mindszenty[39] suggest either that the pre-1944 regime was to be restored or that the socialist organization of the economy and society was to be disassembled. As János Bak has indicated, the bulk of participants looked to restore conditions as they were only a few years before. They looked either to 1953 and the New Course, to 1948 before the imposition of complete Stalinism, or to 1946, after the land reform.[40] It was this intention to maintain the 'best' elements of socialism while jettisoning the oppressive baggage of high Stalinism that impelled István Bibó to look back on 1956 as 'the beginning of one of the most exciting socialist experiments of this century.'[41]

For others, however, 1956 was far from being a benign attempt to give socialism a human face. The British left-wing observer, Dora Scarlett, noted how ÁVH officers were 'hunted down like animals, hung on trees, or just beaten to death. Armed men guard escape routes out of the city.' For Charlie Coutts of the *Daily Worker*, the gangs on the streets presaged the return of right-wing vengeance. It was only by the Soviet intervention that 'fascism was stopped just in time'.[42] Of course, both journalists were caught up in their own vocabulary and political reflexes. But may we not observe the same of those who mouthed platitudes about a new socialist experiment? Were they not

---

36 See Thomas Lorman's essay here, pp. 121–7.
37 But note György Schöpflin's point in his essay here (p. 248) that it was precisely the speed of events and their spontaneity that lent 1956 a revolutionary character.
38 We should not overlook (as historians often do) the enormous changes which overtook Hungarian society in and immediately after October 1944. They truly marked 'the end of a world' – see C.A. Macartney, *October Fifteenth: A History of Modern Hungary 1929–1945*, 2 vols, Edinburgh, 1956, vol 1, p. 3.
39 Several witnesses claim to have heard Mindszenty demanding on the radio the return of church property. The text of his radio address delivered on 3 November (given in Mindszenty, *Memoirs*, London, 1974, pp. 331–3) indicates, however, that he said no such thing. See János Berecz (ed.), *Visszaemlékezések 1956*, Budapest, 1986, pp. 33, 227 (citing the recollections of Antal Apró and Judit Máriássy).
40 See János Bak's essay here, pp. 215–9.
41 István Kemény and Mátyás Sárközi (eds), *Bibó István. Összegyűjtött munkái*, vol 3, Bern, 1983, p. 888.
42 Bill Lomax (ed.), *Eyewitness in Hungary: The Soviet Invasion of 1956*, Nottingham, 1981, pp. 53, 121; A.J.P. Taylor's similar view is given here by György Schöpflin, p. 247.

themselves caught up in the same sort of institutionalized discourse as guided English political debate in the 1640s or Hungarian peasant responses to emancipation in 1848?[43] And would not a 'free Hungary', had it so emerged in 1956, have rapidly acquired from the West a new type of discourse centred, as after 1989, on varieties of capitalist triumphalism? In short, might it not be that after a brief lingering on the socialist plain, our agoraphobic Hungarians would have mounted the same train as thirty years later?[44] On account of the Soviet re-conquest, we cannot know. But neither can we judge whether what happened in October and November 1956 amounted from its content to a revolution.

*   *   *

1956 was not a revolution that was 'made' by revolutionaries. As a consequence both of this and of the speed of its suppression, it was an event singularly lacking in ideological content. Unlike 1789, it left no great doctrine or idea around which revolutionary forces might later gather. The sense of revolutionary selfhood aroused by the act of snatching up a gun was suppressed either physically in the crackdown that followed, or psychologically by the act of emigration, or morally by later complicity in the Kádárist compromise. We may smirk at the rituals of Romania's interwar legionaries, denounce the killing in which they engaged, and marvel at their union with Orthodox mysticism.[45] Clearly, though, the sense of selfhood engendered by participation in legionary ritual and practice sustained an insurrectionary tradition of enormous strength that survived the communist takeover. As the latest Romanian research shows,[46] legionary 'nests' led a prolonged and active resistance to communism that carried on until well into the 1960s, and opposition to the regime was never as weak in Romania as commentators have usually averred.[47] Elsewhere, in Eastern Europe, however, resistance was muted. Just as the SOE found it hard during the Second World War to set the region ablaze – the Czechoslovak case is considered in this volume by Martin Brown – so resistance and opposition to communist rule were marked either by passivity or by strategies of personal opportunism and manipulation.[48] Observers of Hungarian affairs accordingly reported, even on the eve of 1956, that 'there is no tradition or history of active resistance in Hungary and all evidence indicates that this tradition has not been broken' and that what resistance there was in the country was 'more or less restricted to passive unorganized manifestations'.[49]

---

43 See the essays here by Michael Braddick (pp. 4–5) and Robert Gray (pp. 101, 105).
44 The metaphor builds on Tim Beasley-Murray's essay, given here on pp. 23–39 (pp. 31–2).
45 See Rebecca Haynes's essay here, pp. 129–42.
46 See thus the important series of documents on resistance to communism in Romania published by the National Institute for the Study of Totalitarianism in Bucharest. I am grateful to Marian Cojoc of the University of Constanța, the author of *Rezistența Armată din Dobrogea 1945–1960* (Bucharest, 2004) for drawing my attention to this series and to his own contribution to it.
47 See thus János Rainer's essay here, p. 192.
48 See thus Gábor Bátonyi's essay here, pp. 159–70. Martin Brown's essay is given here on pp. 145–57.
49 'Study Prepared for US Army Intelligence, "Hungary: Resistance Activities and Potentials"', given in *The Hungarian Revolution: A History in Documents*, pp. 97, 101. See also Tamás Meszerics, 'Independence Before all Else: The Hungarian anti-communist resistance in the East European context', *East European Quarterly*, 41, 2007, 1, pp. 39–59 (p. 49).

Personal strategies again prevailed after 1956. Once the teeth of the post-1956 resistance movement had been drawn by the Kádárist compromise, Hungarians began their own debate of *kicsi vagy kocsi*.[50] In Poland, meanwhile, there took place the Nowa Huta revolt of 1960 (which left several dozen killed), the risings in 1976 in Radom, Łódź, Warsaw and Poznań (the last of these left 53 dead and 300 wounded), and the 1980 Solidarity strikes. Even in 1989, however, Hungarians remained passive, entrusting their future to a small clique of professional dissidents. What emerged may have been (as journalists aver) a 'negotiated' or even 'lawful' revolution, but it was performed without any of the intellectual ferment and discussion that attended 1789, 1848 and 1870, and, as the work of a self-appointed cabal, it was profoundly undemocratic in its making. In short, not only was 1956 not 'made' as a revolution but it was also contextually short. The most we can say is that communist rule in Hungary 'elicit[ed] weak resistance in the longer term, but with a strong, one-off potential for rebellion or revolution.'[51]

A revolution without a pre-existing cadre of revolutionaries, with neither content nor doctrine, that awoke no new sense of the self nor fostered a revolutionary tradition, nor indeed built on one, does not merit the description of a revolution. In its attempt to reverse, even in the name of a new socialism, the radical changes that had taken place in Hungary after 1944, 1956 might, as Jürgen Habermas has described 1989, be realistically considered 'a revolution that is to some degree flowing backwards'[52] and so possibly as a counter-revolution.[53] But such would be to overlook what lent 1956 its purpose and what prompted ordinary Hungarians to extraordinary action. 1956 had one aim and around this it gathered the nation, if not in arms then at least in quiet approval around their radios. It was a national uprising against alien rule and against the Russians and their Hungarian stooges: it was, as Sir Leslie Fry noted only weeks after its suppression, 'a revolt by a nation'.[54] In view of the interest of many of its participants in retaining socialism, 1956 hardly merits the description of a 'war for freedom'. After all, did not Bibó himself recommend that only socialist parties be permitted to contest any future multi-party elections?[55] But 1956 may still join with the Bocskai Revolt, Rákóczi rebellion and the struggle against the Habsburgs in 1848–49 as being a 'war of independence'.

---

50 See thus Géza Jeszenszky's essay here, pp. 253–69 (p. 259).
51 See János Rainer's essay here, p. 192.
52 Jürgen Habermas, 'What does Socialism mean Today? The Rectifying Revolution and the Need for New Thinking on the Left', *New Left Review*, 183, 1990, pp. 3–21 (p. 4).
53 See thus Mikko Lagerspetz's view of 1989 as an 'anti-modernist' revolution, in 'Postsocialism as a Return: Notes on a Discursive Strategy', *East European Politics and Societies*, 13, 1999, 2, pp. 377–90.
54 See Éva Figder's essay here, pp. 221–6. See also Gabor Gyani's discussion here of Ferenc Vali's *Rift and Revolt in Hungary: Nationalism versus Communism* (Oxford, 1961), pp. 209–13.
55 *Bibó István. Összegyűjtött munkái*, vol 3, p. 890.

Contributors

János M. Bak	Professor Emeritus of the University of British Columbia (Vancouver, BC) and the Central European University, Budapest
Gábor Bátonyi	Lecturer in History, University of Bradford
Tim Beasley-Murray	Lecturer in Slovak Studies, UCL-SSEES
Rachel Beckles-Willson	Reader in Music, Royal Holloway, University of London
Grzegorz Berendt	Assistant Professor in the Institute of History, University of Gdańsk
Michael Braddick	Professor of History, University of Sheffield
Martin D. Brown	Assistant Professor in International History, Richmond: The American University in London
Ágnes Deák	Associate Professor, Institute of History, University of Szeged
László Eörsi	Research Fellow at the 1956 Institute, Budapest
Éva Figder	formerly of the Contemporary History Section of the Historical Institute of the Hungarian Academy of Sciences
Robert Gray	PhD History student, UCL-SSEES
Gábor Gyáni	Senior Research Fellow, Institute of History of the Hungarian Academy of Sciences
Rebecca Ann Haynes	Senior Lecturer in Romanian History, UCL-SSEES
Róbert Hermann	Chief of the Hungarian Archive-Delegation in the Austrian Military Archive, Vienna
Paul Hollander	Professor of Sociology at the University of Massachusetts, Amherst, and Associate of the Davis Center for Russian and Eurasian Studies at Harvard University

355

Géza Jeszenszky	teaches at the Corvinus University, Budapest; formerly Foreign Minister of Hungary, 1990–94
Thomas Kabdebo	writer and historian
György Litván (1929–2006)	formerly Director of the 1956 Institute, Budapest
Thomas Lorman	Assistant Professor of History, University of Cincinnati
Alan McDougall	Associate Professor in Modern European History and European Studies, Guelph University, Canada
László Péter	Professor Emeritus of Hungarian History, UCL-SSEES
Attila Pók	Deputy Director of the Institute of History of the Hungarian Academy of Sciences
Martyn Rady	Professor of Central European History, UCL-SSEES
János Rainer	Director of the 1956 Institute, Budapest
Brodie Richards	PhD History student, University of Guelph, Canada
I.W. Roberts	former member of Her Majesty's Diplomatic Service (1951–84)
Gabriel Ronay	writer, broadcaster and journalist, formerly of *The Times*, now of the *Sunday Herald*
György Schöpflin	MEP for Hungary (FIDESZ – Hungarian Civic Union); formerly Jean Monnet Professor of Politics, UCL-SSEES
Peter Sherwood	First Distinguished László Birinyi Professor of Hungarian Language and Culture, University of North Carolina at Chapel Hill
Alan Sked	Senior Lecturer in International History, LSE
Orsolya Szakály	Lecturer in European Society and Thought, SOAS, London
István M. Szijártó	Assistant Professor, Department of Economic and Social History, Eötvös University
Krisztián Ungváry	Research Fellow at the 1956 Institute, Budapest
Zsuzsanna Vajda	teaches Psychology at the University of Miskolc

Index